MONSTROUS

A TRANSRACIAL ADOPTION STORY

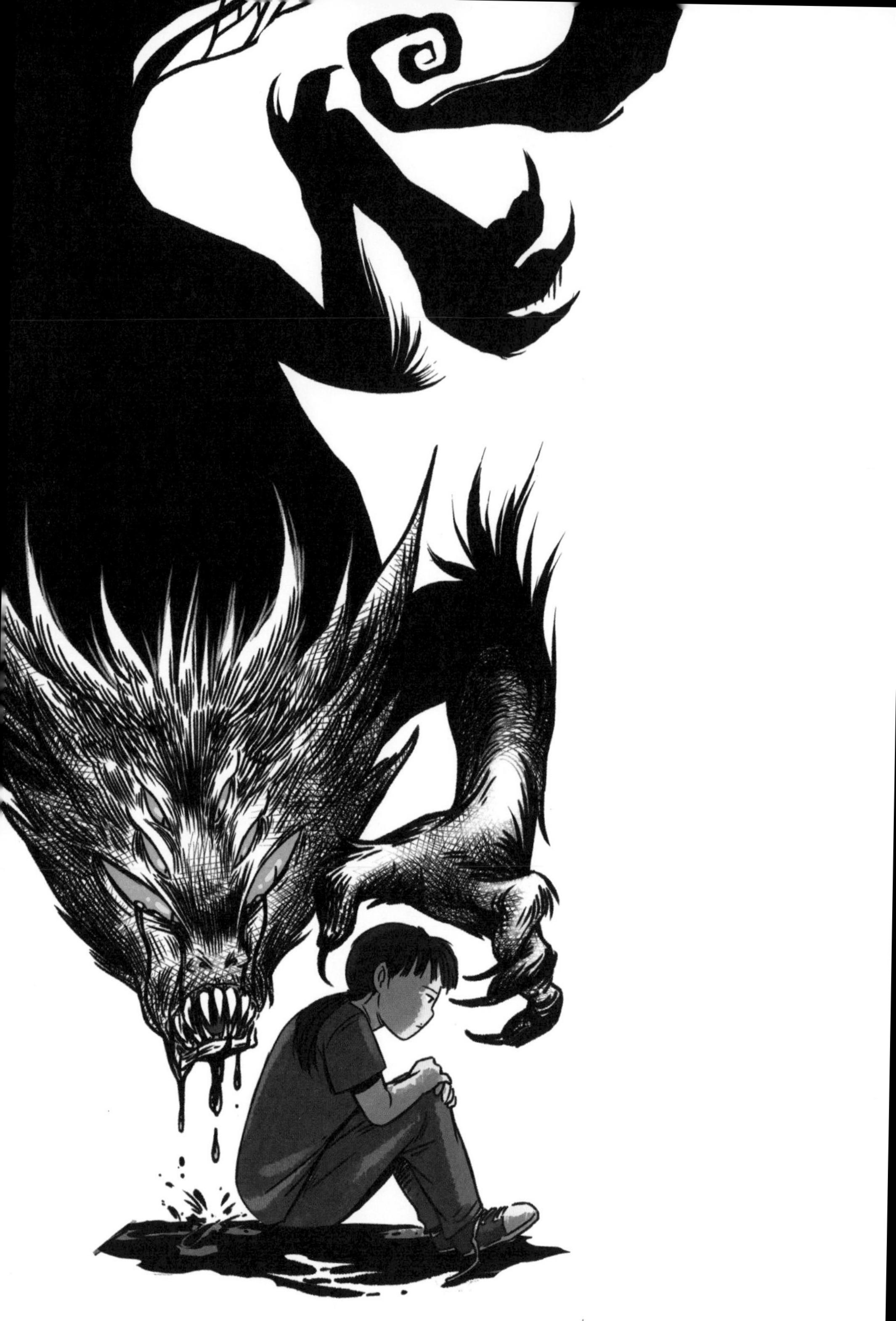

MONSTROUS

A TRANSRACIAL ADOPTION STORY

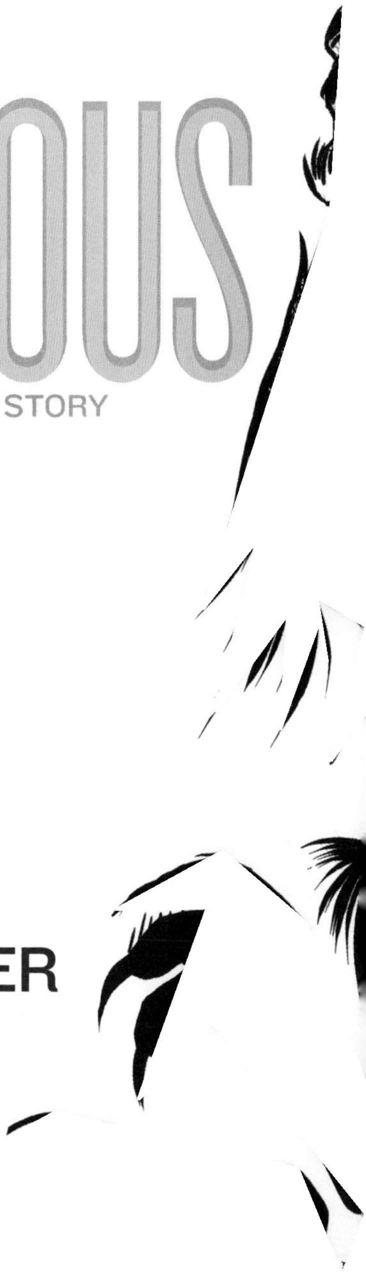

SARAH MYER

First Second

Published by First Second
First Second is an imprint of Roaring Brook Press,
a division of Holtzbrinck Publishing Holdings Limited Partnership
120 Broadway, New York, NY 10271
firstsecondbooks.com

Library of Congress Control Number: 2022920214

Our books may be purchased in bulk for promotional, educational, or business use. Please
contact your local bookseller or the Macmillan Corporate and Premium Sales Department at
(800) 221-7945 ext. 5442 or by email at MacmillanSpecialMarkets@macmillan.com.

First edition, 2023
Edited by Robyn Chapman and Michael Moccio
Cover design by Kirk Benshoff and Molly Johanson
Interior book design by Molly Johanson and Yan L. Moy
Production editing by Sarah Gompper and Kelly Markus
With special thanks to Susan Chang

Penciled, inked, and colored digitally with sketch pencil–style brushes in
Clip Studio Paint.

Printed in China.

ISBN 978-1-250-26880-8 (paperback)
10 9 8 7 6 5 4 3 2 1

ISBN 978-1-250-26879-2 (hardcover)
10 9 8 7 6 5 4 3 2 1

Don't miss your next favorite book from First Second!
For the latest updates go to firstsecondnewsletter.com and sign up for our enewsletter.

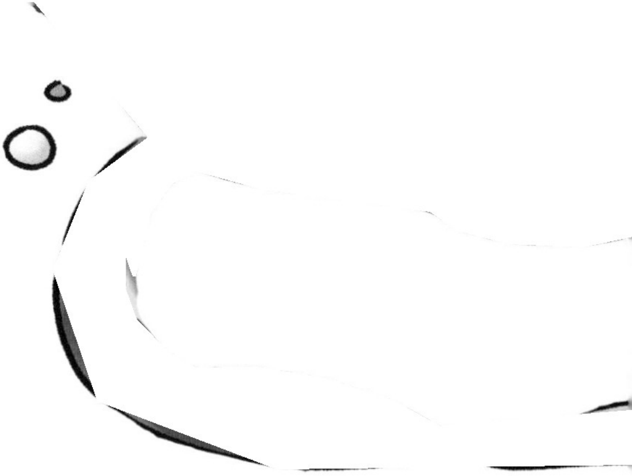

For Mom and Dad—MARY ANN and STEVE MYER

For those who feel unwanted

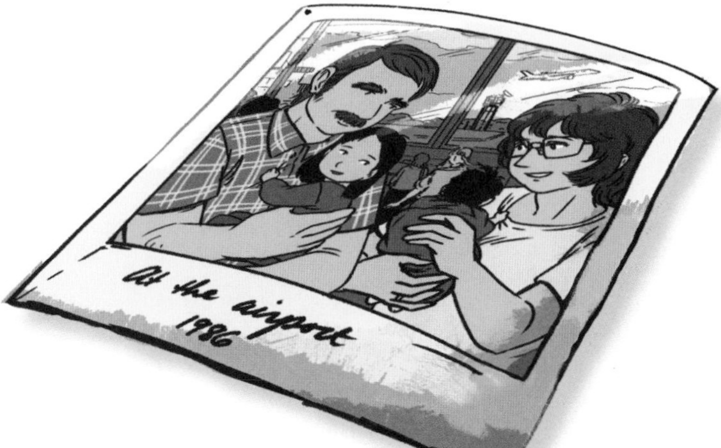
At the airport
1986

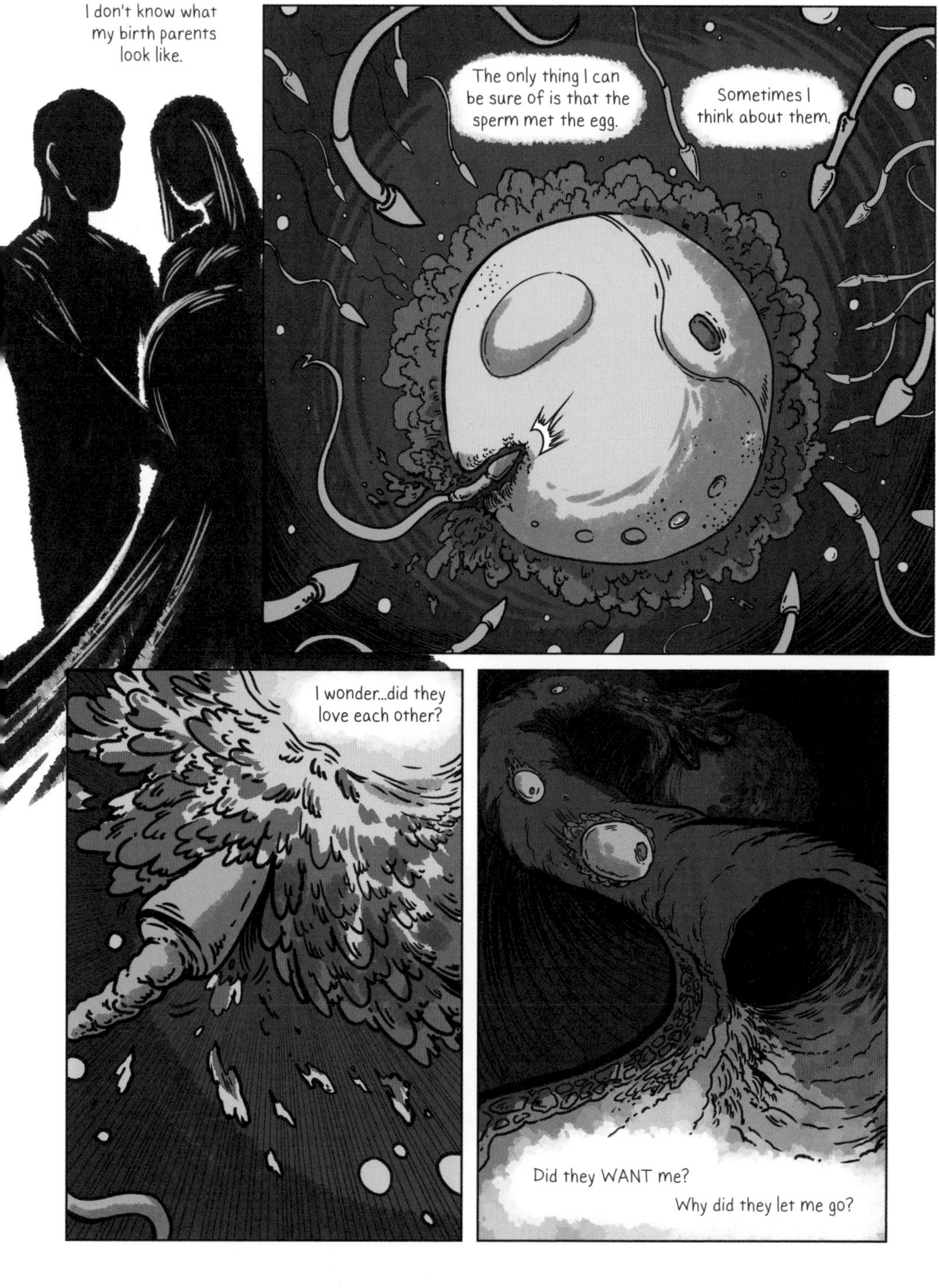
I don't know what my birth parents look like.
The only thing I can be sure of is that the sperm met the egg.
Sometimes I think about them.
I wonder...did they love each other?
Did they WANT me?
Why did they let me go?

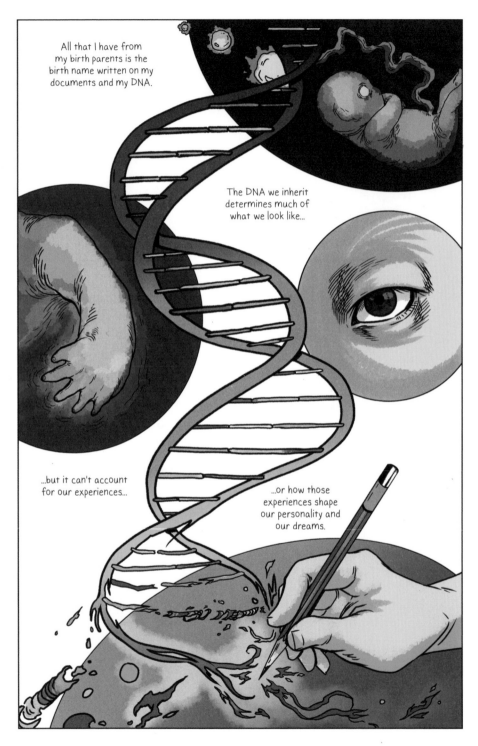

All that I have from my birth parents is the birth name written on my documents and my DNA.

The DNA we inherit determines much of what we look like...

...but it can't account for our experiences...

...or how those experiences shape our personality and our dreams.

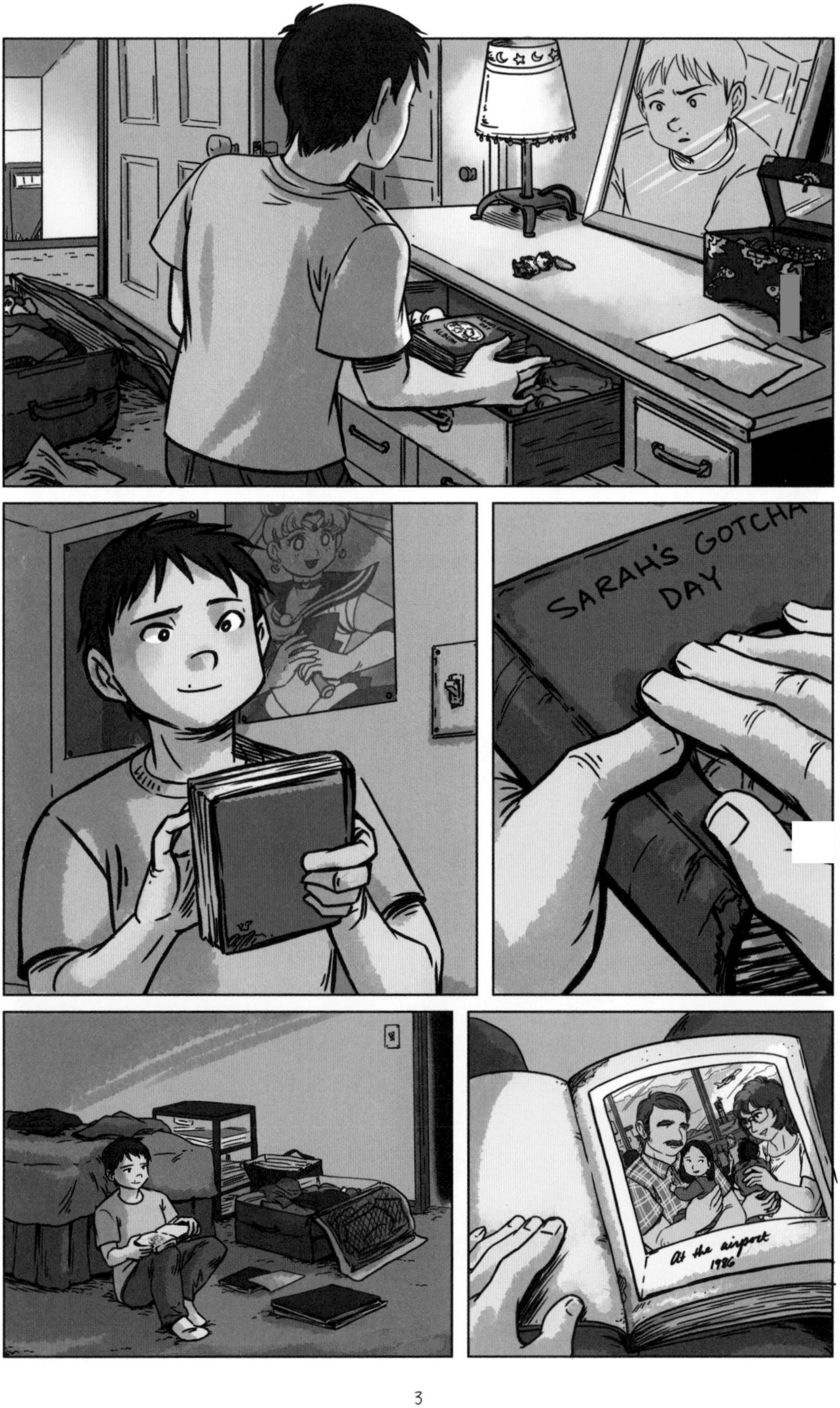
SARAH'S GOTCHA DAY
At the airport
1986

The South Korean Ministry of Health and Welfare reports that there were 66,511 intercountry adoptions out of South Korea between 1980 and 1989.

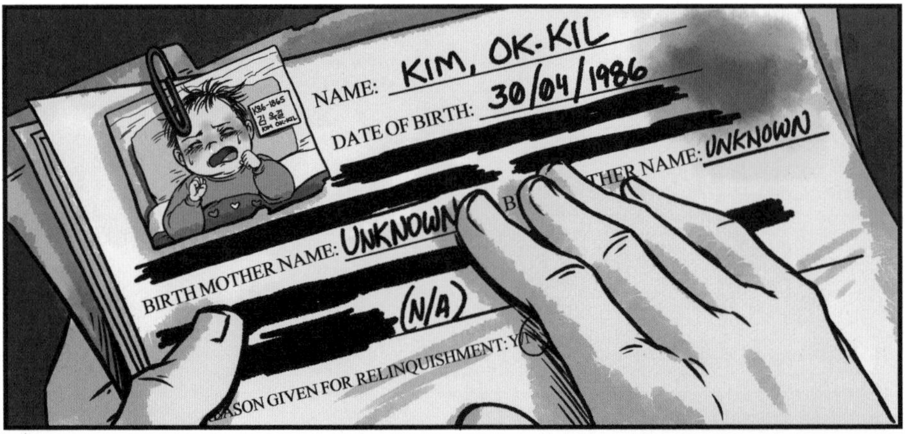

NAME: KIM, OK-KIL
DATE OF BIRTH: 30/04/1986
[redacted]
THER NAME: UNKNOWN
BIRTH MOTHER NAME: UNKNOWN
[redacted]
(N/A)
[redacted]
ASON GIVEN FOR RELINQUISHMENT:

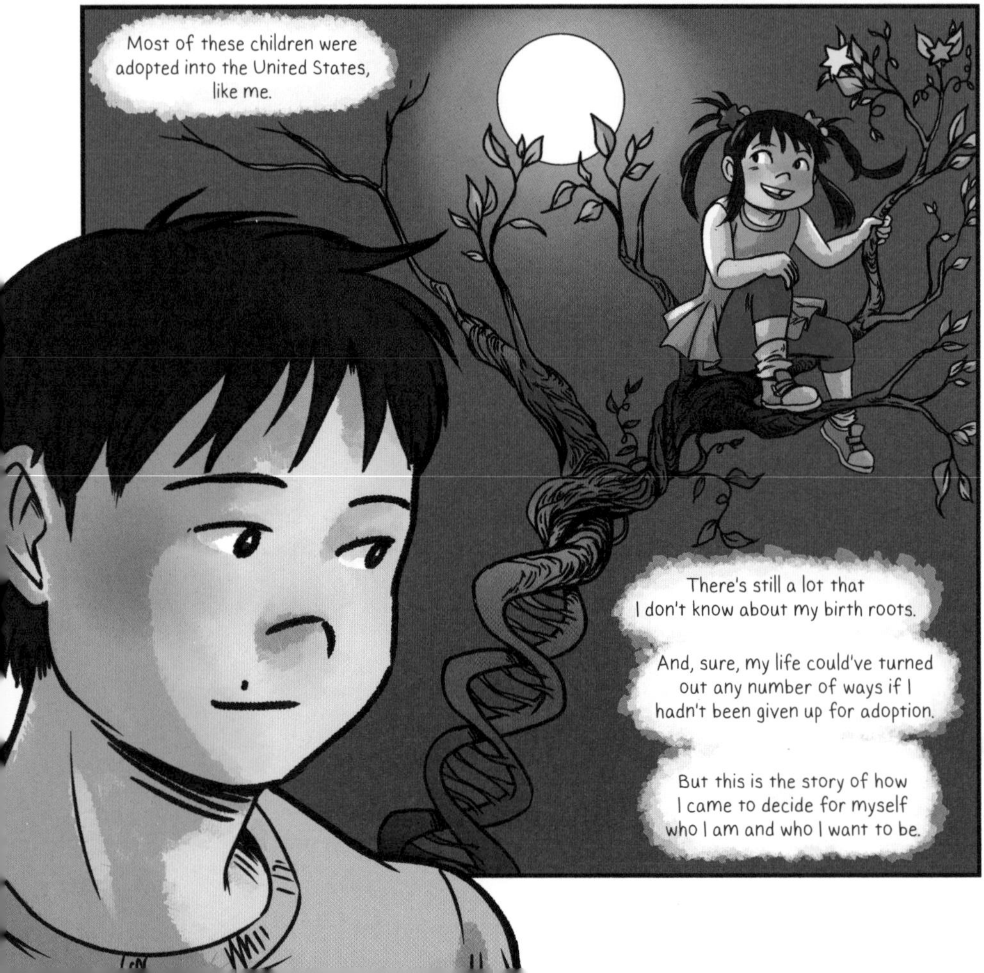

Most of these children were adopted into the United States, like me.
There's still a lot that I don't know about my birth roots.
And, sure, my life could've turned out any number of ways if I hadn't been given up for adoption.
But this is the story of how I came to decide for myself who I am and who I want to be.

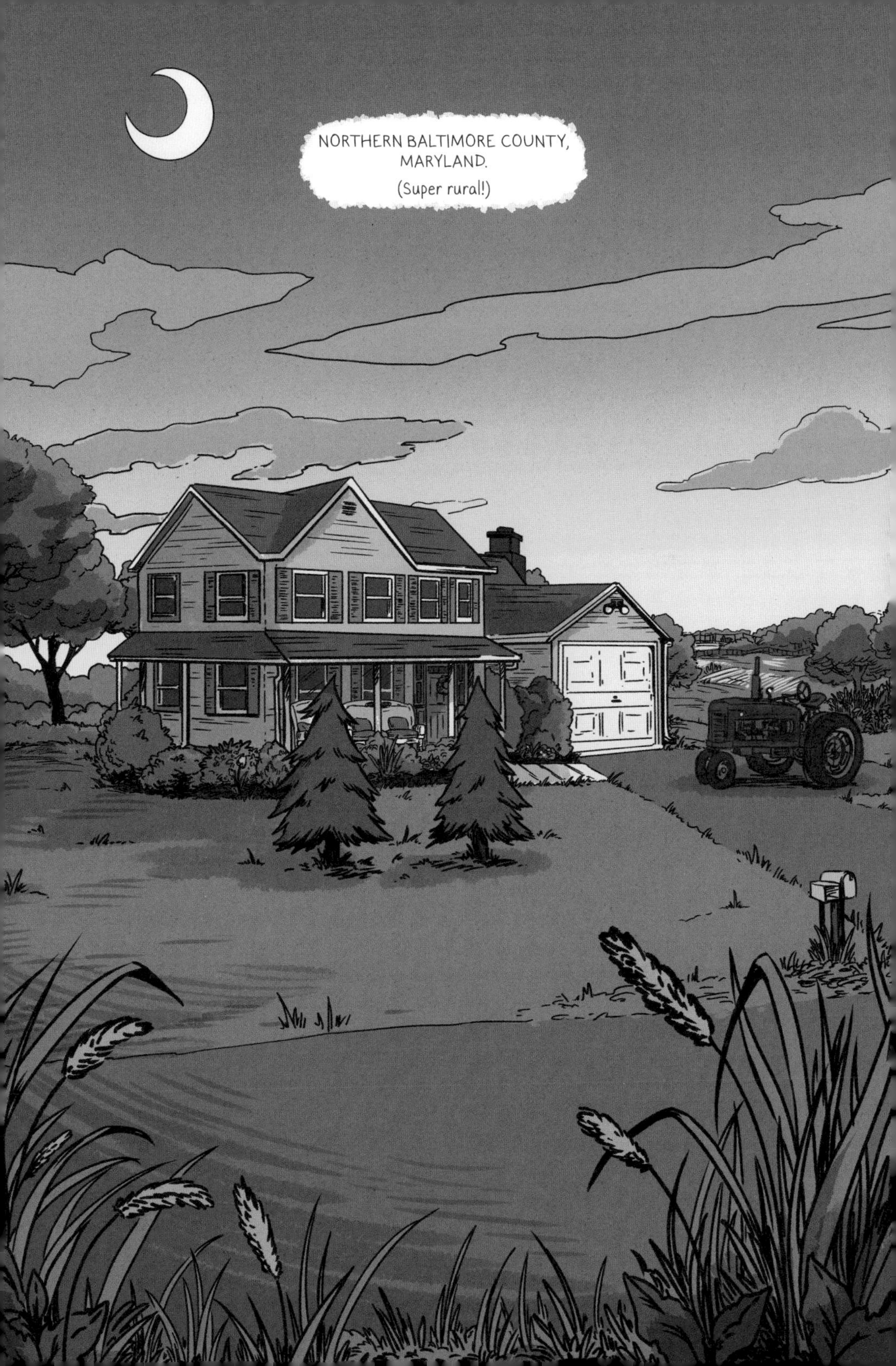
NORTHERN BALTIMORE COUNTY, MARYLAND.
(Super rural!)

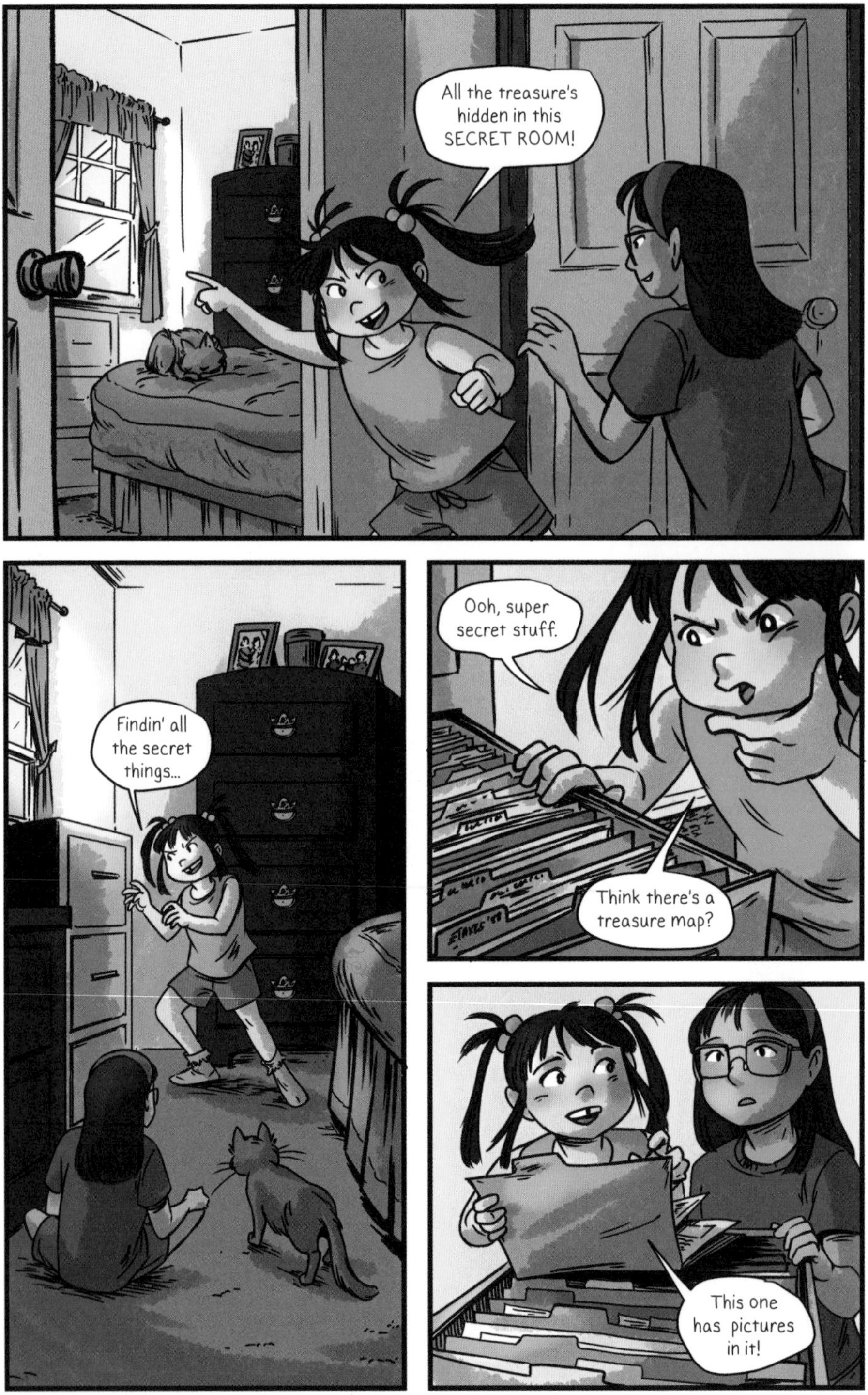
All the treasure's hidden in this SECRET ROOM!
Findin' all the secret things...
Ooh, super secret stuff.
Think there's a treasure map?
This one has pictures in it!

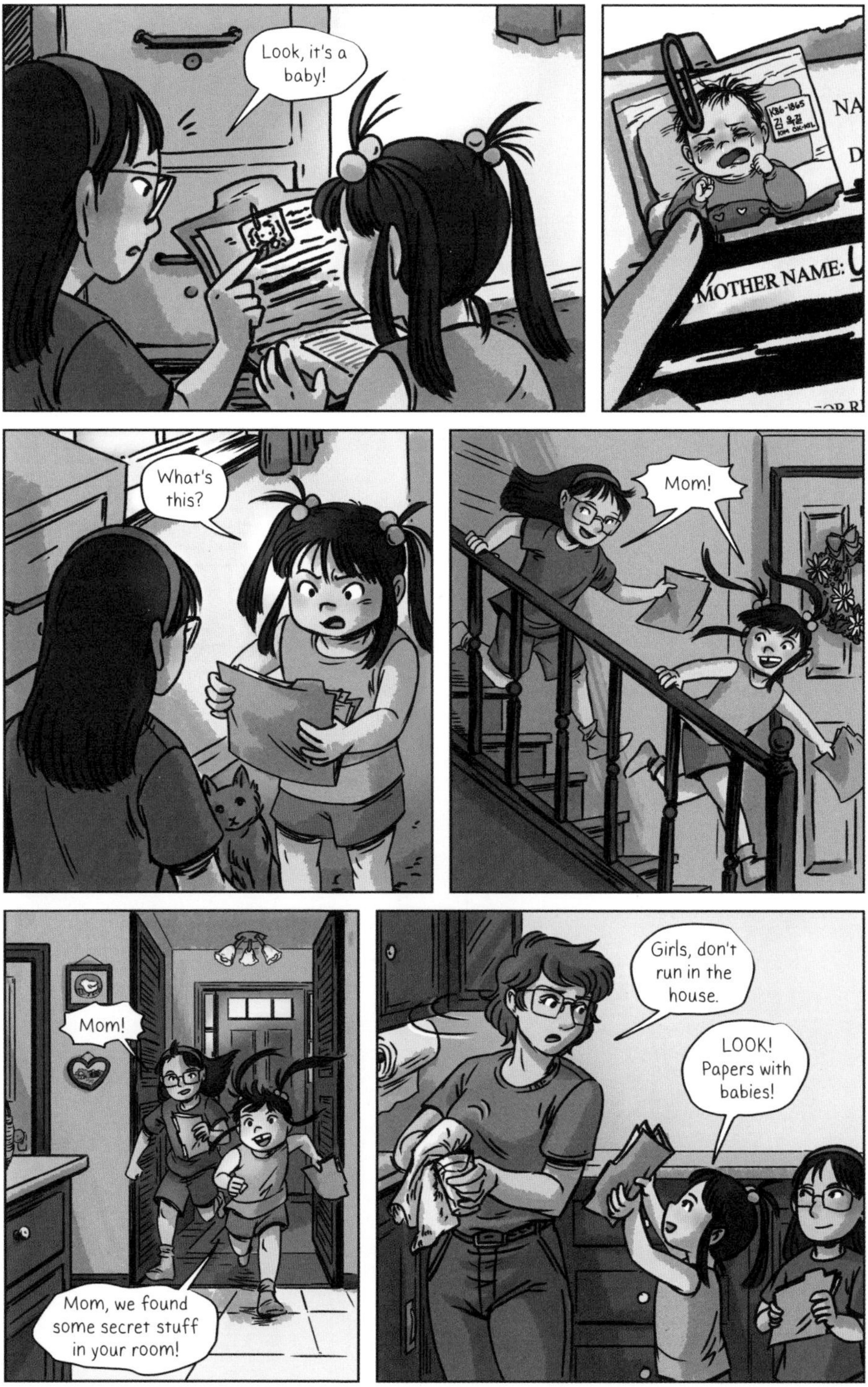
Look, it's a baby!
MOTHER NAME:
What's this?
Mom!
Mom!
Mom, we found some secret stuff in your room!
Girls, don't run in the house.
LOOK! Papers with babies!

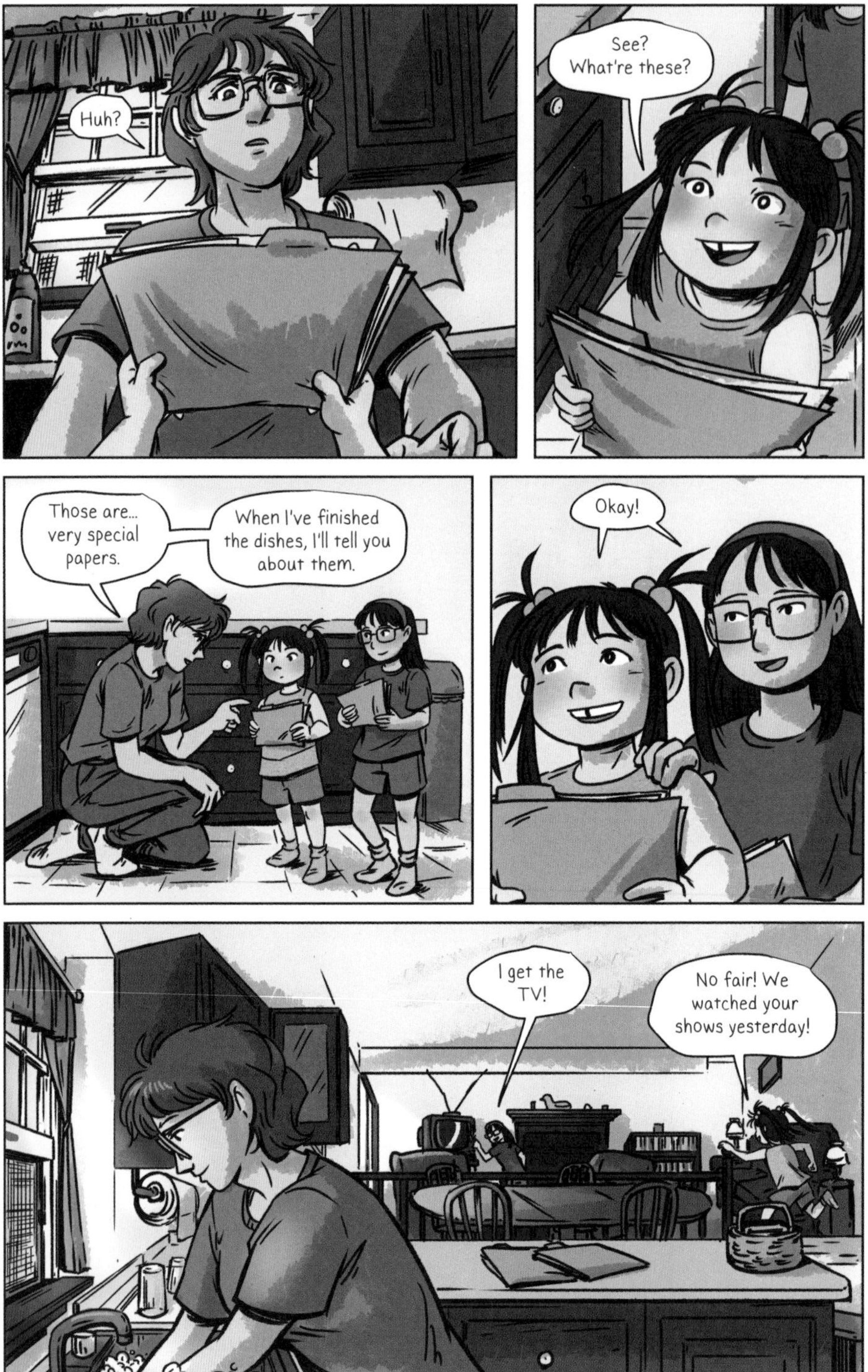
Huh?
See? What're these?
Those are... very special papers.
When I've finished the dishes, I'll tell you about them.
Okay!
I get the TV!
No fair! We watched your shows yesterday!

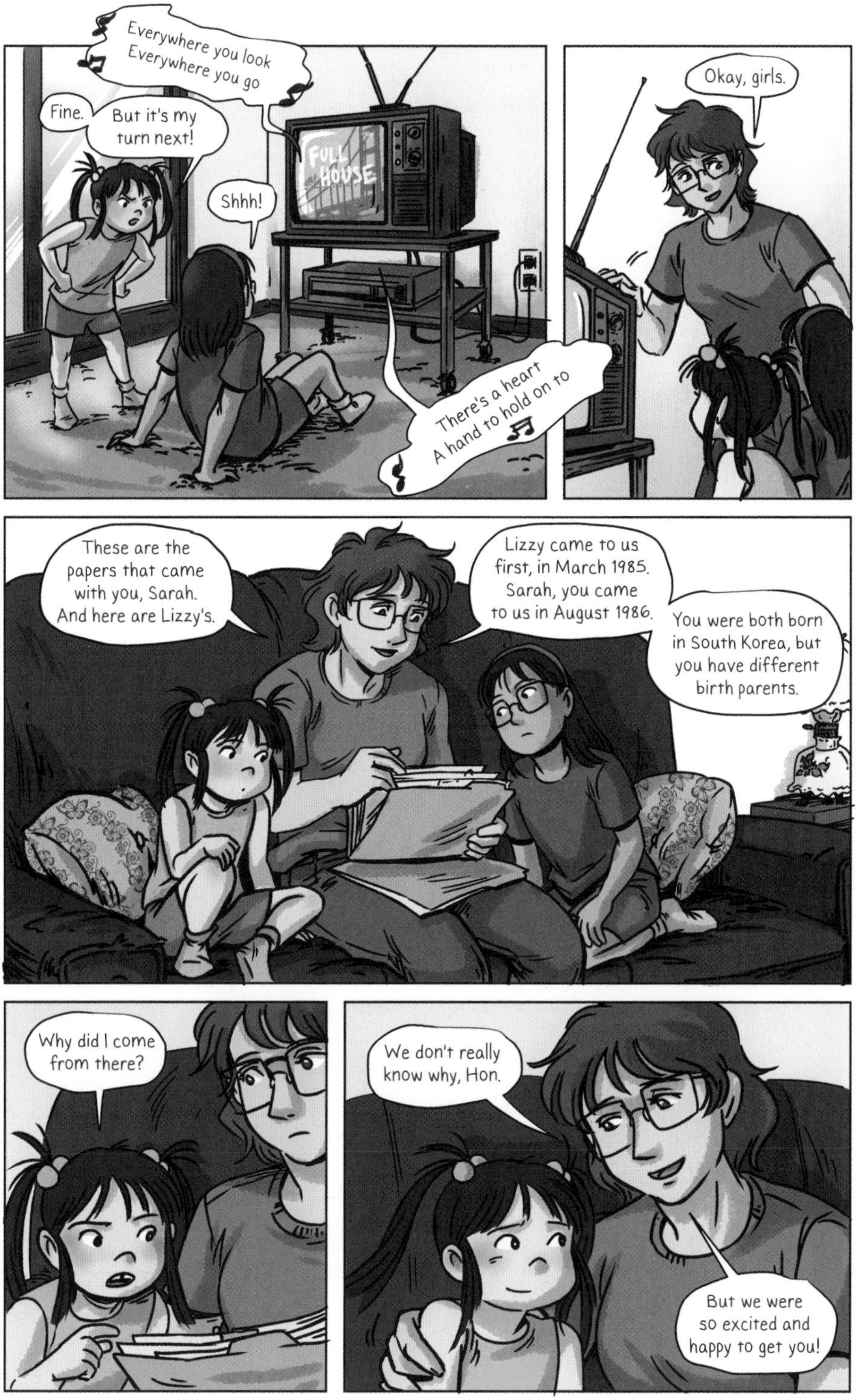
Everywhere you look
Everywhere you go
Fine.
But it's my turn next!
FULL HOUSE
Shhh!
There's a heart
A hand to hold on to
Okay, girls.
These are the papers that came with you, Sarah. And here are Lizzy's.
Lizzy came to us first, in March 1985. Sarah, you came to us in August 1986.
You were both born in South Korea, but you have different birth parents.
Why did I come from there?
We don't really know why, Hon.
But we were so excited and happy to get you!

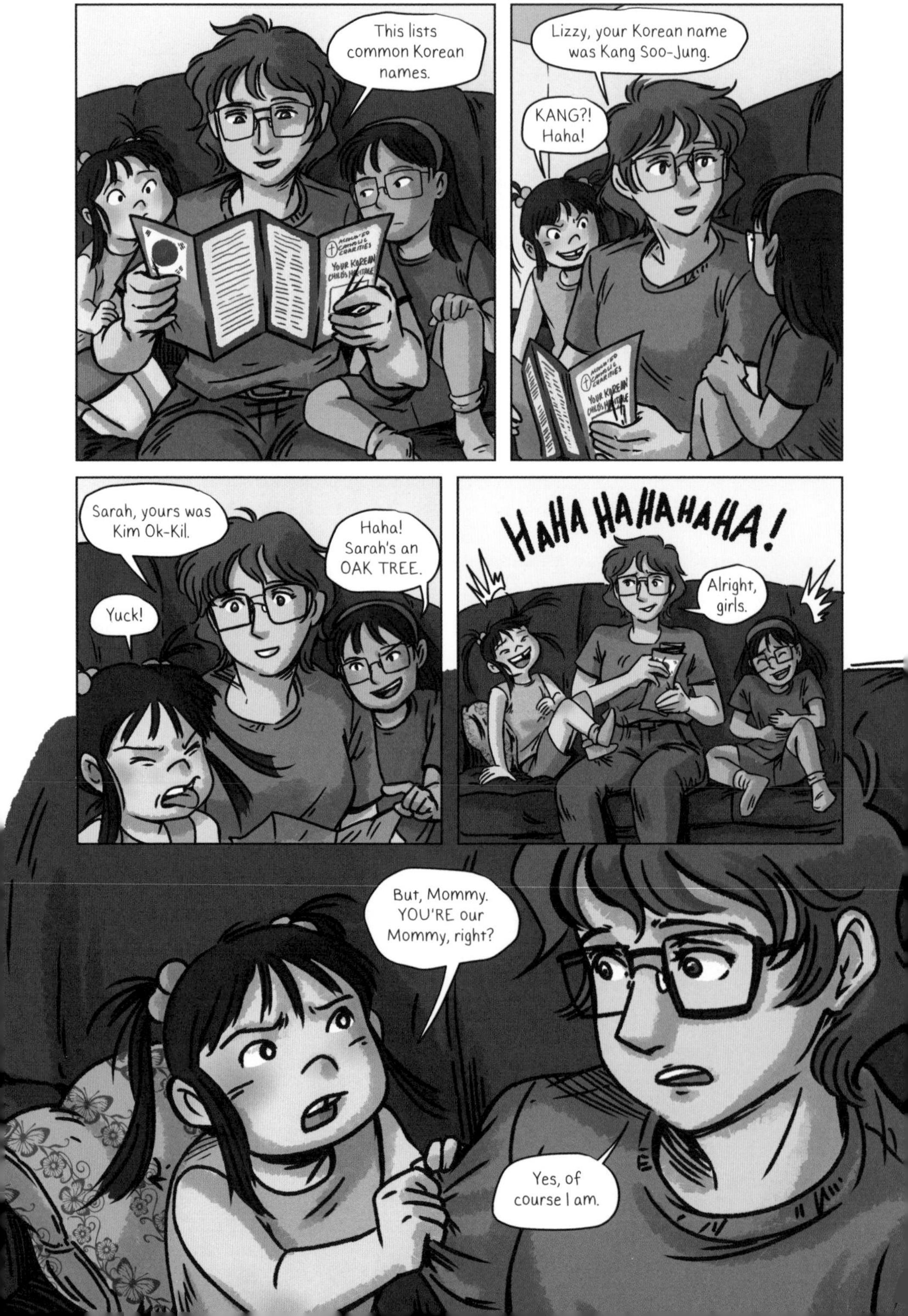
This lists common Korean names.
Lizzy, your Korean name was Kang Soo-Jung.
KANG?! Haha!
YOUR KOREAN CHILD'S HERITAGE
Sarah, yours was Kim Ok-Kil.
Haha! Sarah's an OAK TREE.
Yuck!
HAHA HAHAHAHA!
Alright, girls.
But, Mommy. YOU'RE our Mommy, right?
Yes, of course I am.

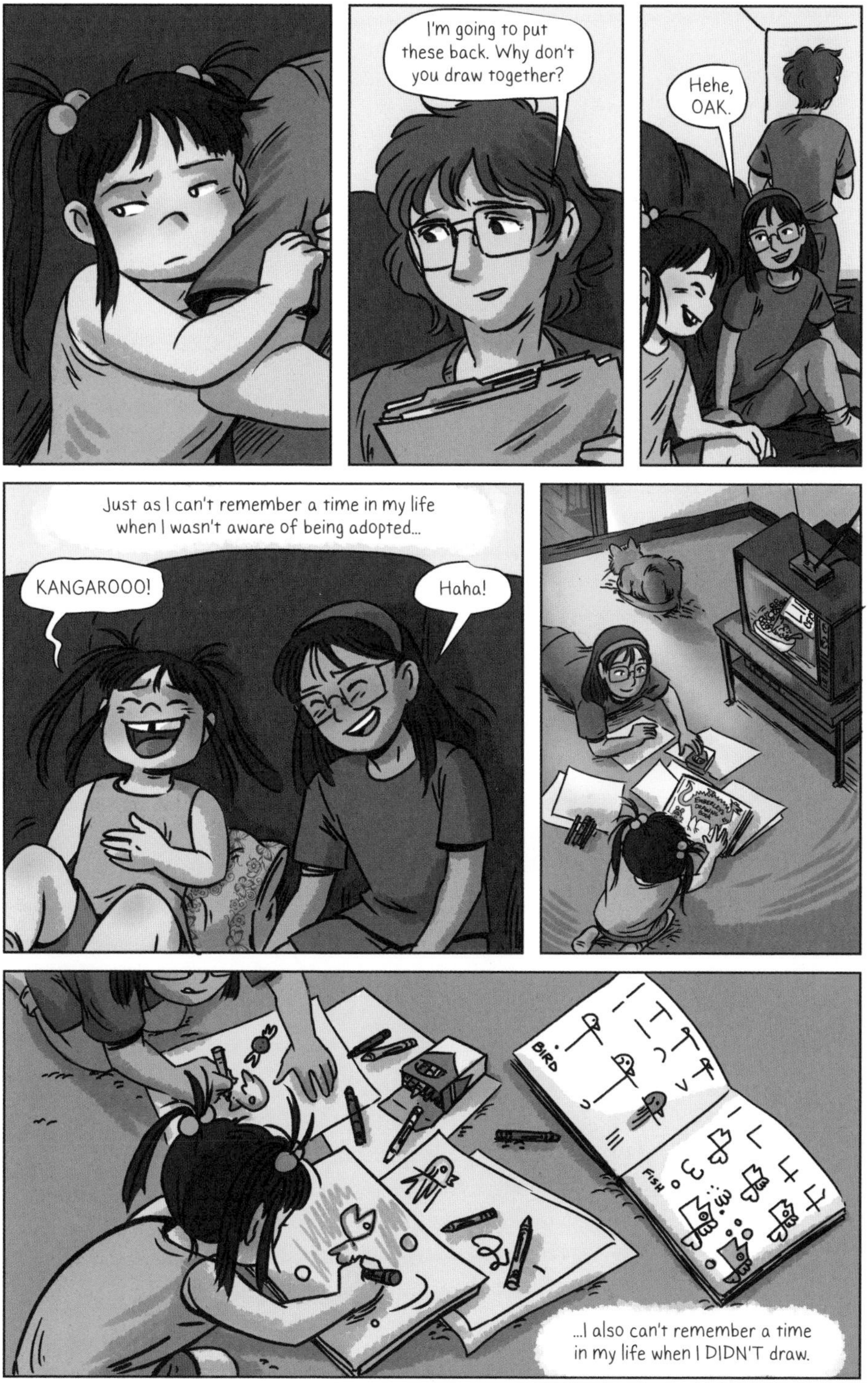
I'm going to put these back. Why don't you draw together?
Hehe, OAK.
Just as I can't remember a time in my life when I wasn't aware of being adopted...
KANGAROOO!
Haha!
BIRD
FISH
...I also can't remember a time in my life when I DIDN'T draw.

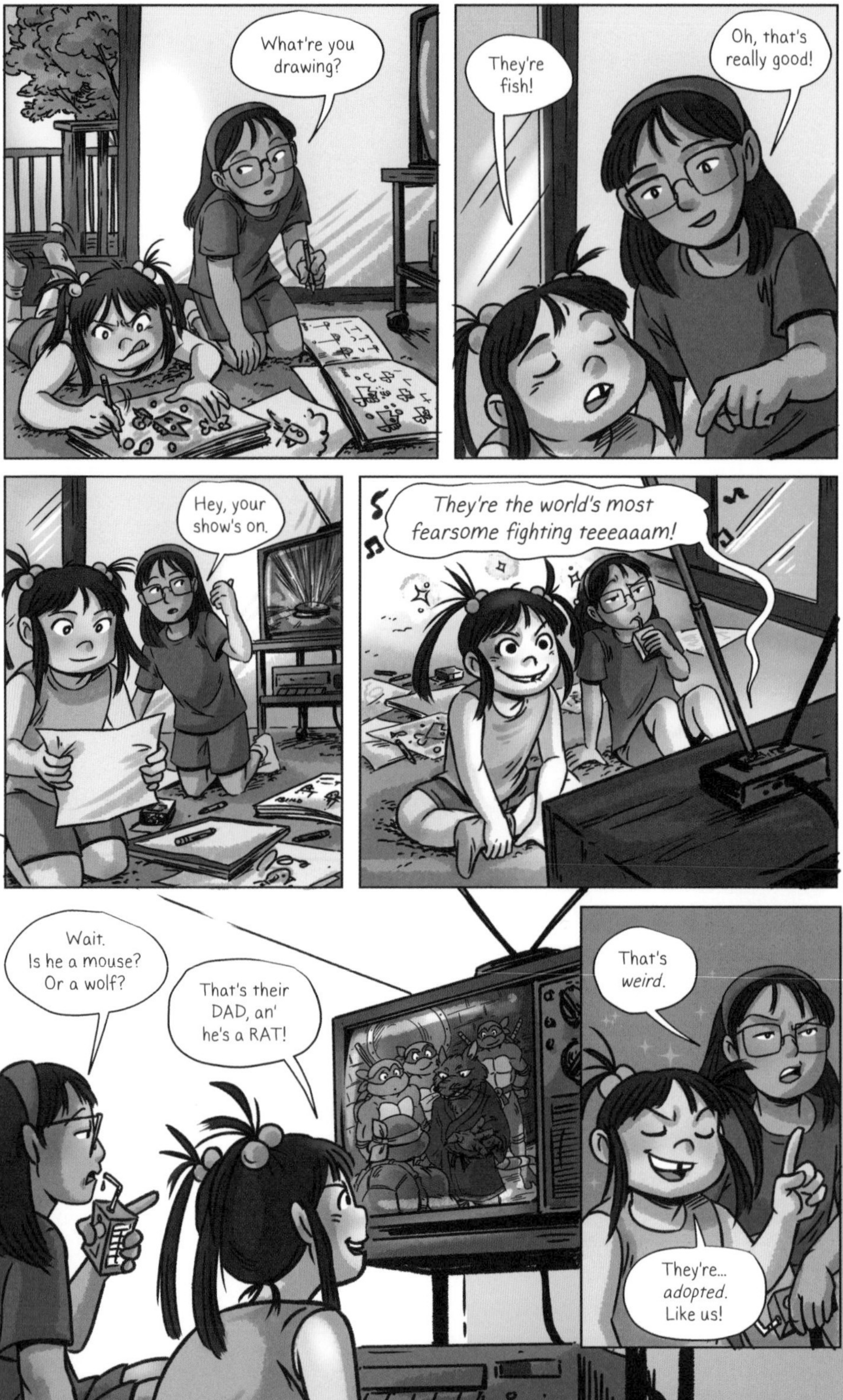

What're you drawing?
They're fish!
Oh, that's really good!
Hey, your show's on.
They're the world's most fearsome fighting teeeaaam!
Wait. Is he a mouse? Or a wolf?
That's their DAD, an' he's a RAT!
That's weird.
They're... adopted. Like us!

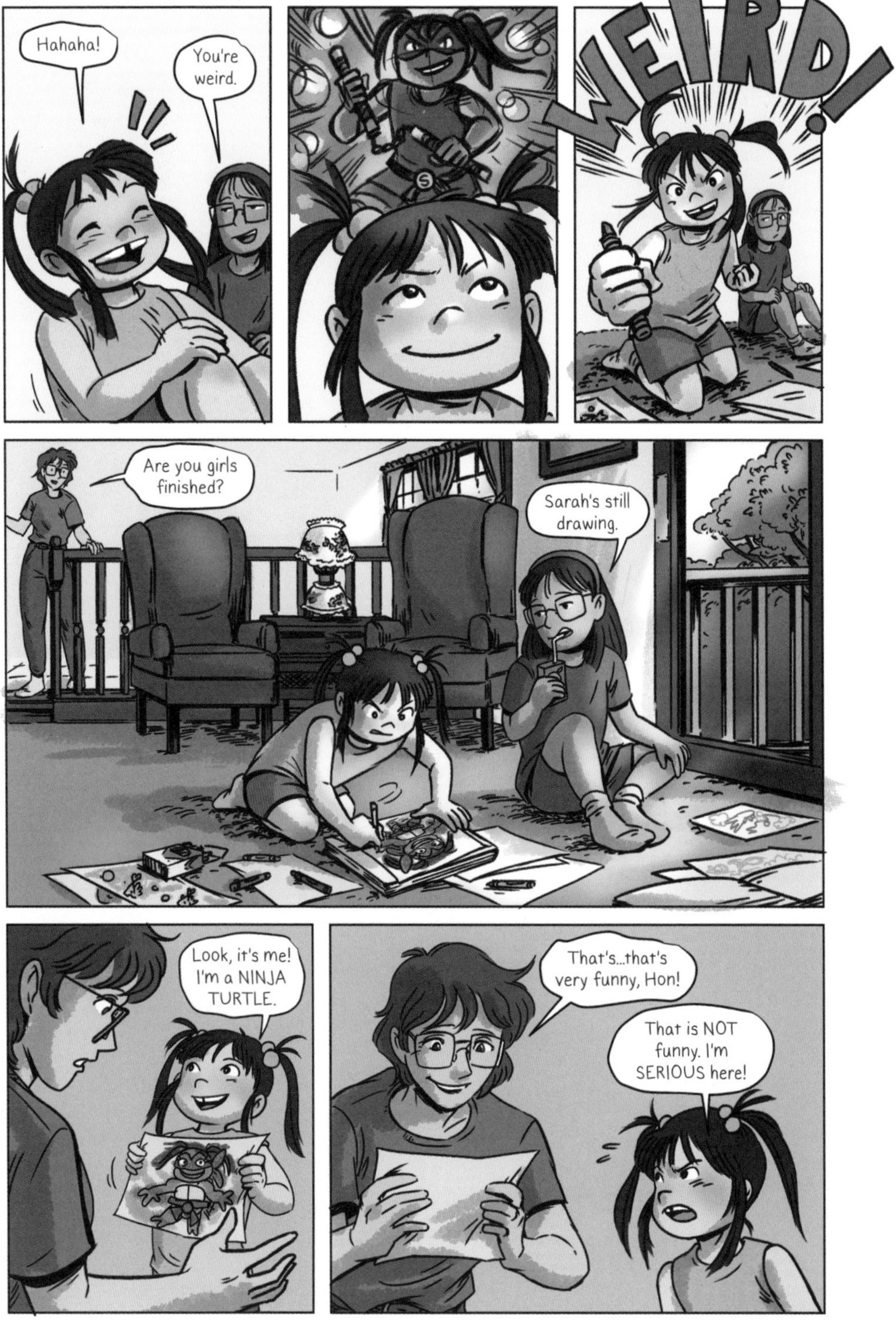
Hahaha!
You're weird.
WEIRD!
Are you girls finished?
Sarah's still drawing.
Look, it's me! I'm a NINJA TURTLE.
That's...that's very funny, Hon!
That is NOT funny. I'm SERIOUS here!

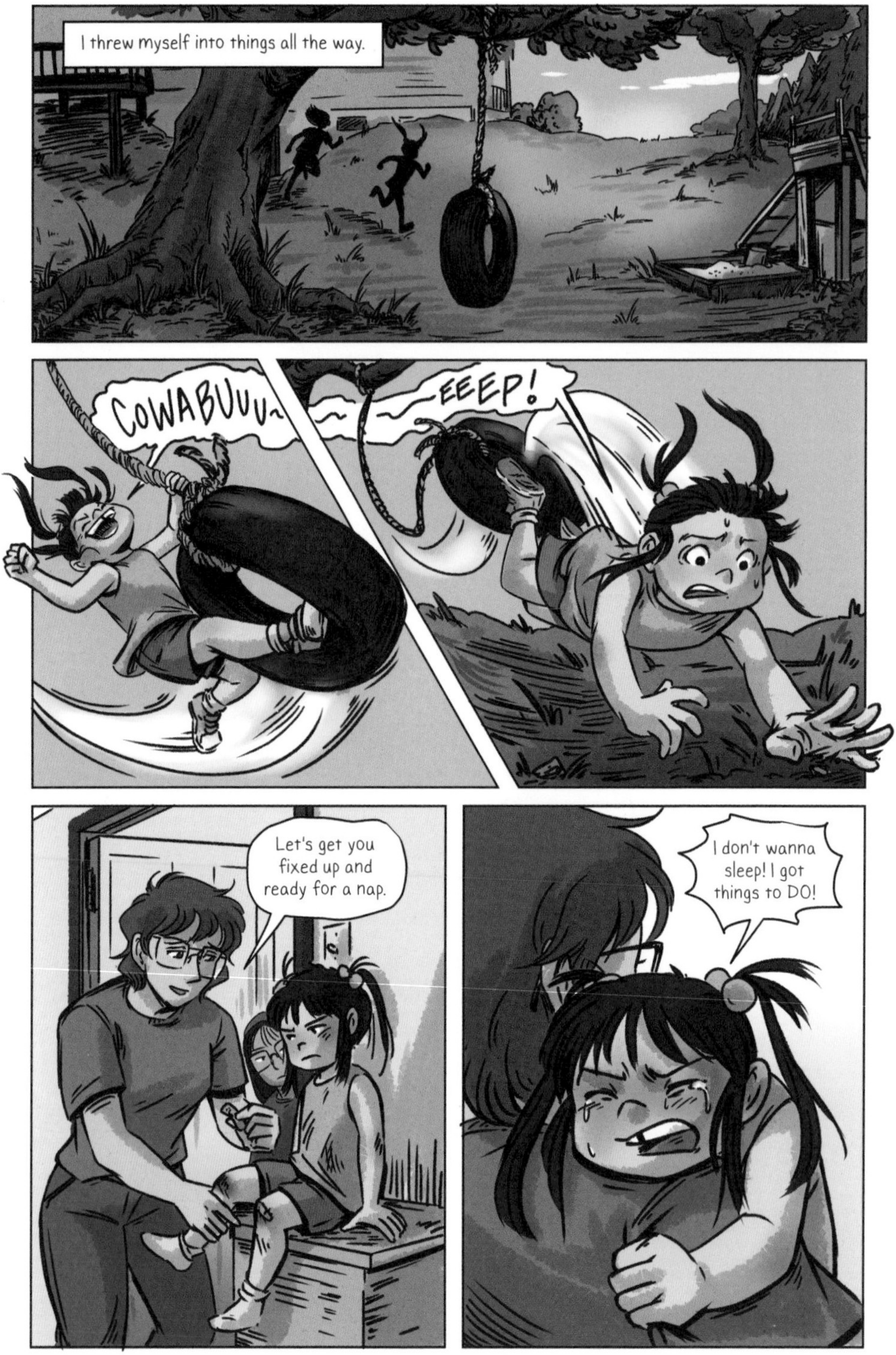
I threw myself into things all the way.
COWABUUU~
~—EEEP!
Let's get you fixed up and ready for a nap.
I don't wanna sleep! I got things to DO!

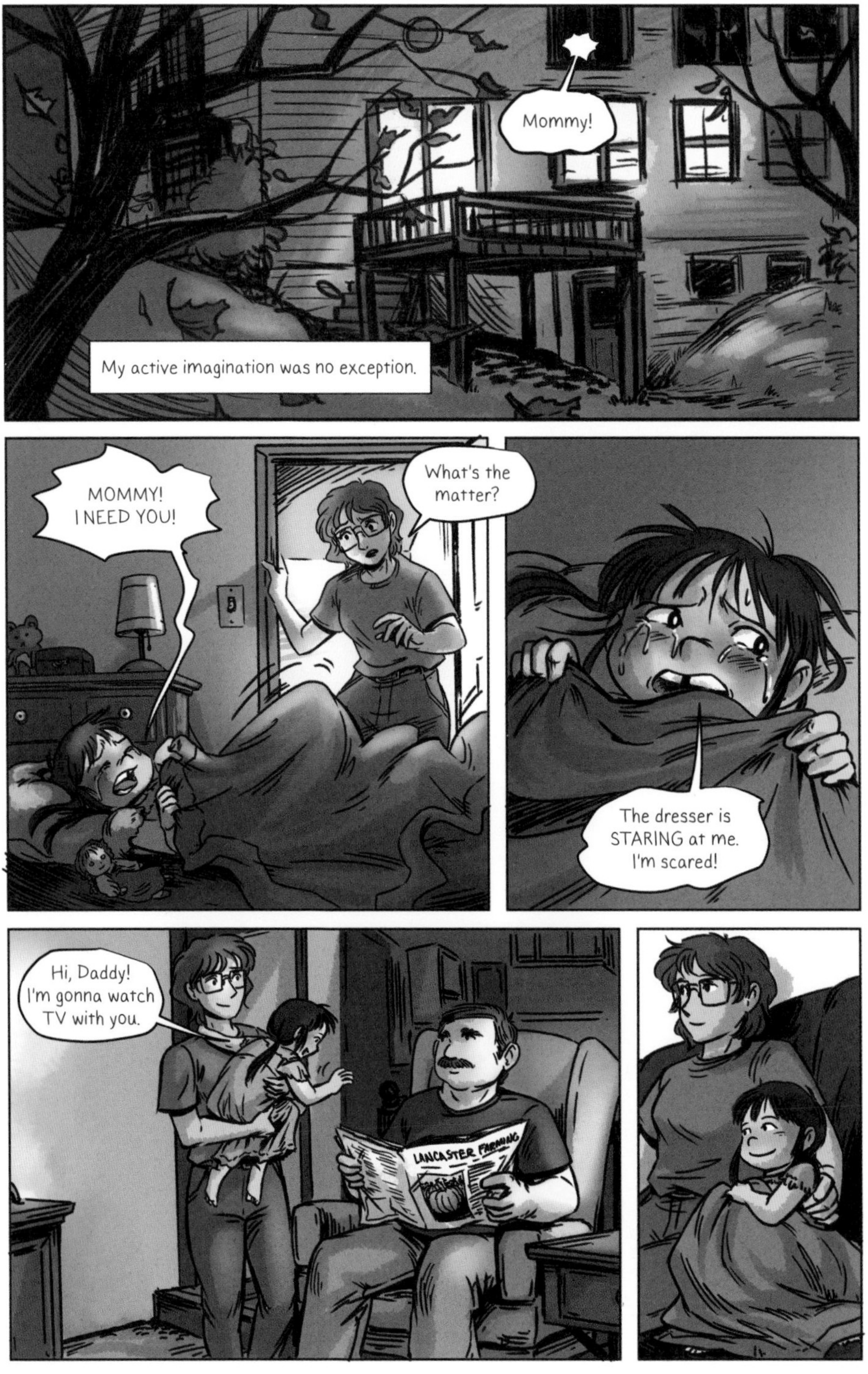
Mommy!
My active imagination was no exception.
MOMMY! I NEED YOU!
What's the matter?
The dresser is STARING at me. I'm scared!
Hi, Daddy! I'm gonna watch TV with you.
LANCASTER FARMING

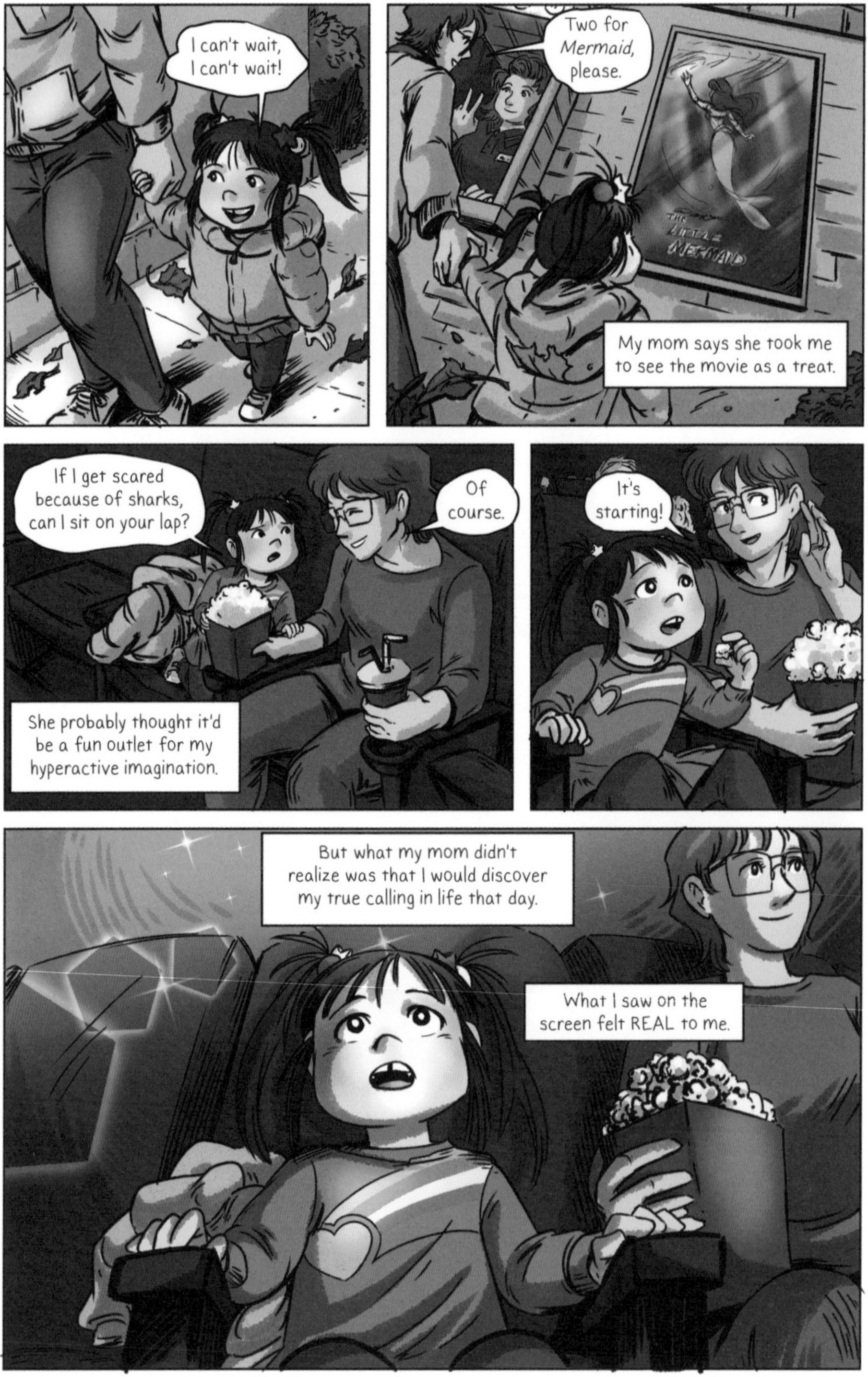
I can't wait, I can't wait!
Two for *Mermaid*, please.
THE LITTLE MERMAID
My mom says she took me to see the movie as a treat.
If I get scared because of sharks, can I sit on your lap?
Of course.
She probably thought it'd be a fun outlet for my hyperactive imagination.
It's starting!
But what my mom didn't realize was that I would discover my true calling in life that day.
What I saw on the screen felt REAL to me.

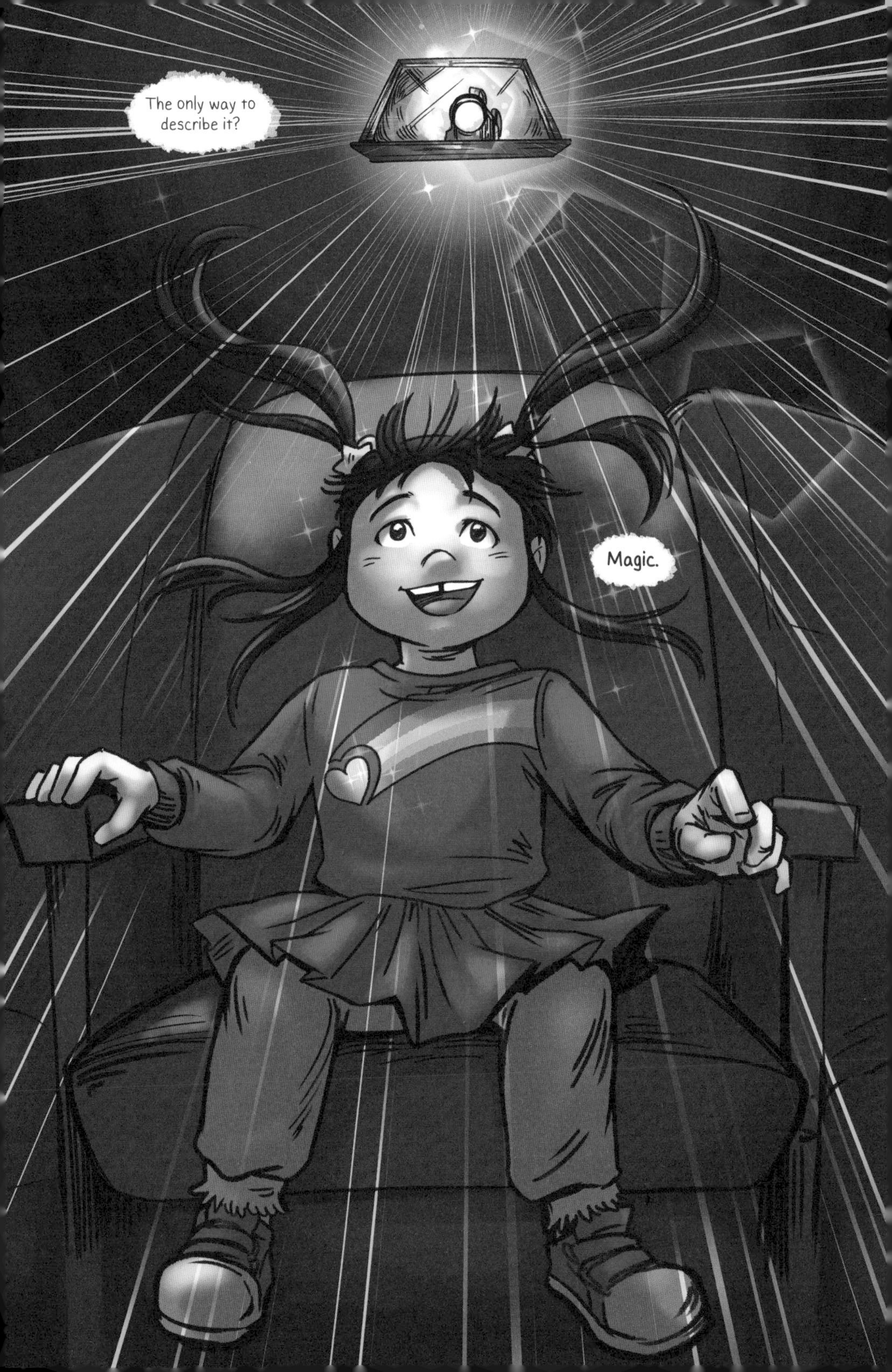
The only way to describe it?
Magic.

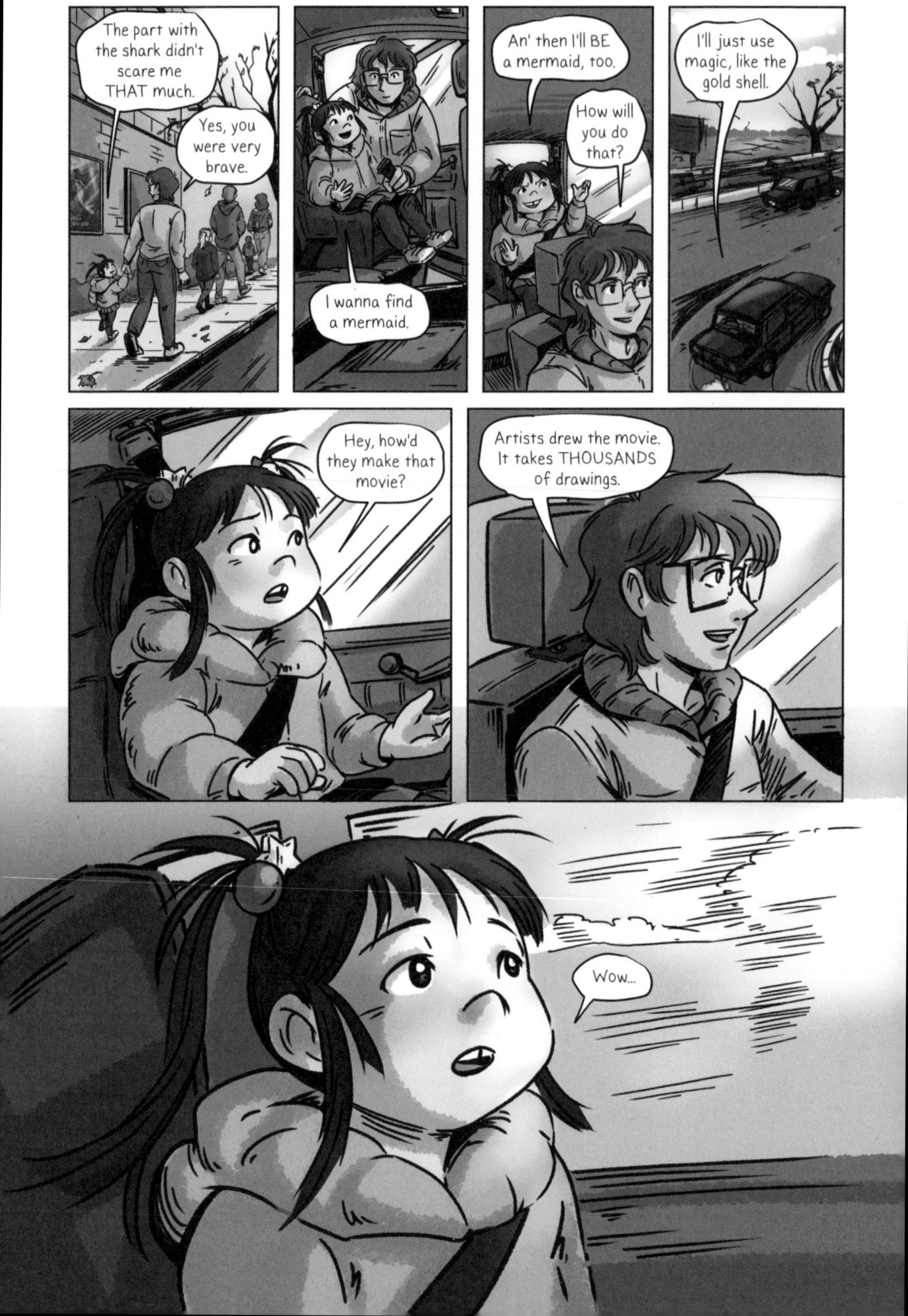
The part with the shark didn't scare me THAT much.
Yes, you were very brave.
I wanna find a mermaid.
An' then I'll BE a mermaid, too.
How will you do that?
I'll just use magic, like the gold shell.
Hey, how'd they make that movie?
Artists drew the movie. It takes THOUSANDS of drawings.
Wow...

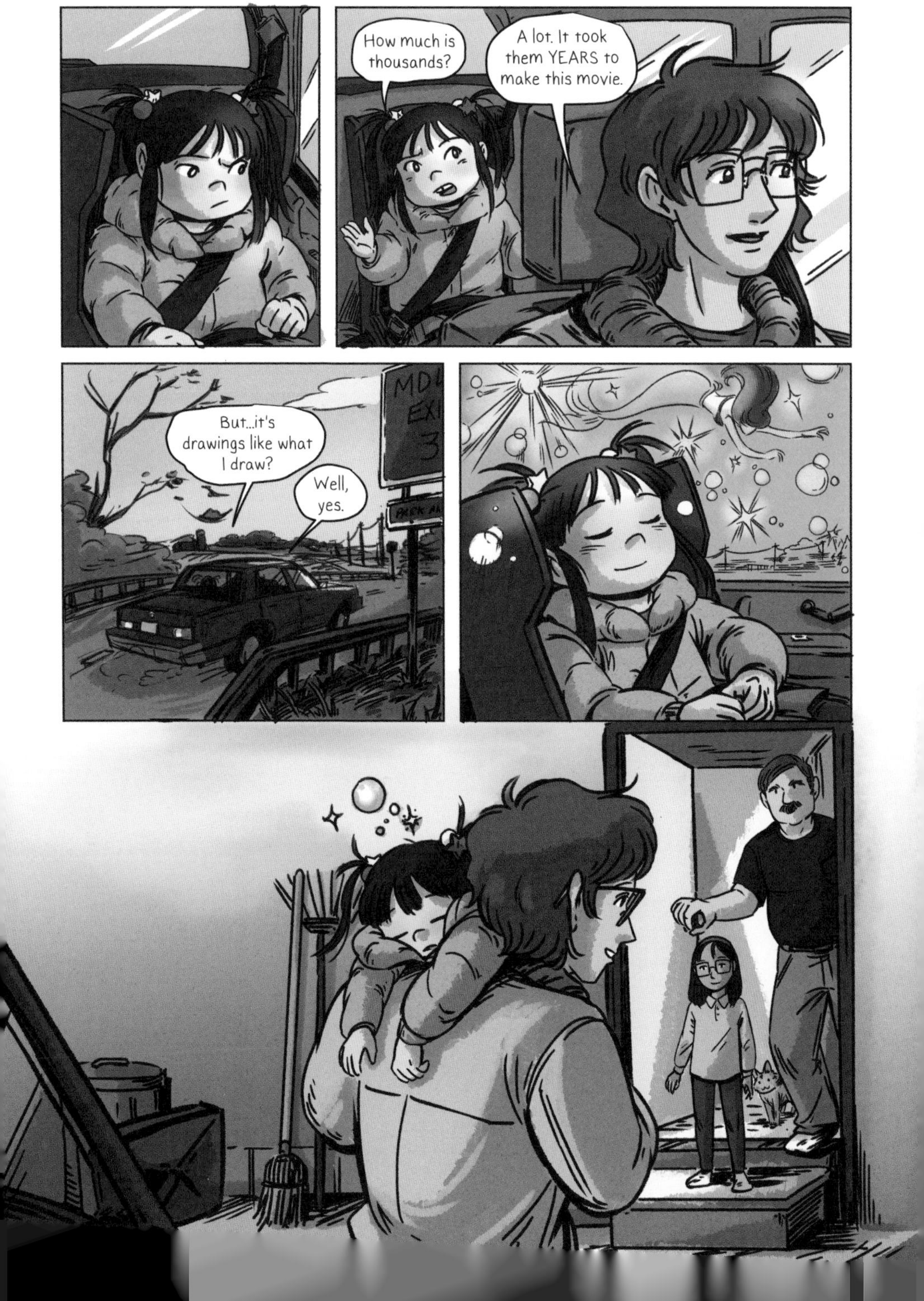
How much is thousands?
A lot. It took them YEARS to make this movie.
But...it's drawings like what I draw?
Well, yes.

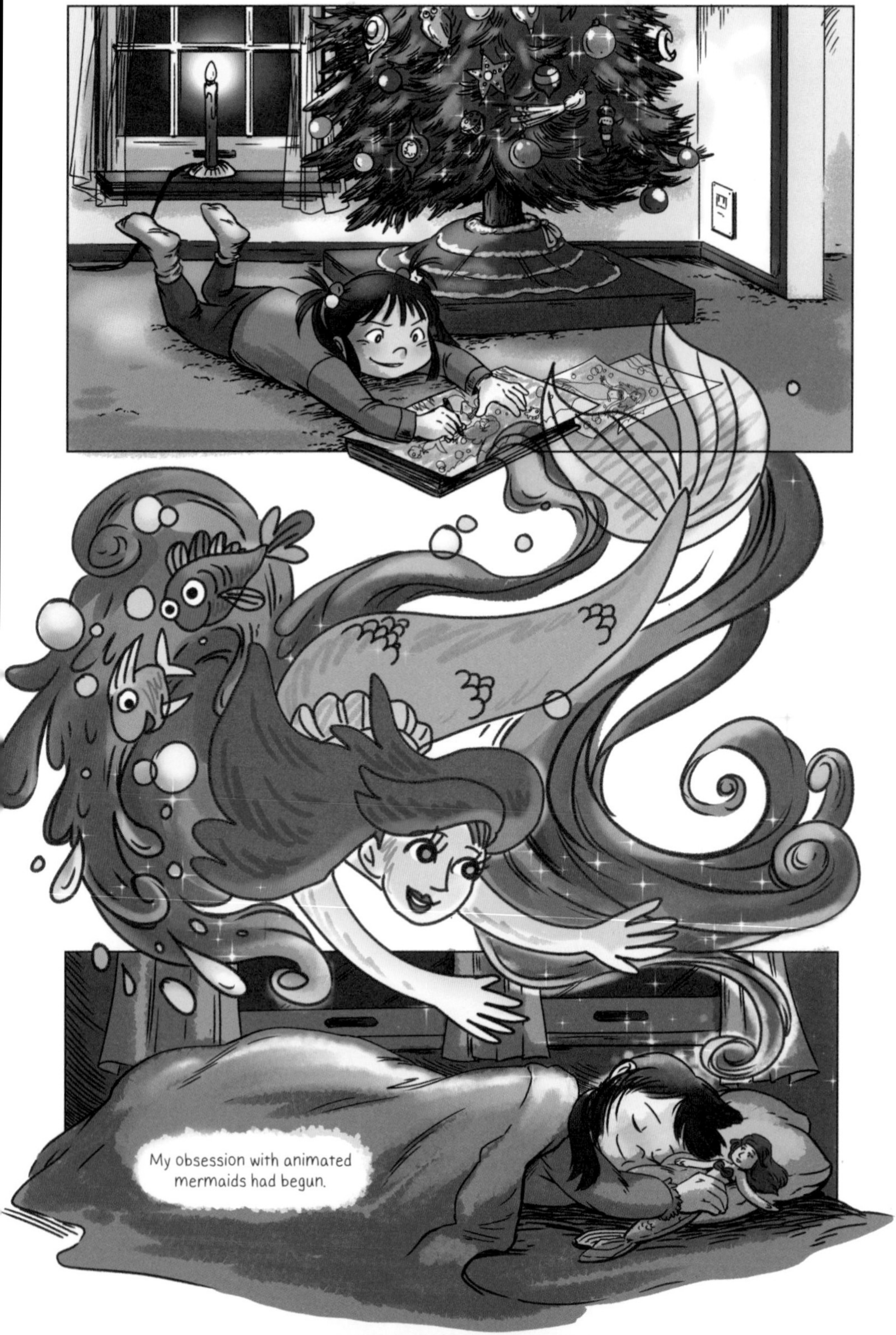
My obsession with animated mermaids had begun.

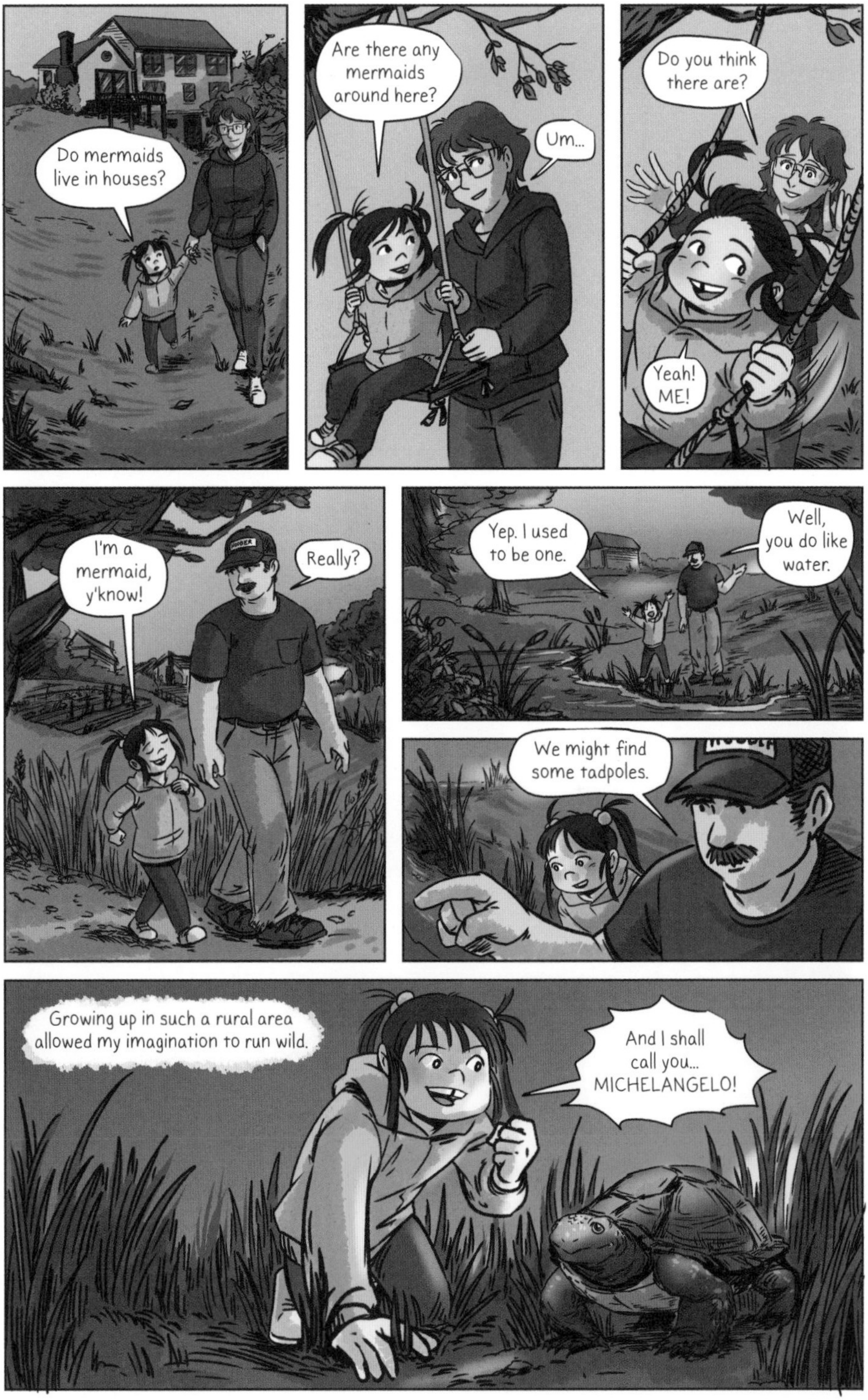
Do mermaids live in houses?
Are there any mermaids around here?
Um...
Do you think there are?
Yeah! ME!
I'm a mermaid, y'know!
Really?
Yep. I used to be one.
Well, you do like water.
We might find some tadpoles.
Growing up in such a rural area allowed my imagination to run wild.
And I shall call you... MICHELANGELO!

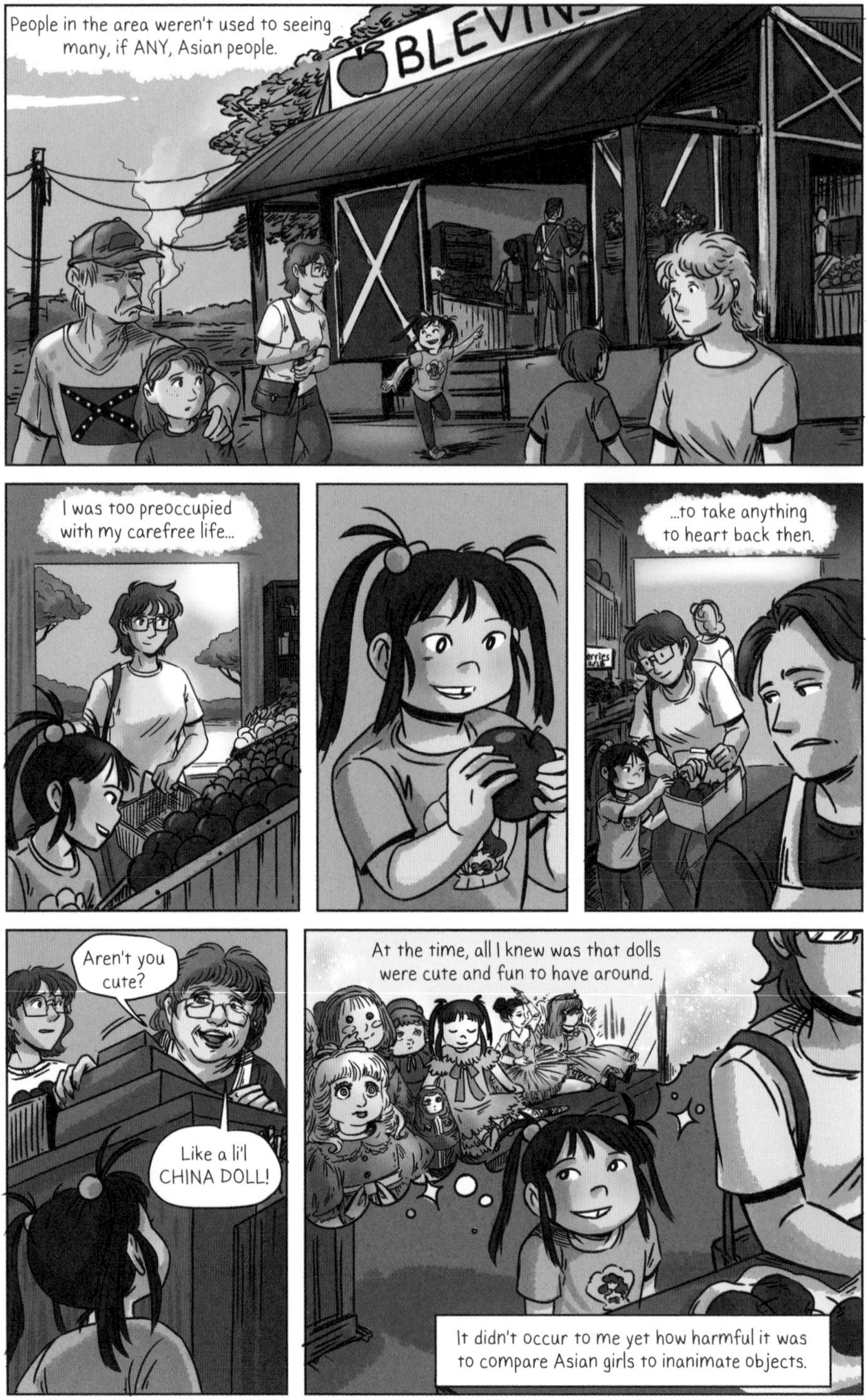
People in the area weren't used to seeing many, if ANY, Asian people.
BLEVINS
I was too preoccupied with my carefree life...
...to take anything to heart back then.
Aren't you cute?
Like a li'l CHINA DOLL!
At the time, all I knew was that dolls were cute and fun to have around.
It didn't occur to me yet how harmful it was to compare Asian girls to inanimate objects.

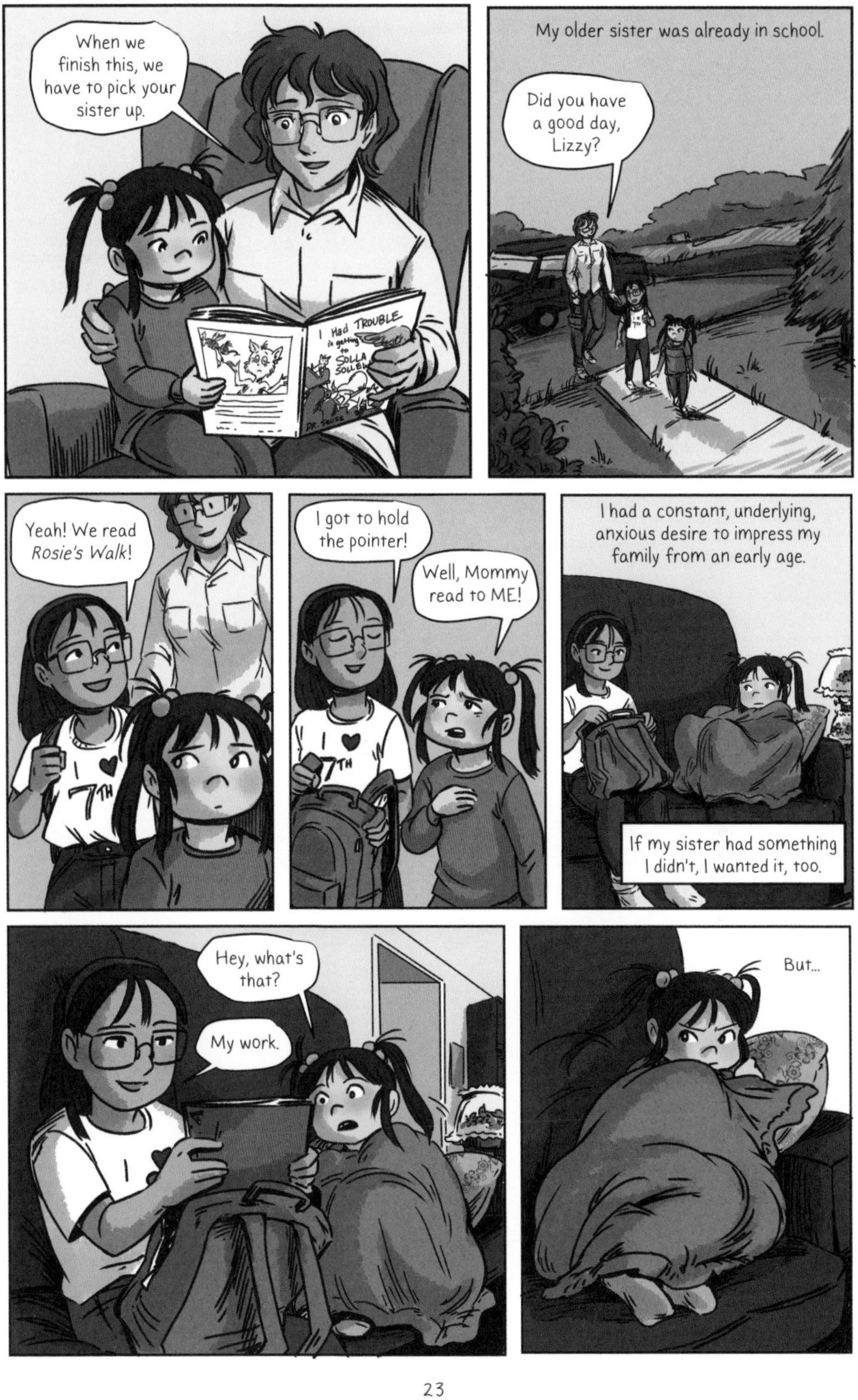
When we finish this, we have to pick your sister up.
I Had TROUBLE in getting to SOLLA SOLLEW
DR. SEUSS
My older sister was already in school.
Did you have a good day, Lizzy?
Yeah! We read *Rosie's Walk*!
I got to hold the pointer!
Well, Mommy read to ME!
I had a constant, underlying, anxious desire to impress my family from an early age.
If my sister had something I didn't, I wanted it, too.
Hey, what's that?
My work.
But...

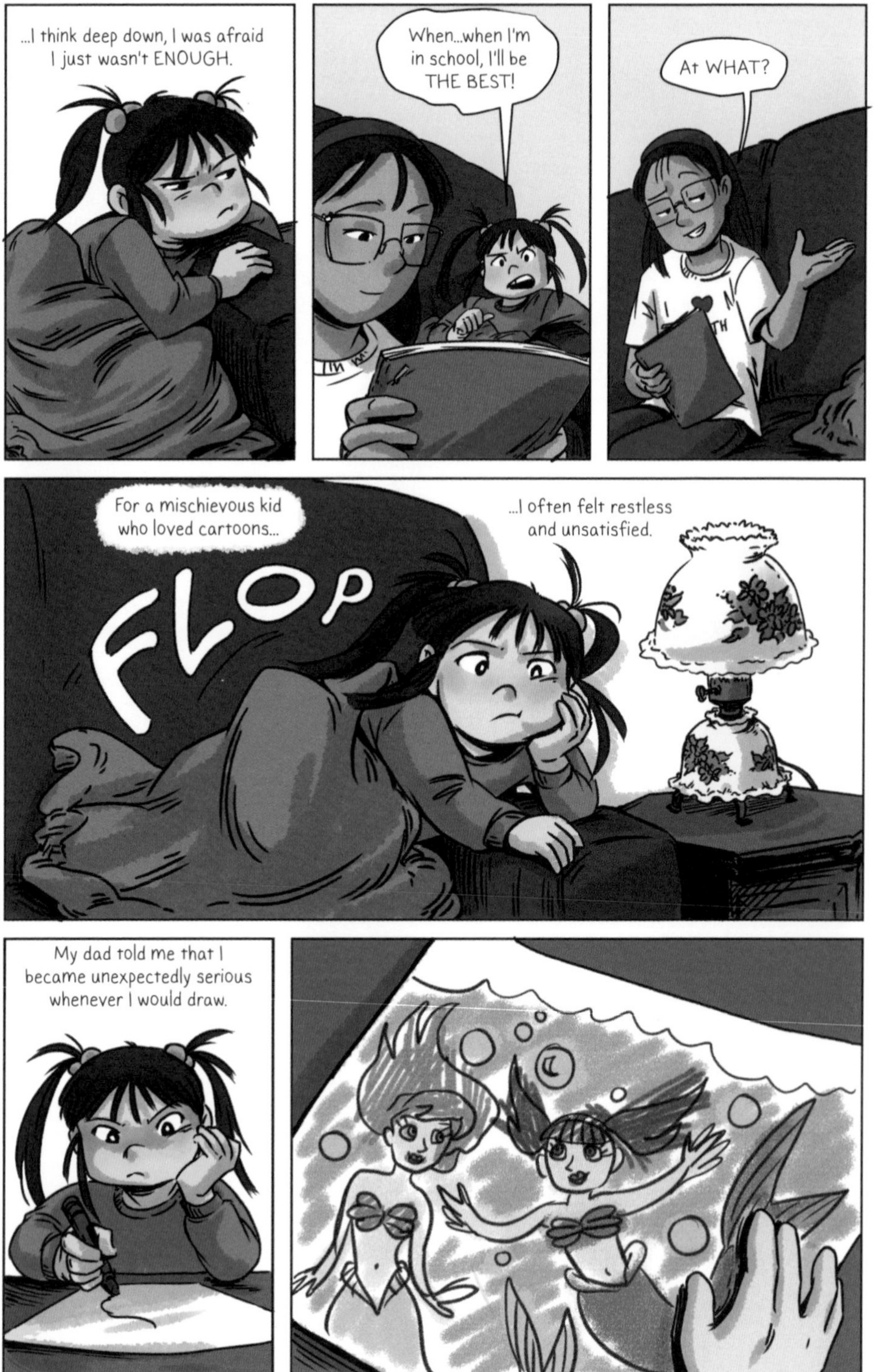
...I think deep down, I was afraid I just wasn't ENOUGH.
When...when I'm in school, I'll be THE BEST!
At WHAT?
For a mischievous kid who loved cartoons...
...I often felt restless and unsatisfied.
FLOP
My dad told me that I became unexpectedly serious whenever I would draw.

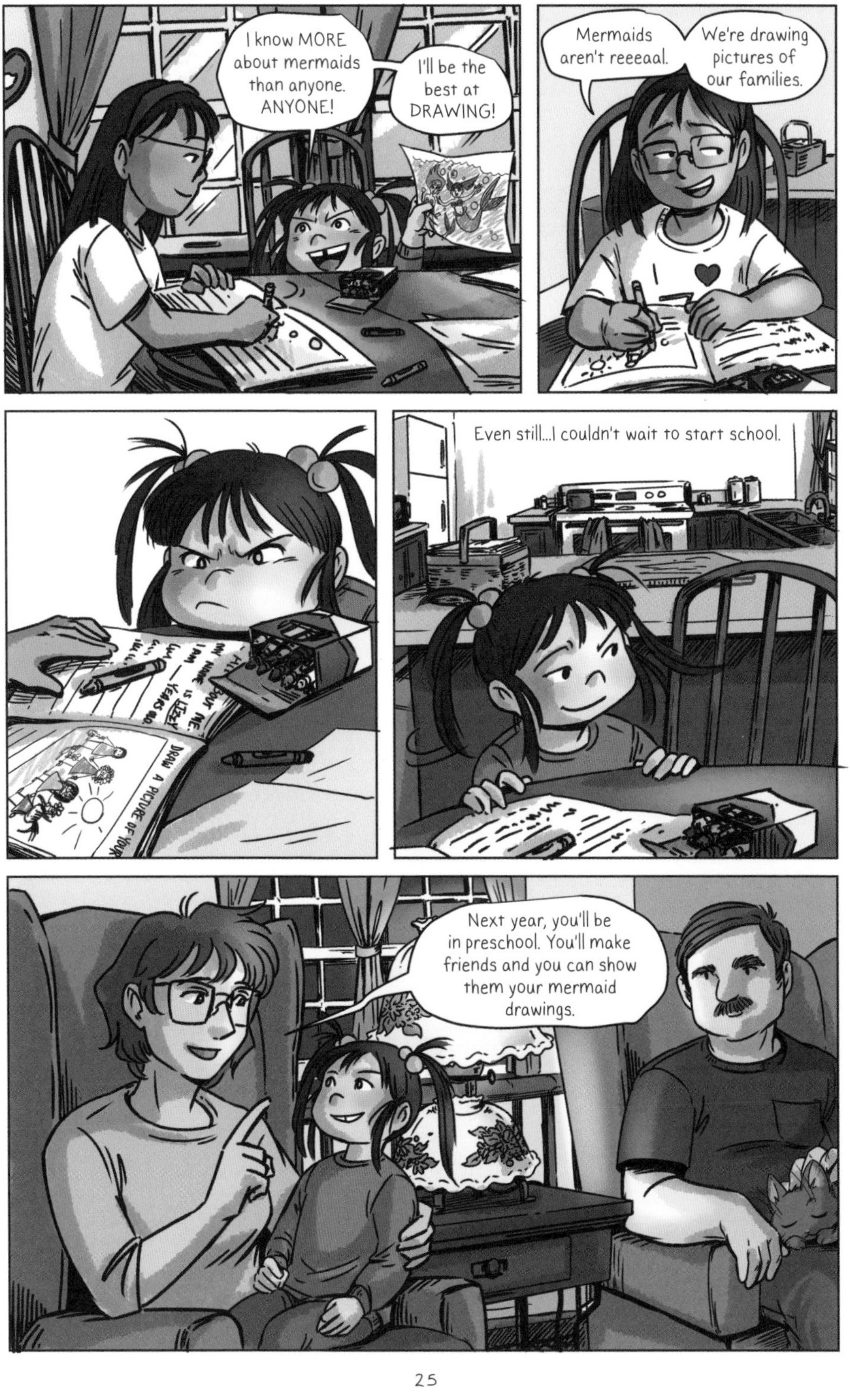
I know MORE about mermaids than anyone. ANYONE!
I'll be the best at DRAWING!
Mermaids aren't reeeaal.
We're drawing pictures of our families.
DRAW A PICTURE OF YOUR
Even still...I couldn't wait to start school.
Next year, you'll be in preschool. You'll make friends and you can show them your mermaid drawings.

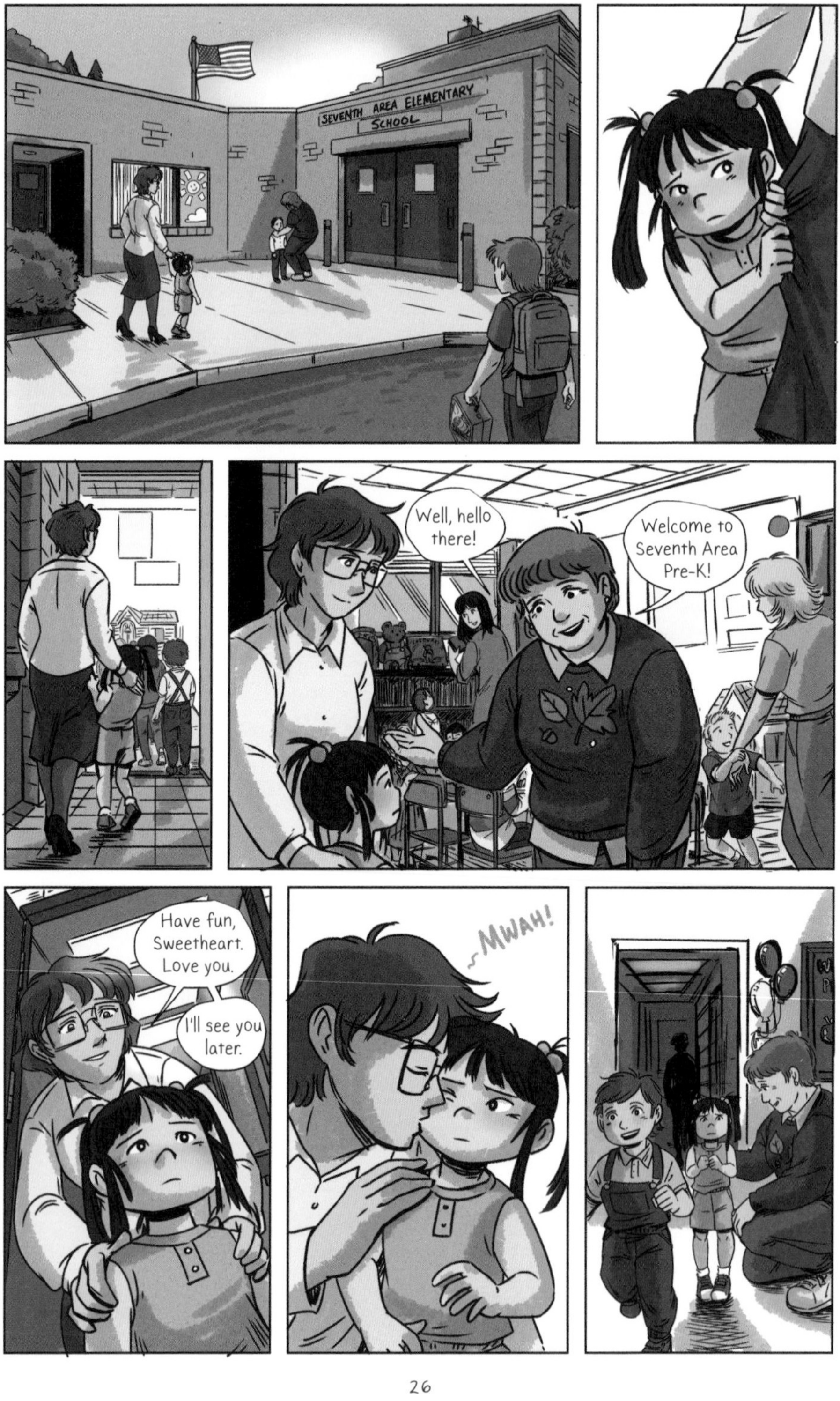
SEVENTH AREA ELEMENTARY
SCHOOL
Well, hello there!
Welcome to Seventh Area Pre-K!
Have fun, Sweetheart. Love you.
I'll see you later.
MWAH!

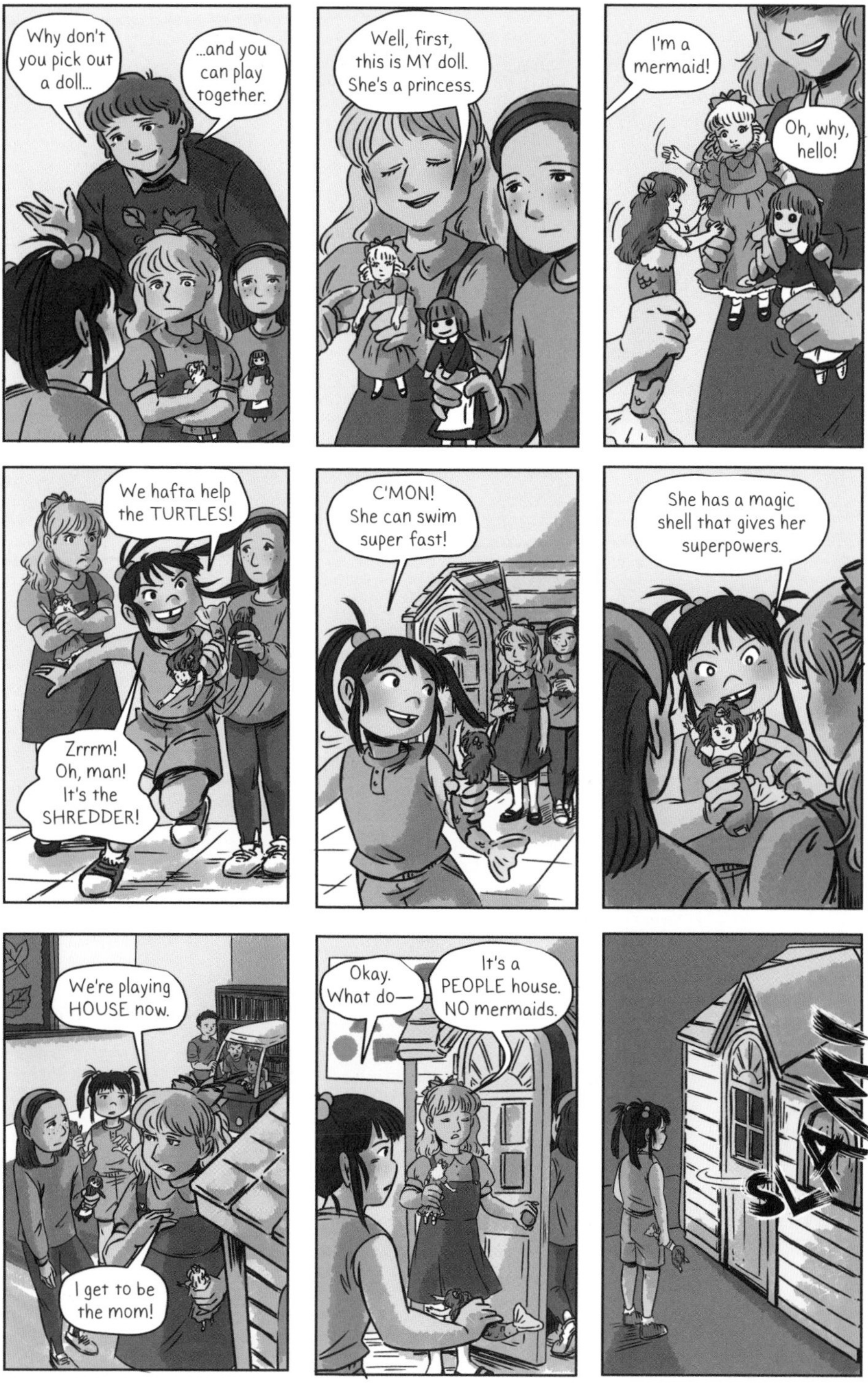
Why don't you pick out a doll...
...and you can play together.
Well, first, this is MY doll. She's a princess.
I'm a mermaid!
Oh, why, hello!
We hafta help the TURTLES!
Zrrrm! Oh, man! It's the SHREDDER!
C'MON! She can swim super fast!
She has a magic shell that gives her superpowers.
We're playing HOUSE now.
I get to be the mom!
Okay. What do—
It's a PEOPLE house. NO mermaids.
SLAM!

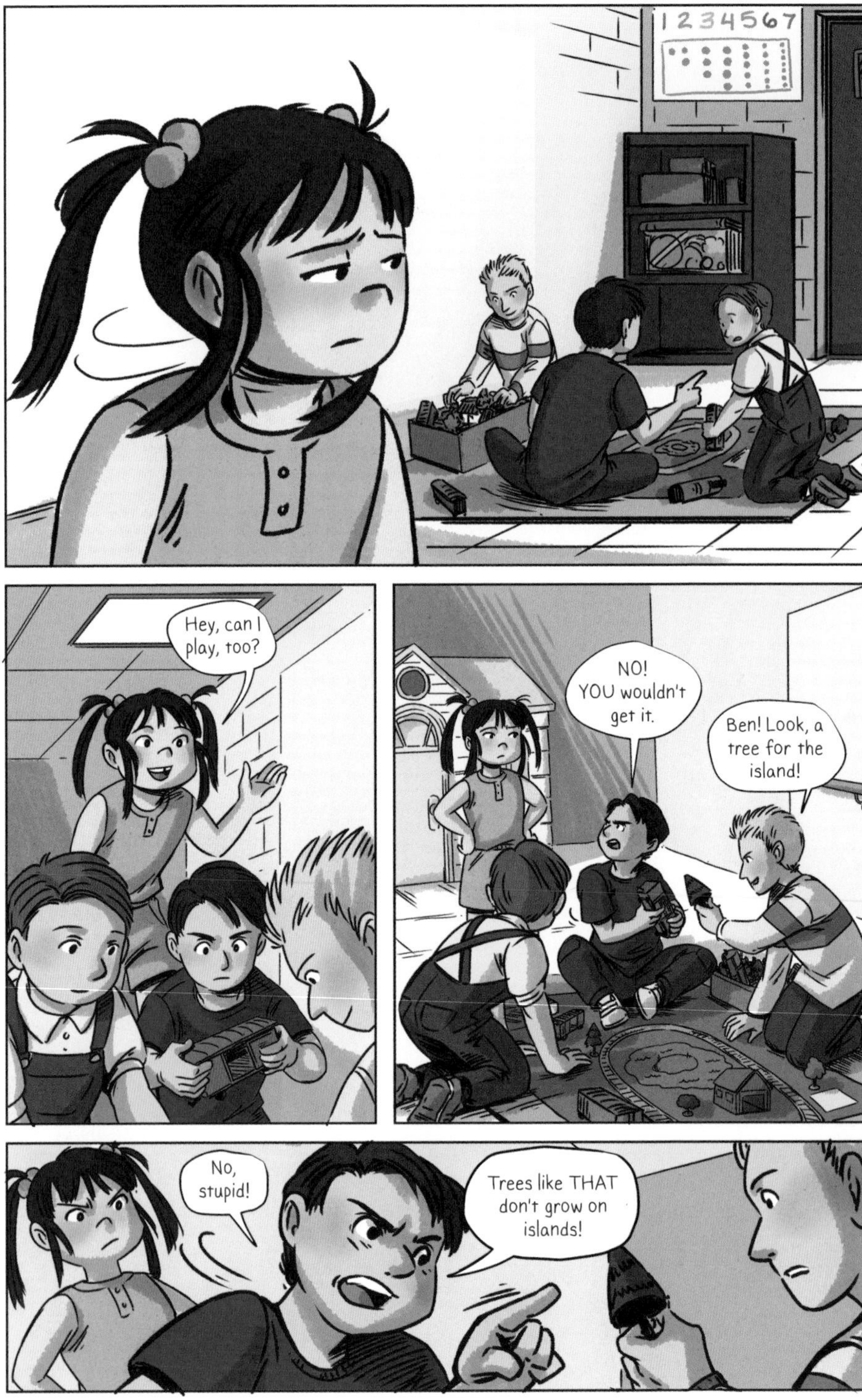
1234567
Hey, can I play, too?
NO! YOU wouldn't get it.
Ben! Look, a tree for the island!
No, stupid!
Trees like THAT don't grow on islands!

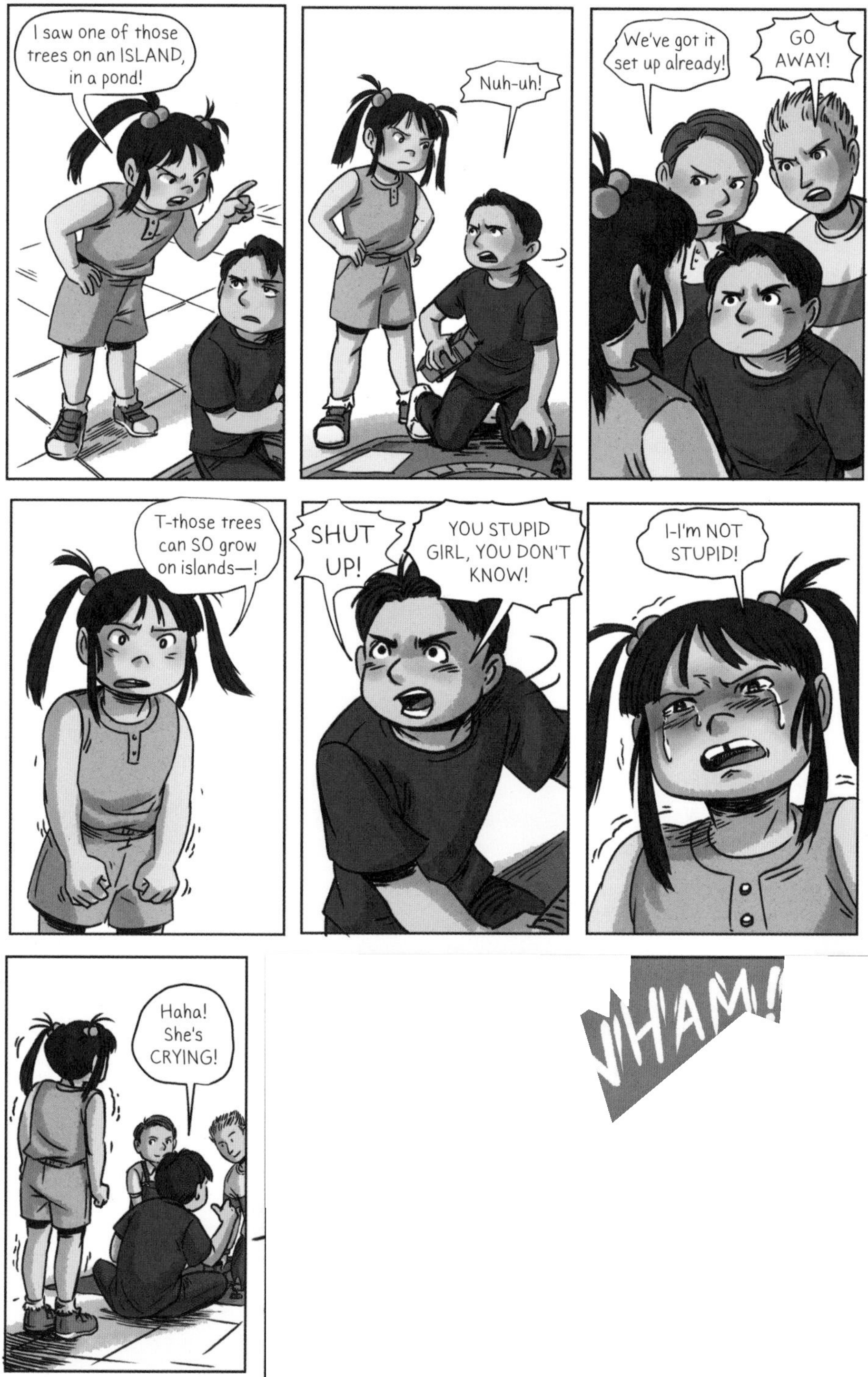
I saw one of those trees on an ISLAND, in a pond!
Nuh-uh!
We've got it set up already!
GO AWAY!
T-those trees can SO grow on islands—!
SHUT UP!
YOU STUPID GIRL, YOU DON'T KNOW!
I-I'm NOT STUPID!
Haha! She's CRYING!
WHAM!

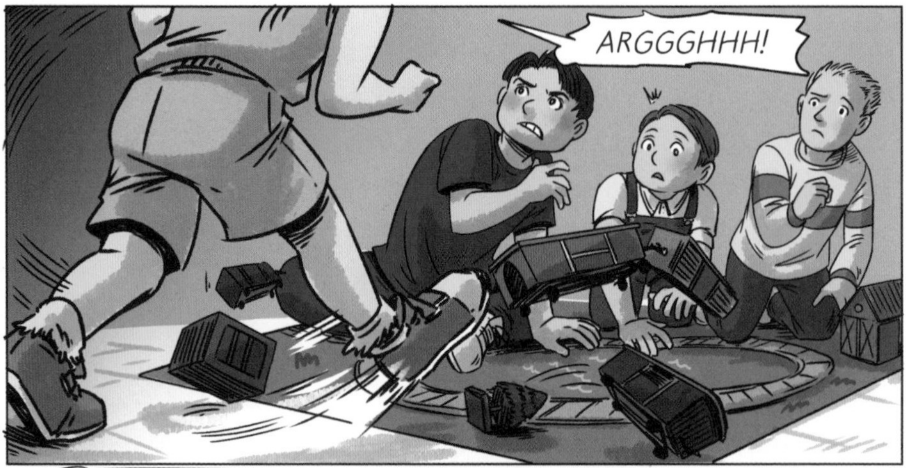
ARGGGHHH!

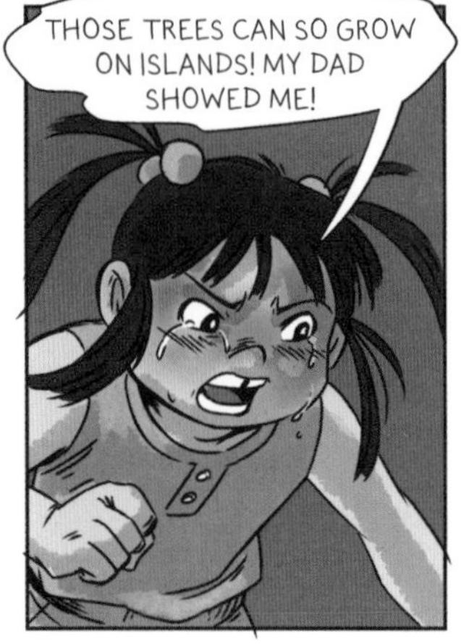
THOSE TREES CAN SO GROW ON ISLANDS! MY DAD SHOWED ME!

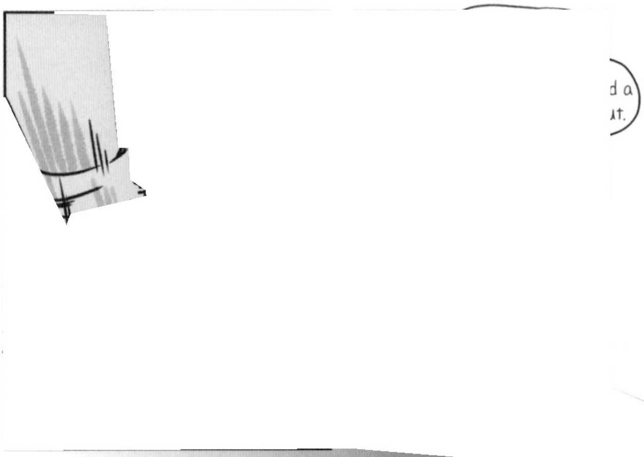

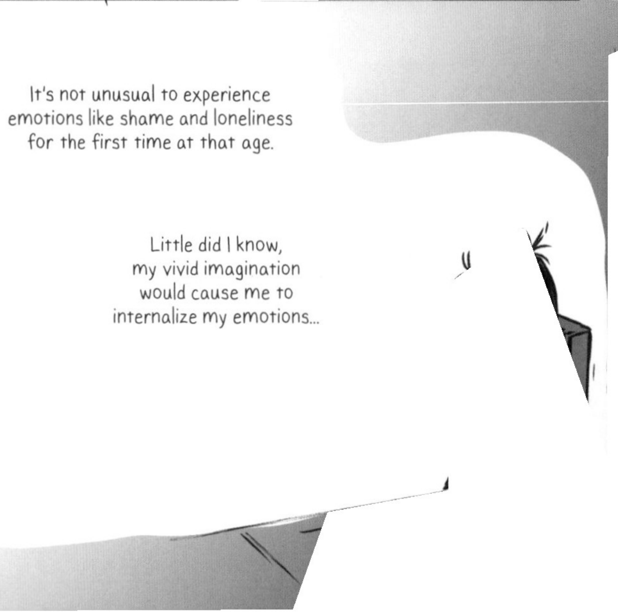
It's not unusual to experience emotions like shame and loneliness for the first time at that age.
Little did I know, my vivid imagination would cause me to internalize my emotions...

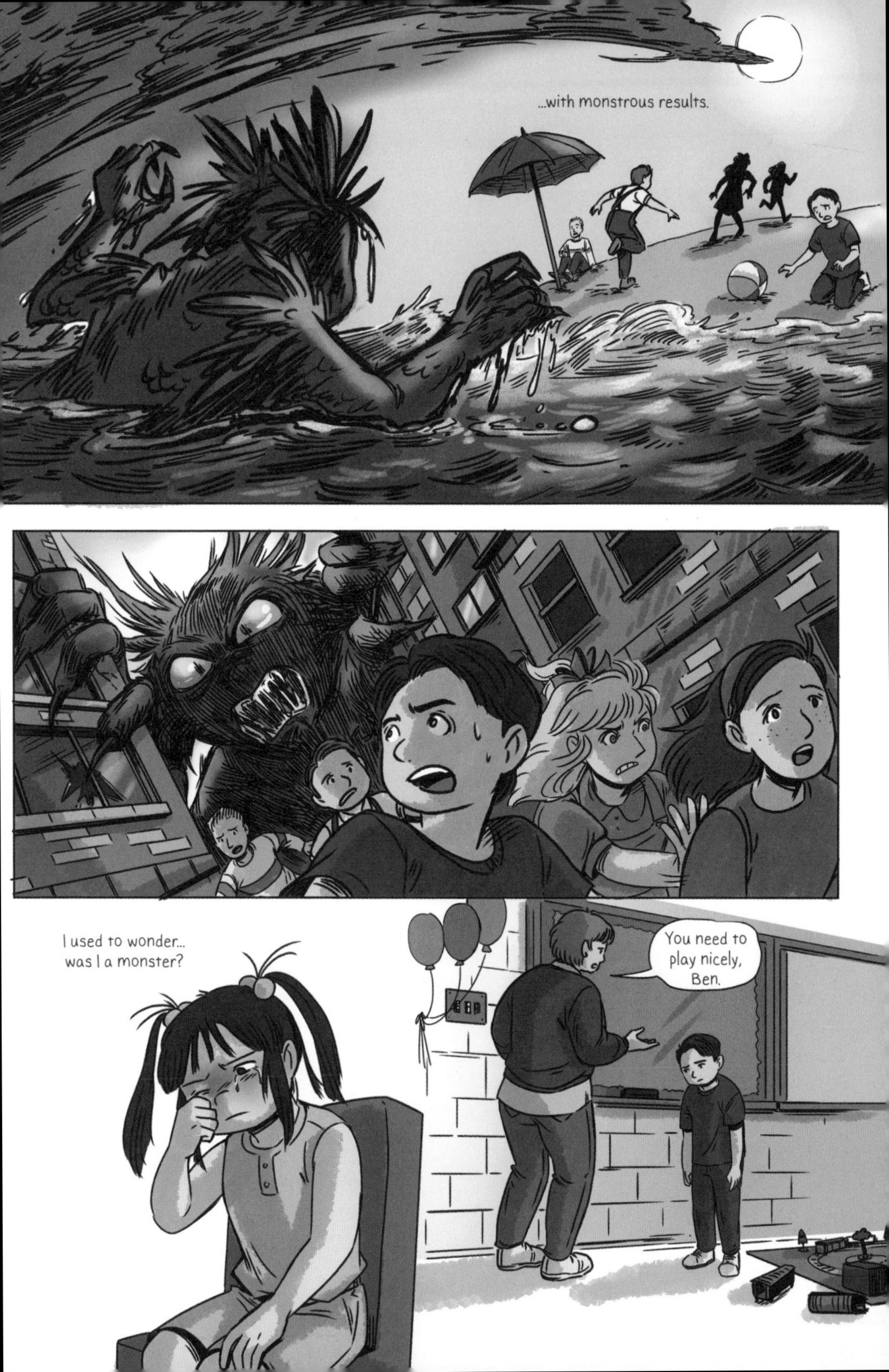
...with monstrous results.
I used to wonder... was I a monster?
You need to play nicely, Ben.

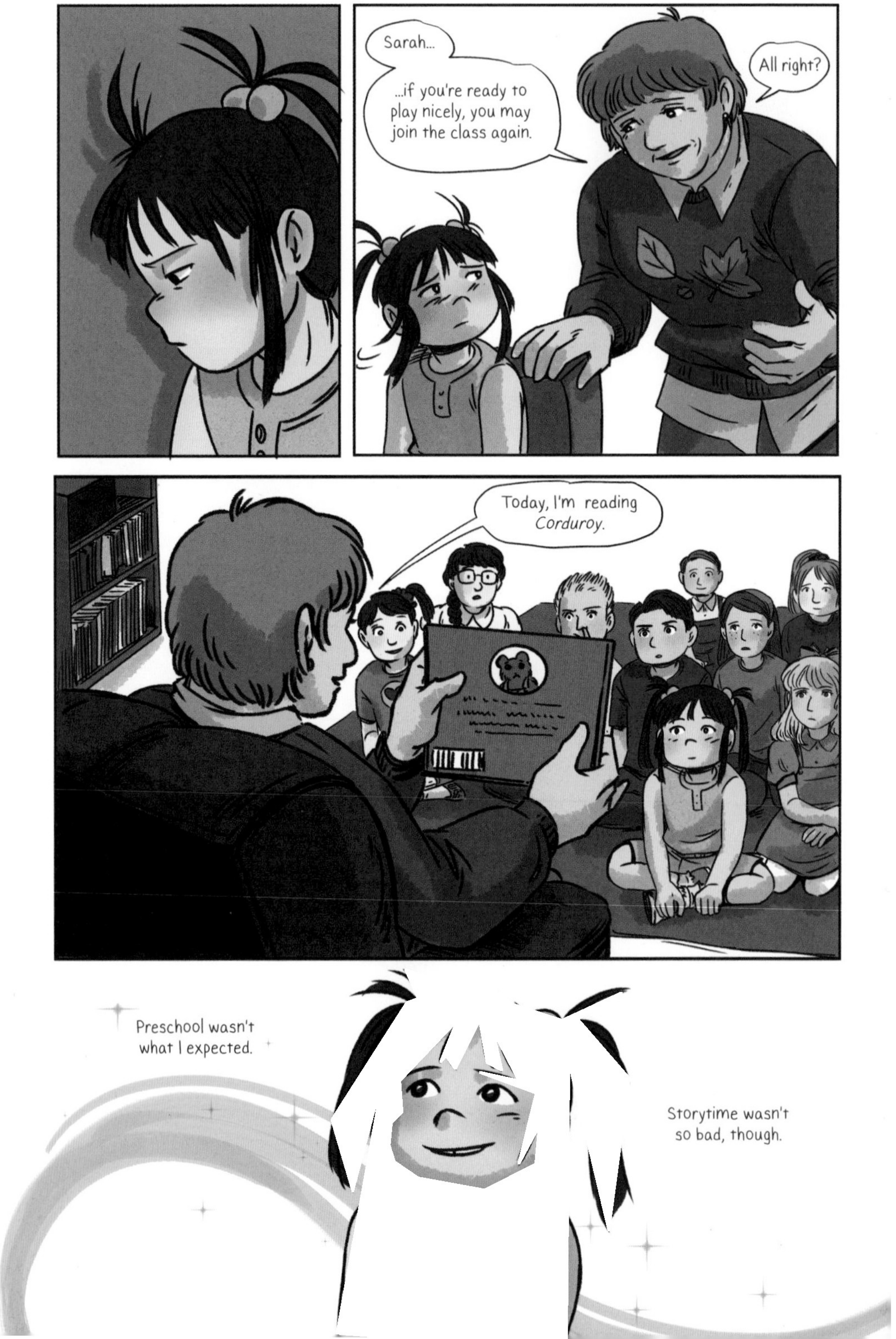

Sarah...
...if you're ready to play nicely, you may join the class again.
All right?
Today, I'm reading *Corduroy*.
Preschool wasn't what I expected.
Storytime wasn't so bad, though.

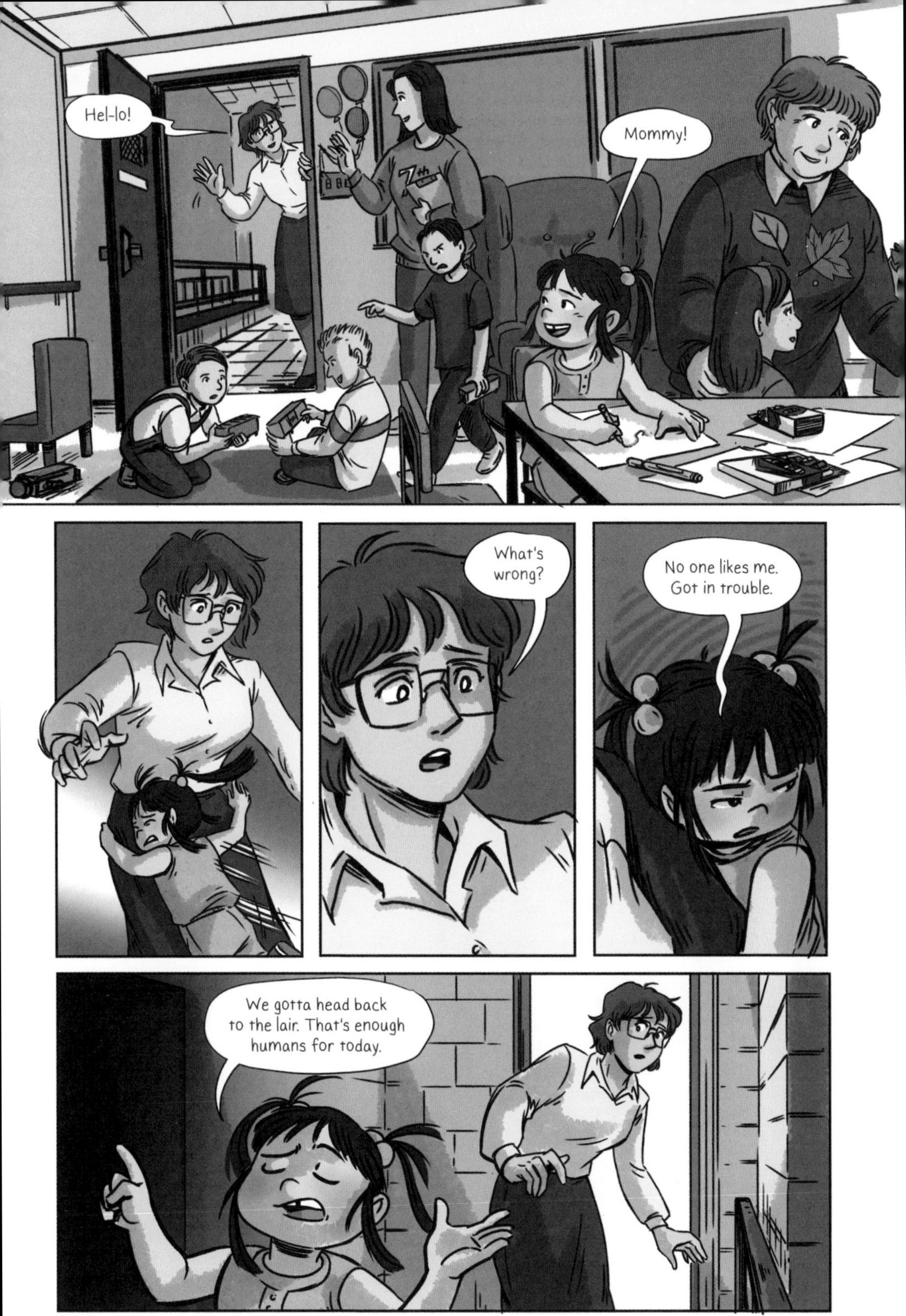
Hel-lo!
Mommy!
What's wrong?
No one likes me. Got in trouble.
We gotta head back to the lair. That's enough humans for today.

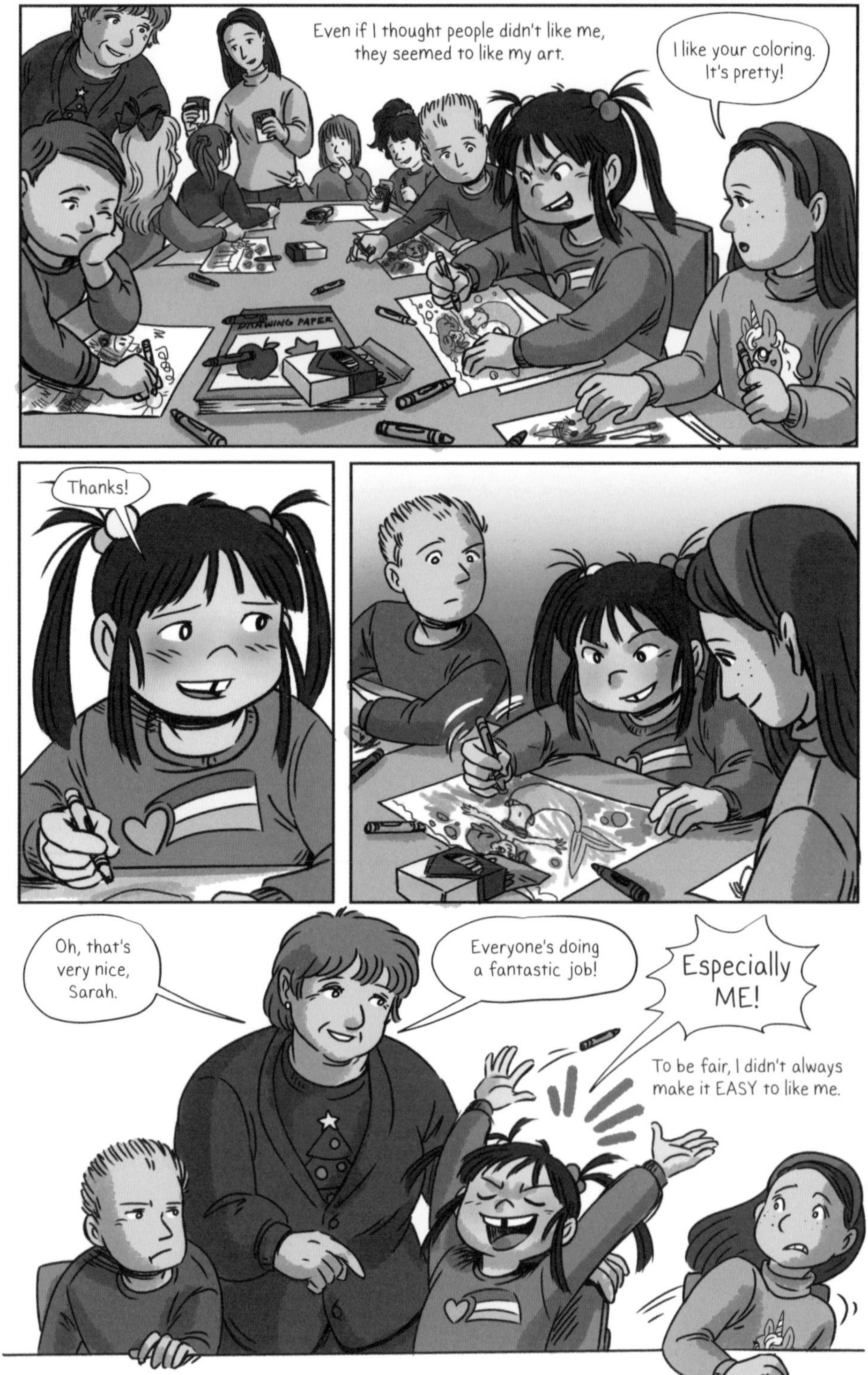
Even if I thought people didn't like me, they seemed to like my art.
I like your coloring. It's pretty!
DRAWING PAPER
Thanks!
Oh, that's very nice, Sarah.
Everyone's doing a fantastic job!
Especially ME!
To be fair, I didn't always make it EASY to like me.

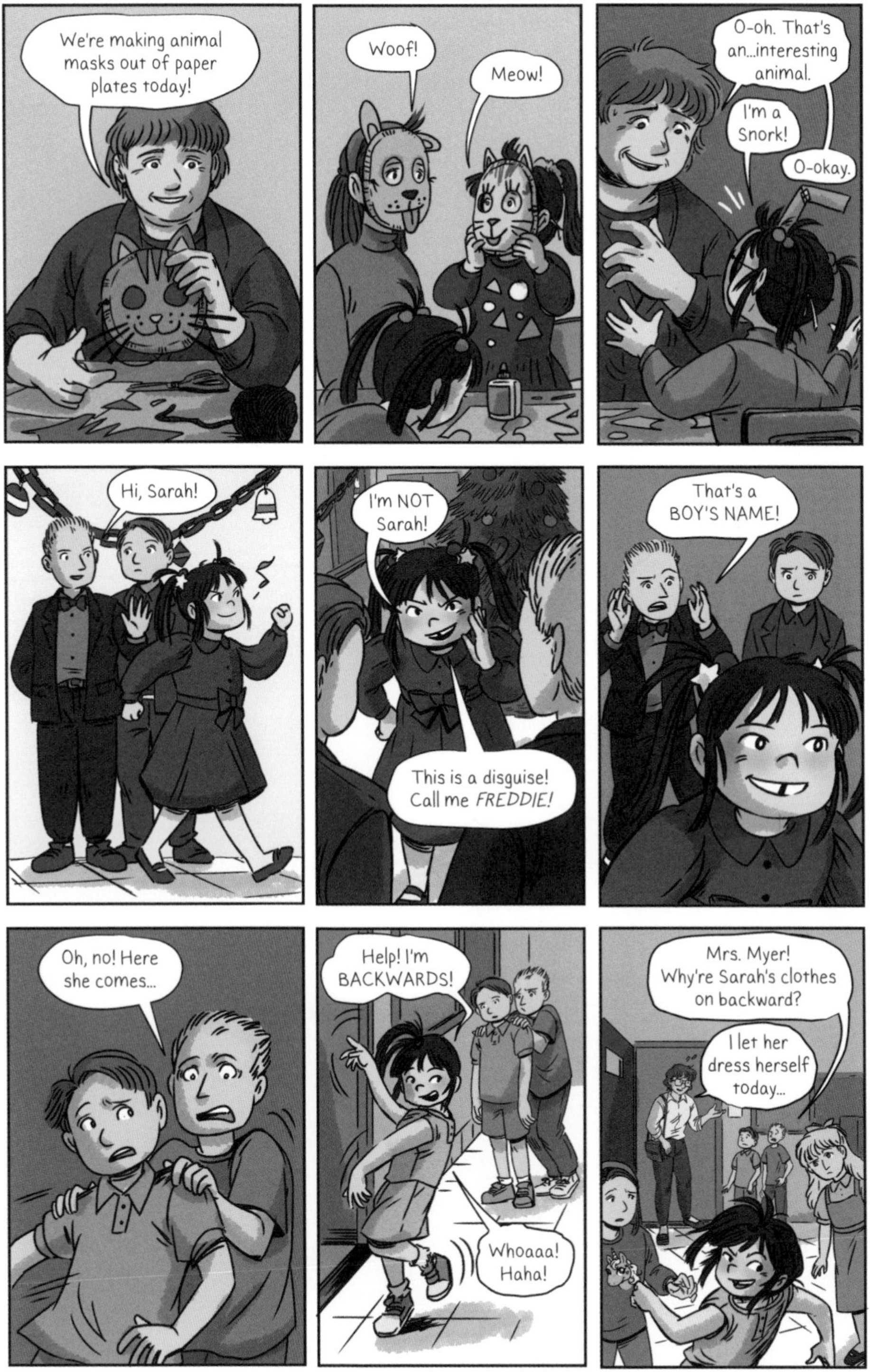
We're making animal masks out of paper plates today!
Woof!
Meow!
O-oh. That's an...interesting animal.
I'm a Snork!
O-okay.
Hi, Sarah!
I'm NOT Sarah!
This is a disguise! Call me FREDDIE!
That's a BOY'S NAME!
Oh, no! Here she comes...
Help! I'm BACKWARDS!
Whoaaa! Haha!
Mrs. Myer! Why're Sarah's clothes on backward?
I let her dress herself today...

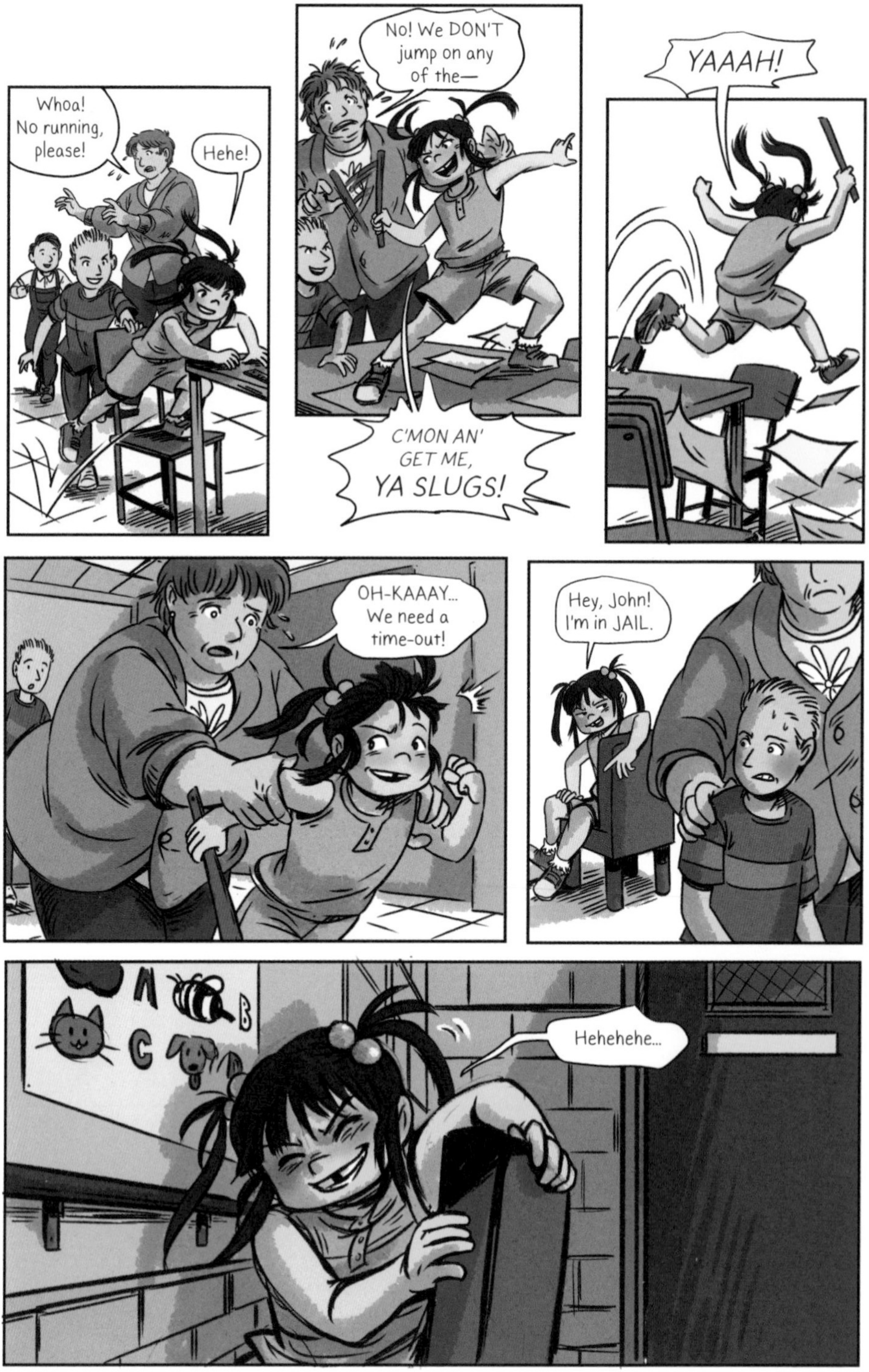
Whoa!
No running,
please!
Hehe!
No! We DON'T
jump on any
of the—
C'MON AN'
GET ME,
YA SLUGS!
YAAAH!
OH-KAAAY...
We need a
time-out!
Hey, John!
I'm in JAIL.
Hehehehe...

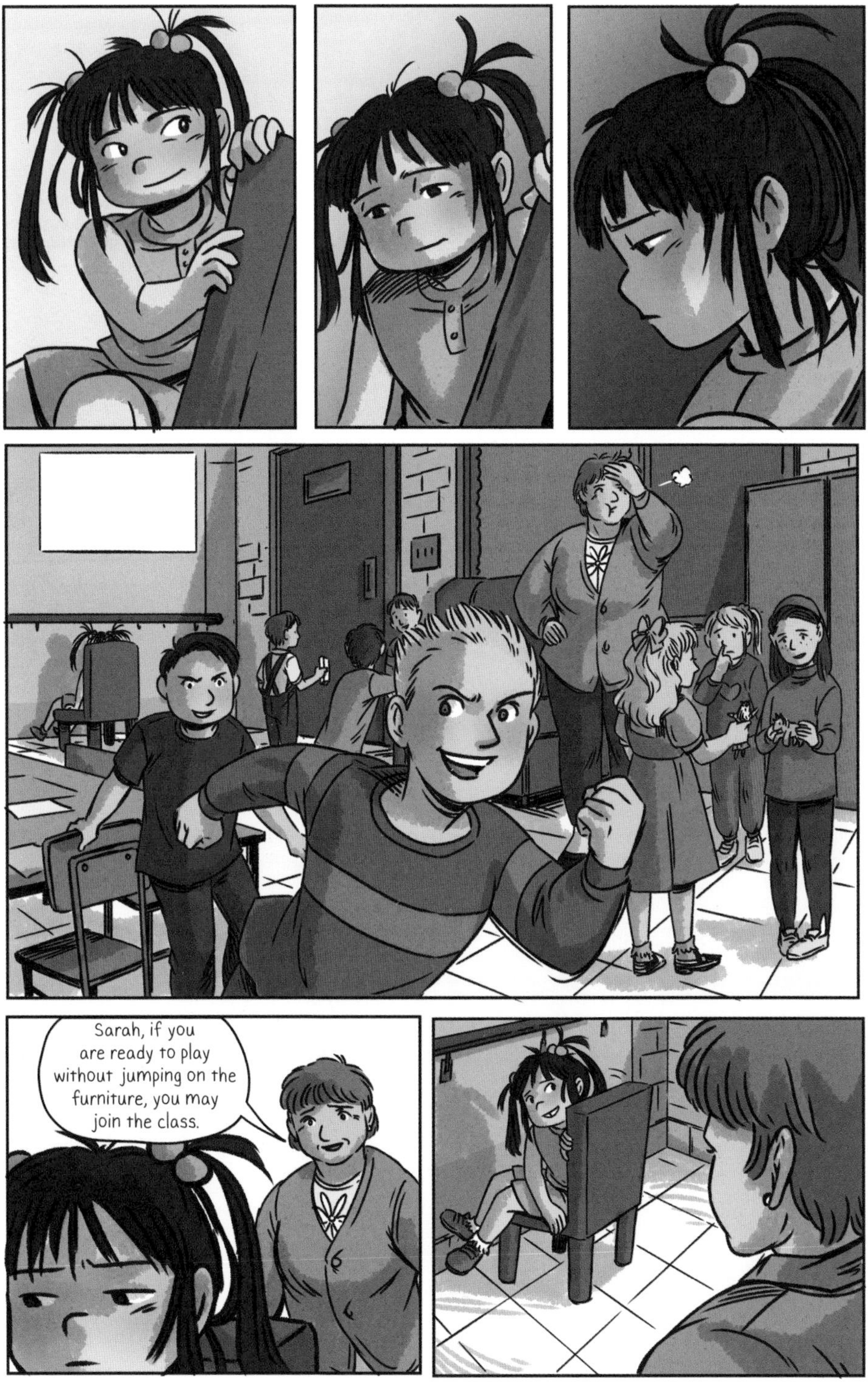
Sarah, if you are ready to play without jumping on the furniture, you may join the class.

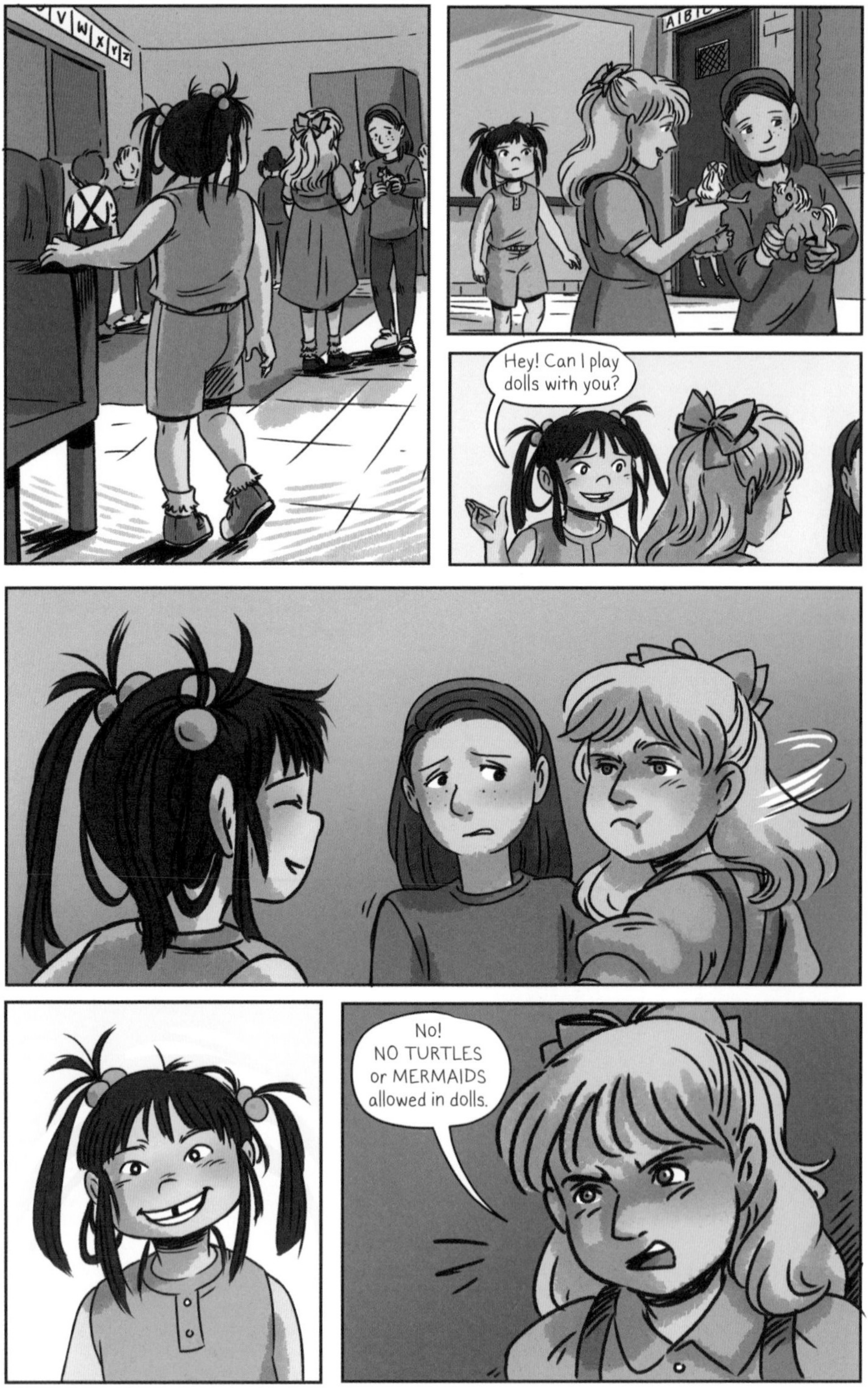
Hey! Can I play dolls with you?
No! NO TURTLES or MERMAIDS allowed in dolls.

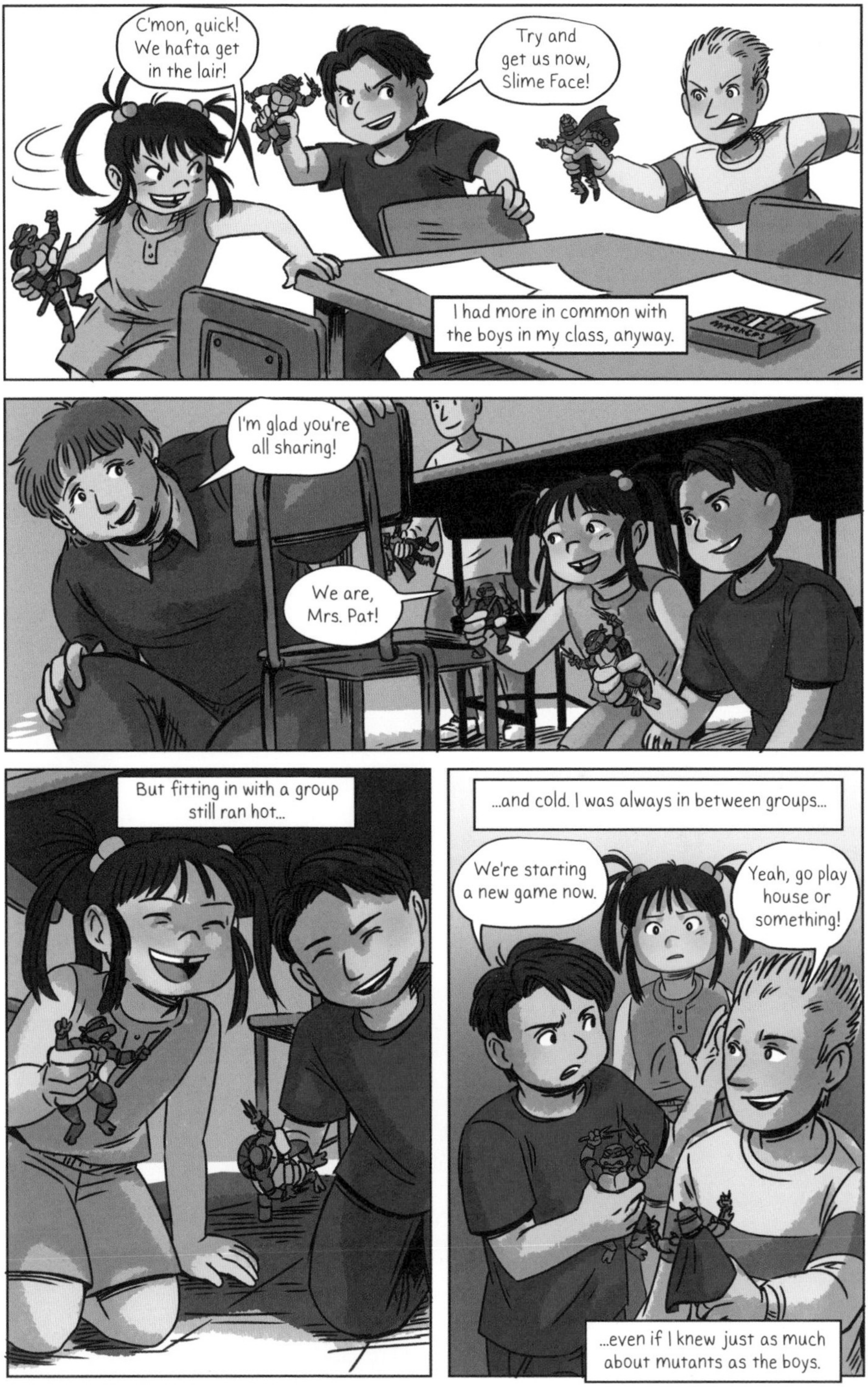
C'mon, quick! We hafta get in the lair!
Try and get us now, Slime Face!
I had more in common with the boys in my class, anyway.
I'm glad you're all sharing!
We are, Mrs. Pat!
But fitting in with a group still ran hot...
...and cold. I was always in between groups...
We're starting a new game now.
Yeah, go play house or something!
...even if I knew just as much about mutants as the boys.

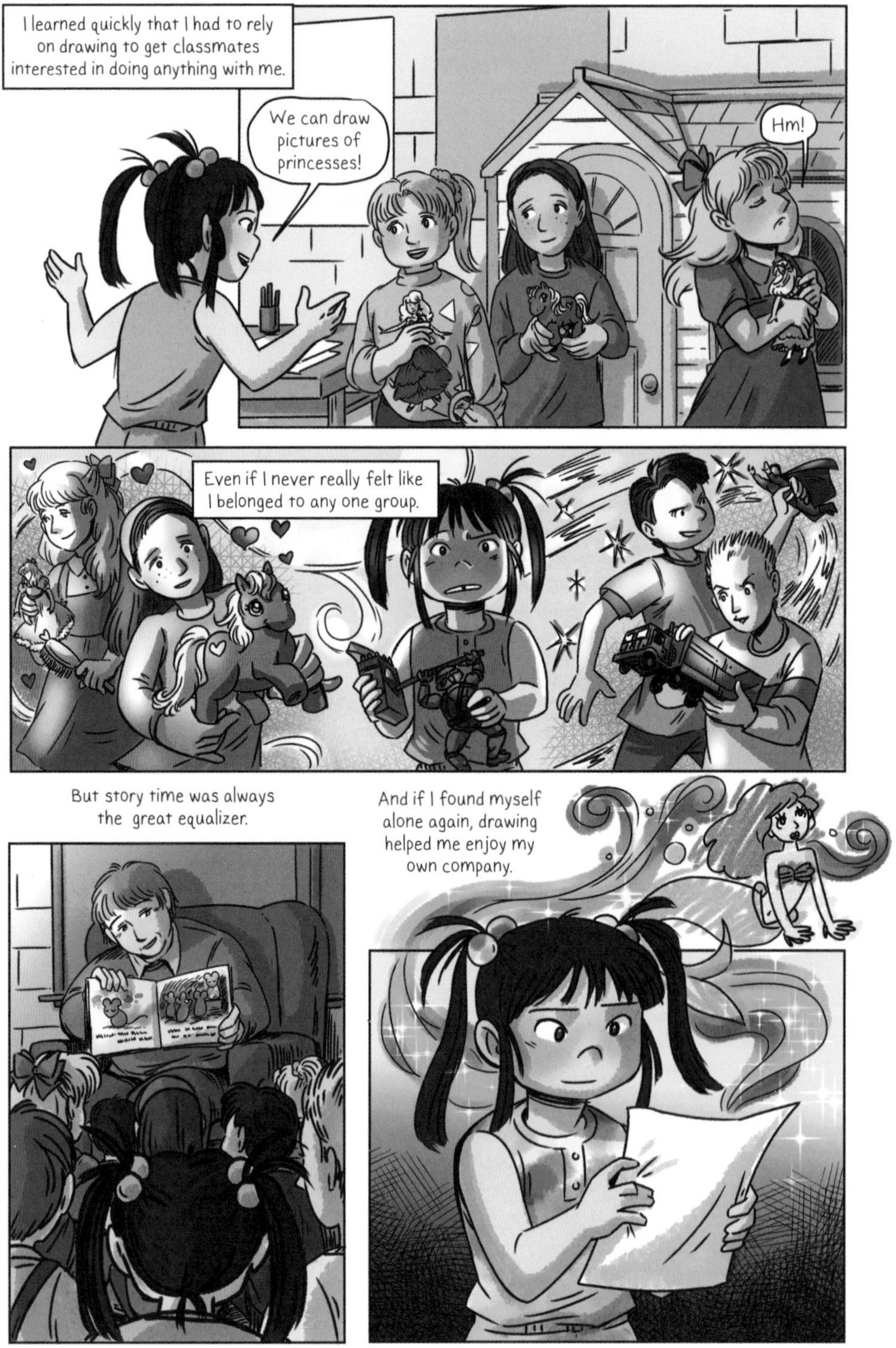
I learned quickly that I had to rely on drawing to get classmates interested in doing anything with me.
We can draw pictures of princesses!
Hm!
Even if I never really felt like I belonged to any one group.
But story time was always the great equalizer.
And if I found myself alone again, drawing helped me enjoy my own company.

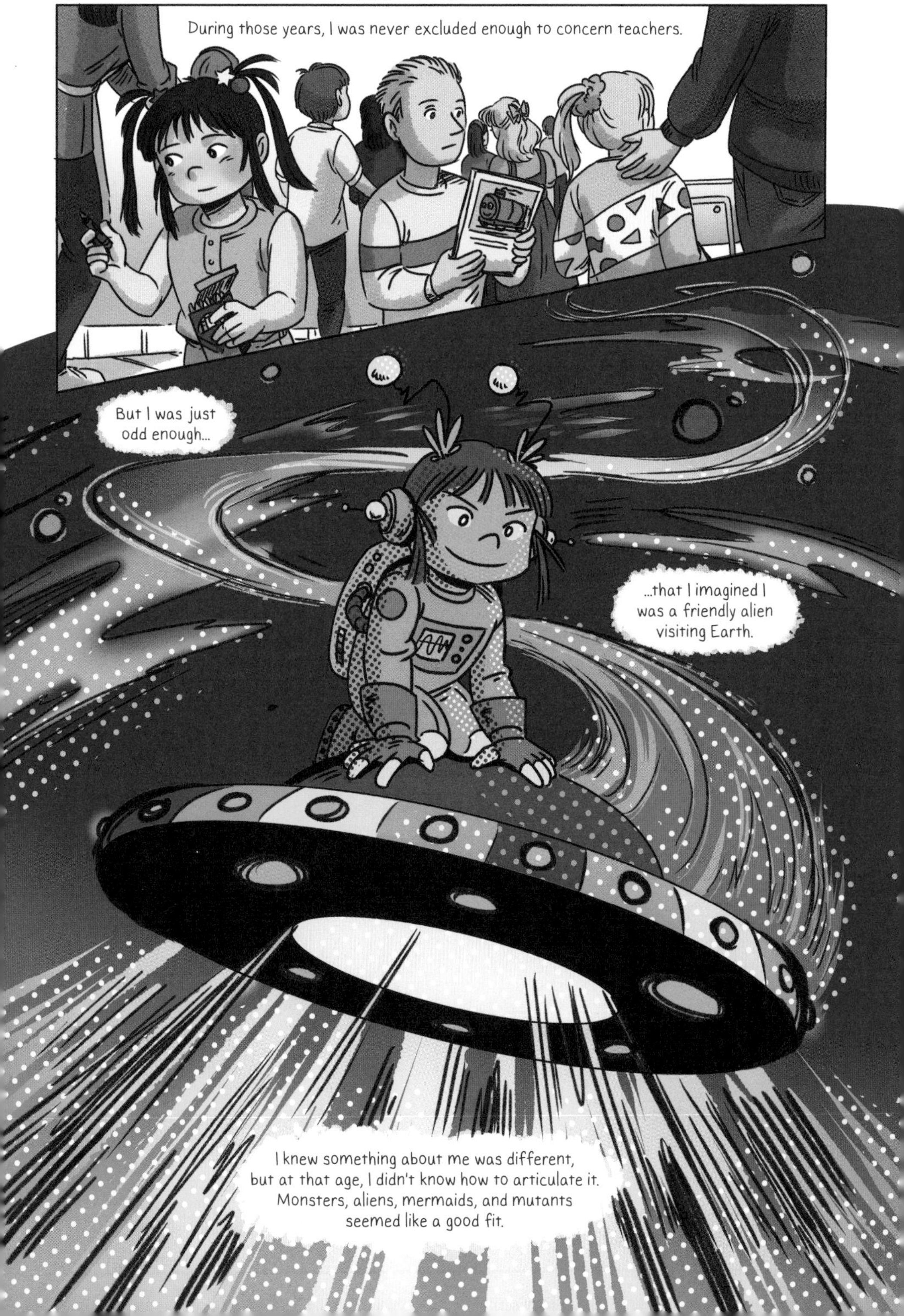
During those years, I was never excluded enough to concern teachers.
But I was just odd enough...
...that I imagined I was a friendly alien visiting Earth.
I knew something about me was different, but at that age, I didn't know how to articulate it. Monsters, aliens, mermaids, and mutants seemed like a good fit.

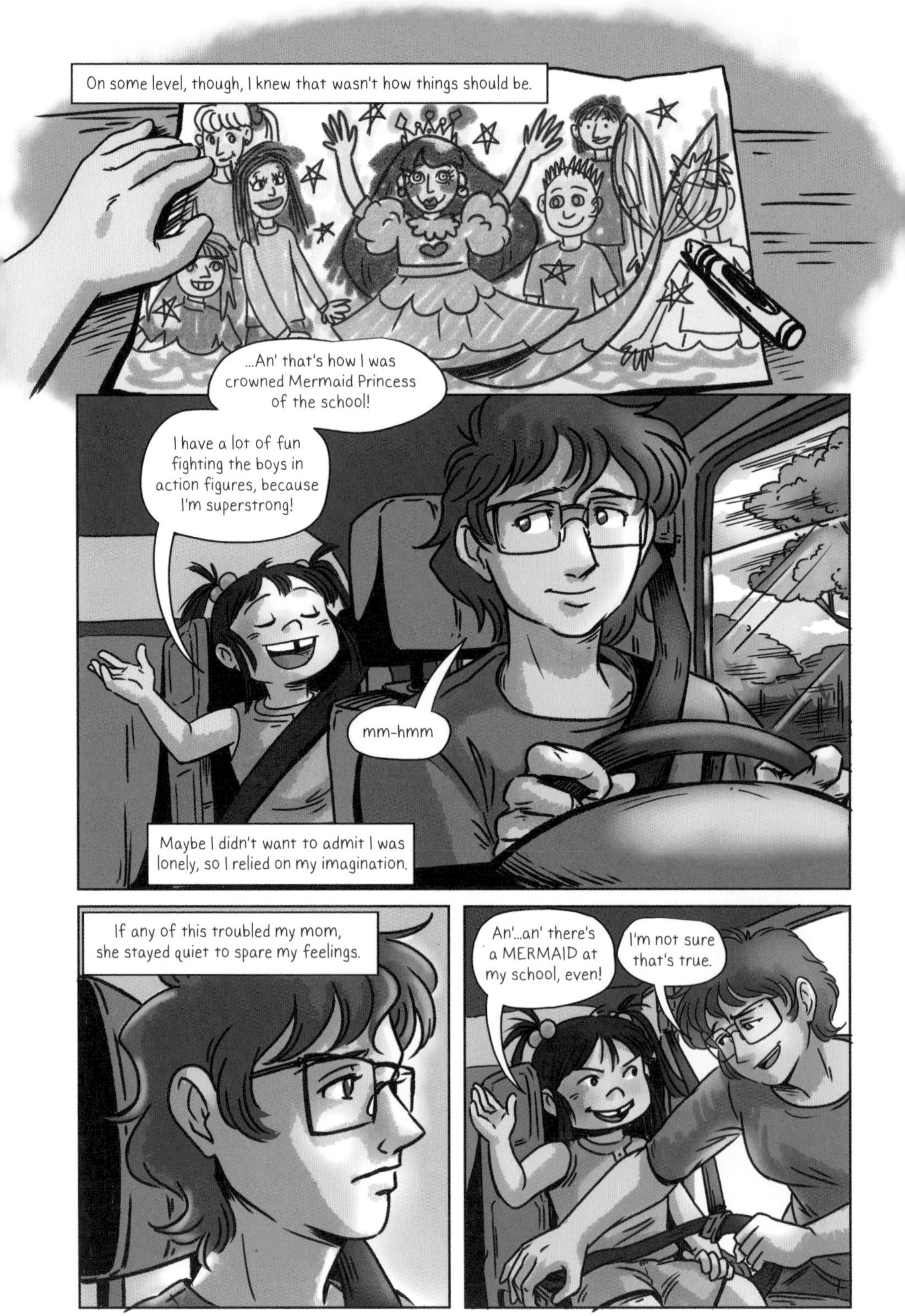

On some level, though, I knew that wasn't how things should be.
...An' that's how I was crowned Mermaid Princess of the school!
I have a lot of fun fighting the boys in action figures, because I'm superstrong!
mm-hmm
Maybe I didn't want to admit I was lonely, so I relied on my imagination.
If any of this troubled my mom, she stayed quiet to spare my feelings.
An'...an' there's a MERMAID at my school, even!
I'm not sure that's true.

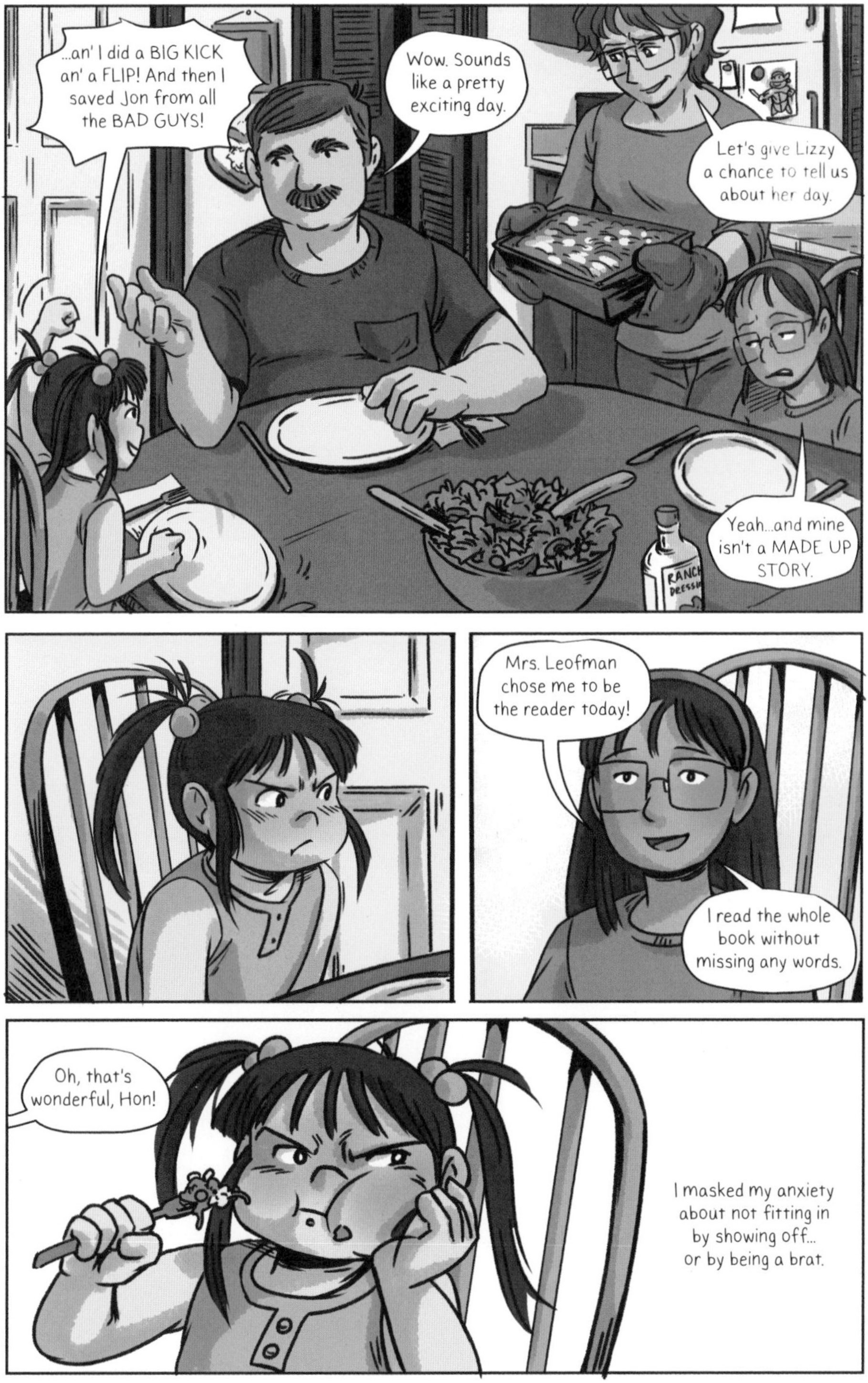
...an' I did a BIG KICK an' a FLIP! And then I saved Jon from all the BAD GUYS!
Wow. Sounds like a pretty exciting day.
Let's give Lizzy a chance to tell us about her day.
Yeah...and mine isn't a MADE UP STORY.
RANCH DRESSING
Mrs. Leofman chose me to be the reader today!
I read the whole book without missing any words.
Oh, that's wonderful, Hon!
I masked my anxiety about not fitting in by showing off... or by being a brat.

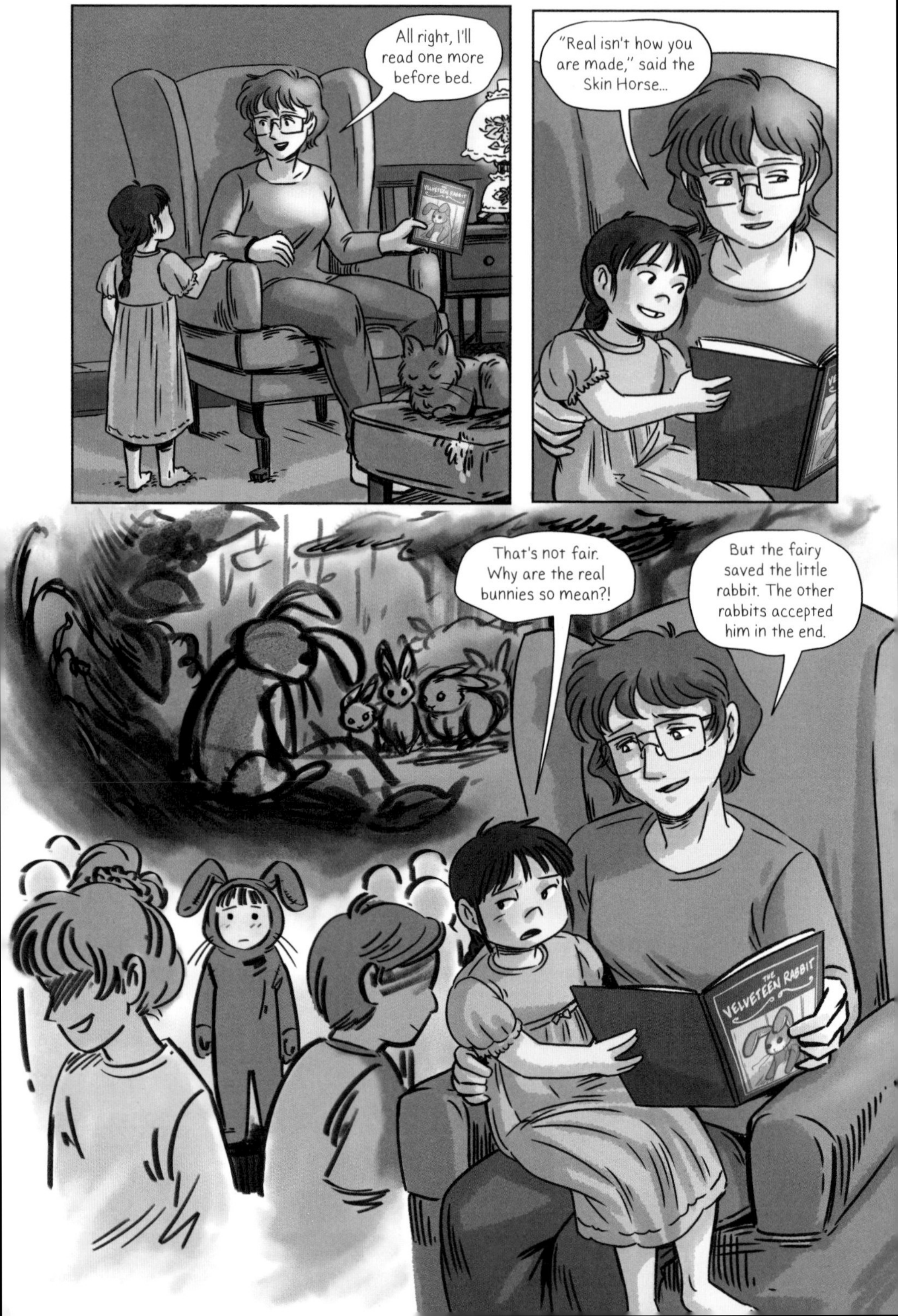
All right, I'll read one more before bed.
"Real isn't how you are made," said the Skin Horse...
That's not fair. Why are the real bunnies so mean?!
But the fairy saved the little rabbit. The other rabbits accepted him in the end.
THE VELVETEEN RABBIT

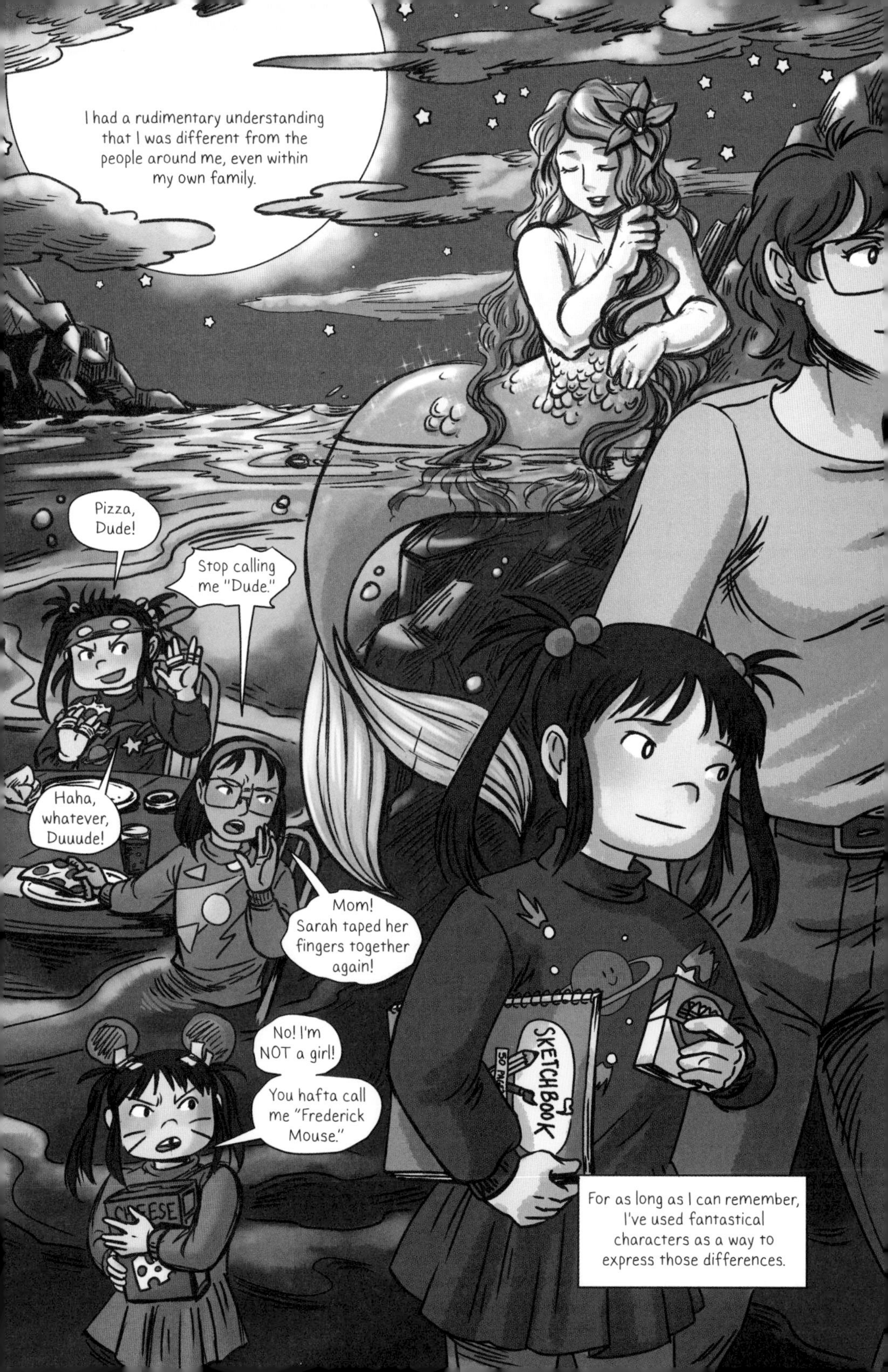

I had a rudimentary understanding that I was different from the people around me, even within my own family.
Pizza, Dude!
Stop calling me "Dude."
Haha, whatever, Duuude!
Mom! Sarah taped her fingers together again!
No! I'm NOT a girl!
You hafta call me "Frederick Mouse."
CHEESE
SKETCHBOOK
For as long as I can remember, I've used fantastical characters as a way to express those differences.

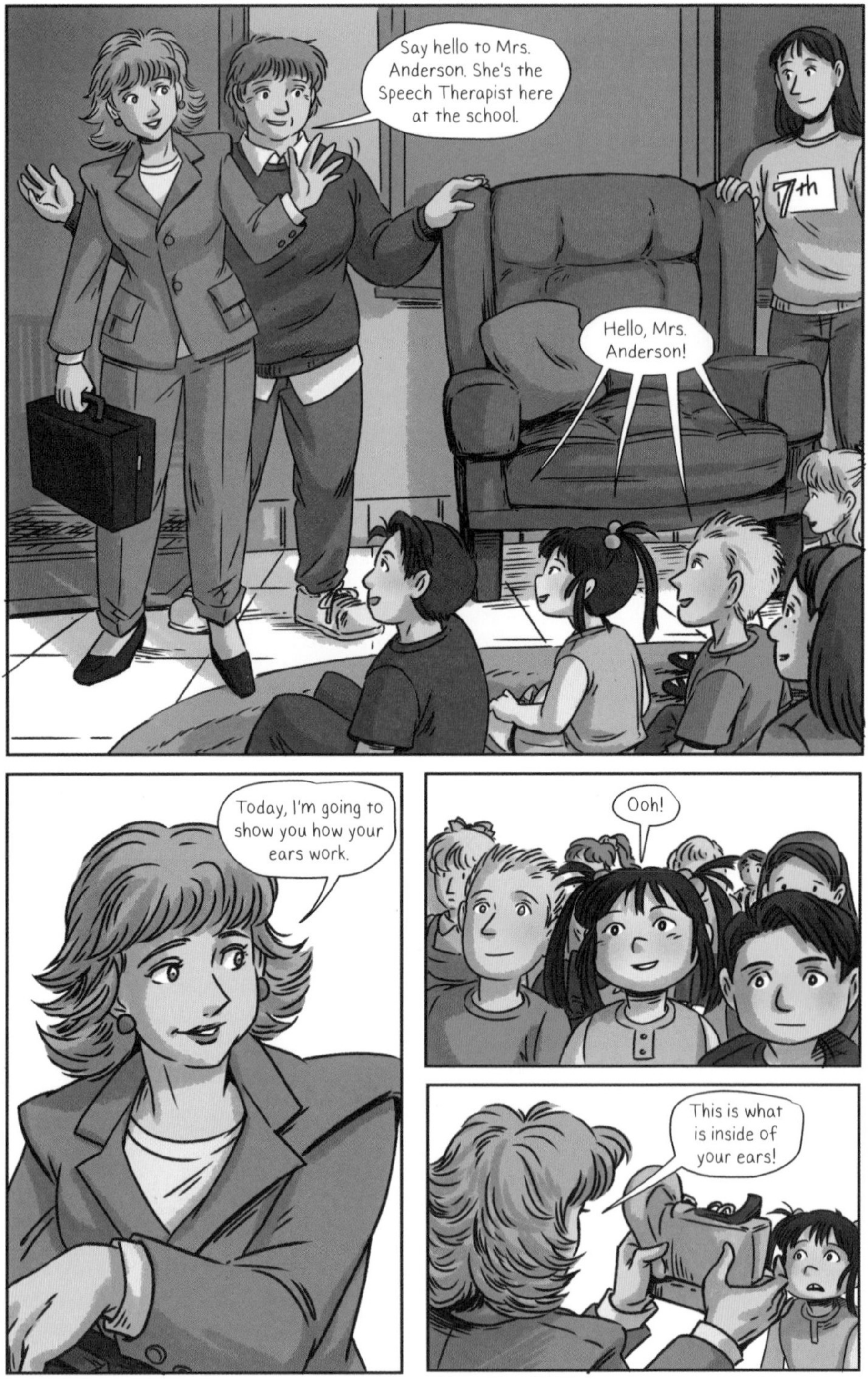
Say hello to Mrs. Anderson. She's the Speech Therapist here at the school.
7th
Hello, Mrs. Anderson!
Today, I'm going to show you how your ears work.
Ooh!
This is what is inside of your ears!

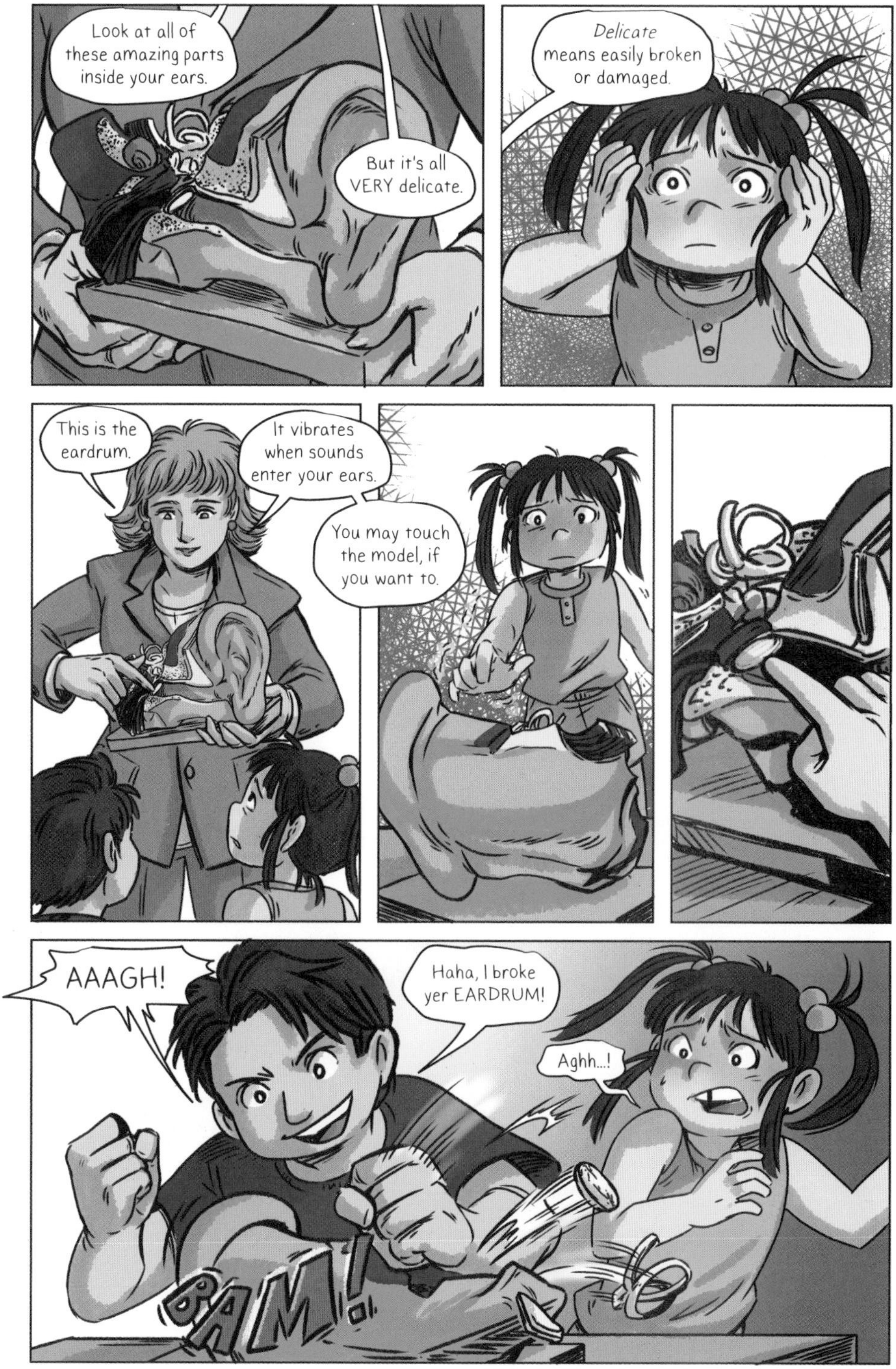
Look at all of these amazing parts inside your ears.
But it's all VERY delicate.
Delicate means easily broken or damaged.
This is the eardrum.
It vibrates when sounds enter your ears.
You may touch the model, if you want to.
AAAGH!
Haha, I broke yer EARDRUM!
Aghh...!
BAM!

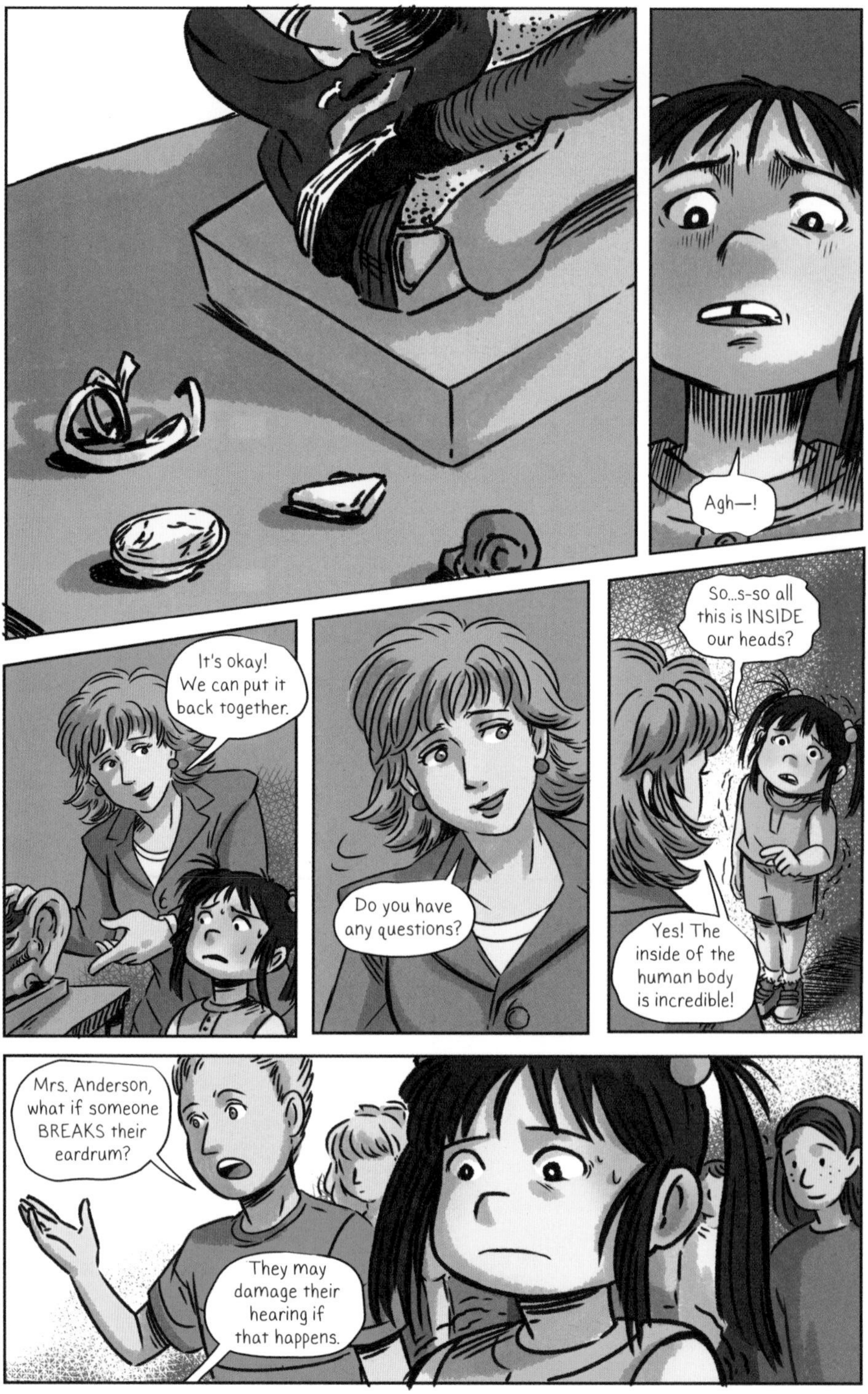
Agh—!
It's okay! We can put it back together.
Do you have any questions?
So...s-so all this is INSIDE our heads?
Yes! The inside of the human body is incredible!
Mrs. Anderson, what if someone BREAKS their eardrum?
They may damage their hearing if that happens.

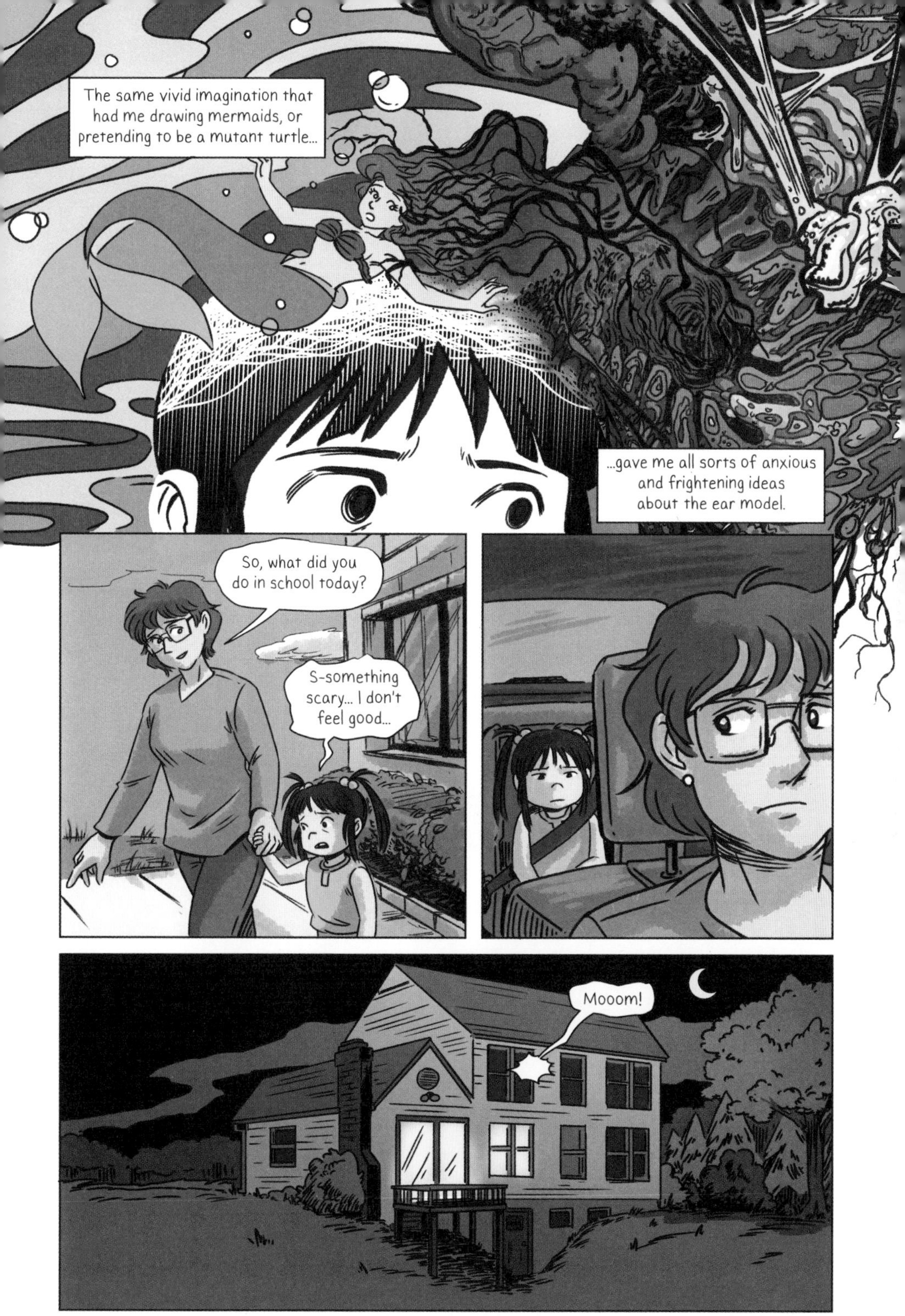
The same vivid imagination that had me drawing mermaids, or pretending to be a mutant turtle...
...gave me all sorts of anxious and frightening ideas about the ear model.
So, what did you do in school today?
S-something scary... I don't feel good...
Mooom!

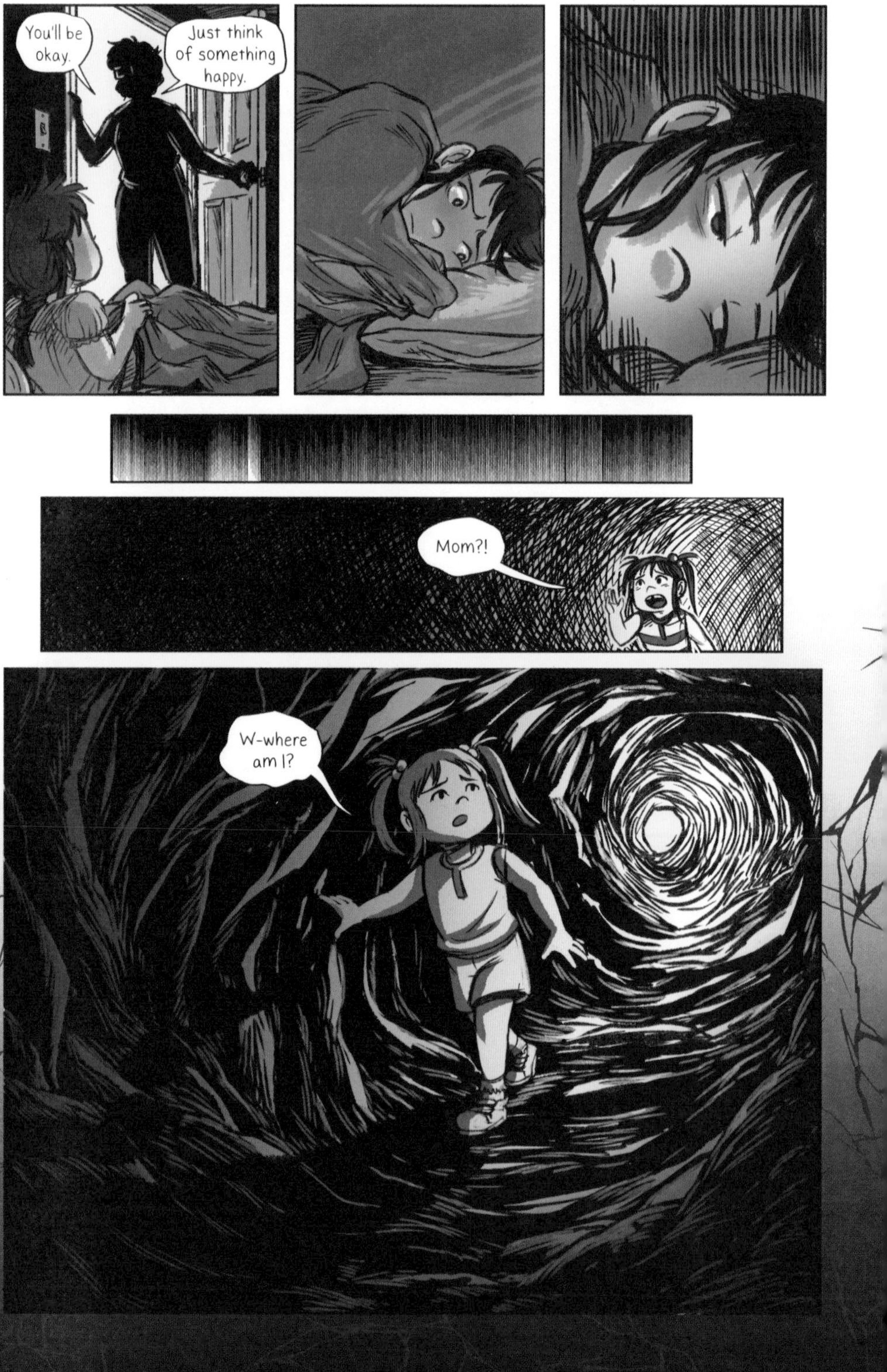
You'll be okay.
Just think of something happy.
Mom?!
W-where am I?

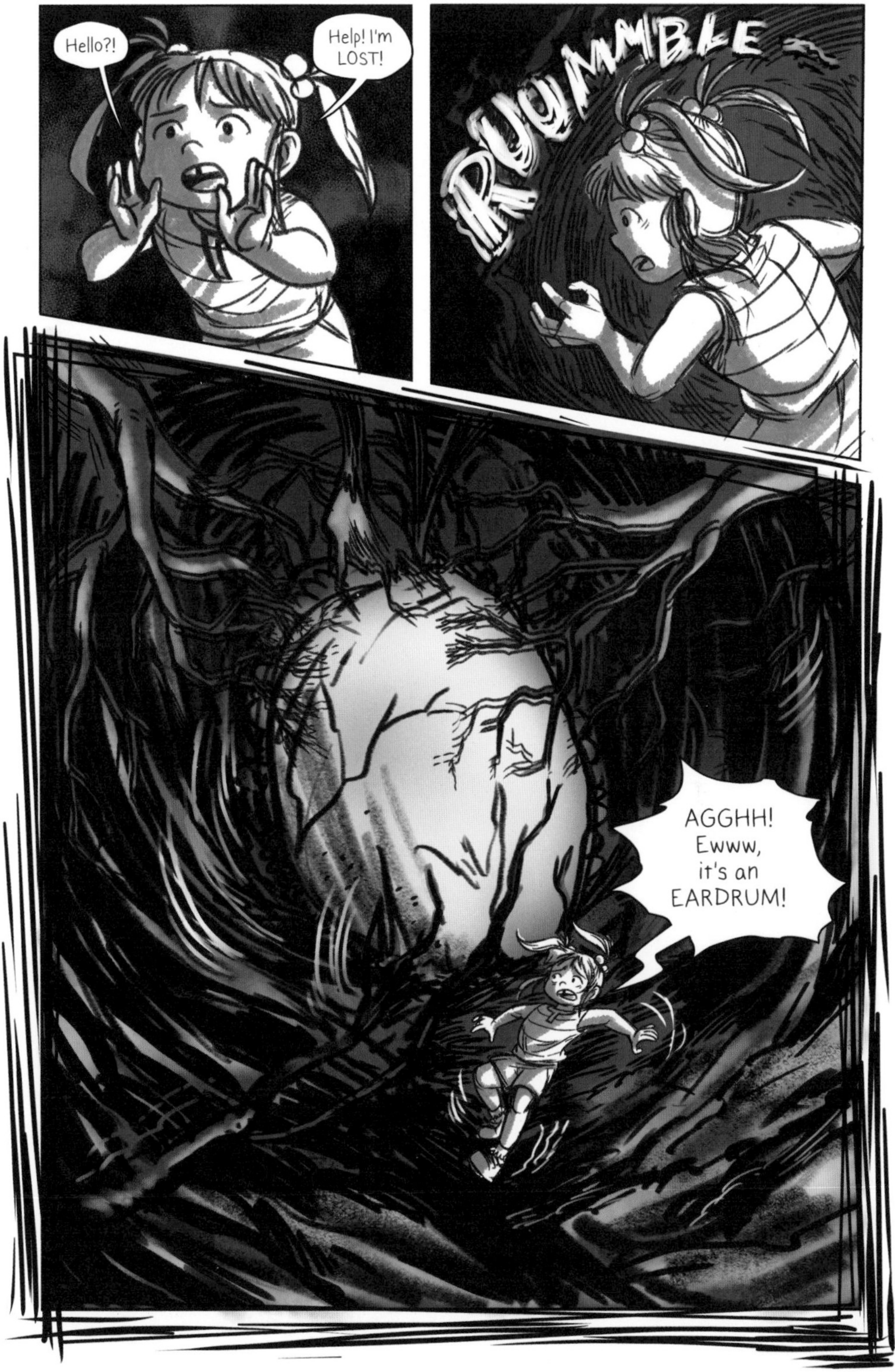
Hello?!
Help! I'm LOST!
RUMMBLE
AGGHH! Ewww, it's an EARDRUM!

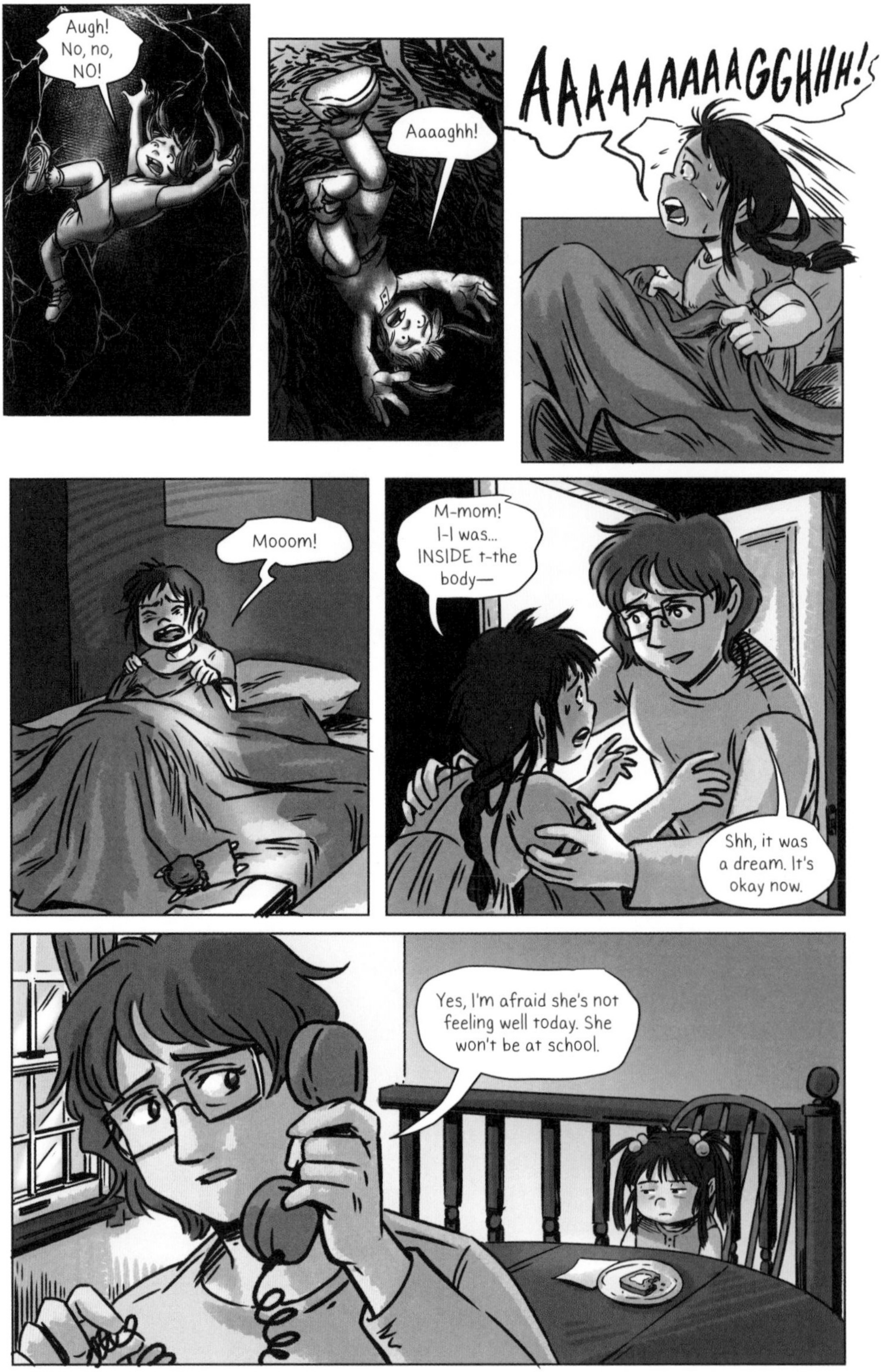
Augh! No, no, NO!
Aaaaghh!
AAAAAAAAGGHHH!
Mooom!
M-mom! I-I was... INSIDE t-the body—
Shh, it was a dream. It's okay now.
Yes, I'm afraid she's not feeling well today. She won't be at school.

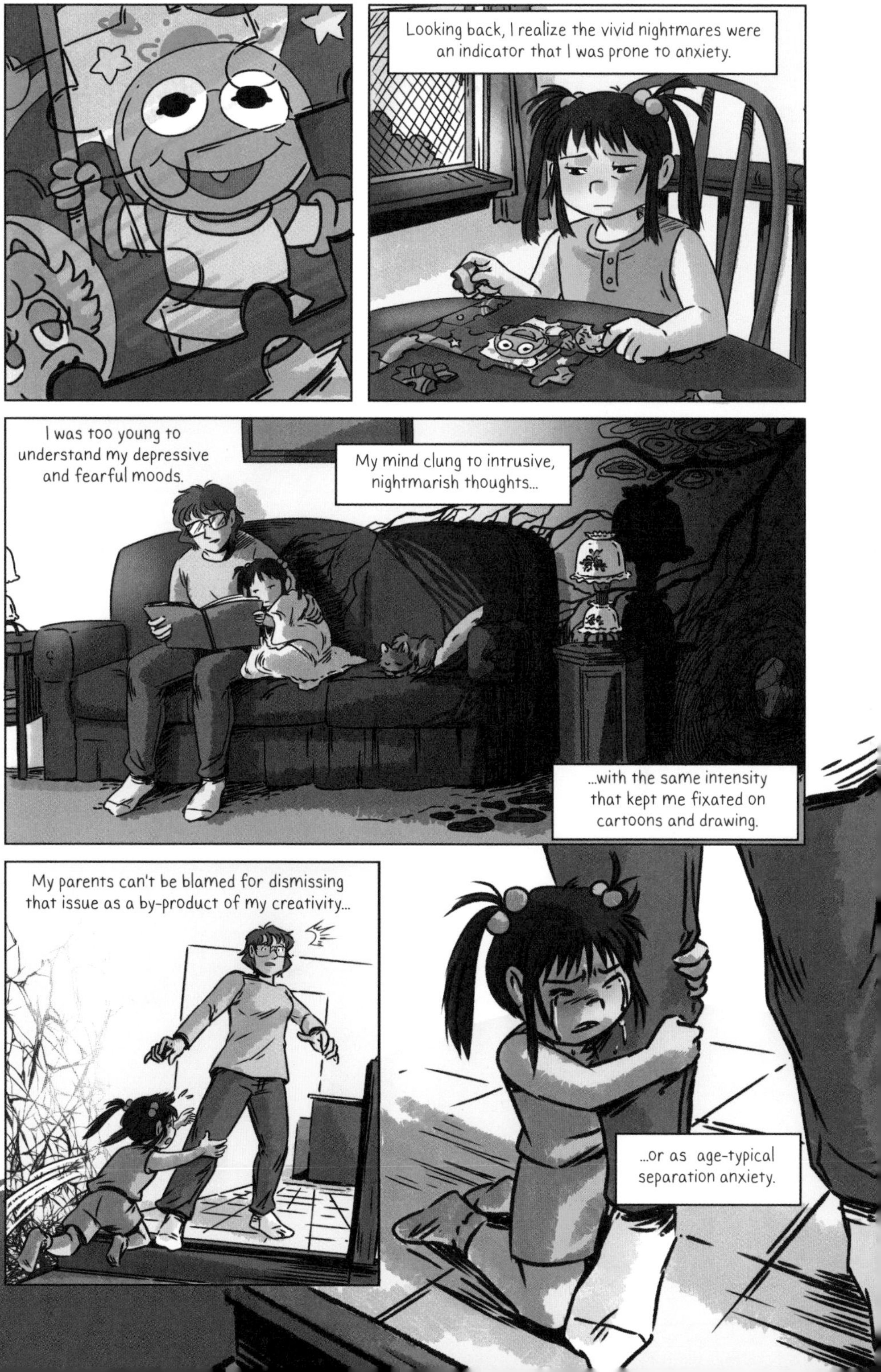
Looking back, I realize the vivid nightmares were an indicator that I was prone to anxiety.
I was too young to understand my depressive and fearful moods.
My mind clung to intrusive, nightmarish thoughts...
...with the same intensity that kept me fixated on cartoons and drawing.
My parents can't be blamed for dismissing that issue as a by-product of my creativity...
...or as age-typical separation anxiety.

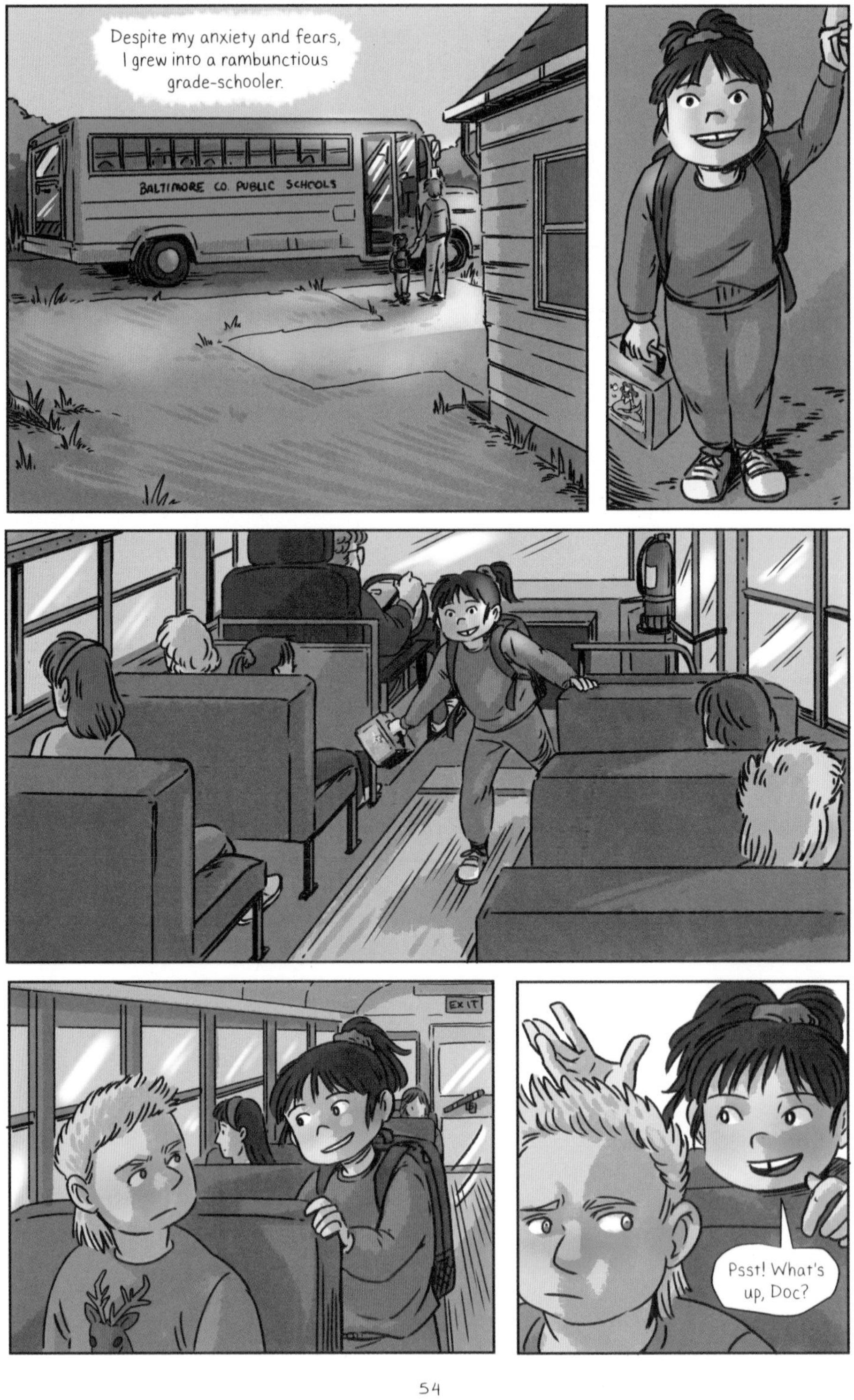
Despite my anxiety and fears, I grew into a rambunctious grade-schooler.
BALTIMORE CO. PUBLIC SCHOOLS
EXIT
Psst! What's up, Doc?

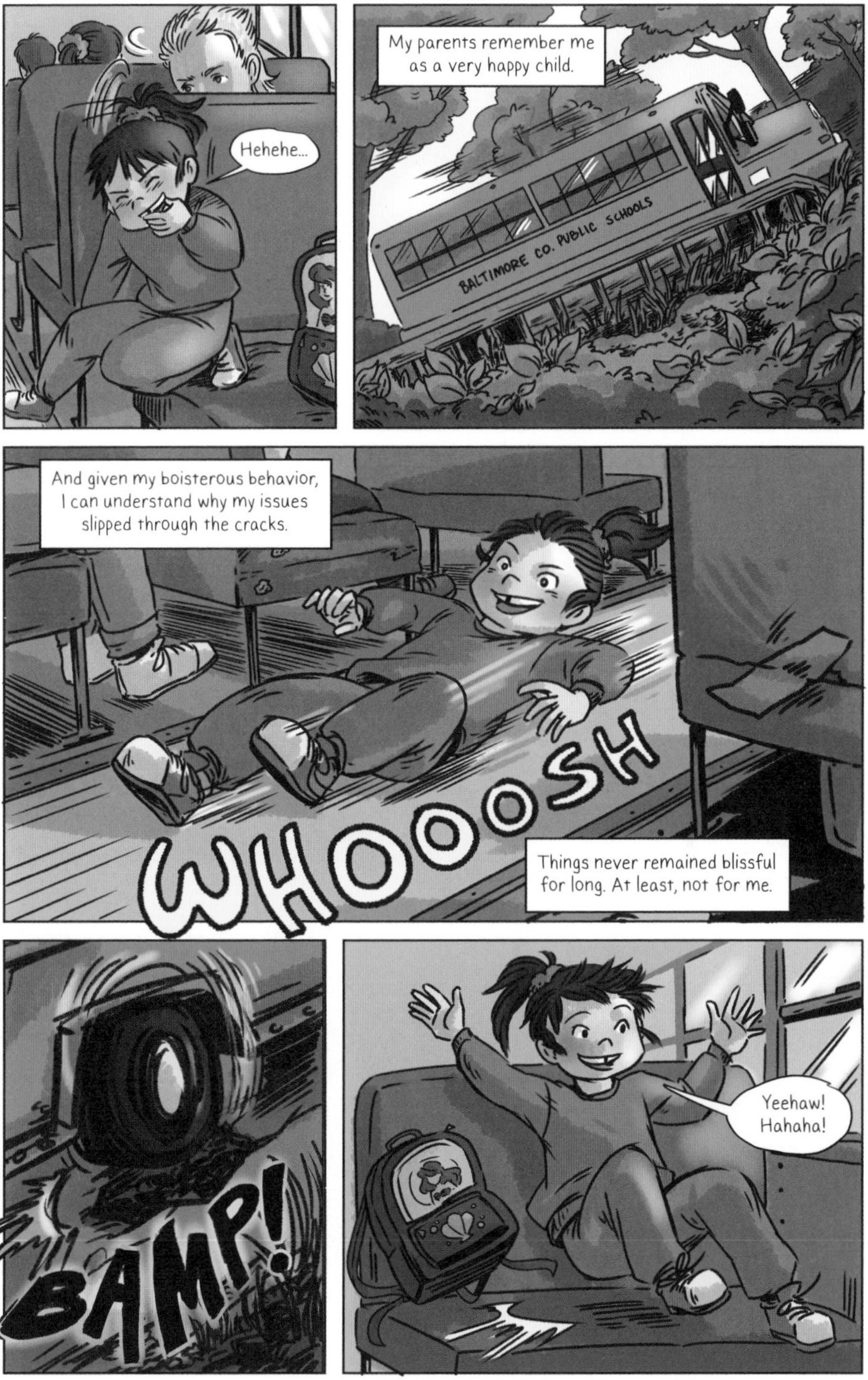
Hehehe...
My parents remember me as a very happy child.
BALTIMORE CO. PUBLIC SCHOOLS
And given my boisterous behavior, I can understand why my issues slipped through the cracks.
WHOOOSH
Things never remained blissful for long. At least, not for me.
BAMP!
Yeehaw! Hahaha!

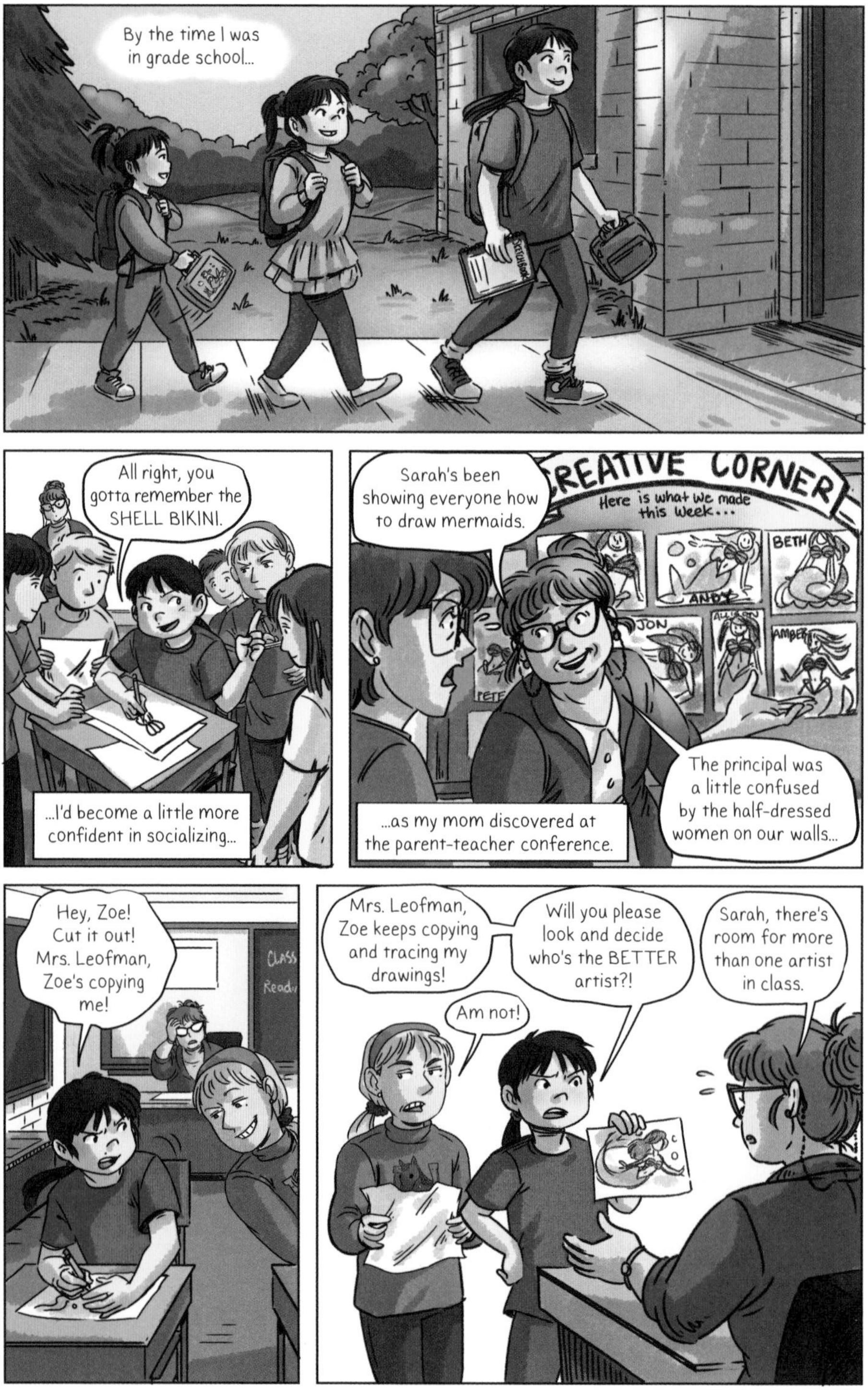

By the time I was in grade school...
All right, you gotta remember the SHELL BIKINI.
...I'd become a little more confident in socializing...
CREATIVE CORNER
Here is what we made this week...
BETH
ANDY
JON
ALLISON
AMBER
PETE
Sarah's been showing everyone how to draw mermaids.
...as my mom discovered at the parent-teacher conference.
The principal was a little confused by the half-dressed women on our walls...
Hey, Zoe! Cut it out! Mrs. Leofman, Zoe's copying me!
Mrs. Leofman, Zoe keeps copying and tracing my drawings!
Will you please look and decide who's the BETTER artist?!
Am not!
Sarah, there's room for more than one artist in class.

Unfortunately, the energy and confidence that at times earned me praise, especially when it came to drawing, also made me short-tempered and restless.

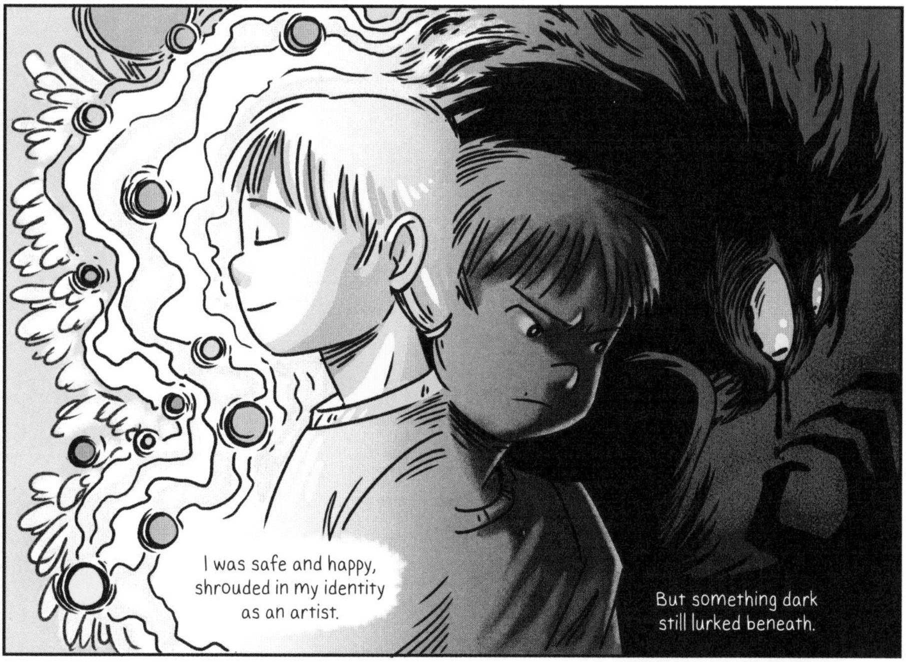
I was safe and happy, shrouded in my identity as an artist.
But something dark still lurked beneath.

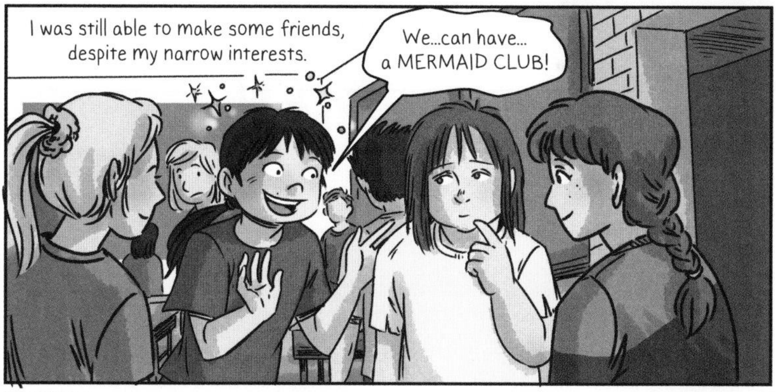
I was still able to make some friends, despite my narrow interests.
We...can have... a MERMAID CLUB!

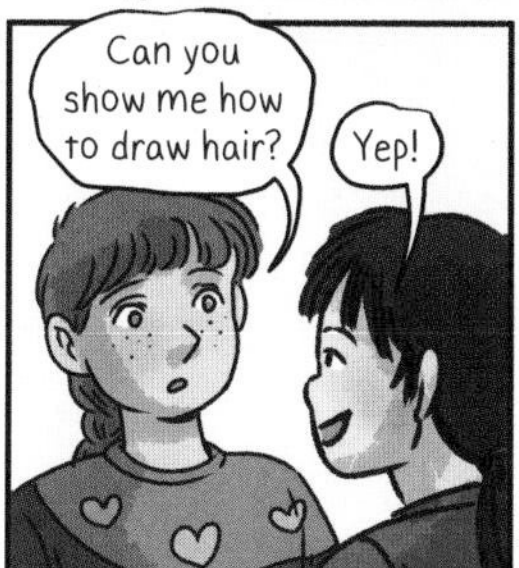
Can you show me how to draw hair?
Yep!

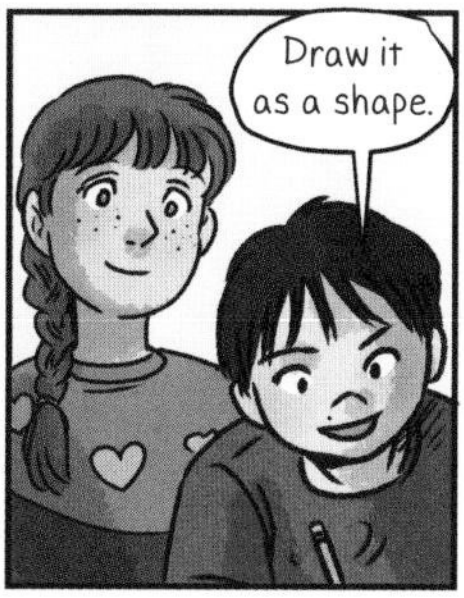
Draw it as a shape.

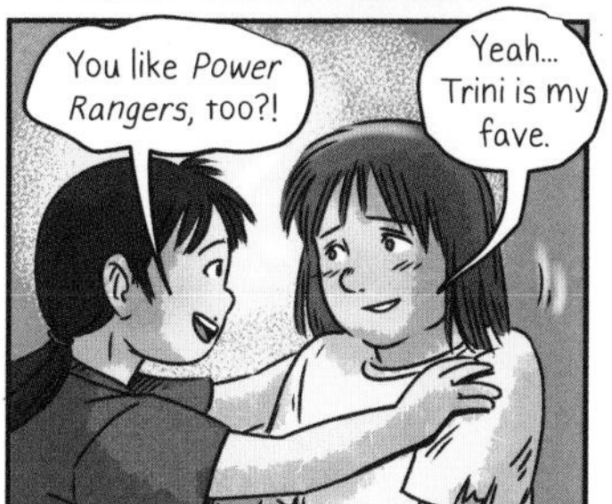
You like *Power Rangers*, too?!
Yeah... Trini is my fave.

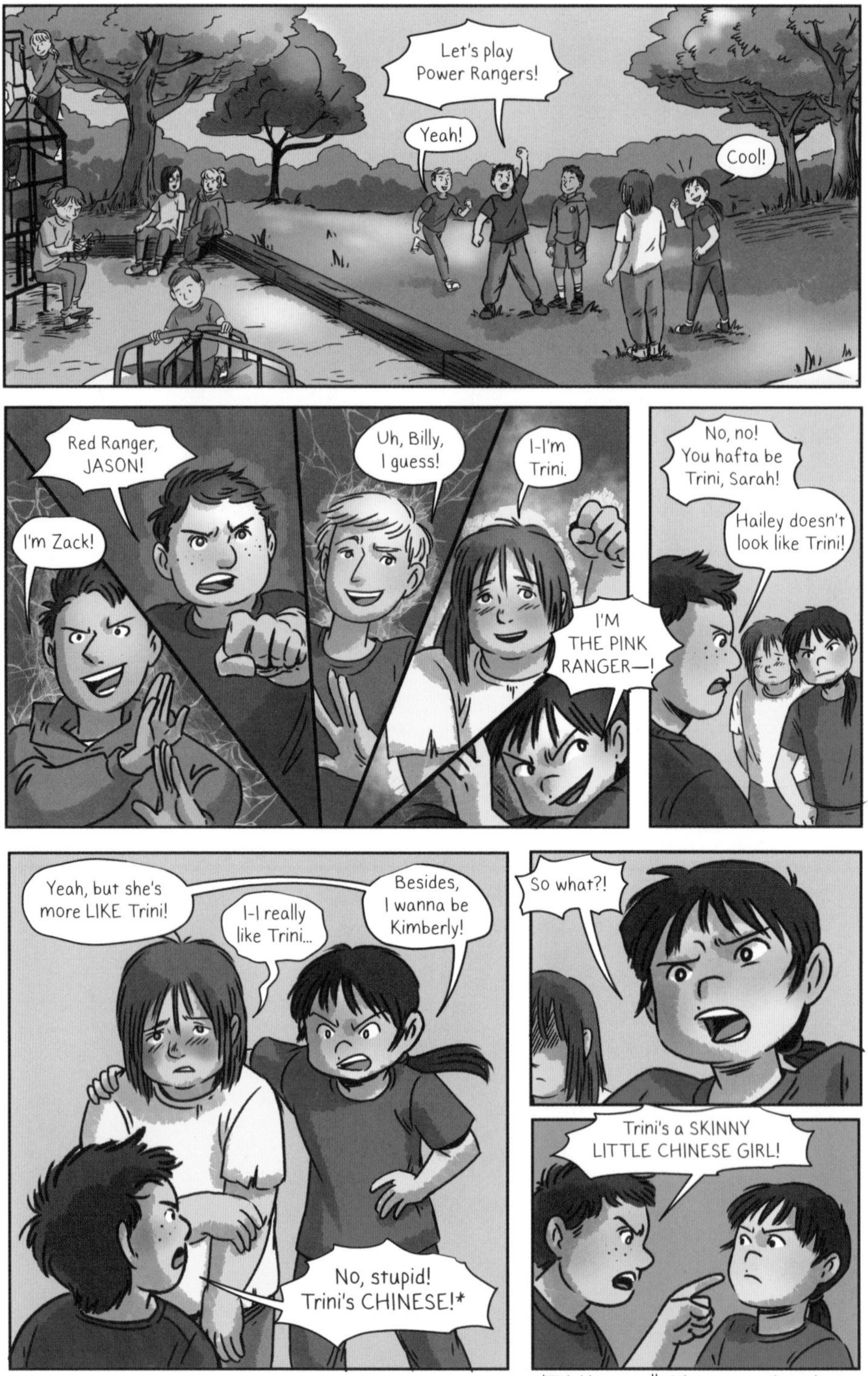
Let's play Power Rangers!
Yeah!
Cool!
Red Ranger, JASON!
I'm Zack!
Uh, Billy, I guess!
I-I'm Trini.
I'M THE PINK RANGER—!
No, no! You hafta be Trini, Sarah!
Hailey doesn't look like Trini!
Yeah, but she's more LIKE Trini!
I-I really like Trini...
Besides, I wanna be Kimberly!
No, stupid! Trini's CHINESE!*
So what?!
Trini's a SKINNY LITTLE CHINESE GIRL!

*Trini is actually Vietnamese American.

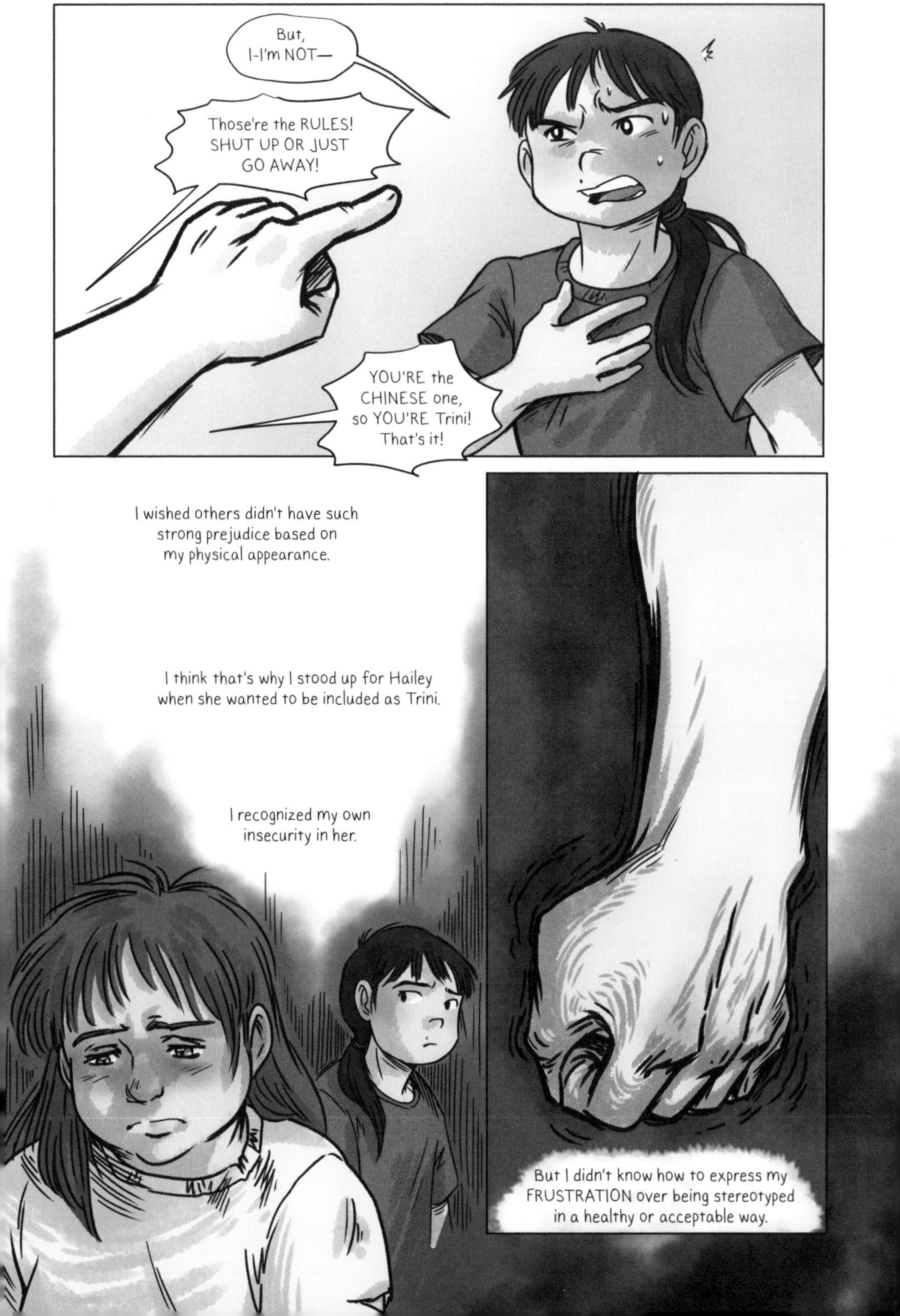
But, I-I'm NOT—
Those're the RULES! SHUT UP OR JUST GO AWAY!
YOU'RE the CHINESE one, so YOU'RE Trini! That's it!
I wished others didn't have such strong prejudice based on my physical appearance.
I think that's why I stood up for Hailey when she wanted to be included as Trini.
I recognized my own insecurity in her.
But I didn't know how to express my FRUSTRATION over being stereotyped in a healthy or acceptable way.

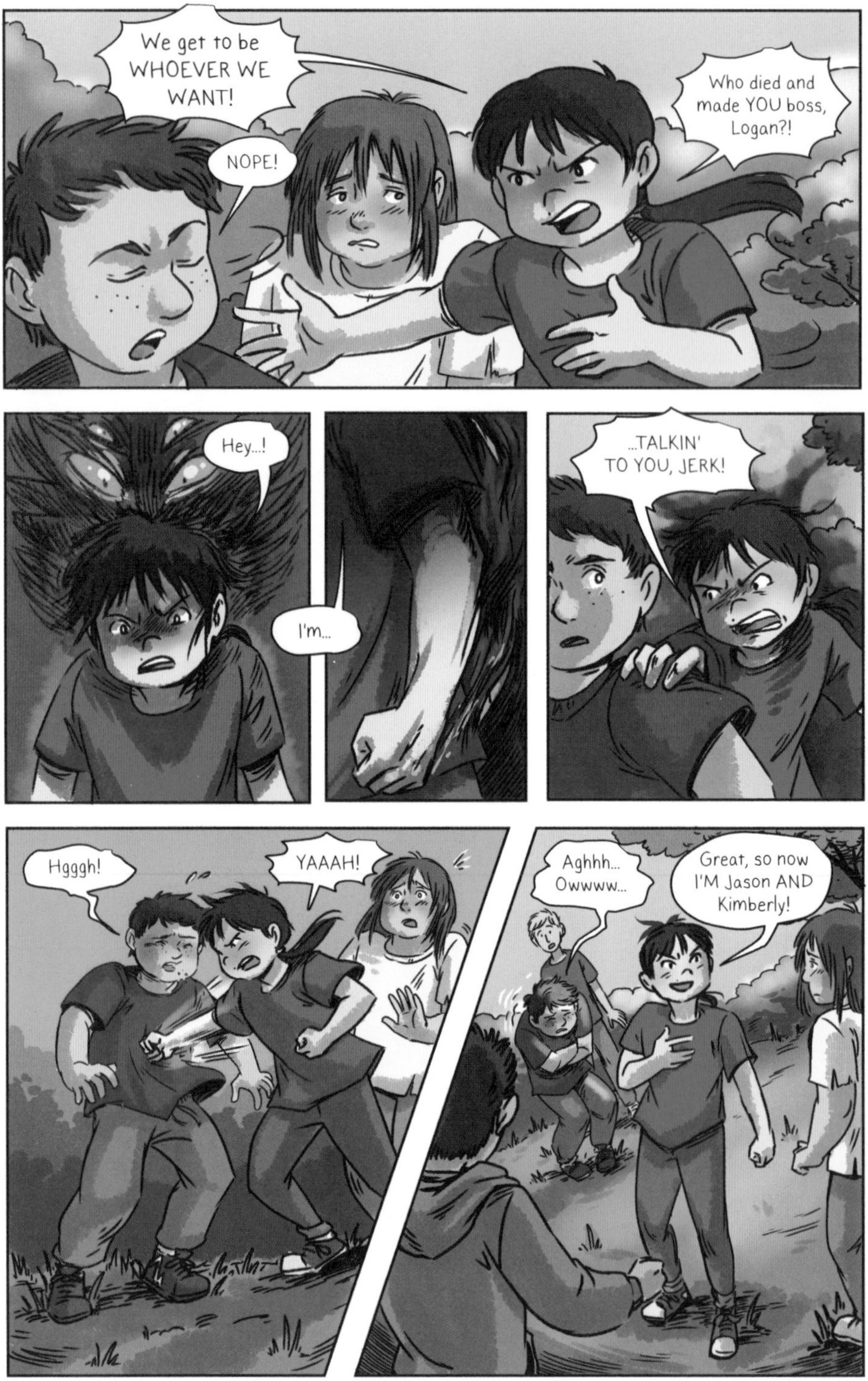
We get to be WHOEVER WE WANT!
NOPE!
Who died and made YOU boss, Logan?!
Hey...!
I'm...
...TALKIN' TO YOU, JERK!
Hgggh!
YAAAH!
Aghhh... Owwww...
Great, so now I'M Jason AND Kimberly!

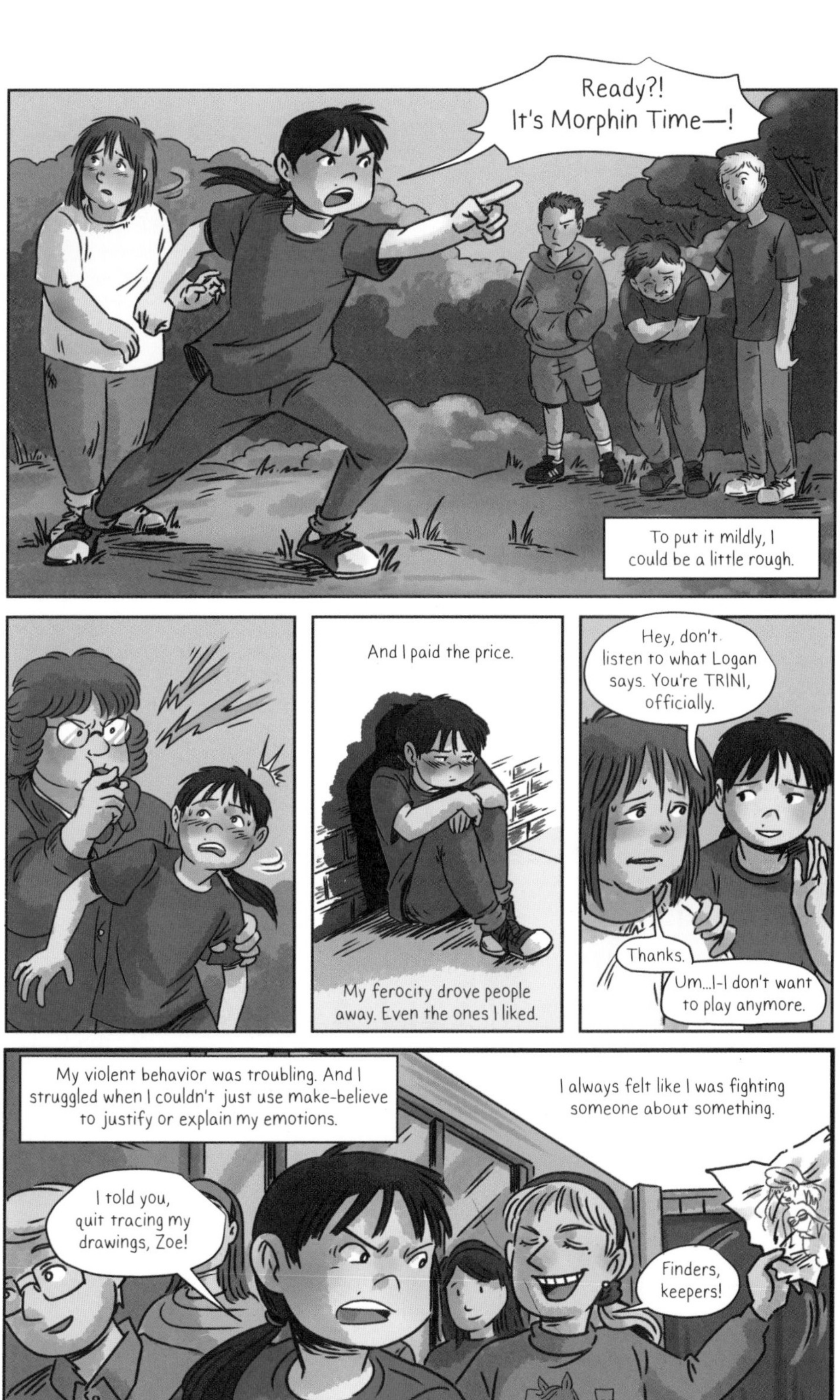
Ready?! It's Morphin Time—!
To put it mildly, I could be a little rough.
And I paid the price.
My ferocity drove people away. Even the ones I liked.
Hey, don't listen to what Logan says. You're TRINI, officially.
Thanks.
Um...I-I don't want to play anymore.
My violent behavior was troubling. And I struggled when I couldn't just use make-believe to justify or explain my emotions.
I always felt like I was fighting someone about something.
I told you, quit tracing my drawings, Zoe!
Finders, keepers!

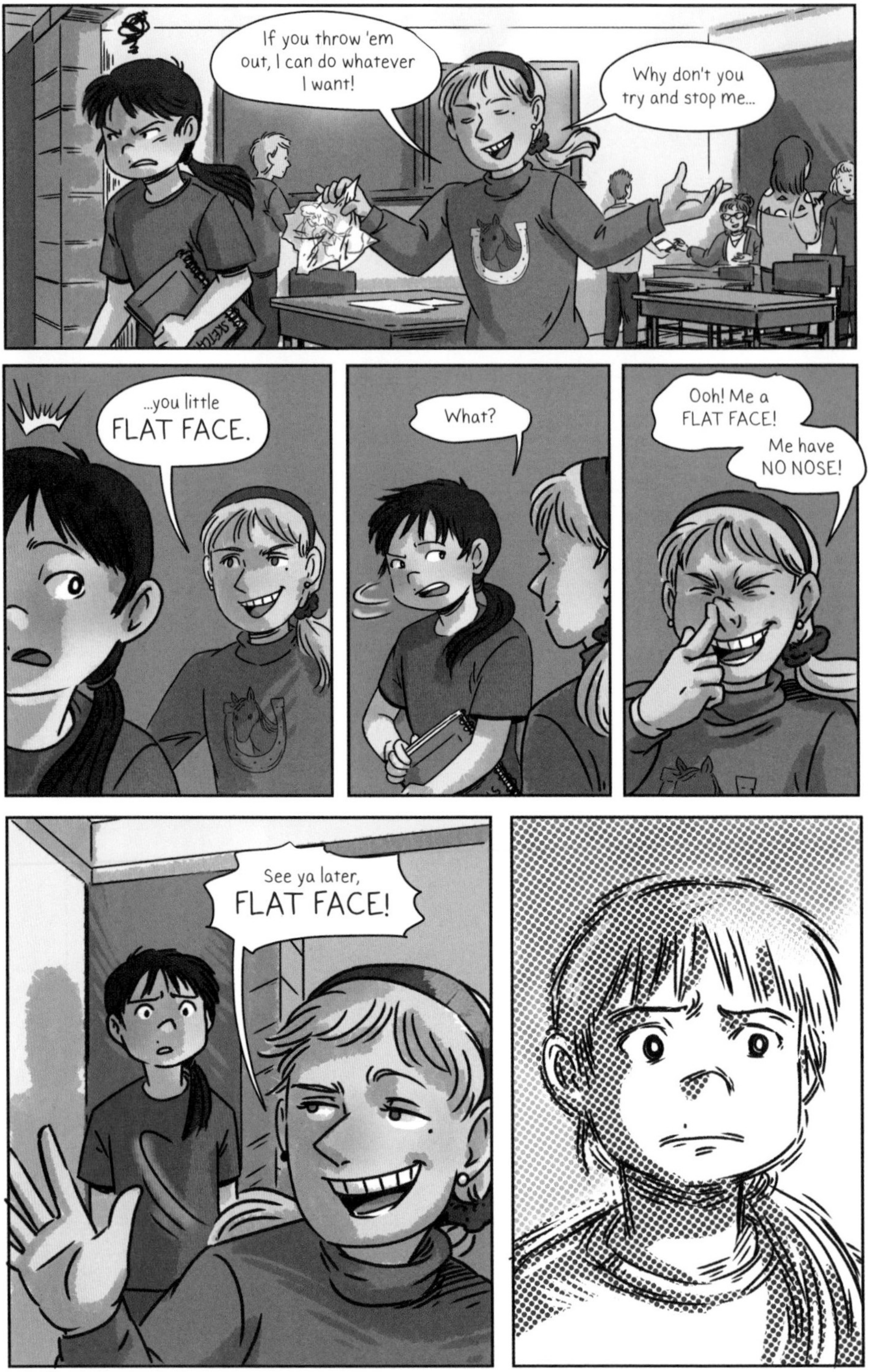
If you throw 'em out, I can do whatever I want!
Why don't you try and stop me...
...you little FLAT FACE.
What?
Ooh! Me a FLAT FACE!
Me have NO NOSE!
See ya later, FLAT FACE!

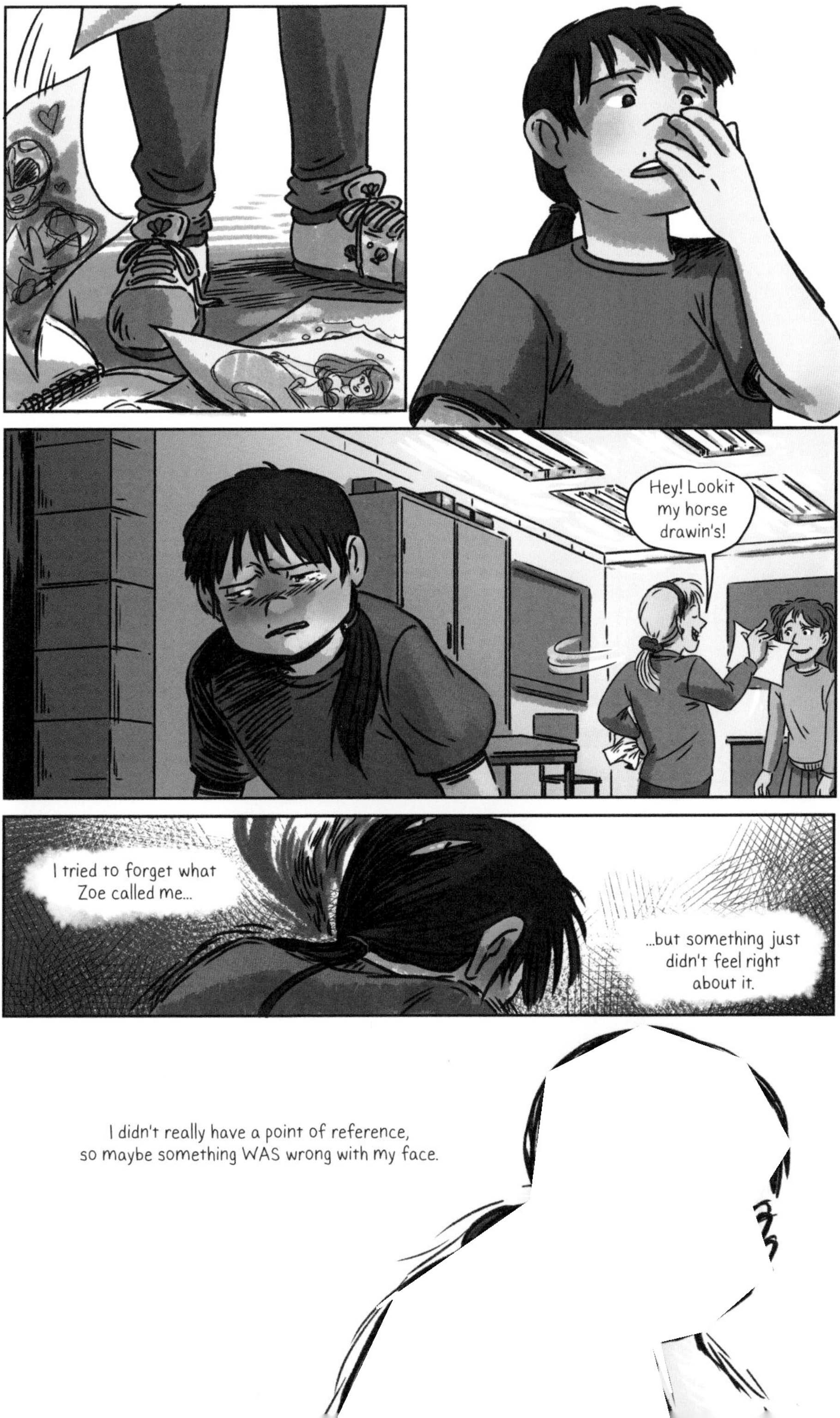
Hey! Lookit my horse drawin's!
I tried to forget what Zoe called me...
...but something just didn't feel right about it.
I didn't really have a point of reference, so maybe something WAS wrong with my face.

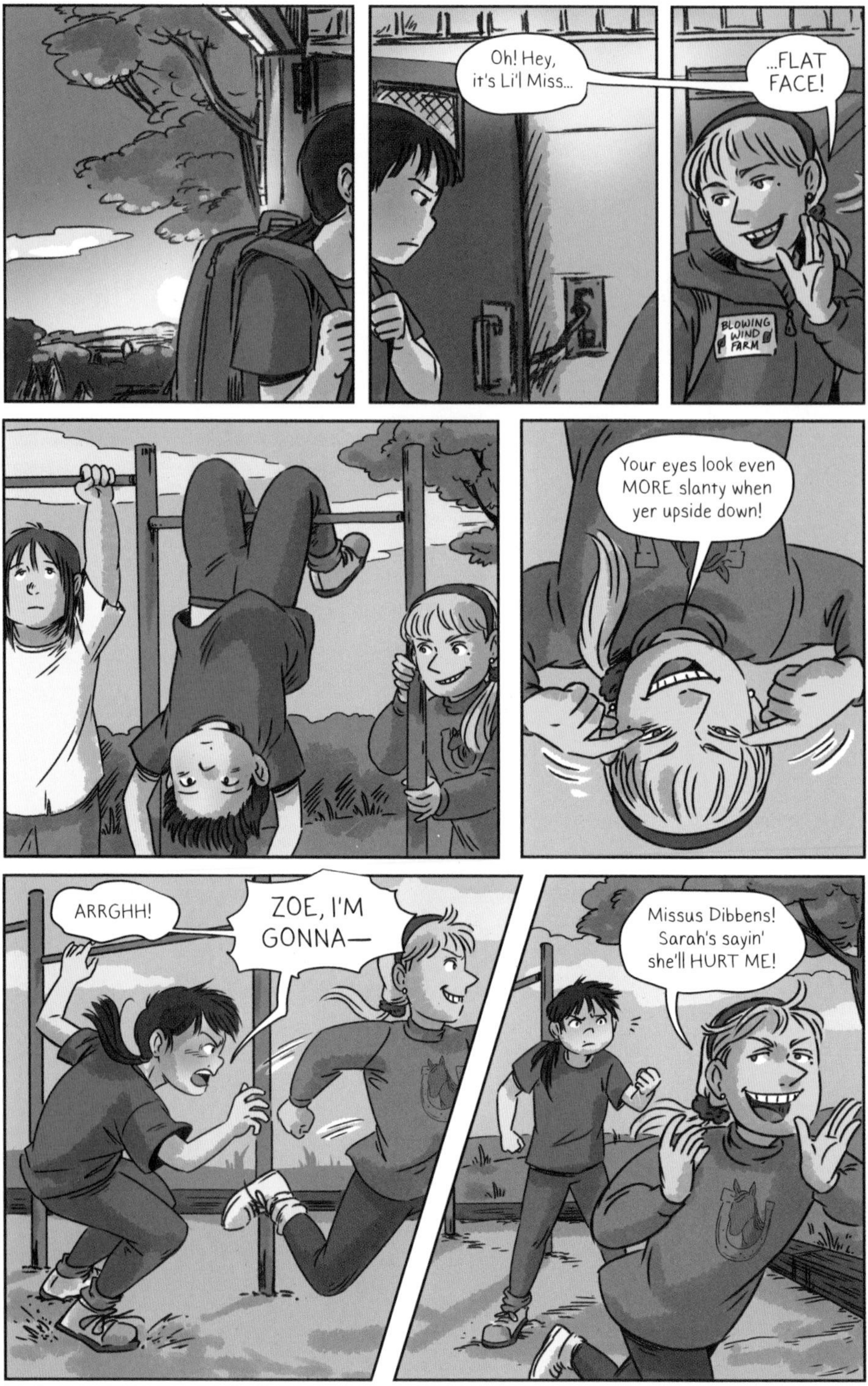
Oh! Hey, it's Li'l Miss...
...FLAT FACE!
BLOWING WIND FARM
Your eyes look even MORE slanty when yer upside down!
ARRGHH!
ZOE, I'M GONNA—
Missus Dibbens! Sarah's sayin' she'll HURT ME!

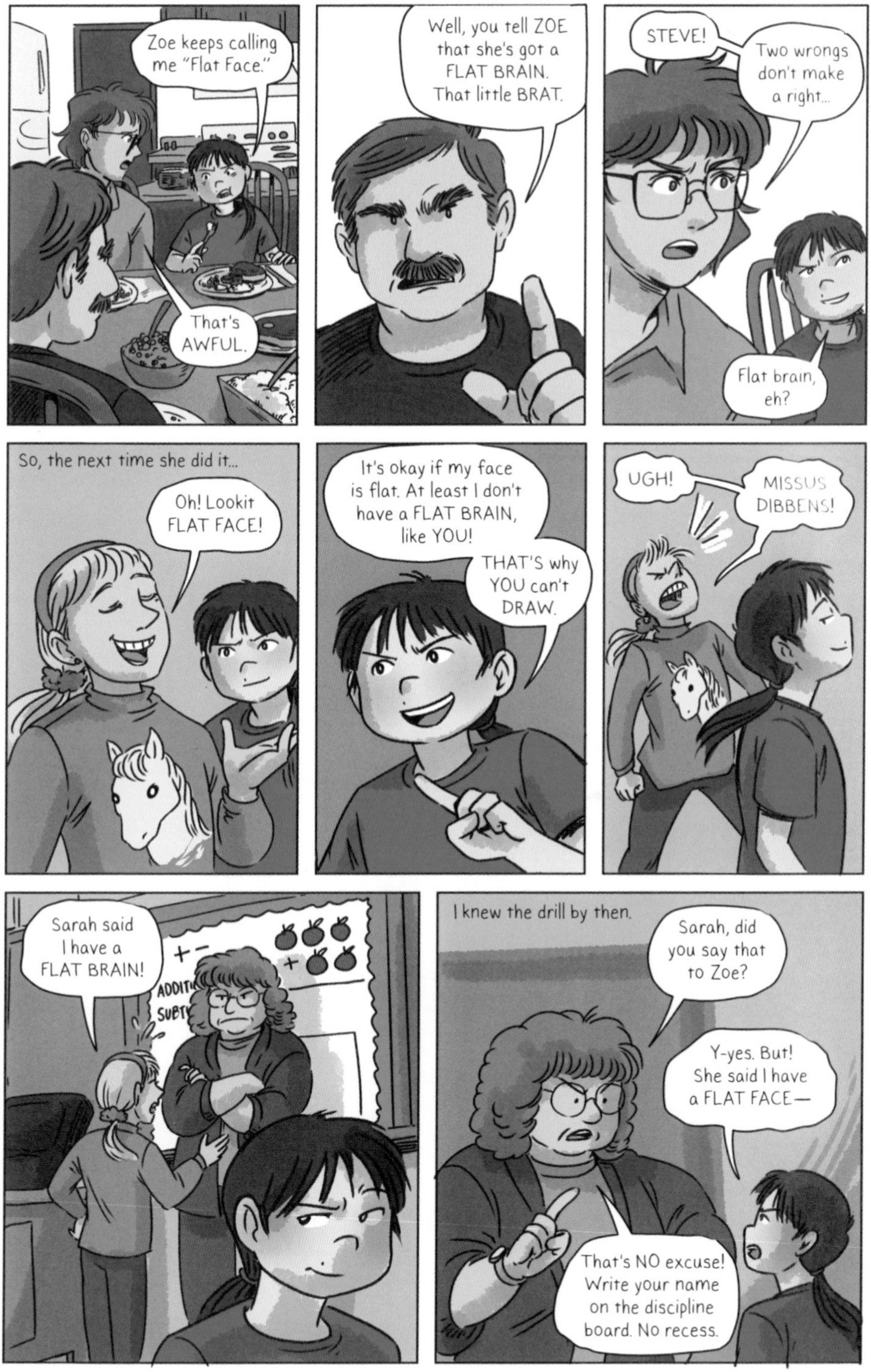
Zoe keeps calling me "Flat Face."
That's AWFUL.
Well, you tell ZOE that she's got a FLAT BRAIN. That little BRAT.
STEVE!
Two wrongs don't make a right...
Flat brain, eh?
So, the next time she did it...
Oh! Lookit FLAT FACE!
It's okay if my face is flat. At least I don't have a FLAT BRAIN, like YOU!
THAT'S why YOU can't DRAW.
UGH!
MISSUS DIBBENS!
Sarah said I have a FLAT BRAIN!
I knew the drill by then.
Sarah, did you say that to Zoe?
Y-yes. But! She said I have a FLAT FACE—
That's NO excuse! Write your name on the discipline board. No recess.

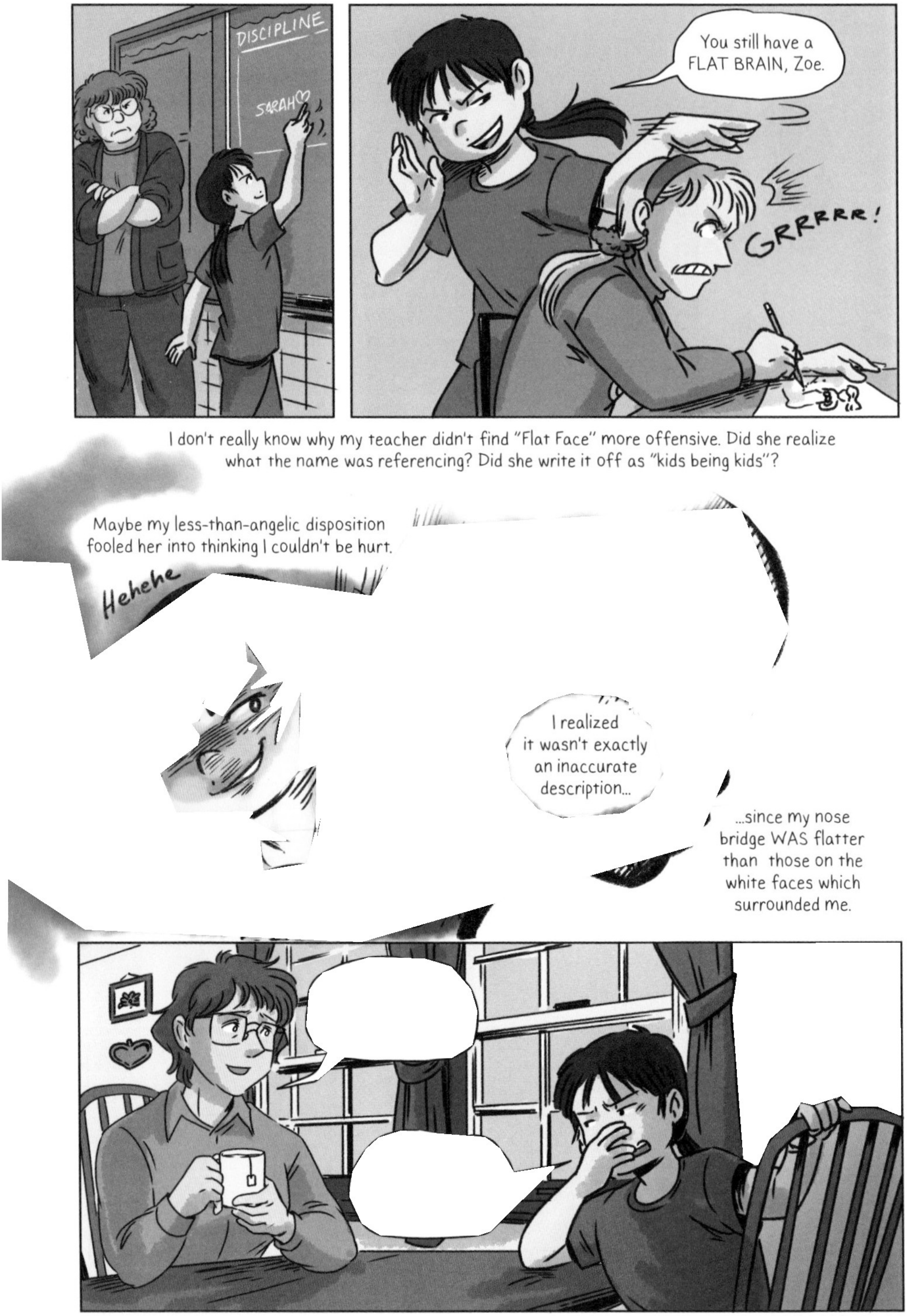
DISCIPLINE
SARAH
You still have a FLAT BRAIN, Zoe.
GRRRRR!
I don't really know why my teacher didn't find "Flat Face" more offensive. Did she realize what the name was referencing? Did she write it off as "kids being kids"?
Maybe my less-than-angelic disposition fooled her into thinking I couldn't be hurt.
Hehehe
I realized it wasn't exactly an inaccurate description...
...since my nose bridge WAS flatter than those on the white faces which surrounded me.

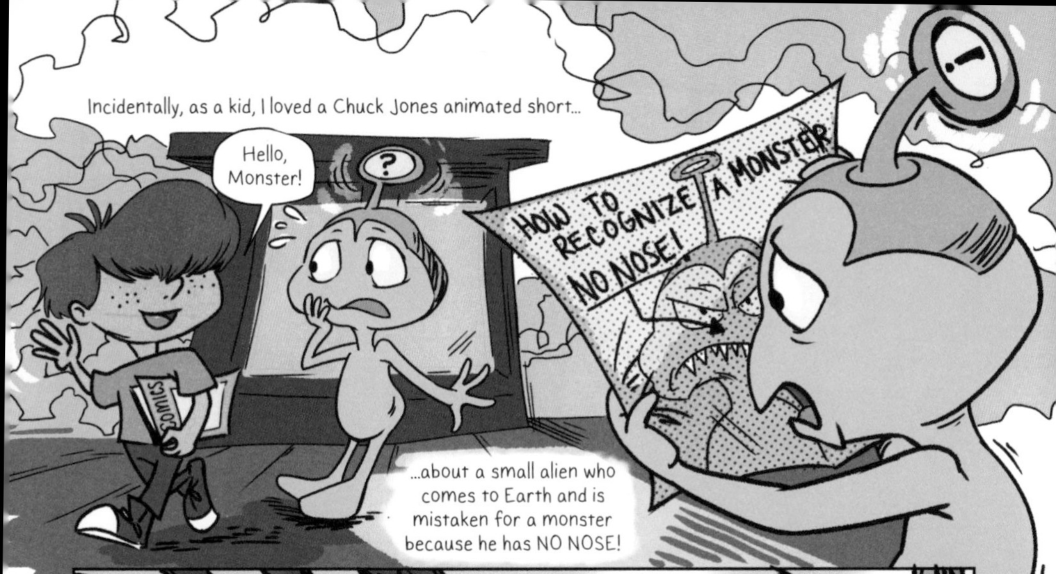
Incidentally, as a kid, I loved a Chuck Jones animated short...
Hello, Monster!
?
COMICS
HOW TO RECOGNIZE A MONSTER NO NOSE!
...about a small alien who comes to Earth and is mistaken for a monster because he has NO NOSE!

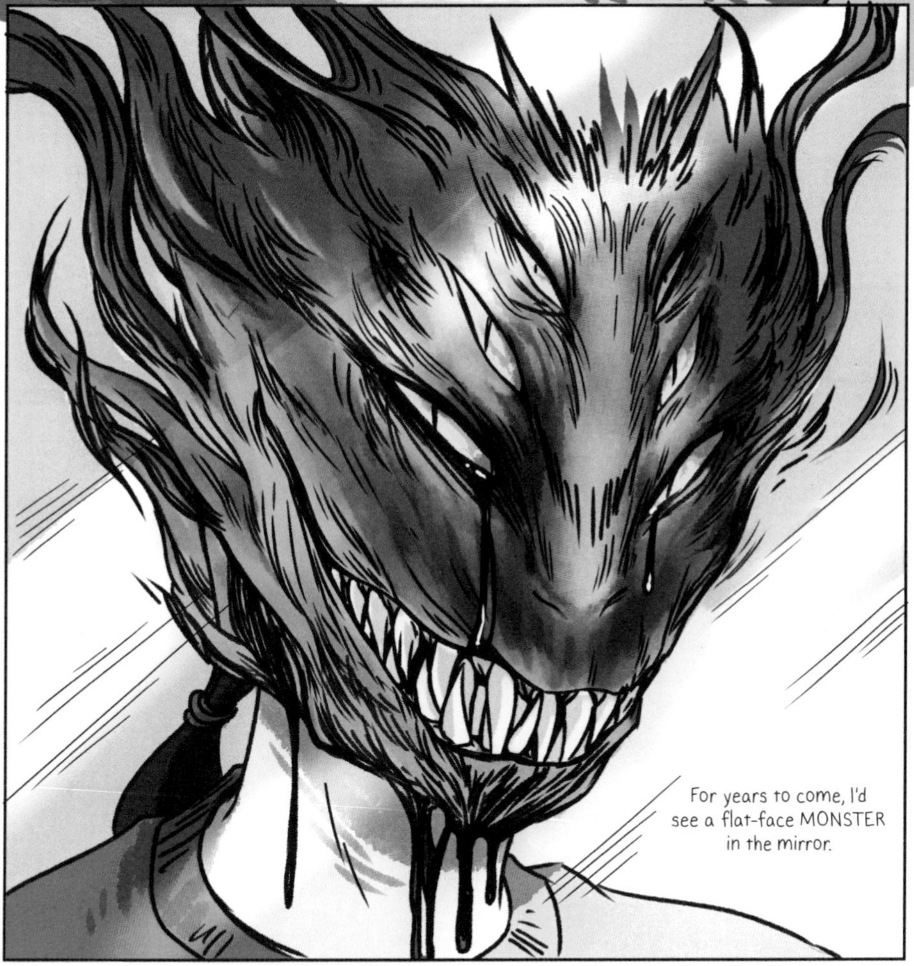
For years to come, I'd see a flat-face MONSTER in the mirror.

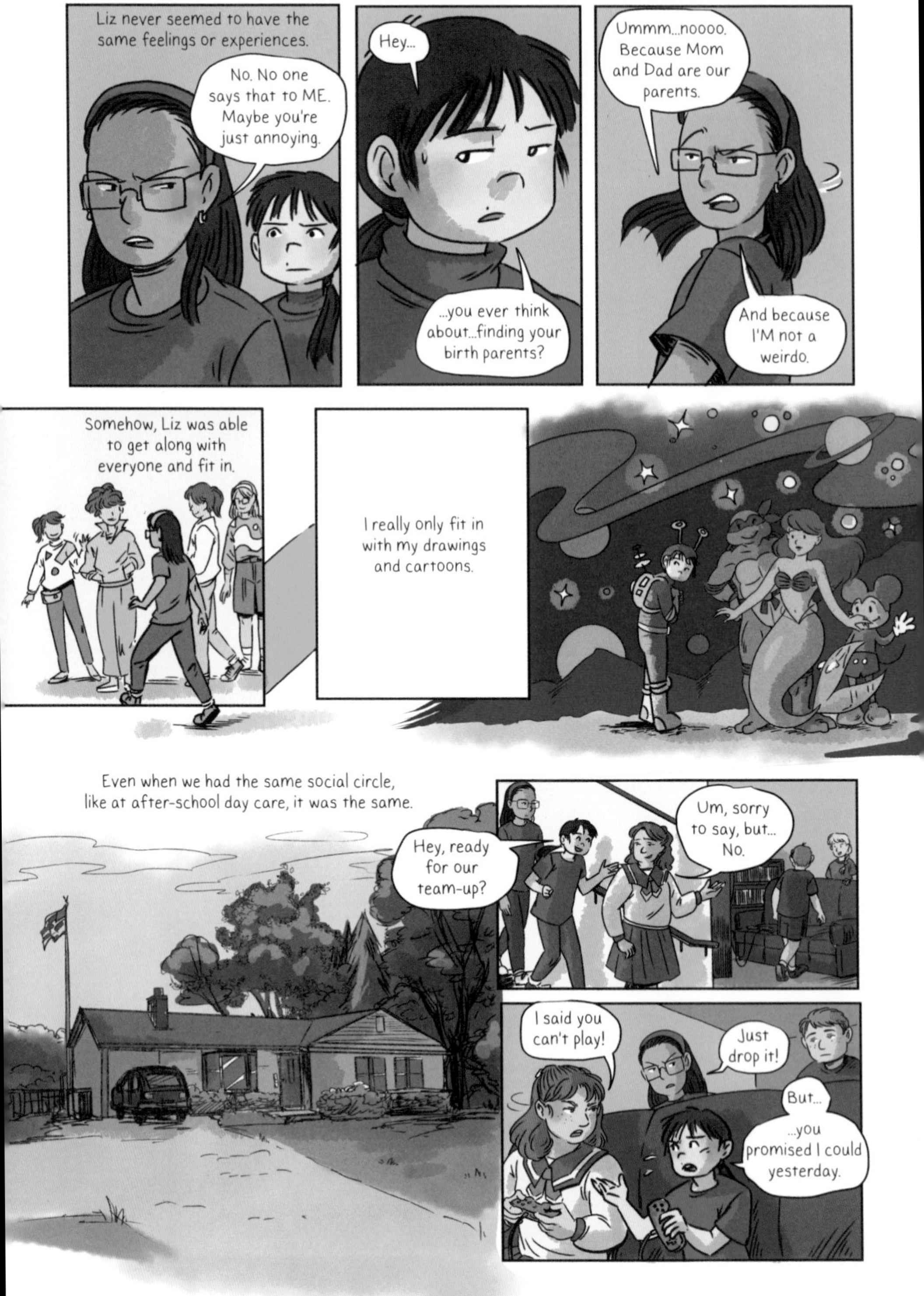
Liz never seemed to have the same feelings or experiences.
No. No one says that to ME. Maybe you're just annoying.
Hey...
...you ever think about...finding your birth parents?
Ummm...noooo. Because Mom and Dad are our parents.
And because I'M not a weirdo.
Somehow, Liz was able to get along with everyone and fit in.
I really only fit in with my drawings and cartoons.
Even when we had the same social circle, like at after-school day care, it was the same.
Hey, ready for our team-up?
Um, sorry to say, but... No.
I said you can't play!
Just drop it!
But...
...you promised I could yesterday.

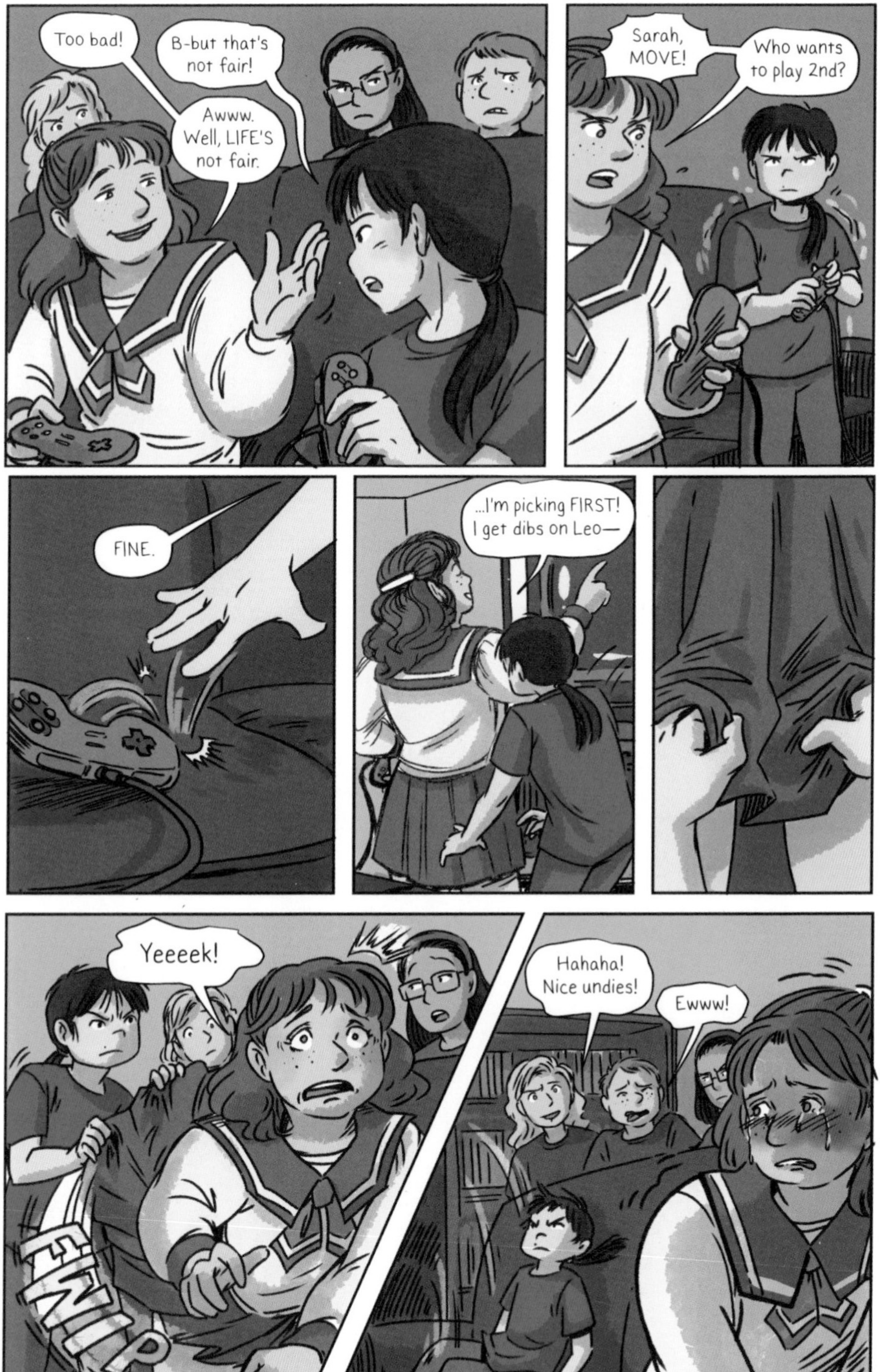
Too bad!
B-but that's not fair!
Awww. Well, LIFE'S not fair.
Sarah, MOVE!
Who wants to play 2nd?
FINE.
...I'm picking FIRST! I get dibs on Leo—
Yeeeek!
FWIP
Hahaha! Nice undies!
Ewww!

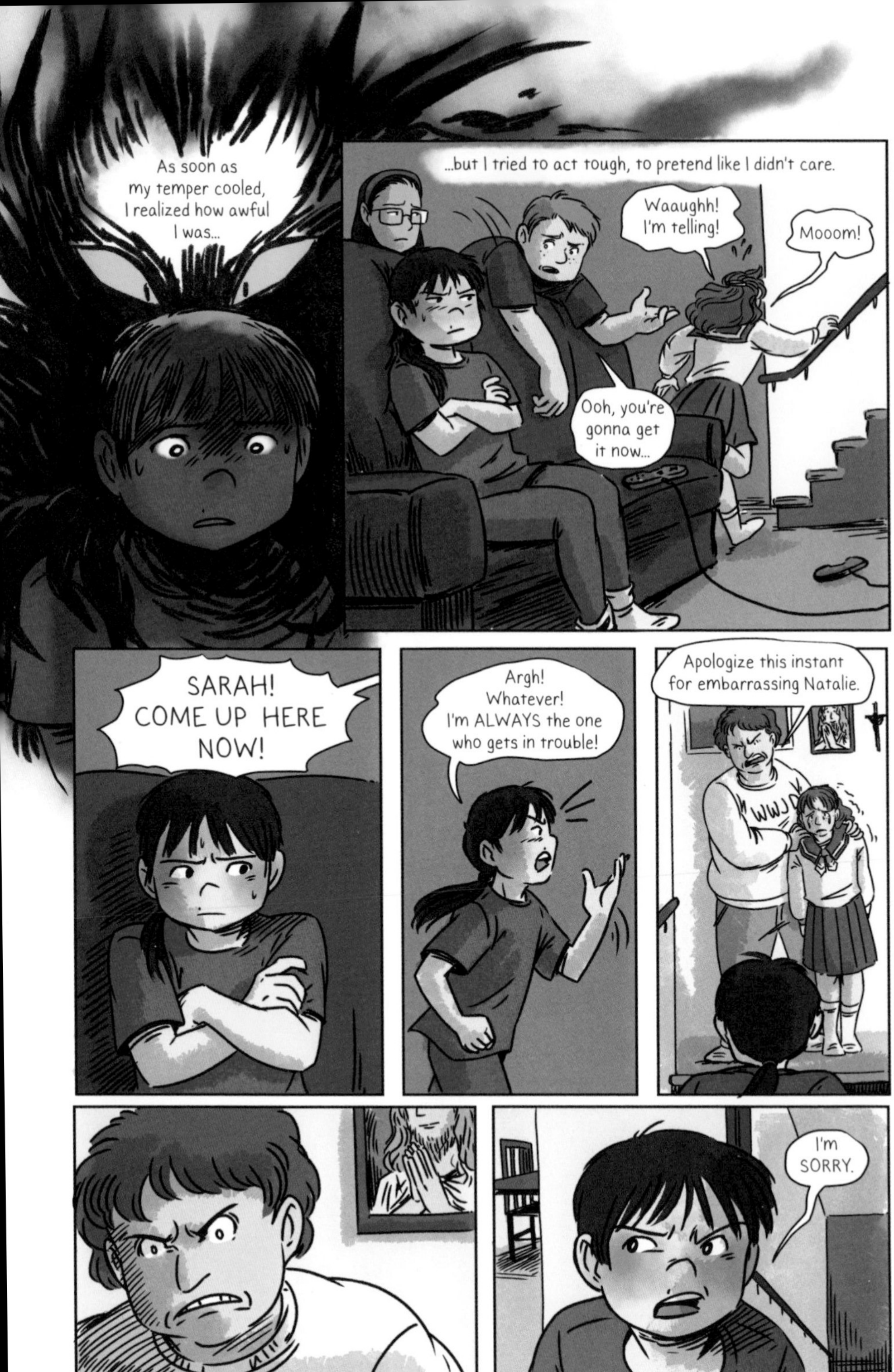
As soon as my temper cooled, I realized how awful I was...
...but I tried to act tough, to pretend like I didn't care.
Waaughh! I'm telling!
Mooom!
Ooh, you're gonna get it now...
SARAH! COME UP HERE NOW!
Argh! Whatever! I'm ALWAYS the one who gets in trouble!
Apologize this instant for embarrassing Natalie.
WWJD
I'm SORRY.

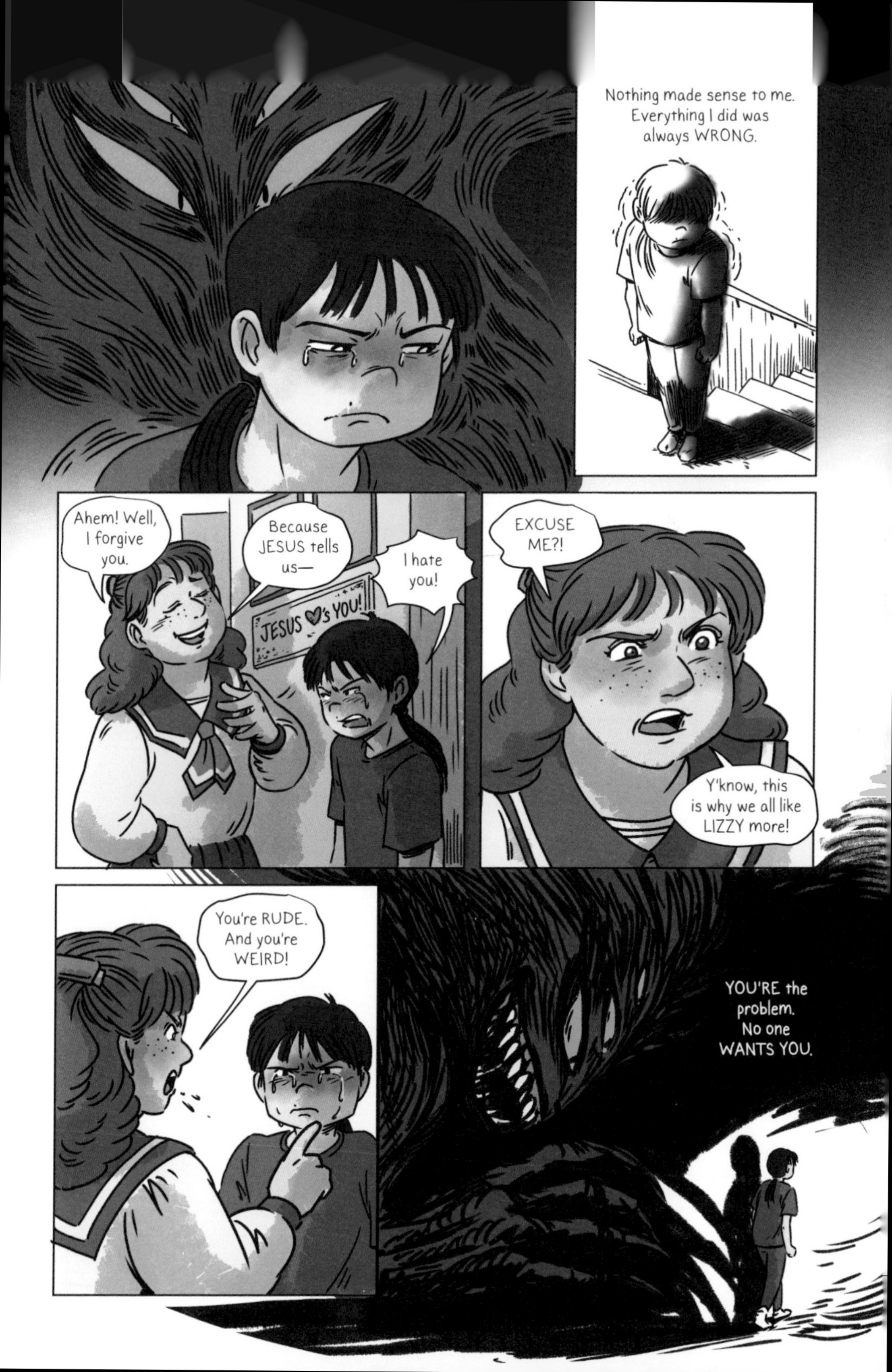
Nothing made sense to me. Everything I did was always WRONG.
Ahem! Well, I forgive you.
Because JESUS tells us—
I hate you!
JESUS ♡'s YOU!
EXCUSE ME?!
Y'know, this is why we all like LIZZY more!
You're RUDE. And you're WEIRD!
YOU'RE the problem. No one WANTS YOU.

I didn't fit the "Asian American Whiz Kid" stereotype, which had been popularized by *Time* magazine in the '80s.

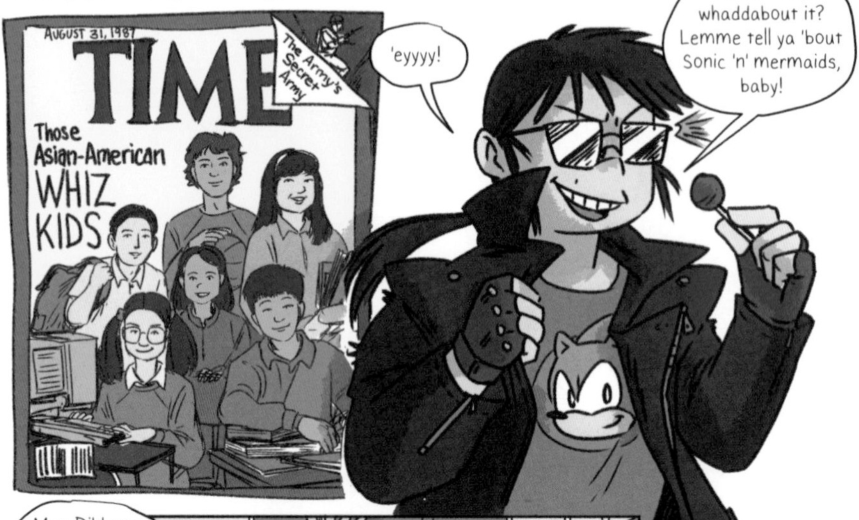
AUGUST 31, 1987
TIME
The Army's Secret Army
Those Asian-American WHIZ KIDS
'eyyyy!
Math? Yeh, whaddabout it? Lemme tell ya 'bout Sonic 'n' mermaids, baby!

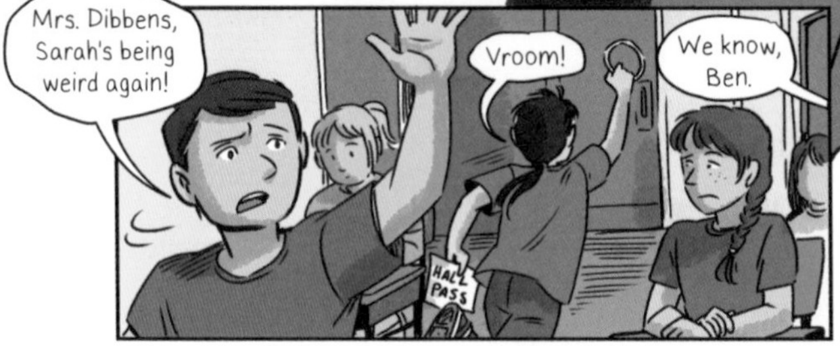
Mrs. Dibbens, Sarah's being weird again!
Vroom!
HALL PASS
We know, Ben.

The more attention I got for drawing, the more it became part of my social identity.

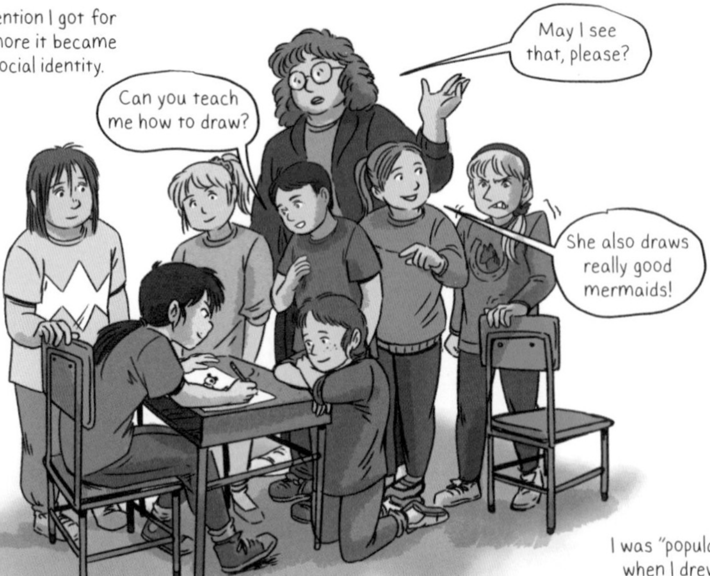
Can you teach me how to draw?
May I see that, please?
She also draws really good mermaids!

I was "popular" when I drew.

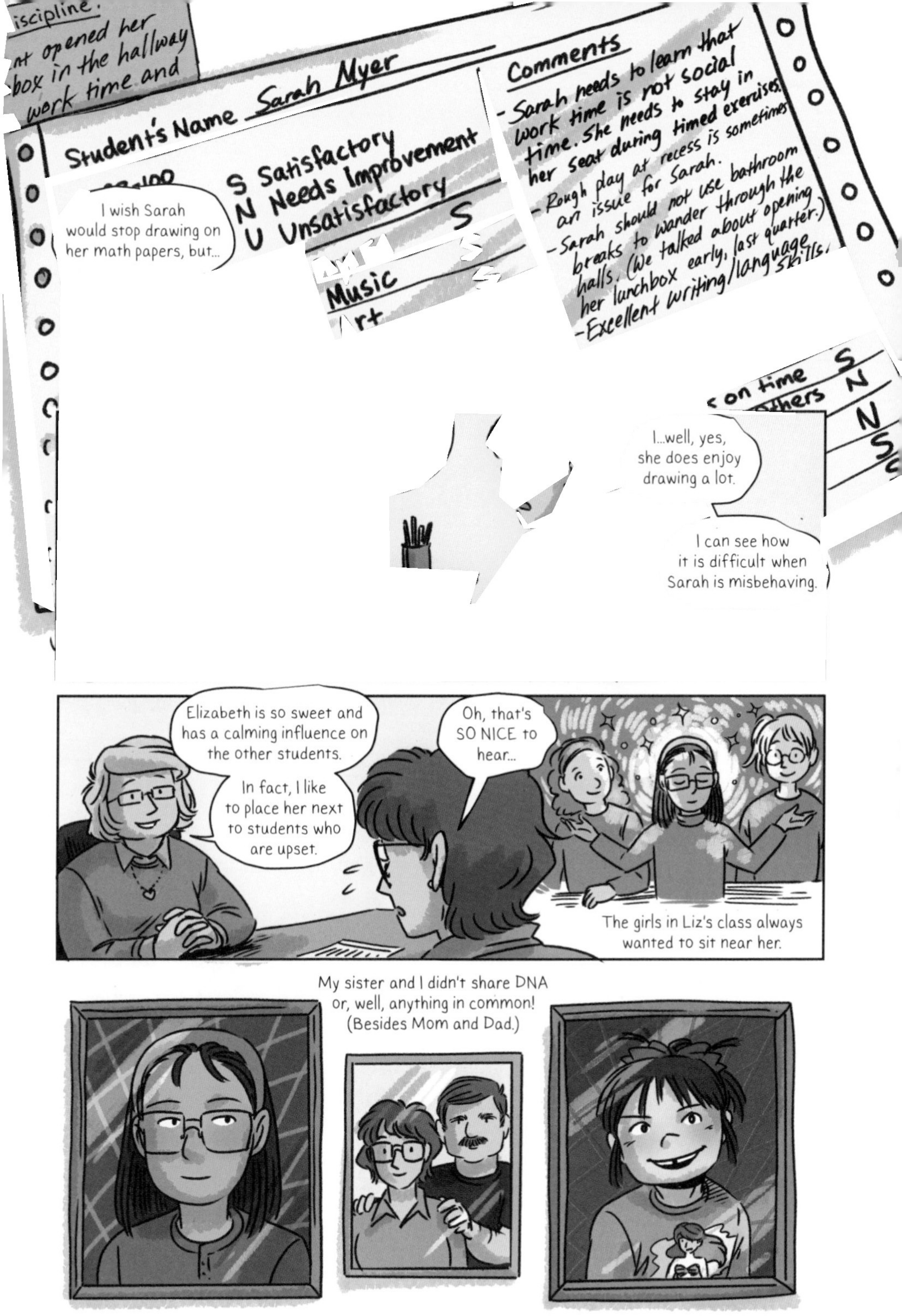

iscipline:
nt opened her
box in the hallway
work time and
Student's Name Sarah Myer
S Satisfactory
N Needs Improvement
U Unsatisfactory
Music
Comments
-Sarah needs to learn that work time is not social time. She needs to stay in her seat during timed exercises.
-Rough play at recess is sometimes an issue for Sarah.
-Sarah should not use bathroom breaks to wander through the halls. (We talked about opening her lunchbox early, last quarter.)
-Excellent writing/language skills.
I wish Sarah would stop drawing on her math papers, but...
I...well, yes, she does enjoy drawing a lot.
I can see how it is difficult when Sarah is misbehaving.
Elizabeth is so sweet and has a calming influence on the other students.
In fact, I like to place her next to students who are upset.
Oh, that's SO NICE to hear...
The girls in Liz's class always wanted to sit near her.
My sister and I didn't share DNA or, well, anything in common! (Besides Mom and Dad.)

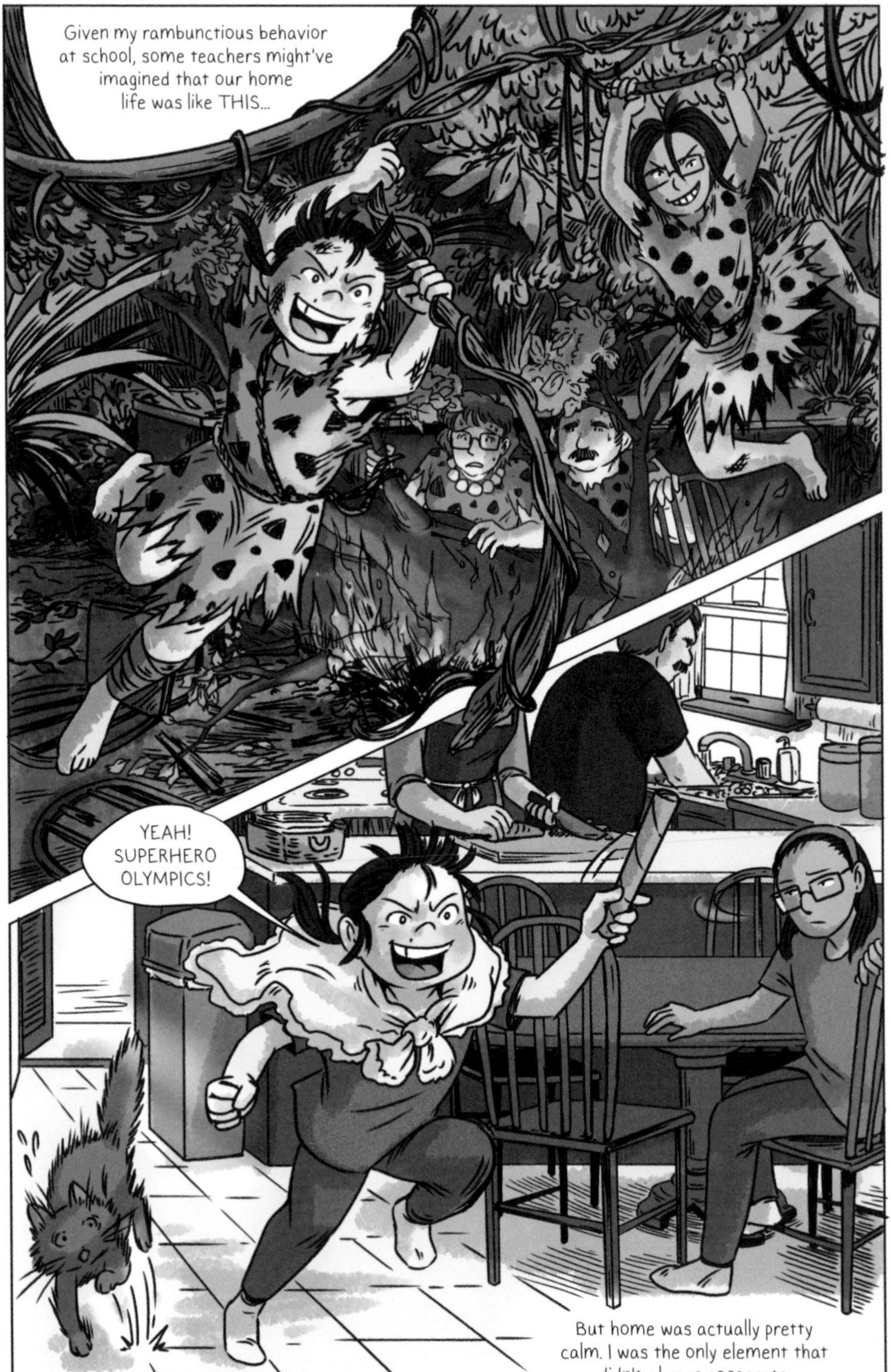
Given my rambunctious behavior at school, some teachers might've imagined that our home life was like THIS...
YEAH! SUPERHERO OLYMPICS!
But home was actually pretty calm. I was the only element that didn't always cooperate.

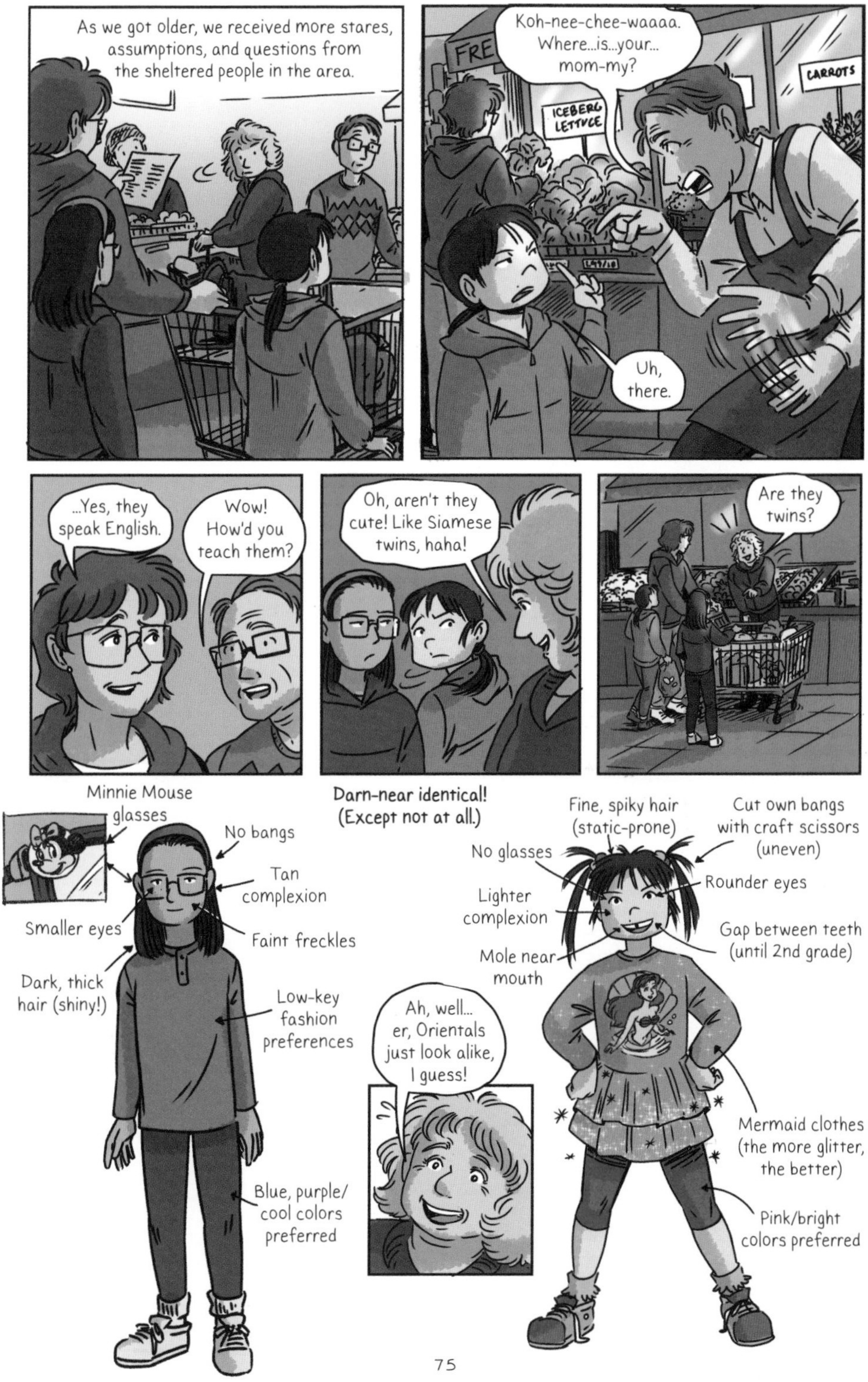

As we got older, we received more stares, assumptions, and questions from the sheltered people in the area.
Koh-nee-chee-waaaa. Where...is...your... mom-my?
ICEBERG LETTUCE
CARROTS
Uh, there.
...Yes, they speak English.
Wow! How'd you teach them?
Oh, aren't they cute! Like Siamese twins, haha!
Are they twins?
Darn-near identical! (Except not at all.)
Minnie Mouse glasses
No bangs
Tan complexion
Smaller eyes
Faint freckles
Dark, thick hair (shiny!)
Low-key fashion preferences
Blue, purple/ cool colors preferred
Fine, spiky hair (static-prone)
Cut own bangs with craft scissors (uneven)
No glasses
Rounder eyes
Lighter complexion
Gap between teeth (until 2nd grade)
Mole near mouth
Ah, well... er, Orientals just look alike, I guess!
Mermaid clothes (the more glitter, the better)
Pink/bright colors preferred

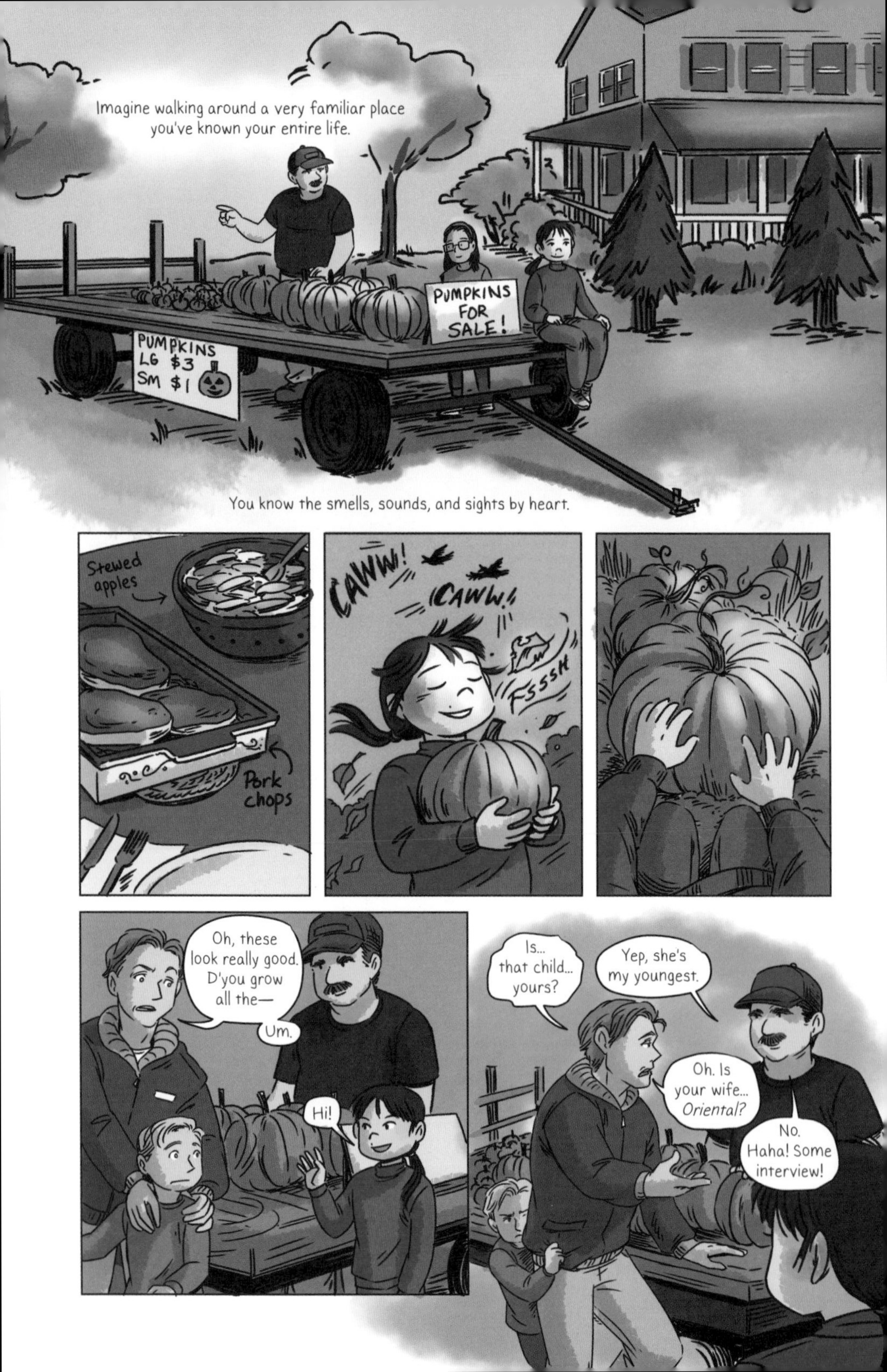
Imagine walking around a very familiar place you've known your entire life.
PUMPKINS FOR SALE!
PUMPKINS LG $3 SM $1
You know the smells, sounds, and sights by heart.
Stewed apples
Pork chops
CAWW!
CAWW!
FSSSH
Oh, these look really good. D'you grow all the—
Um.
Hi!
Is... that child... yours?
Yep, she's my youngest.
Oh. Is your wife... *Oriental?*
No. Haha! Some interview!

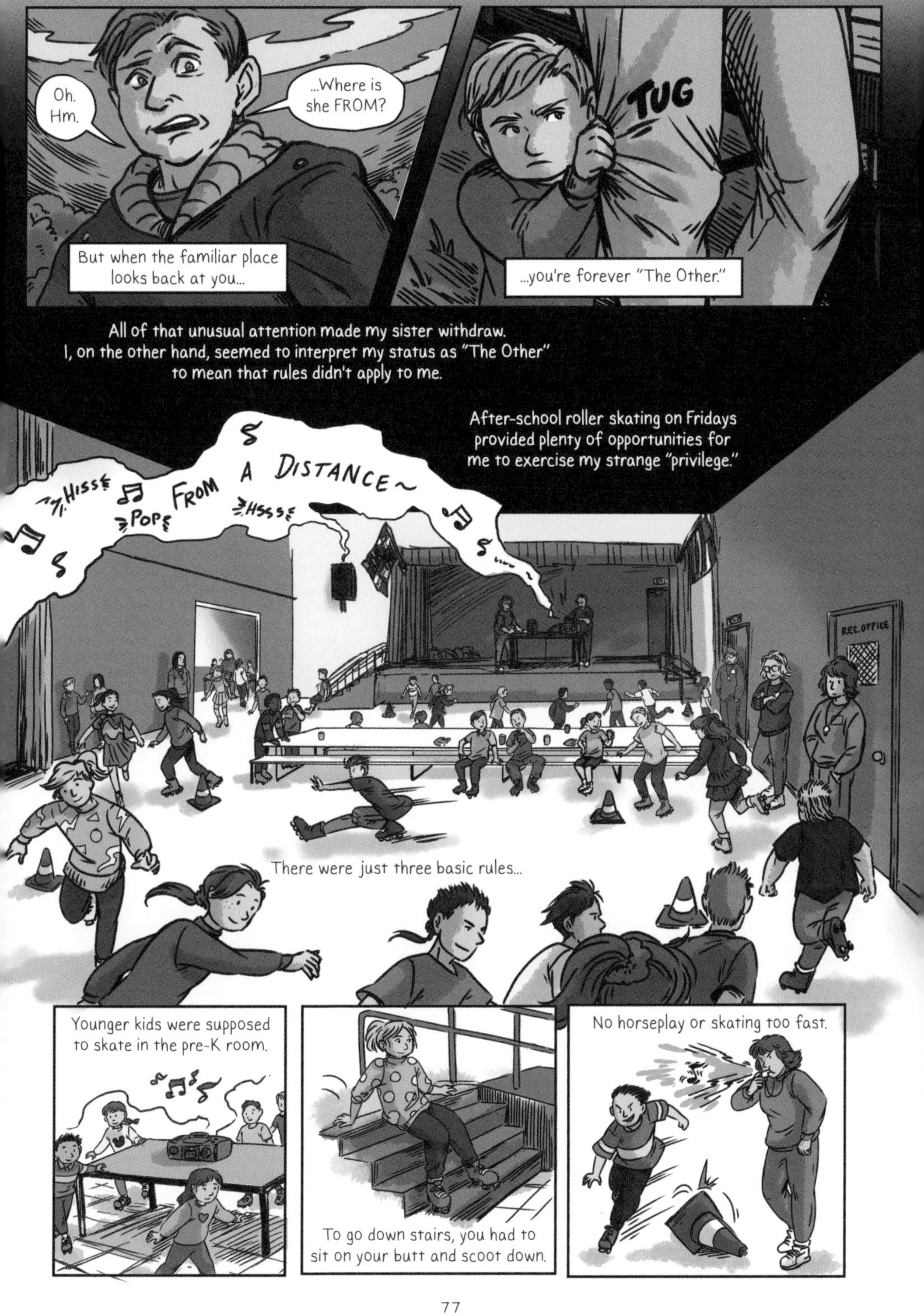
Oh.
Hm.
...Where is
she FROM?
But when the familiar place
looks back at you...
TUG
...you're forever "The Other."
All of that unusual attention made my sister withdraw.
I, on the other hand, seemed to interpret my status as "The Other"
to mean that rules didn't apply to me.
After-school roller skating on Fridays
provided plenty of opportunities for
me to exercise my strange "privilege."
HISS
POP
FROM A DISTANCE~
HSSS
REC. OFFICE
There were just three basic rules...
Younger kids were supposed
to skate in the pre-K room.
To go down stairs, you had to
sit on your butt and scoot down.
No horseplay or skating too fast.

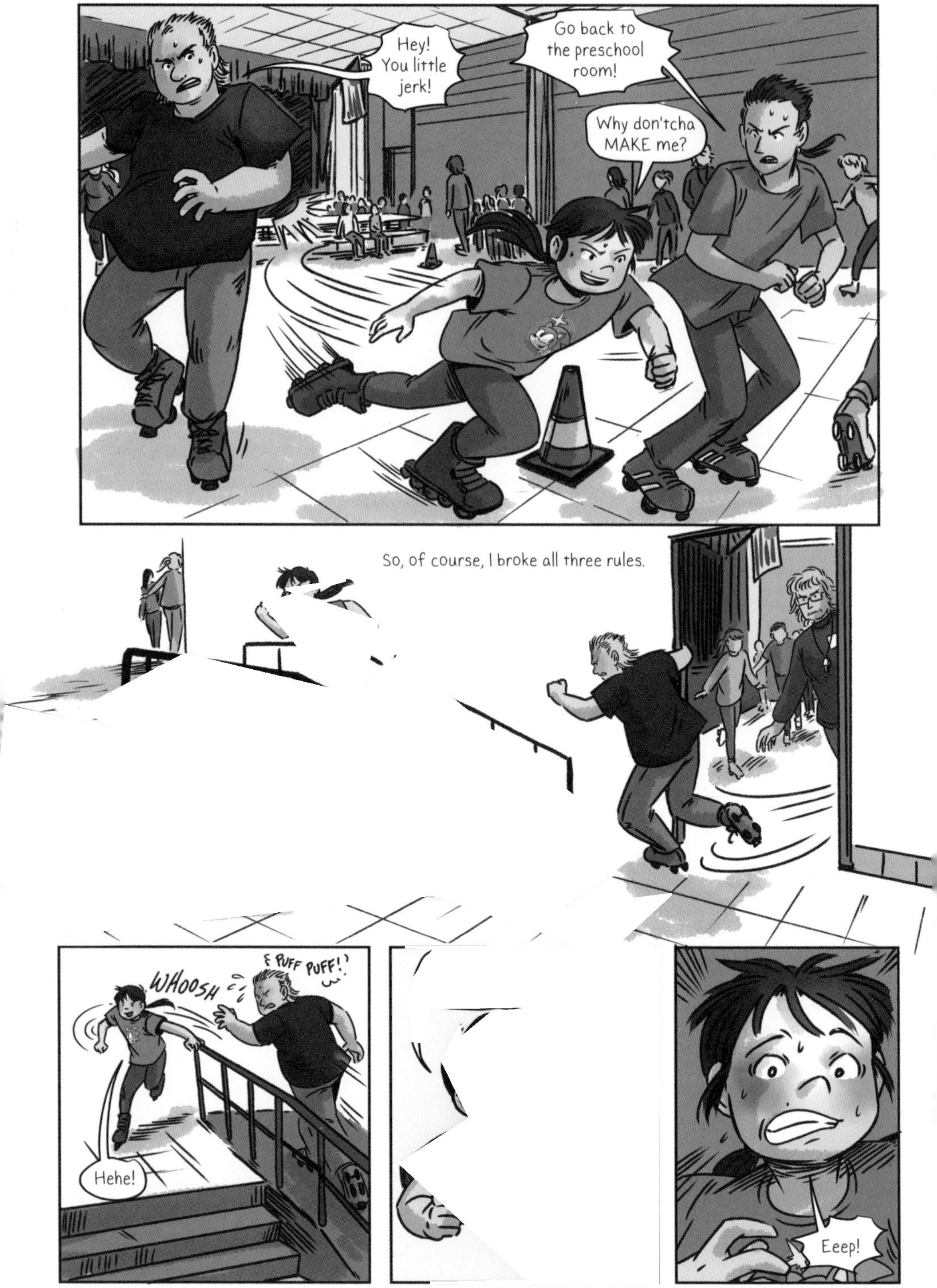
Hey! You little jerk!
Go back to the preschool room!
Why don'tcha MAKE me?
So, of course, I broke all three rules.
WHOOSH
PUFF PUFF!
Hehe!
Eeep!

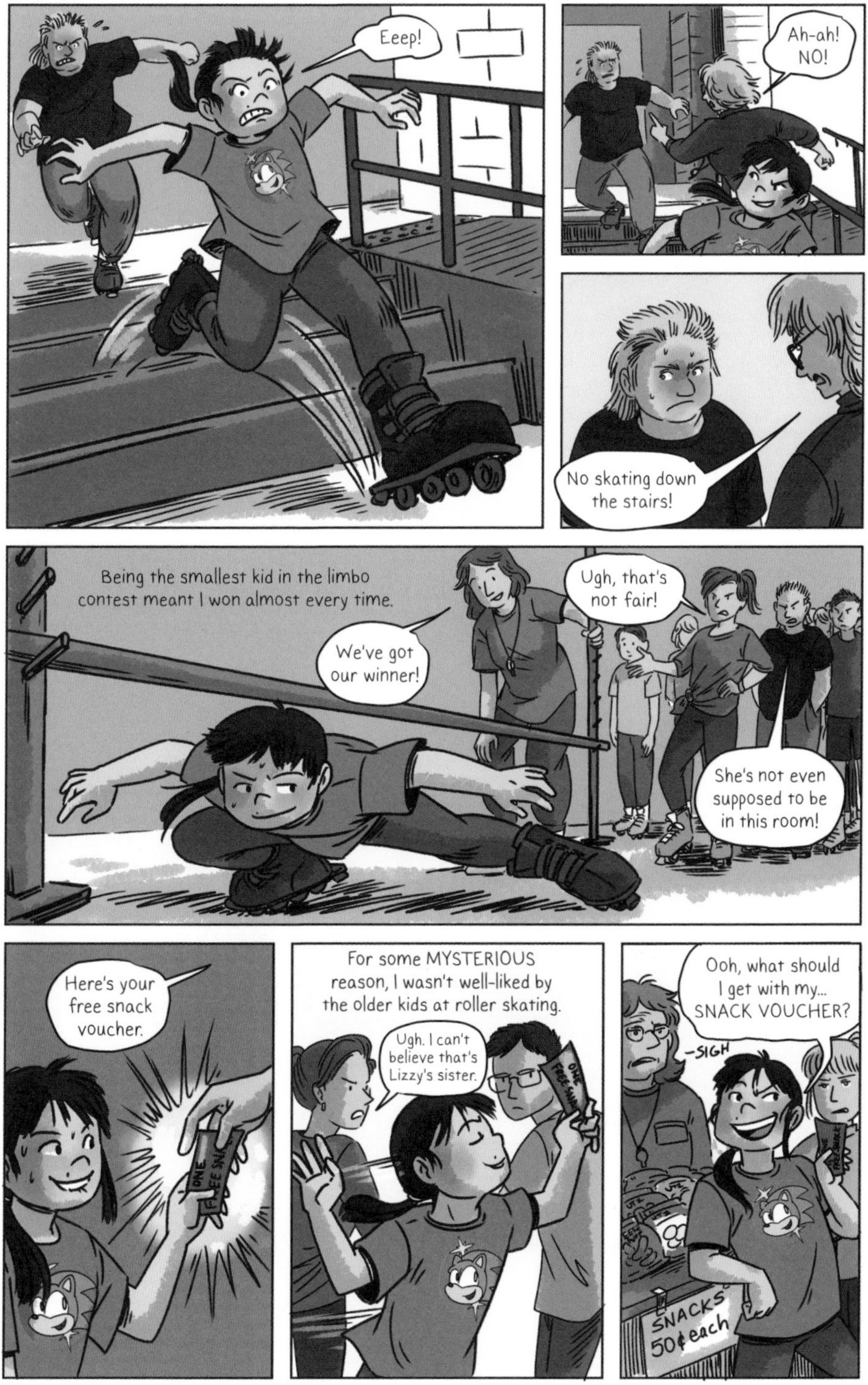
Eeep!
Ah-ah! NO!
No skating down the stairs!
Being the smallest kid in the limbo contest meant I won almost every time.
We've got our winner!
Ugh, that's not fair!
She's not even supposed to be in this room!
Here's your free snack voucher.
For some MYSTERIOUS reason, I wasn't well-liked by the older kids at roller skating.
Ugh. I can't believe that's Lizzy's sister.
Ooh, what should I get with my... SNACK VOUCHER?
-SIGH
SNACKS 50¢ each

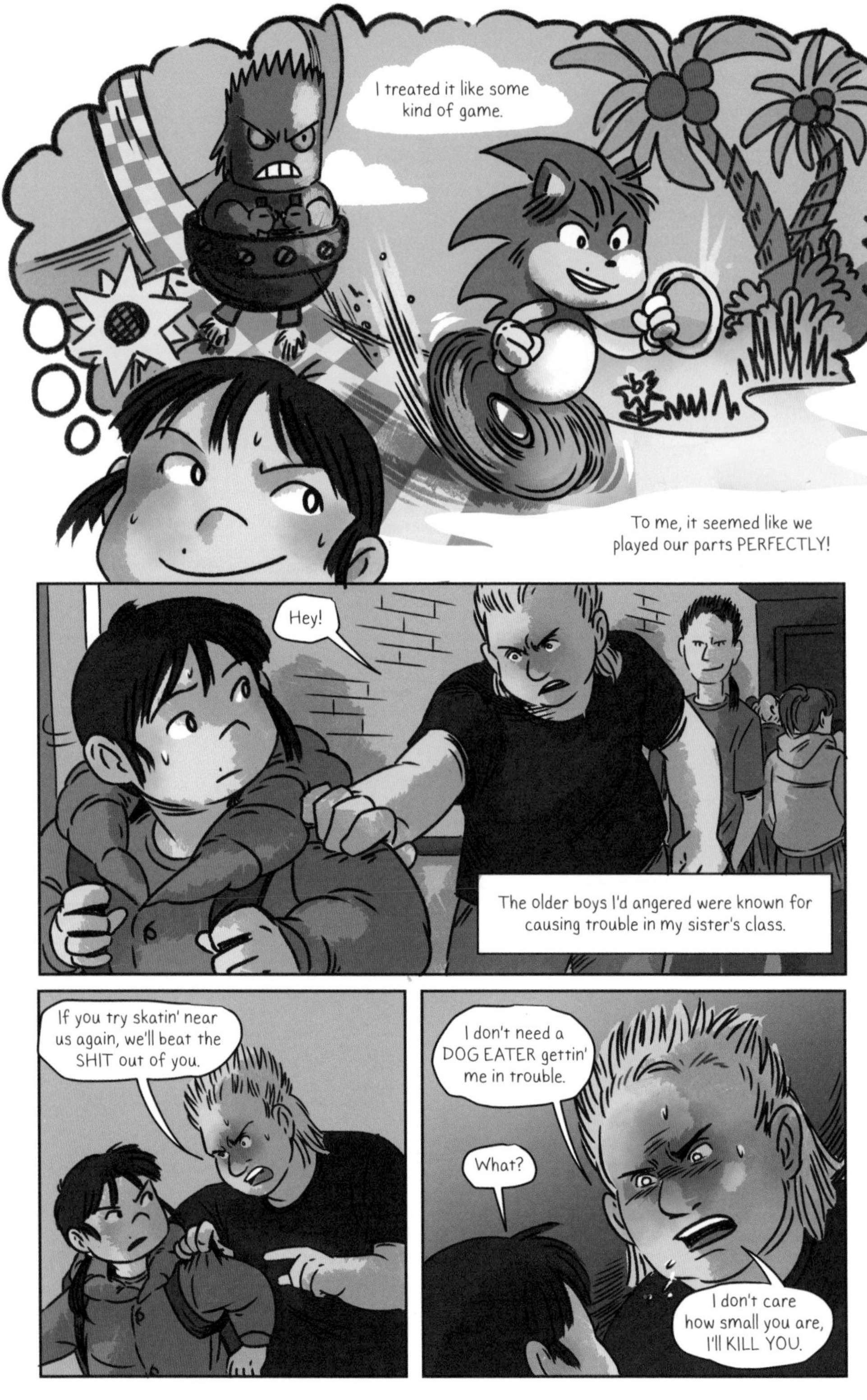

I treated it like some kind of game.
To me, it seemed like we played our parts PERFECTLY!
Hey!
The older boys I'd angered were known for causing trouble in my sister's class.
If you try skatin' near us again, we'll beat the SHIT out of you.
I don't need a DOG EATER gettin' me in trouble.
What?
I don't care how small you are, I'll KILL YOU.

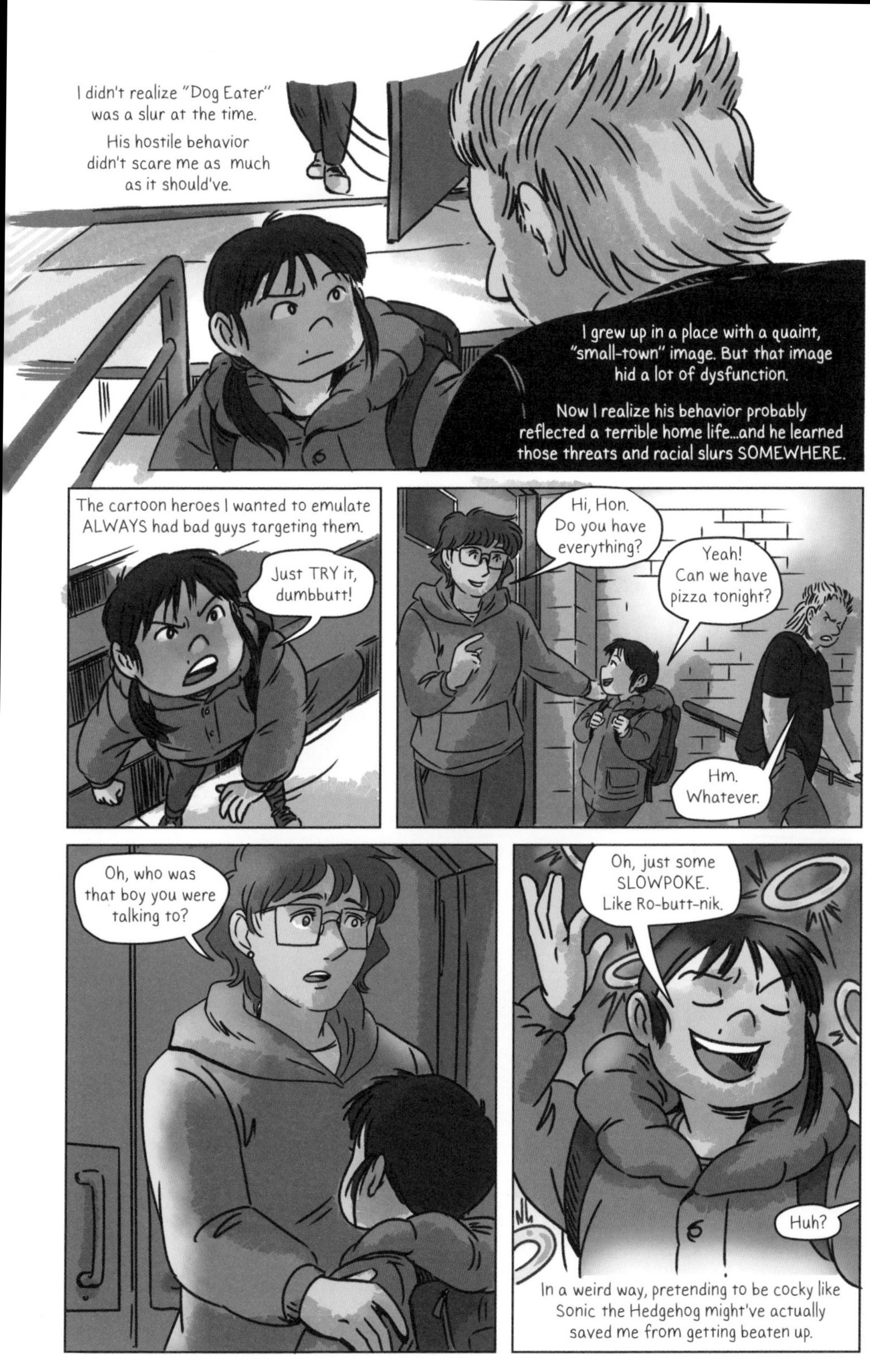
I didn't realize "Dog Eater" was a slur at the time.
His hostile behavior didn't scare me as much as it should've.
I grew up in a place with a quaint, "small-town" image. But that image hid a lot of dysfunction.
Now I realize his behavior probably reflected a terrible home life...and he learned those threats and racial slurs SOMEWHERE.
The cartoon heroes I wanted to emulate ALWAYS had bad guys targeting them.
Just TRY it, dumbbutt!
Hi, Hon. Do you have everything?
Yeah! Can we have pizza tonight?
Hm. Whatever.
Oh, who was that boy you were talking to?
Oh, just some SLOWPOKE. Like Ro-butt-nik.
Huh?
In a weird way, pretending to be cocky like Sonic the Hedgehog might've actually saved me from getting beaten up.

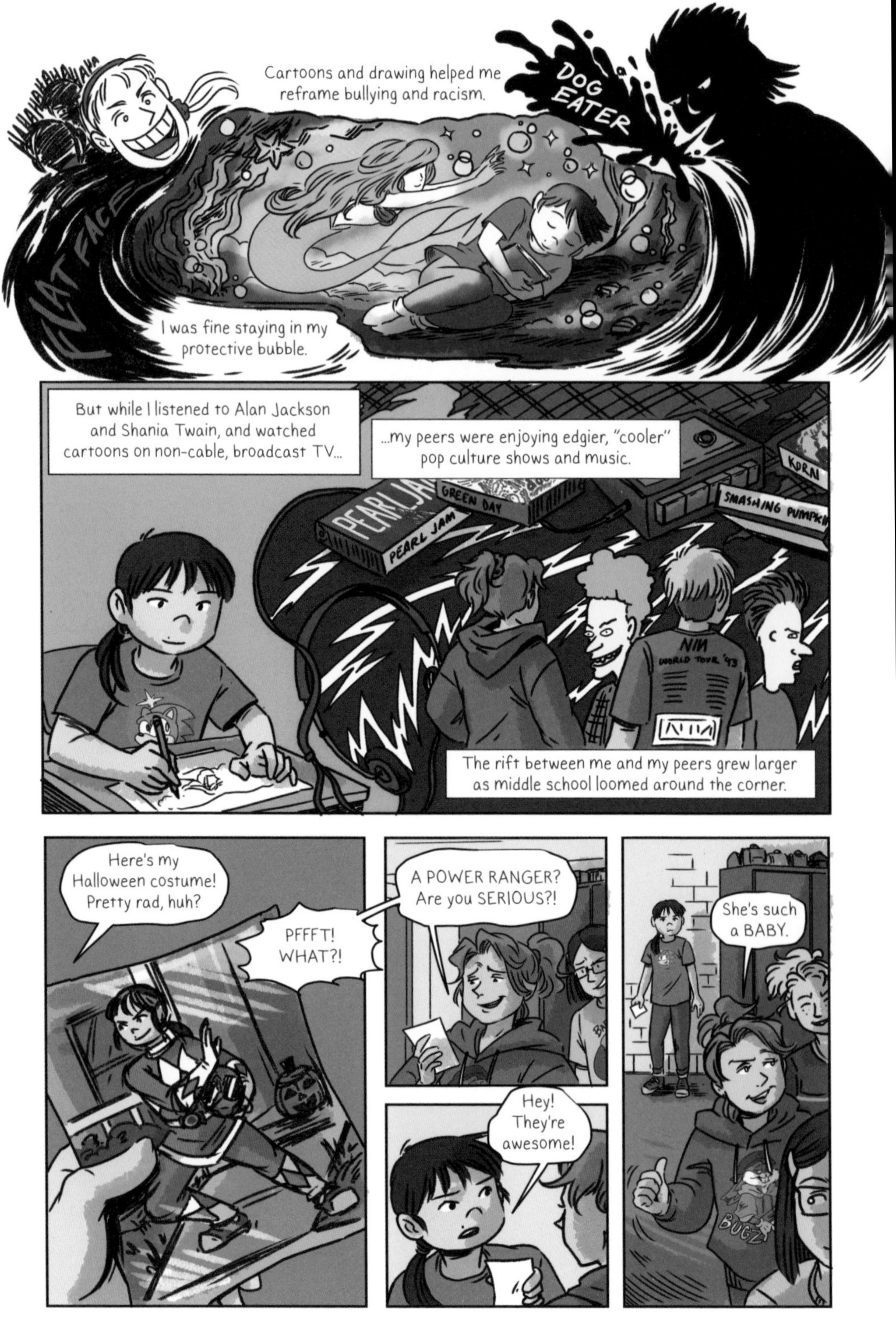
HAHAHAHAHAHAHA
Cartoons and drawing helped me reframe bullying and racism.
DOG EATER
FLAT FACE
I was fine staying in my protective bubble.
But while I listened to Alan Jackson and Shania Twain, and watched cartoons on non-cable, broadcast TV...
...my peers were enjoying edgier, "cooler" pop culture shows and music.
PEARL JAM
PEARL JAM
GREEN DAY
KORN
SMASHING PUMPKI
NIN
WORLD TOUR '93
The rift between me and my peers grew larger as middle school loomed around the corner.
Here's my Halloween costume! Pretty rad, huh?
PFFFT! WHAT?!
A POWER RANGER? Are you SERIOUS?!
Hey! They're awesome!
She's such a BABY.
BUGZ

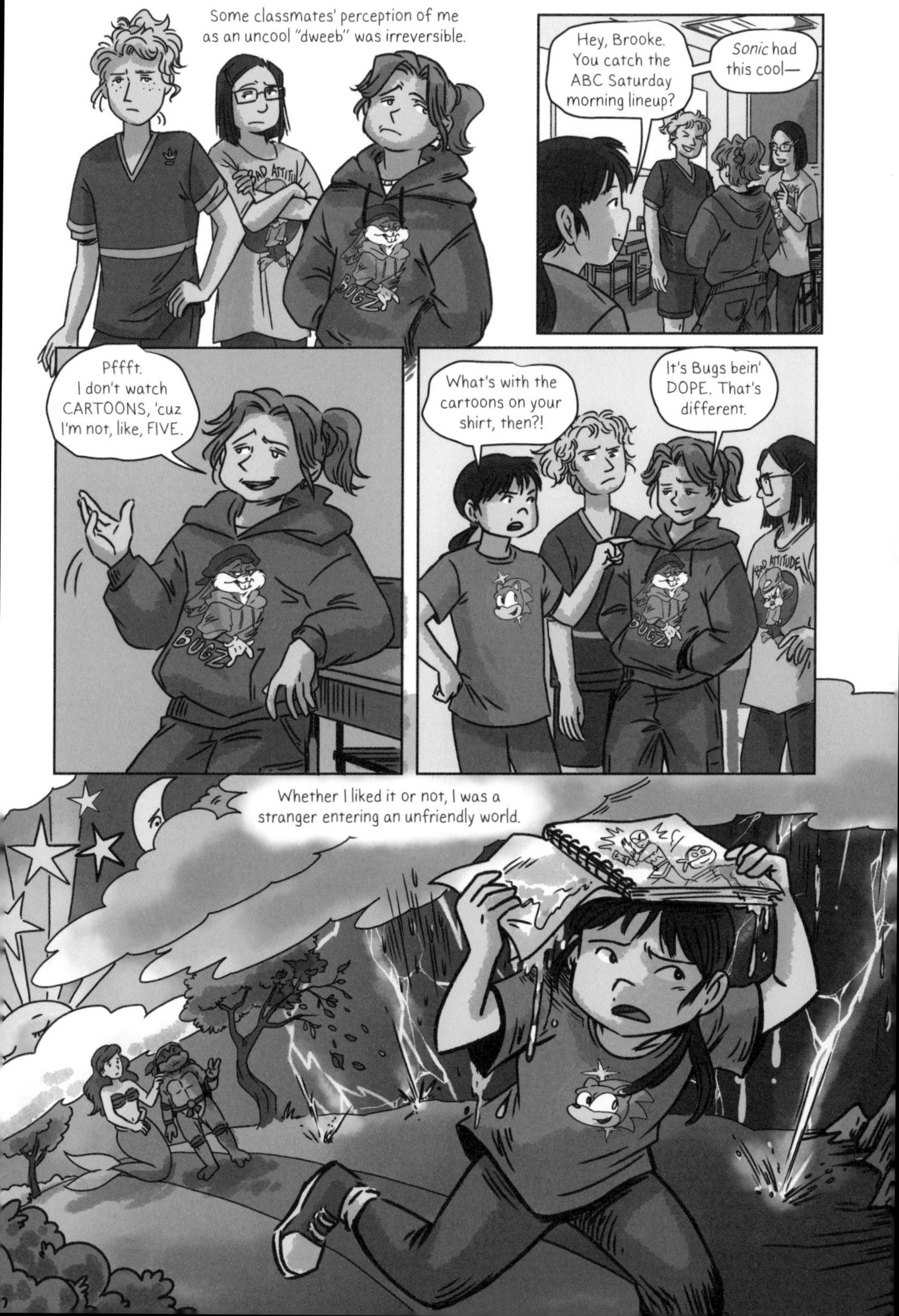
Some classmates' perception of me as an uncool "dweeb" was irreversible.
BAD ATTITUDE
BUGZ
Hey, Brooke. You catch the ABC Saturday morning lineup?
Sonic had this cool—
Pffft. I don't watch CARTOONS, 'cuz I'm not, like, FIVE.
BUGZ
What's with the cartoons on your shirt, then?!
It's Bugs bein' DOPE. That's different.
BUGZ
BAD ATTITUDE
Whether I liked it or not, I was a stranger entering an unfriendly world.

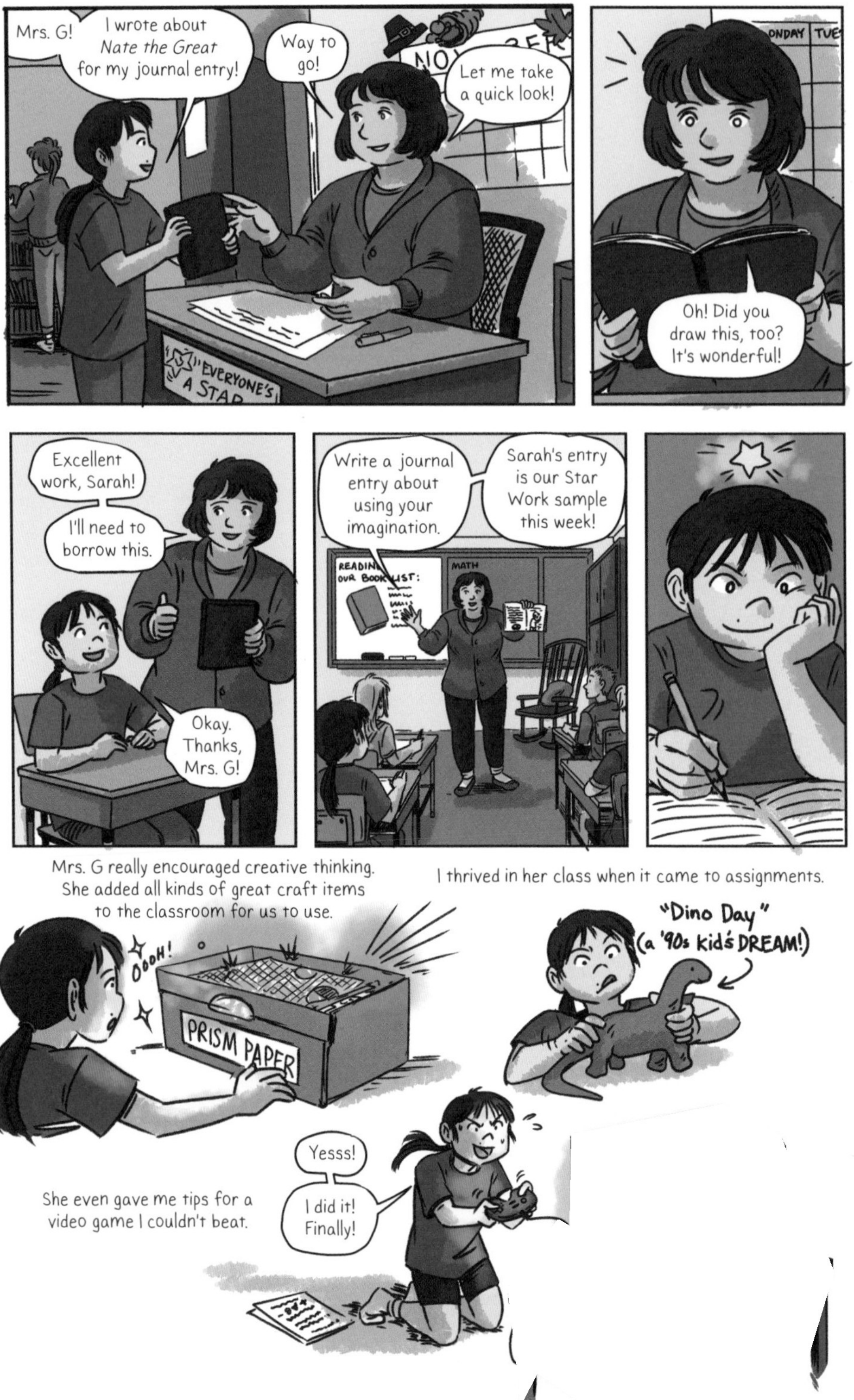

Mrs. G!
I wrote about *Nate the Great* for my journal entry!
Way to go!
Let me take a quick look!
"EVERYONE'S A STAR
Oh! Did you draw this, too? It's wonderful!
Excellent work, Sarah!
I'll need to borrow this.
Okay. Thanks, Mrs. G!
Write a journal entry about using your imagination.
Sarah's entry is our Star Work sample this week!
READING OUR BOOK LIST:
MATH
Mrs. G really encouraged creative thinking. She added all kinds of great craft items to the classroom for us to use.
OOOH!
PRISM PAPER
I thrived in her class when it came to assignments.
"Dino Day" (a '90s kid's DREAM!)
She even gave me tips for a video game I couldn't beat.
Yesss!
I did it! Finally!

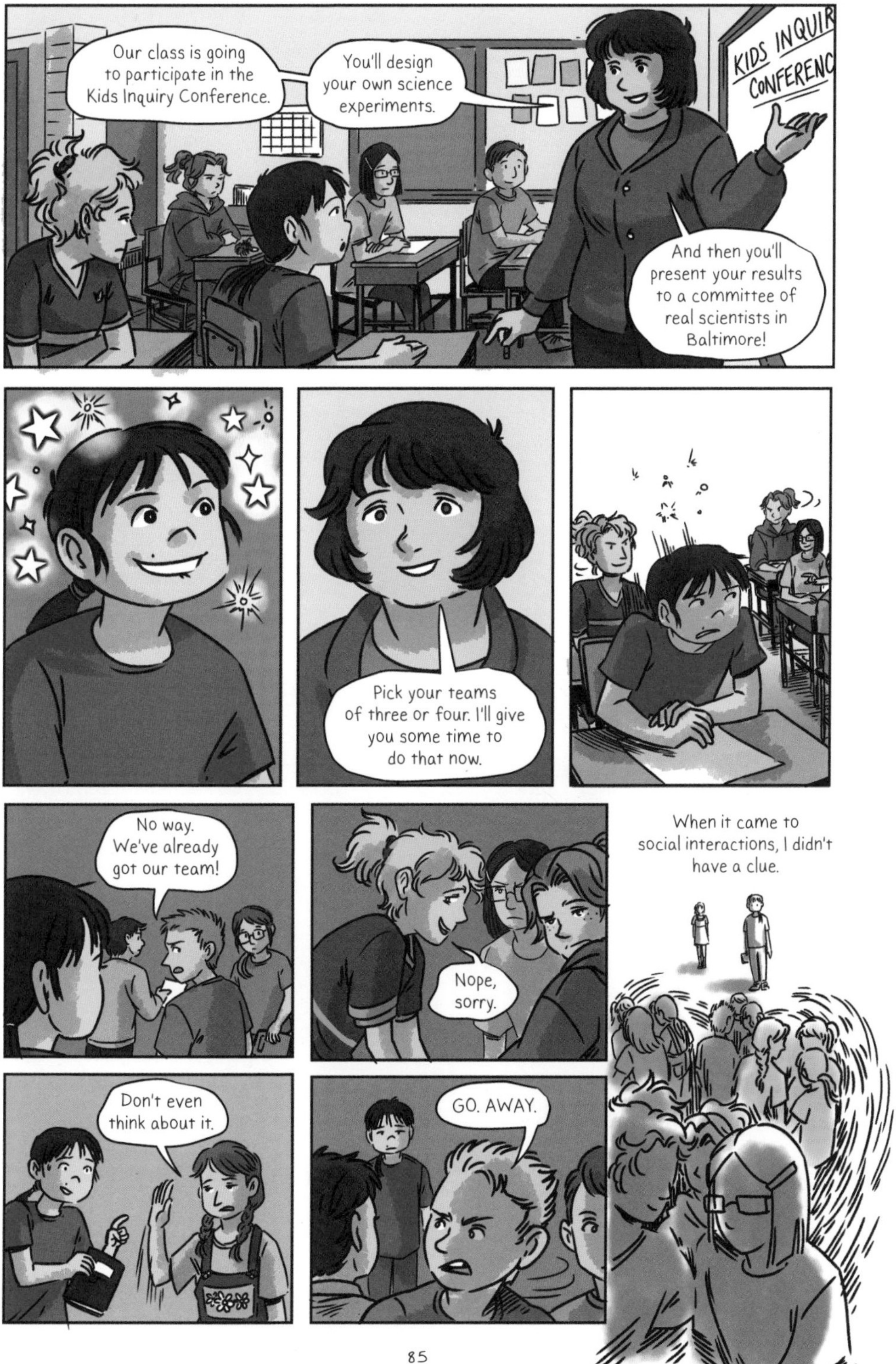

Our class is going to participate in the Kids Inquiry Conference.
You'll design your own science experiments.
KIDS INQUIR CONFERENC
And then you'll present your results to a committee of real scientists in Baltimore!
Pick your teams of three or four. I'll give you some time to do that now.
No way. We've already got our team!
Nope, sorry.
When it came to social interactions, I didn't have a clue.
Don't even think about it.
GO. AWAY.

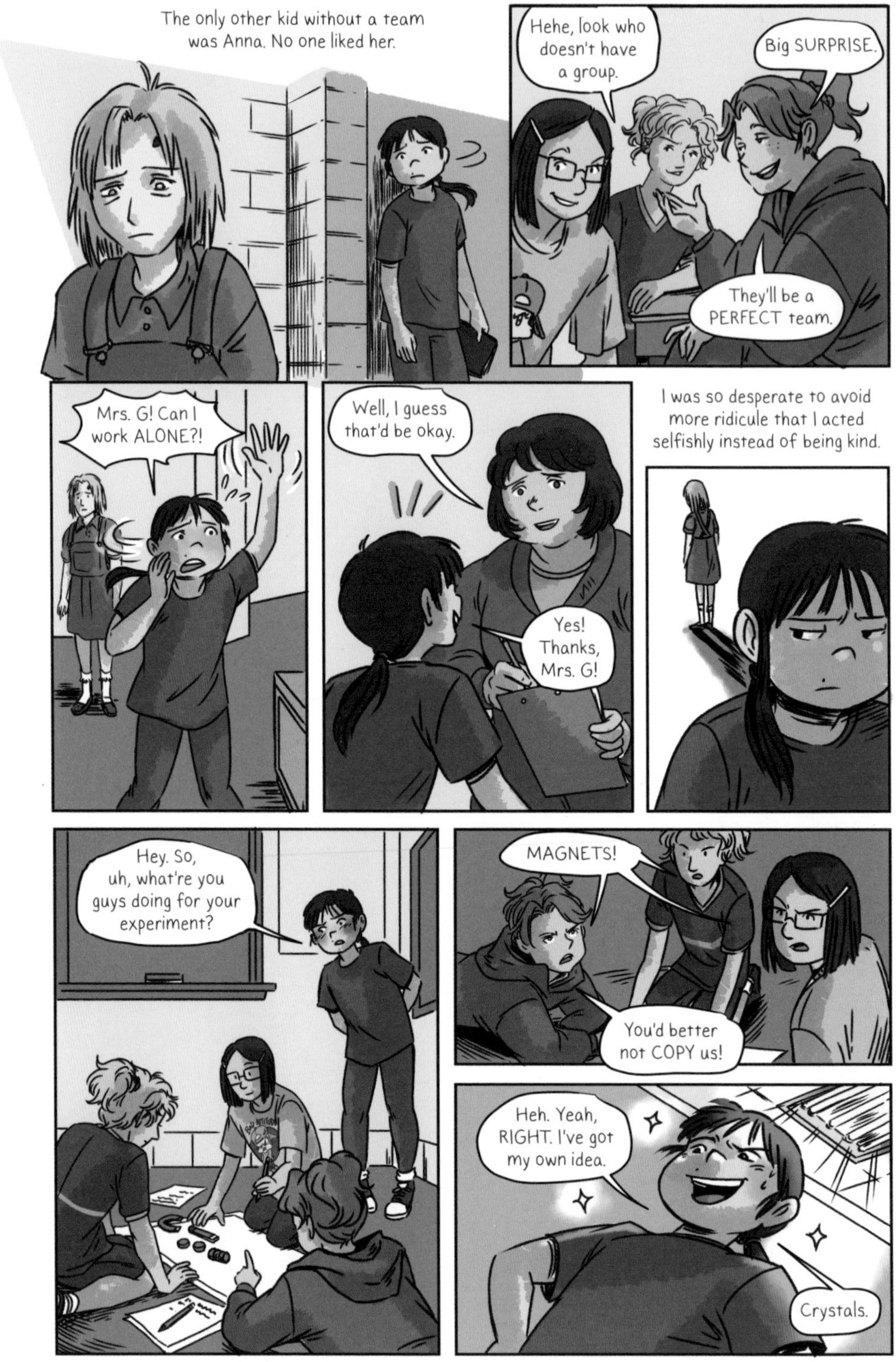

The only other kid without a team was Anna. No one liked her.
Hehe, look who doesn't have a group.
Big SURPRISE.
They'll be a PERFECT team.
Mrs. G! Can I work ALONE?!
Well, I guess that'd be okay.
Yes! Thanks, Mrs. G!
I was so desperate to avoid more ridicule that I acted selfishly instead of being kind.
Hey. So, uh, what're you guys doing for your experiment?
MAGNETS!
You'd better not COPY us!
Heh. Yeah, RIGHT. I've got my own idea.
Crystals.

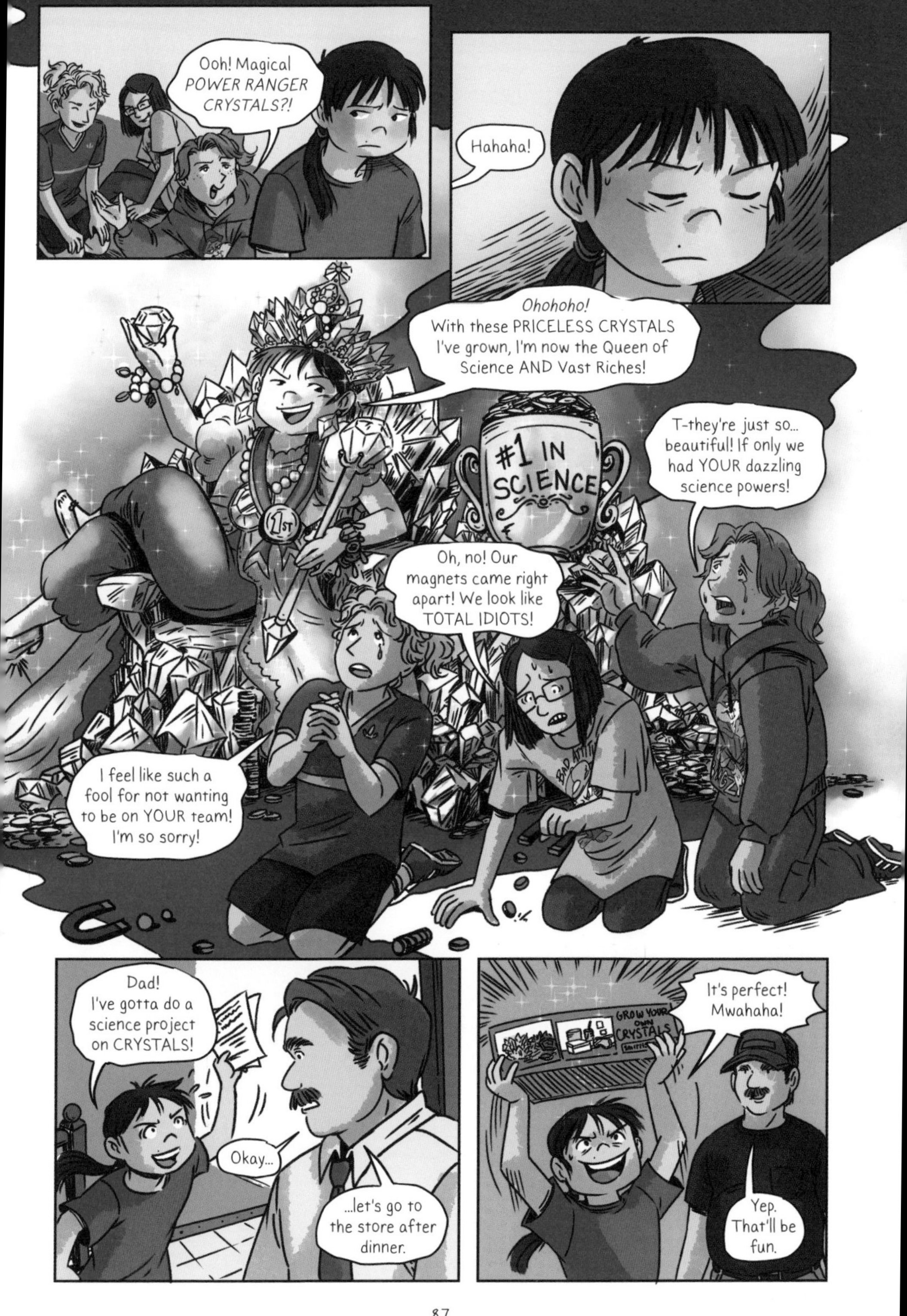
Ooh! Magical *POWER RANGER CRYSTALS?!*
Hahaha!
Ohohoho! With these PRICELESS CRYSTALS I've grown, I'm now the Queen of Science AND Vast Riches!
#1 IN SCIENCE
1st
T-they're just so... beautiful! If only we had YOUR dazzling science powers!
Oh, no! Our magnets came right apart! We look like TOTAL IDIOTS!
I feel like such a fool for not wanting to be on YOUR team! I'm so sorry!
Dad! I've gotta do a science project on CRYSTALS!
Okay...
...let's go to the store after dinner.
GROW YOUR OWN CRYSTALS
It's perfect! Mwahaha!
Yep. That'll be fun.

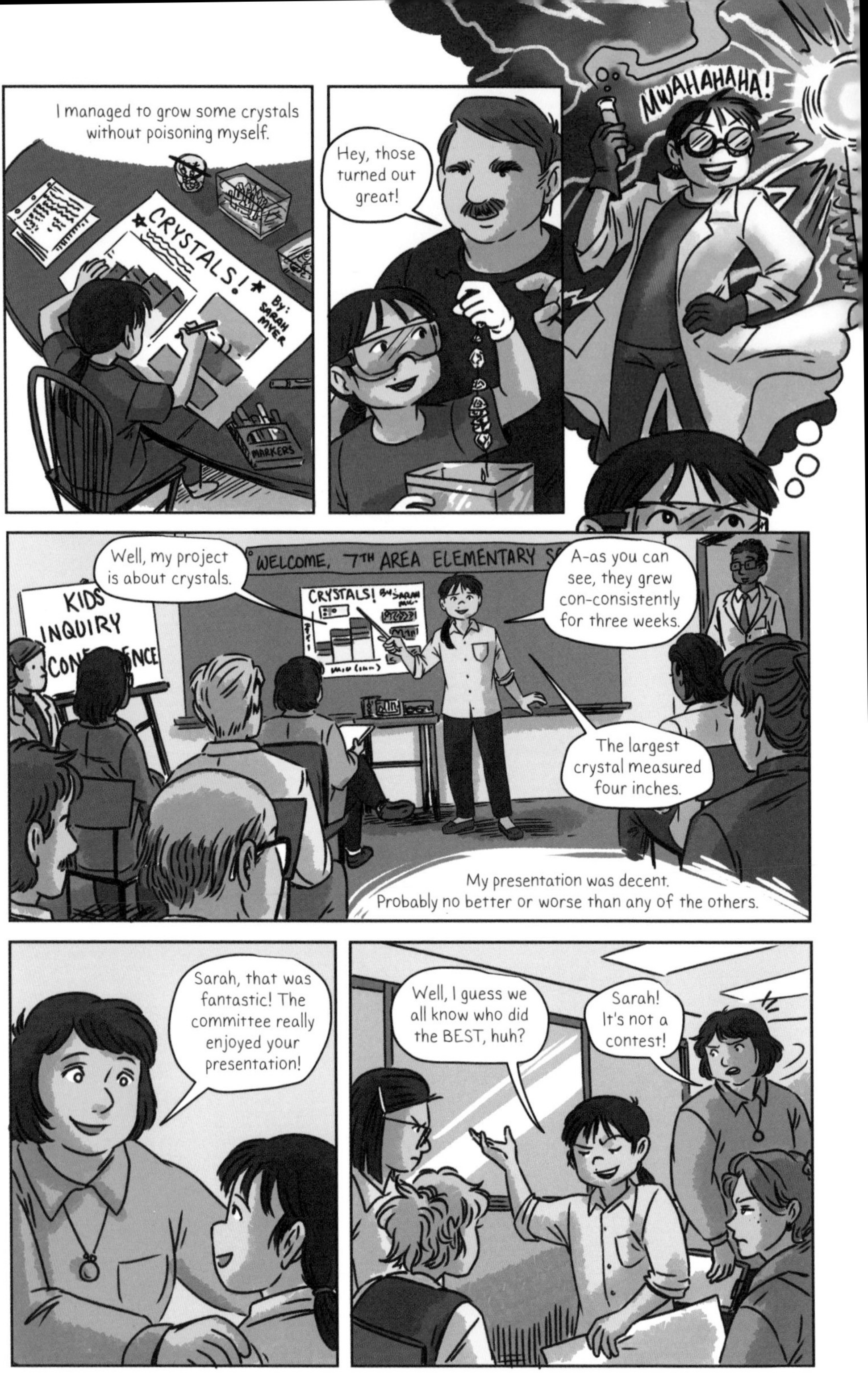
I managed to grow some crystals without poisoning myself.
CRYSTALS!
By: SARAH MYER
MARKERS
Hey, those turned out great!
MWAHAHAHA!
Well, my project is about crystals.
WELCOME, 7TH AREA ELEMENTARY S
KIDS INQUIRY
A-as you can see, they grew con-consistently for three weeks.
The largest crystal measured four inches.
My presentation was decent. Probably no better or worse than any of the others.
Sarah, that was fantastic! The committee really enjoyed your presentation!
Well, I guess we all know who did the BEST, huh?
Sarah! It's not a contest!

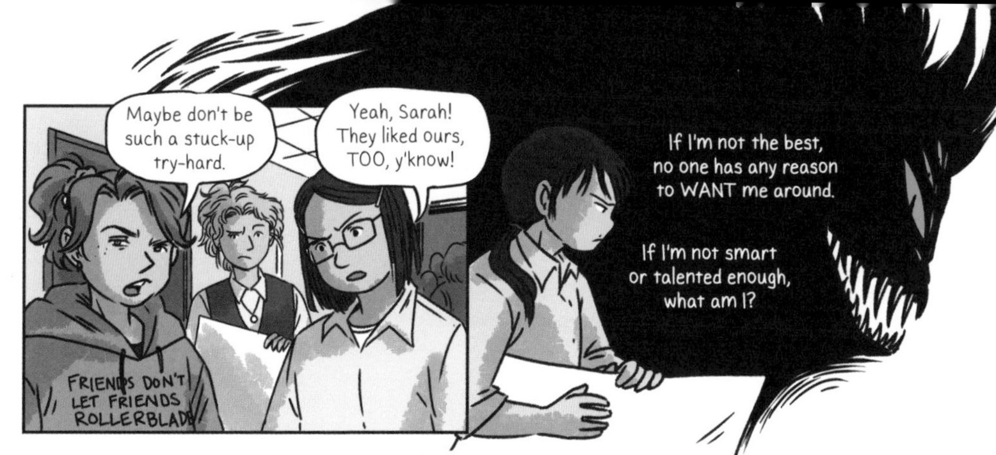
Maybe don't be such a stuck-up try-hard.
Yeah, Sarah! They liked ours, TOO, y'know!
FRIENDS DON'T LET FRIENDS ROLLERBLADE
If I'm not the best, no one has any reason to WANT me around.
If I'm not smart or talented enough, what am I?

Family dinners were seldom true, round-table discussions.
I craved attention and praise, and often monopolized the conversation.

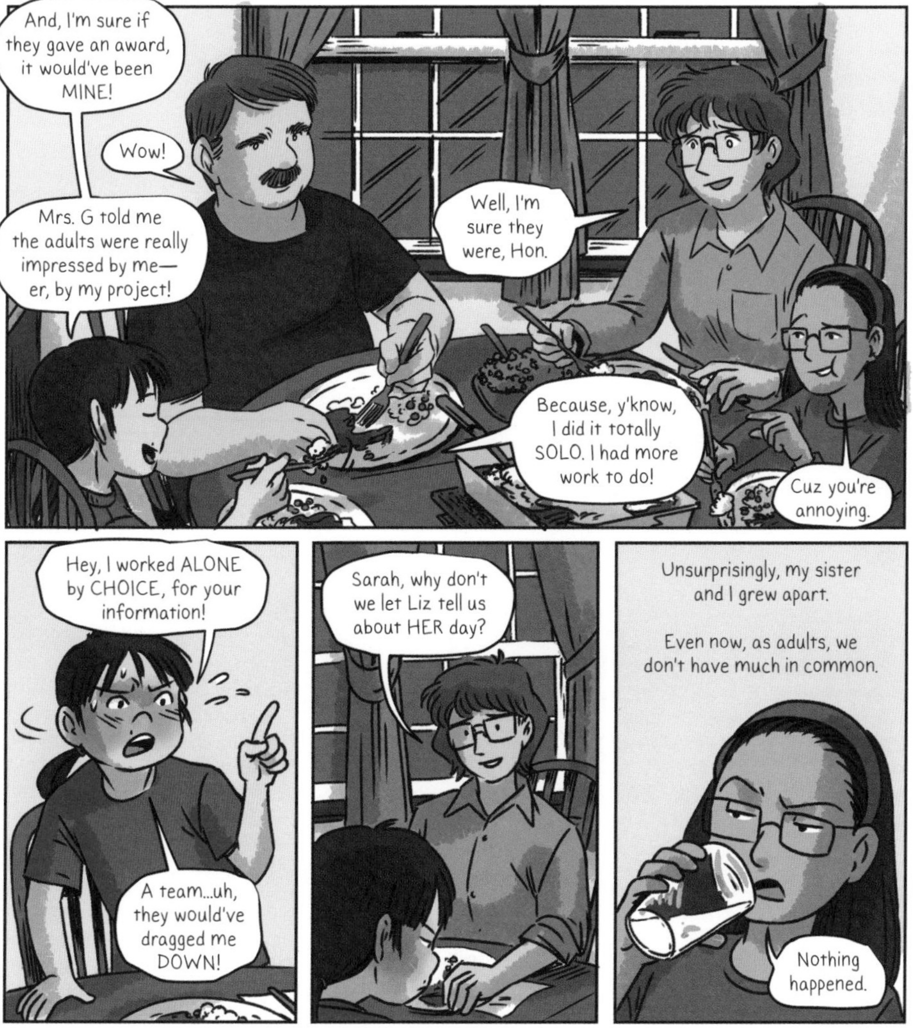
And, I'm sure if they gave an award, it would've been MINE!
Wow!
Mrs. G told me the adults were really impressed by me— er, by my project!
Well, I'm sure they were, Hon.
Because, y'know, I did it totally SOLO. I had more work to do!
Cuz you're annoying.
Hey, I worked ALONE by CHOICE, for your information!
A team...uh, they would've dragged me DOWN!
Sarah, why don't we let Liz tell us about HER day?
Unsurprisingly, my sister and I grew apart.
Even now, as adults, we don't have much in common.
Nothing happened.

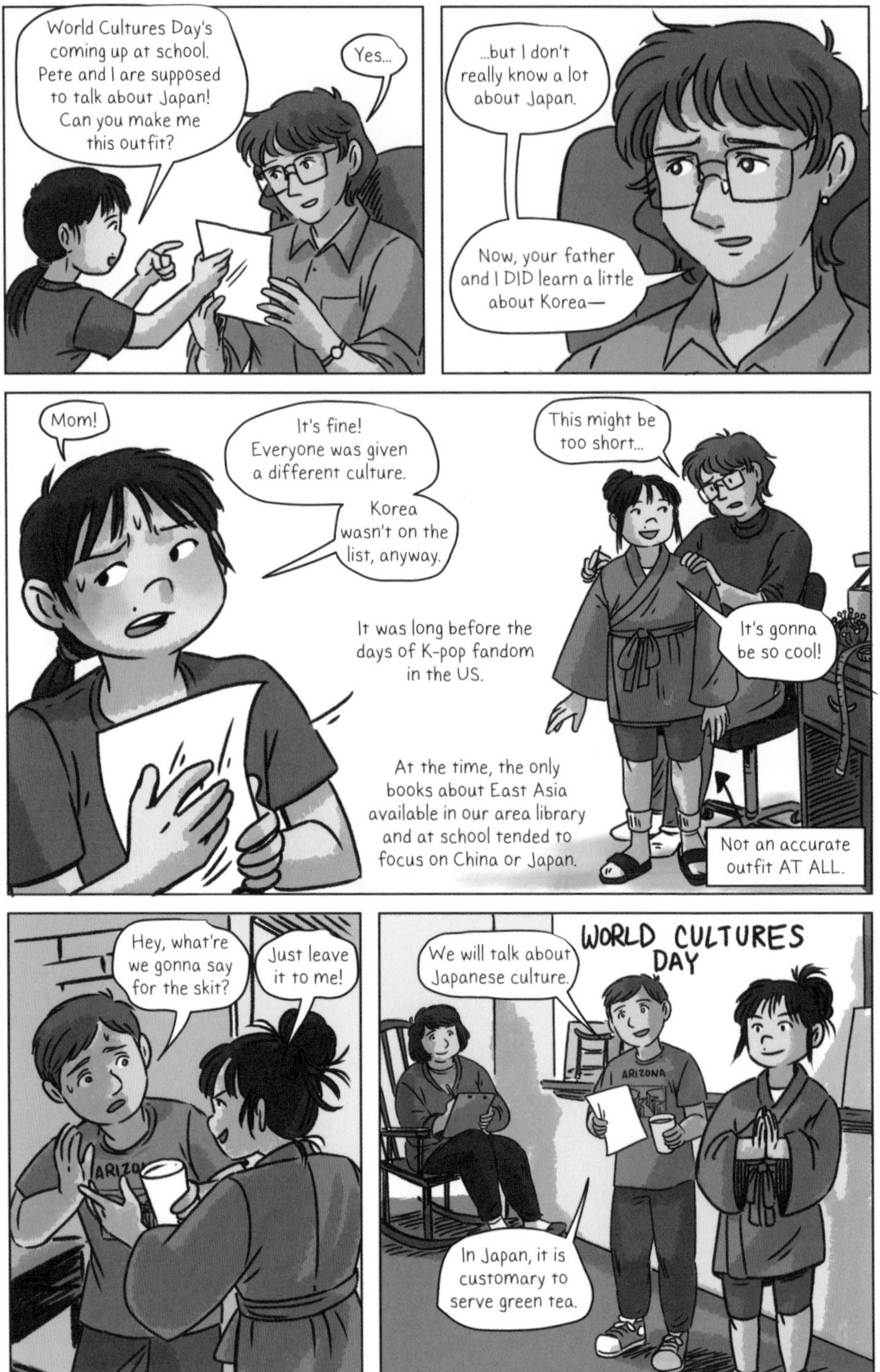

World Cultures Day's coming up at school. Pete and I are supposed to talk about Japan! Can you make me this outfit?
Yes...
...but I don't really know a lot about Japan.
Now, your father and I DID learn a little about Korea—
Mom!
It's fine! Everyone was given a different culture.
Korea wasn't on the list, anyway.
It was long before the days of K-pop fandom in the US.
At the time, the only books about East Asia available in our area library and at school tended to focus on China or Japan.
This might be too short...
It's gonna be so cool!
Not an accurate outfit AT ALL.
Hey, what're we gonna say for the skit?
Just leave it to me!
WORLD CULTURES DAY
We will talk about Japanese culture.
ARIZONA
In Japan, it is customary to serve green tea.

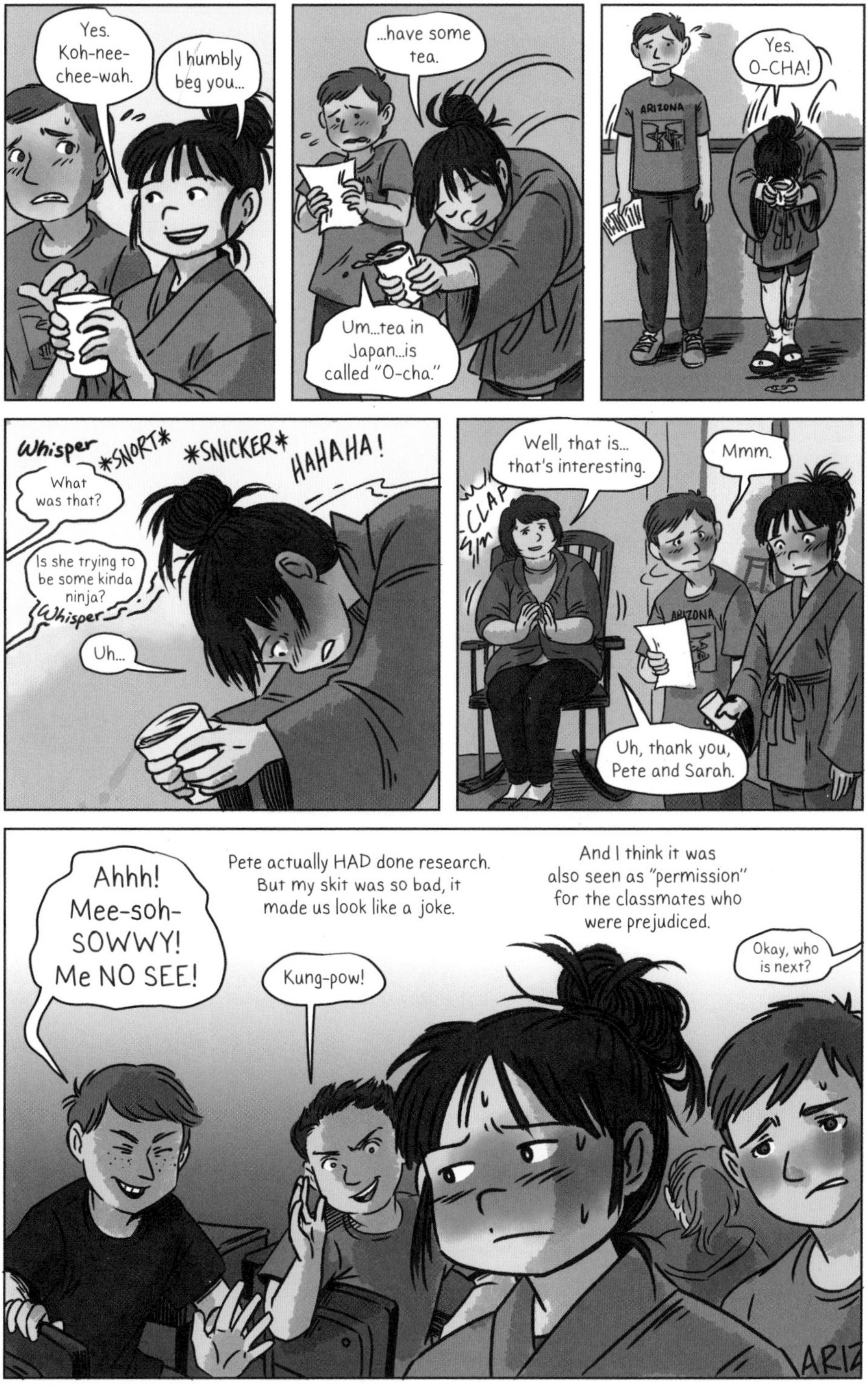

Yes. Koh-nee-chee-wah.
I humbly beg you...
...have some tea.
Um...tea in Japan...is called "O-cha."
Yes. O-CHA!
ARIZONA
Whisper
SNORT
SNICKER
HAHAHA!
What was that?
Is she trying to be some kinda ninja?
Whisper
Uh...
CLAP
Well, that is... that's interesting.
Mmm.
Uh, thank you, Pete and Sarah.
Ahhh! Mee-soh-SOWWY! Me NO SEE!
Pete actually HAD done research. But my skit was so bad, it made us look like a joke.
Kung-pow!
And I think it was also seen as "permission" for the classmates who were prejudiced.
Okay, who is next?
ARIZ

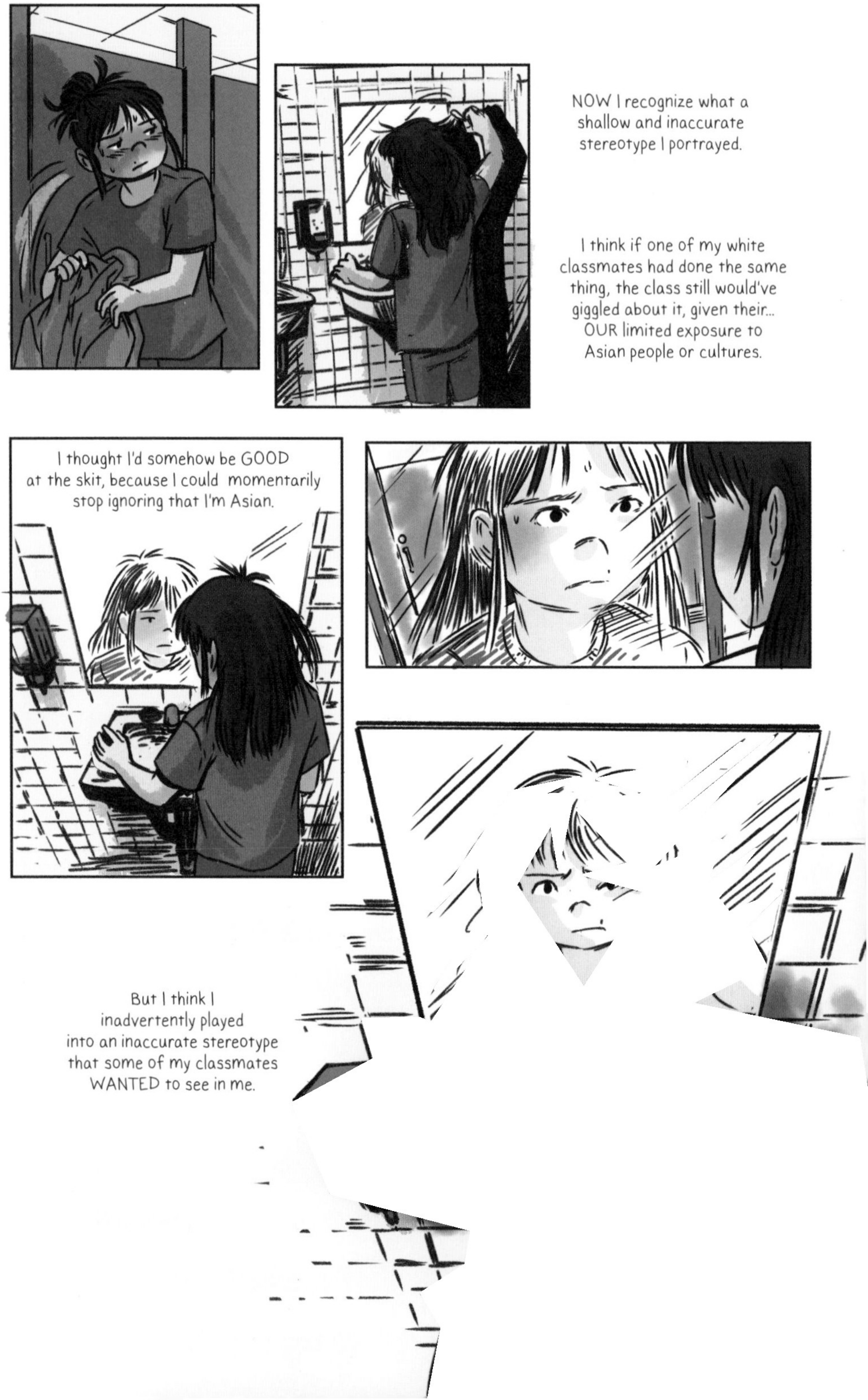
NOW I recognize what a shallow and inaccurate stereotype I portrayed.
I think if one of my white classmates had done the same thing, the class still would've giggled about it, given their... OUR limited exposure to Asian people or cultures.
I thought I'd somehow be GOOD at the skit, because I could momentarily stop ignoring that I'm Asian.
But I think I inadvertently played into an inaccurate stereotype that some of my classmates WANTED to see in me.

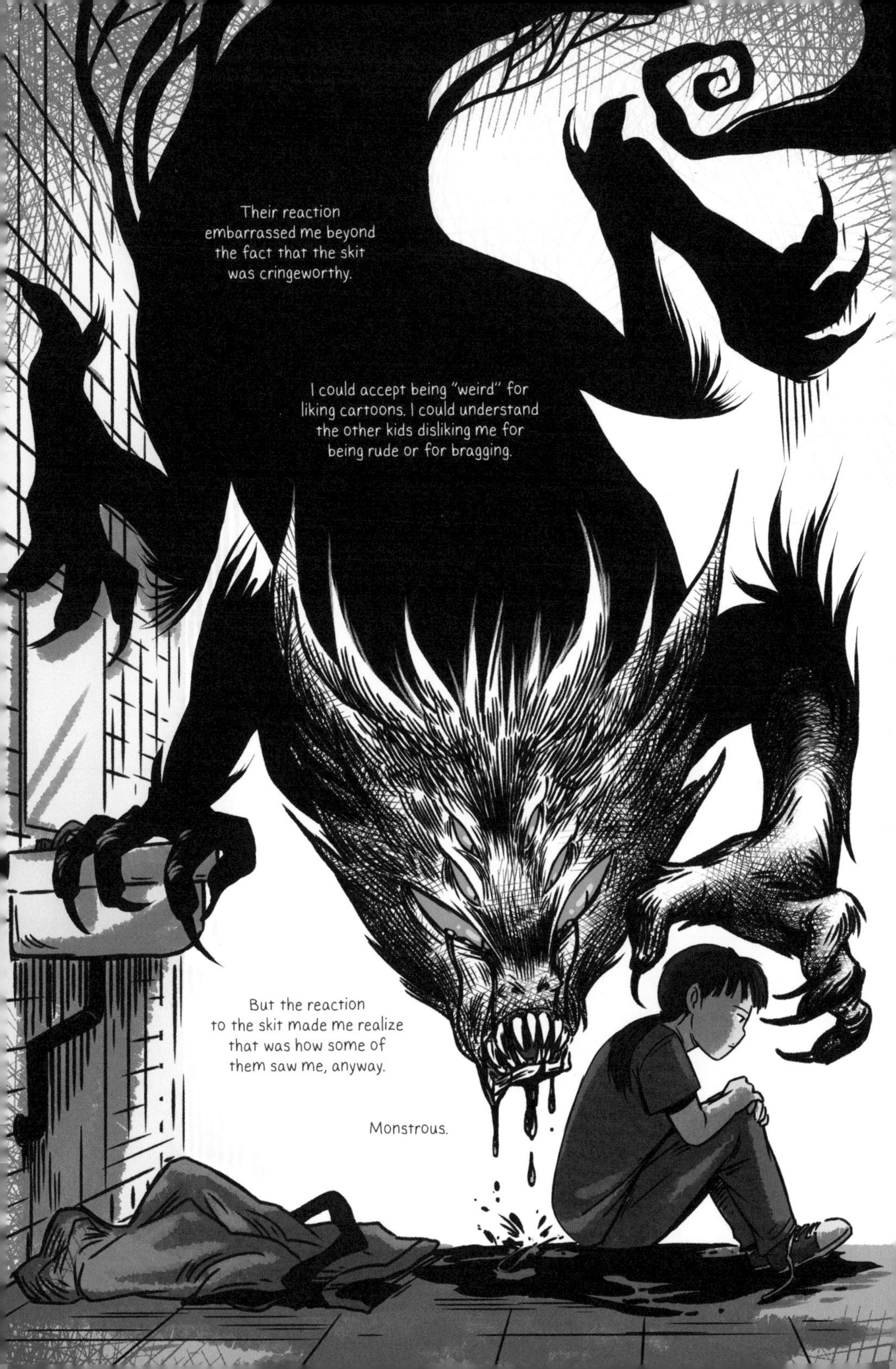
Their reaction embarrassed me beyond the fact that the skit was cringeworthy.
I could accept being "weird" for liking cartoons. I could understand the other kids disliking me for being rude or for bragging.
But the reaction to the skit made me realize that was how some of them saw me, anyway.
Monstrous.

My parents had decided not to raise my sister and I with ANY Korean culture.

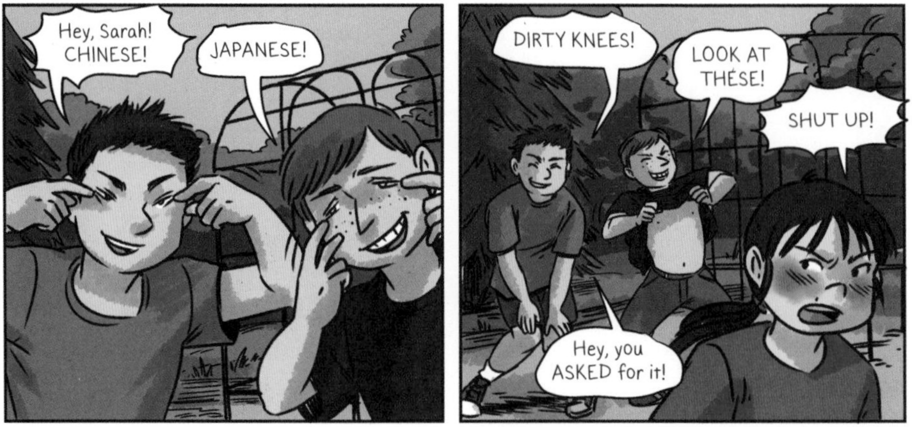

Hey, Sarah! CHINESE!
JAPANESE!
DIRTY KNEES!
LOOK AT THESE!
SHUT UP!
Hey, you ASKED for it!

As it was brought up more and more by my peers,
I started to get curious (and confused) about WHAT I actually WAS.

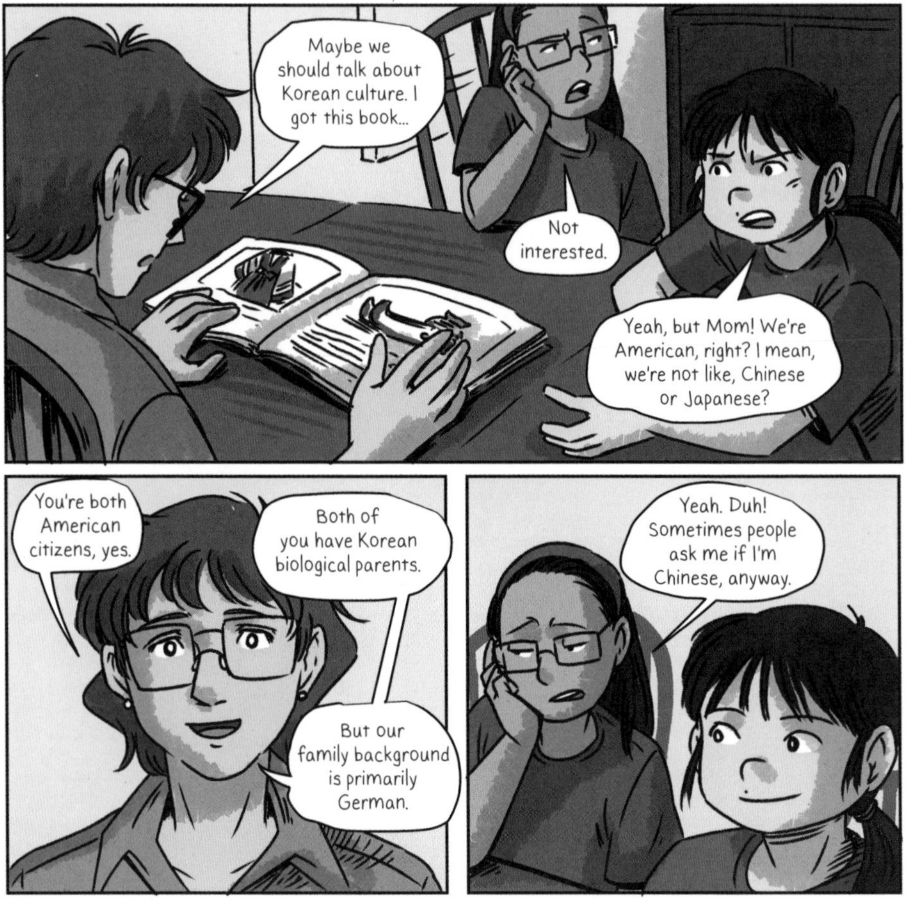

Maybe we should talk about Korean culture. I got this book...
Not interested.
Yeah, but Mom! We're American, right? I mean, we're not like, Chinese or Japanese?
You're both American citizens, yes.
Both of you have Korean biological parents.
But our family background is primarily German.
Yeah. Duh! Sometimes people ask me if I'm Chinese, anyway.

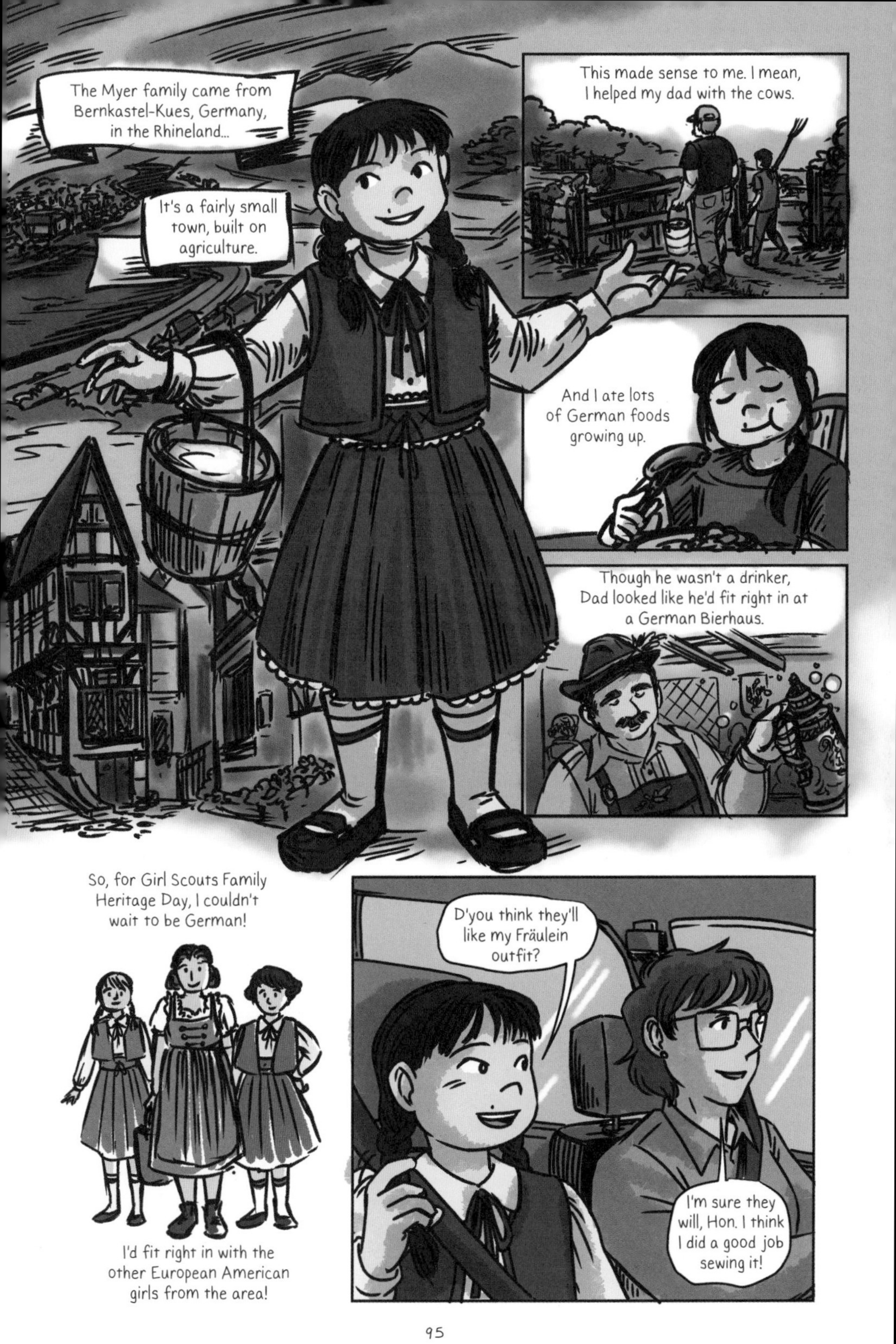

The Myer family came from Bernkastel-Kues, Germany, in the Rhineland...
It's a fairly small town, built on agriculture.
This made sense to me. I mean, I helped my dad with the cows.
And I ate lots of German foods growing up.
Though he wasn't a drinker, Dad looked like he'd fit right in at a German Bierhaus.
So, for Girl Scouts Family Heritage Day, I couldn't wait to be German!
I'd fit right in with the other European American girls from the area!
D'you think they'll like my Fräulein outfit?
I'm sure they will, Hon. I think I did a good job sewing it!

Most of the foods and ethnicities represented at the festival were European.

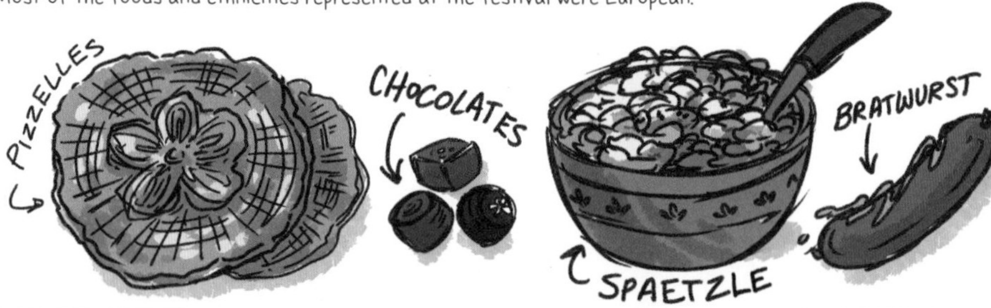
PIZZELLES
CHOCOLATES
SPAETZLE
BRATWURST

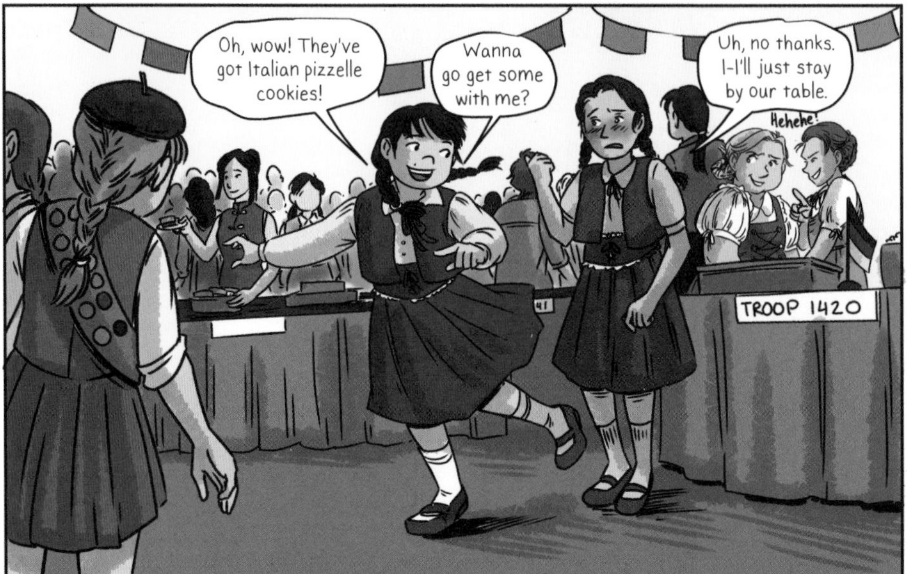
Oh, wow! They've got Italian pizzelle cookies!
Wanna go get some with me?
Uh, no thanks. I-I'll just stay by our table.
Hehehe!
TROOP 1420

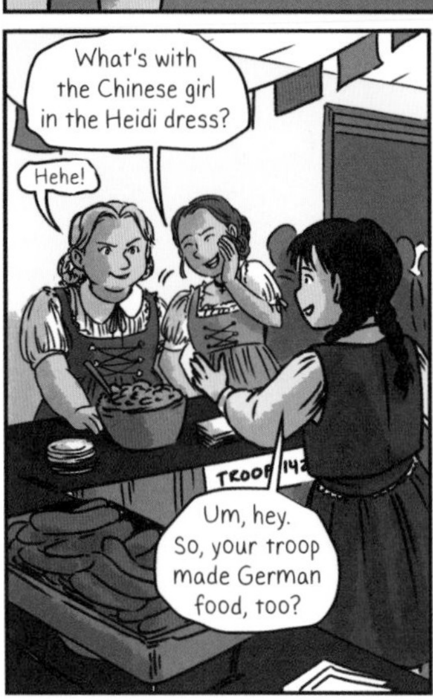
What's with the Chinese girl in the Heidi dress?
Hehe!
Um, hey. So, your troop made German food, too?

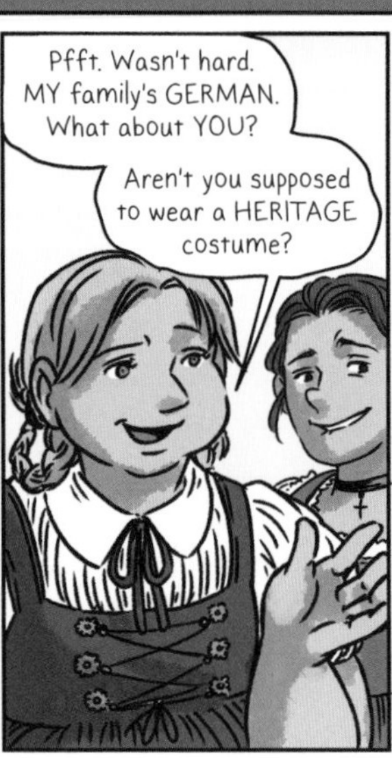
Pfft. Wasn't hard. MY family's GERMAN. What about YOU?
Aren't you supposed to wear a HERITAGE costume?

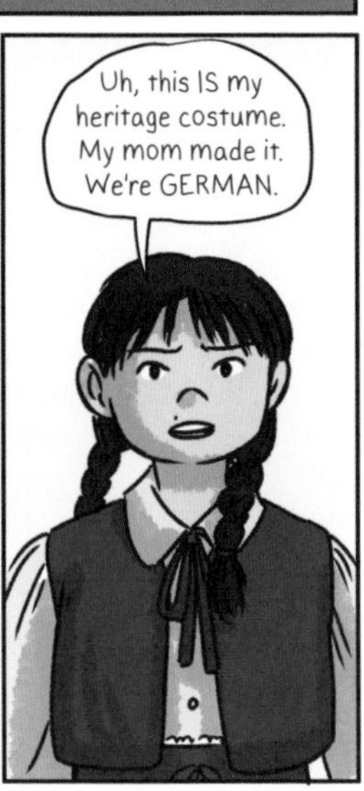
Uh, this IS my heritage costume. My mom made it. We're GERMAN.

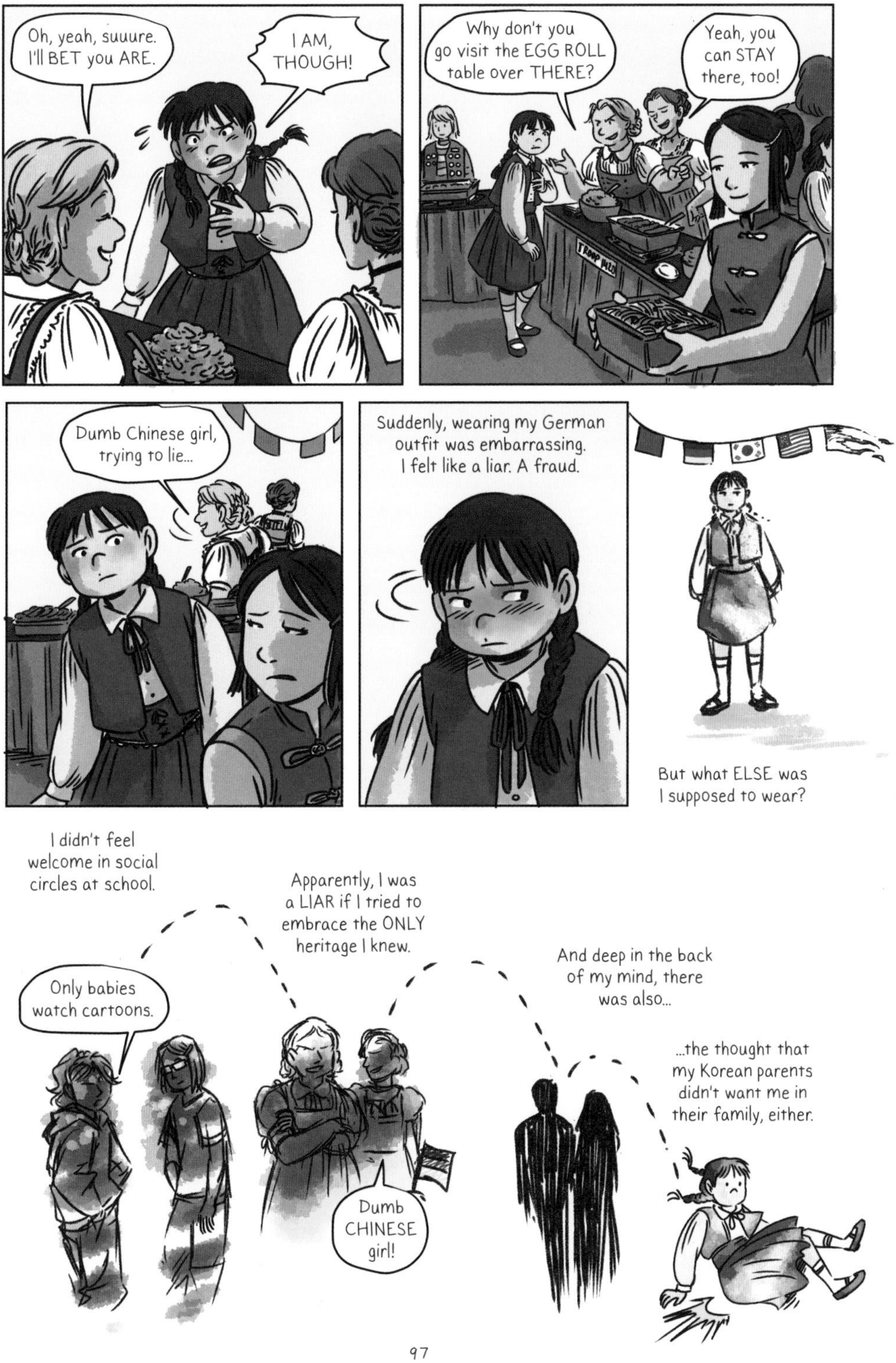

Oh, yeah, suuure. I'll BET you ARE.
I AM, THOUGH!
Why don't you go visit the EGG ROLL table over THERE?
Yeah, you can STAY there, too!
Dumb Chinese girl, trying to lie...
Suddenly, wearing my German outfit was embarrassing. I felt like a liar. A fraud.
But what ELSE was I supposed to wear?
I didn't feel welcome in social circles at school.
Apparently, I was a LIAR if I tried to embrace the ONLY heritage I knew.
And deep in the back of my mind, there was also...
Only babies watch cartoons.
...the thought that my Korean parents didn't want me in their family, either.
Dumb CHINESE girl!

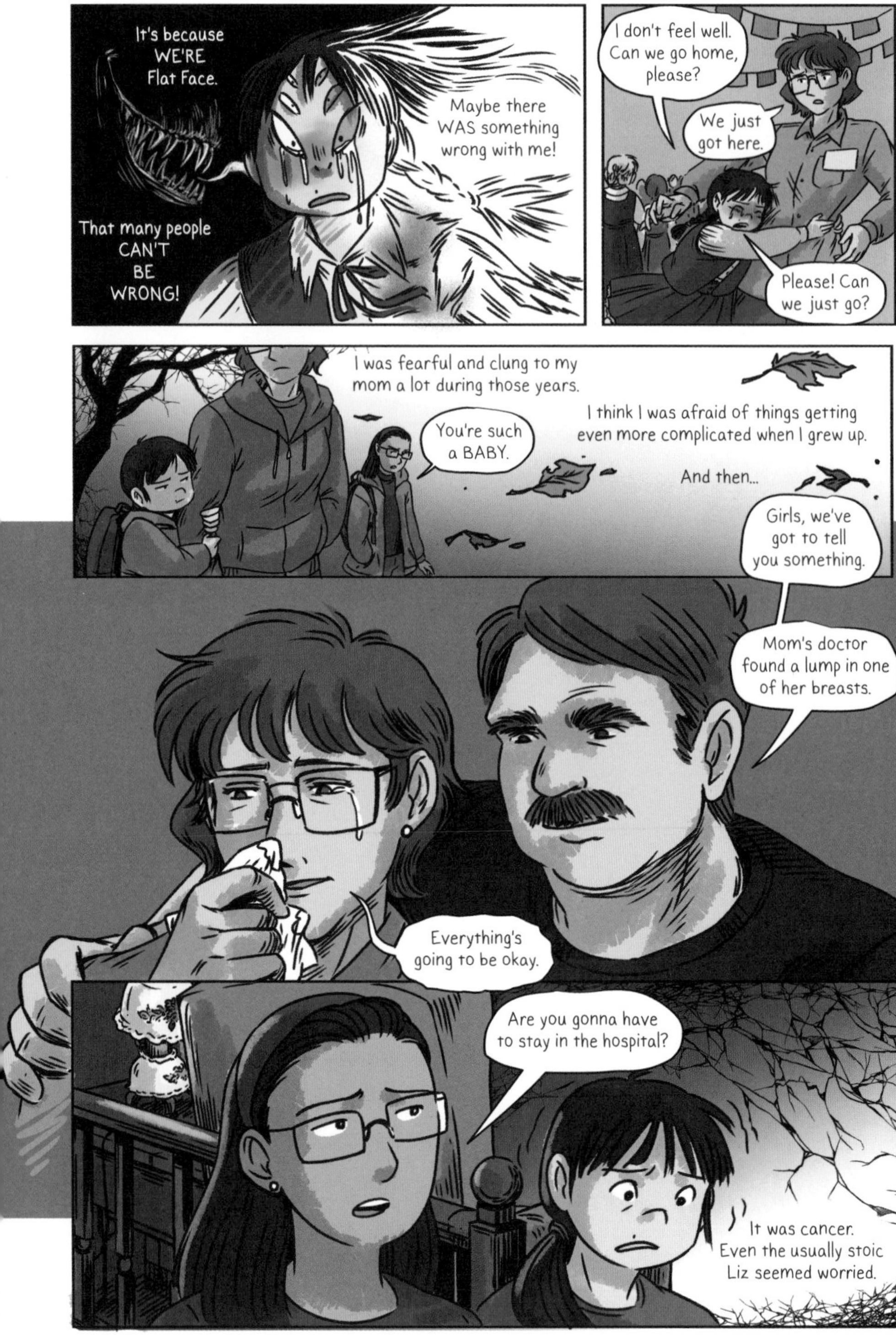
It's because WE'RE Flat Face.
Maybe there WAS something wrong with me!
That many people CAN'T BE WRONG!
I don't feel well. Can we go home, please?
We just got here.
Please! Can we just go?
I was fearful and clung to my mom a lot during those years.
You're such a BABY.
I think I was afraid of things getting even more complicated when I grew up.
And then...
Girls, we've got to tell you something.
Mom's doctor found a lump in one of her breasts.
Everything's going to be okay.
Are you gonna have to stay in the hospital?
It was cancer. Even the usually stoic Liz seemed worried.

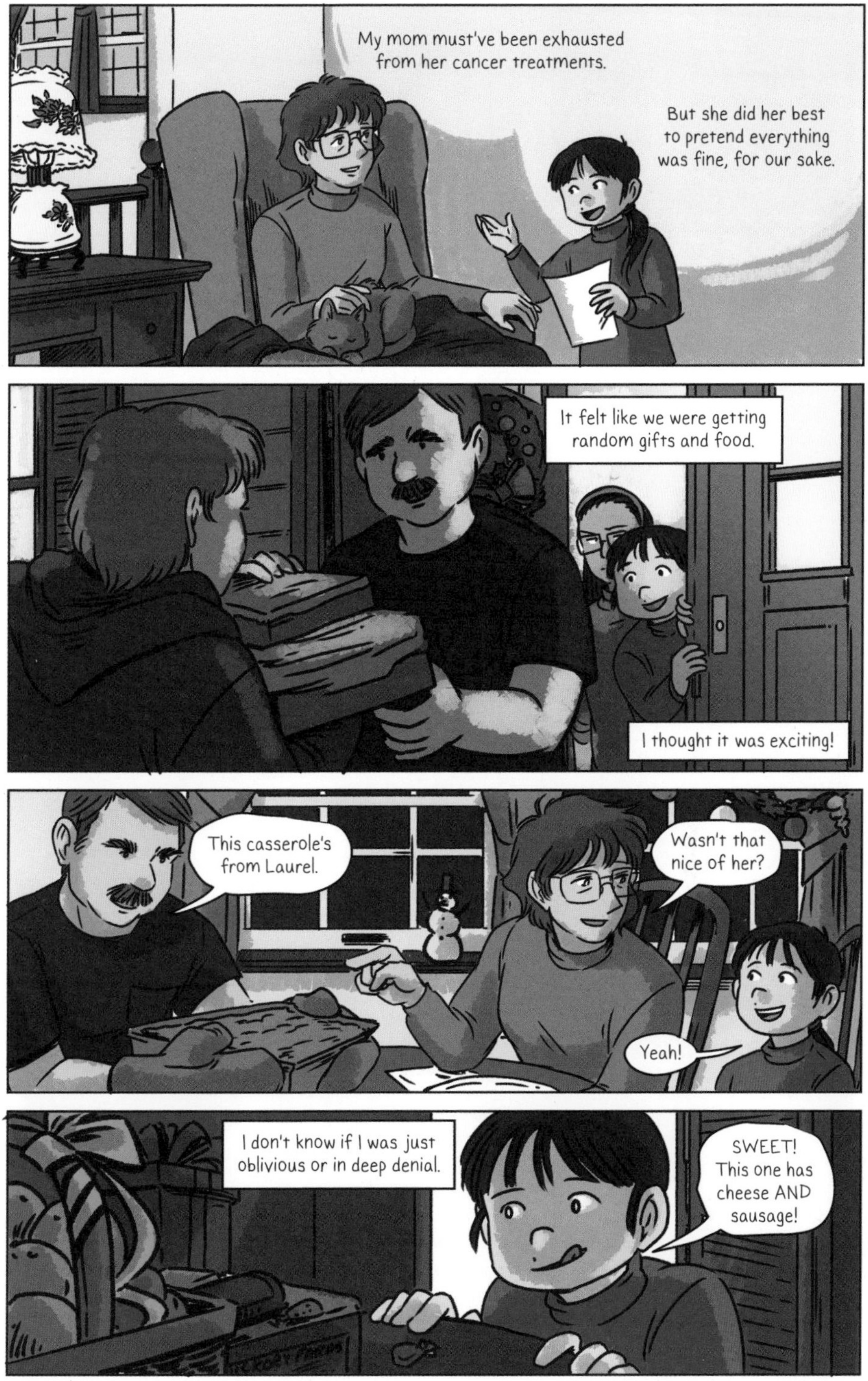
My mom must've been exhausted from her cancer treatments.
But she did her best to pretend everything was fine, for our sake.
It felt like we were getting random gifts and food.
I thought it was exciting!
This casserole's from Laurel.
Wasn't that nice of her?
Yeah!
I don't know if I was just oblivious or in deep denial.
SWEET! This one has cheese AND sausage!

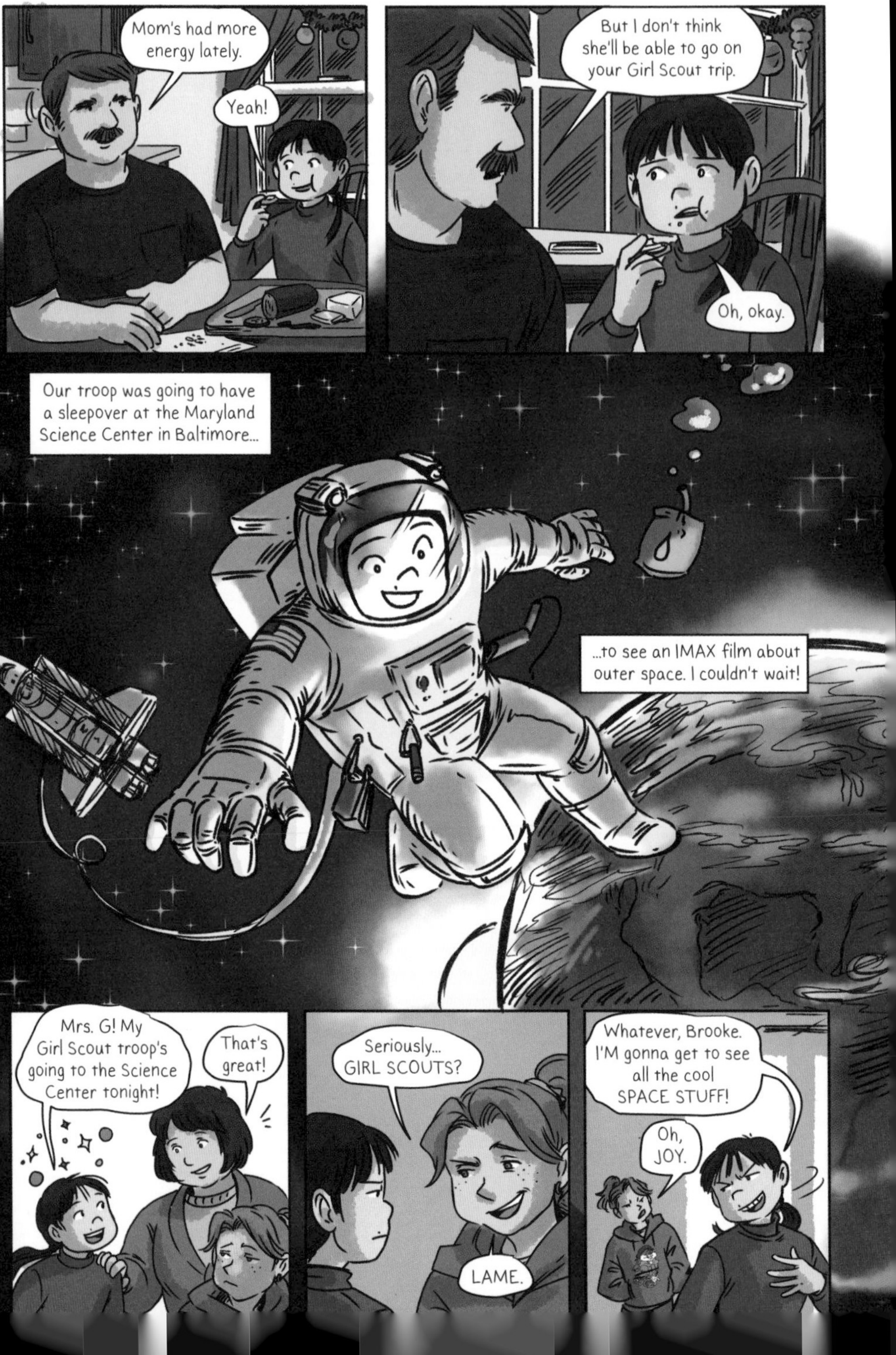
Mom's had more energy lately.
Yeah!
But I don't think she'll be able to go on your Girl Scout trip.
Oh, okay.
Our troop was going to have a sleepover at the Maryland Science Center in Baltimore...
...to see an IMAX film about outer space. I couldn't wait!
Mrs. G! My Girl Scout troop's going to the Science Center tonight!
That's great!
Seriously... GIRL SCOUTS?
LAME.
Whatever, Brooke. I'M gonna get to see all the cool SPACE STUFF!
Oh, JOY.

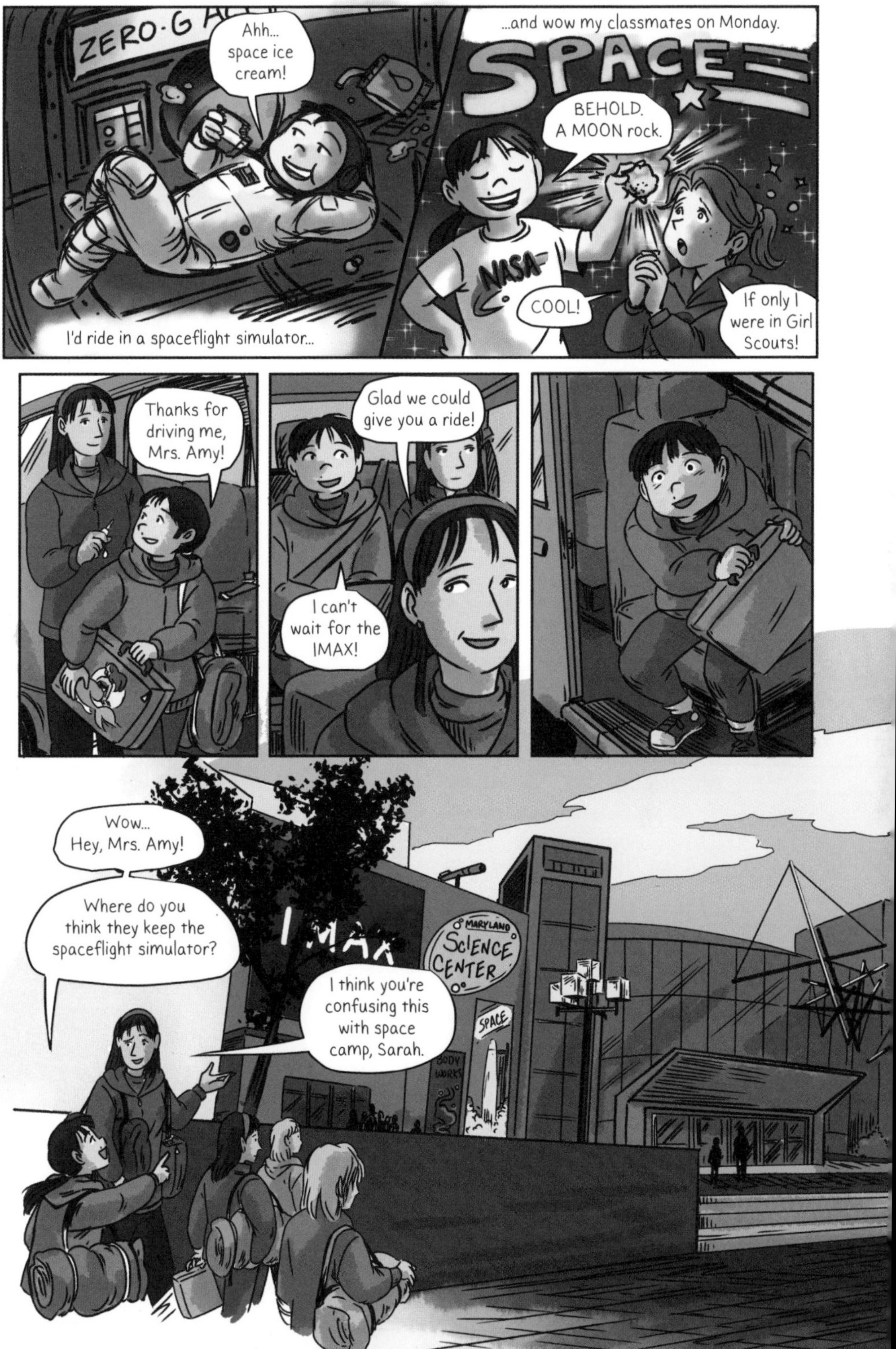
ZERO-G
Ahh... space ice cream!
I'd ride in a spaceflight simulator...
...and wow my classmates on Monday.
SPACE
BEHOLD. A MOON rock.
NASA
COOL!
If only I were in Girl Scouts!
Thanks for driving me, Mrs. Amy!
Glad we could give you a ride!
I can't wait for the IMAX!
Wow... Hey, Mrs. Amy!
Where do you think they keep the spaceflight simulator?
IMAX
MARYLAND SCIENCE CENTER
I think you're confusing this with space camp, Sarah.
SPACE
BODY WORKS

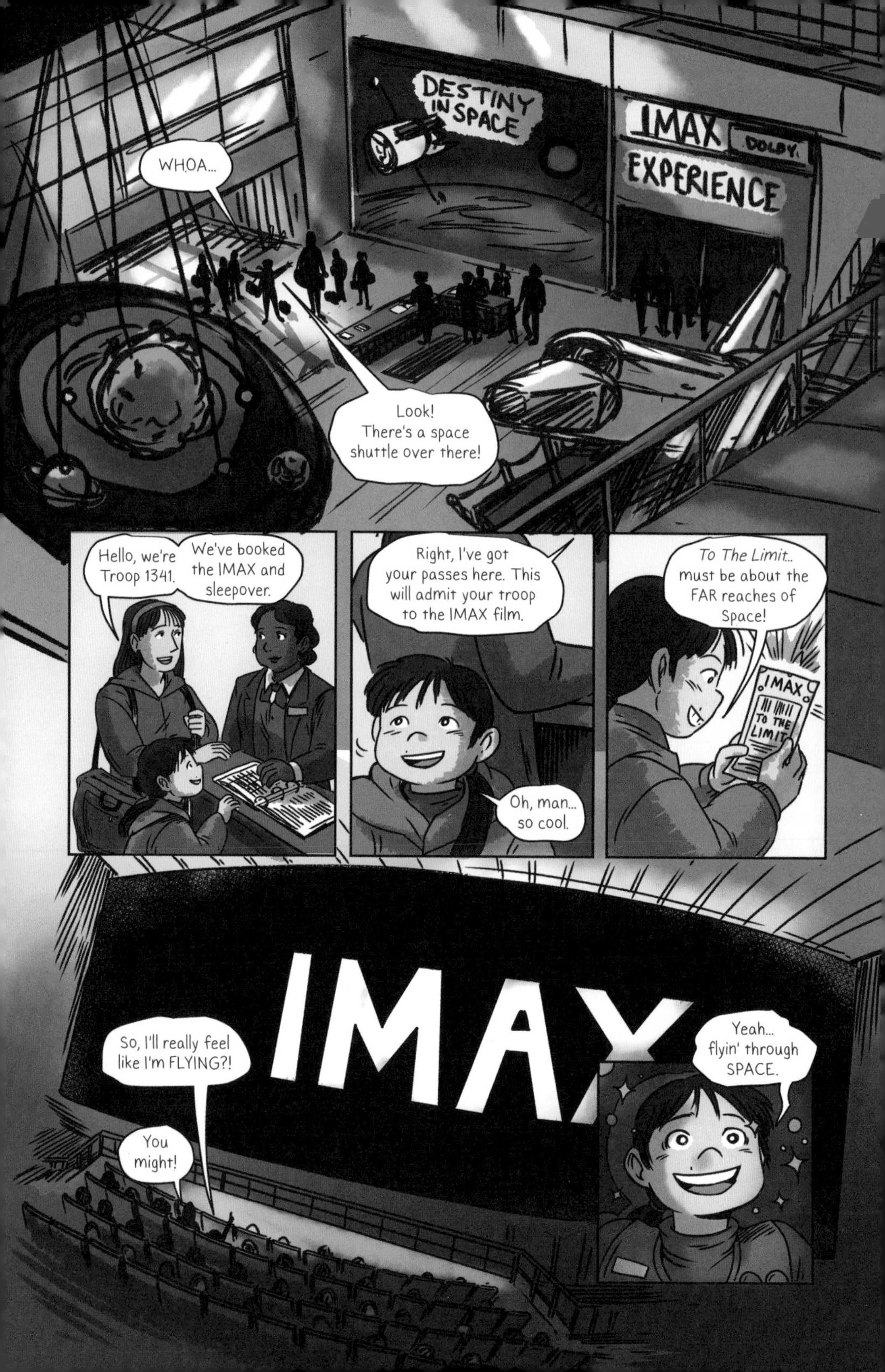
DESTINY IN SPACE
IMAX DOLBY EXPERIENCE
WHOA...
Look! There's a space shuttle over there!
Hello, we're Troop 1341.
We've booked the IMAX and sleepover.
Right, I've got your passes here. This will admit your troop to the IMAX film.
Oh, man... so cool.
To The Limit... must be about the FAR reaches of Space!
IMAX TO THE LIMIT
IMAX
So, I'll really feel like I'm FLYING?!
You might!
Yeah... flyin' through SPACE.

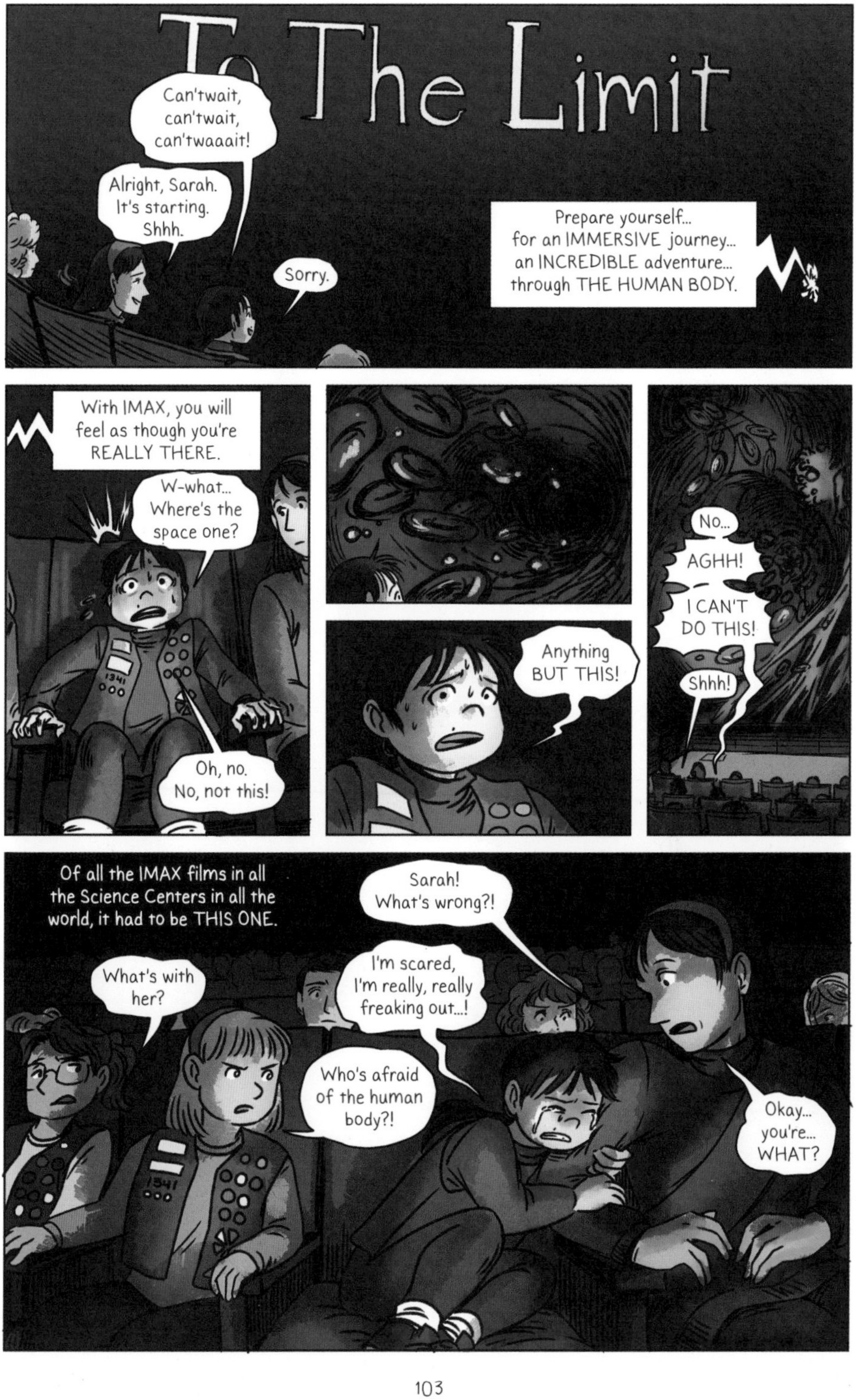

To The Limit
Can'twait, can'twait, can'twaaait!
Alright, Sarah. It's starting. Shhh.
Sorry.
Prepare yourself... for an IMMERSIVE journey... an INCREDIBLE adventure... through THE HUMAN BODY.
With IMAX, you will feel as though you're REALLY THERE.
W-what... Where's the space one?
Oh, no. No, not this!
Anything BUT THIS!
No...
AGHH!
I CAN'T DO THIS!
Shhh!
Of all the IMAX films in all the Science Centers in all the world, it had to be THIS ONE.
What's with her?
Sarah! What's wrong?!
I'm scared, I'm really, really freaking out...!
Who's afraid of the human body?!
Okay... you're... WHAT?

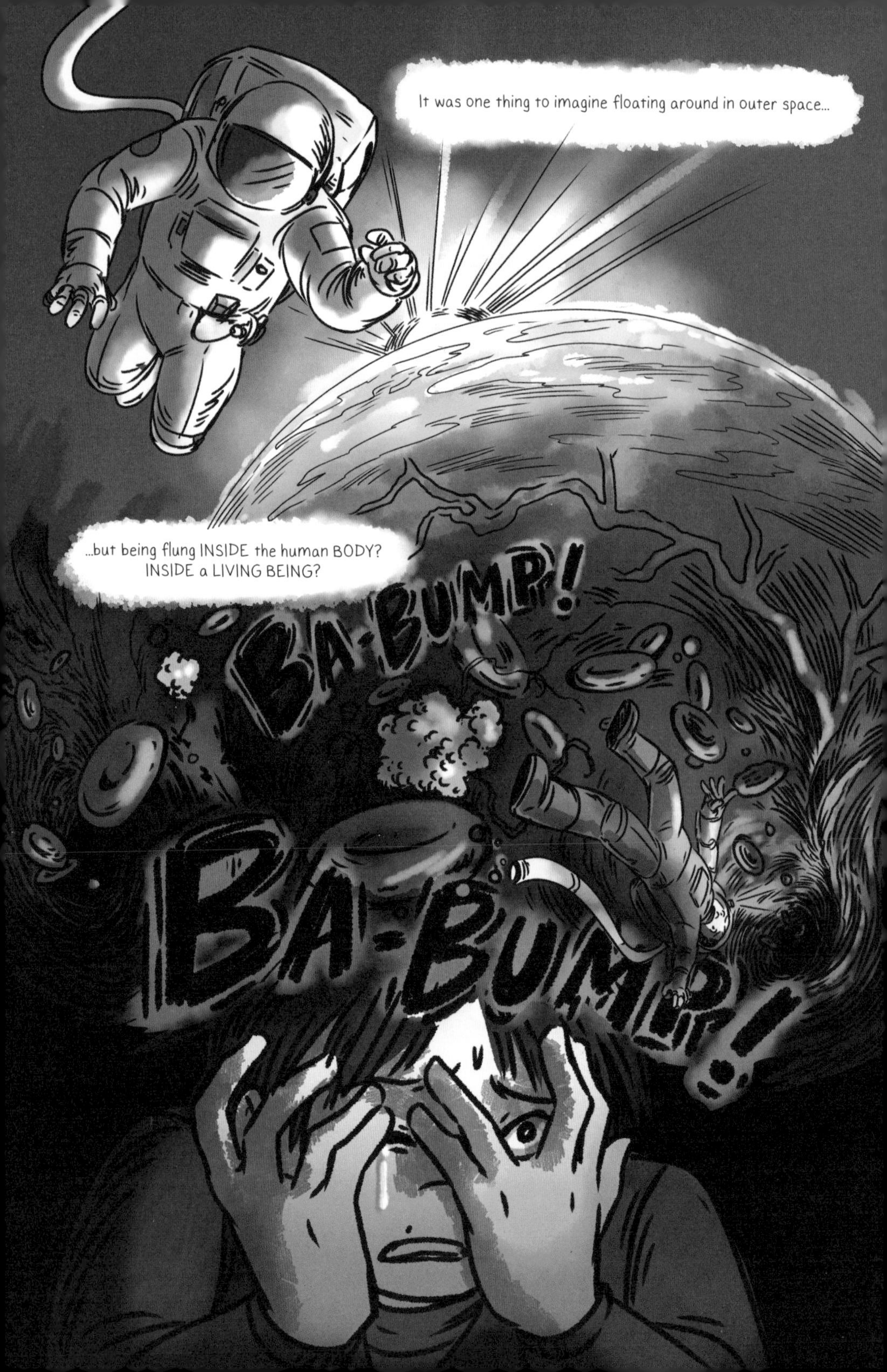
It was one thing to imagine floating around in outer space...
...but being flung INSIDE the human BODY? INSIDE a LIVING BEING?
BA-BUMP!
BA-BUMP!

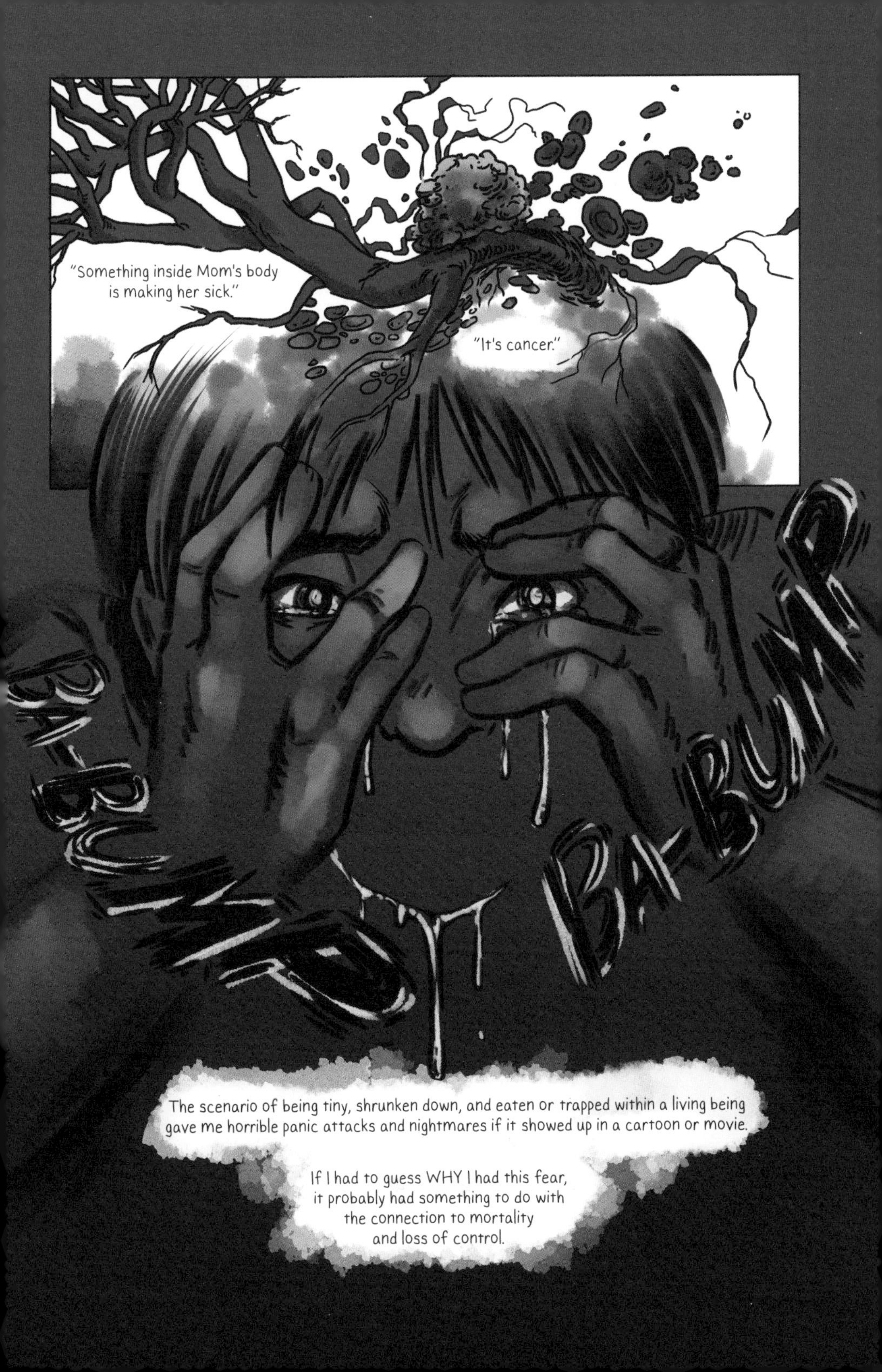
"Something inside Mom's body is making her sick."
"It's cancer."
BA-BUMP
BA-BUMP
The scenario of being tiny, shrunken down, and eaten or trapped within a living being gave me horrible panic attacks and nightmares if it showed up in a cartoon or movie.
If I had to guess WHY I had this fear, it probably had something to do with the connection to mortality and loss of control.

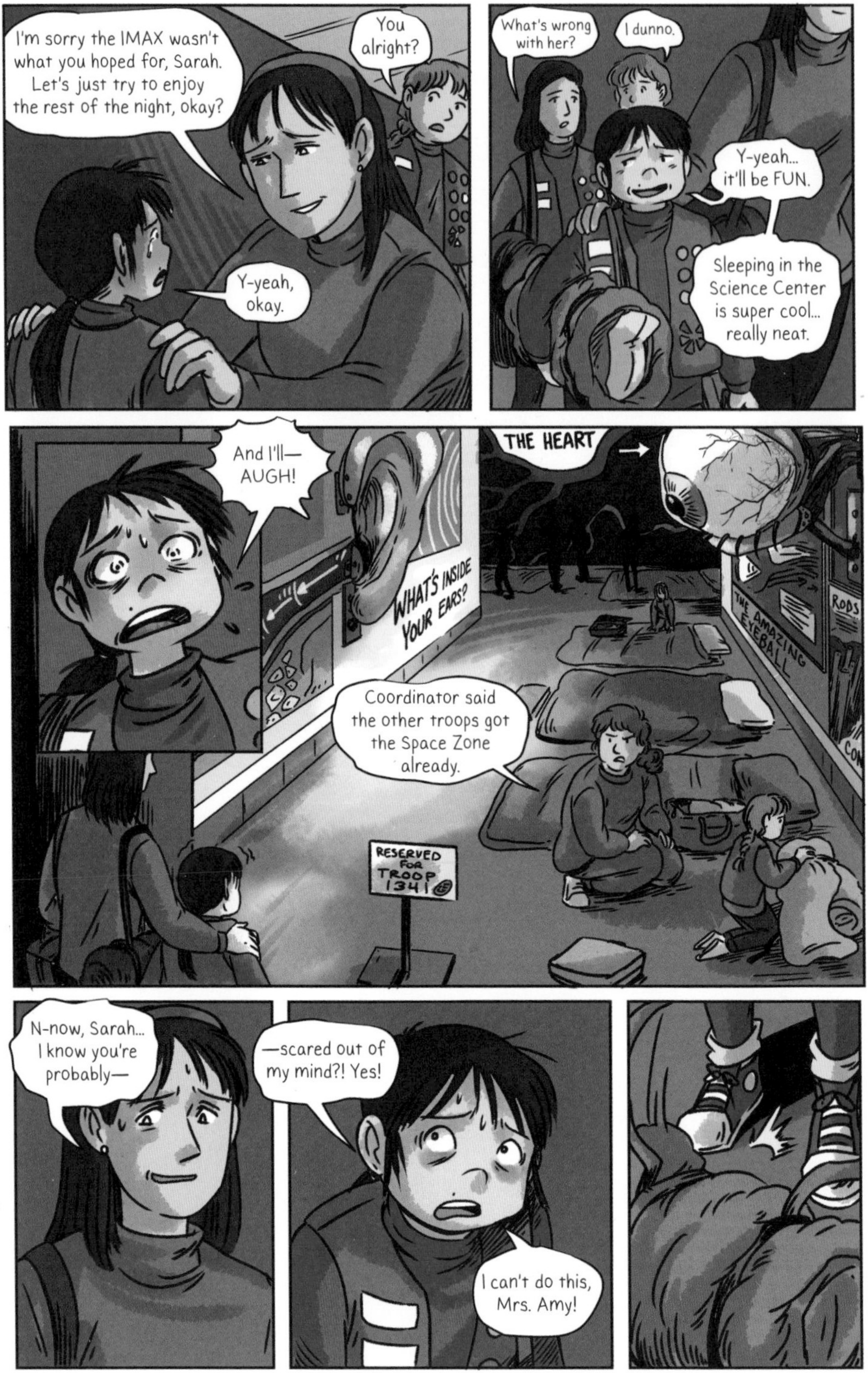
I'm sorry the IMAX wasn't what you hoped for, Sarah. Let's just try to enjoy the rest of the night, okay?
You alright?
Y-yeah, okay.
What's wrong with her?
I dunno.
Y-yeah... it'll be FUN.
Sleeping in the Science Center is super cool... really neat.
And I'll— AUGH!
WHAT'S INSIDE YOUR EARS?
THE HEART
THE AMAZING EYEBALL
RODS
Coordinator said the other troops got the Space Zone already.
RESERVED FOR TROOP 1341
N-now, Sarah... I know you're probably—
—scared out of my mind?! Yes!
I can't do this, Mrs. Amy!

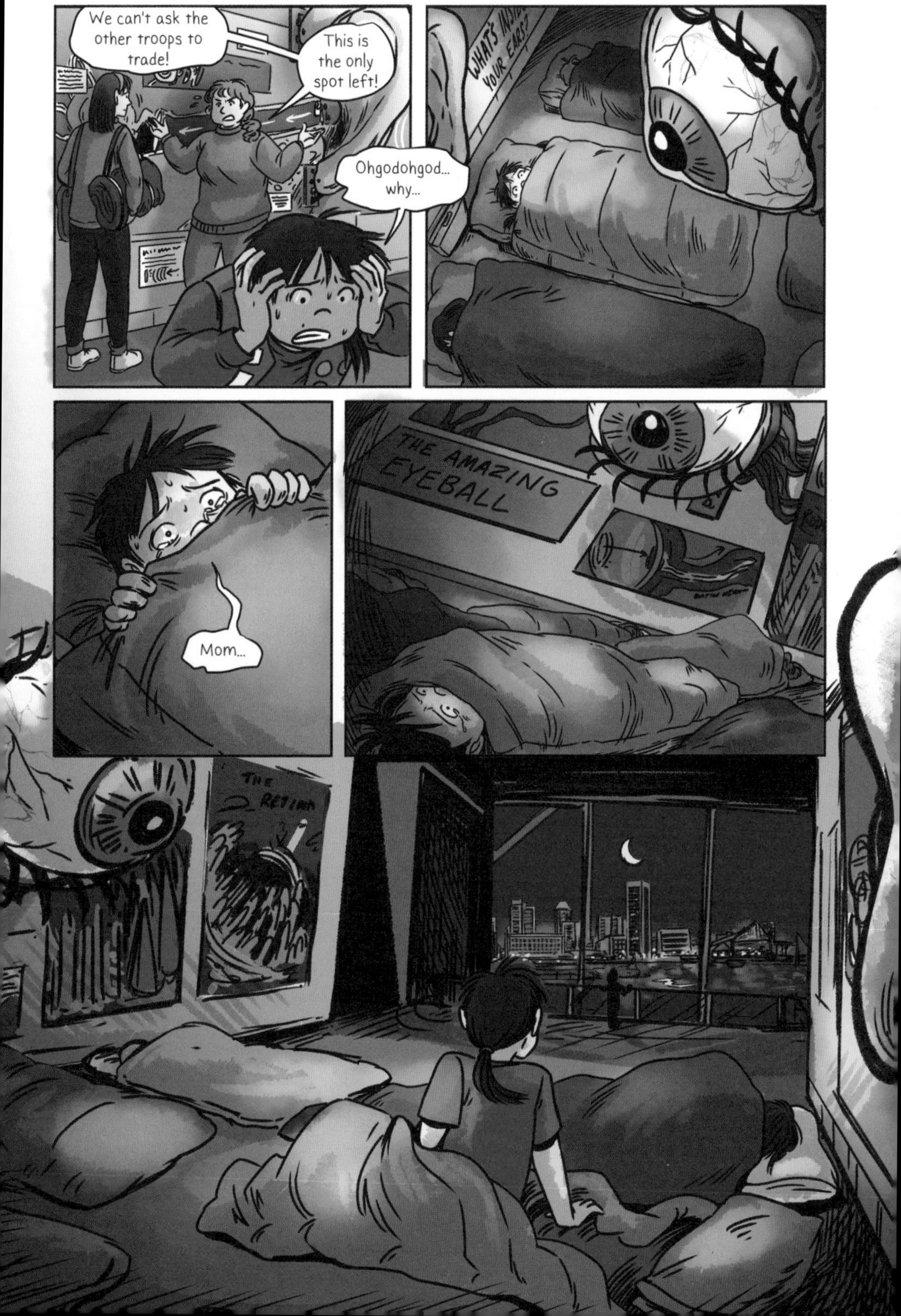
We can't ask the other troops to trade!
This is the only spot left!
Ohgodohgod... why...
WHAT'S INSIDE YOUR EARS?
Mom...
THE AMAZING EYEBALL
THE RETINA

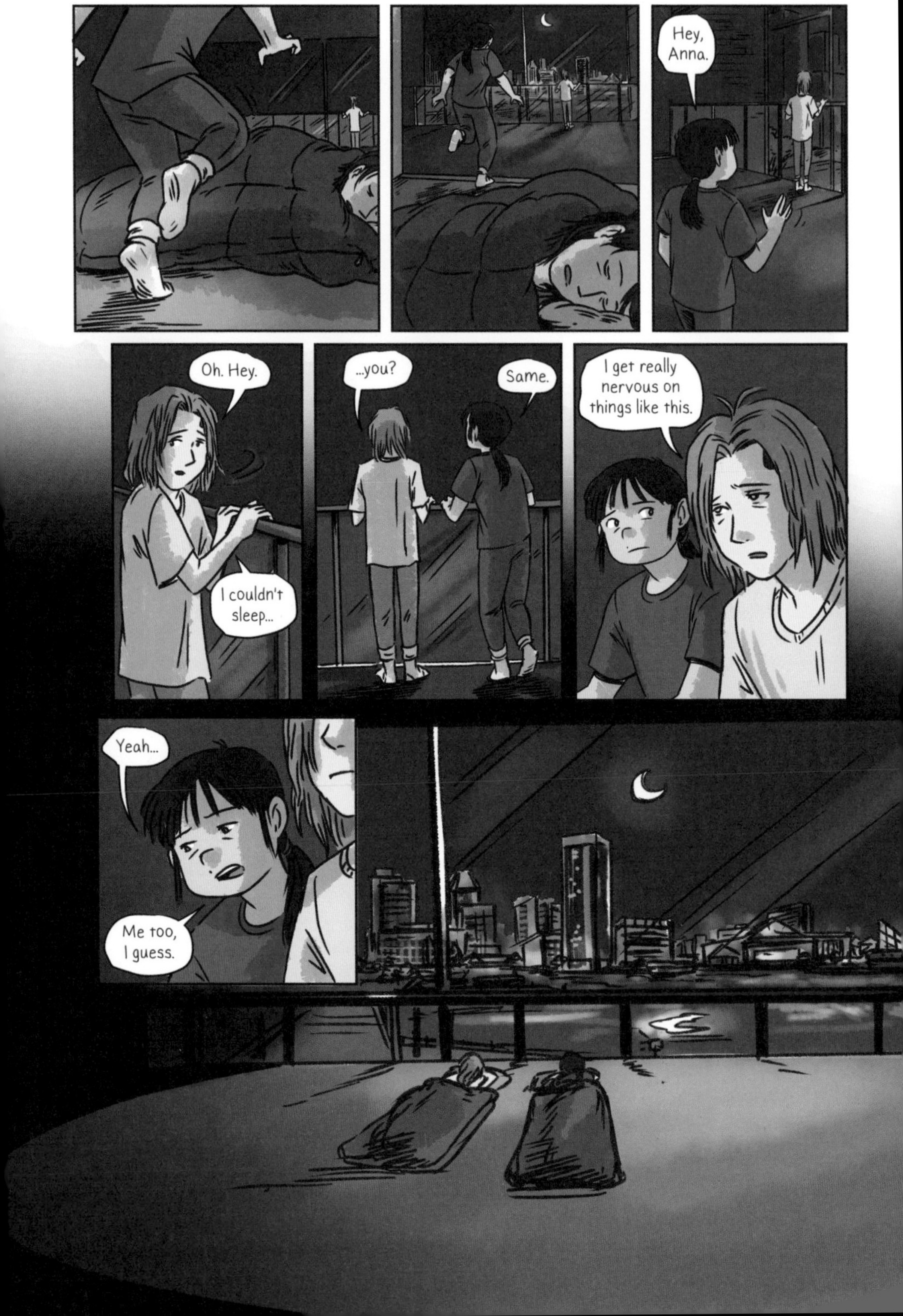
Hey, Anna.
Oh. Hey.
I couldn't sleep...
...you?
Same.
I get really nervous on things like this.
Yeah...
Me too, I guess.

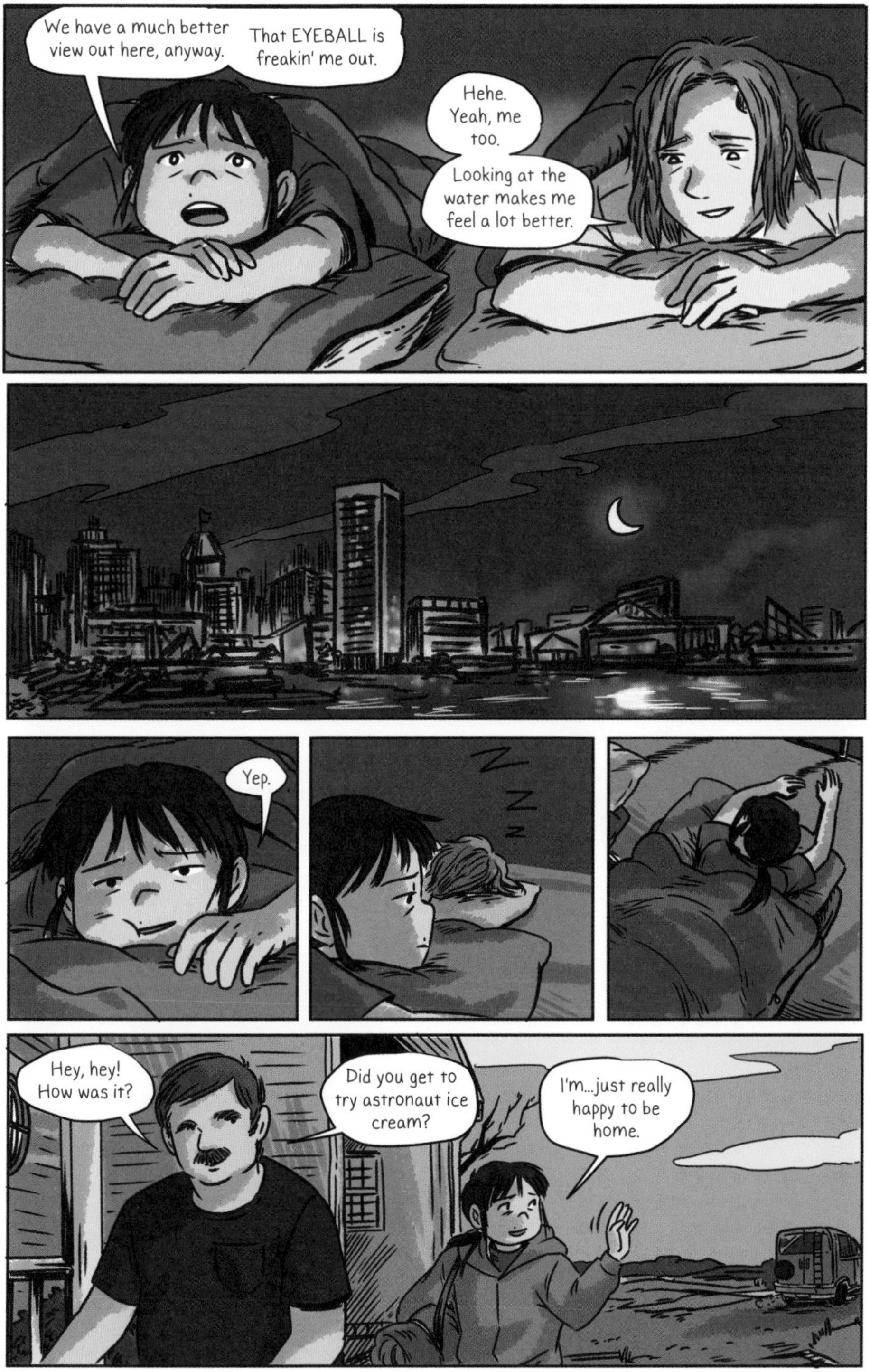
We have a much better view out here, anyway.
That EYEBALL is freakin' me out.
Hehe. Yeah, me too.
Looking at the water makes me feel a lot better.
Yep.
Z Z Z
Hey, hey! How was it?
Did you get to try astronaut ice cream?
I'm...just really happy to be home.

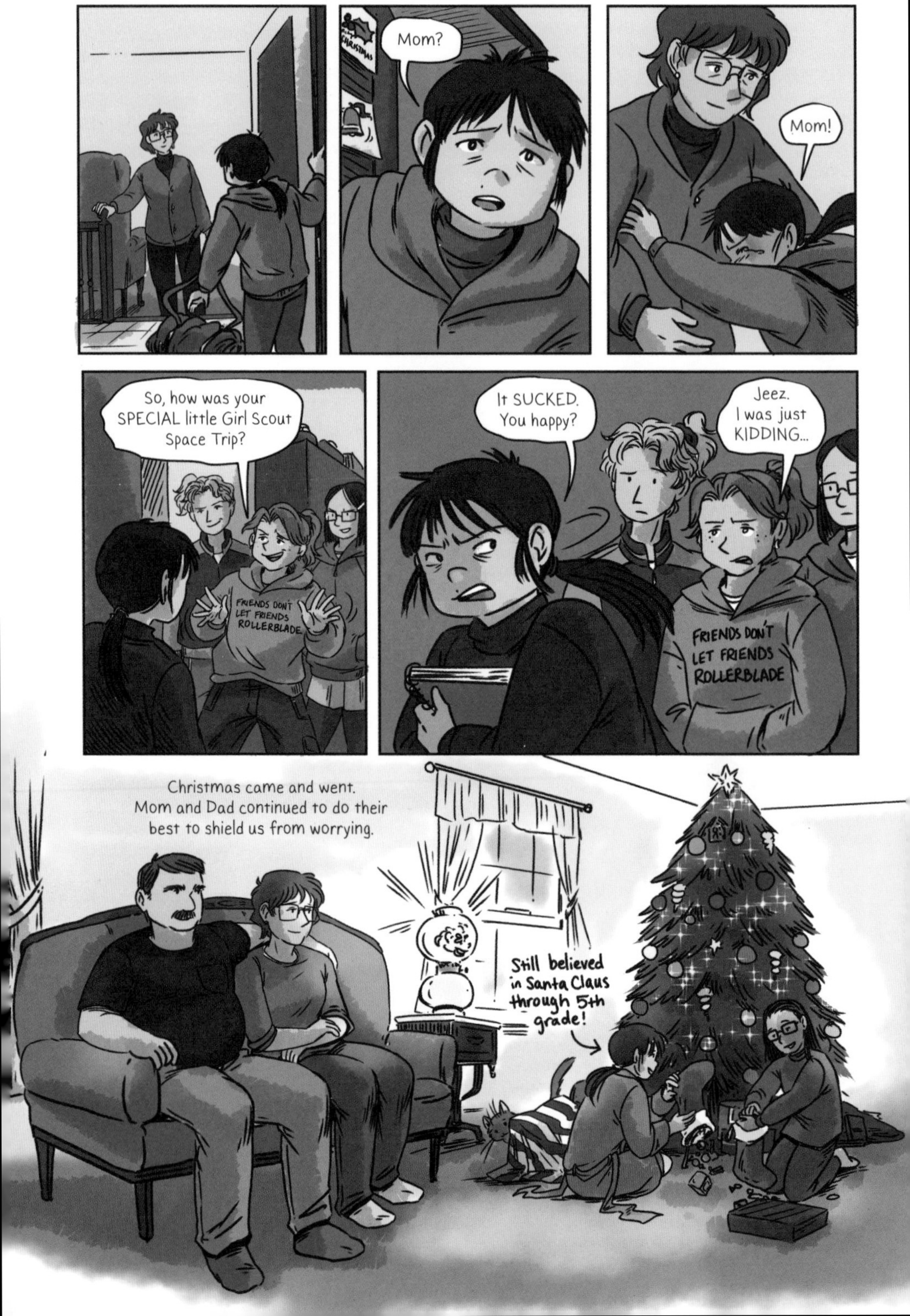

Mom?
Mom!
So, how was your SPECIAL little Girl Scout Space Trip?
FRIENDS DON'T LET FRIENDS ROLLERBLADE
It SUCKED. You happy?
Jeez. I was just KIDDING...
FRIENDS DON'T LET FRIENDS ROLLERBLADE
Christmas came and went. Mom and Dad continued to do their best to shield us from worrying.
Still believed in Santa Claus through 5th grade!

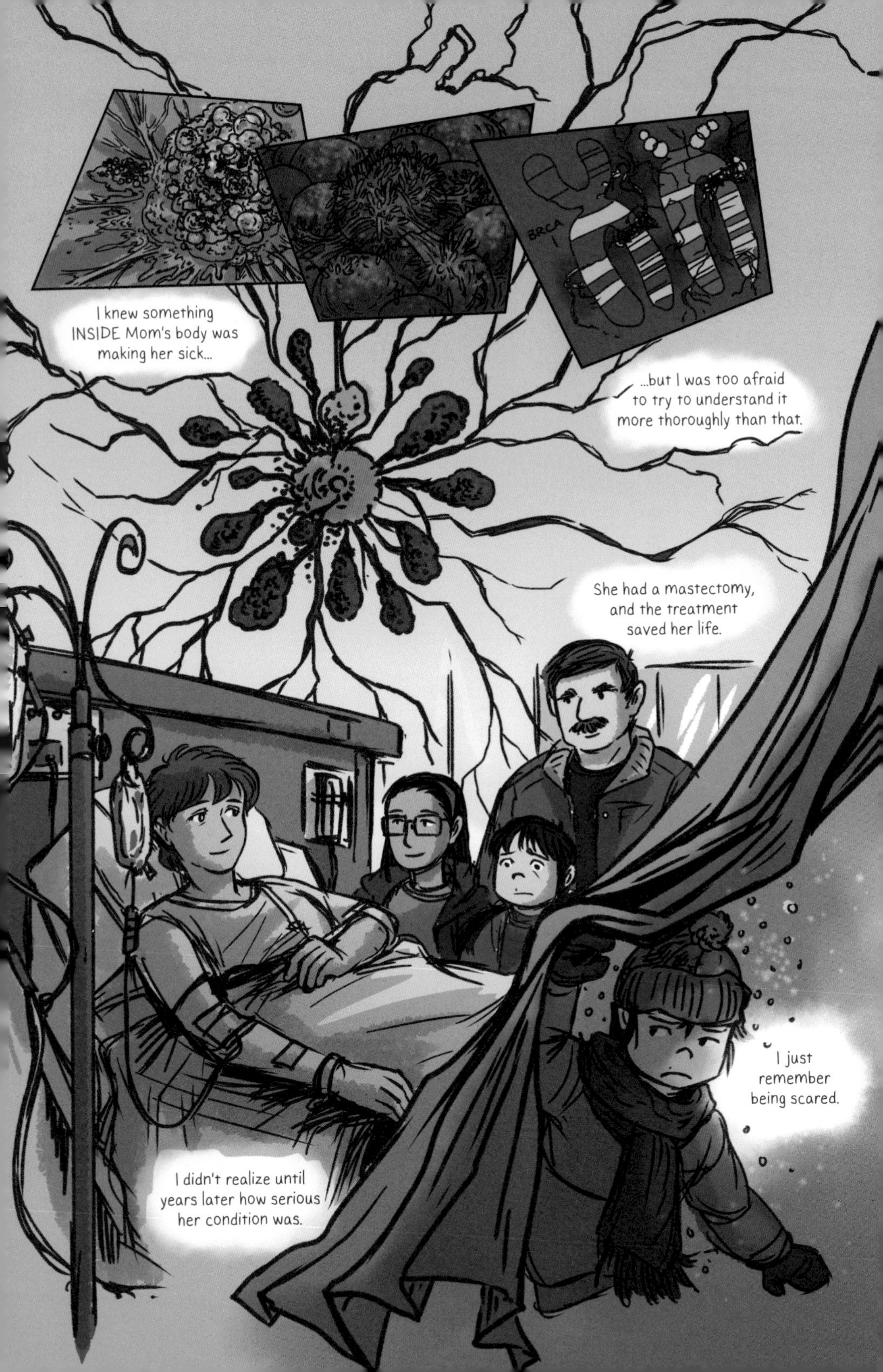
BRCA
I knew something INSIDE Mom's body was making her sick...
...but I was too afraid to try to understand it more thoroughly than that.
She had a mastectomy, and the treatment saved her life.
I just remember being scared.
I didn't realize until years later how serious her condition was.

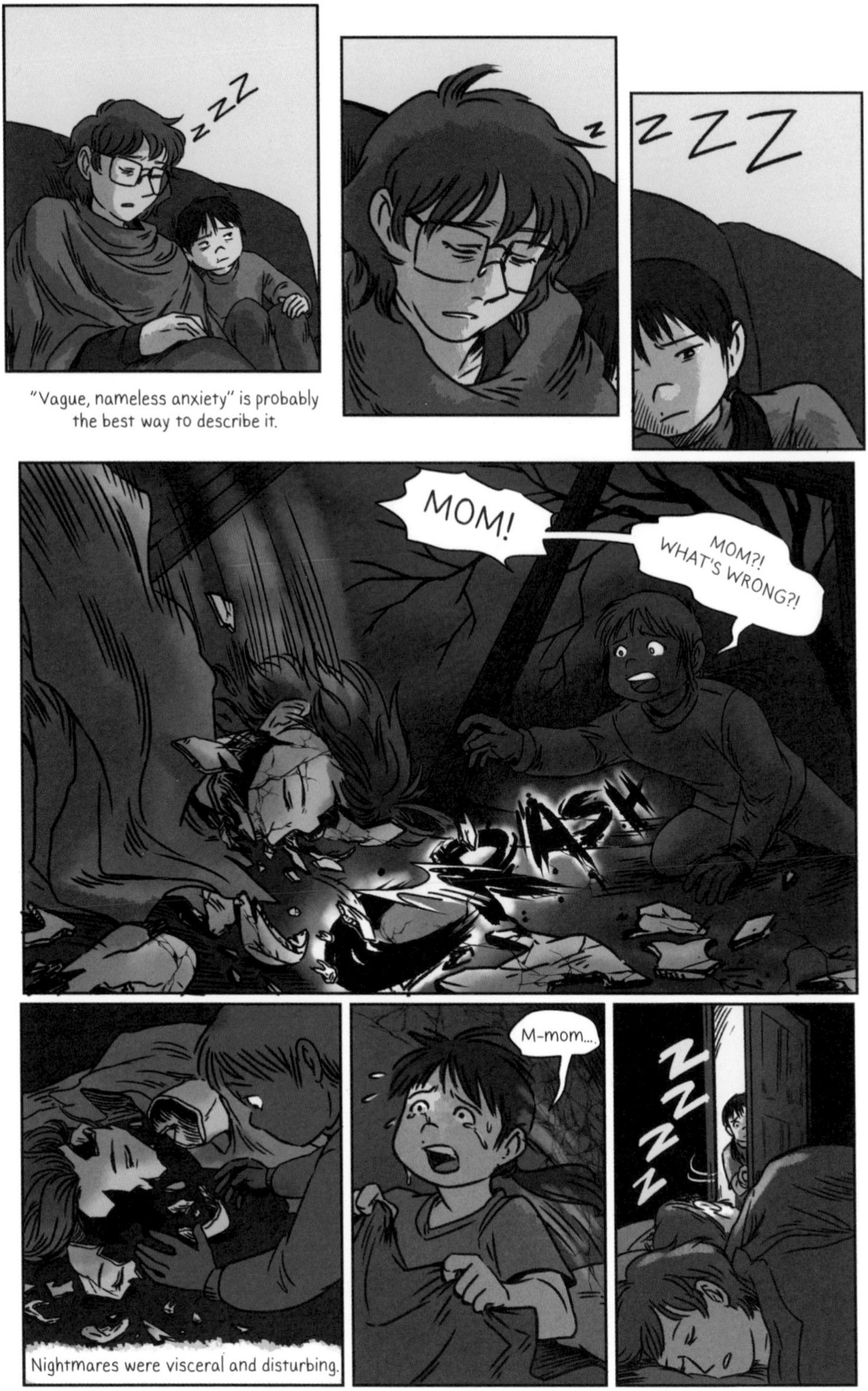

zZZ
"Vague, nameless anxiety" is probably the best way to describe it.
z
ZZZ
MOM!
MOM?! WHAT'S WRONG?!
CRASH
Nightmares were visceral and disturbing.
M-mom...
ZZZZ

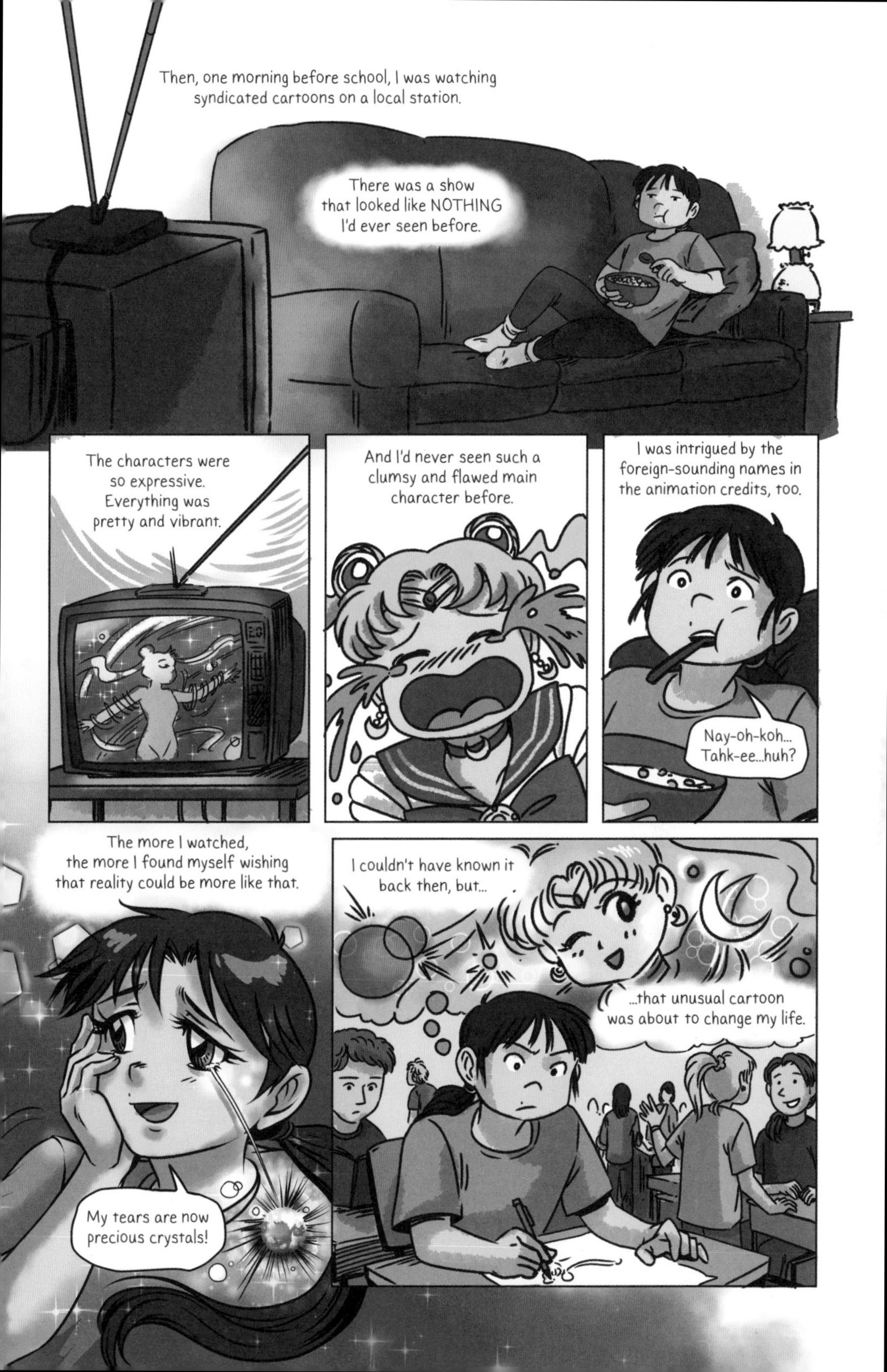
Then, one morning before school, I was watching syndicated cartoons on a local station.
There was a show that looked like NOTHING I'd ever seen before.
The characters were so expressive. Everything was pretty and vibrant.
And I'd never seen such a clumsy and flawed main character before.
I was intrigued by the foreign-sounding names in the animation credits, too.
Nay-oh-koh... Tahk-ee...huh?
The more I watched, the more I found myself wishing that reality could be more like that.
My tears are now precious crystals!
I couldn't have known it back then, but...
...that unusual cartoon was about to change my life.

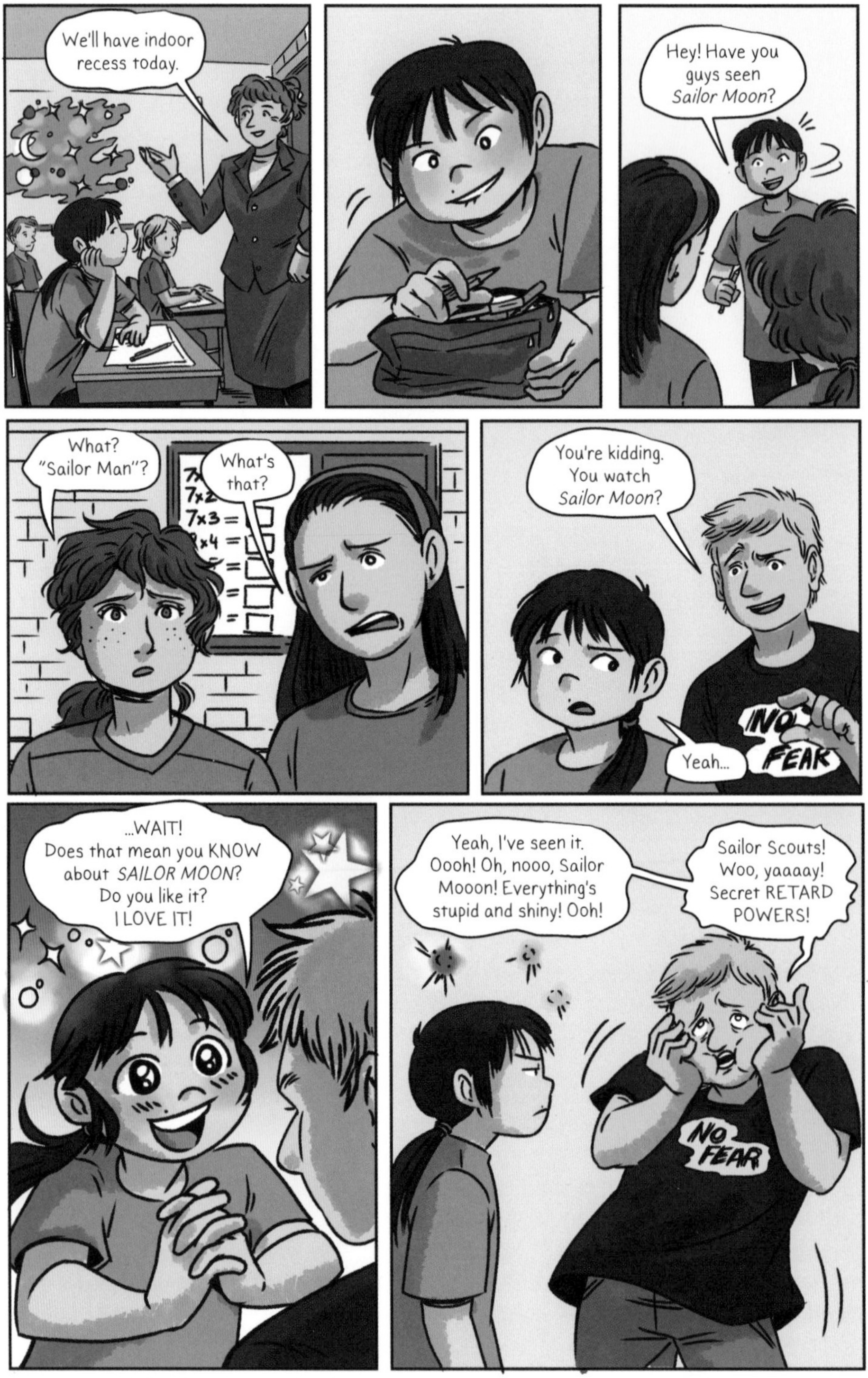
We'll have indoor recess today.
Hey! Have you guys seen Sailor Moon?
What? "Sailor Man"?
What's that?
You're kidding. You watch Sailor Moon?
Yeah...
NO FEAR
...WAIT! Does that mean you KNOW about SAILOR MOON? Do you like it? I LOVE IT!
Yeah, I've seen it. Oooh! Oh, nooo, Sailor Mooon! Everything's stupid and shiny! Ooh!
Sailor Scouts! Woo, yaaaay! Secret RETARD POWERS!
NO FEAR

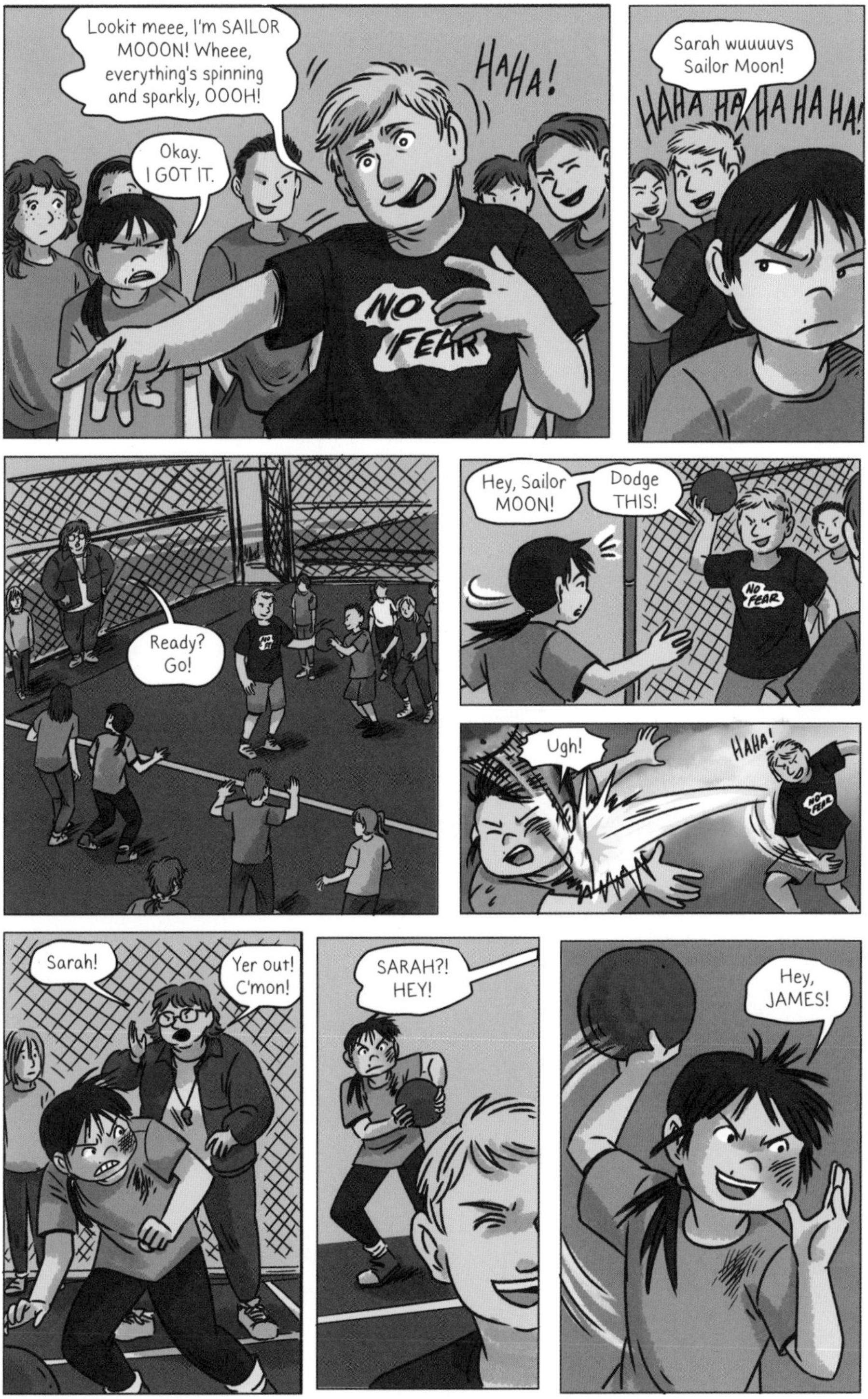
Lookit meee, I'm SAILOR MOOON! Wheee, everything's spinning and sparkly, OOOH!
HAHA!
Okay. I GOT IT.
NO FEAR
Sarah wuuuuvs Sailor Moon!
HAHA HAHA HA HA HA!
Ready? Go!
Hey, Sailor MOON!
Dodge THIS!
NO FEAR
Ugh!
HAHA!
NO FEAR
Sarah!
Yer out! C'mon!
SARAH?! HEY!
Hey, JAMES!

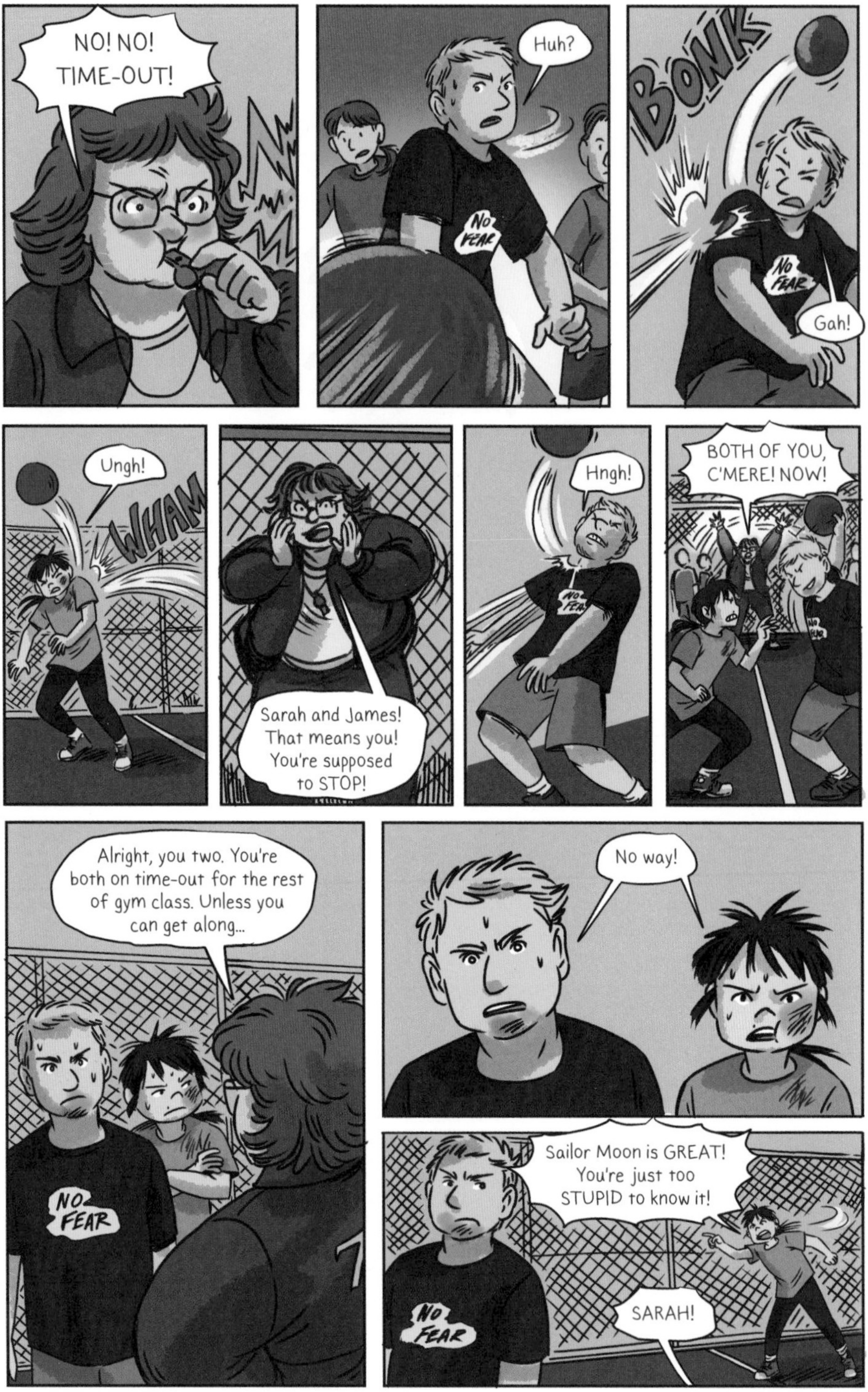
NO! NO! TIME-OUT!
Huh?
BONK
Gah!
Ungh!
WHAM
Sarah and James! That means you! You're supposed to STOP!
Hngh!
BOTH OF YOU, C'MERE! NOW!
Alright, you two. You're both on time-out for the rest of gym class. Unless you can get along...
NO FEAR
No way!
Sailor Moon is GREAT! You're just too STUPID to know it!
SARAH!

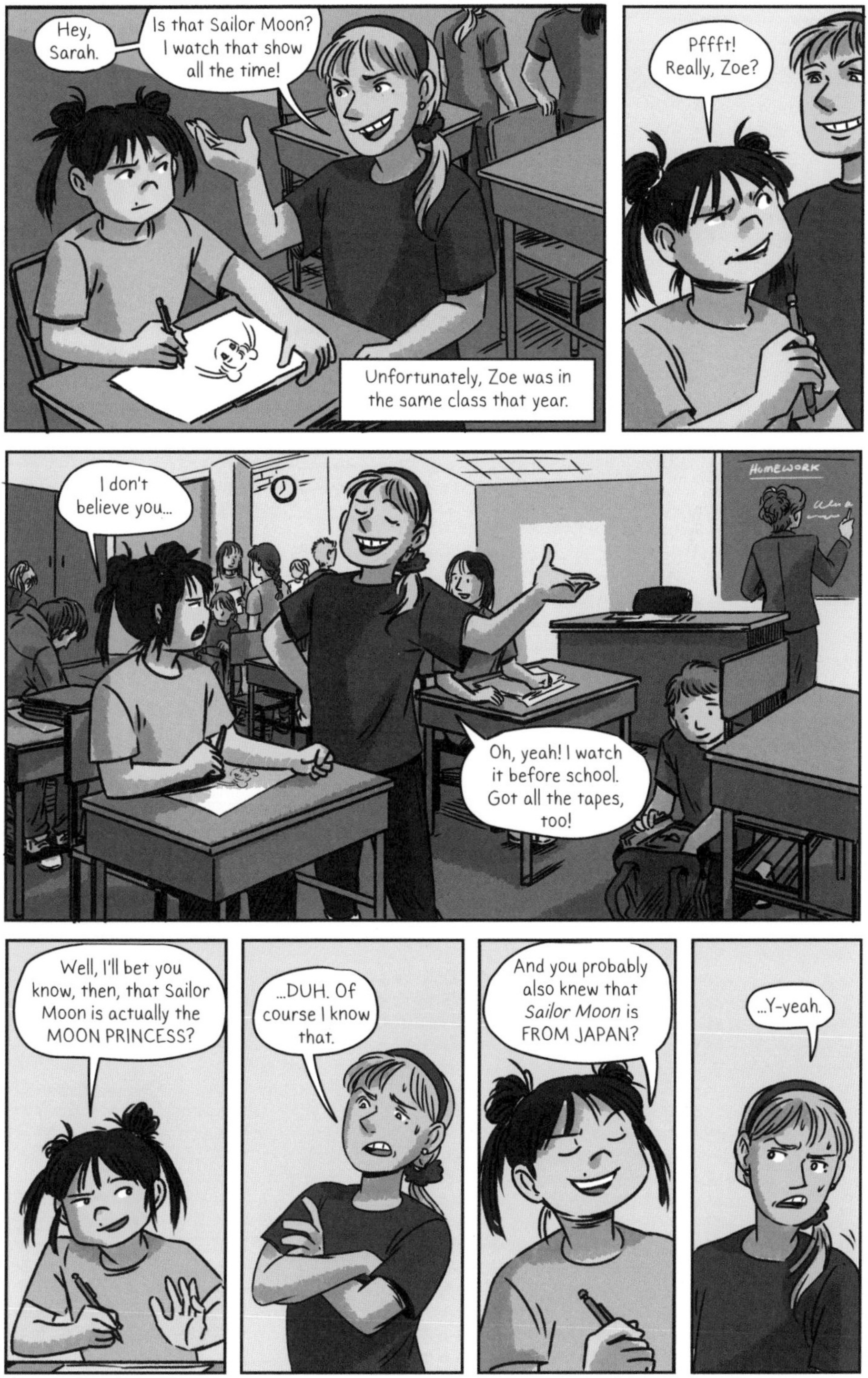
Hey, Sarah.
Is that Sailor Moon? I watch that show all the time!
Unfortunately, Zoe was in the same class that year.
Pffft! Really, Zoe?
I don't believe you...
HOMEWORK
Oh, yeah! I watch it before school. Got all the tapes, too!
Well, I'll bet you know, then, that Sailor Moon is actually the MOON PRINCESS?
...DUH. Of course I know that.
And you probably also knew that *Sailor Moon* is FROM JAPAN?
...Y-yeah.

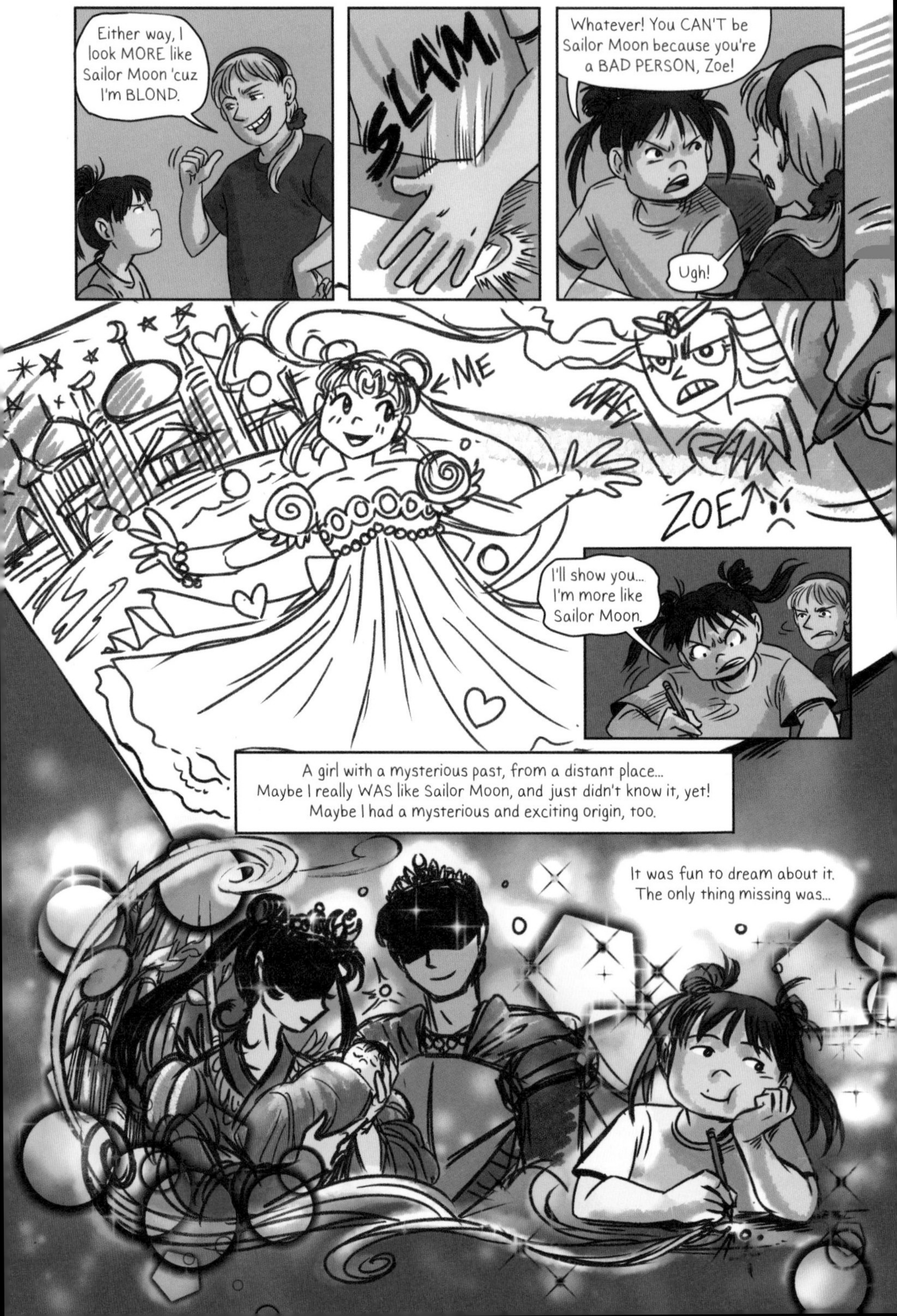
Either way, I look MORE like Sailor Moon 'cuz I'm BLOND.
SLAM
Whatever! You CAN'T be Sailor Moon because you're a BAD PERSON, Zoe!
Ugh!
ME
ZOE
I'll show you... I'm more like Sailor Moon.
A girl with a mysterious past, from a distant place...
Maybe I really WAS like Sailor Moon, and just didn't know it, yet!
Maybe I had a mysterious and exciting origin, too.
It was fun to dream about it.
The only thing missing was...

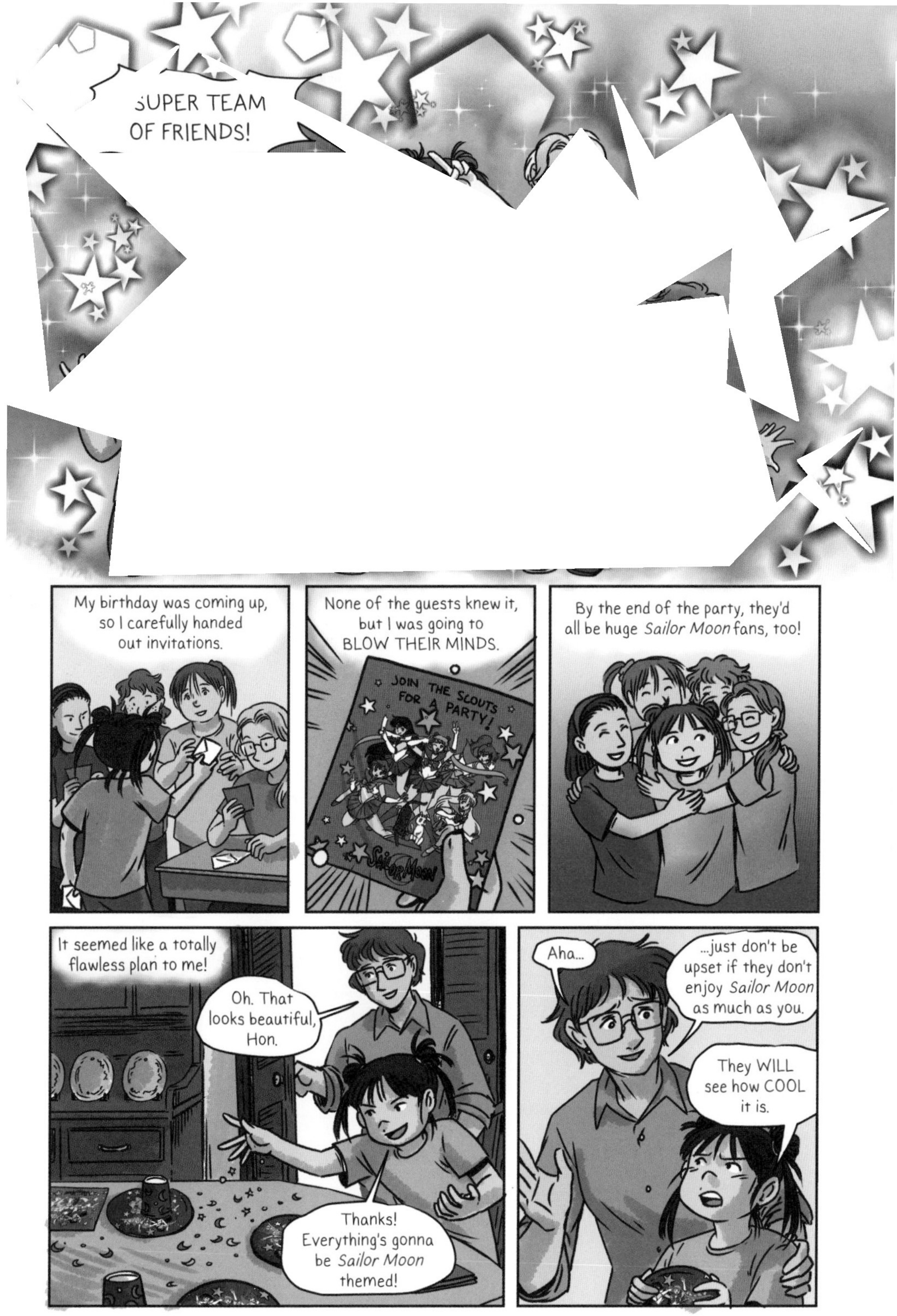
SUPER TEAM OF FRIENDS!
My birthday was coming up, so I carefully handed out invitations.
None of the guests knew it, but I was going to BLOW THEIR MINDS.
JOIN THE SCOUTS FOR A PARTY!
SAILOR MOON
By the end of the party, they'd all be huge *Sailor Moon* fans, too!
It seemed like a totally flawless plan to me!
Oh. That looks beautiful, Hon.
Thanks! Everything's gonna be *Sailor Moon* themed!
Aha...
...just don't be upset if they don't enjoy *Sailor Moon* as much as you.
They WILL see how COOL it is.

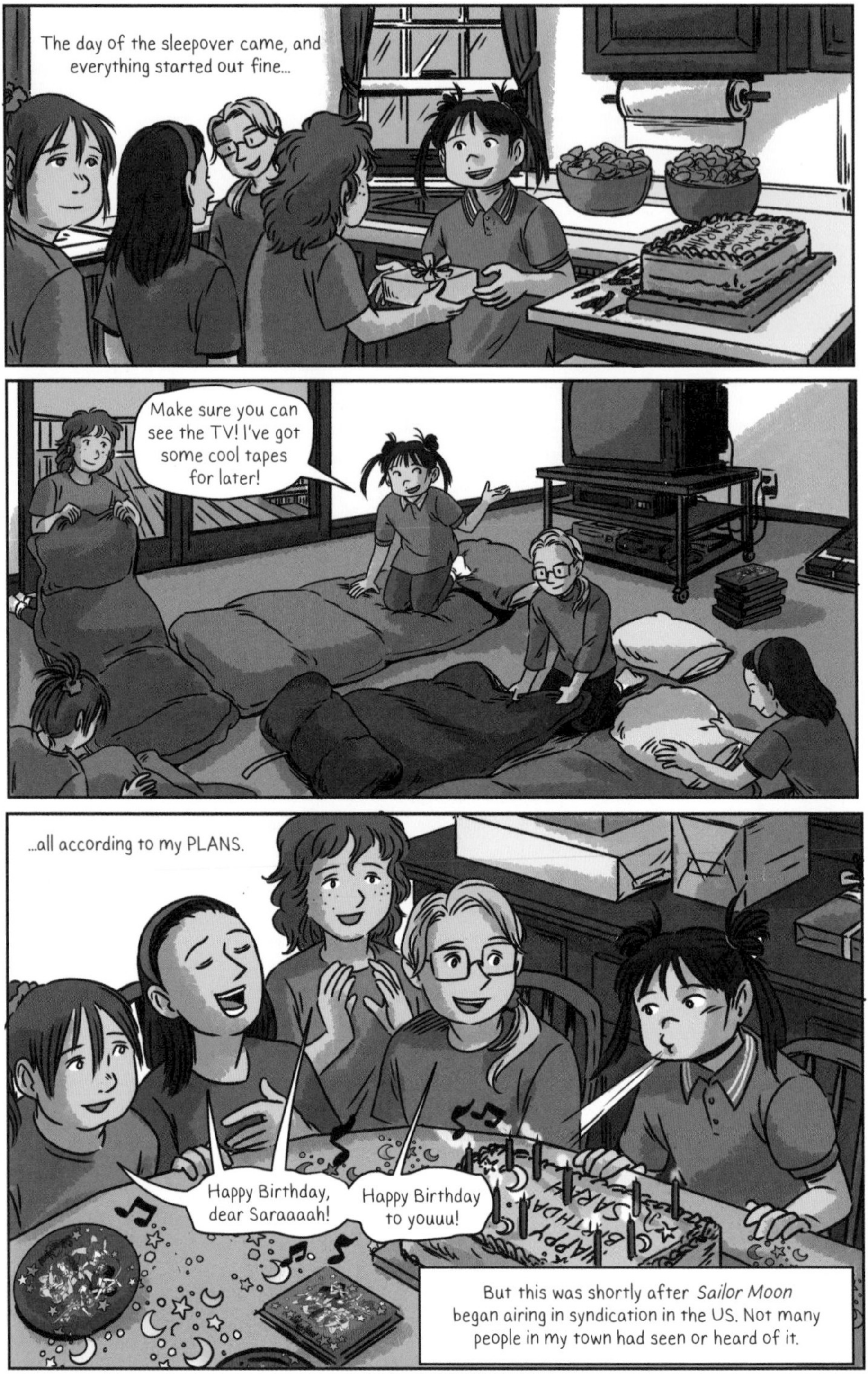
The day of the sleepover came, and everything started out fine...
Make sure you can see the TV! I've got some cool tapes for later!
...all according to my PLANS.
Happy Birthday, dear Saraaaah!
Happy Birthday to youuu!
But this was shortly after *Sailor Moon* began airing in syndication in the US. Not many people in my town had seen or heard of it.

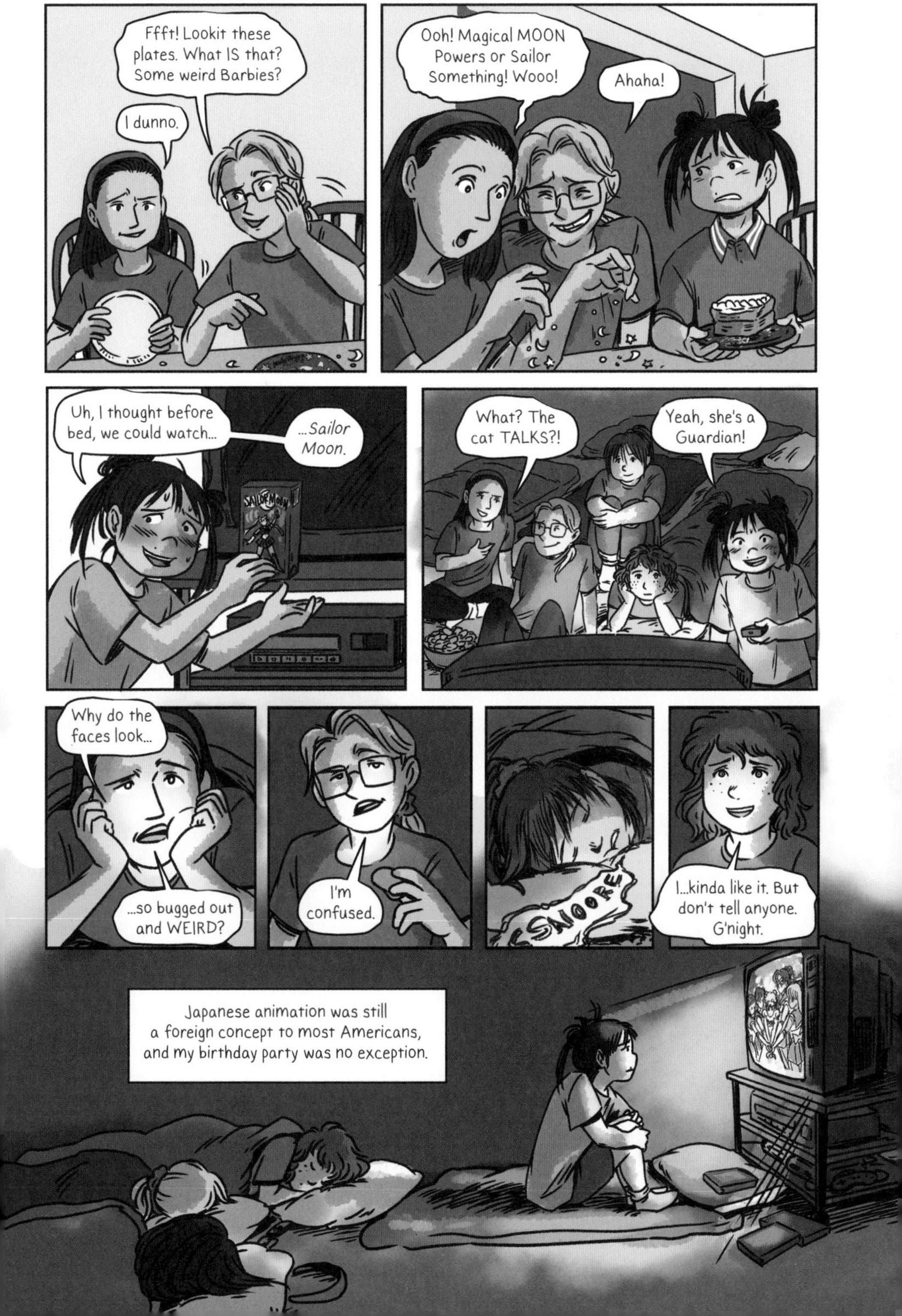
Ffft! Lookit these plates. What IS that? Some weird Barbies?
I dunno.
Ooh! Magical MOON Powers or Sailor Something! Wooo!
Ahaha!
Uh, I thought before bed, we could watch...
...Sailor Moon.
SAILOR MOON
What? The cat TALKS?!
Yeah, she's a Guardian!
Why do the faces look...
...so bugged out and WEIRD?
I'm confused.
SNOORE
I...kinda like it. But don't tell anyone. G'night.
Japanese animation was still a foreign concept to most Americans, and my birthday party was no exception.

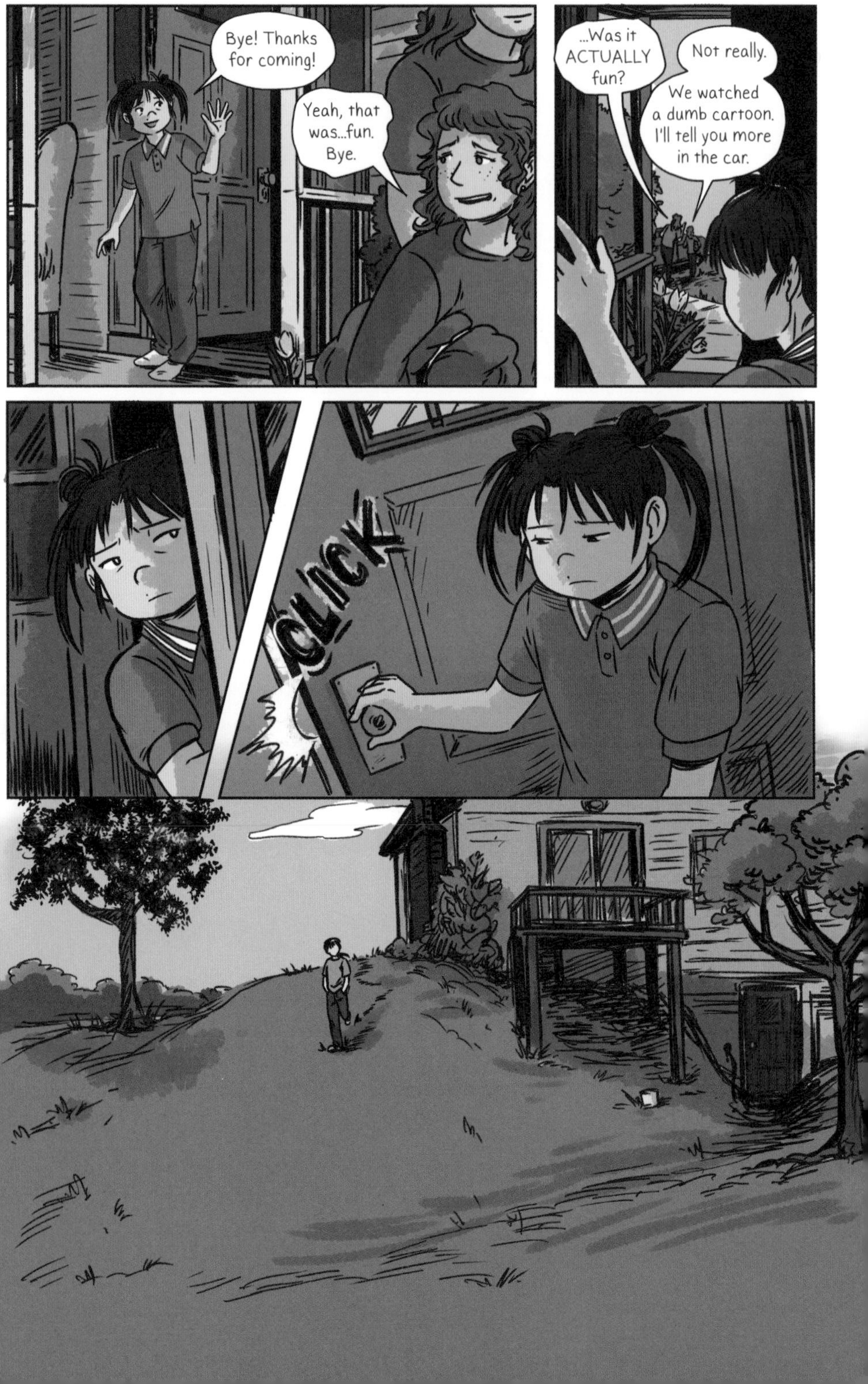
Bye! Thanks for coming!
Yeah, that was...fun. Bye.
...Was it ACTUALLY fun?
Not really.
We watched a dumb cartoon. I'll tell you more in the car.
CLICK

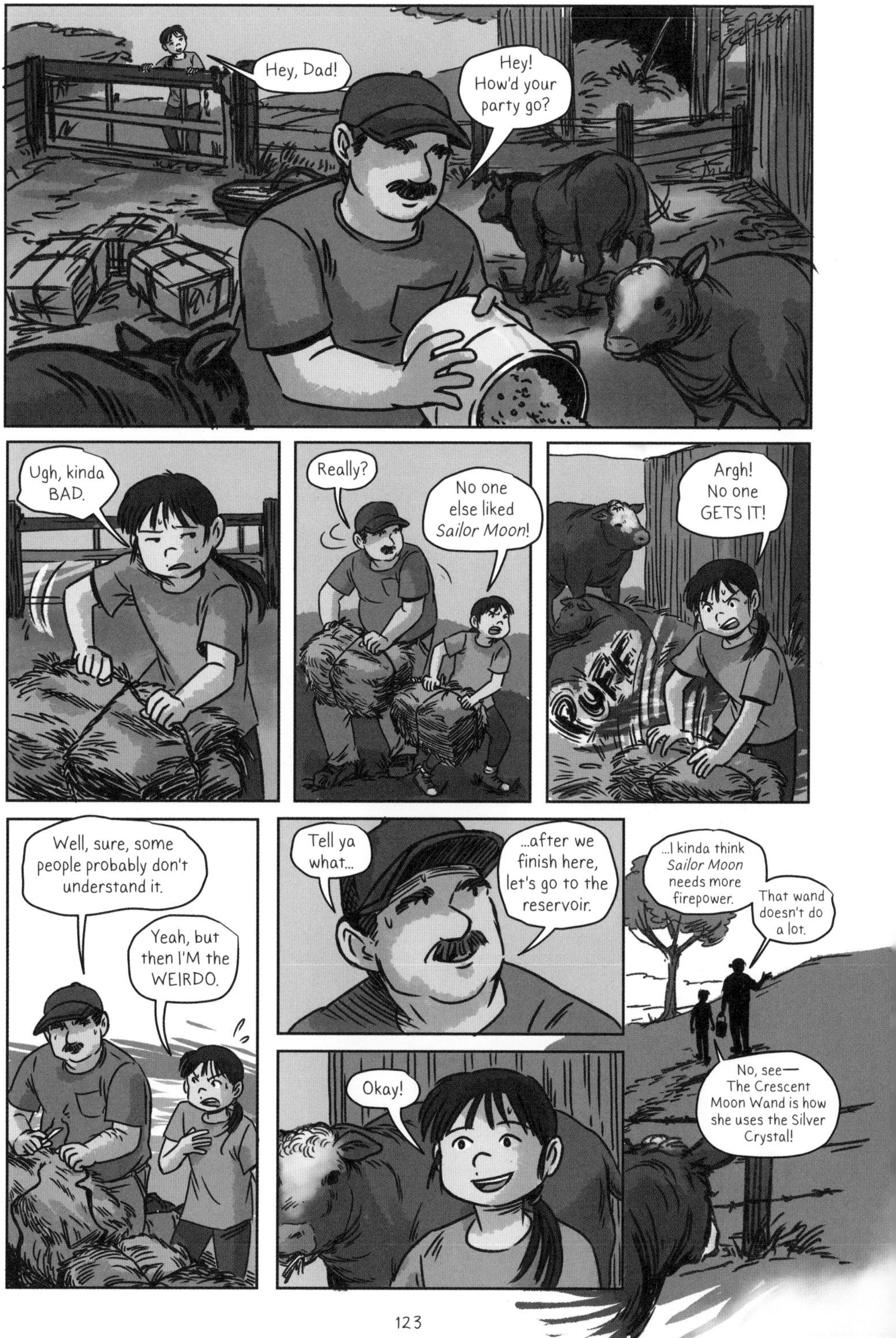
Hey, Dad!
Hey! How'd your party go?
Ugh, kinda BAD.
Really?
No one else liked *Sailor Moon*!
Argh! No one GETS IT!
PUFF
Well, sure, some people probably don't understand it.
Yeah, but then I'M the WEIRDO.
Tell ya what...
...after we finish here, let's go to the reservoir.
Okay!
...I kinda think *Sailor Moon* needs more firepower.
That wand doesn't do a lot.
No, see— The Crescent Moon Wand is how she uses the Silver Crystal!

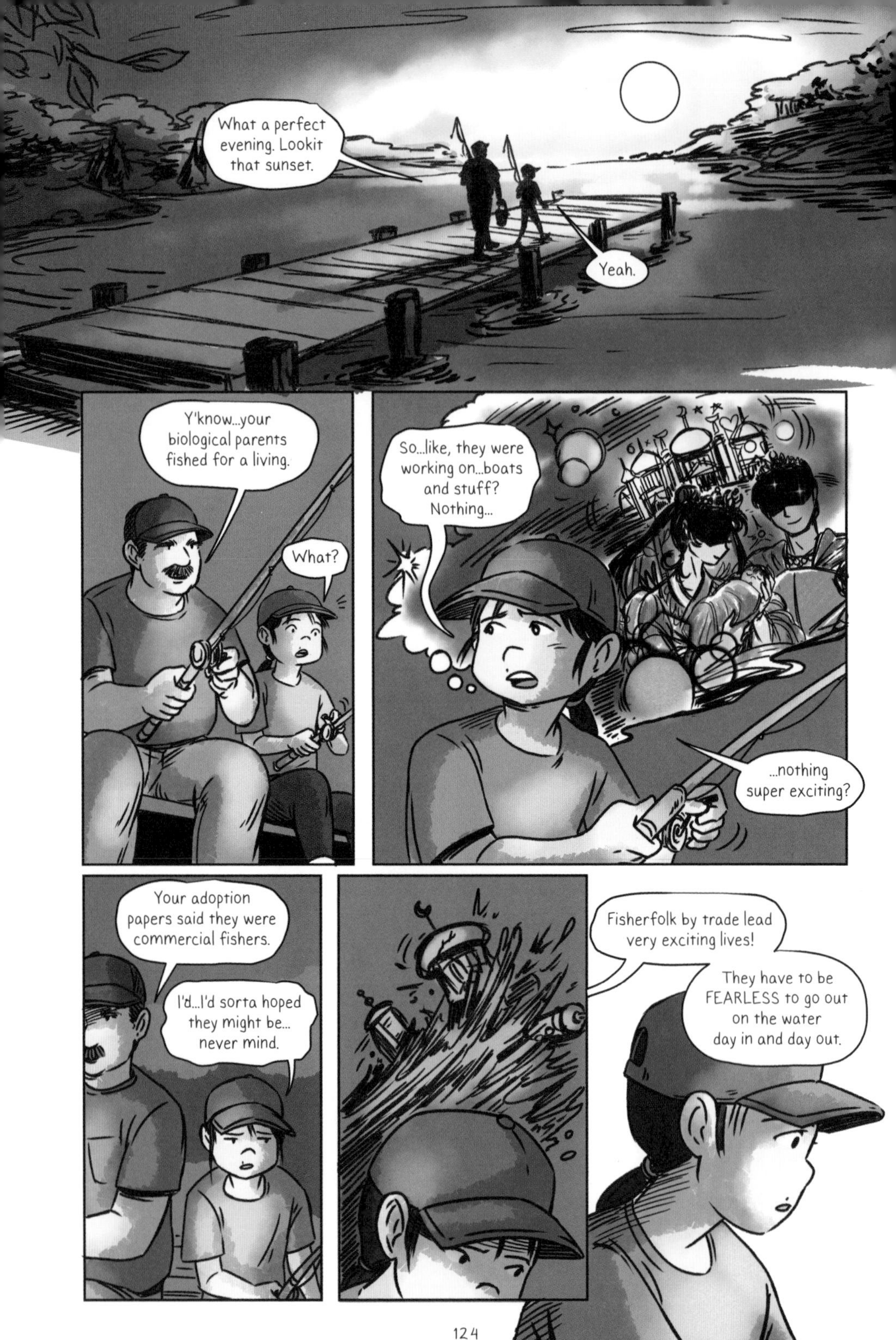
What a perfect evening. Lookit that sunset.
Yeah.
Y'know...your biological parents fished for a living.
What?
So...like, they were working on...boats and stuff? Nothing...
...nothing super exciting?
Your adoption papers said they were commercial fishers.
I'd...I'd sorta hoped they might be... never mind.
Fisherfolk by trade lead very exciting lives!
They have to be FEARLESS to go out on the water day in and day out.

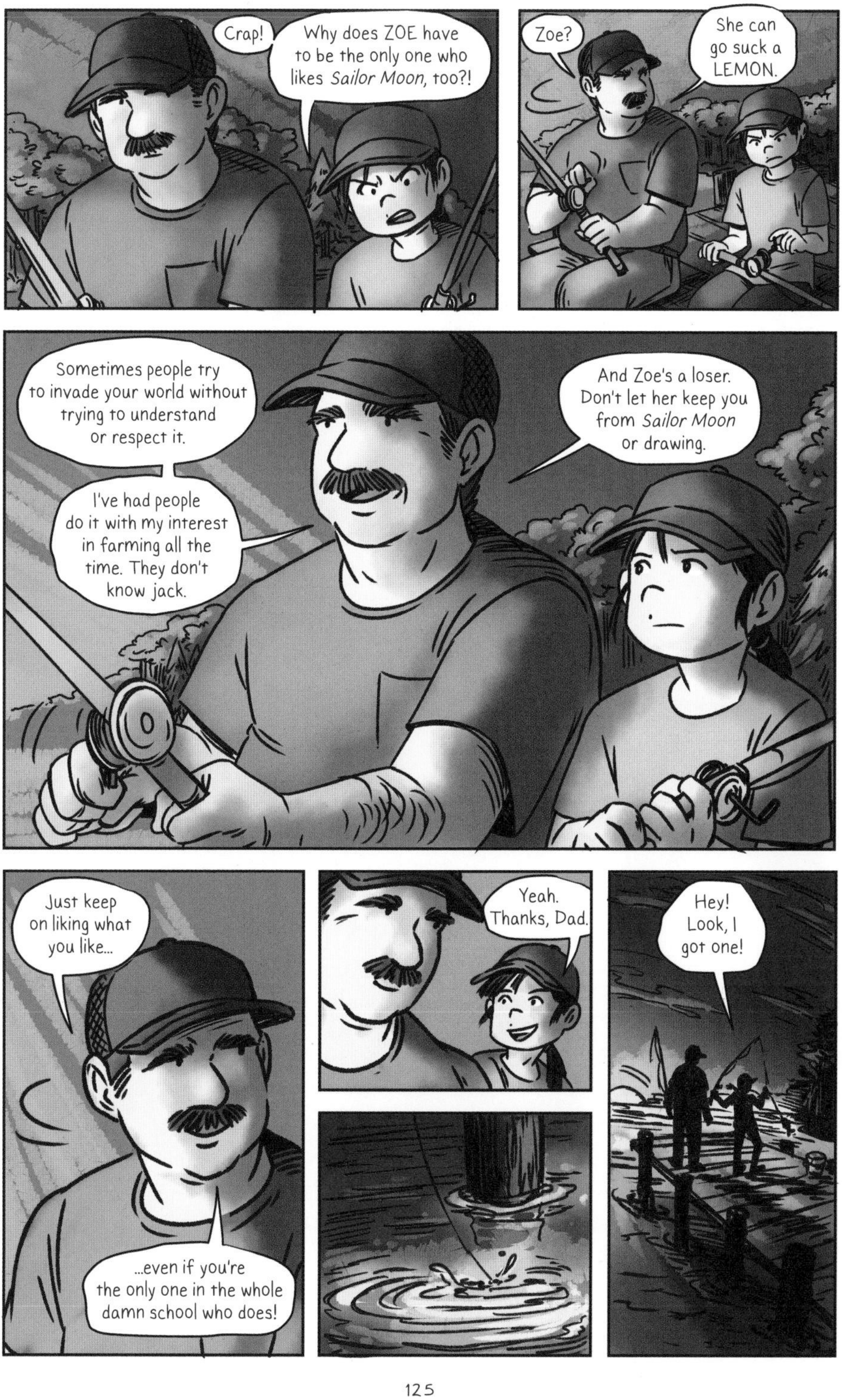
Crap!
Why does ZOE have to be the only one who likes *Sailor Moon*, too?!
Zoe?
She can go suck a LEMON.
Sometimes people try to invade your world without trying to understand or respect it.
I've had people do it with my interest in farming all the time. They don't know jack.
And Zoe's a loser. Don't let her keep you from *Sailor Moon* or drawing.
Just keep on liking what you like...
...even if you're the only one in the whole damn school who does!
Yeah. Thanks, Dad.
Hey! Look, I got one!

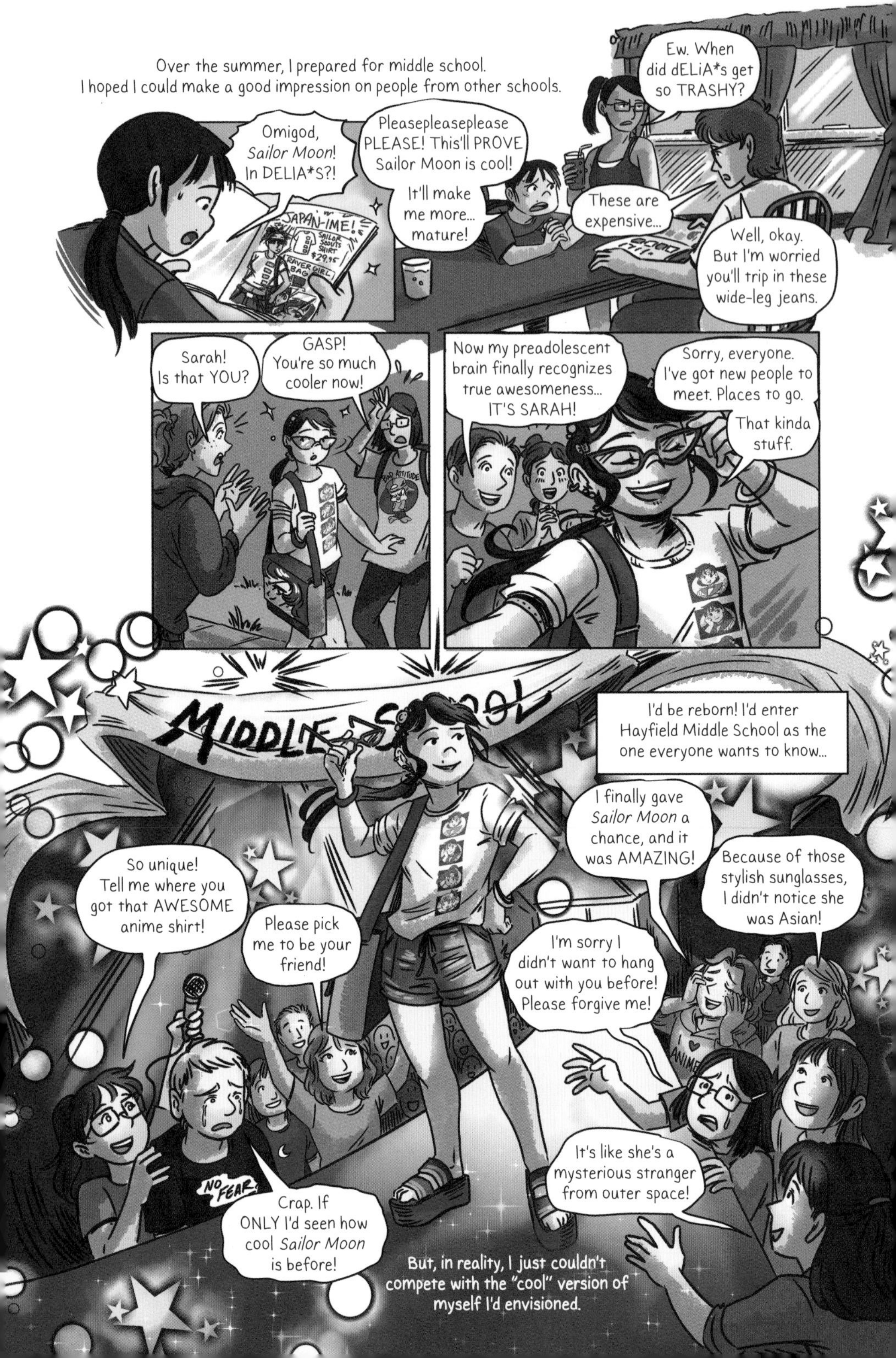
Over the summer, I prepared for middle school.
I hoped I could make a good impression on people from other schools.
Omigod, Sailor Moon! In DELIA*S?!
JAPAN-IME!
SAILOR SCOUTS SHIRT $29.95
RAVER GIRL BAG
Pleasepleaseplease PLEASE! This'll PROVE Sailor Moon is cool!
It'll make me more... mature!
Ew. When did dELiA*s get so TRASHY?
These are expensive...
Well, okay. But I'm worried you'll trip in these wide-leg jeans.
Sarah! Is that YOU?
GASP! You're so much cooler now!
BAD ATTITUDE
Now my preadolescent brain finally recognizes true awesomeness... IT'S SARAH!
Sorry, everyone. I've got new people to meet. Places to go.
That kinda stuff.
MIDDLE SCHOOL
I'd be reborn! I'd enter Hayfield Middle School as the one everyone wants to know...
I finally gave Sailor Moon a chance, and it was AMAZING!
Because of those stylish sunglasses, I didn't notice she was Asian!
So unique! Tell me where you got that AWESOME anime shirt!
Please pick me to be your friend!
I'm sorry I didn't want to hang out with you before! Please forgive me!
NO FEAR
Crap. If ONLY I'd seen how cool Sailor Moon is before!
It's like she's a mysterious stranger from outer space!
But, in reality, I just couldn't compete with the "cool" version of myself I'd envisioned.

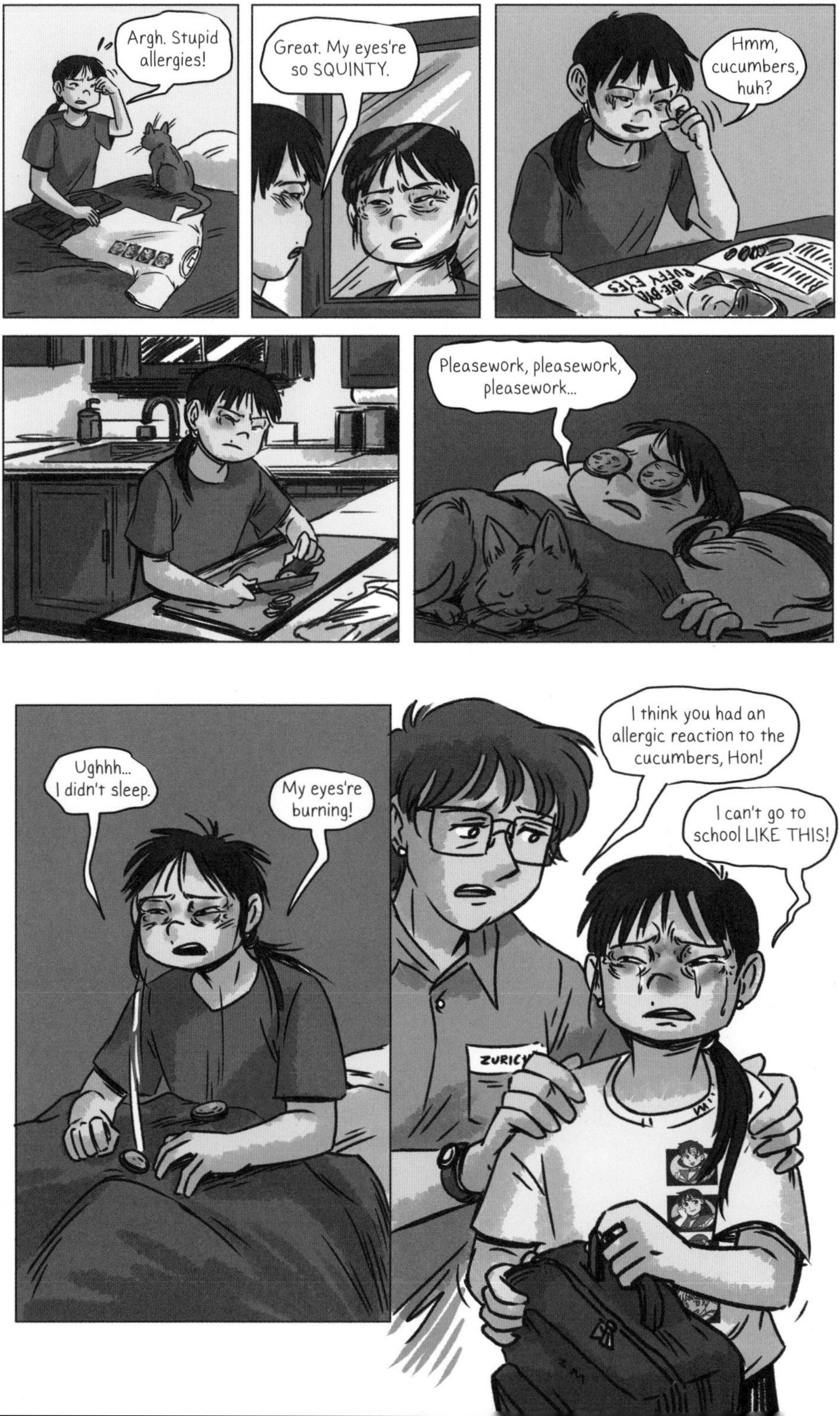
Argh. Stupid allergies!
Great. My eyes're so SQUINTY.
Hmm, cucumbers, huh?
BYE-BYE PUFFY EYES
Pleasework, pleasework, pleasework...
Ughhh... I didn't sleep.
My eyes're burning!
I think you had an allergic reaction to the cucumbers, Hon!
I can't go to school LIKE THIS!

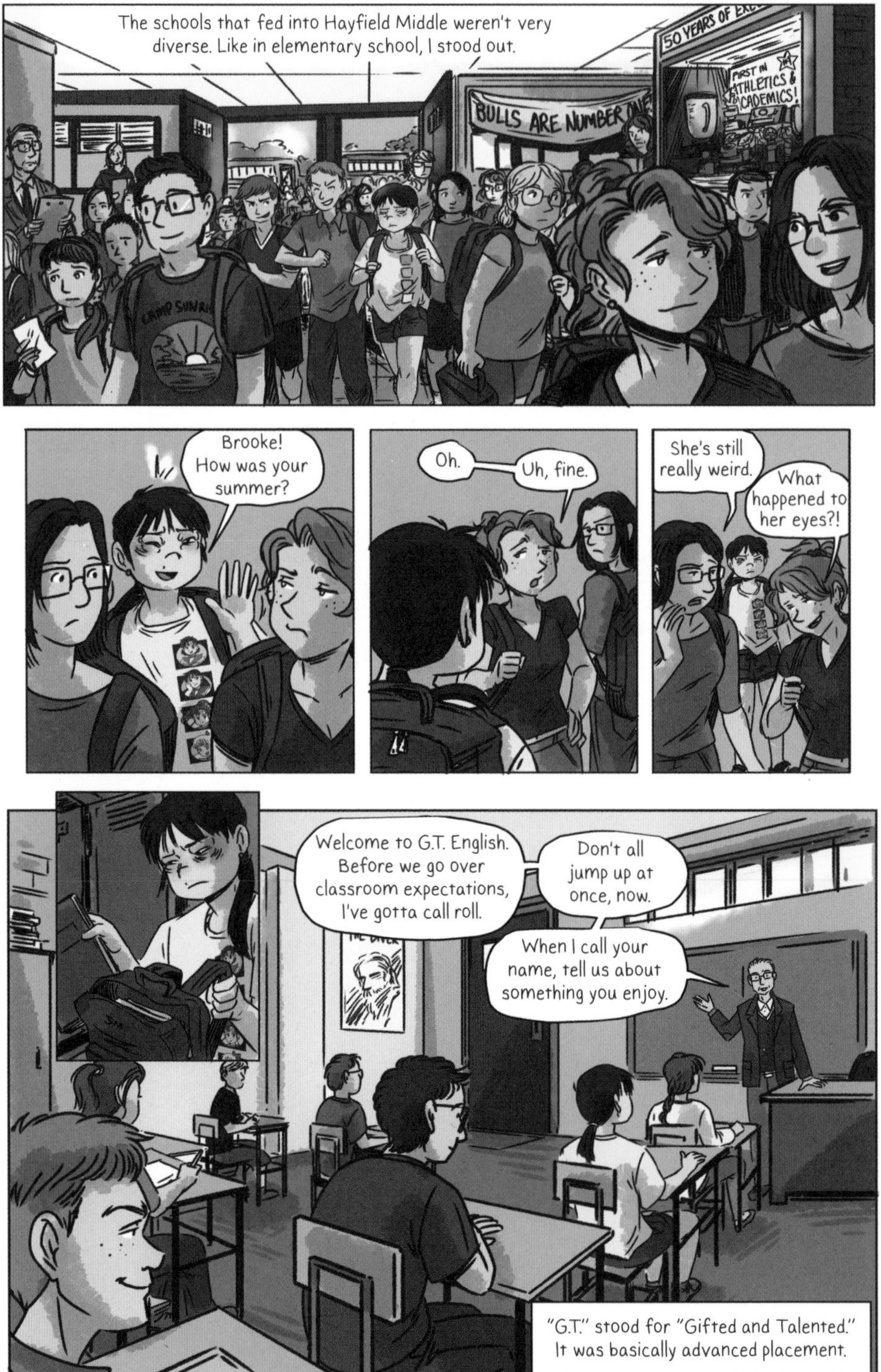

The schools that fed into Hayfield Middle weren't very diverse. Like in elementary school, I stood out.
Brooke! How was your summer?
Oh.
Uh, fine.
She's still really weird.
What happened to her eyes?!
Welcome to G.T. English. Before we go over classroom expectations, I've gotta call roll.
Don't all jump up at once, now.
When I call your name, tell us about something you enjoy.
"G.T." stood for "Gifted and Talented." It was basically advanced placement.

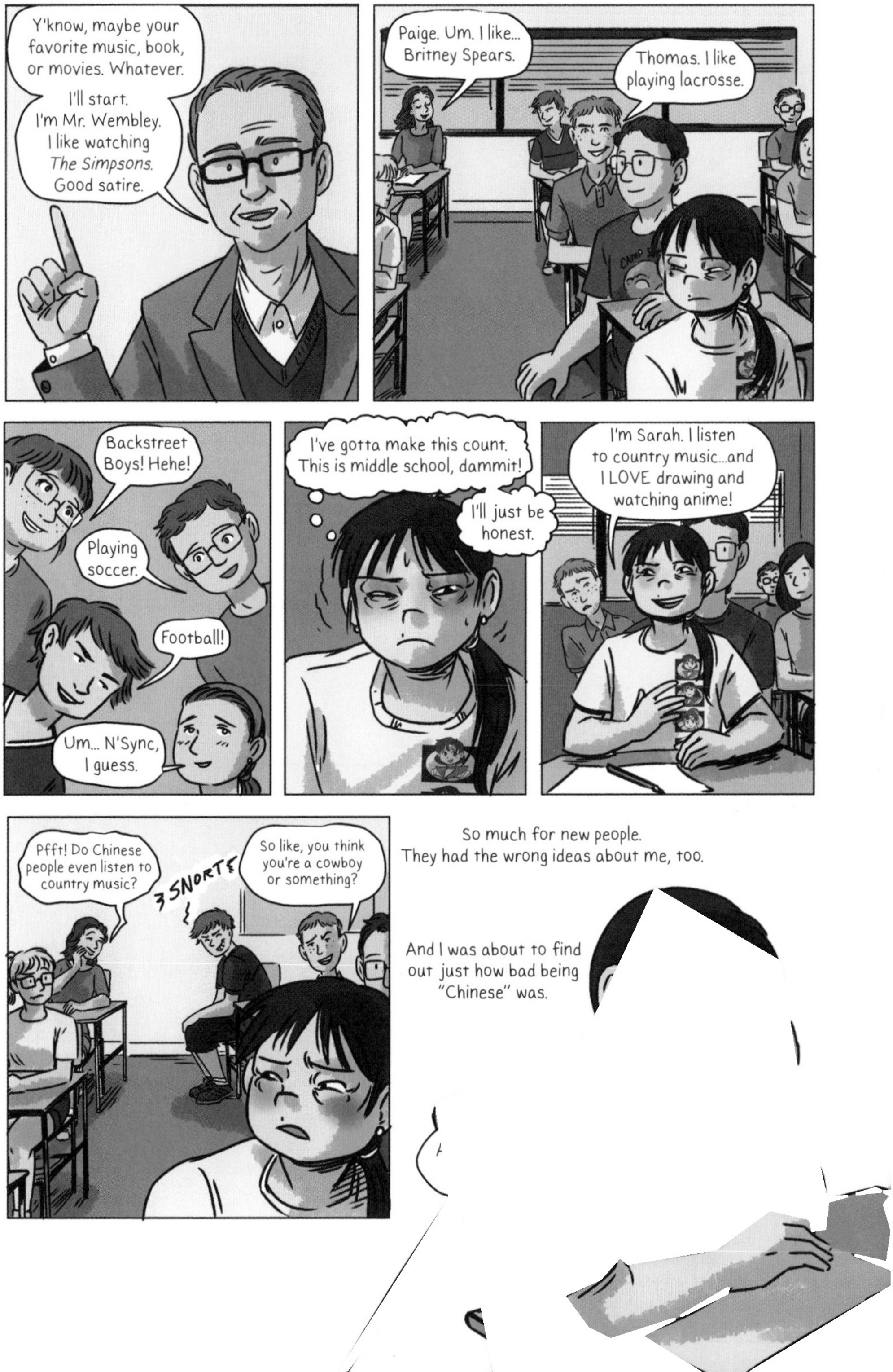
Y'know, maybe your favorite music, book, or movies. Whatever.
I'll start. I'm Mr. Wembley. I like watching The Simpsons. Good satire.
Paige. Um. I like... Britney Spears.
Thomas. I like playing lacrosse.
Backstreet Boys! Hehe!
Playing soccer.
Football!
Um... N'Sync, I guess.
I've gotta make this count. This is middle school, dammit!
I'll just be honest.
I'm Sarah. I listen to country music...and I LOVE drawing and watching anime!
Pfft! Do Chinese people even listen to country music?
SNORT
So like, you think you're a cowboy or something?
So much for new people. They had the wrong ideas about me, too.
And I was about to find out just how bad being "Chinese" was.

Once they were out of earshot of the teacher, some of my classmates made it clear how unwelcome I was.

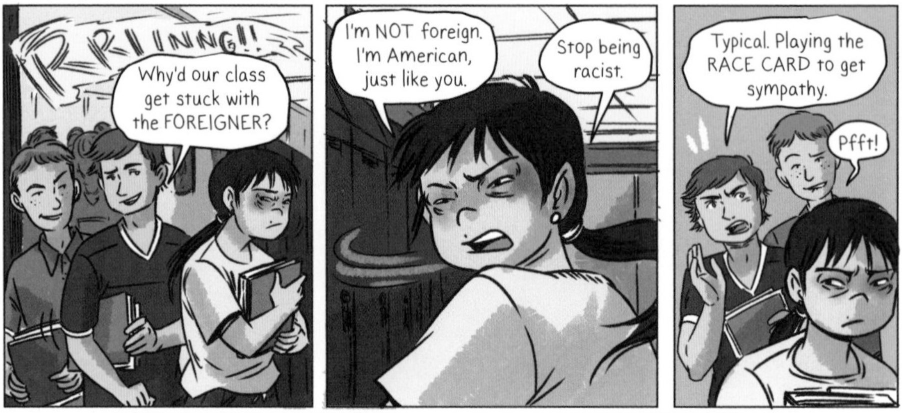
R-RIINNG!!
Why'd our class get stuck with the FOREIGNER?
I'm NOT foreign. I'm American, just like you.
Stop being racist.
Typical. Playing the RACE CARD to get sympathy.
Pfft!

That was the first time I'd heard the term "Race Card."
In hindsight, he was likely parroting terms he'd heard his parents use.

I was convinced I could still be accepted, even if I was different. Thus began...

OPERATION: BE KEWL

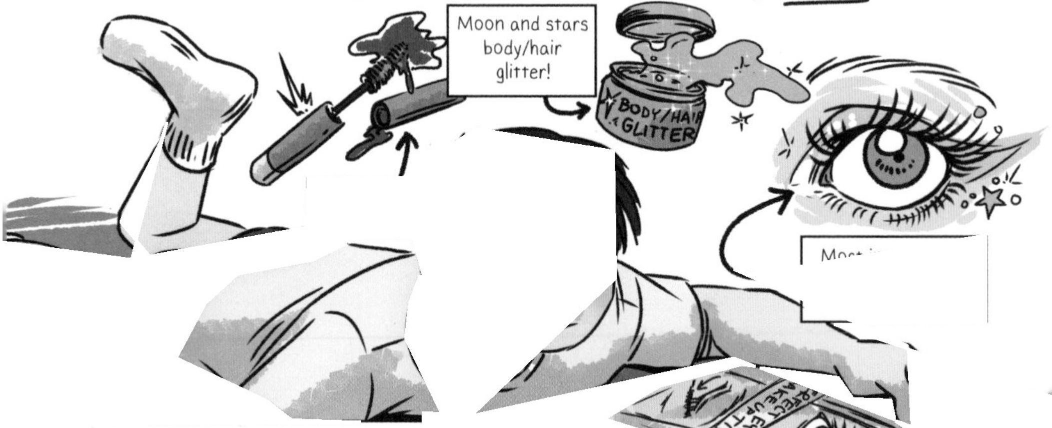
Moon and stars body/hair glitter!
BODY/HAIR GLITTER

Most beauty and style resources back then were almost entirely Eurocentric.

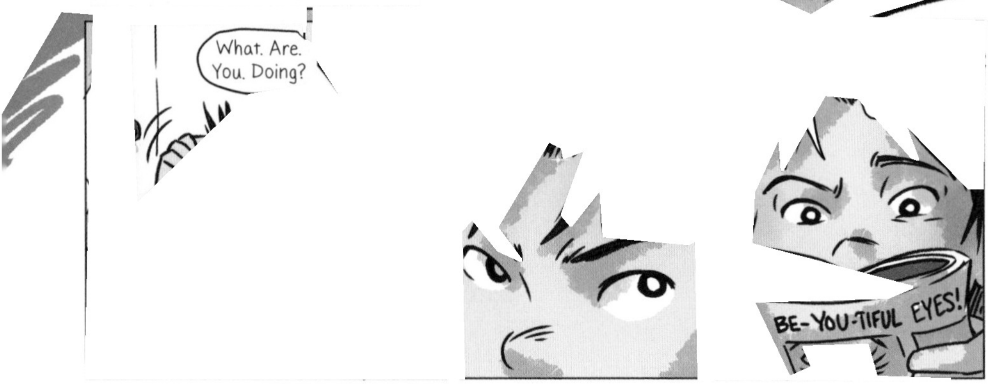
What. Are. You. Doing?
BE-YOU-TIFUL EYES!

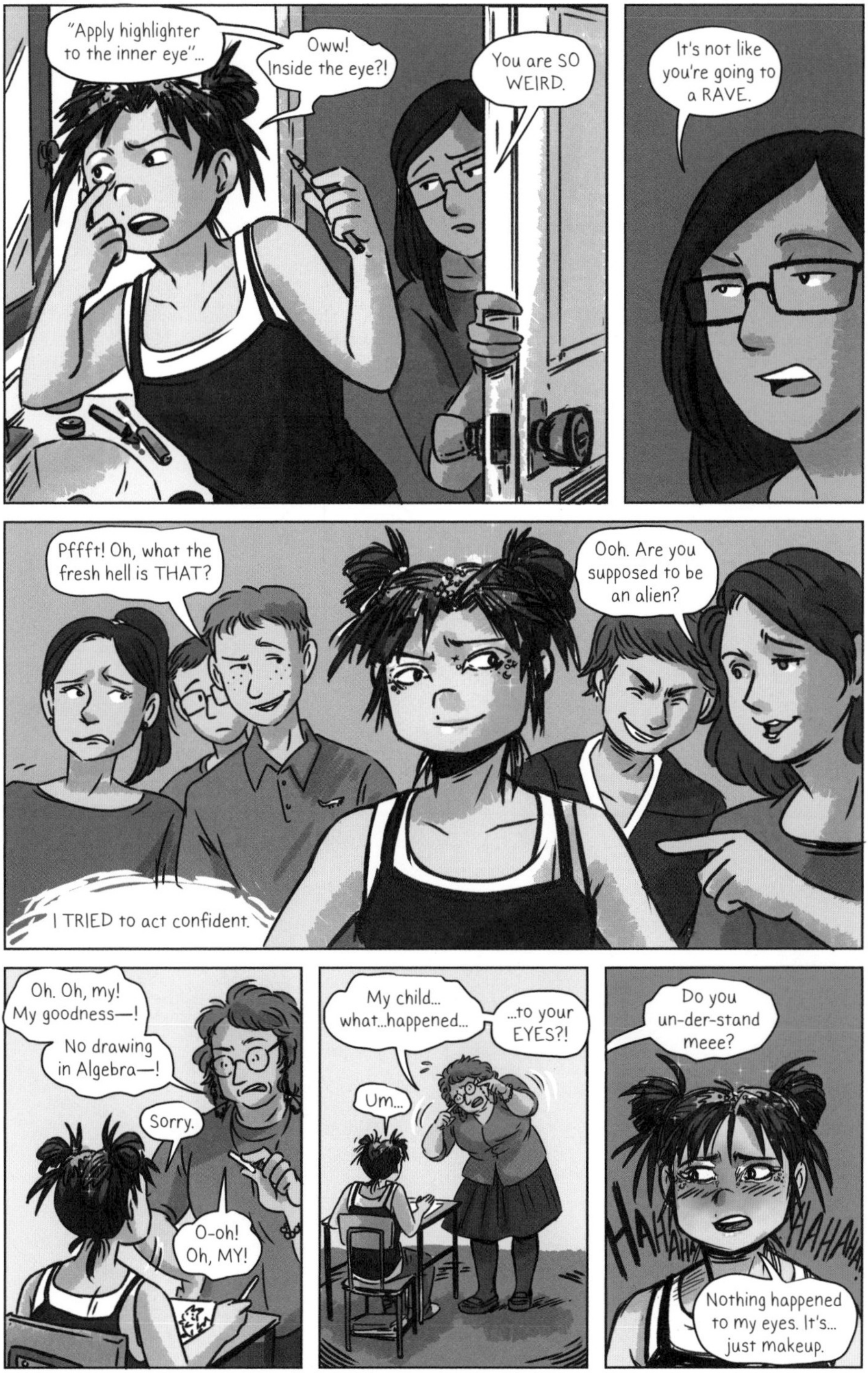
"Apply highlighter to the inner eye"...
Oww! Inside the eye?!
You are SO WEIRD.
It's not like you're going to a RAVE.
Pffft! Oh, what the fresh hell is THAT?
Ooh. Are you supposed to be an alien?
I TRIED to act confident.
Oh. Oh, my! My goodness—!
No drawing in Algebra—!
Sorry.
O-oh! Oh, MY!
My child... what...happened...
...to your EYES?!
Um...
Do you un-der-stand meee?
HAHAHA
HAHAHA
Nothing happened to my eyes. It's... just makeup.

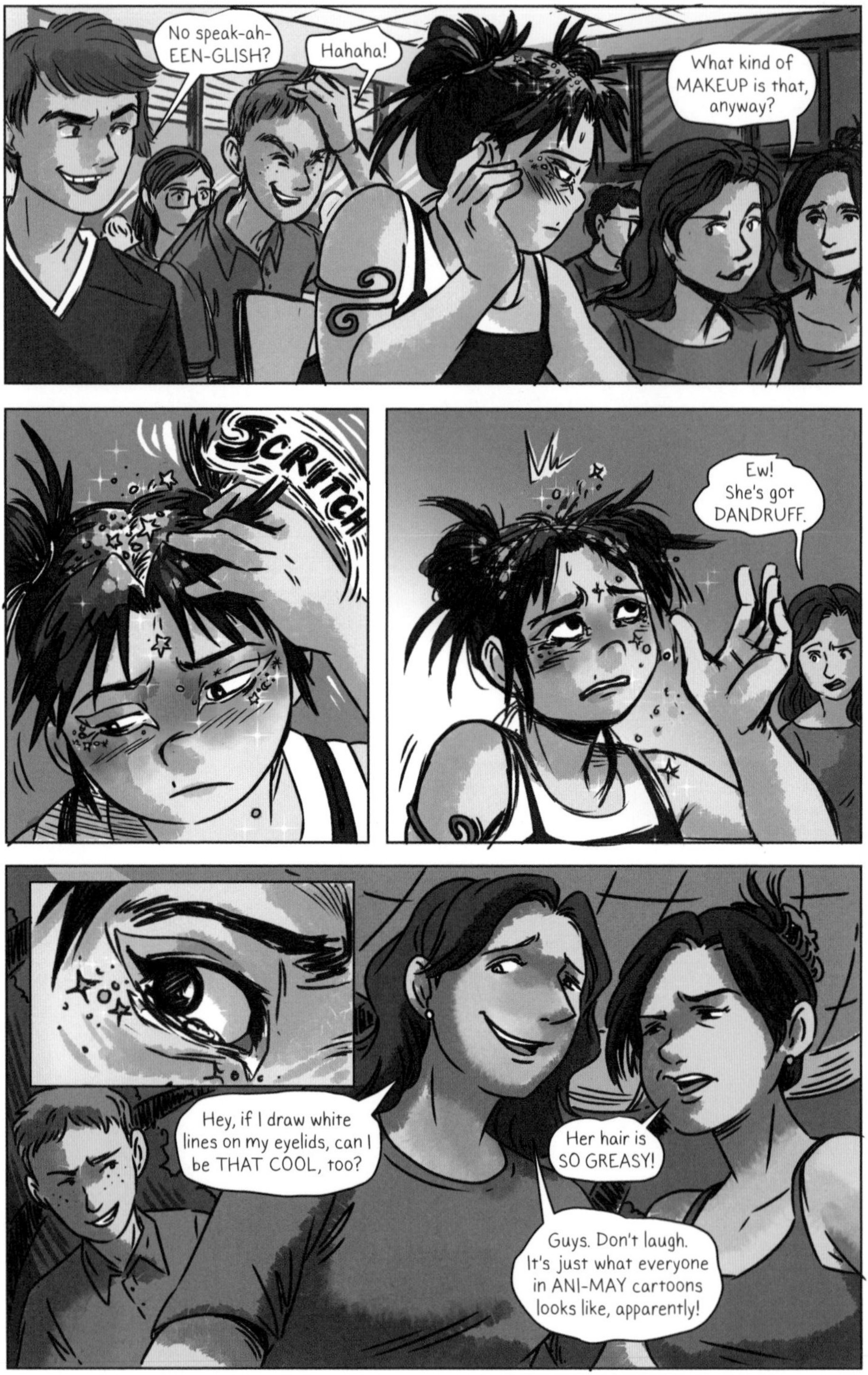
No speak-ah-EEN-GLISH?
Hahaha!
What kind of MAKEUP is that, anyway?
SCRITCH
Ew! She's got DANDRUFF.
Hey, if I draw white lines on my eyelids, can I be THAT COOL, too?
Her hair is SO GREASY!
Guys. Don't laugh. It's just what everyone in ANI-MAY cartoons looks like, apparently!

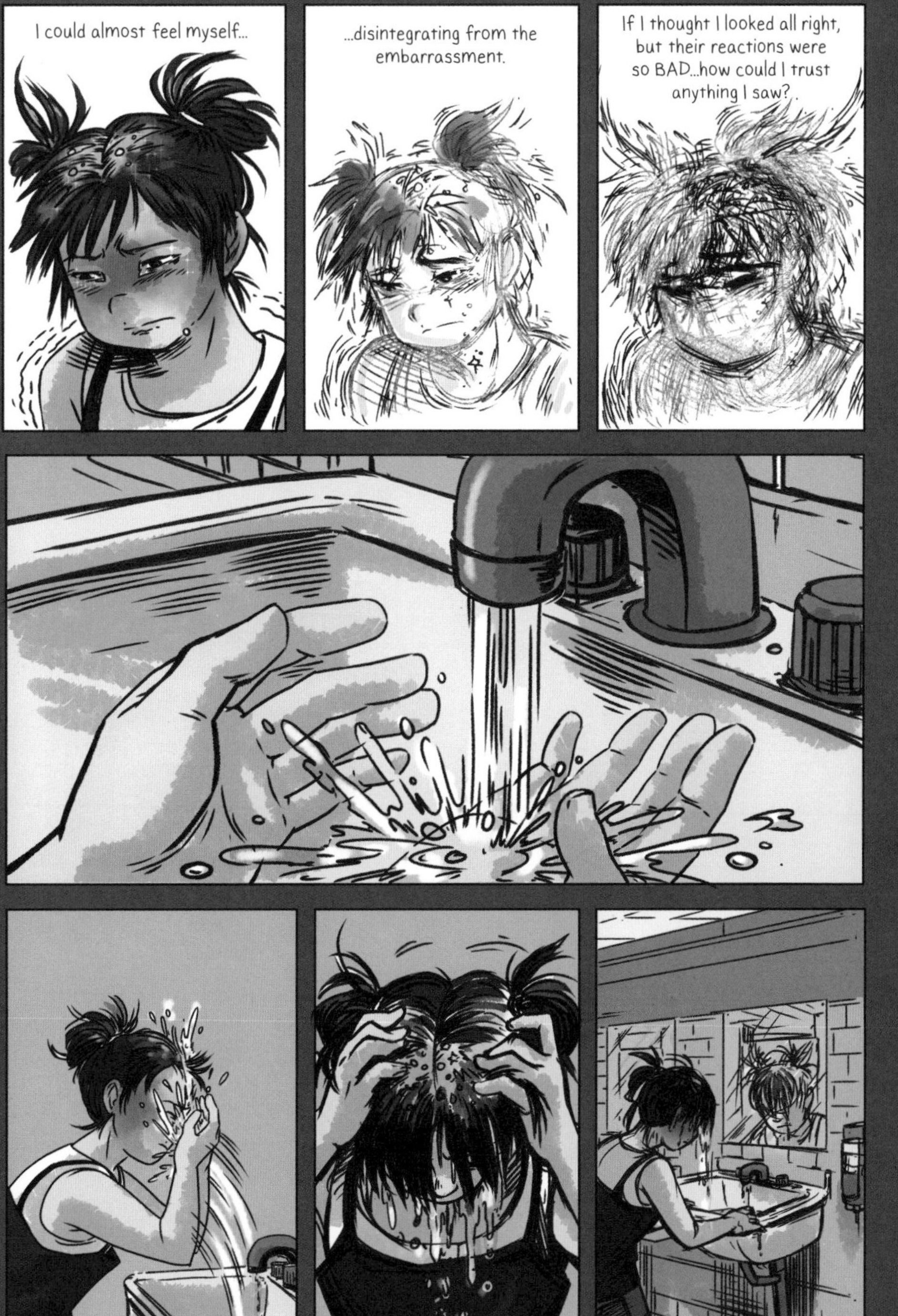
I could almost feel myself...
...disintegrating from the embarrassment.
If I thought I looked all right, but their reactions were so BAD...how could I trust anything I saw?

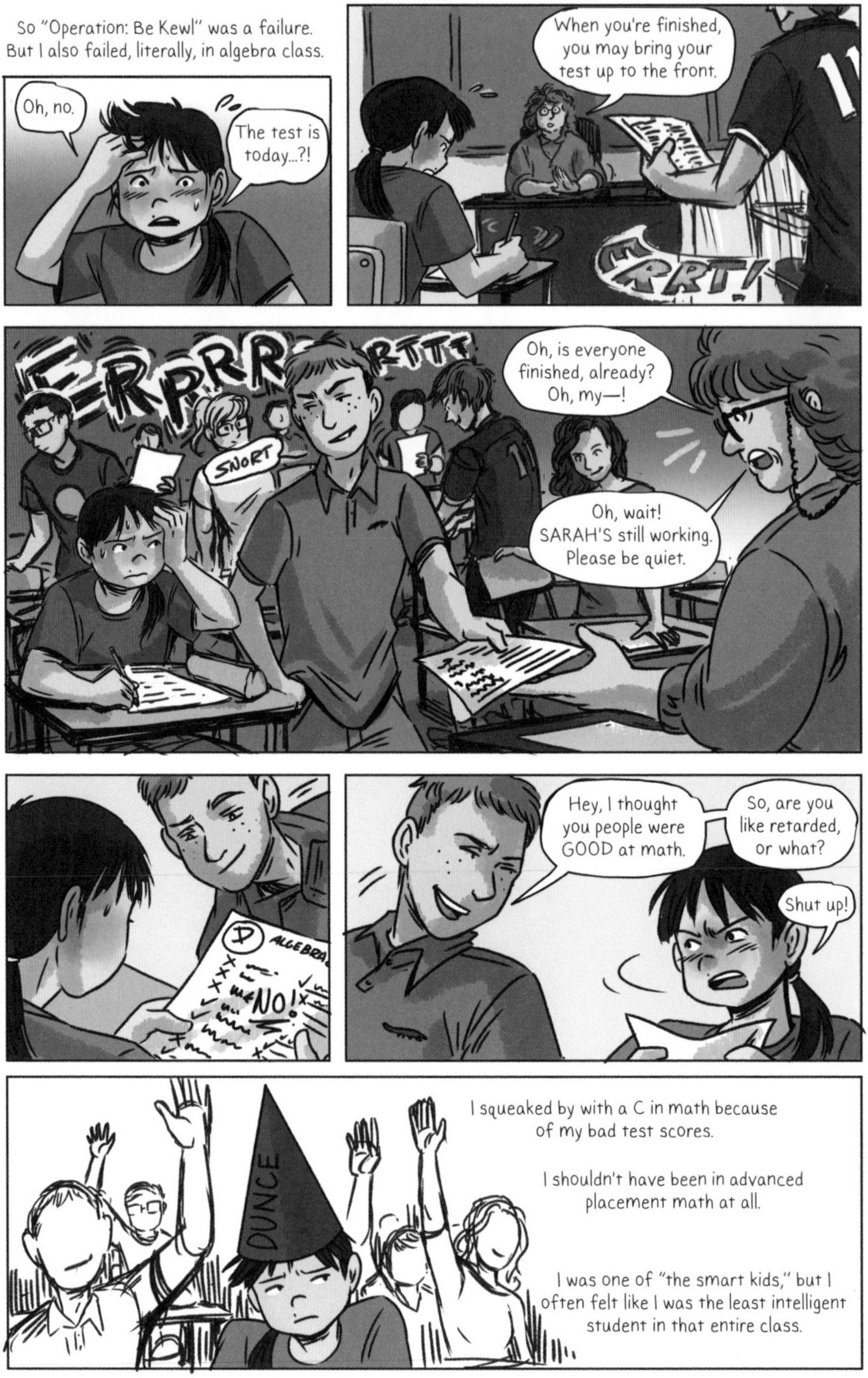
So "Operation: Be Kewl" was a failure.
But I also failed, literally, in algebra class.
Oh, no.
The test is today...?!
When you're finished, you may bring your test up to the front.
RRT!
ERRRR-RTTT
SNORT
Oh, is everyone finished, already? Oh, my—!
Oh, wait! SARAH'S still working. Please be quiet.
D
ALGEBRA
NO!
Hey, I thought you people were GOOD at math.
So, are you like retarded, or what?
Shut up!
DUNCE
I squeaked by with a C in math because of my bad test scores.
I shouldn't have been in advanced placement math at all.
I was one of "the smart kids," but I often felt like I was the least intelligent student in that entire class.

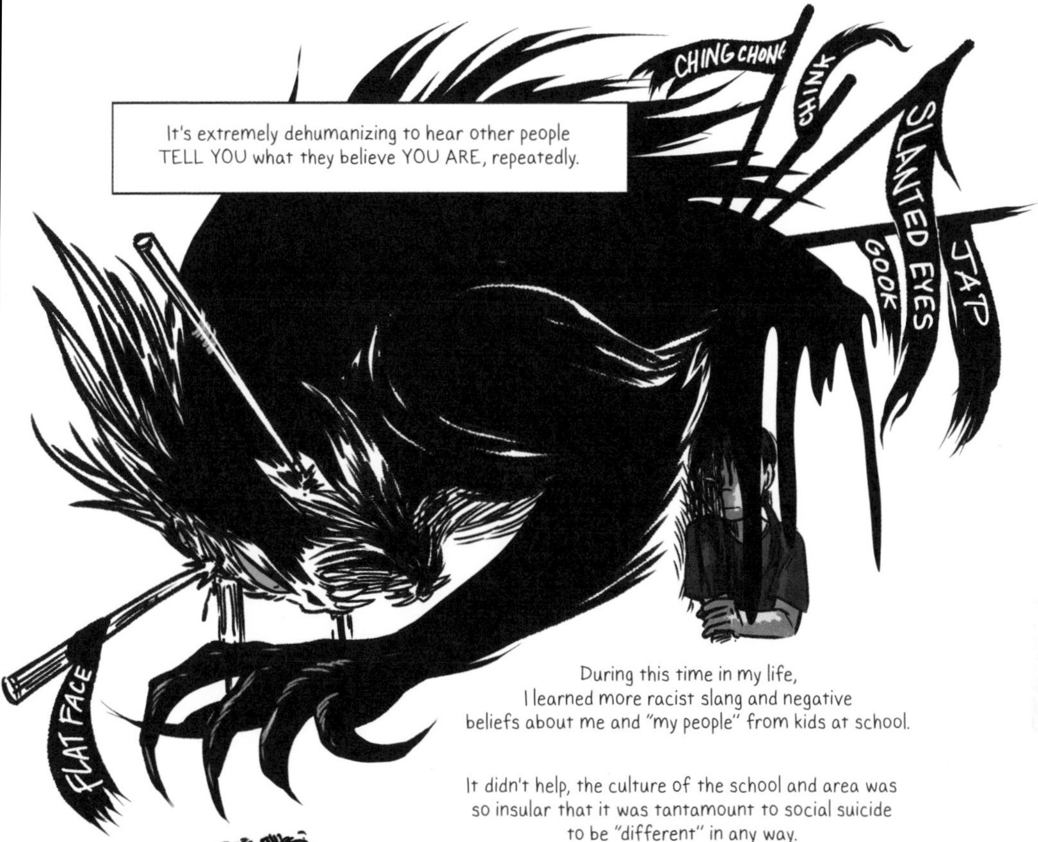
It's extremely dehumanizing to hear other people TELL YOU what they believe YOU ARE, repeatedly.
CHING CHONG
CHINK
SLANTED EYES
GOOK
JAP
FLAT FACE
During this time in my life, I learned more racist slang and negative beliefs about me and "my people" from kids at school.
It didn't help, the culture of the school and area was so insular that it was tantamount to social suicide to be "different" in any way.

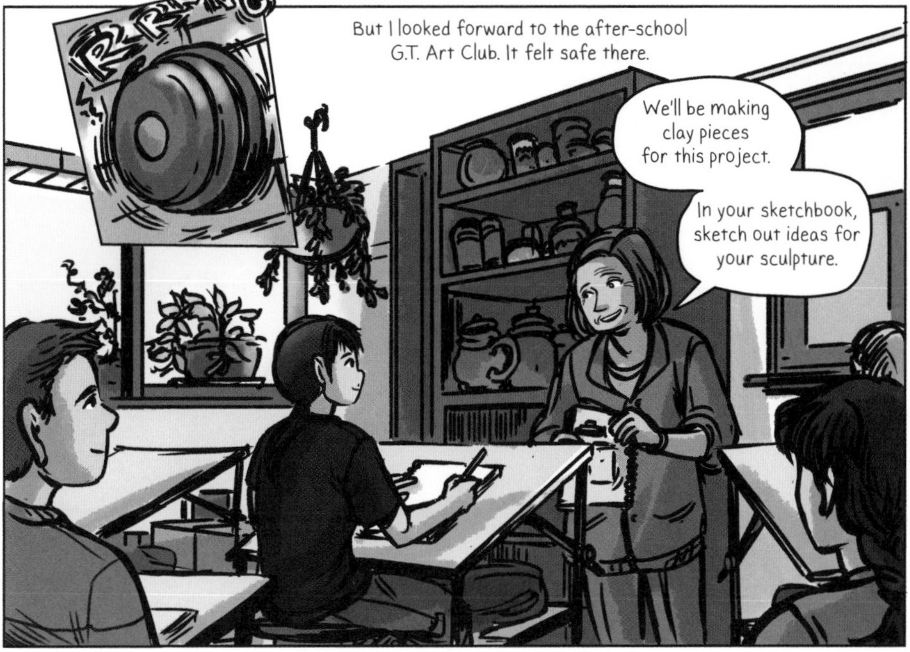
RRRNG
But I looked forward to the after-school G.T. Art Club. It felt safe there.
We'll be making clay pieces for this project.
In your sketchbook, sketch out ideas for your sculpture.

I could explore other cultures, including South Korea, for my project.

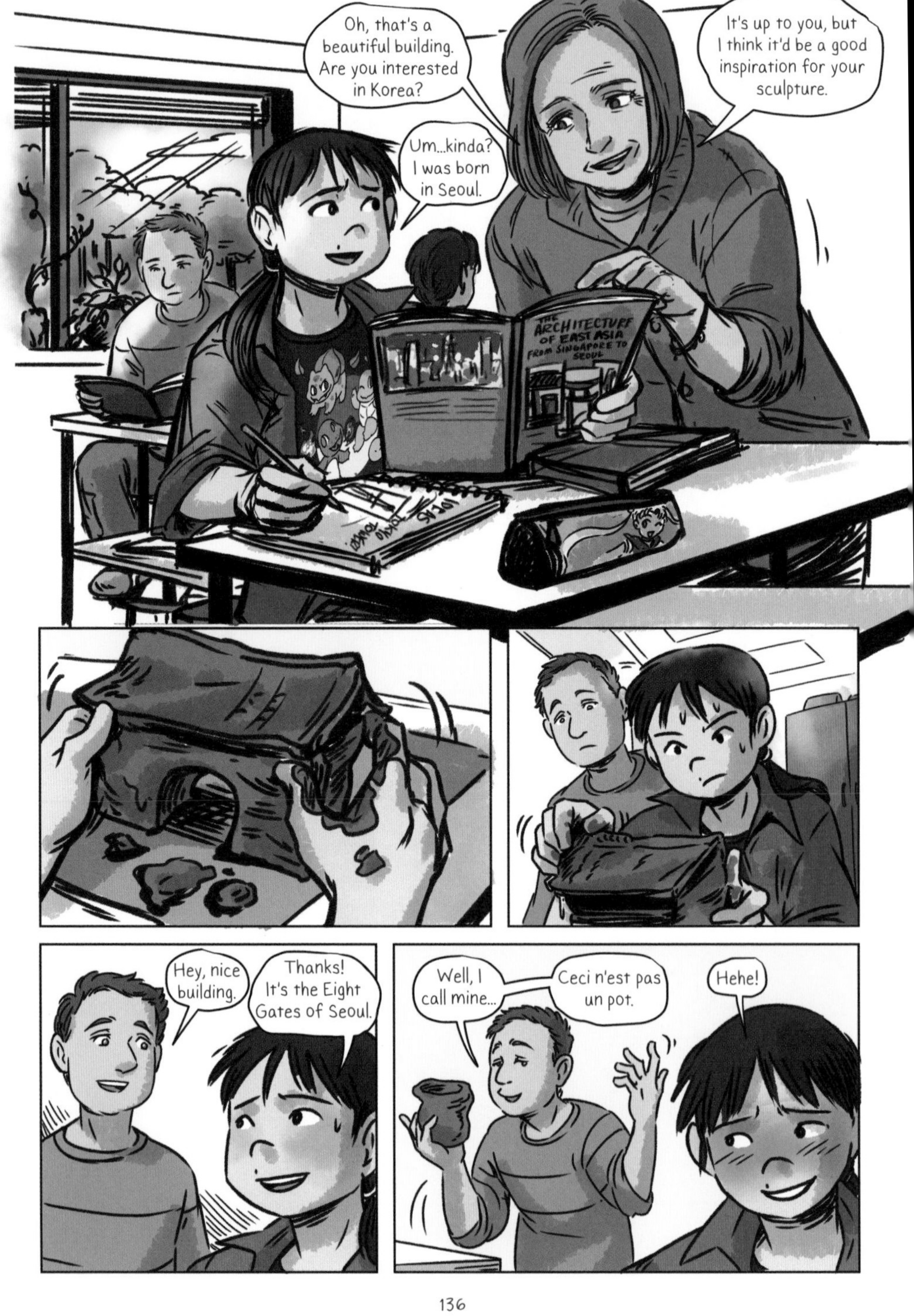
Oh, that's a beautiful building. Are you interested in Korea?
Um...kinda? I was born in Seoul.
It's up to you, but I think it'd be a good inspiration for your sculpture.
THE ARCHITECTURE OF EAST ASIA FROM SINGAPORE TO SEOUL
Hey, nice building.
Thanks! It's the Eight Gates of Seoul.
Well, I call mine...
Ceci n'est pas un pot.
Hehe!

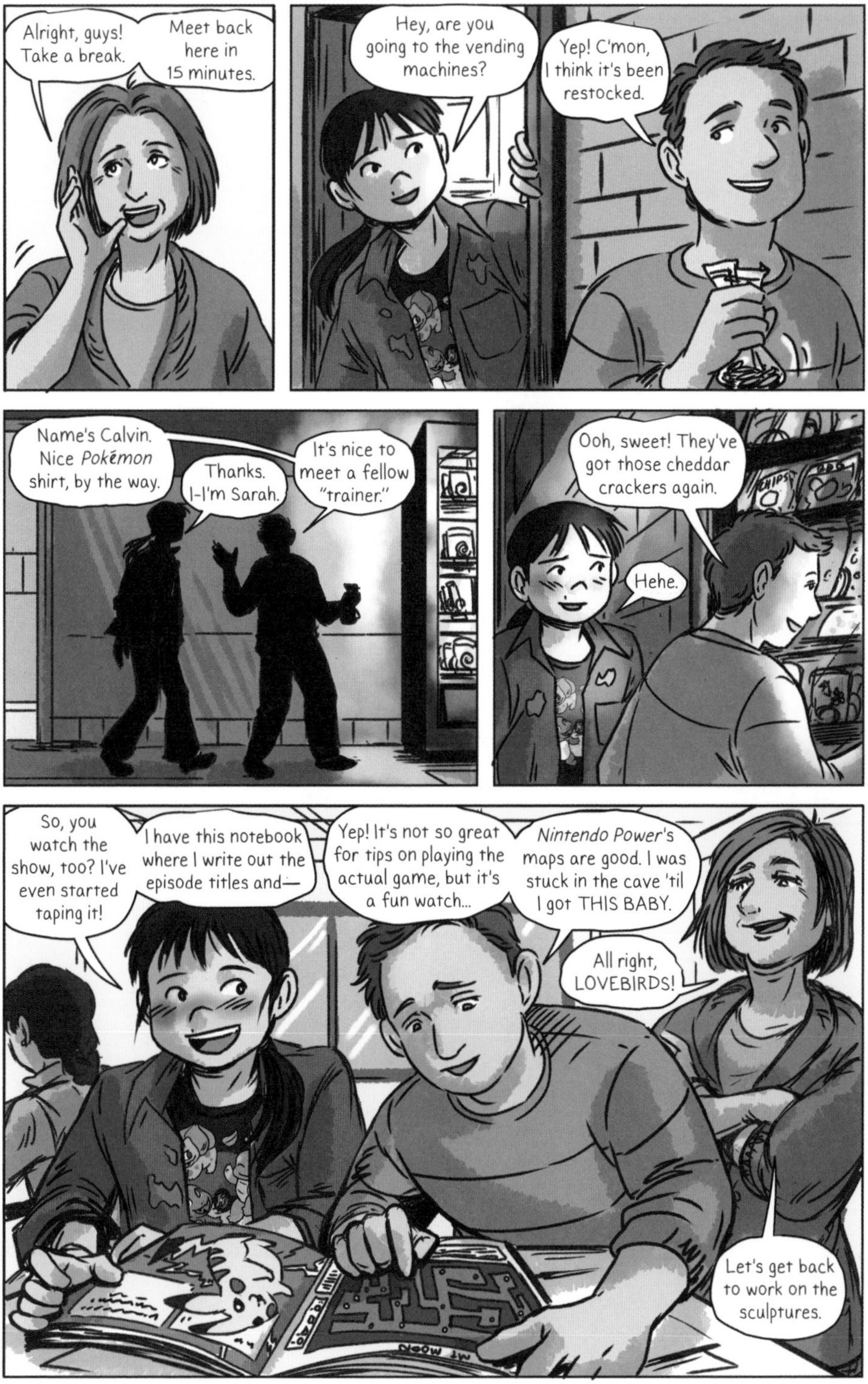
Alright, guys! Take a break.
Meet back here in 15 minutes.
Hey, are you going to the vending machines?
Yep! C'mon, I think it's been restocked.
Name's Calvin. Nice *Pokémon* shirt, by the way.
Thanks. I-I'm Sarah.
It's nice to meet a fellow "trainer."
Ooh, sweet! They've got those cheddar crackers again.
Hehe.
So, you watch the show, too? I've even started taping it!
I have this notebook where I write out the episode titles and—
Yep! It's not so great for tips on playing the actual game, but it's a fun watch...
Nintendo Power's maps are good. I was stuck in the cave 'til I got THIS BABY.
All right, LOVEBIRDS!
Let's get back to work on the sculptures.
MT MOON

Outside of G.T. Art meetings after school, though...

...things began to take a darker turn.

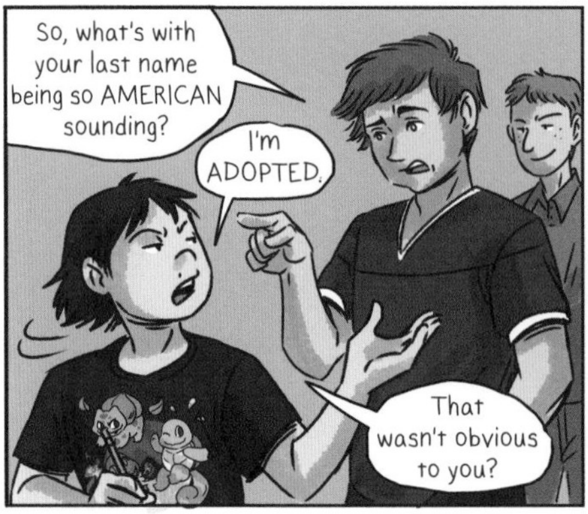
So, what's with your last name being so AMERICAN sounding?
I'm ADOPTED.
That wasn't obvious to you?

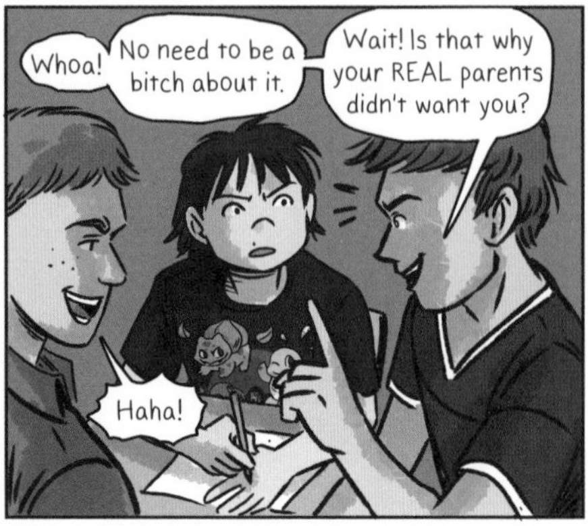
Whoa!
No need to be a bitch about it.
Wait! Is that why your REAL parents didn't want you?
Haha!

Sometimes people don't realize just how backward things were, even in the late '90s.

The murder of Matthew Shepard, a gay university student, was national news when I was 12.

My English teacher in seventh grade tried to discuss the incident with my class.

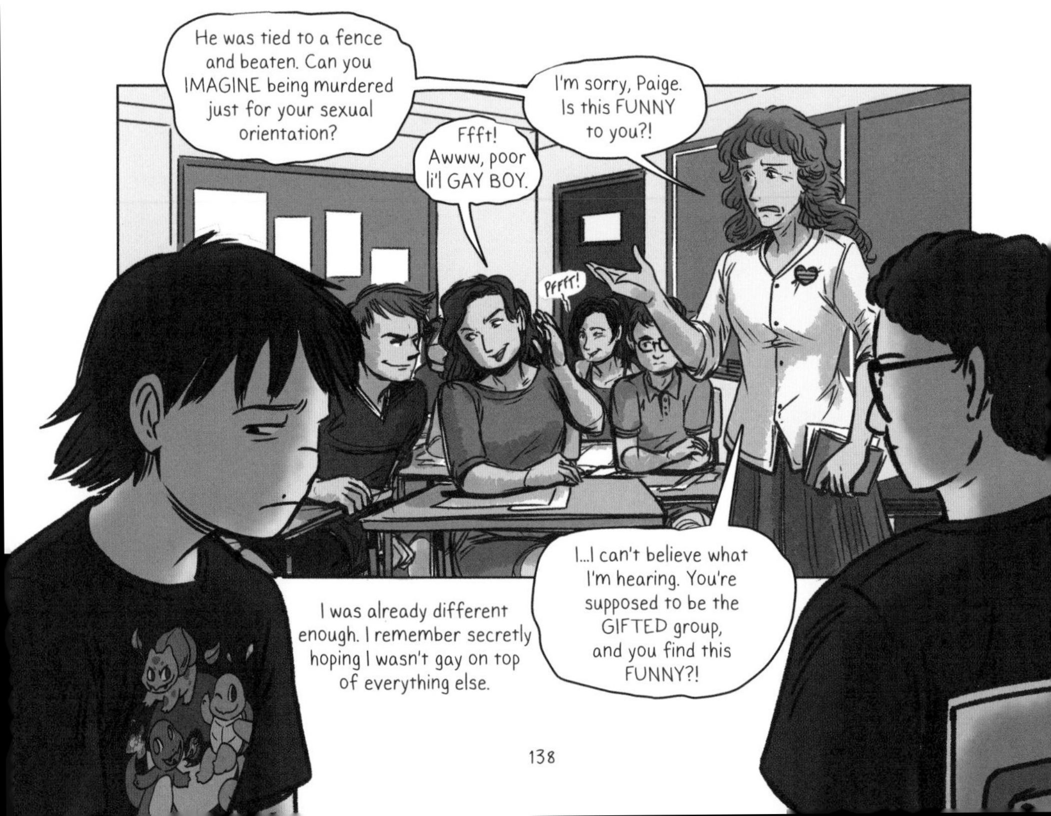
He was tied to a fence and beaten. Can you IMAGINE being murdered just for your sexual orientation?
Ffft! Awww, poor li'l GAY BOY.
I'm sorry, Paige. Is this FUNNY to you?!
PFFFT!
I was already different enough. I remember secretly hoping I wasn't gay on top of everything else.
I...I can't believe what I'm hearing. You're supposed to be the GIFTED group, and you find this FUNNY?!

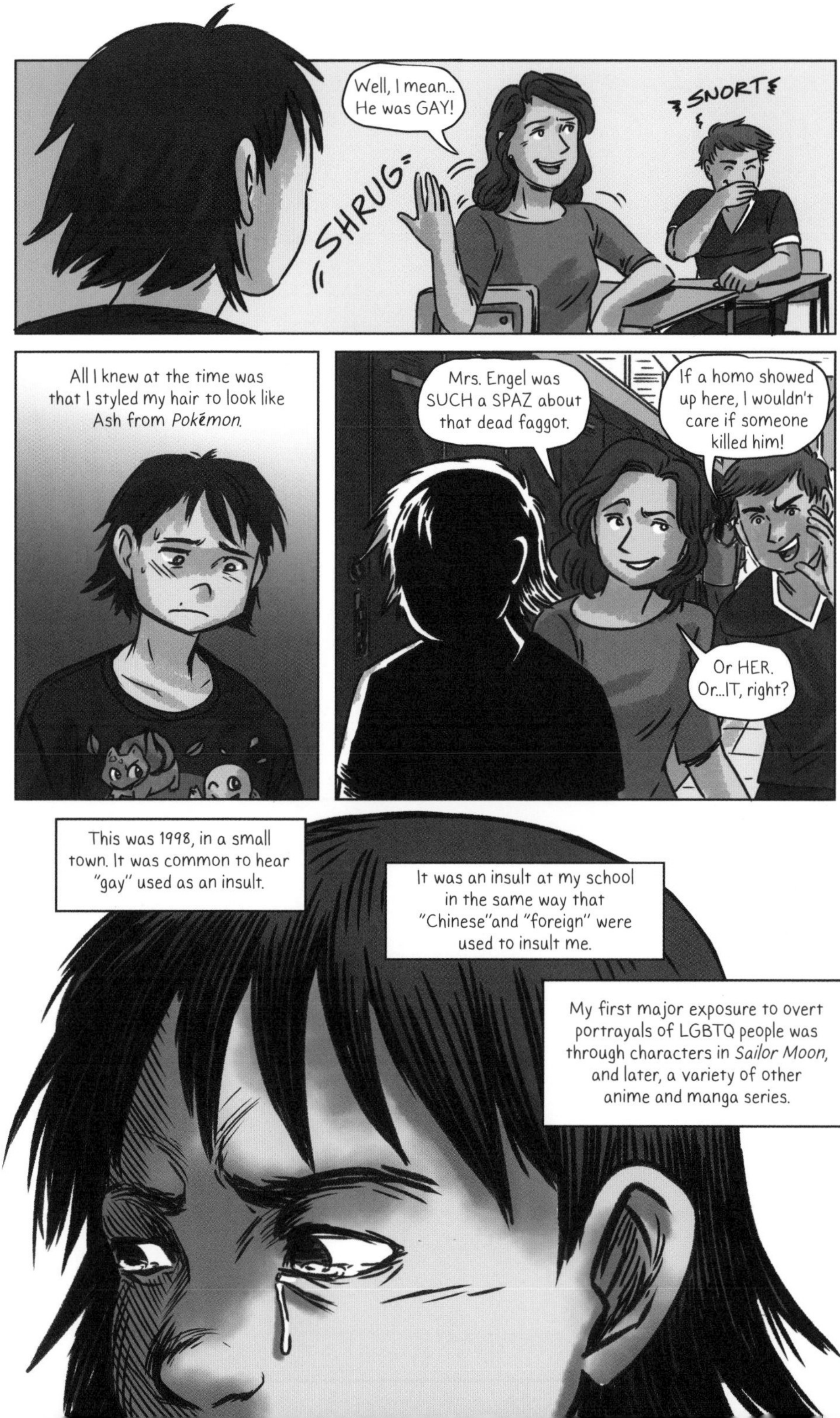
Well, I mean...
He was GAY!
SHRUG
SNORT
All I knew at the time was that I styled my hair to look like Ash from *Pokémon*.
Mrs. Engel was SUCH a SPAZ about that dead faggot.
If a homo showed up here, I wouldn't care if someone killed him!
Or HER.
Or...IT, right?
This was 1998, in a small town. It was common to hear "gay" used as an insult.
It was an insult at my school in the same way that "Chinese" and "foreign" were used to insult me.
My first major exposure to overt portrayals of LGBTQ people was through characters in *Sailor Moon*, and later, a variety of other anime and manga series.

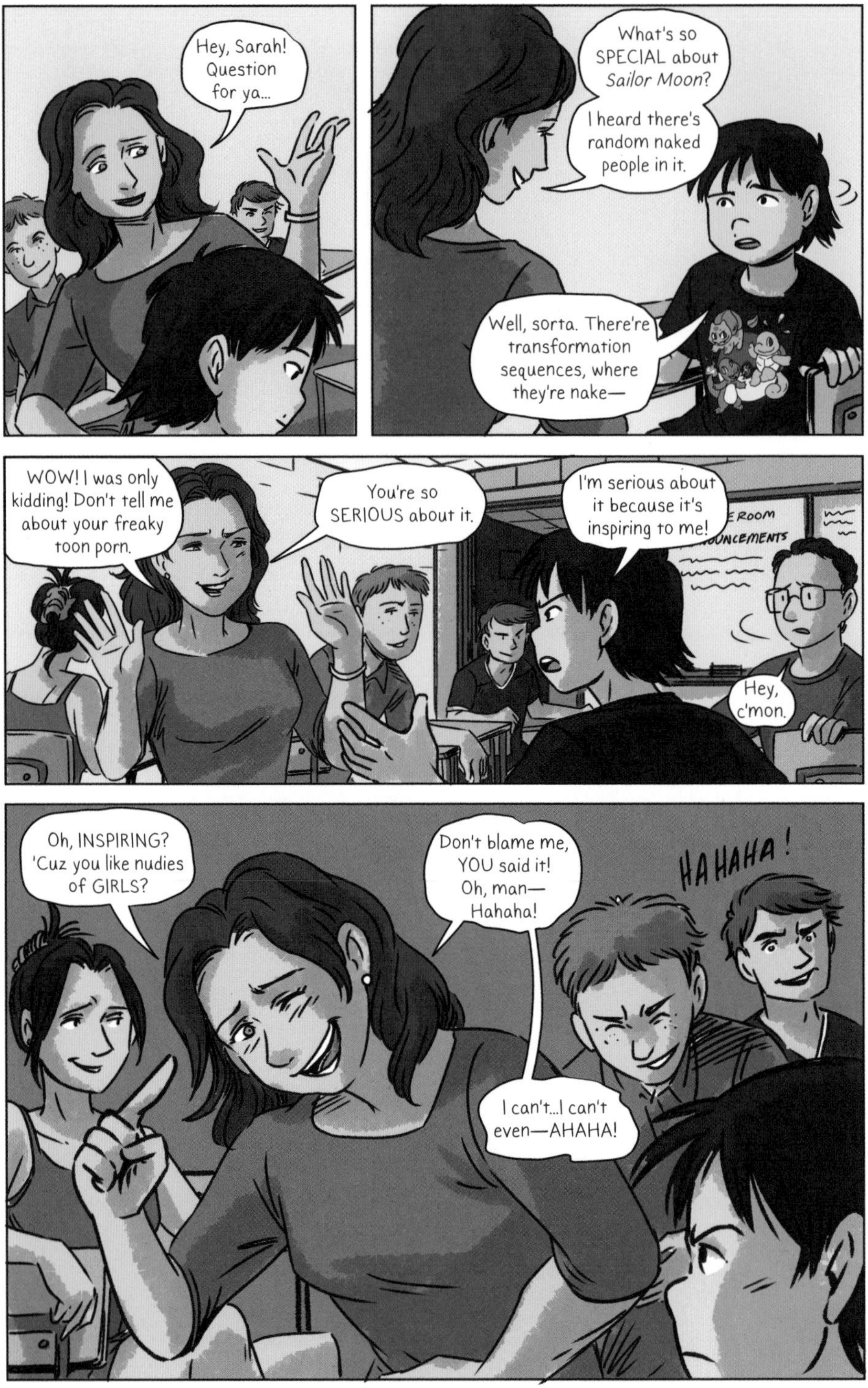

Hey, Sarah! Question for ya...
What's so SPECIAL about *Sailor Moon*?
I heard there's random naked people in it.
Well, sorta. There're transformation sequences, where they're nake—
WOW! I was only kidding! Don't tell me about your freaky toon porn.
You're so SERIOUS about it.
I'm serious about it because it's inspiring to me!
Hey, c'mon.
Oh, INSPIRING? 'Cuz you like nudies of GIRLS?
Don't blame me, YOU said it! Oh, man— Hahaha!
HAHAHA!
I can't...I can't even—AHAHA!

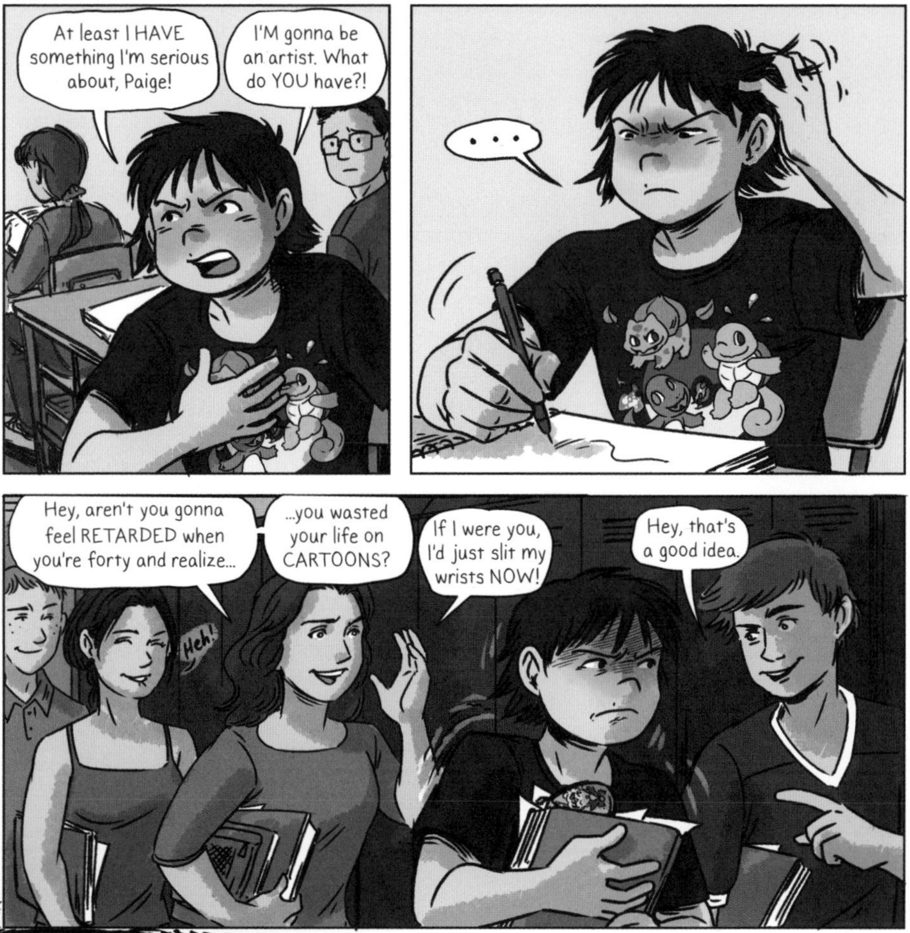
At least I HAVE something I'm serious about, Paige!
I'M gonna be an artist. What do YOU have?!
...
Hey, aren't you gonna feel RETARDED when you're forty and realize...
...you wasted your life on CARTOONS?
Heh!
If I were you, I'd just slit my wrists NOW!
Hey, that's a good idea.

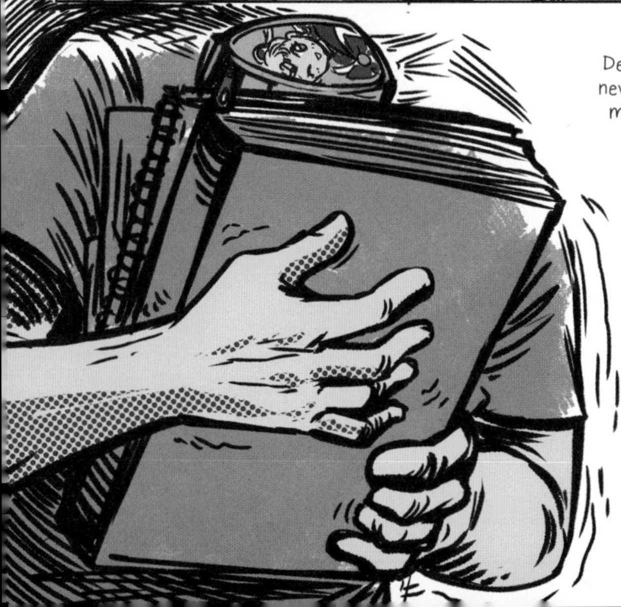

Despite their ridicule, though, I never even considered giving up my interests in art or anime.

Not once.

Still...I felt angry at how they treated me because I knew they were wrong.

Even when I stood up for myself, I felt like I couldn't win.

Inside me, the anger grew into boiling RAGE.

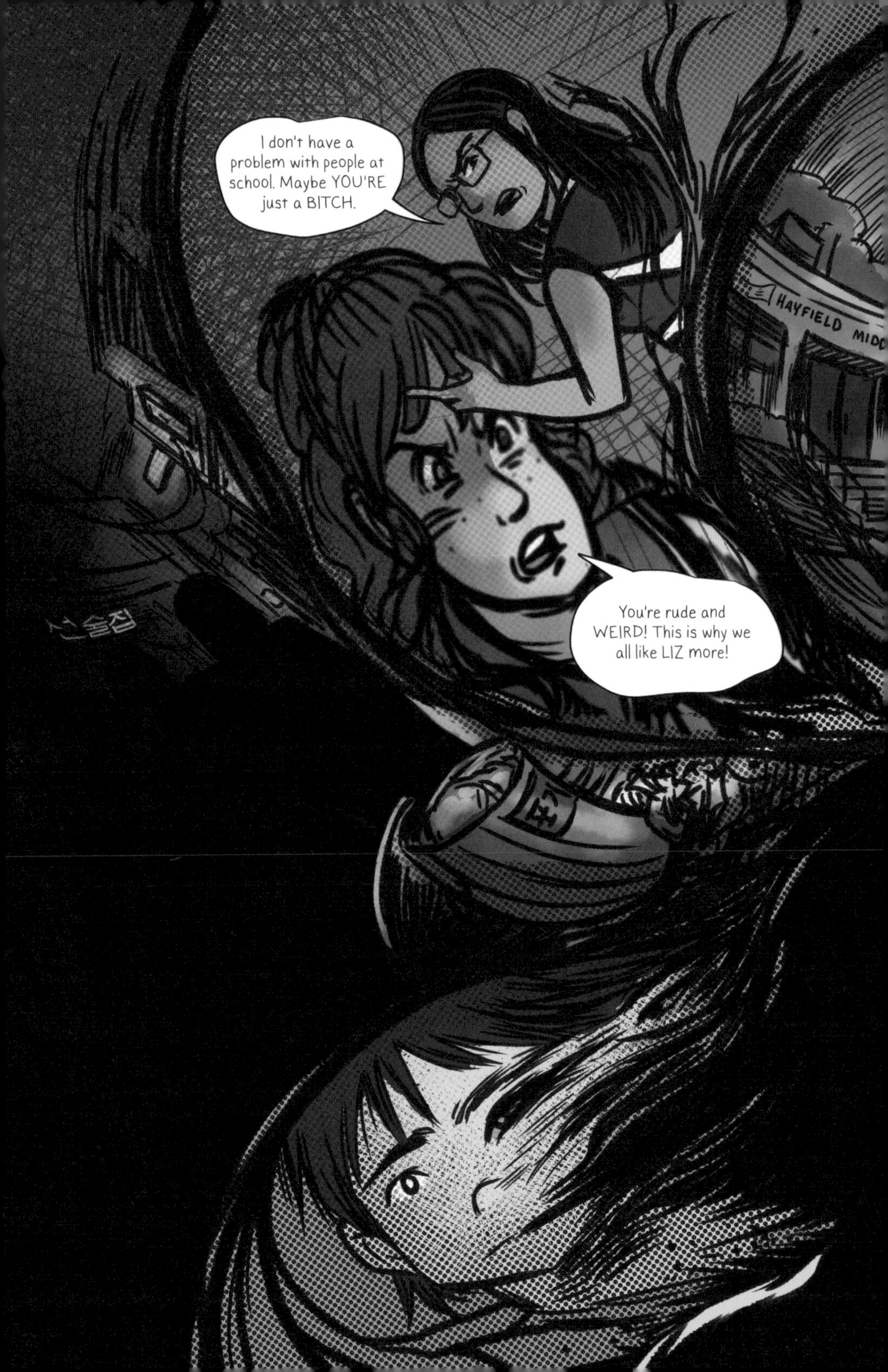
I don't have a problem with people at school. Maybe YOU'RE just a BITCH.
HAYFIELD
You're rude and WEIRD! This is why we all like LIZ more!

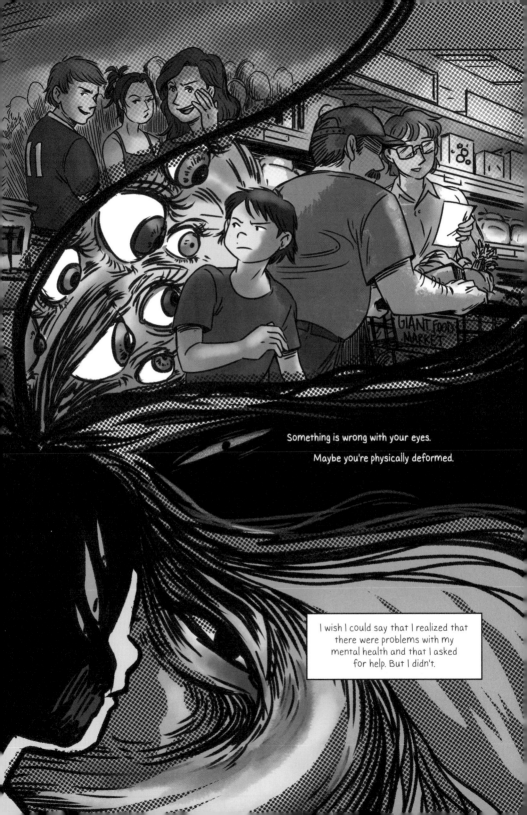

Something is wrong with your eyes.

Maybe you're physically deformed.

I wish I could say that I realized that there were problems with my mental health and that I asked for help. But I didn't.

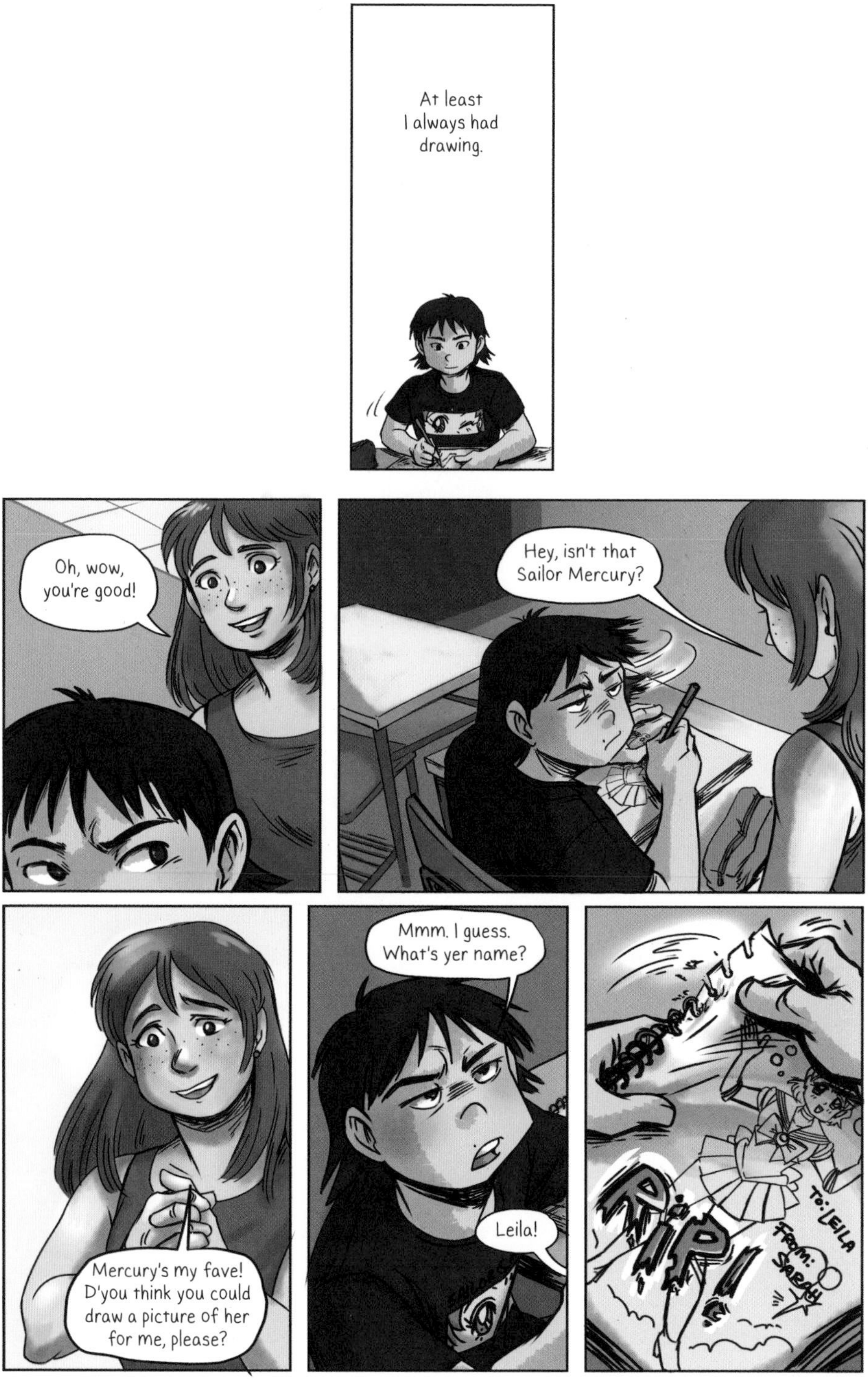
At least I always had drawing.
Oh, wow, you're good!
Hey, isn't that Sailor Mercury?
Mercury's my fave! D'you think you could draw a picture of her for me, please?
Mmm. I guess. What's yer name?
Leila!
RIP!
To: LEILA
FROM: SARAH

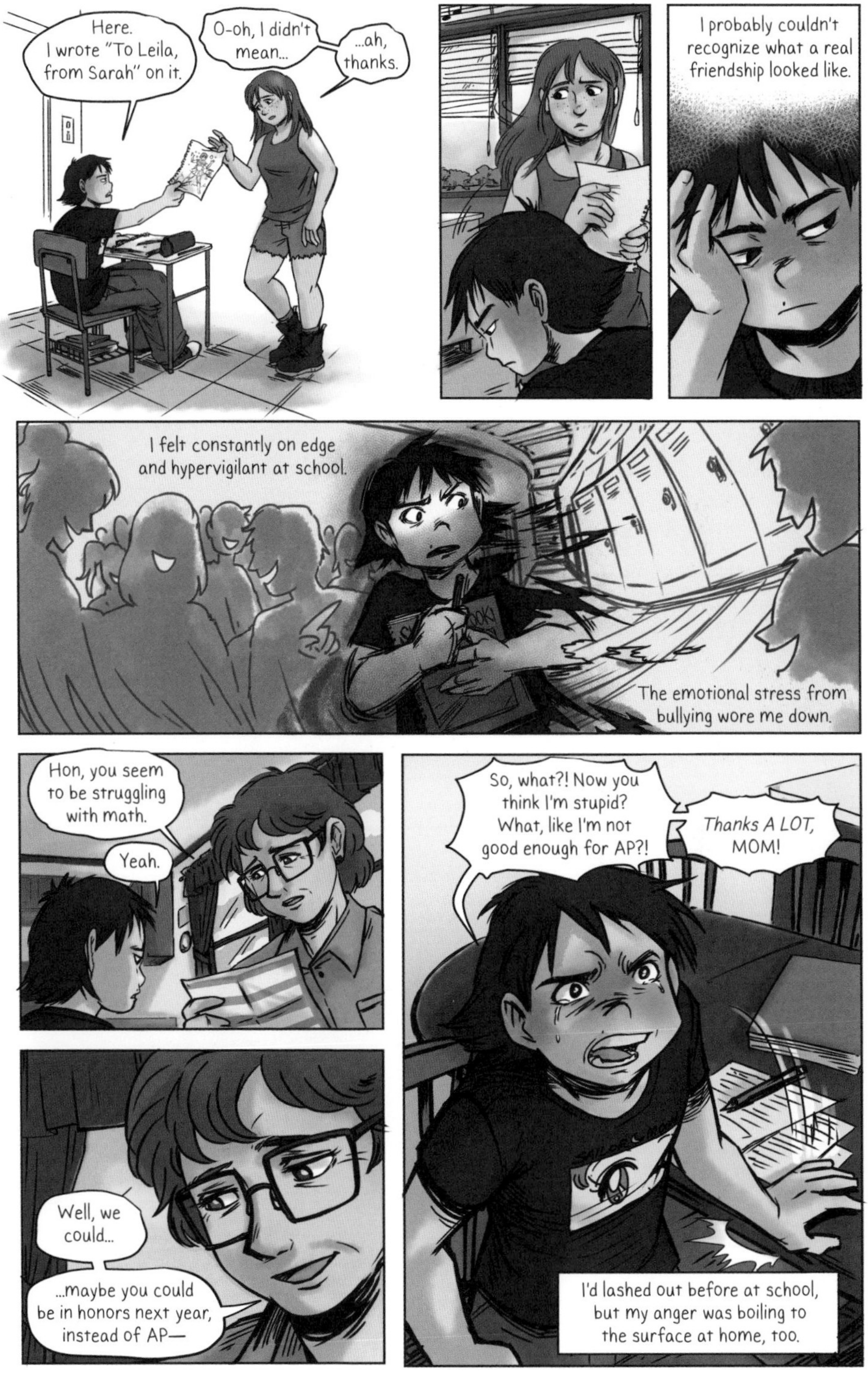
Here. I wrote "To Leila, from Sarah" on it.
O-oh, I didn't mean...
...ah, thanks.
I probably couldn't recognize what a real friendship looked like.
I felt constantly on edge and hypervigilant at school.
The emotional stress from bullying wore me down.
Hon, you seem to be struggling with math.
Yeah.
Well, we could...
...maybe you could be in honors next year, instead of AP—
So, what?! Now you think I'm stupid? What, like I'm not good enough for AP?!
Thanks A LOT, MOM!
I'd lashed out before at school, but my anger was boiling to the surface at home, too.

I'd found some people with similar interests in my grade. Calvin's friends.

But sometimes, I let them treat me badly.

I wasn't confident enough to face the alternative.

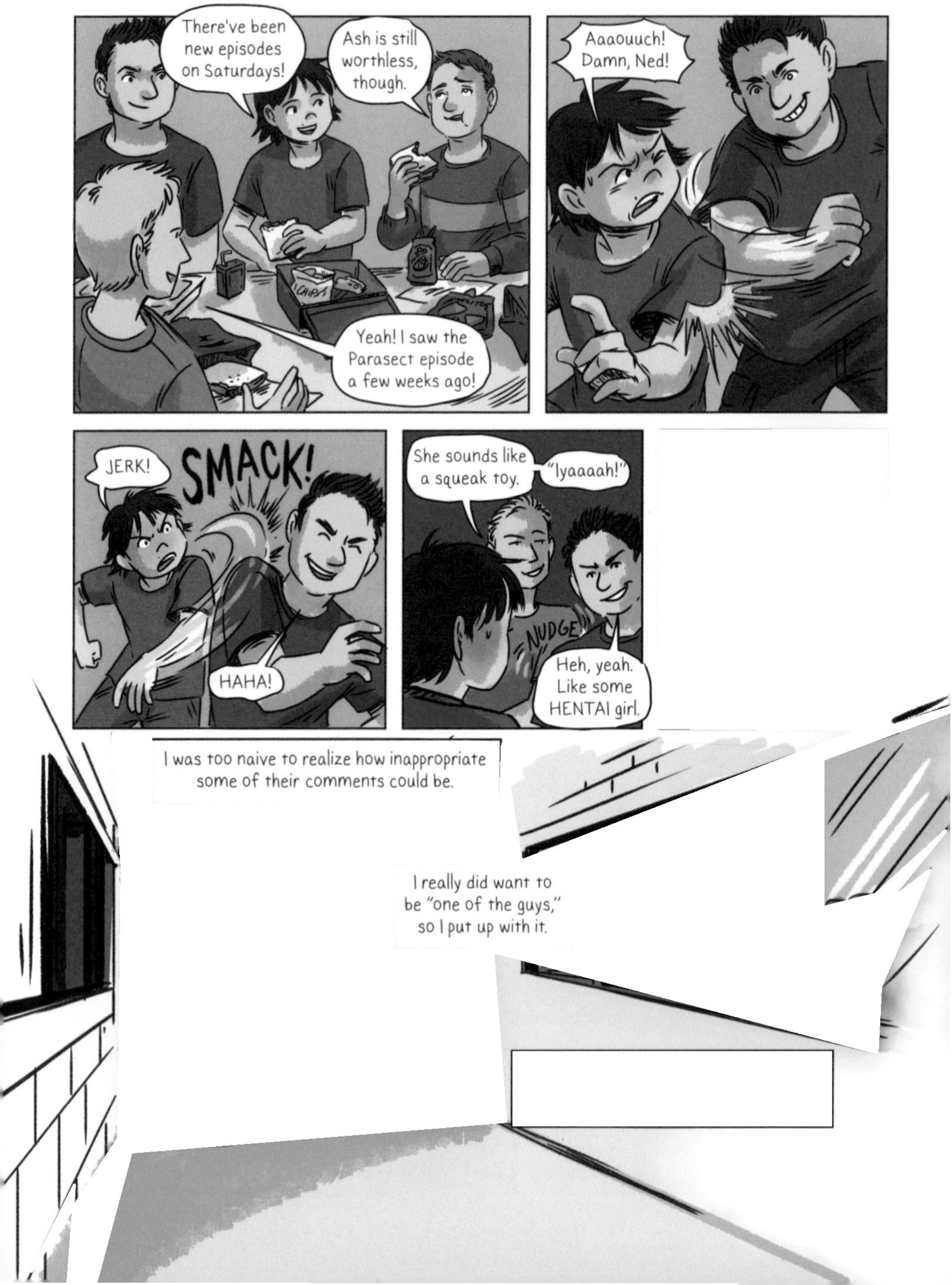

There've been new episodes on Saturdays!
Ash is still worthless, though.
Yeah! I saw the Parasect episode a few weeks ago!
Aaaouuch! Damn, Ned!
JERK!
SMACK!
HAHA!
She sounds like a squeak toy.
"Iyaaaah!"
NUDGE
Heh, yeah. Like some HENTAI girl.
I was too naive to realize how inappropriate some of their comments could be.
I really did want to be "one of the guys," so I put up with it.

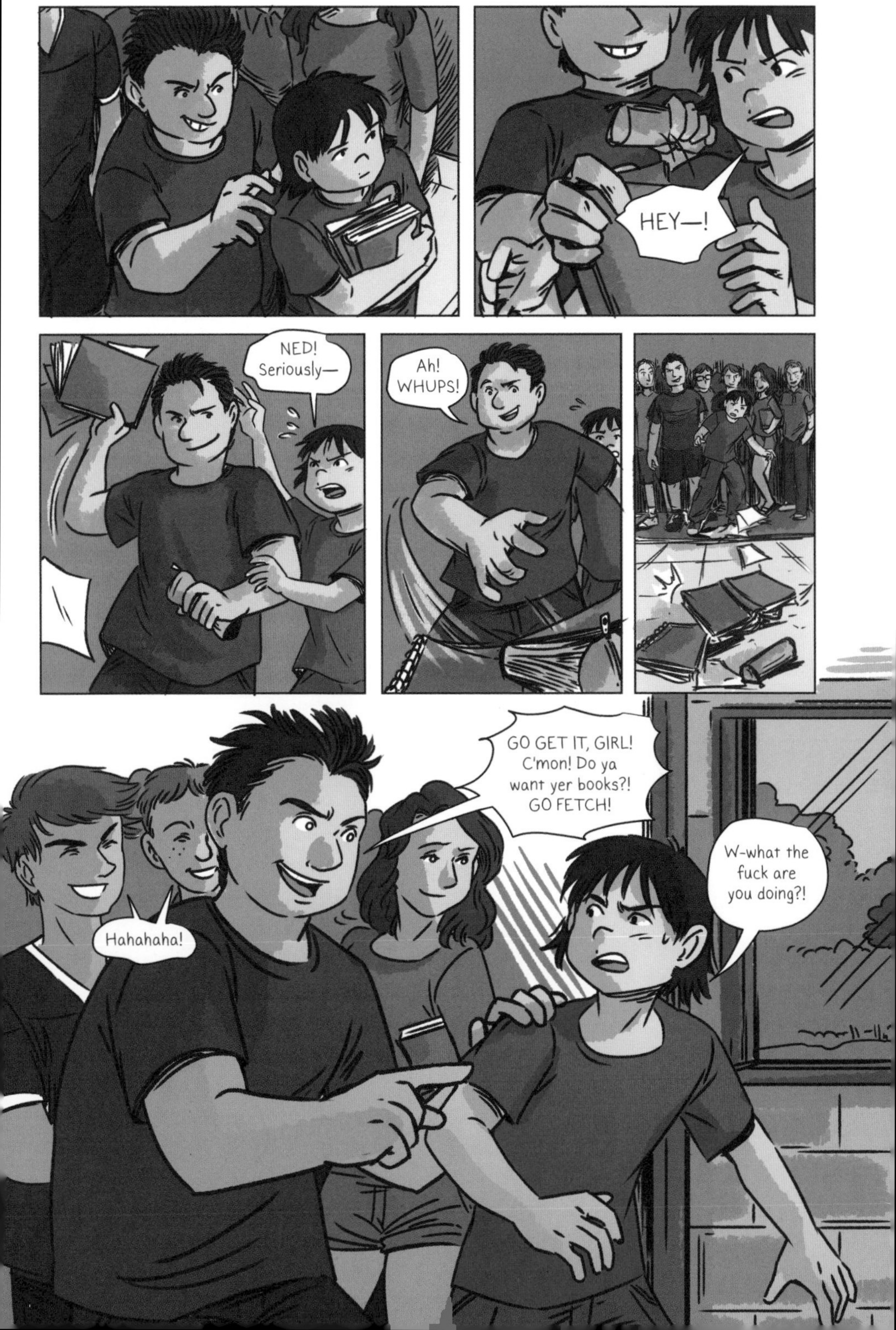
HEY—!
NED! Seriously—
Ah! WHUPS!
GO GET IT, GIRL! C'mon! Do ya want yer books?! GO FETCH!
Hahahaha!
W-what the fuck are you doing?!

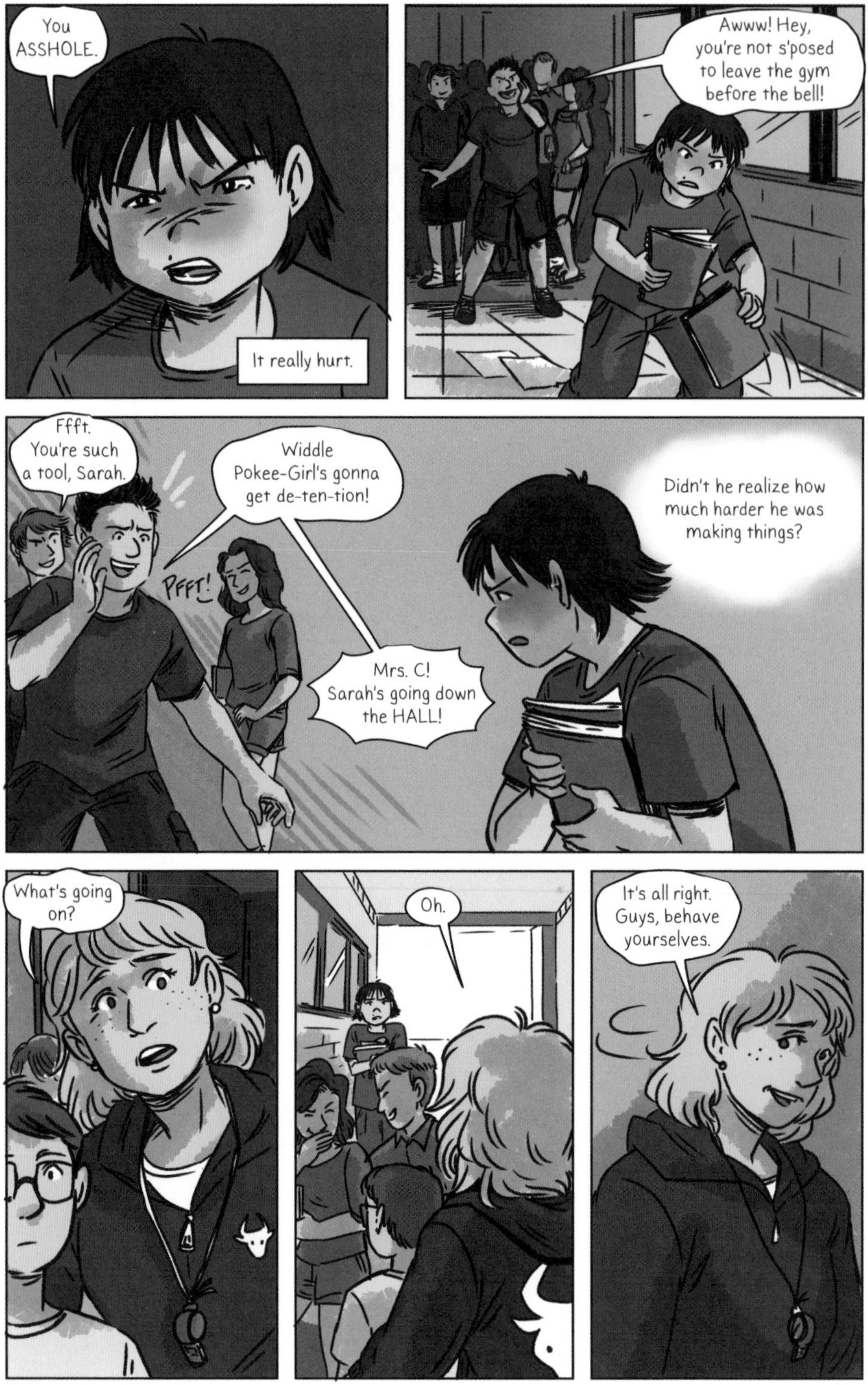
You ASSHOLE.
It really hurt.
Awww! Hey, you're not s'posed to leave the gym before the bell!
Ffft. You're such a tool, Sarah.
Widdle Pokee-Girl's gonna get de-ten-tion!
PFFT!
Mrs. C! Sarah's going down the HALL!
Didn't he realize how much harder he was making things?
What's going on?
Oh.
It's all right. Guys, behave yourselves.

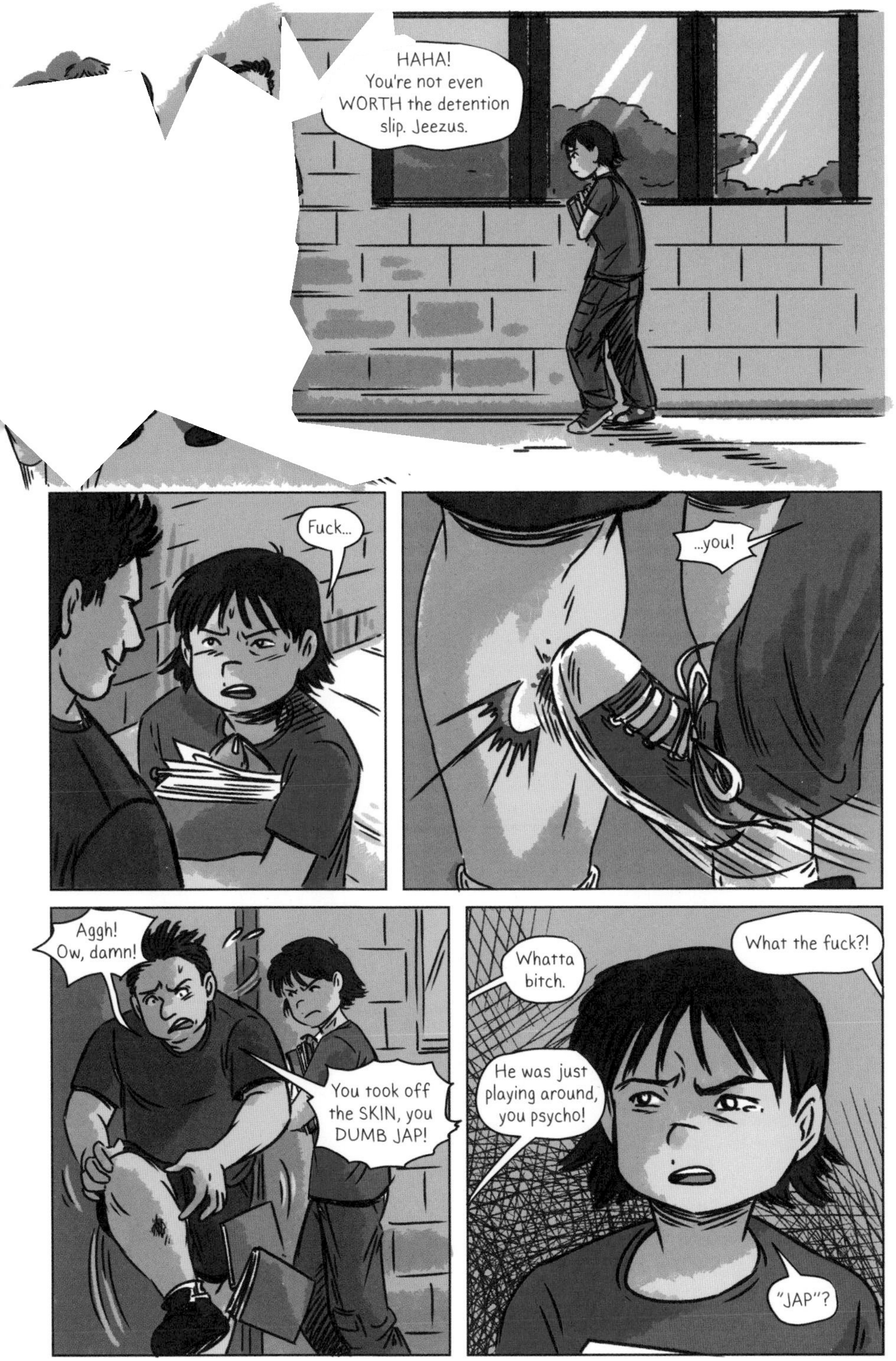
HAHA! You're not even WORTH the detention slip. Jeezus.
Fuck...
...you!
Aggh! Ow, damn!
You took off the SKIN, you DUMB JAP!
Whatta bitch.
What the fuck?!
He was just playing around, you psycho!
"JAP"?

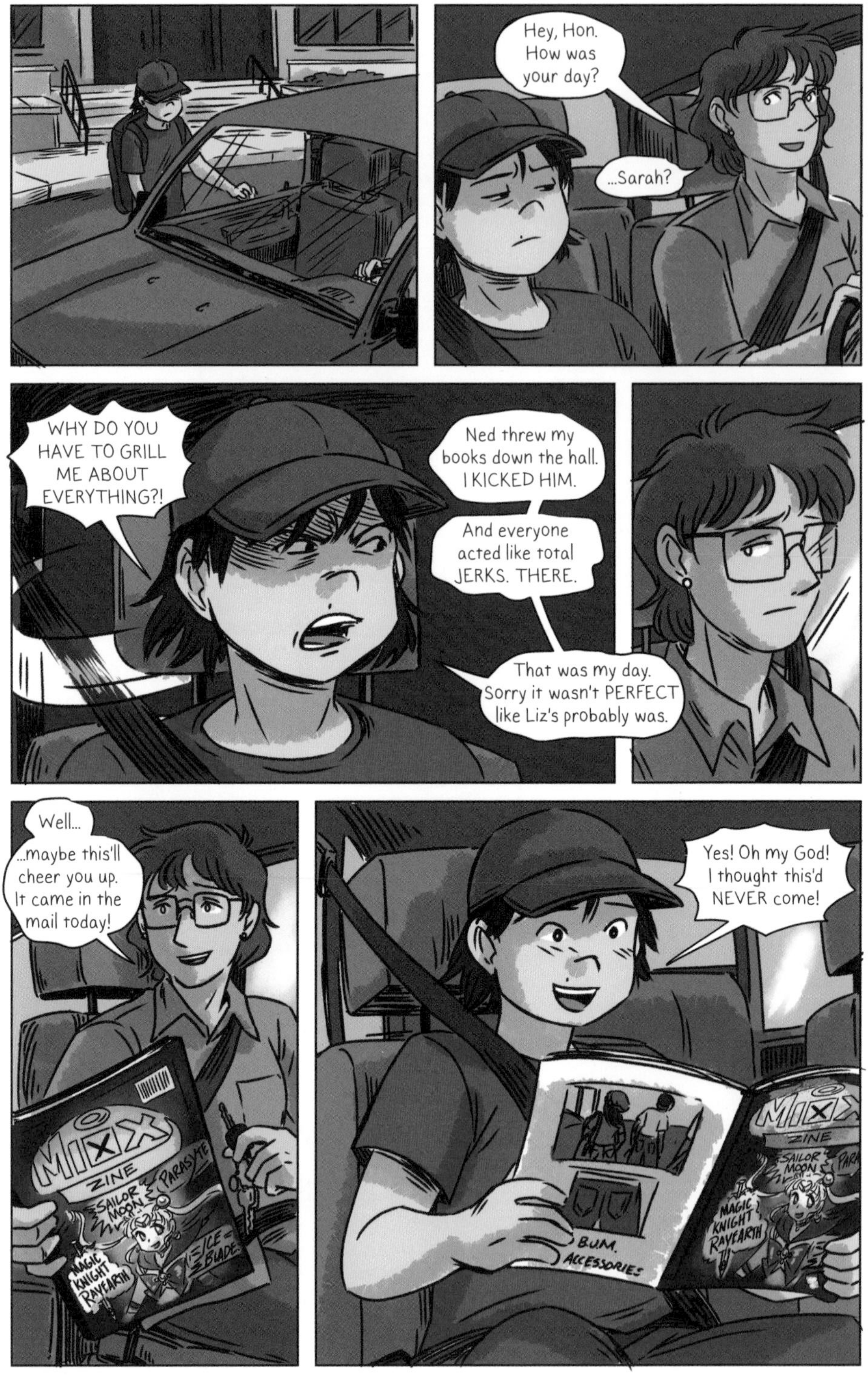
Hey, Hon. How was your day?
...Sarah?
WHY DO YOU HAVE TO GRILL ME ABOUT EVERYTHING?!
Ned threw my books down the hall. I KICKED HIM.
And everyone acted like total JERKS. THERE.
That was my day. Sorry it wasn't PERFECT like Liz's probably was.
Well...
...maybe this'll cheer you up. It came in the mail today!
MIXX ZINE
SAILOR MOON
PARASYTE
MAGIC KNIGHT RAYEARTH
ICE BLADE
Yes! Oh my God! I thought this'd NEVER come!
B.U.M. ACCESSORIES

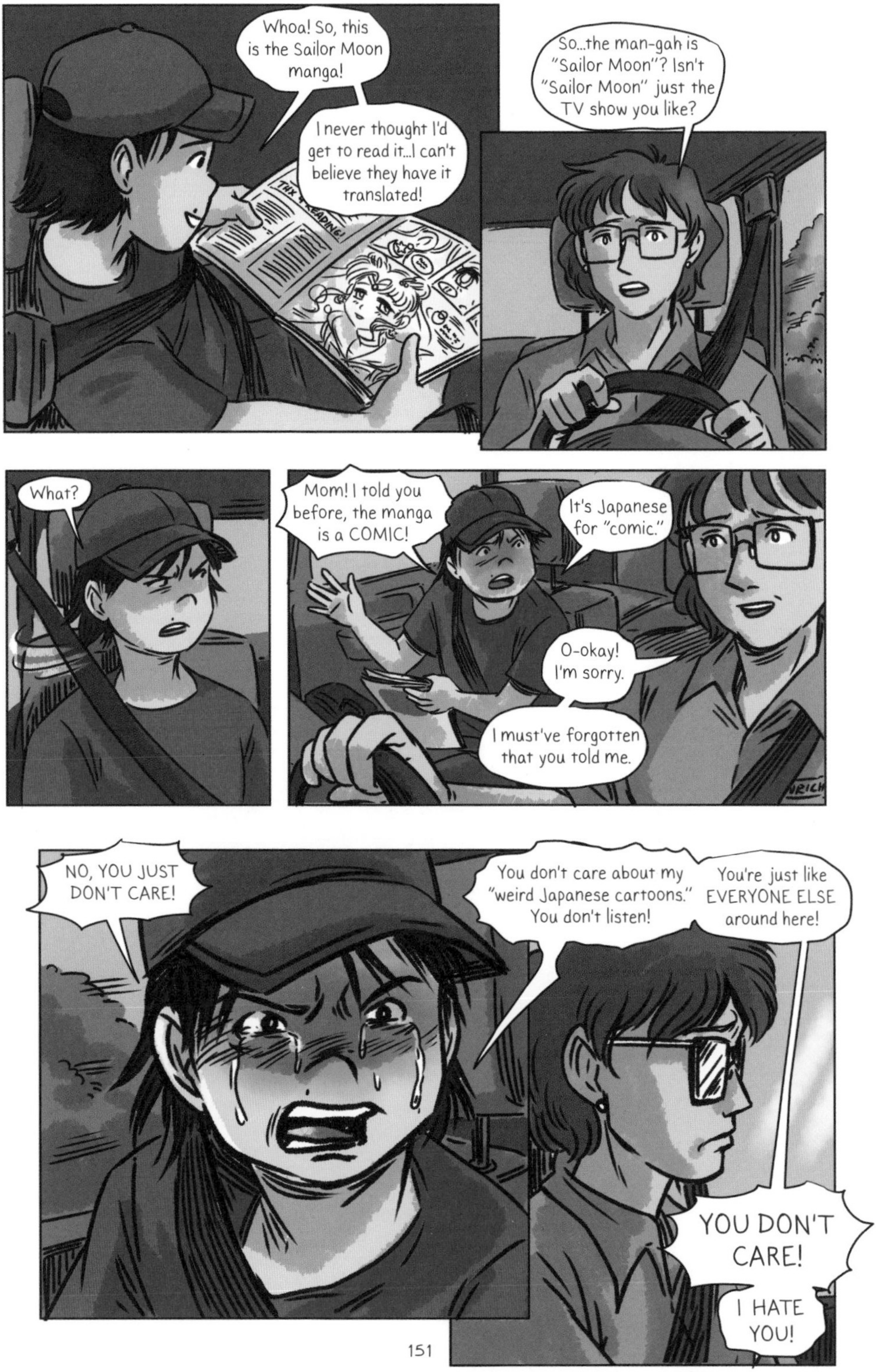
Whoa! So, this is the Sailor Moon manga!
I never thought I'd get to read it...I can't believe they have it translated!
THX 4 READING!
So...the man-gah is "Sailor Moon"? Isn't "Sailor Moon" just the TV show you like?
What?
Mom! I told you before, the manga is a COMIC!
It's Japanese for "comic."
O-okay! I'm sorry.
I must've forgotten that you told me.
NO, YOU JUST DON'T CARE!
You don't care about my "weird Japanese cartoons." You don't listen!
You're just like EVERYONE ELSE around here!
YOU DON'T CARE!
I HATE YOU!

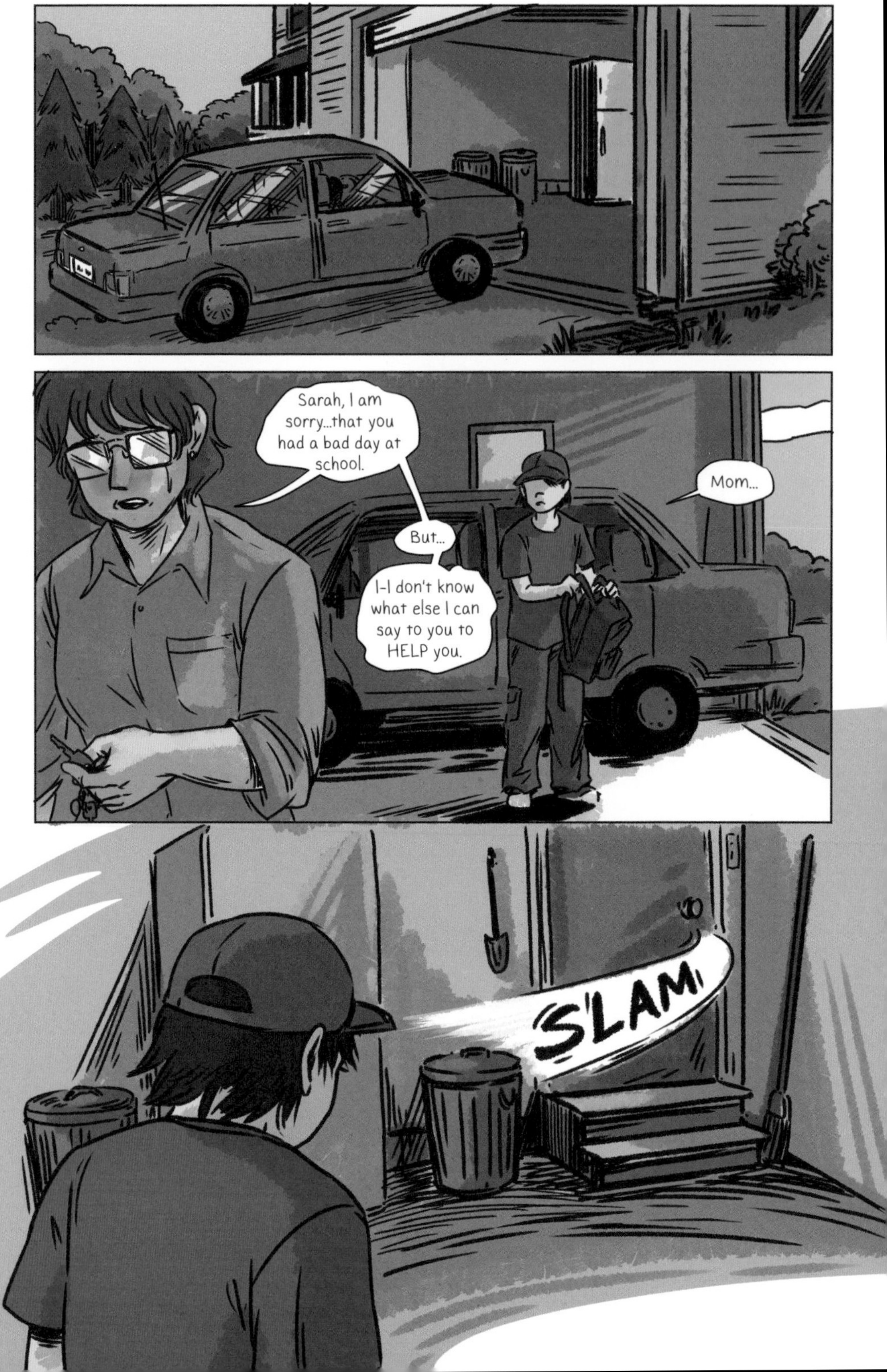
Sarah, I am sorry...that you had a bad day at school.
But...
I-I don't know what else I can say to you to HELP you.
Mom...
SLAM

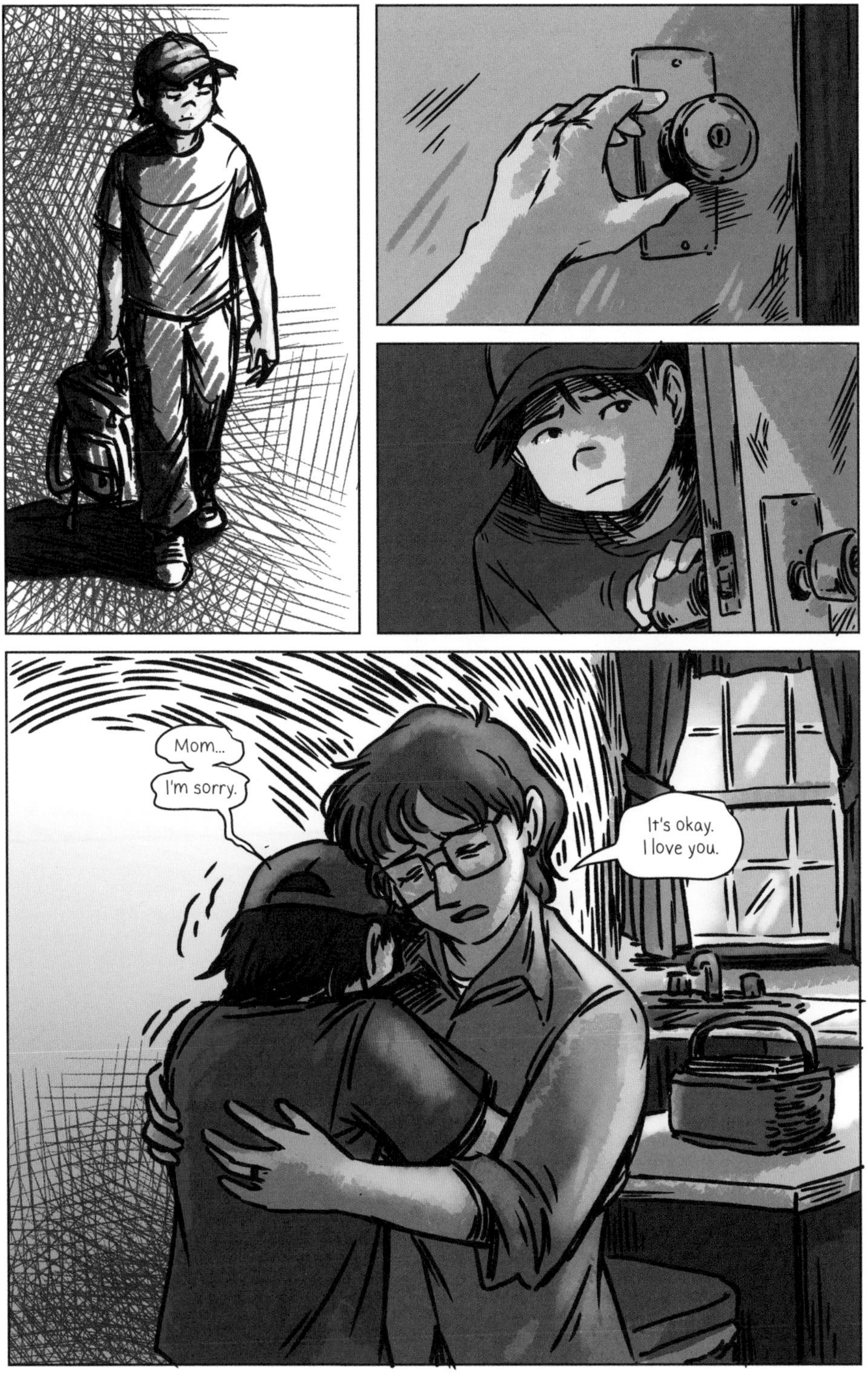
Mom...
I'm sorry.
It's okay.
I love you.

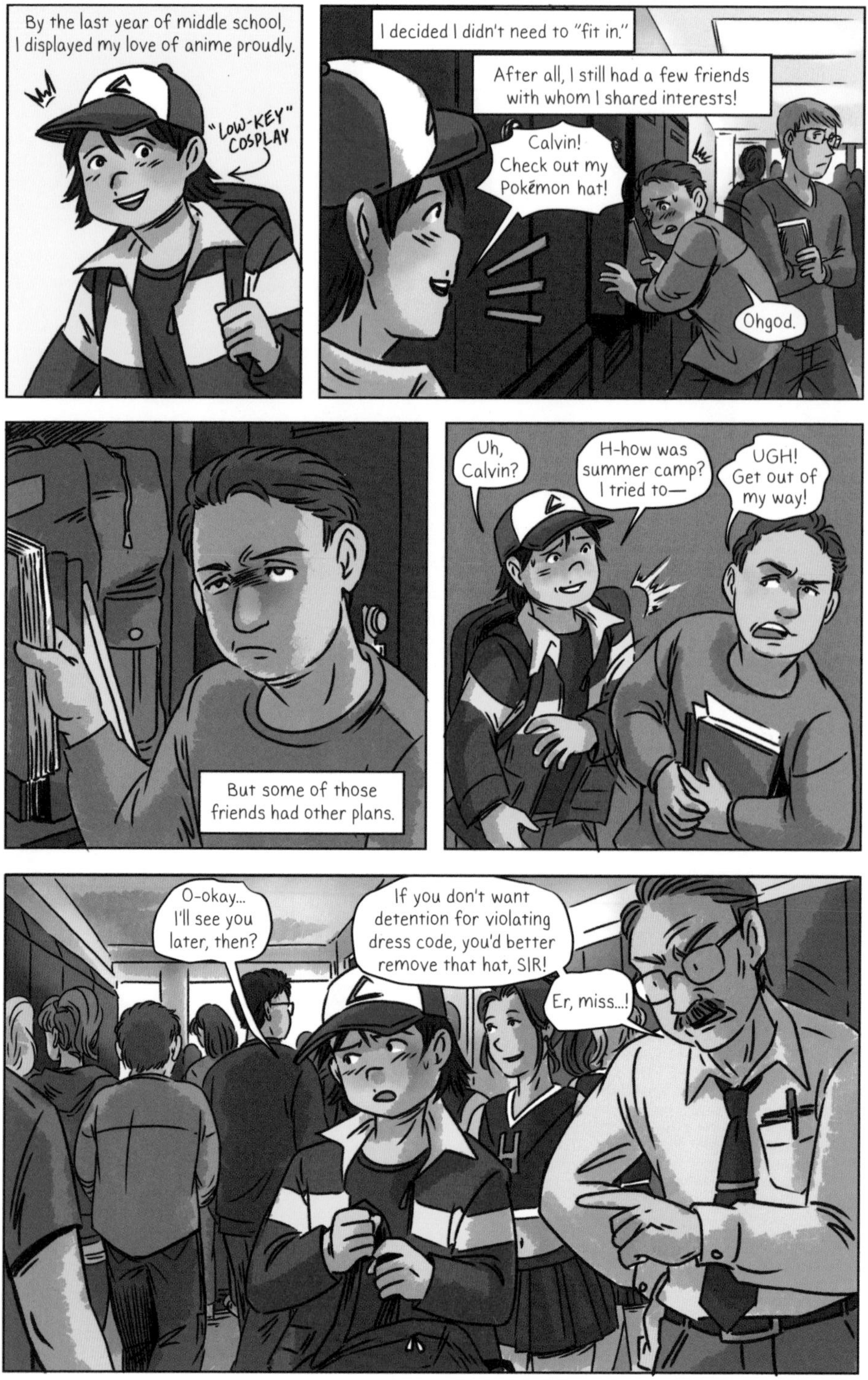
By the last year of middle school, I displayed my love of anime proudly.
"LOW-KEY" COSPLAY
I decided I didn't need to "fit in."
After all, I still had a few friends with whom I shared interests!
Calvin! Check out my Pokémon hat!
Ohgod.
But some of those friends had other plans.
Uh, Calvin?
H-how was summer camp? I tried to—
UGH! Get out of my way!
O-okay... I'll see you later, then?
If you don't want detention for violating dress code, you'd better remove that hat, SIR!
Er, miss...!

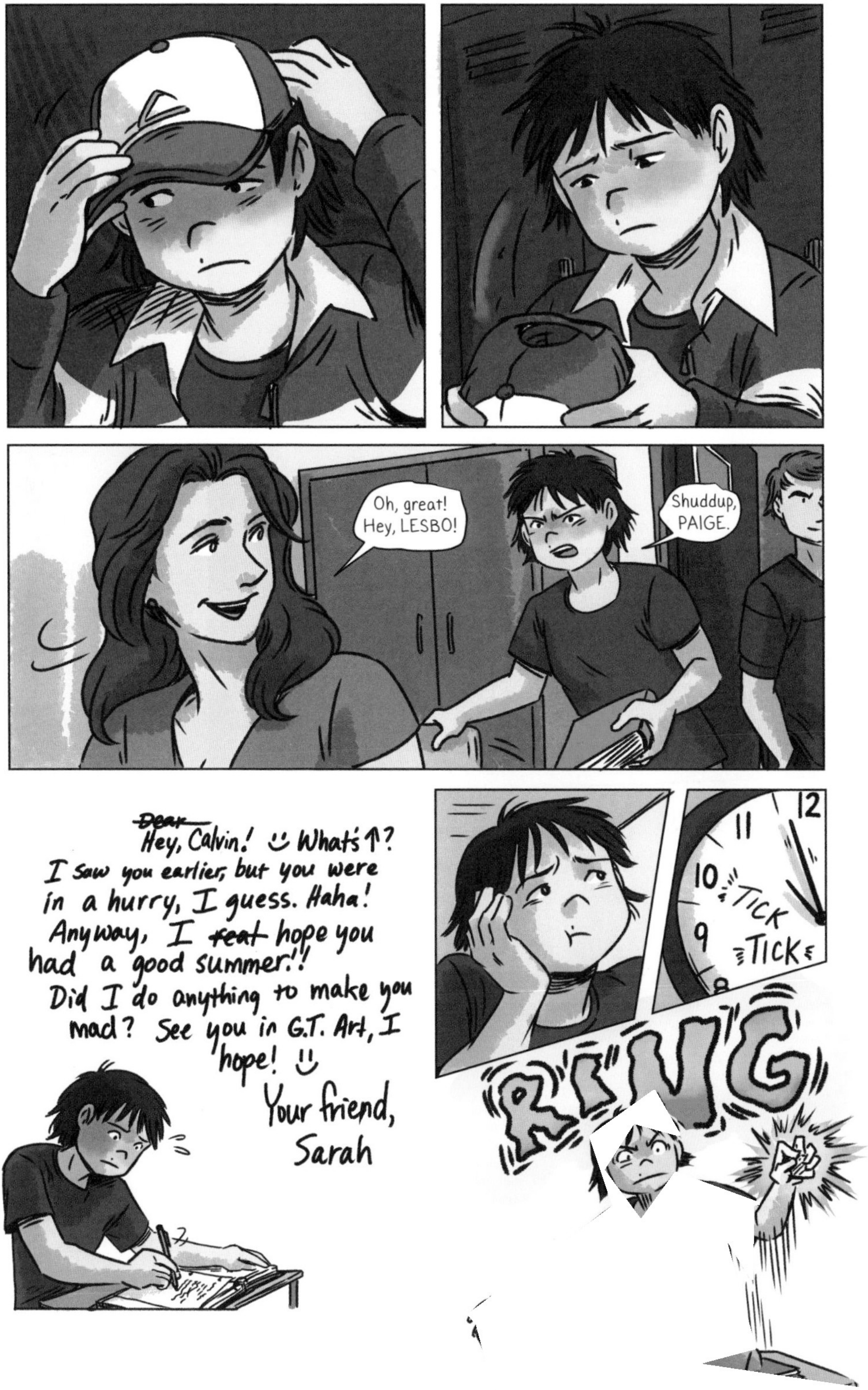

Oh, great! Hey, LESBO!
Shuddup, PAIGE.
TICK
TICK
~~Dear~~ Hey, Calvin! ☺ What's ↑? I saw you earlier, but you were in a hurry, I guess. Haha! Anyway, I ~~feel~~ hope you had a good summer!! Did I do anything to make you mad? See you in G.T. Art, I hope! ☺
Your friend, Sarah
RING

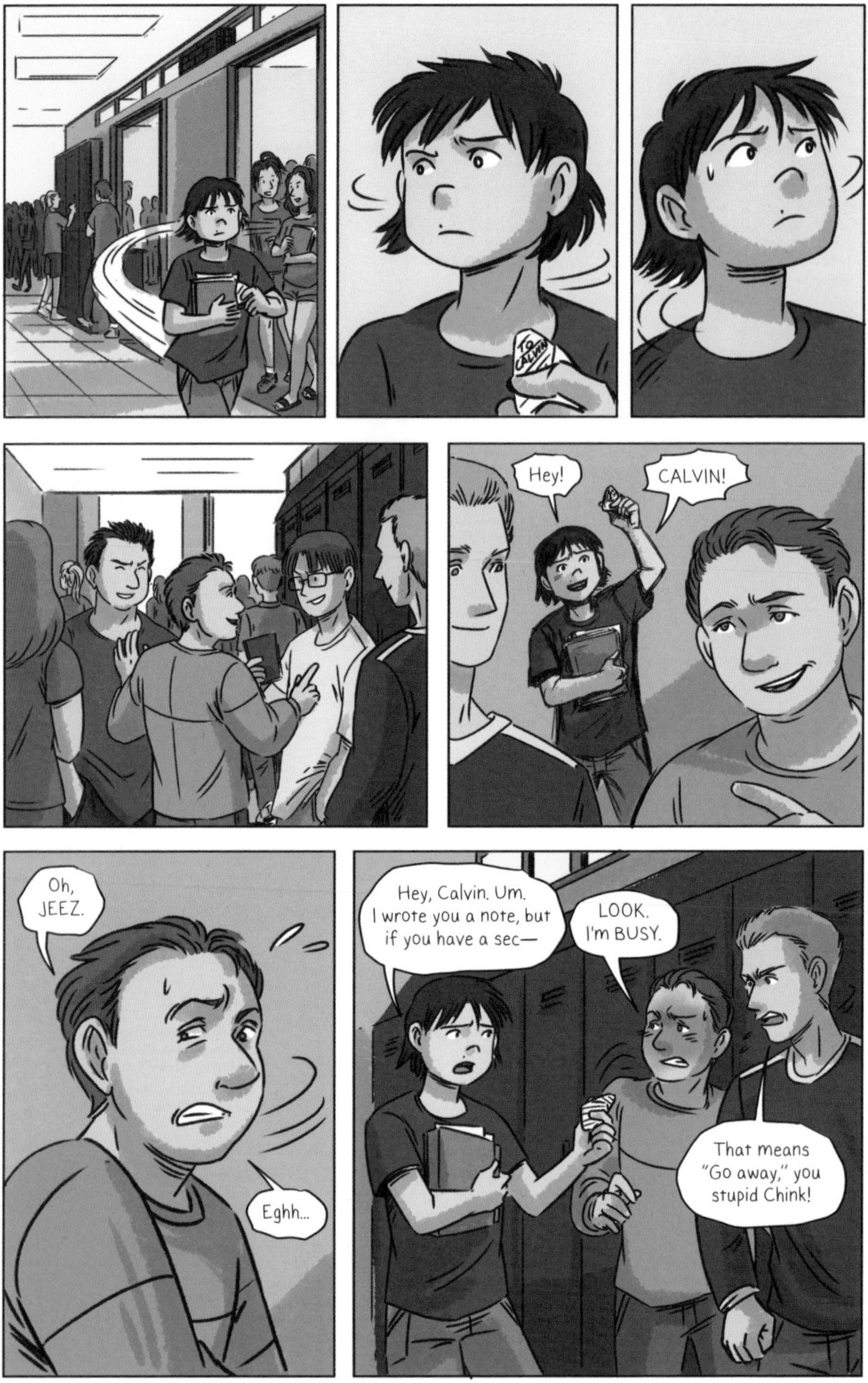

TO CALVIN
Hey!
CALVIN!
Oh, JEEZ.
Eghh...
Hey, Calvin. Um. I wrote you a note, but if you have a sec—
LOOK. I'm BUSY.
That means "Go away," you stupid Chink!

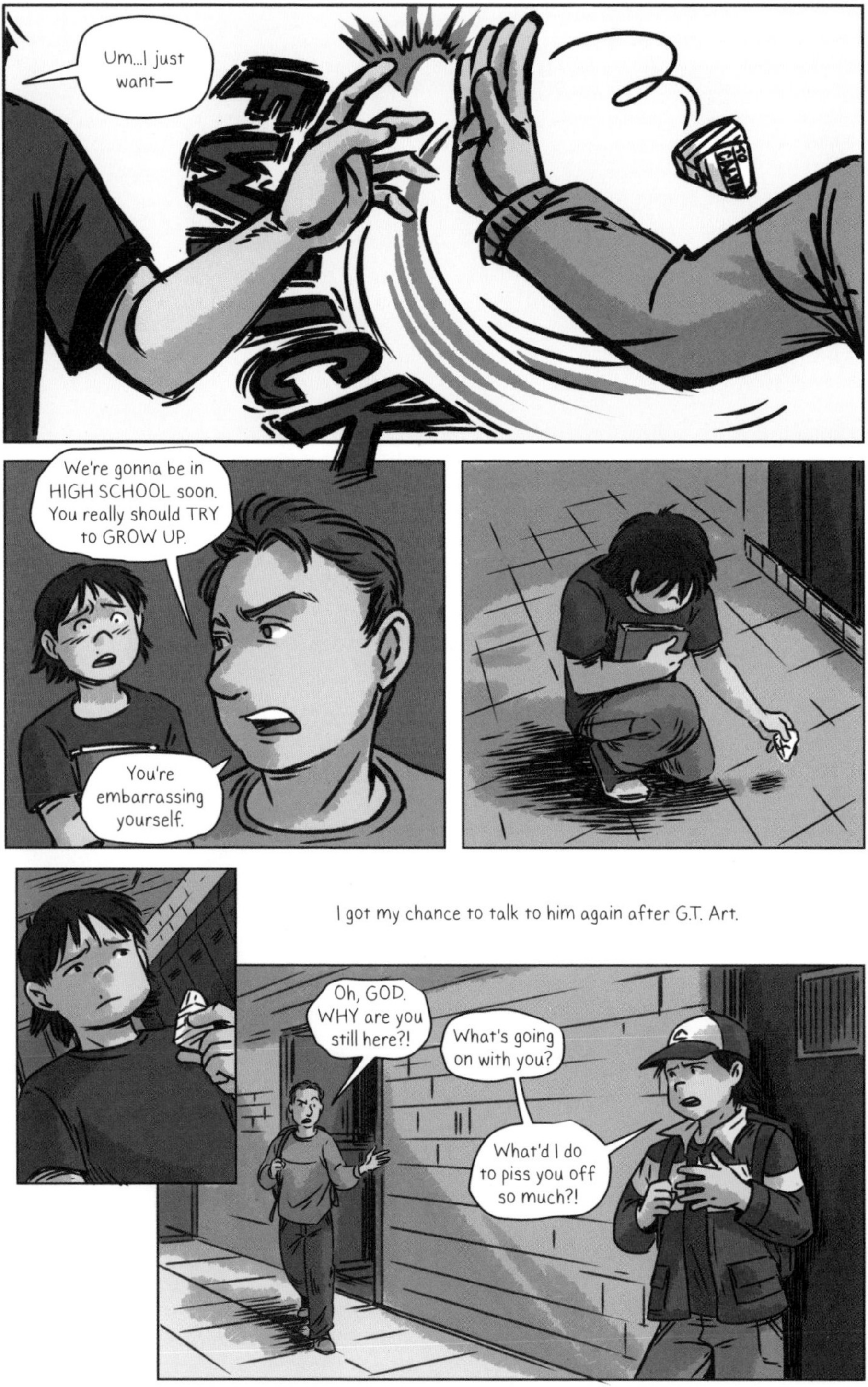
Um...I just want—
We're gonna be in HIGH SCHOOL soon. You really should TRY to GROW UP.
You're embarrassing yourself.
I got my chance to talk to him again after G.T. Art.
Oh, GOD. WHY are you still here?!
What's going on with you?
What'd I do to piss you off so much?!

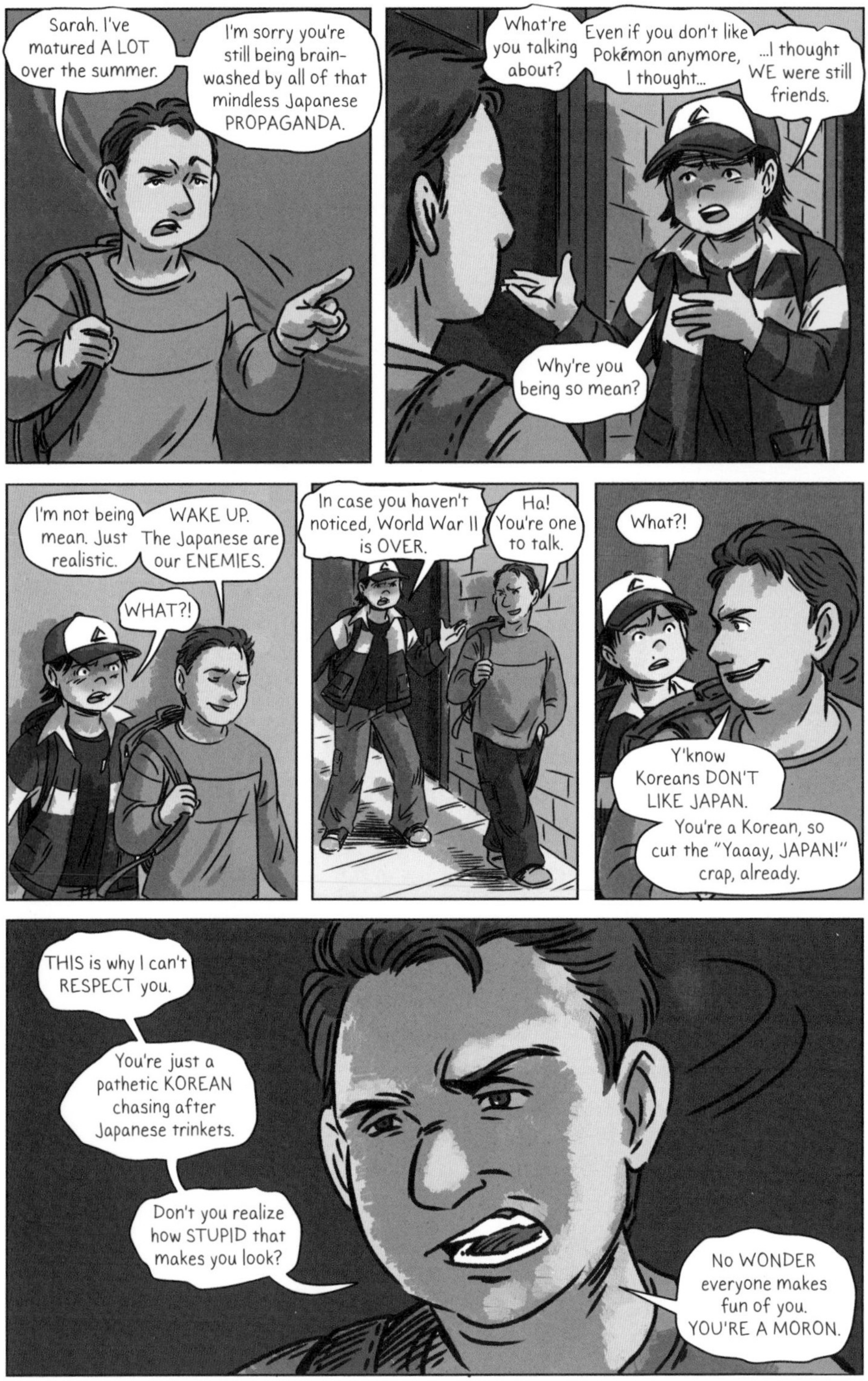
Sarah. I've matured A LOT over the summer.
I'm sorry you're still being brain-washed by all of that mindless Japanese PROPAGANDA.
What're you talking about?
Even if you don't like Pokémon anymore, I thought...
...I thought WE were still friends.
Why're you being so mean?
I'm not being mean. Just realistic.
WAKE UP. The Japanese are our ENEMIES.
WHAT?!
In case you haven't noticed, World War II is OVER.
Ha! You're one to talk.
What?!
Y'know Koreans DON'T LIKE JAPAN.
You're a Korean, so cut the "Yaaay, JAPAN!" crap, already.
THIS is why I can't RESPECT you.
You're just a pathetic KOREAN chasing after Japanese trinkets.
Don't you realize how STUPID that makes you look?
No WONDER everyone makes fun of you. YOU'RE A MORON.

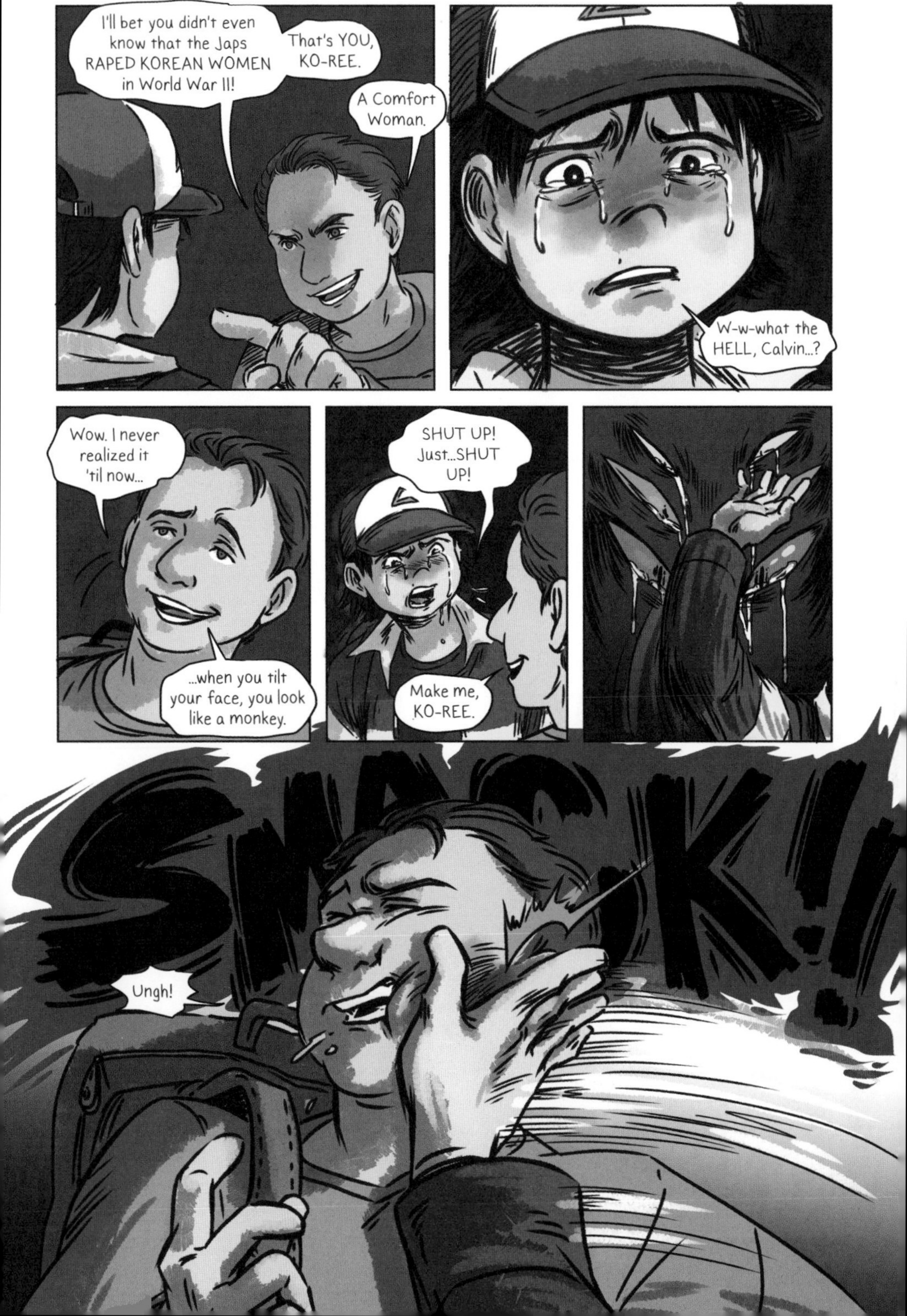
I'll bet you didn't even know that the Japs RAPED KOREAN WOMEN in World War II!
That's YOU, KO-REE.
A Comfort Woman.
W-w-what the HELL, Calvin...?
Wow. I never realized it 'til now...
...when you tilt your face, you look like a monkey.
SHUT UP! Just...SHUT UP!
Make me, KO-REE.
Unghl!

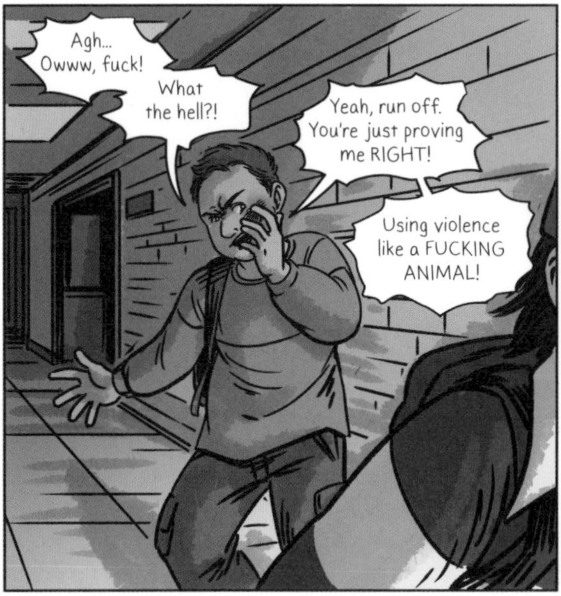
Agh... Owww, fuck!
What the hell?!
Yeah, run off. You're just proving me RIGHT!
Using violence like a FUCKING ANIMAL!
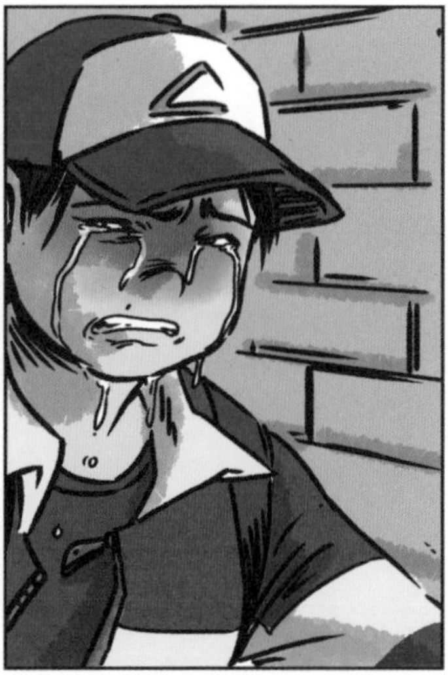
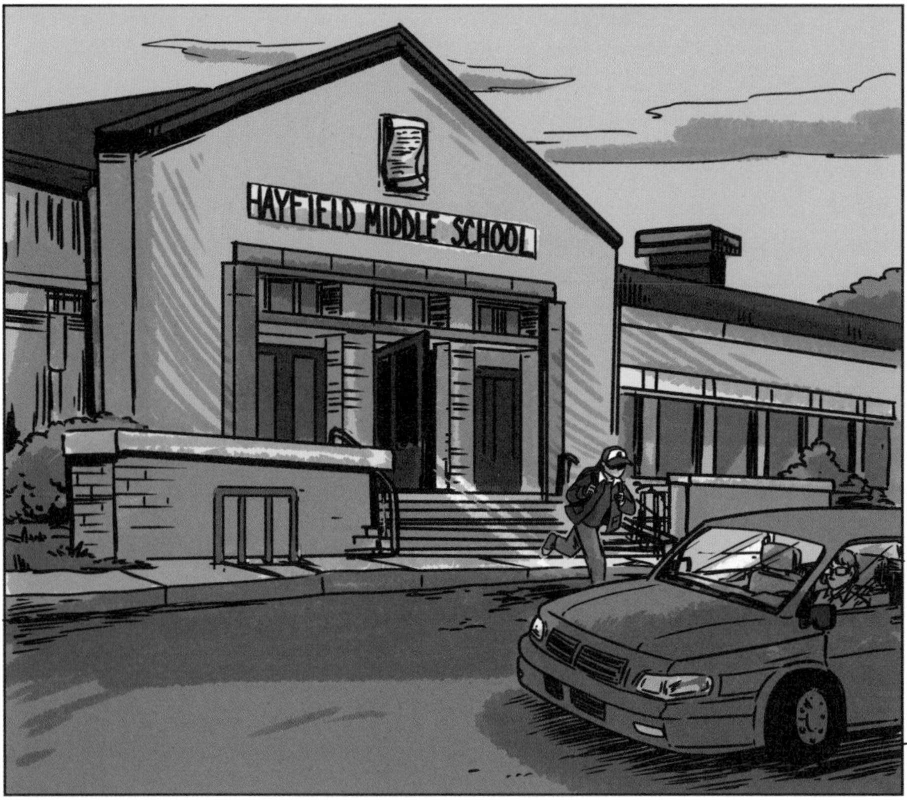
HAYFIELD MIDDLE SCHOOL

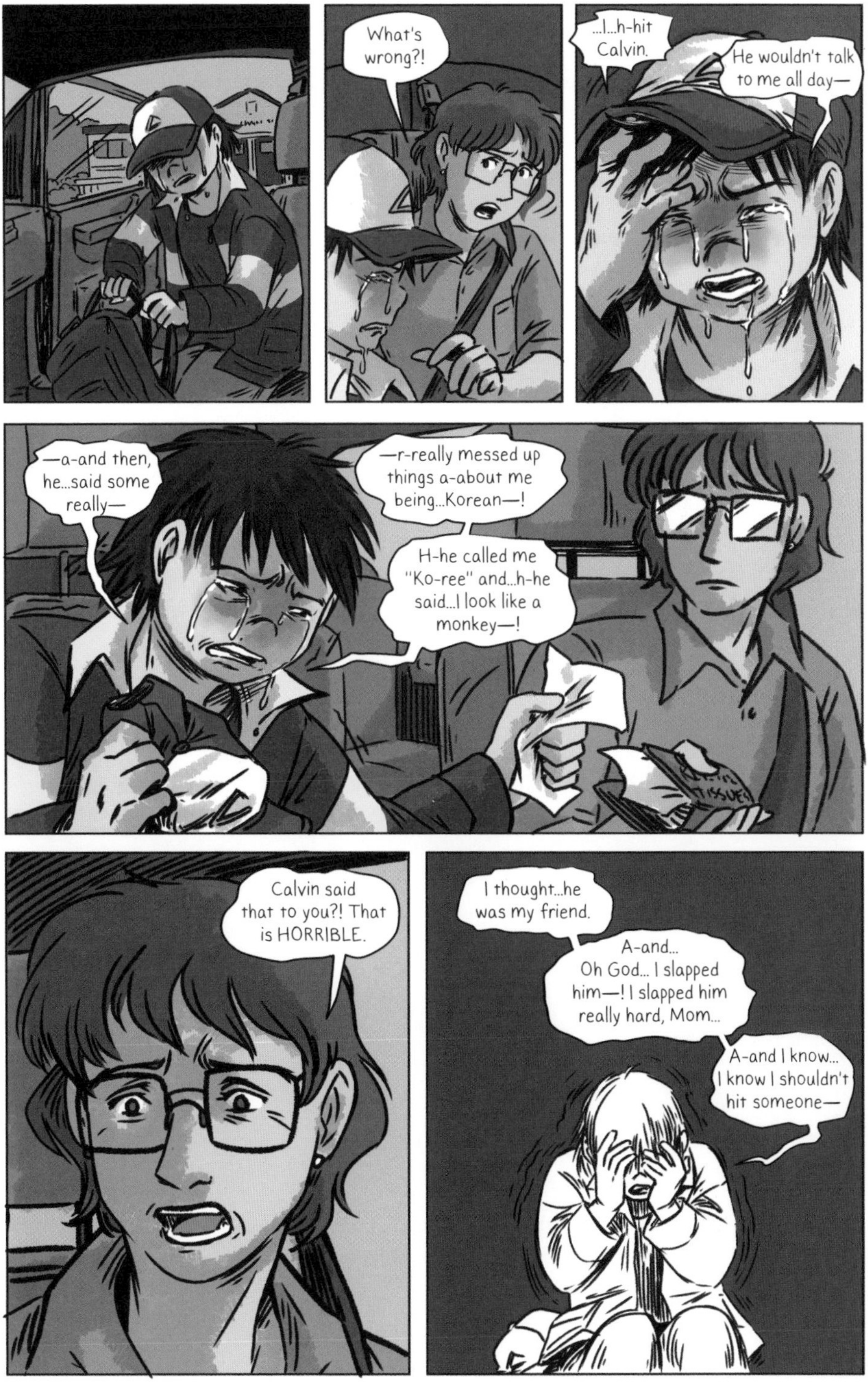
What's wrong?!
...I...h-hit Calvin.
He wouldn't talk to me all day—
—a-and then, he...said some really—
—r-really messed up things a-about me being...Korean—!
H-he called me "Ko-ree" and...h-he said...I look like a monkey—!
TISSUES
Calvin said that to you?! That is HORRIBLE.
I thought...he was my friend.
A-and... Oh God... I slapped him—! I slapped him really hard, Mom...
A-and I know... I know I shouldn't hit someone—

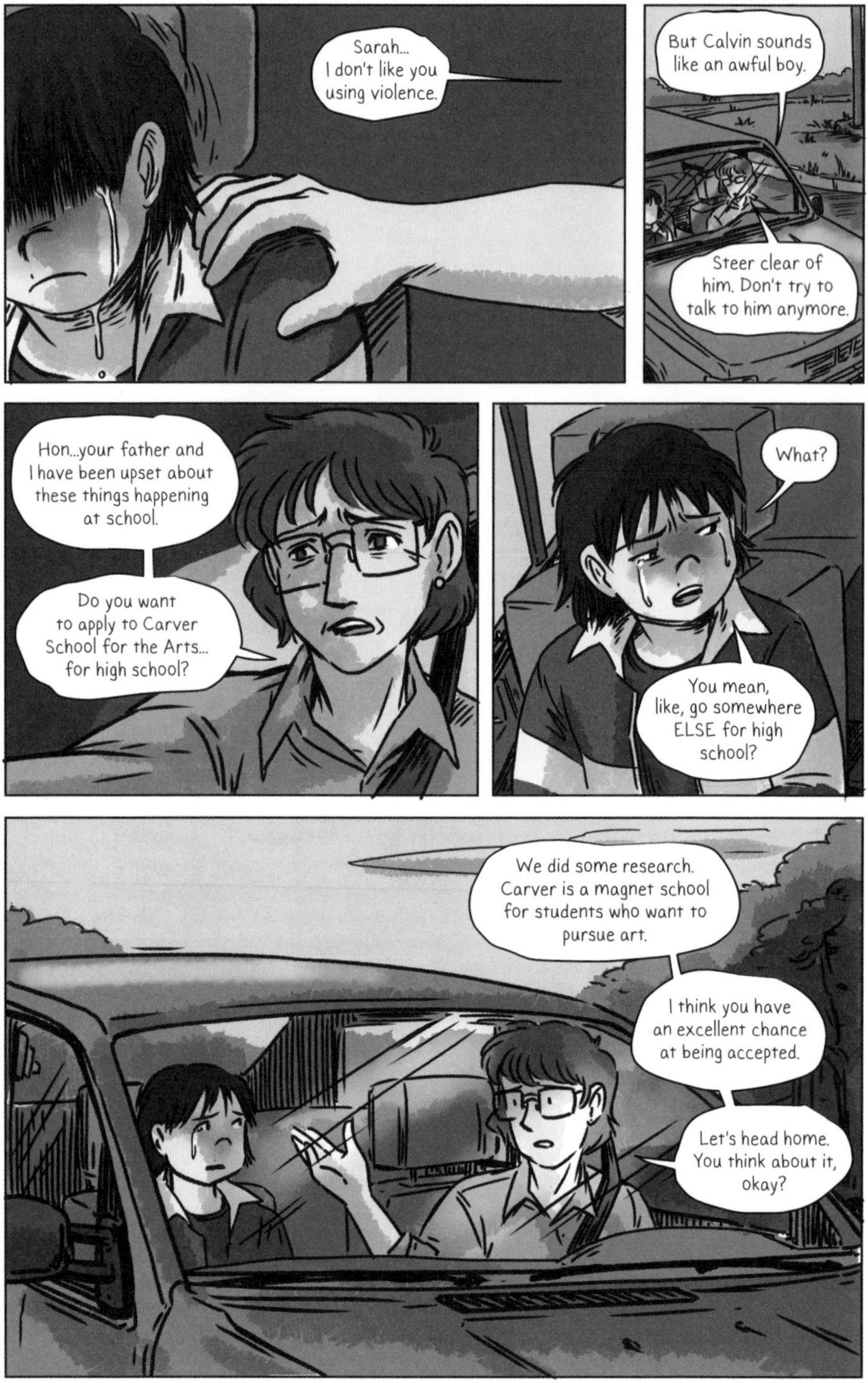
Sarah... I don't like you using violence.
But Calvin sounds like an awful boy.
Steer clear of him. Don't try to talk to him anymore.
Hon...your father and I have been upset about these things happening at school.
Do you want to apply to Carver School for the Arts... for high school?
What?
You mean, like, go somewhere ELSE for high school?
We did some research. Carver is a magnet school for students who want to pursue art.
I think you have an excellent chance at being accepted.
Let's head home. You think about it, okay?

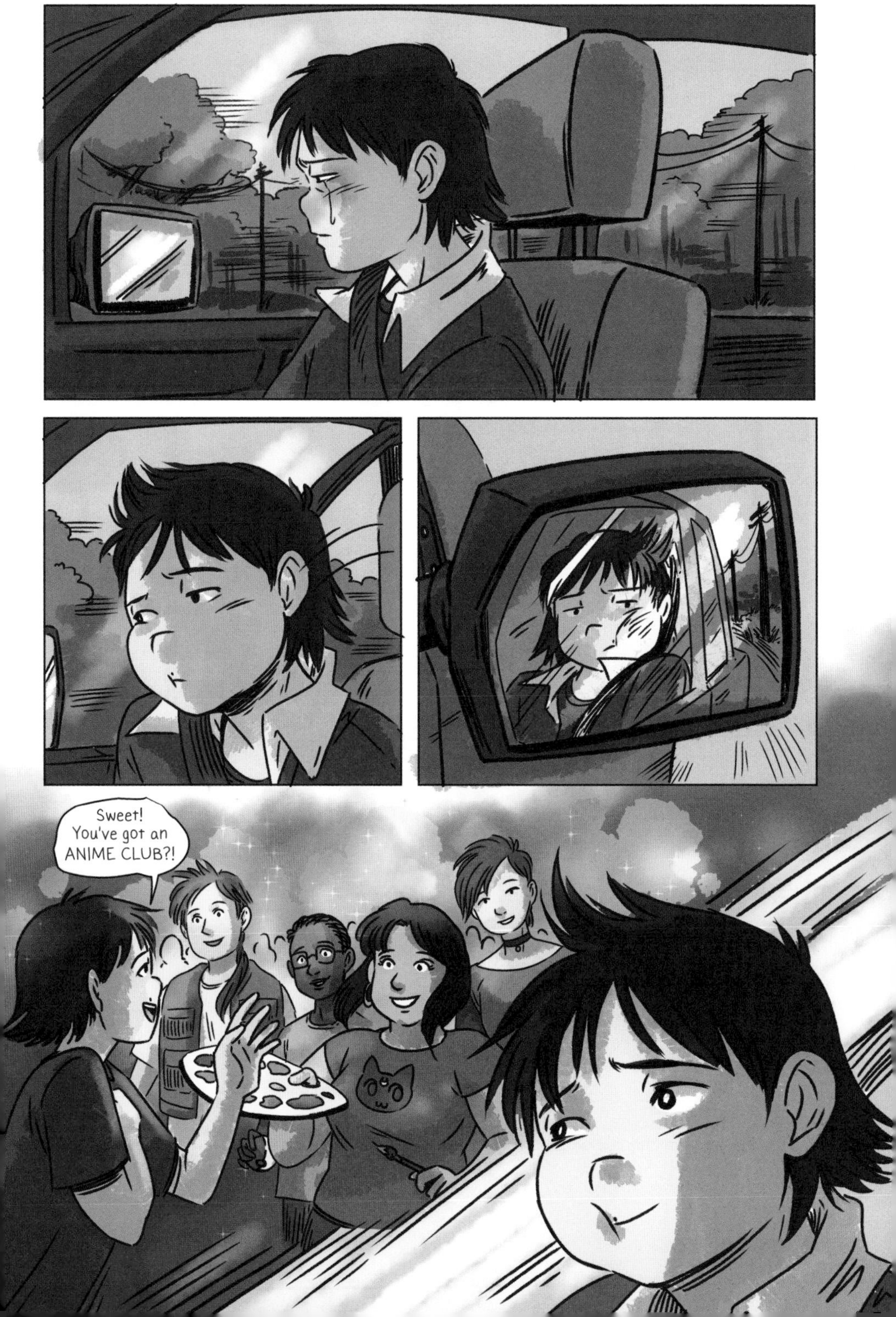
Sweet!
You've got an
ANIME CLUB?!

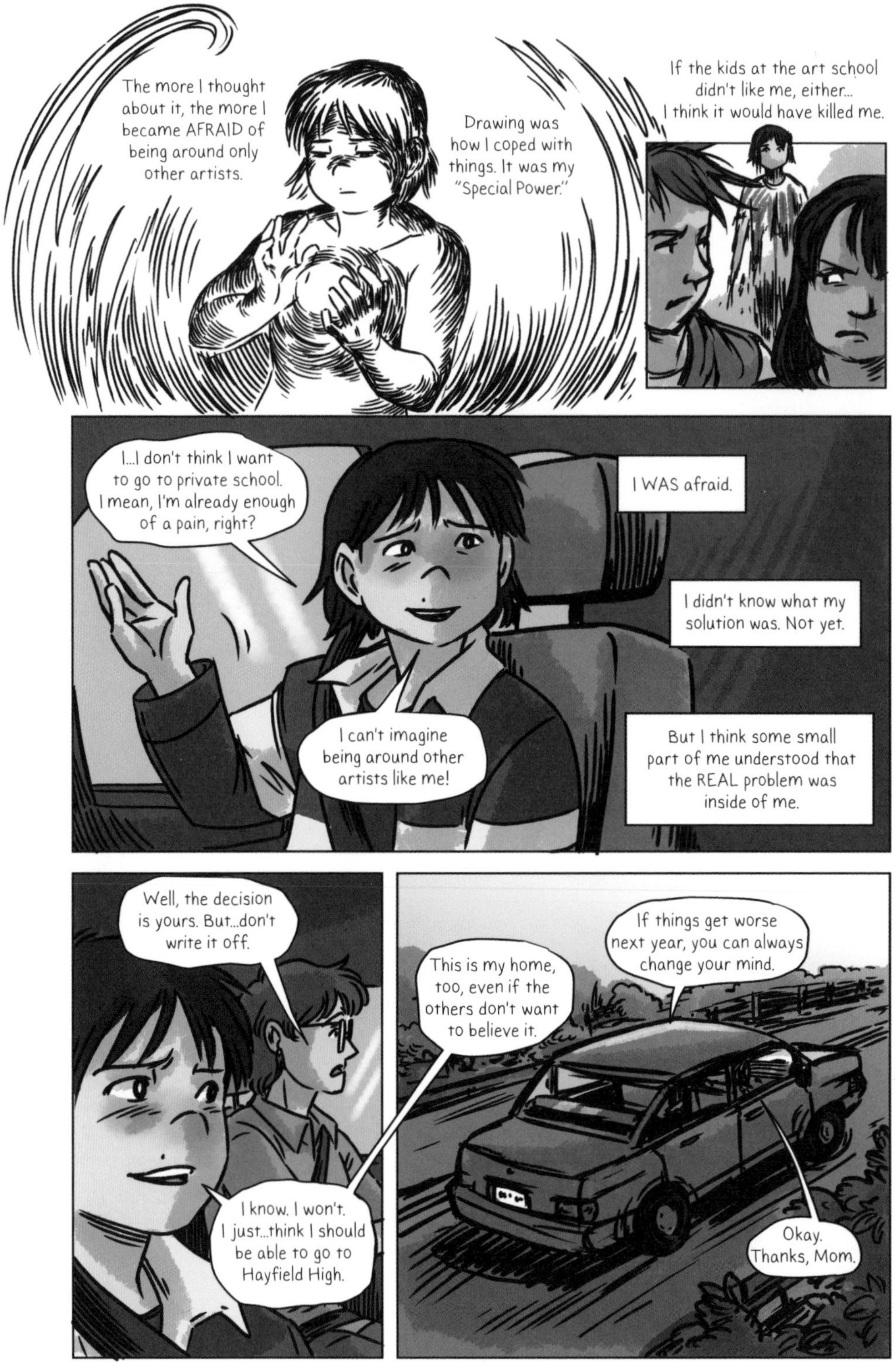

The more I thought about it, the more I became AFRAID of being around only other artists.
Drawing was how I coped with things. It was my "Special Power."
If the kids at the art school didn't like me, either... I think it would have killed me.
I...I don't think I want to go to private school. I mean, I'm already enough of a pain, right?
I WAS afraid.
I didn't know what my solution was. Not yet.
I can't imagine being around other artists like me!
But I think some small part of me understood that the REAL problem was inside of me.
Well, the decision is yours. But...don't write it off.
I know. I won't. I just...think I should be able to go to Hayfield High.
This is my home, too, even if the others don't want to believe it.
If things get worse next year, you can always change your mind.
Okay. Thanks, Mom.

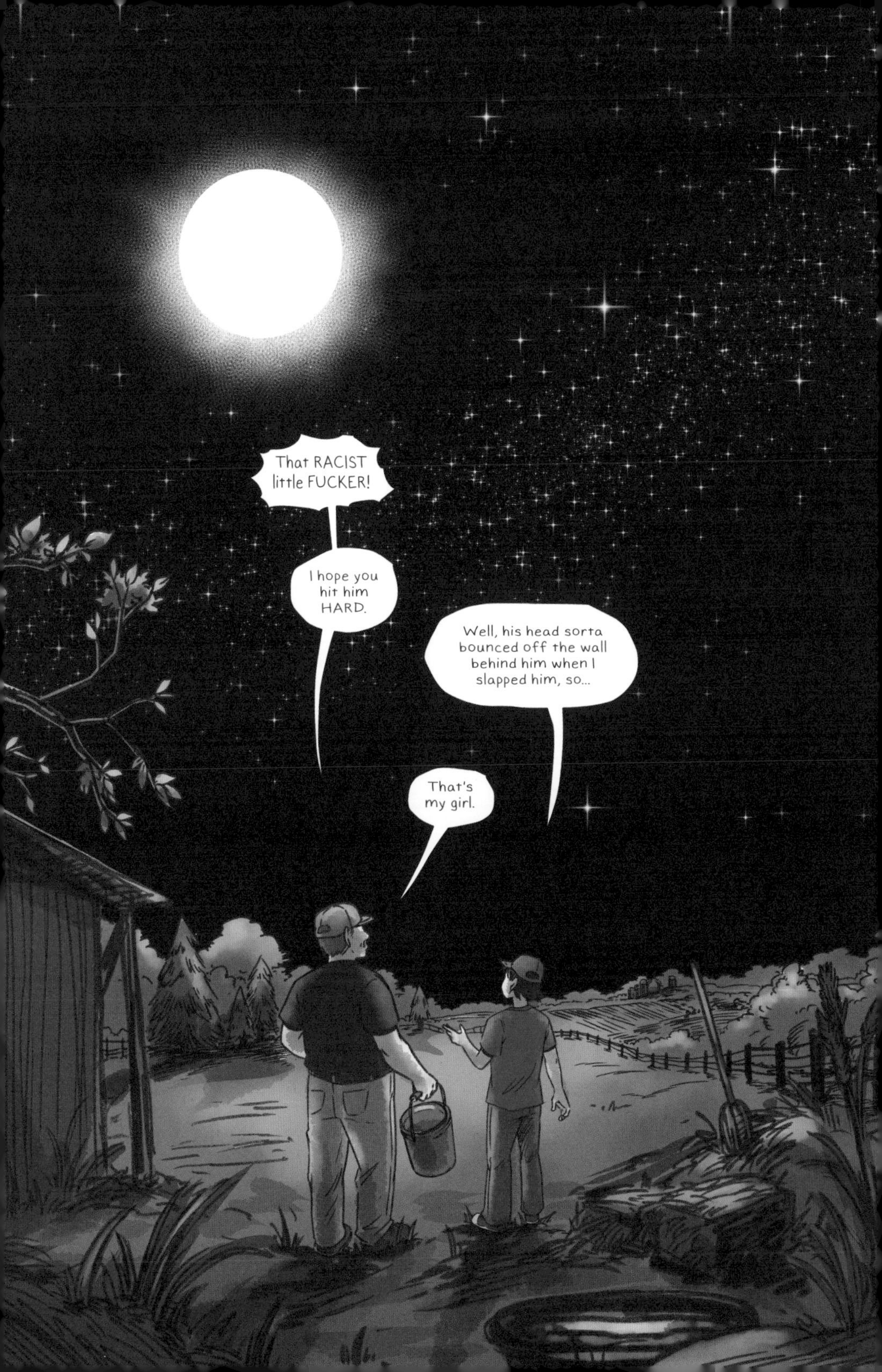
That RACIST little FUCKER!
I hope you hit him HARD.
Well, his head sorta bounced off the wall behind him when I slapped him, so...
That's my girl.

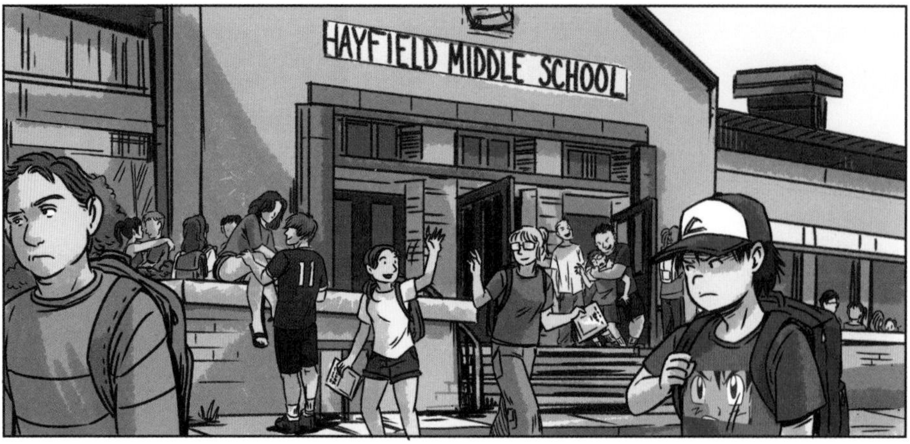
HAYFIELD MIDDLE SCHOOL

As middle school drew to an end, I continued turning to art, animation, and comics to cope.

I didn't have much hope for my experiences at school, but
I found pleasure in pursuing new nuggets of information about anime.

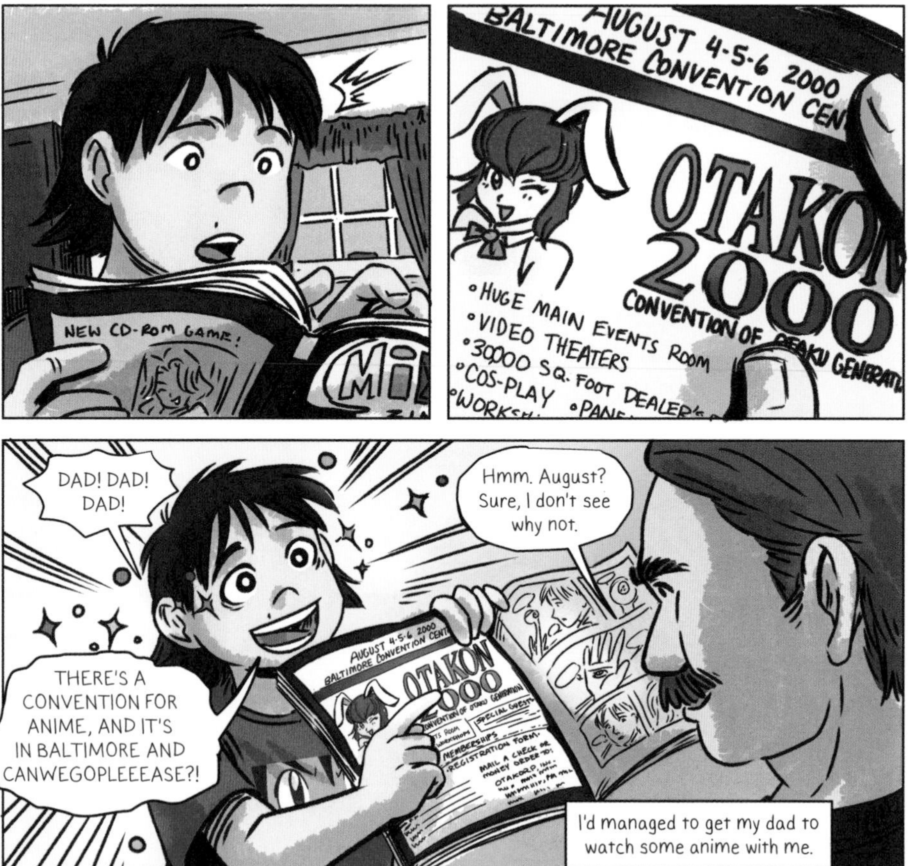
NEW CD-ROM GAME!
AUGUST 4-5-6 2000
BALTIMORE CONVENTION CEN
OTAKON
2000
CONVENTION OF
• HUGE MAIN EVENTS ROOM
• VIDEO THEATERS
• 30,000 SQ. FOOT DEALER'S
• COS-PLAY
DAD! DAD! DAD!
Hmm. August? Sure, I don't see why not.
THERE'S A CONVENTION FOR ANIME, AND IT'S IN BALTIMORE AND CANWEGOPLEEEASE?!
I'd managed to get my dad to watch some anime with me.

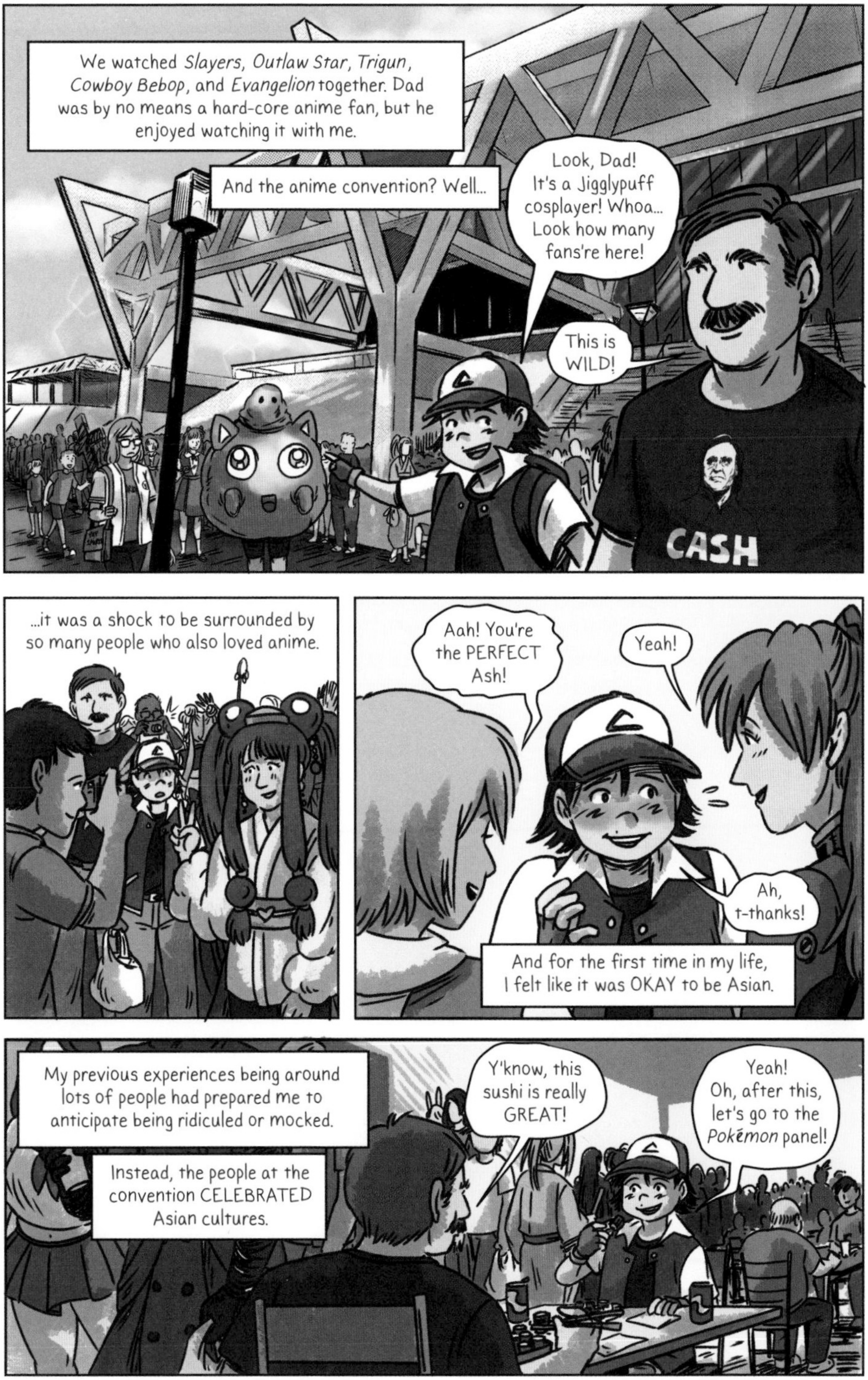
We watched *Slayers*, *Outlaw Star*, *Trigun*, *Cowboy Bebop*, and *Evangelion* together. Dad was by no means a hard-core anime fan, but he enjoyed watching it with me.
And the anime convention? Well...
Look, Dad! It's a Jigglypuff cosplayer! Whoa... Look how many fans're here!
This is WILD!
CASH
...it was a shock to be surrounded by so many people who also loved anime.
Aah! You're the PERFECT Ash!
Yeah!
Ah, t-thanks!
And for the first time in my life, I felt like it was OKAY to be Asian.
My previous experiences being around lots of people had prepared me to anticipate being ridiculed or mocked.
Instead, the people at the convention CELEBRATED Asian cultures.
Y'know, this sushi is really GREAT!
Yeah! Oh, after this, let's go to the *Pokémon* panel!

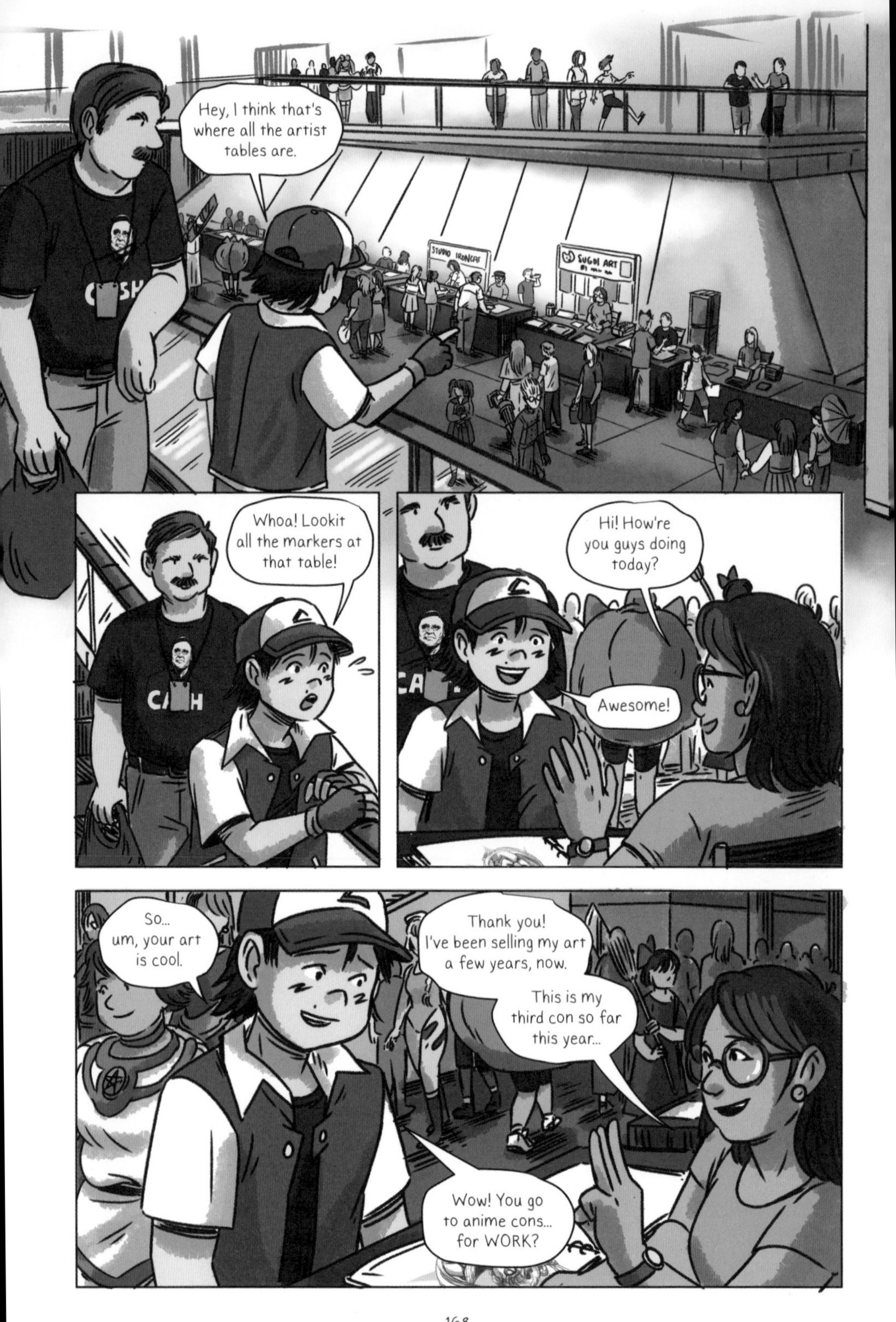
Hey, I think that's where all the artist tables are.
STUDIO IRONCAT
SUGOI ART
Whoa! Lookit all the markers at that table!
Hi! How're you guys doing today?
Awesome!
So... um, your art is cool.
Thank you! I've been selling my art a few years, now.
This is my third con so far this year...
Wow! You go to anime cons... for WORK?

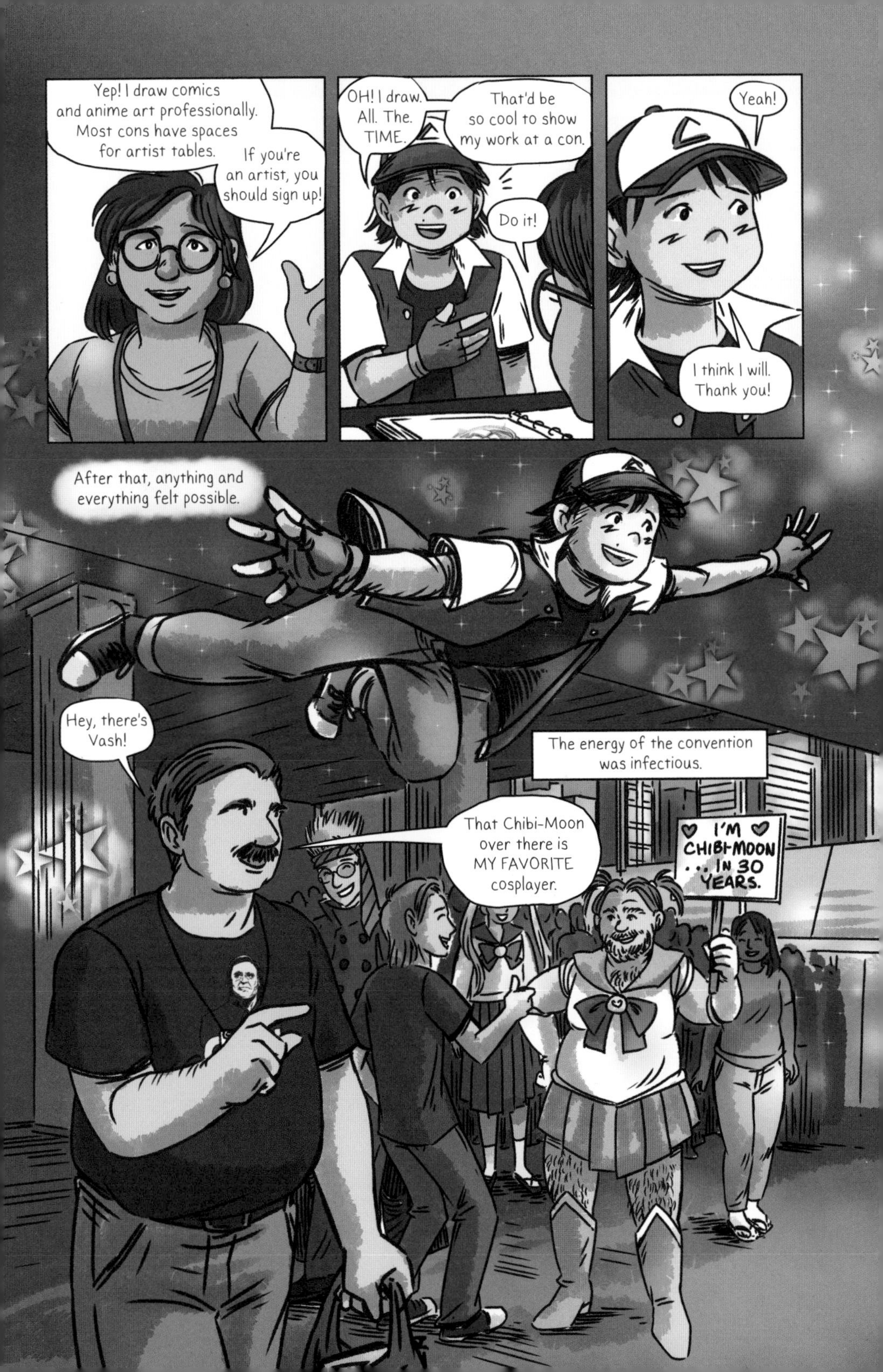
Yep! I draw comics and anime art professionally. Most cons have spaces for artist tables.
If you're an artist, you should sign up!
OH! I draw. All. The. TIME.
That'd be so cool to show my work at a con.
Do it!
Yeah!
I think I will. Thank you!
After that, anything and everything felt possible.
Hey, there's Vash!
The energy of the convention was infectious.
That Chibi-Moon over there is MY FAVORITE cosplayer.
I'M CHIBI-MOON . . . IN 30 YEARS.

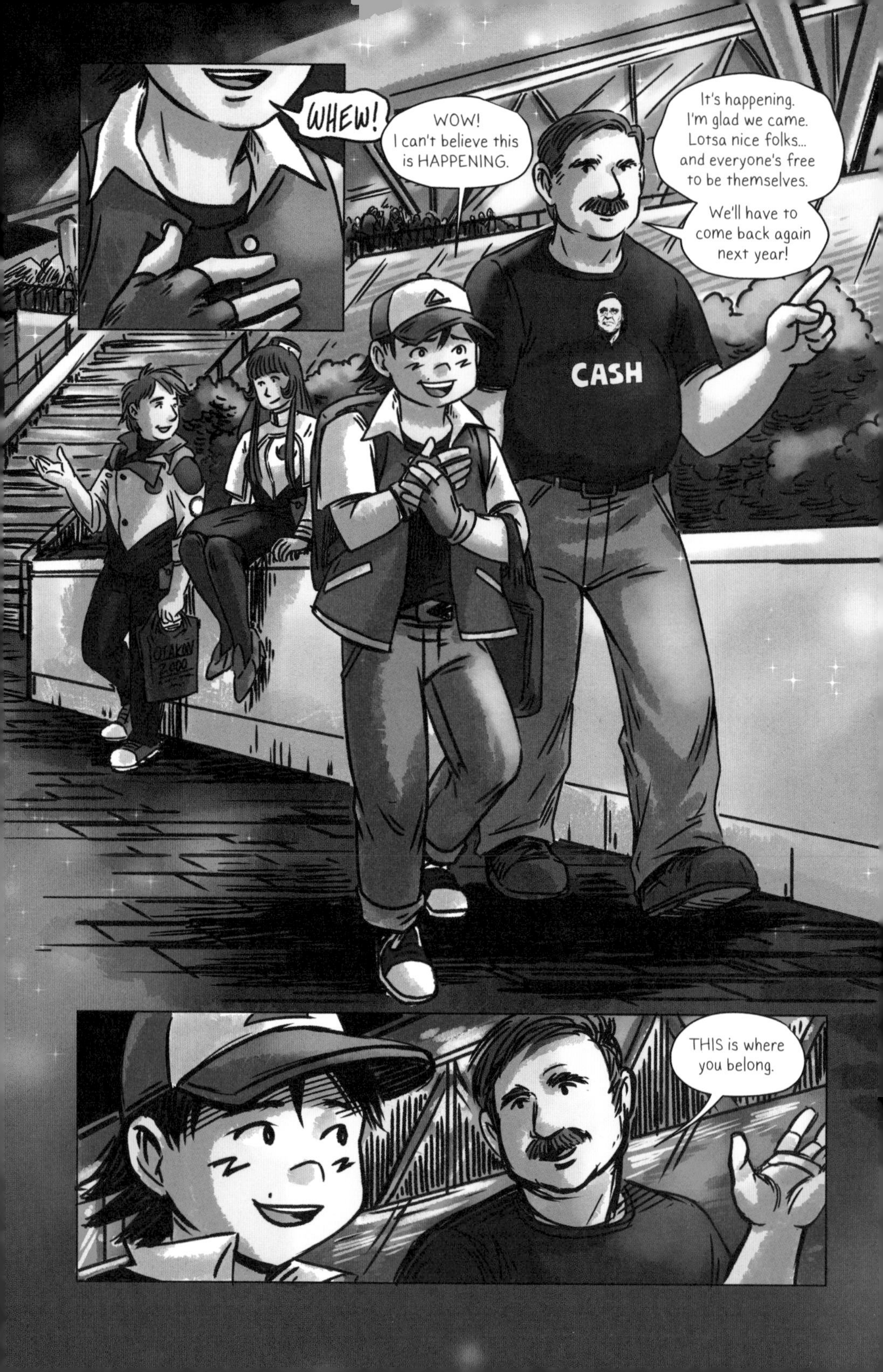
WHEW!
WOW! I can't believe this is HAPPENING.
It's happening. I'm glad we came. Lotsa nice folks... and everyone's free to be themselves.
We'll have to come back again next year!
CASH
THIS is where you belong.

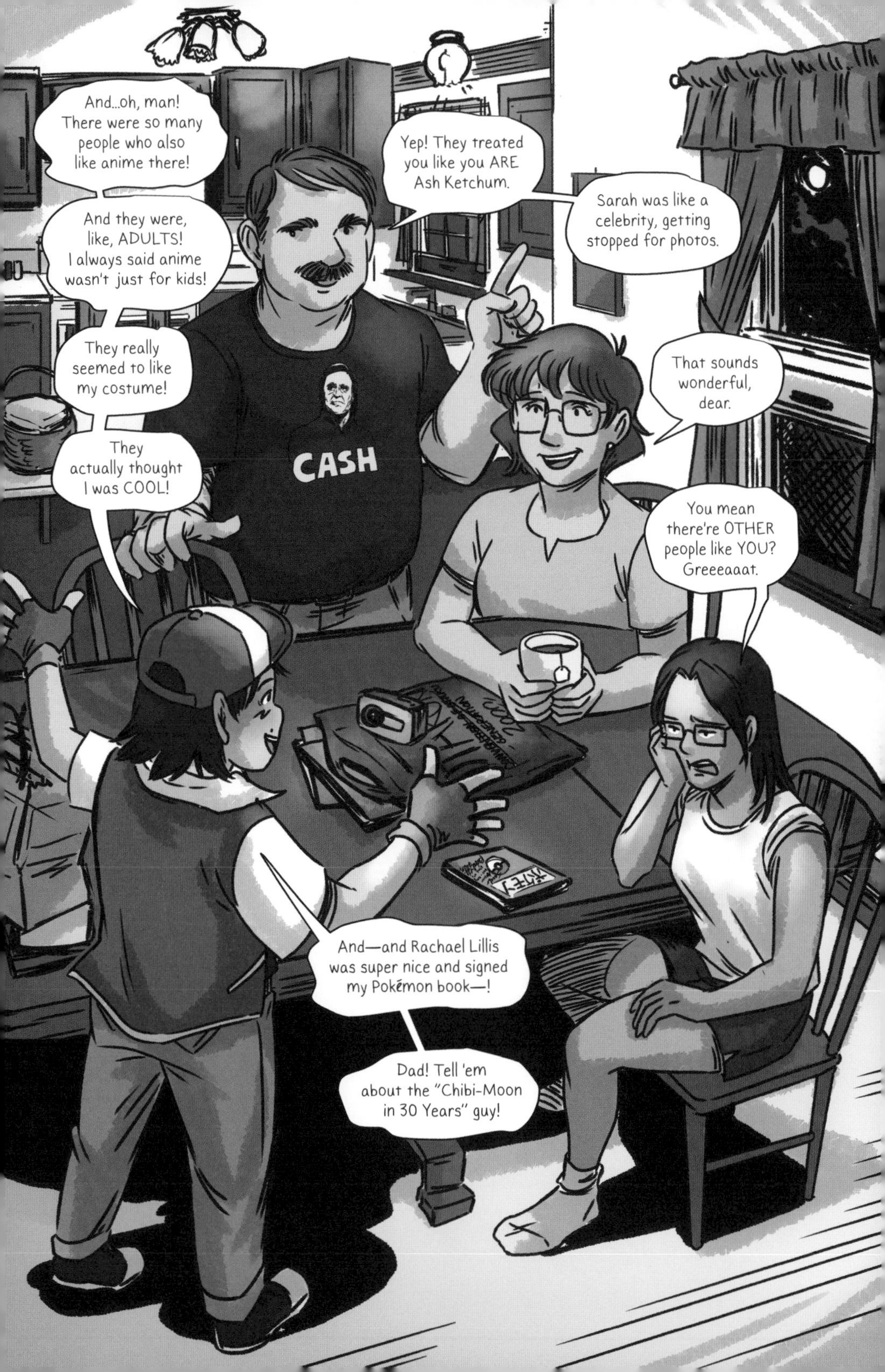
And...oh, man! There were so many people who also like anime there!
And they were, like, ADULTS! I always said anime wasn't just for kids!
They really seemed to like my costume!
They actually thought I was COOL!
Yep! They treated you like you ARE Ash Ketchum.
Sarah was like a celebrity, getting stopped for photos.
CASH
That sounds wonderful, dear.
You mean there're OTHER people like YOU? Greeeaaat.
And—and Rachael Lillis was super nice and signed my Pokémon book—!
Dad! Tell 'em about the "Chibi-Moon in 30 Years" guy!

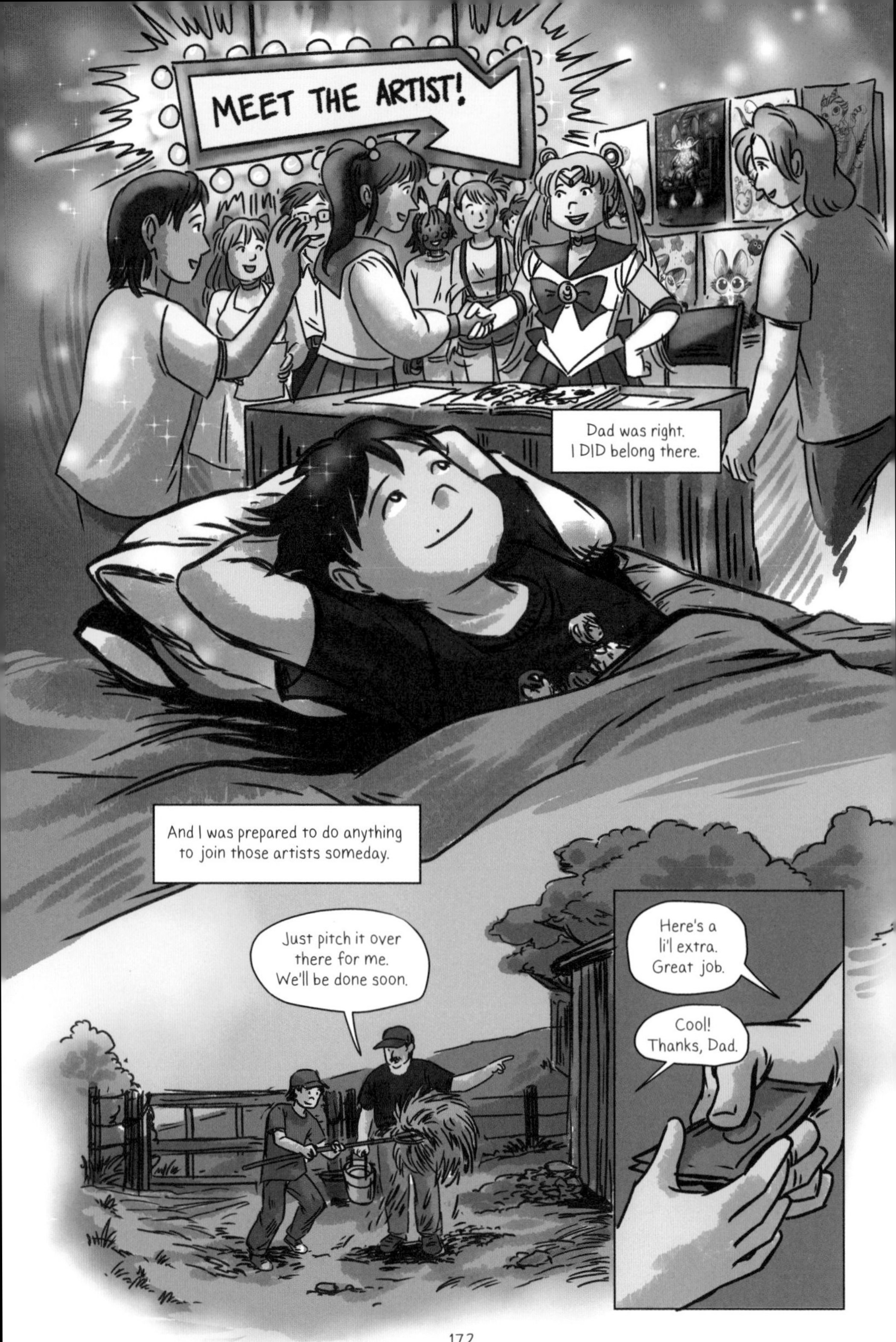
MEET THE ARTIST!
Dad was right.
I DID belong there.
And I was prepared to do anything
to join those artists someday.
Just pitch it over
there for me.
We'll be done soon.
Here's a
li'l extra.
Great job.
Cool!
Thanks, Dad.

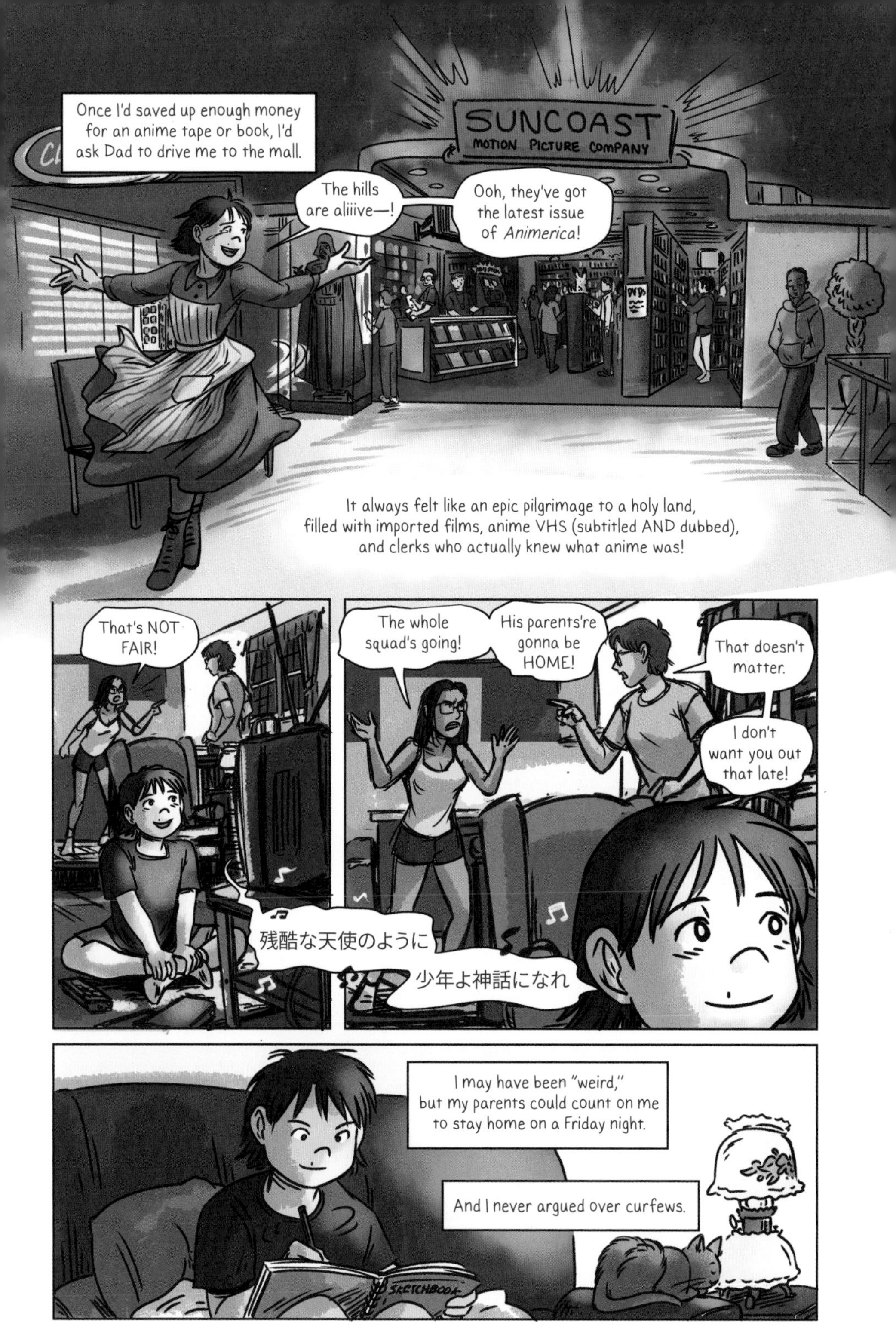
Once I'd saved up enough money for an anime tape or book, I'd ask Dad to drive me to the mall.
SUNCOAST
MOTION PICTURE COMPANY
The hills are aliiive—!
Ooh, they've got the latest issue of *Animerica*!
DVDs
It always felt like an epic pilgrimage to a holy land, filled with imported films, anime VHS (subtitled AND dubbed), and clerks who actually knew what anime was!
That's NOT FAIR!
The whole squad's going!
His parents're gonna be HOME!
That doesn't matter.
I don't want you out that late!
残酷な天使のように
少年よ神話になれ
I may have been "weird," but my parents could count on me to stay home on a Friday night.
And I never argued over curfews.
SKETCHBOOK

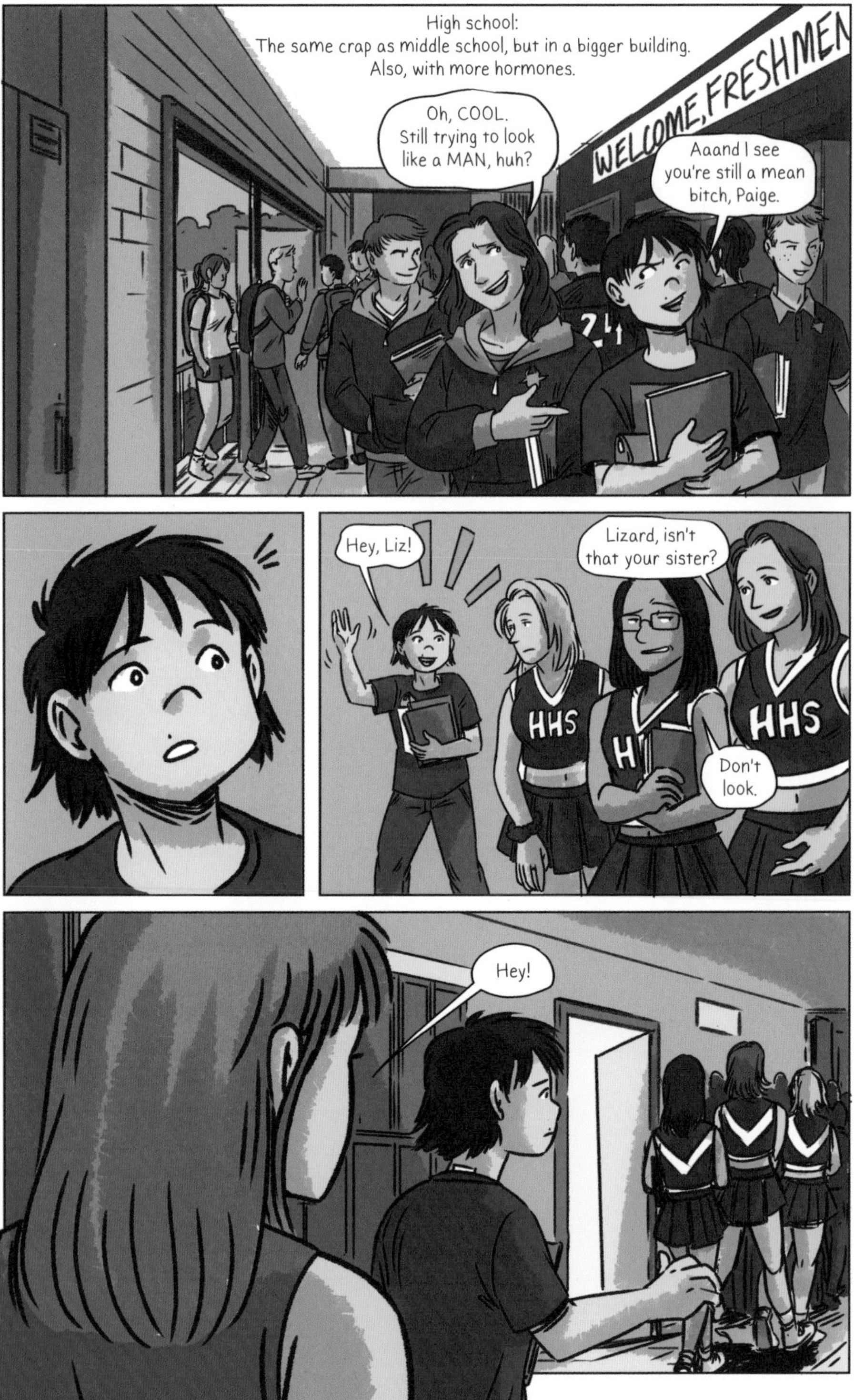
High school:
The same crap as middle school, but in a bigger building.
Also, with more hormones.
WELCOME, FRESHMEN
Oh, COOL. Still trying to look like a MAN, huh?
Aaand I see you're still a mean bitch, Paige.
Hey, Liz!
Lizard, isn't that your sister?
HHS
HHS
Don't look.
Hey!

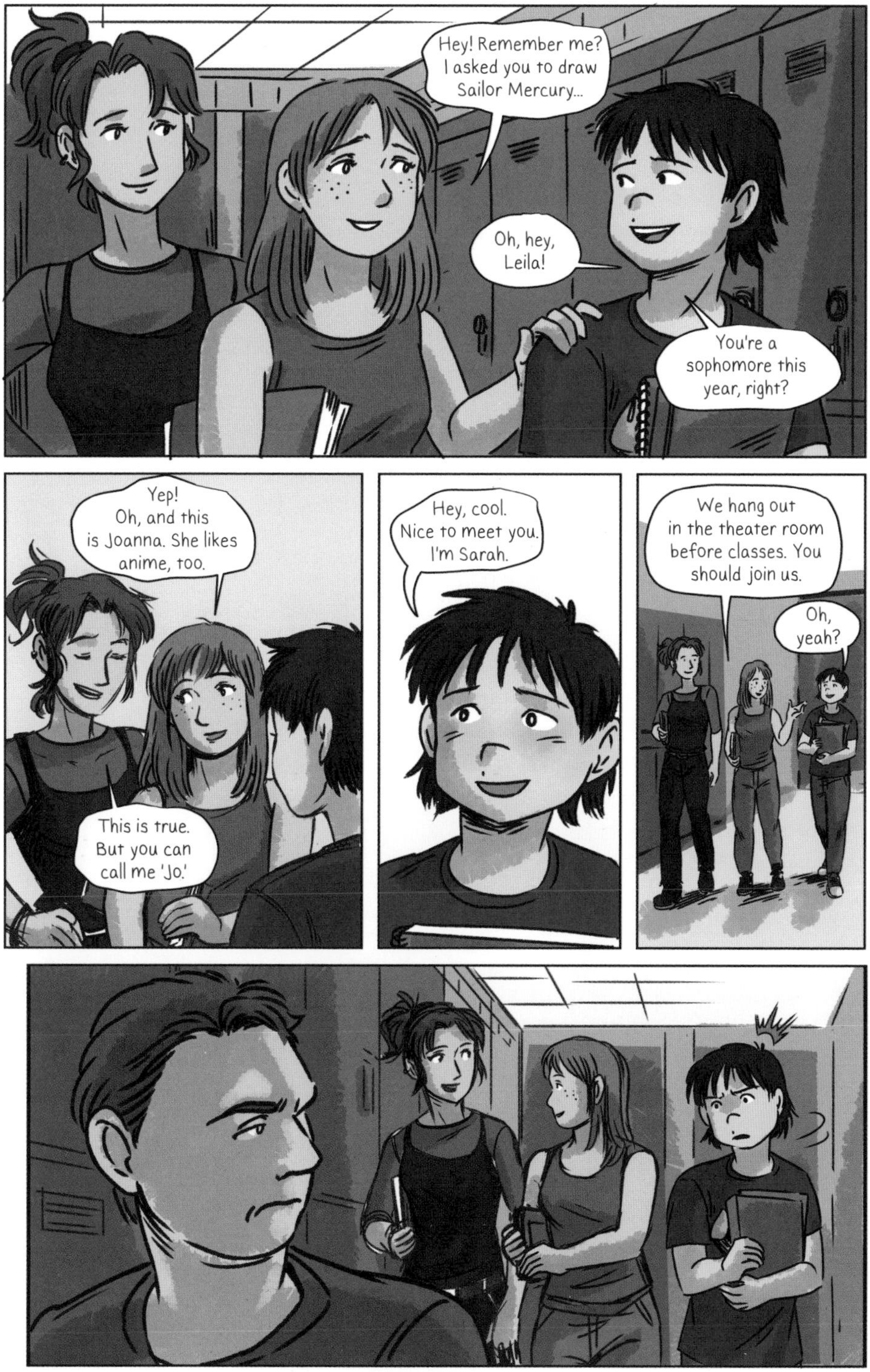
Hey! Remember me? I asked you to draw Sailor Mercury...
Oh, hey, Leila!
You're a sophomore this year, right?
Yep! Oh, and this is Joanna. She likes anime, too.
This is true. But you can call me 'Jo.'
Hey, cool. Nice to meet you. I'm Sarah.
We hang out in the theater room before classes. You should join us.
Oh, yeah?

Seeing Calvin again really hurt.

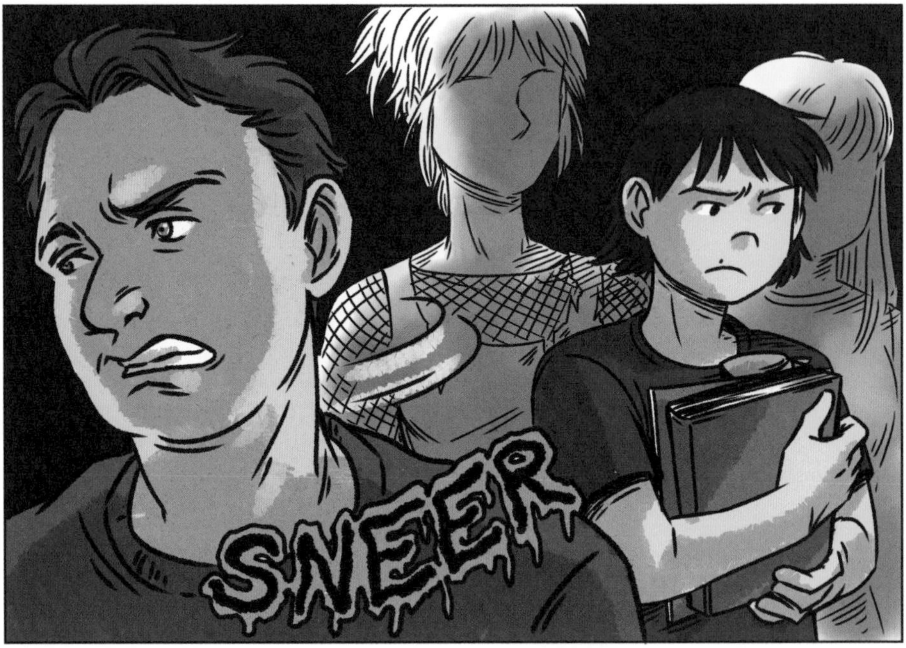
SNEER

Deep down, I wanted to tell him about how much fun I had going to Otakon in my Ash Ketchum costume.

I wanted to ask him what happened to make him hate *Pokémon*, what made him decide I was subhuman.

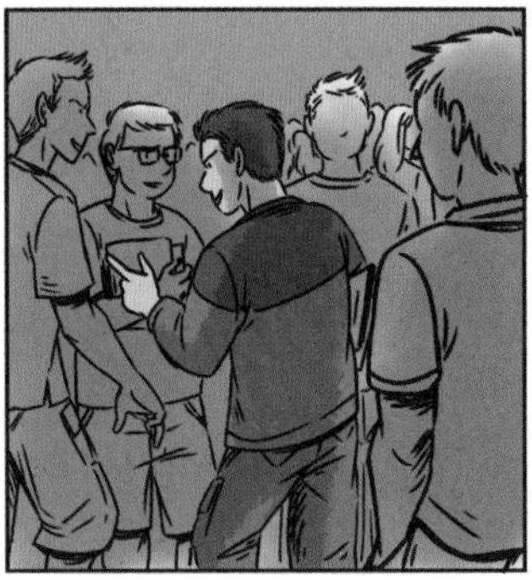

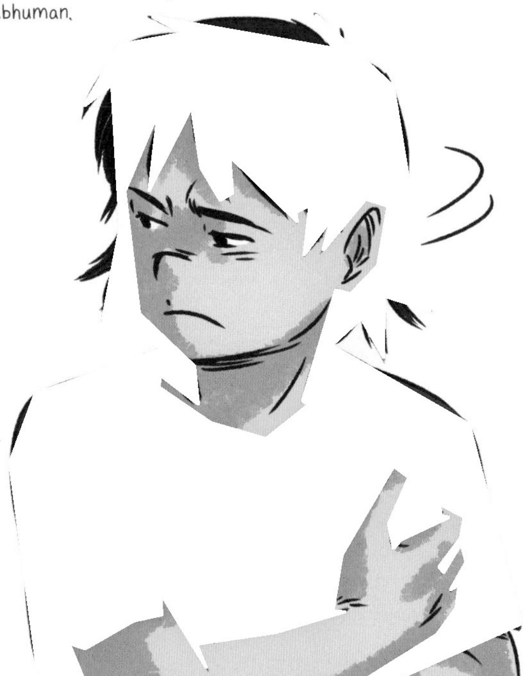

But seeing him again just made me feel shame.

Not just because I'd hit him.

I think he may have been my first crush.

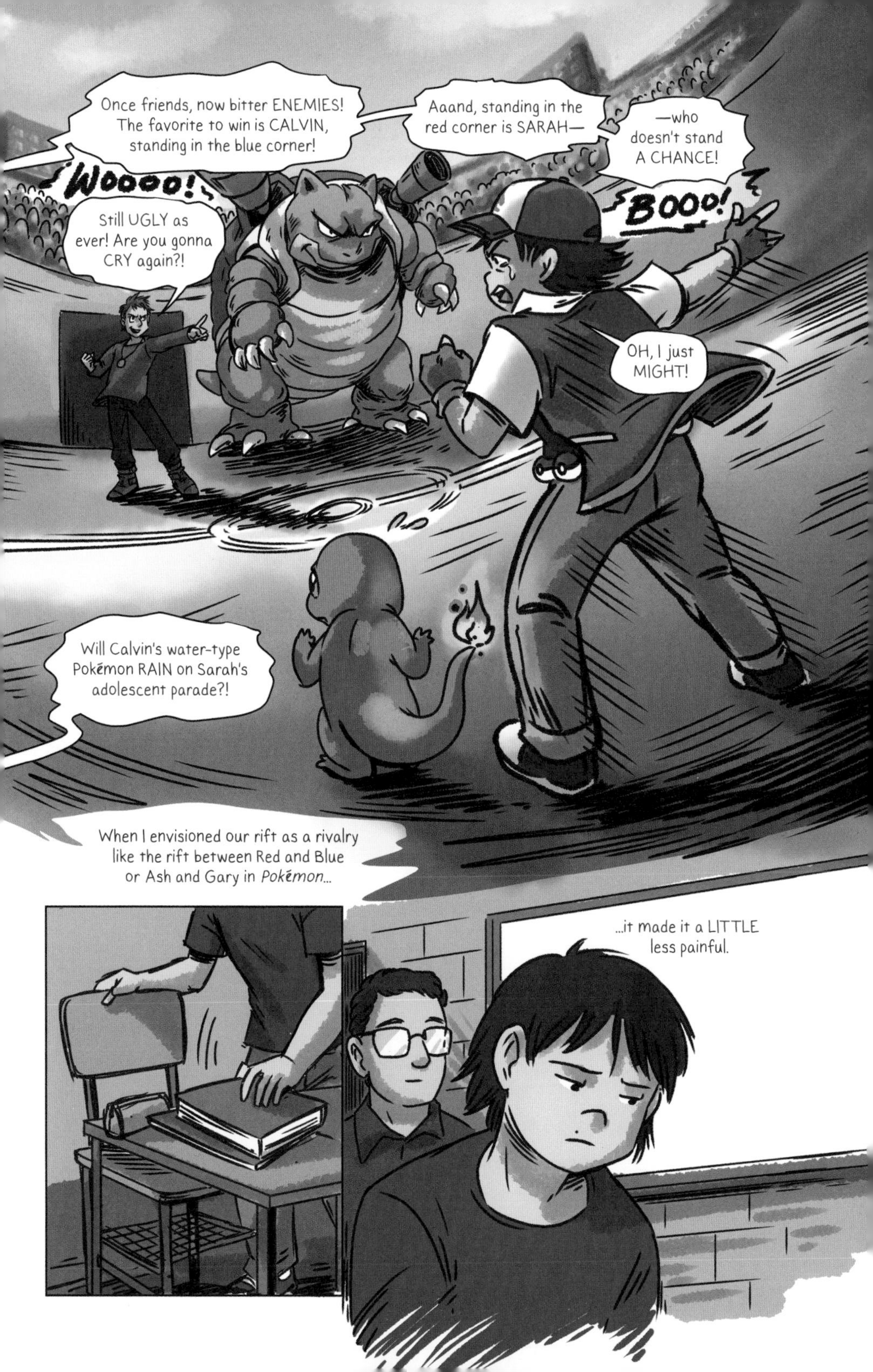
Once friends, now bitter ENEMIES! The favorite to win is CALVIN, standing in the blue corner!
Aaand, standing in the red corner is SARAH—
—who doesn't stand A CHANCE!
WOOOO!
BOOO!
Still UGLY as ever! Are you gonna CRY again?!
OH, I just MIGHT!
Will Calvin's water-type Pokémon RAIN on Sarah's adolescent parade?!
When I envisioned our rift as a rivalry like the rift between Red and Blue or Ash and Gary in *Pokémon*...
...it made it a LITTLE less painful.

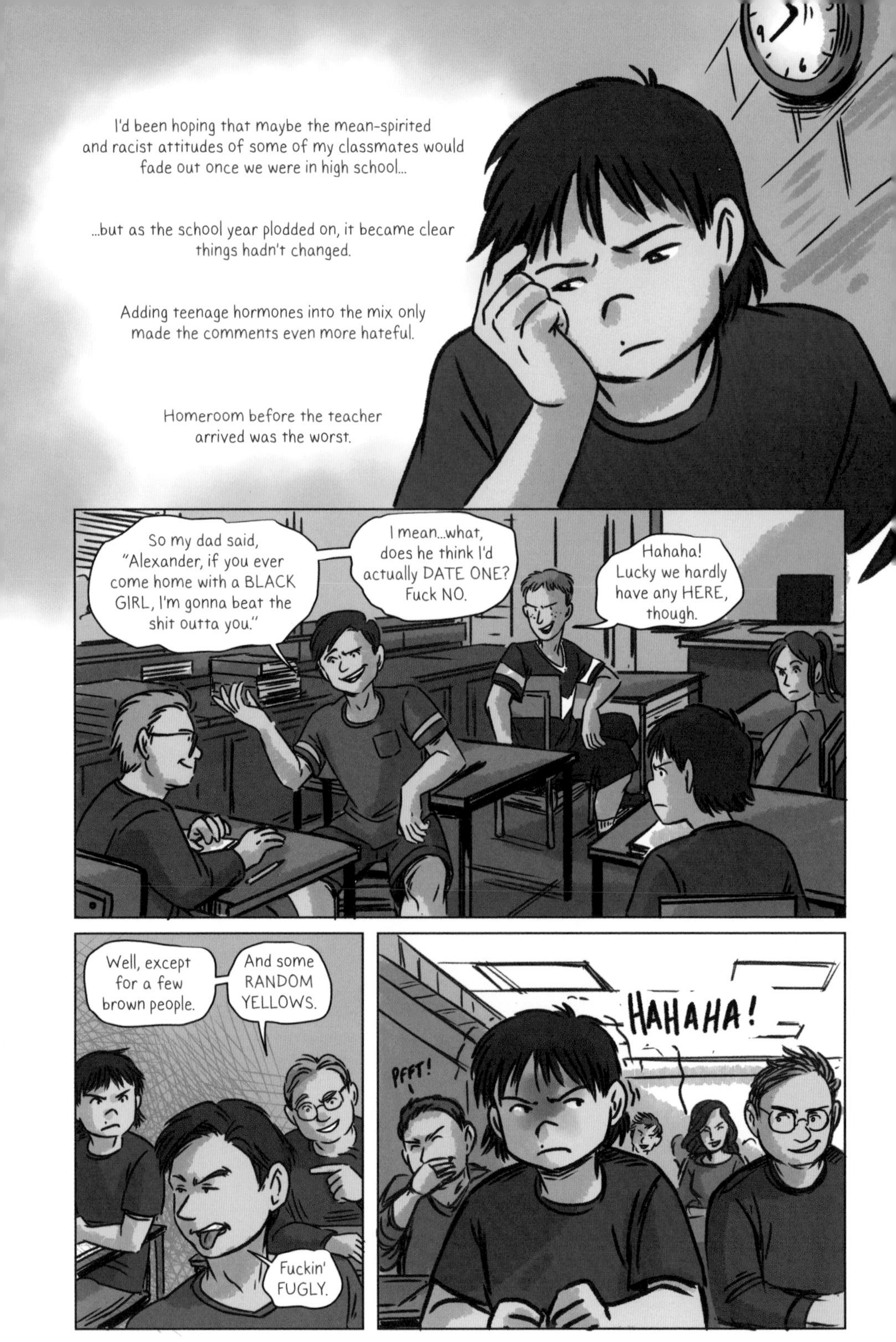
I'd been hoping that maybe the mean-spirited and racist attitudes of some of my classmates would fade out once we were in high school...
...but as the school year plodded on, it became clear things hadn't changed.
Adding teenage hormones into the mix only made the comments even more hateful.
Homeroom before the teacher arrived was the worst.
So my dad said, "Alexander, if you ever come home with a BLACK GIRL, I'm gonna beat the shit outta you."
I mean...what, does he think I'd actually DATE ONE? Fuck NO.
Hahaha! Lucky we hardly have any HERE, though.
Well, except for a few brown people.
And some RANDOM YELLOWS.
Fuckin' FUGLY.
PFFT!
HAHAHA!

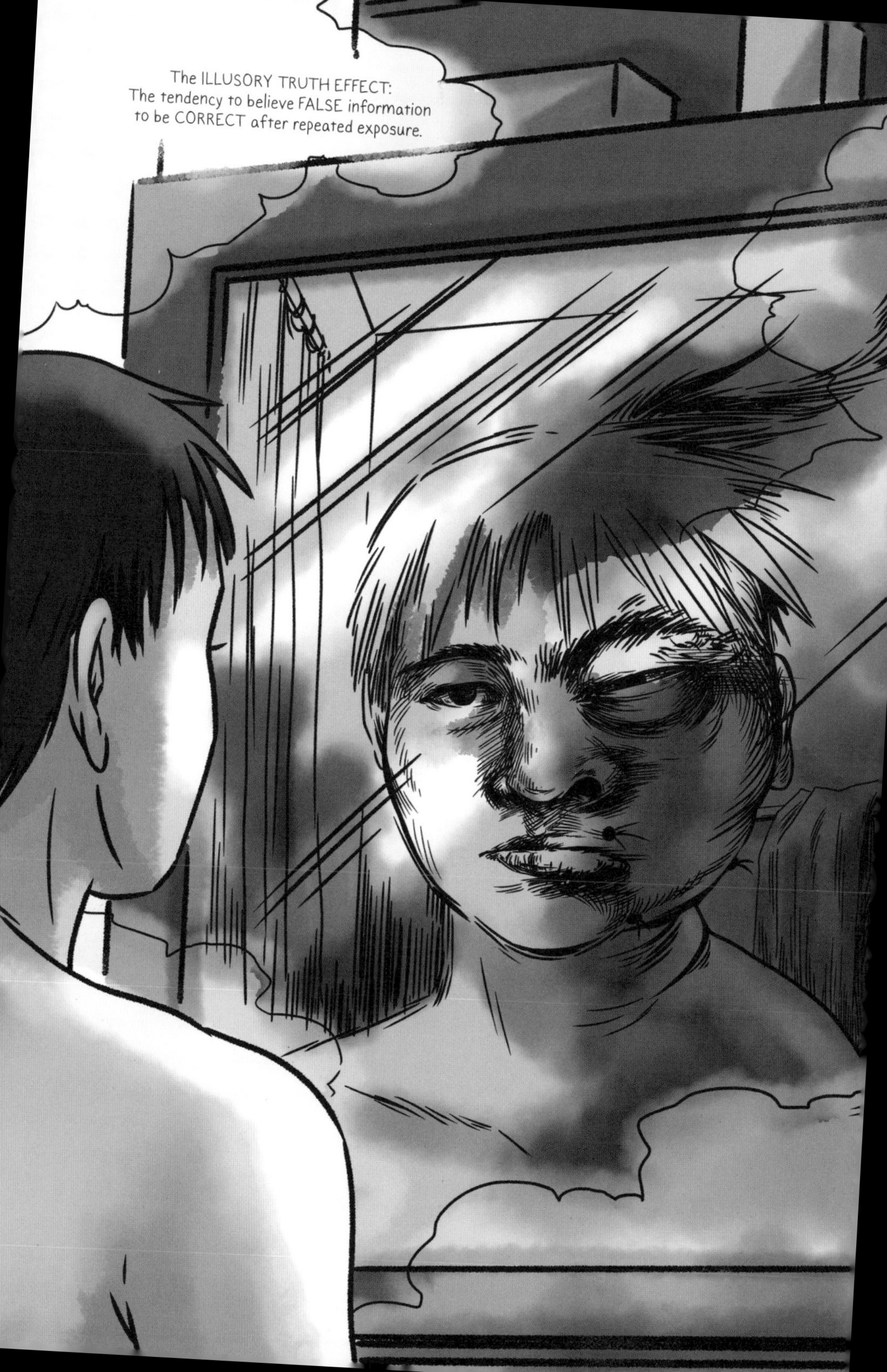
The ILLUSORY TRUTH EFFECT:
The tendency to believe FALSE information
to be CORRECT after repeated exposure.

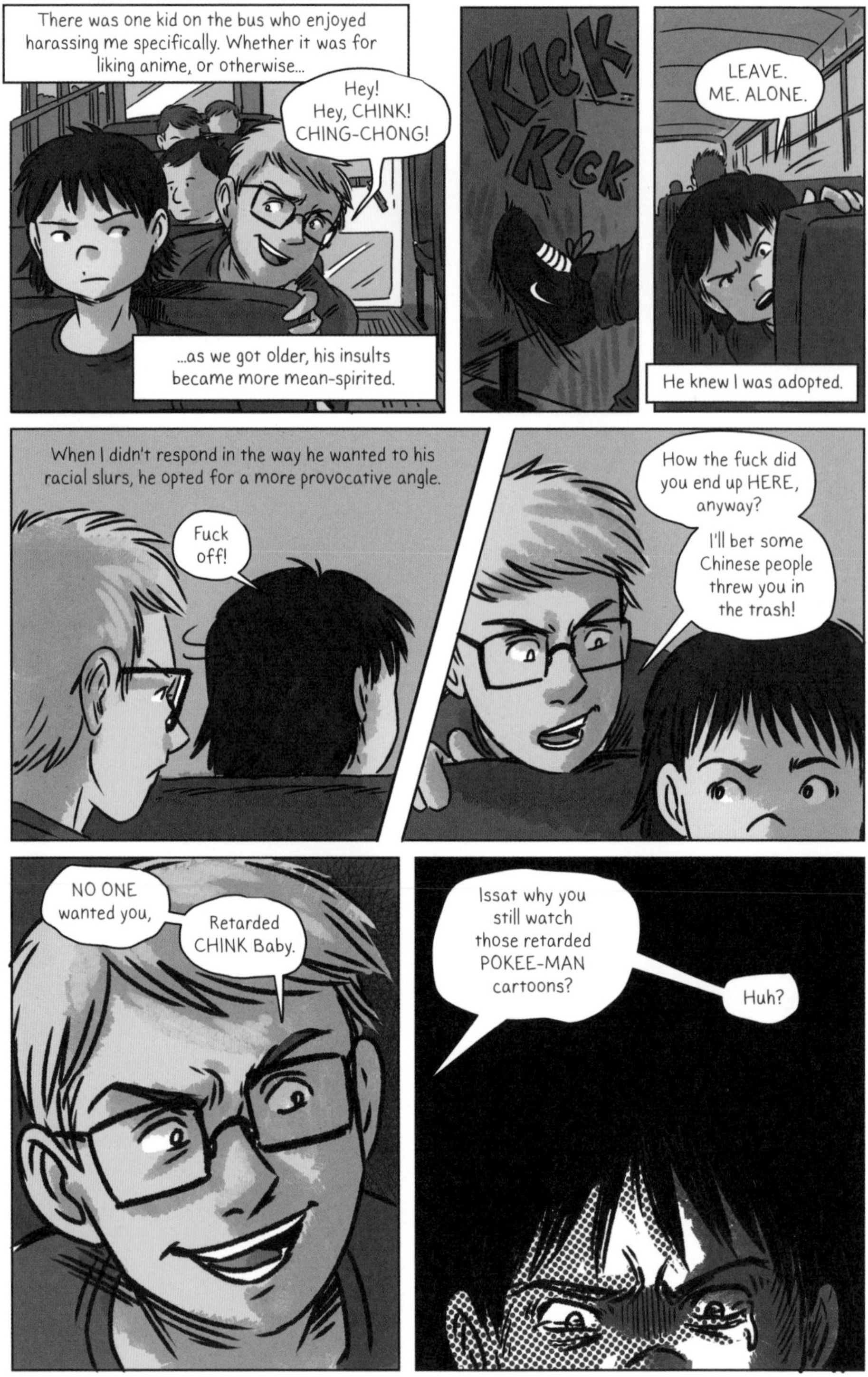
There was one kid on the bus who enjoyed harassing me specifically. Whether it was for liking anime, or otherwise...
Hey! Hey, CHINK! CHING-CHONG!
...as we got older, his insults became more mean-spirited.
KICK
KICK
LEAVE. ME. ALONE.
He knew I was adopted.
When I didn't respond in the way he wanted to his racial slurs, he opted for a more provocative angle.
Fuck off!
How the fuck did you end up HERE, anyway?
I'll bet some Chinese people threw you in the trash!
NO ONE wanted you,
Retarded CHINK Baby.
Issat why you still watch those retarded POKEE-MAN cartoons?
Huh?

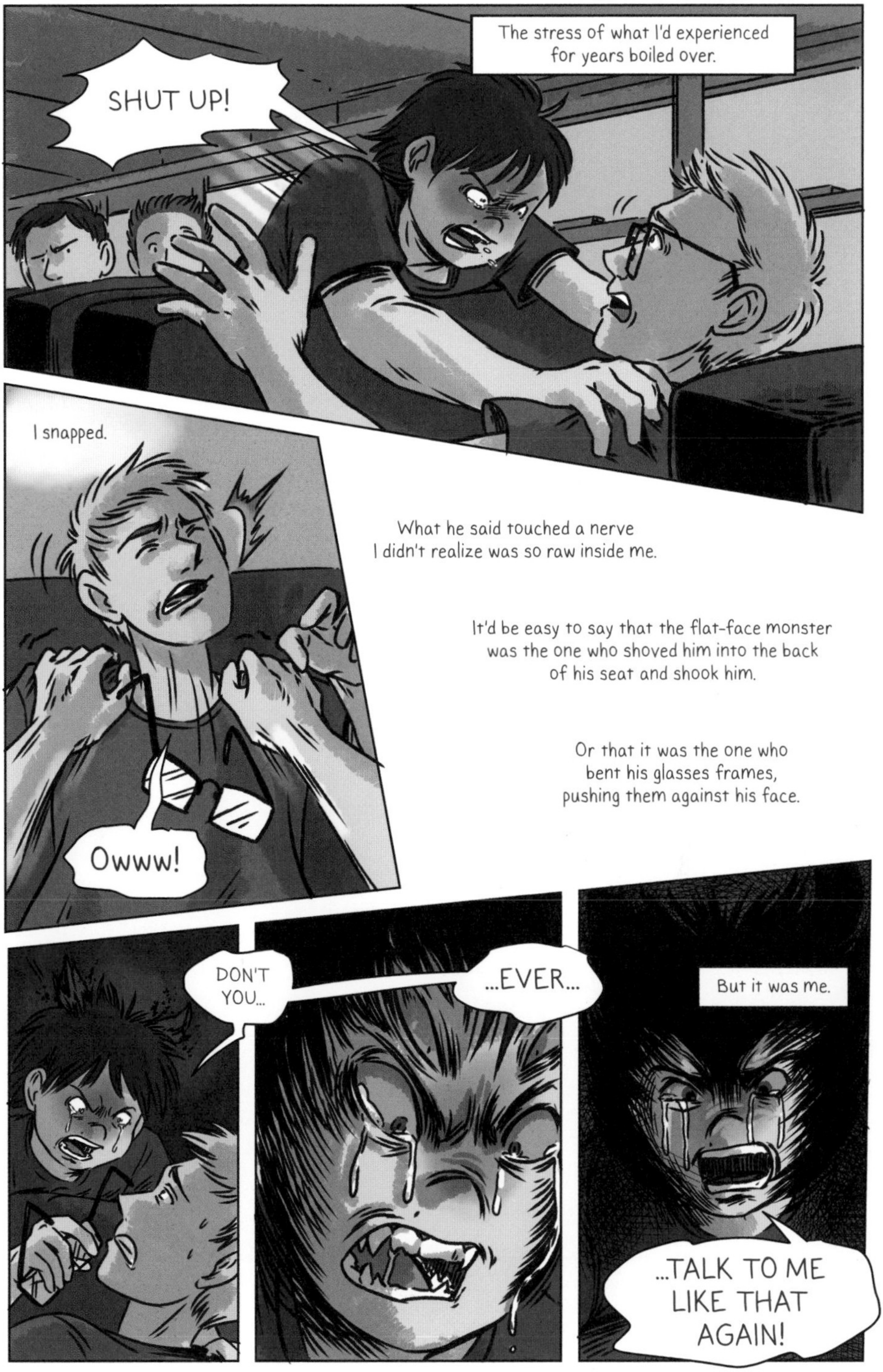
The stress of what I'd experienced for years boiled over.
SHUT UP!
I snapped.
What he said touched a nerve I didn't realize was so raw inside me.
It'd be easy to say that the flat-face monster was the one who shoved him into the back of his seat and shook him.
Or that it was the one who bent his glasses frames, pushing them against his face.
Owww!
DON'T YOU...
...EVER...
But it was me.
...TALK TO ME LIKE THAT AGAIN!

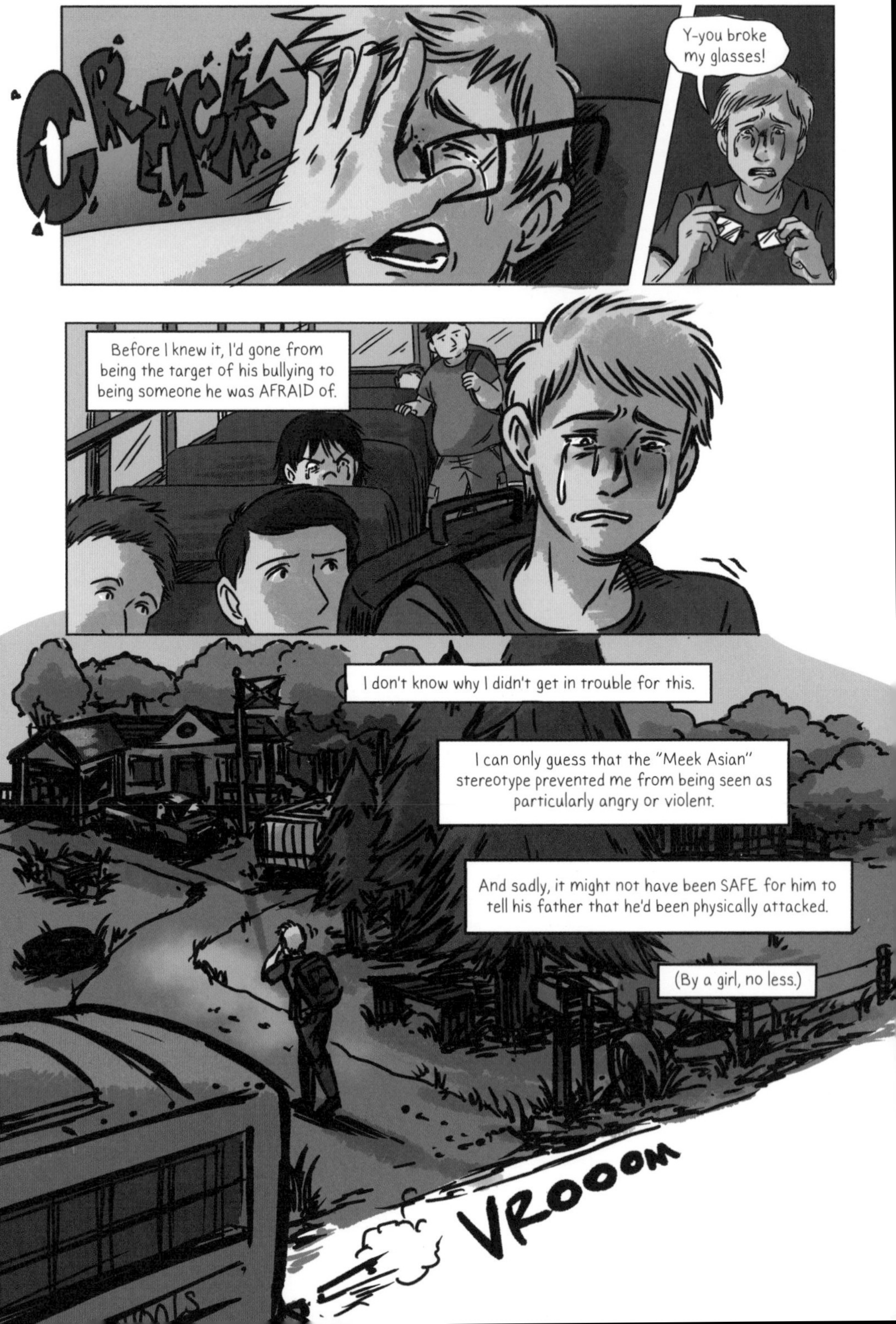
CRACK
Y-you broke my glasses!
Before I knew it, I'd gone from being the target of his bullying to being someone he was AFRAID of.
I don't know why I didn't get in trouble for this.
I can only guess that the "Meek Asian" stereotype prevented me from being seen as particularly angry or violent.
And sadly, it might not have been SAFE for him to tell his father that he'd been physically attacked.
(By a girl, no less.)
VROOOM

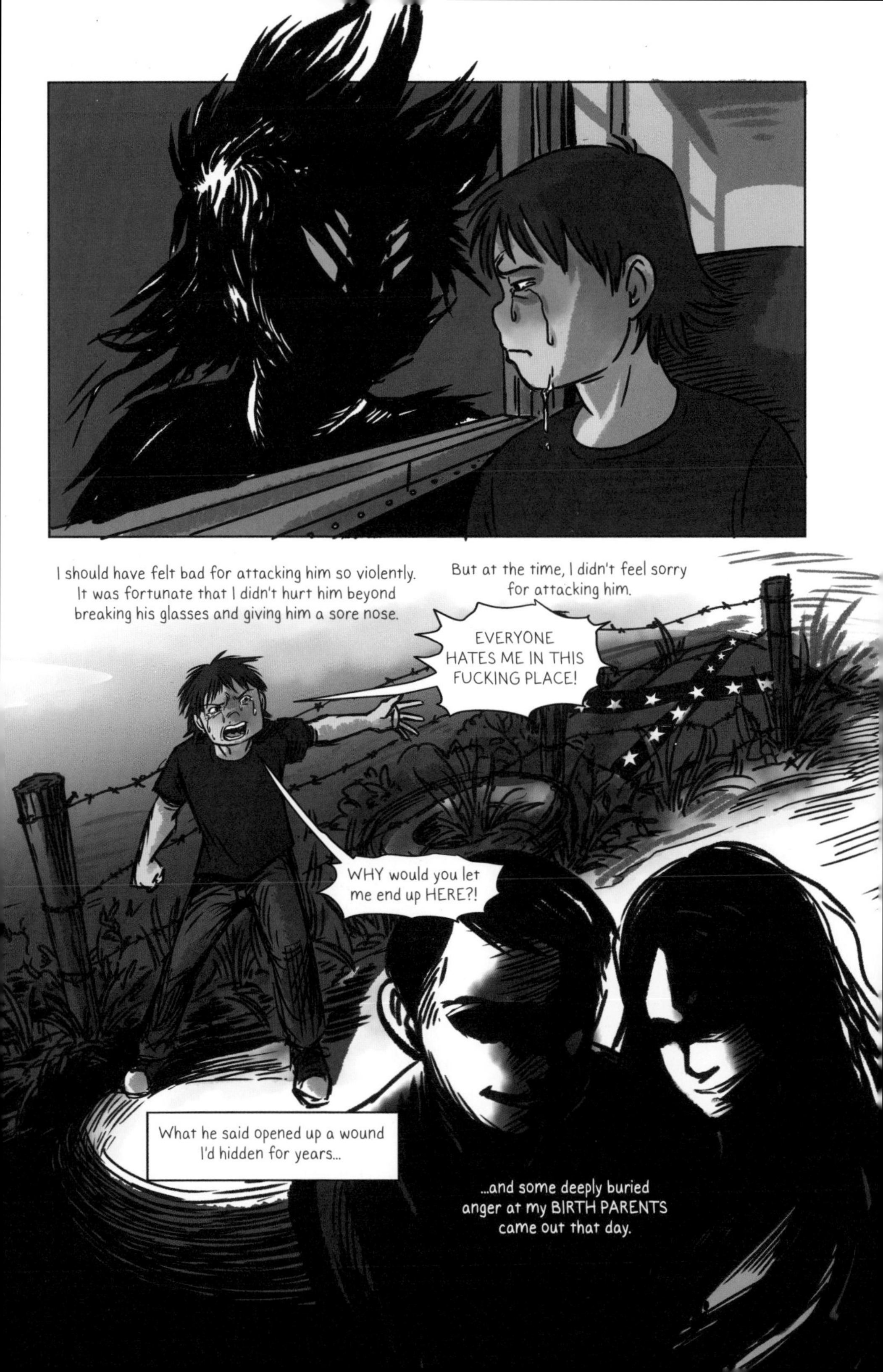
I should have felt bad for attacking him so violently. It was fortunate that I didn't hurt him beyond breaking his glasses and giving him a sore nose.
But at the time, I didn't feel sorry for attacking him.
EVERYONE HATES ME IN THIS FUCKING PLACE!
WHY would you let me end up HERE?!
What he said opened up a wound I'd hidden for years...
...and some deeply buried anger at my BIRTH PARENTS came out that day.

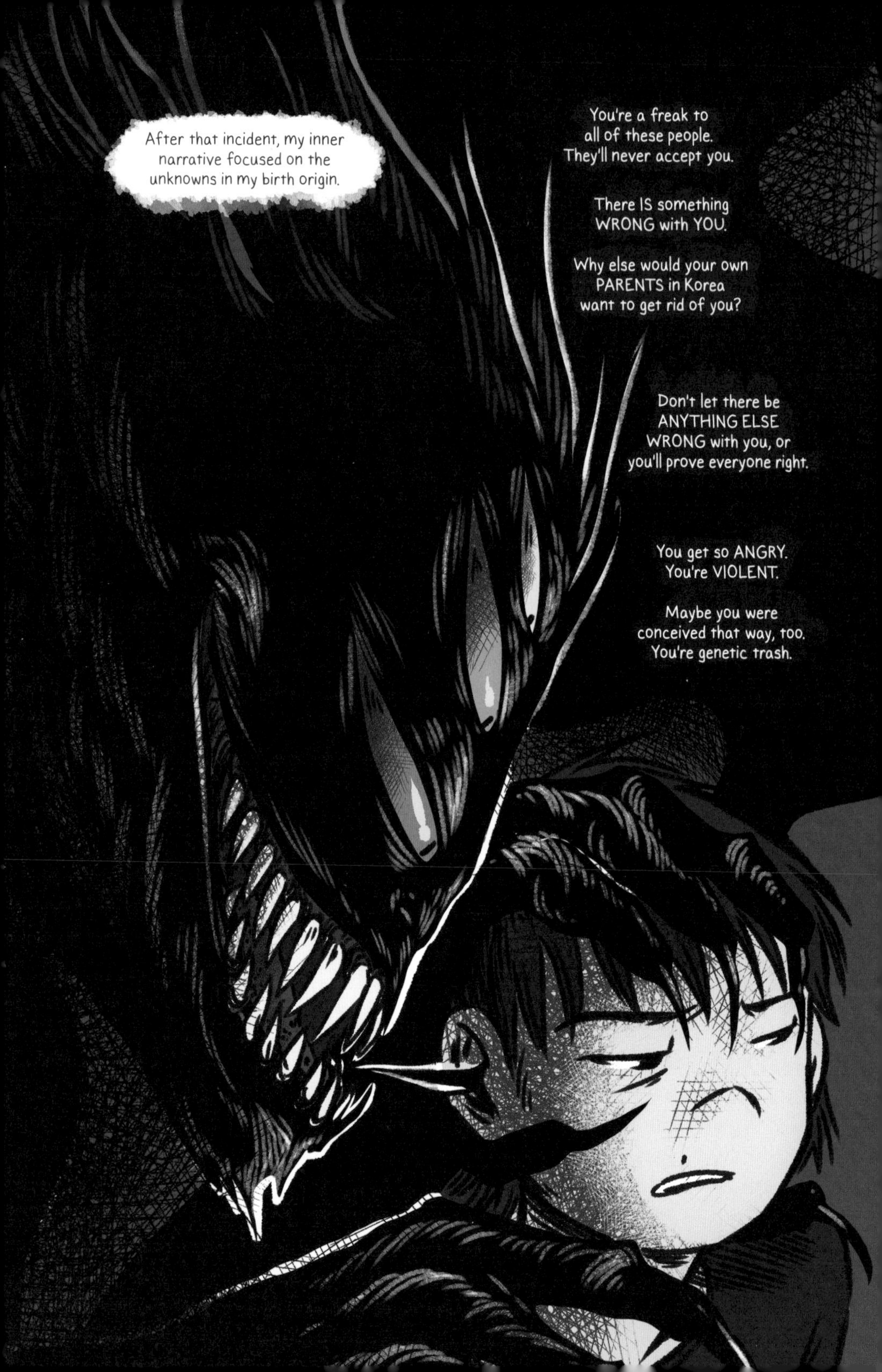
After that incident, my inner narrative focused on the unknowns in my birth origin.
You're a freak to all of these people. They'll never accept you.
There IS something WRONG with YOU.
Why else would your own PARENTS in Korea want to get rid of you?
Don't let there be ANYTHING ELSE WRONG with you, or you'll prove everyone right.
You get so ANGRY. You're VIOLENT.
Maybe you were conceived that way, too. You're genetic trash.

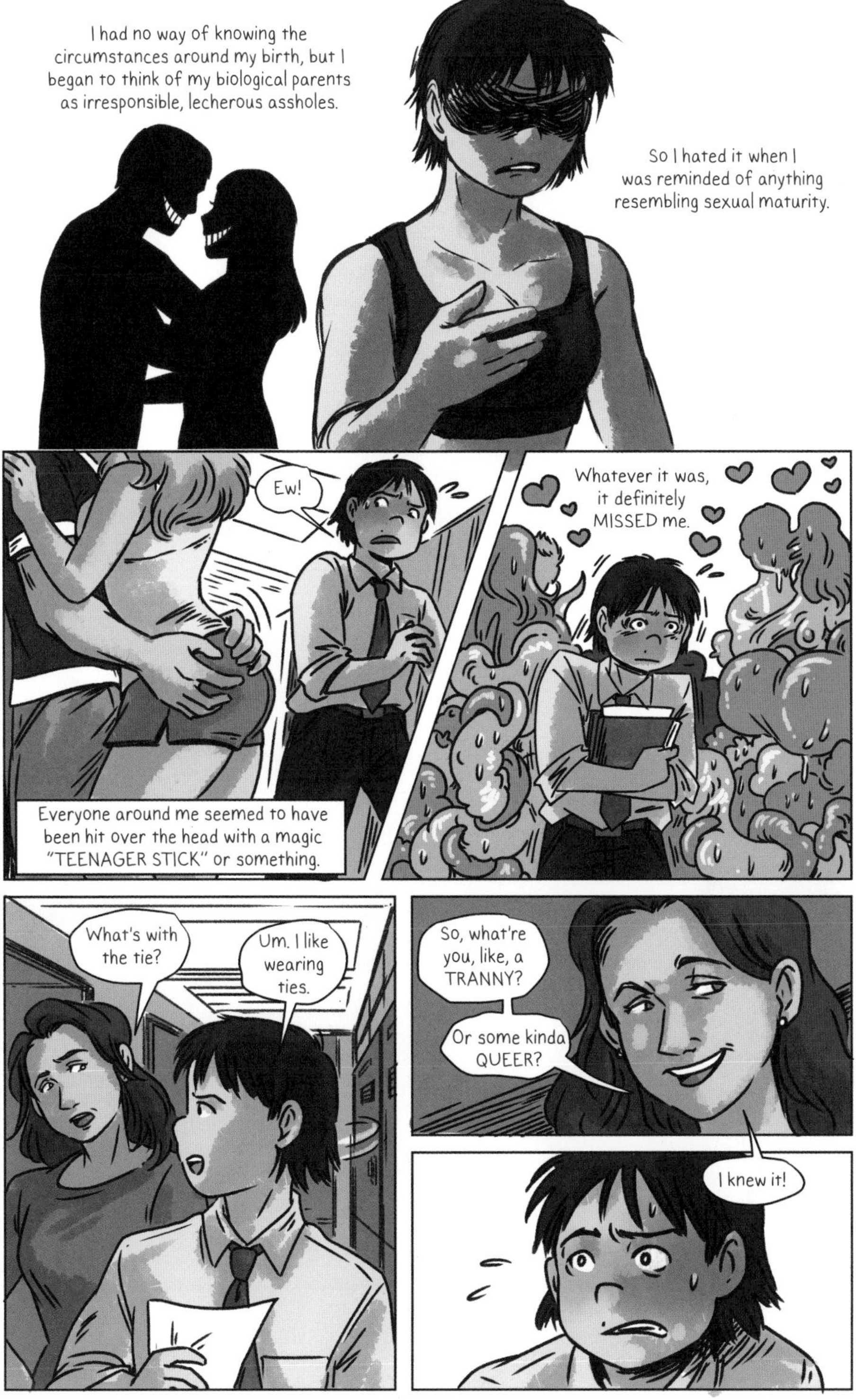
I had no way of knowing the circumstances around my birth, but I began to think of my biological parents as irresponsible, lecherous assholes.
So I hated it when I was reminded of anything resembling sexual maturity.
Ew!
Everyone around me seemed to have been hit over the head with a magic "TEENAGER STICK" or something.
Whatever it was, it definitely MISSED me.
What's with the tie?
Um. I like wearing ties.
So, what're you, like, a TRANNY?
Or some kinda QUEER?
I knew it!

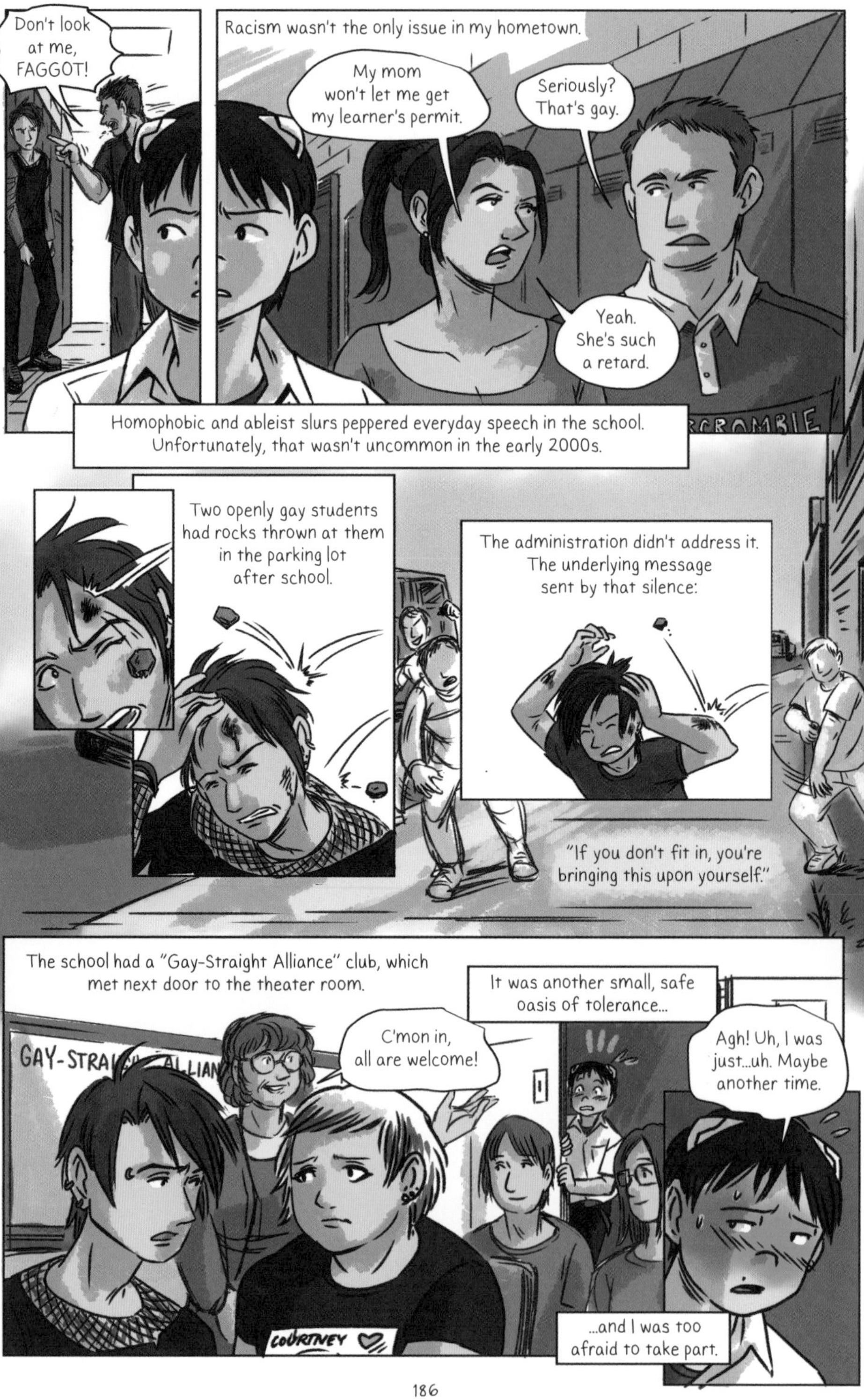
Don't look at me, FAGGOT!
Racism wasn't the only issue in my hometown.
My mom won't let me get my learner's permit.
Seriously? That's gay.
Yeah. She's such a retard.
RCROMBIE
Homophobic and ableist slurs peppered everyday speech in the school. Unfortunately, that wasn't uncommon in the early 2000s.
Two openly gay students had rocks thrown at them in the parking lot after school.
The administration didn't address it. The underlying message sent by that silence:
"If you don't fit in, you're bringing this upon yourself."
The school had a "Gay-Straight Alliance" club, which met next door to the theater room.
It was another small, safe oasis of tolerance...
C'mon in, all are welcome!
Agh! Uh, I was just...uh. Maybe another time.
...and I was too afraid to take part.
COURTNEY

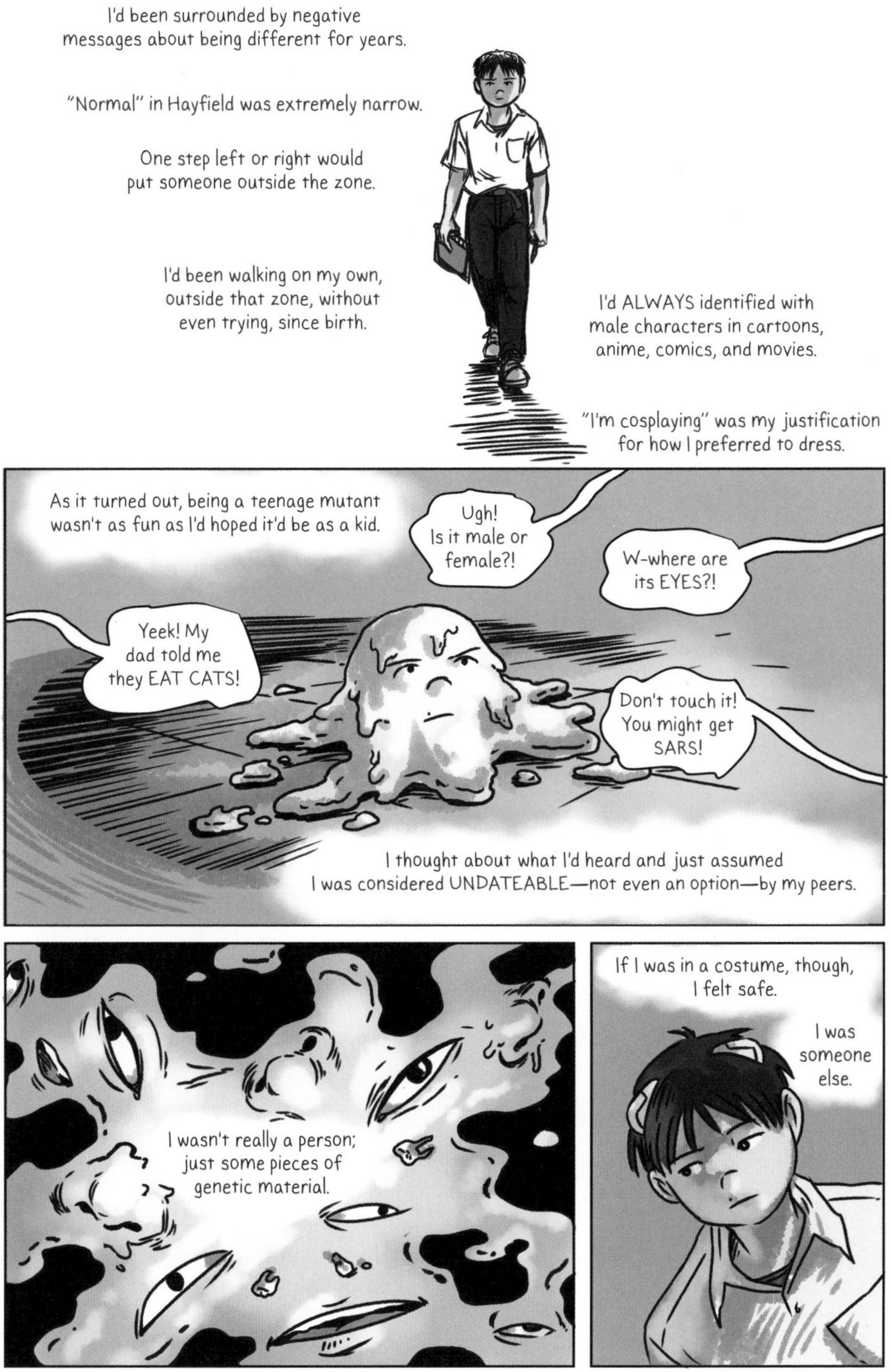
I'd been surrounded by negative messages about being different for years.
"Normal" in Hayfield was extremely narrow.
One step left or right would put someone outside the zone.
I'd been walking on my own, outside that zone, without even trying, since birth.
I'd ALWAYS identified with male characters in cartoons, anime, comics, and movies.
"I'm cosplaying" was my justification for how I preferred to dress.
As it turned out, being a teenage mutant wasn't as fun as I'd hoped it'd be as a kid.
Ugh! Is it male or female?!
W-where are its EYES?!
Yeek! My dad told me they EAT CATS!
Don't touch it! You might get SARS!
I thought about what I'd heard and just assumed I was considered UNDATEABLE—not even an option—by my peers.
I wasn't really a person; just some pieces of genetic material.
If I was in a costume, though, I felt safe.
I was someone else.

The theater room quickly became my before-and-after-class hangout spot.

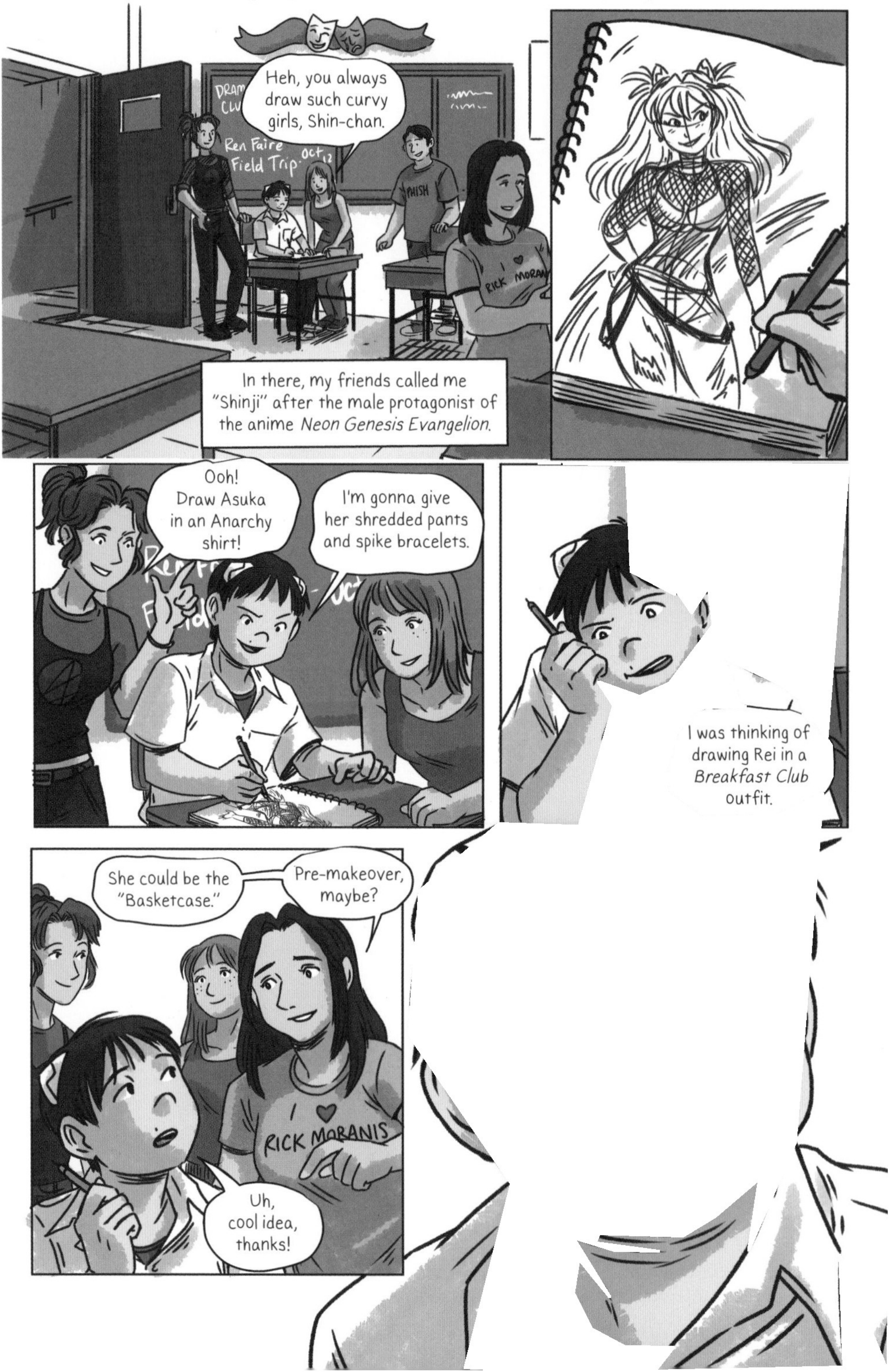
Heh, you always draw such curvy girls, Shin-chan.
Ren Faire Field Trip Oct 12
PHISH
I ♥ RICK MORANIS
In there, my friends called me "Shinji" after the male protagonist of the anime *Neon Genesis Evangelion*.
Ooh! Draw Asuka in an Anarchy shirt!
I'm gonna give her shredded pants and spike bracelets.
I was thinking of drawing Rei in a *Breakfast Club* outfit.
She could be the "Basketcase."
Pre-makeover, maybe?
Uh, cool idea, thanks!

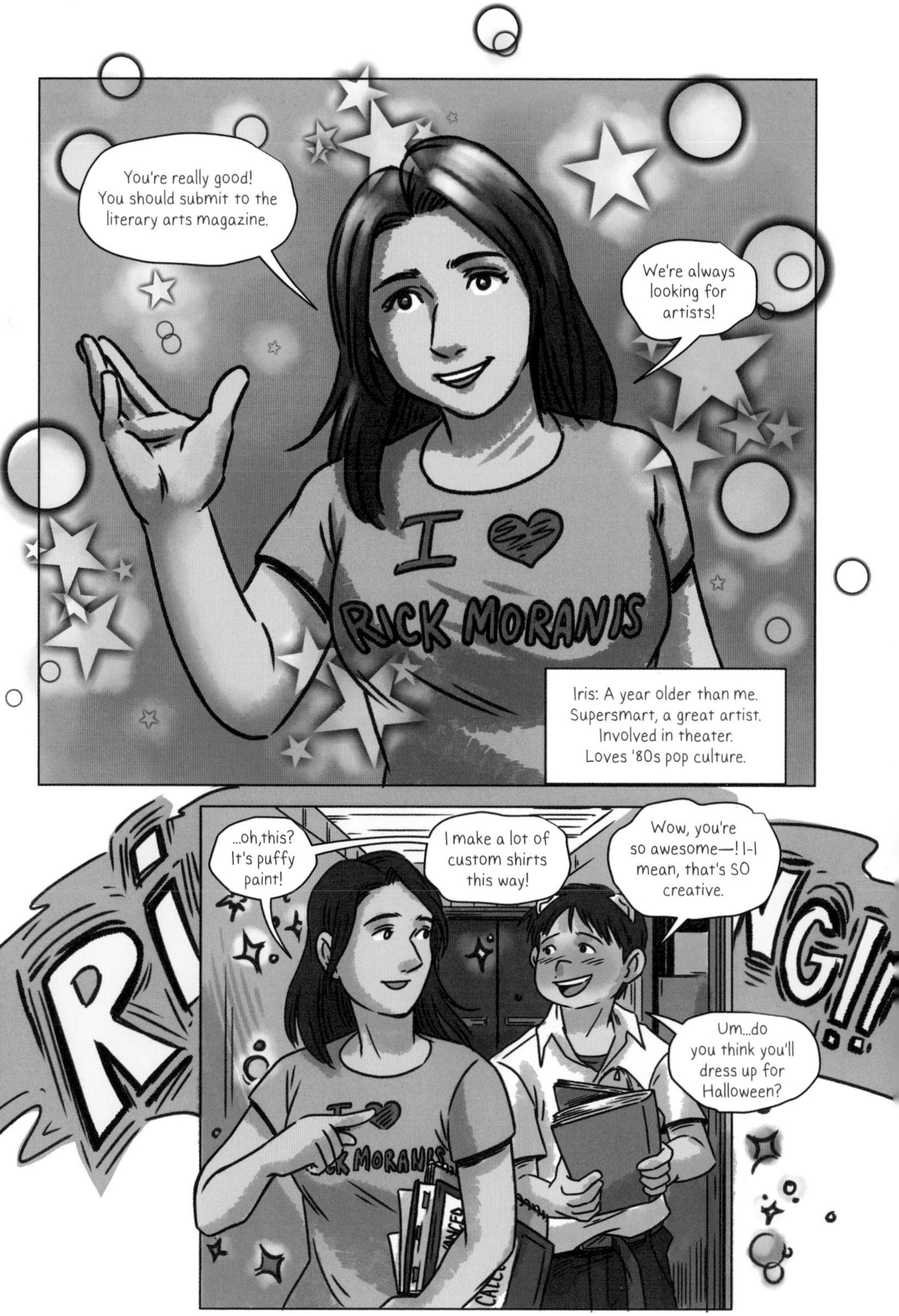
You're really good! You should submit to the literary arts magazine.
We're always looking for artists!
I ♥ RICK MORANIS
Iris: A year older than me. Supersmart, a great artist. Involved in theater. Loves '80s pop culture.
...oh,this? It's puffy paint!
I make a lot of custom shirts this way!
Wow, you're so awesome—! I-I mean, that's SO creative.
Um...do you think you'll dress up for Halloween?

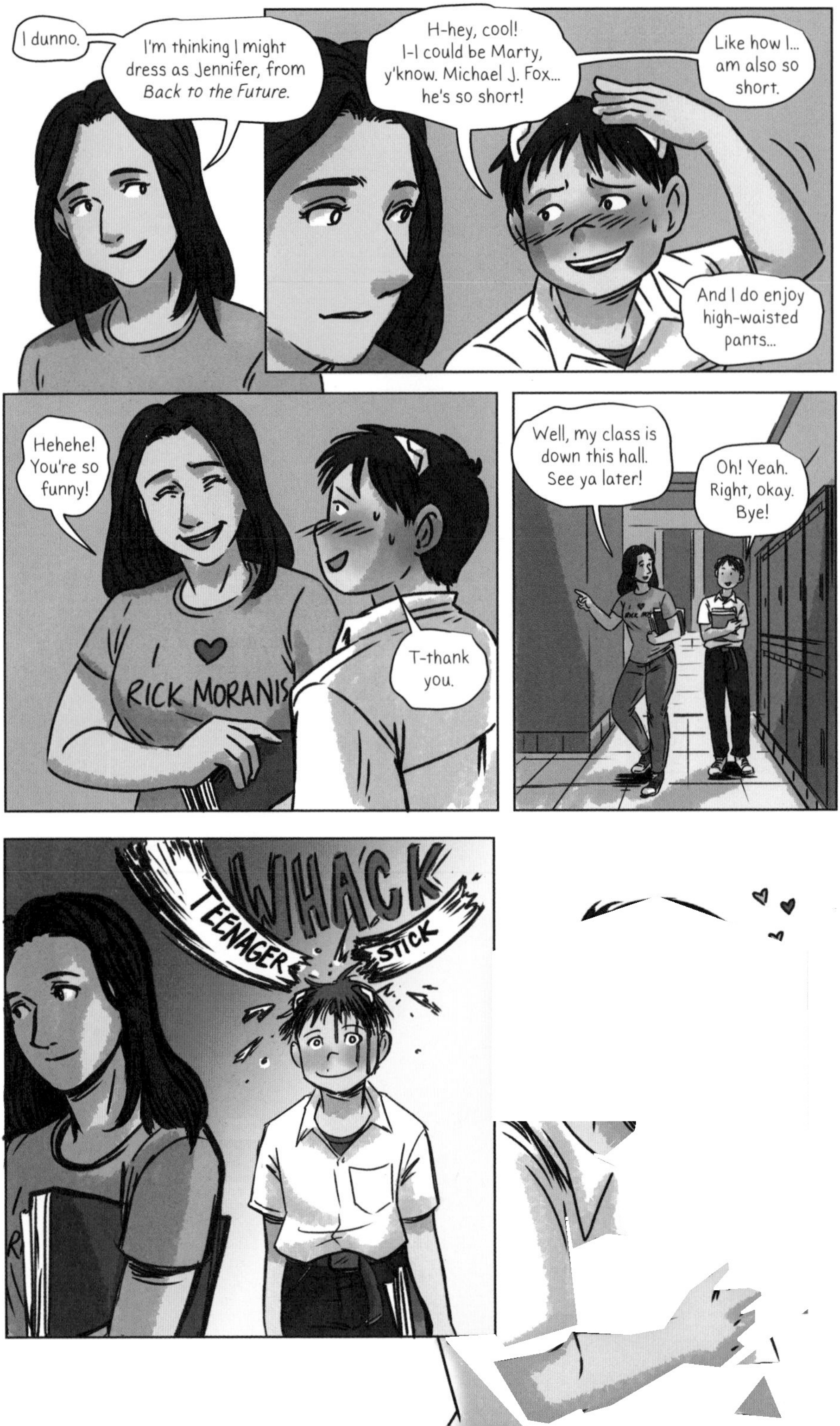
I dunno.
I'm thinking I might dress as Jennifer, from *Back to the Future*.
H-hey, cool! I-I could be Marty, y'know. Michael J. Fox... he's so short!
Like how I... am also so short.
And I do enjoy high-waisted pants...
Hehehe! You're so funny!
I ♥ RICK MORANIS
T-thank you.
Well, my class is down this hall. See ya later!
Oh! Yeah. Right, okay. Bye!
WHACK
TEENAGER STICK

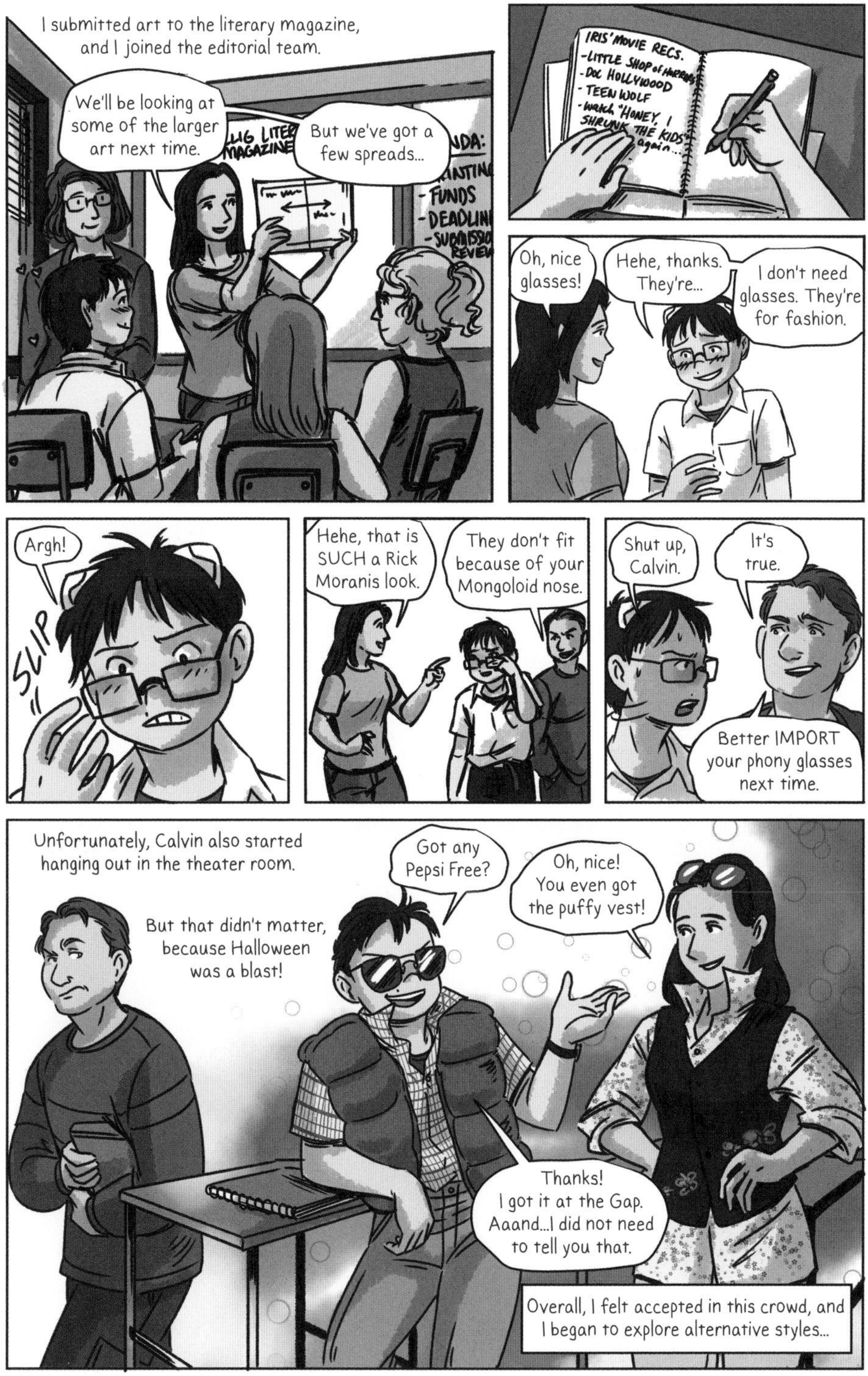
I submitted art to the literary magazine, and I joined the editorial team.
We'll be looking at some of the larger art next time.
But we've got a few spreads...
IRIS' MOVIE RECS.
-LITTLE SHOP of HORRORS
-DOC HOLLYWOOD
-TEEN WOLF
-watch "HONEY, I SHRUNK THE KIDS" again...
Oh, nice glasses!
Hehe, thanks. They're...
I don't need glasses. They're for fashion.
Argh!
SLIP
Hehe, that is SUCH a Rick Moranis look.
They don't fit because of your Mongoloid nose.
Shut up, Calvin.
It's true.
Better IMPORT your phony glasses next time.
Unfortunately, Calvin also started hanging out in the theater room.
But that didn't matter, because Halloween was a blast!
Got any Pepsi Free?
Oh, nice! You even got the puffy vest!
Thanks! I got it at the Gap. Aaand...I did not need to tell you that.
Overall, I felt accepted in this crowd, and I began to explore alternative styles...

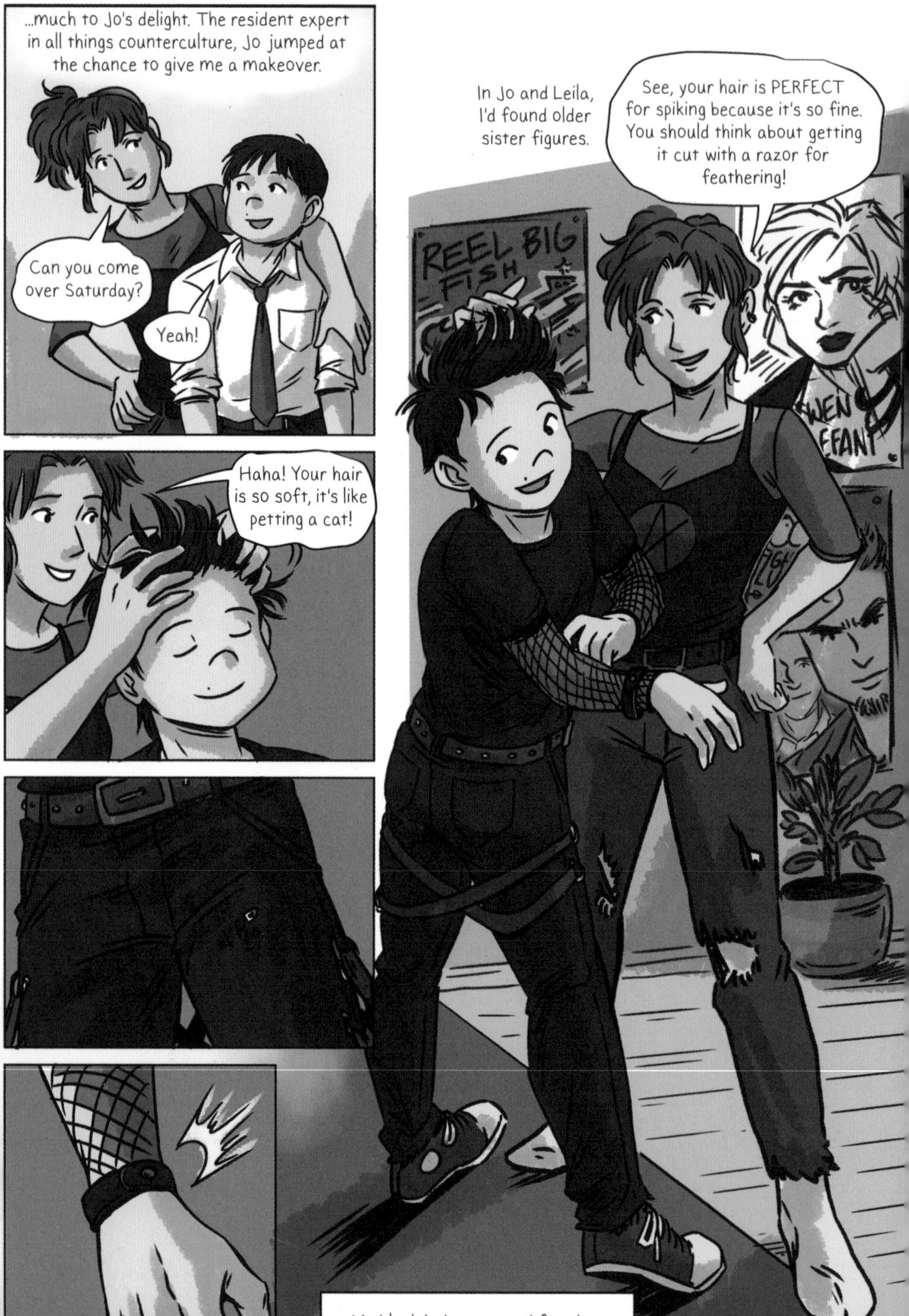
...much to Jo's delight. The resident expert in all things counterculture, Jo jumped at the chance to give me a makeover.
Can you come over Saturday?
Yeah!
Haha! Your hair is so soft, it's like petting a cat!
In Jo and Leila, I'd found older sister figures.
See, your hair is PERFECT for spiking because it's so fine. You should think about getting it cut with a razor for feathering!
REEL BIG FISH
My black hair was good for the punk rock look she had me try out.

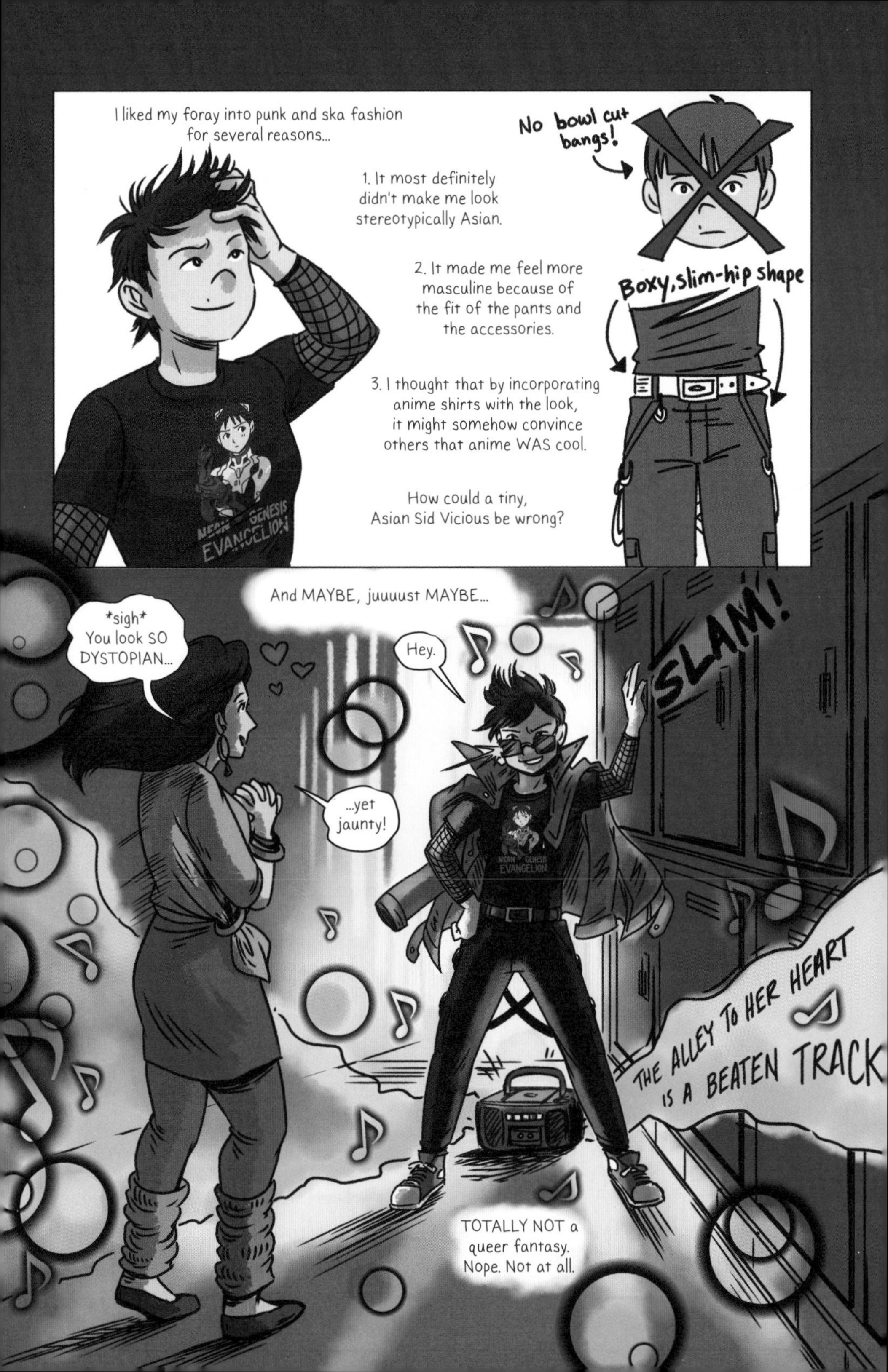
I liked my foray into punk and ska fashion for several reasons...
1. It most definitely didn't make me look stereotypically Asian.
2. It made me feel more masculine because of the fit of the pants and the accessories.
3. I thought that by incorporating anime shirts with the look, it might somehow convince others that anime WAS cool.
How could a tiny, Asian Sid Vicious be wrong?
No bowl cut bangs!
Boxy, slim-hip shape
NEON GENESIS EVANGELION
And MAYBE, juuuust MAYBE...
sigh You look SO DYSTOPIAN...
Hey.
...yet jaunty!
SLAM!
THE ALLEY TO HER HEART IS A BEATEN TRACK
TOTALLY NOT a queer fantasy. Nope. Not at all.

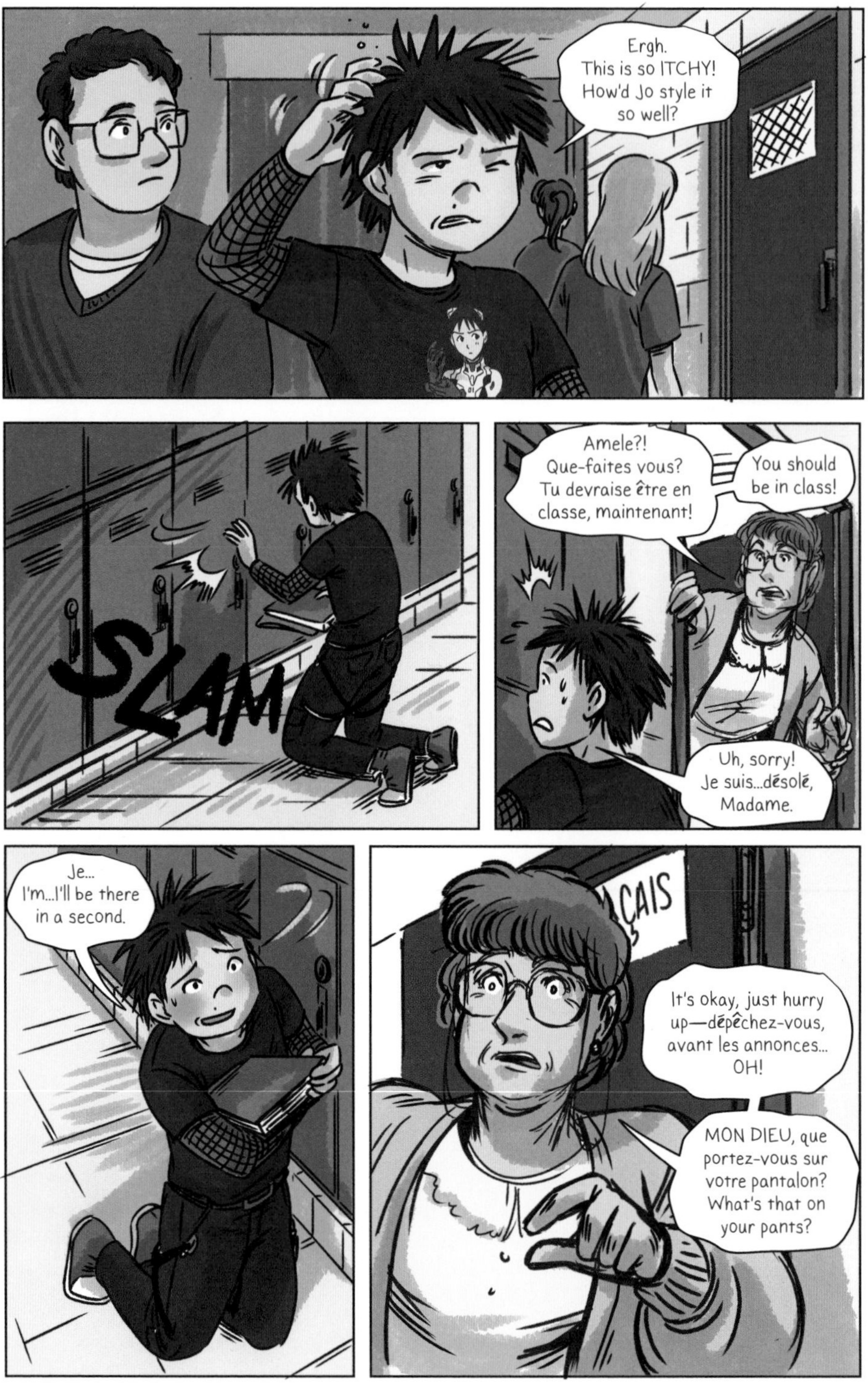
Ergh. This is so ITCHY! How'd Jo style it so well?
SLAM
Amele?! Que-faites vous? Tu devraise être en classe, maintenant!
You should be in class!
Uh, sorry! Je suis...désolé, Madame.
Je... I'm...I'll be there in a second.
ÇAIS
It's okay, just hurry up—dépêchez-vous, avant les annonces... OH!
MON DIEU, que portez-vous sur votre pantalon? What's that on your pants?

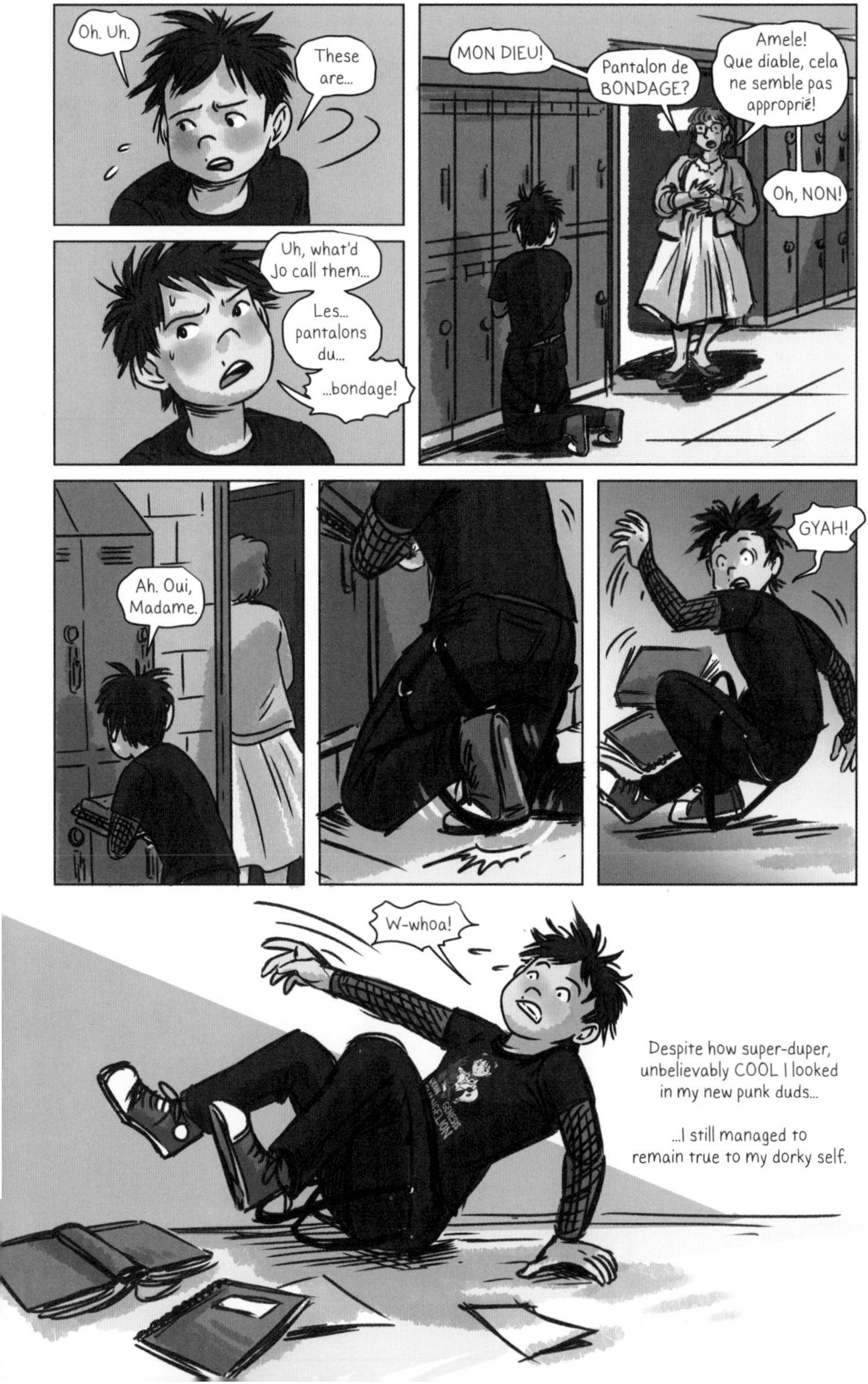

Oh. Uh.
These are...
Uh, what'd Jo call them...
Les... pantalons du...
...bondage!
MON DIEU!
Pantalon de BONDAGE?
Amele! Que diable, cela ne semble pas approprié!
Oh, NON!
Ah. Oui, Madame.
GYAH!
W-whoa!
Despite how super-duper, unbelievably COOL I looked in my new punk duds...
...I still managed to remain true to my dorky self.

But I'd soon find other ways to express my identity...because the auditions for *Les Misérables* were approaching. I'd had a few ensemble parts in theater before this year, but this was the first time I felt a specific role fit me!

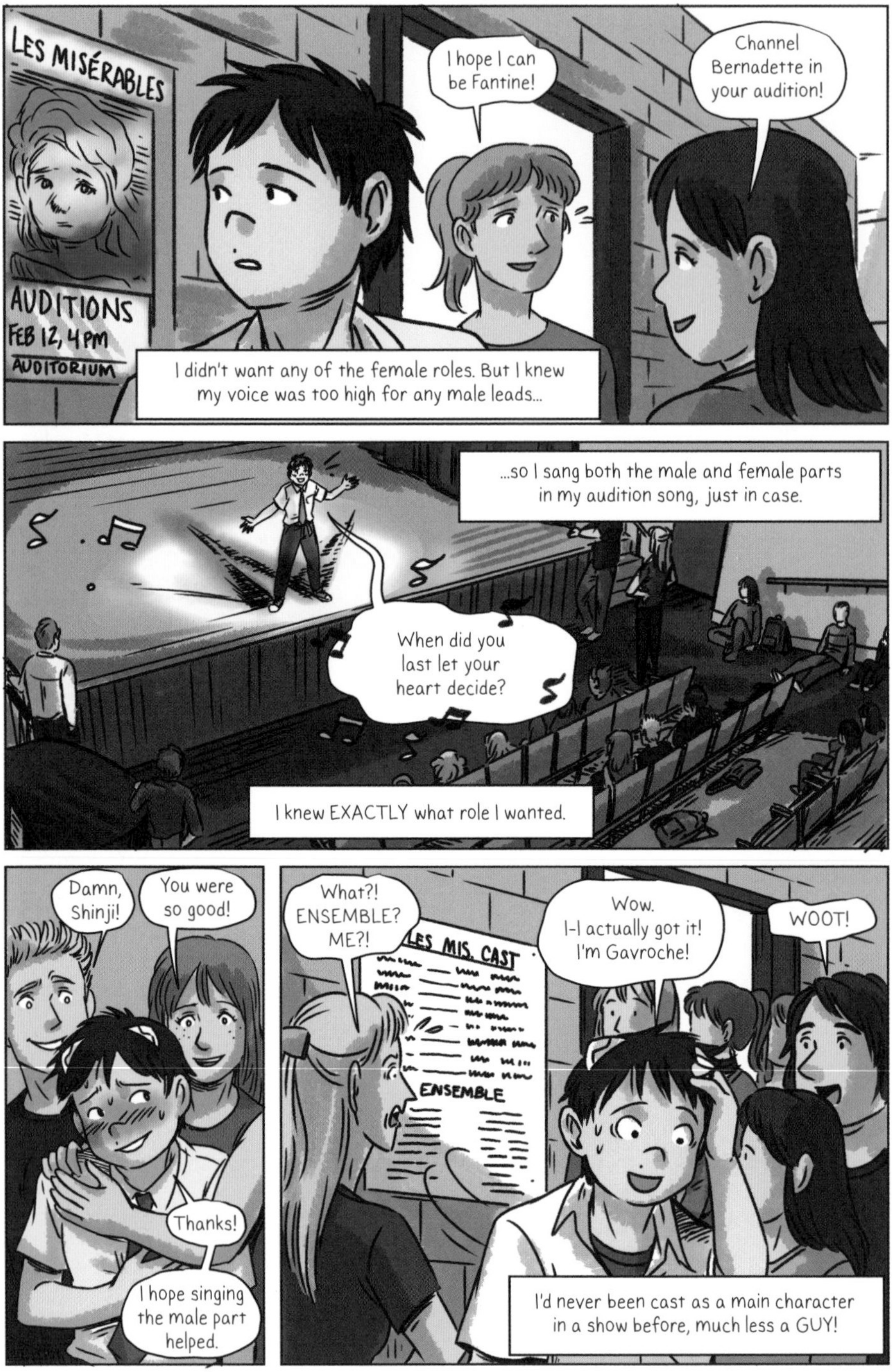

LES MISÉRABLES
AUDITIONS
FEB 12, 4PM
AUDITORIUM
I hope I can be Fantine!
Channel Bernadette in your audition!
I didn't want any of the female roles. But I knew my voice was too high for any male leads...
...so I sang both the male and female parts in my audition song, just in case.
When did you last let your heart decide?
I knew EXACTLY what role I wanted.
Damn, Shinji!
You were so good!
Thanks!
I hope singing the male part helped.
What?! ENSEMBLE? ME?!
LES MIS. CAST
ENSEMBLE
Wow. I-I actually got it! I'm Gavroche!
WOOT!
I'd never been cast as a main character in a show before, much less a GUY!

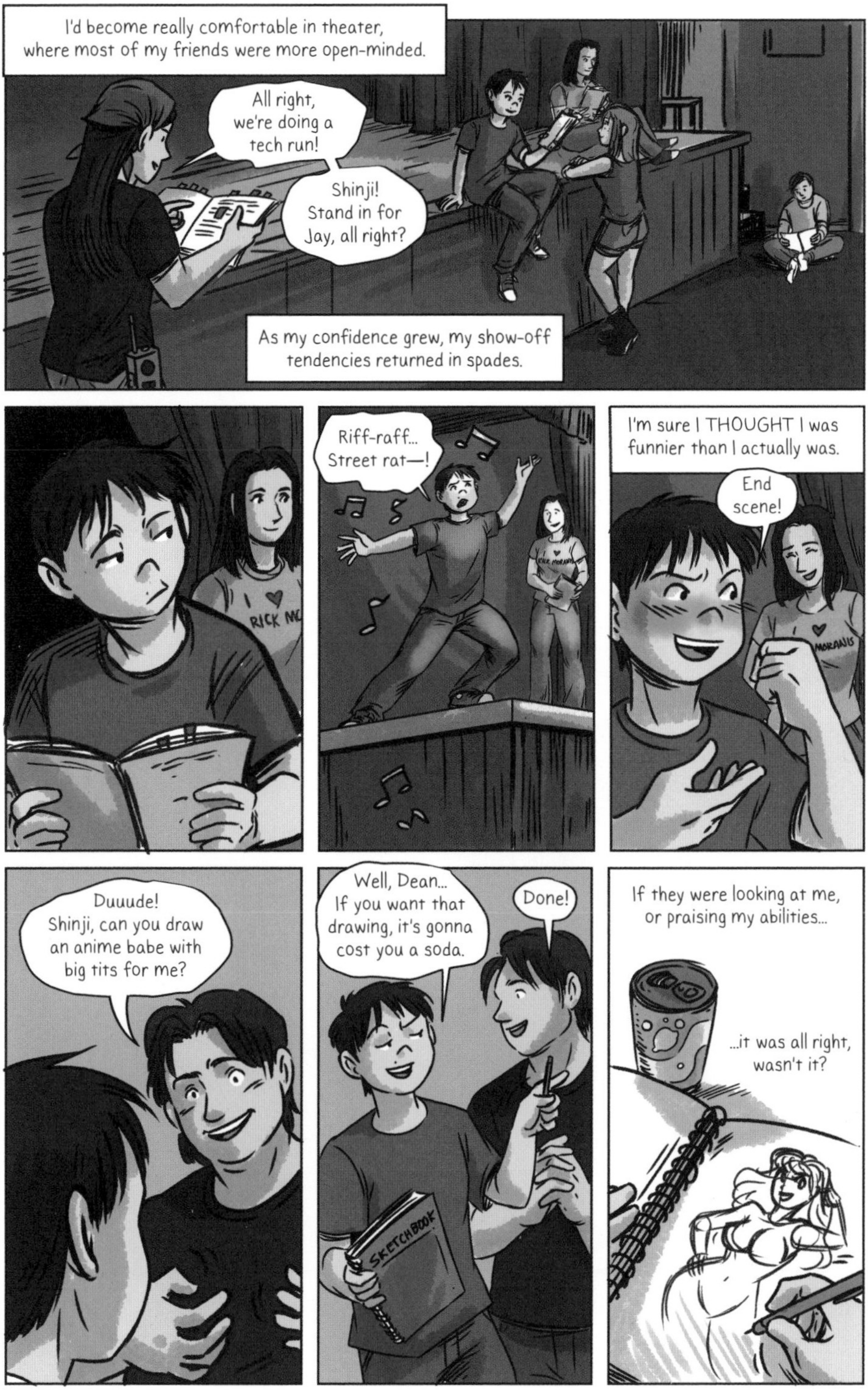
I'd become really comfortable in theater, where most of my friends were more open-minded.
All right, we're doing a tech run!
Shinji! Stand in for Jay, all right?
As my confidence grew, my show-off tendencies returned in spades.
Riff-raff... Street rat—!
I'm sure I THOUGHT I was funnier than I actually was.
End scene!
Duuude! Shinji, can you draw an anime babe with big tits for me?
Well, Dean... If you want that drawing, it's gonna cost you a soda.
Done!
SKETCHBOOK
If they were looking at me, or praising my abilities...
...it was all right, wasn't it?

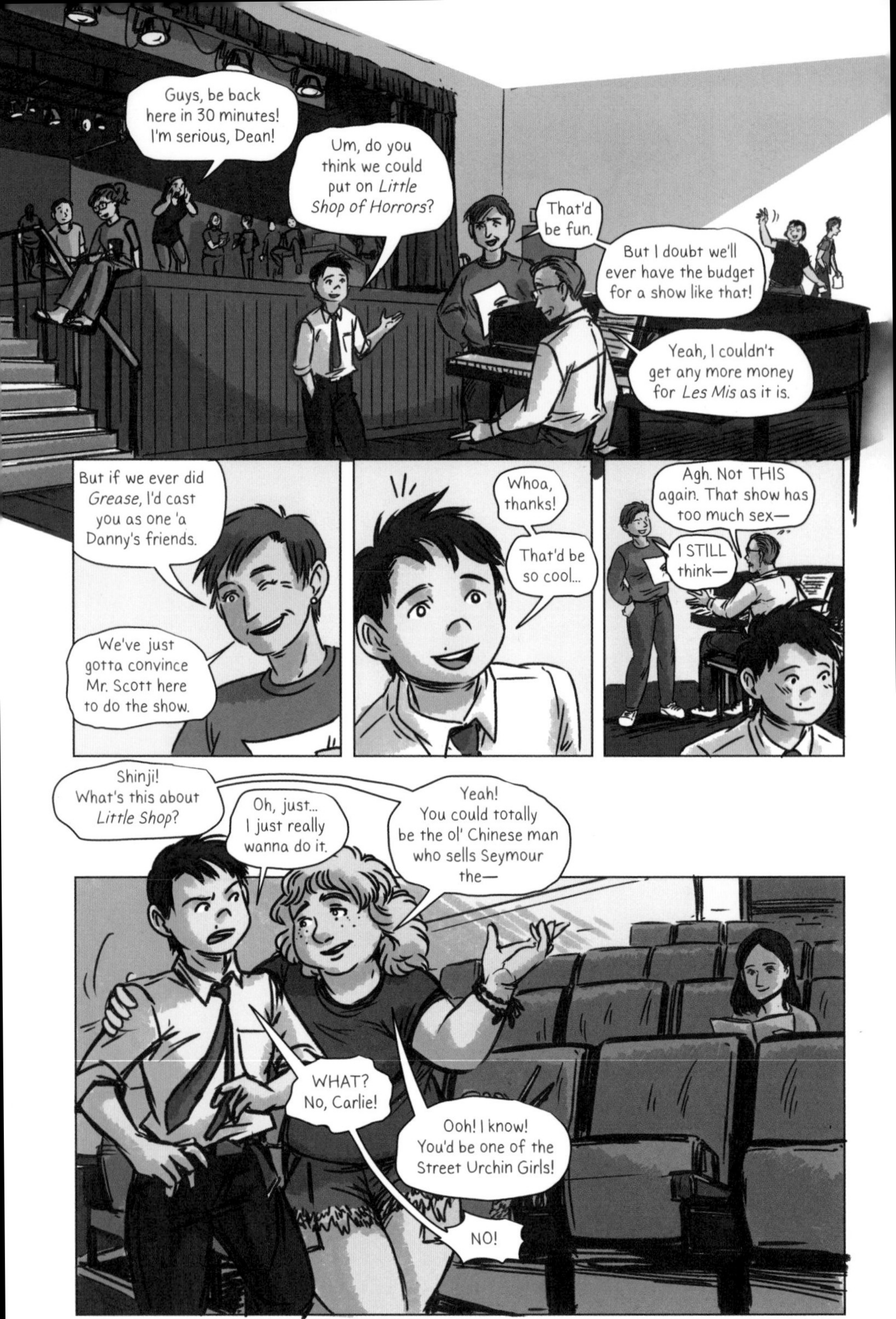

Guys, be back here in 30 minutes! I'm serious, Dean!
Um, do you think we could put on *Little Shop of Horrors*?
That'd be fun.
But I doubt we'll ever have the budget for a show like that!
Yeah, I couldn't get any more money for *Les Mis* as it is.
But if we ever did *Grease*, I'd cast you as one 'a Danny's friends.
We've just gotta convince Mr. Scott here to do the show.
Whoa, thanks!
That'd be so cool...
Agh. Not THIS again. That show has too much sex—
I STILL think—
Shinji! What's this about *Little Shop*?
Oh, just... I just really wanna do it.
Yeah! You could totally be the ol' Chinese man who sells Seymour the—
WHAT? No, Carlie!
Ooh! I know! You'd be one of the Street Urchin Girls!
NO!

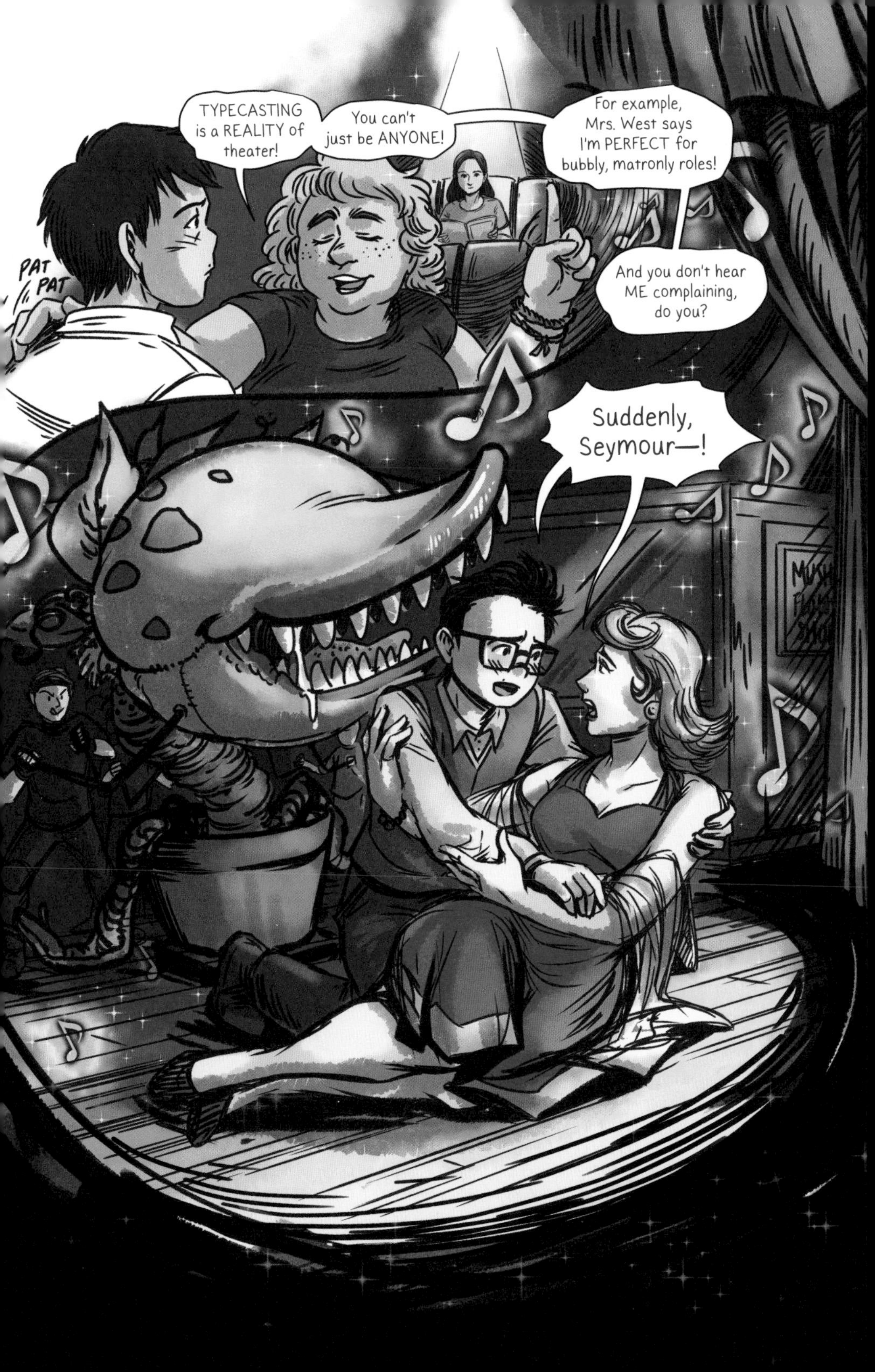
PAT PAT
TYPECASTING is a REALITY of theater!
You can't just be ANYONE!
For example, Mrs. West says I'm PERFECT for bubbly, matronly roles!
And you don't hear ME complaining, do you?
Suddenly, Seymour—!

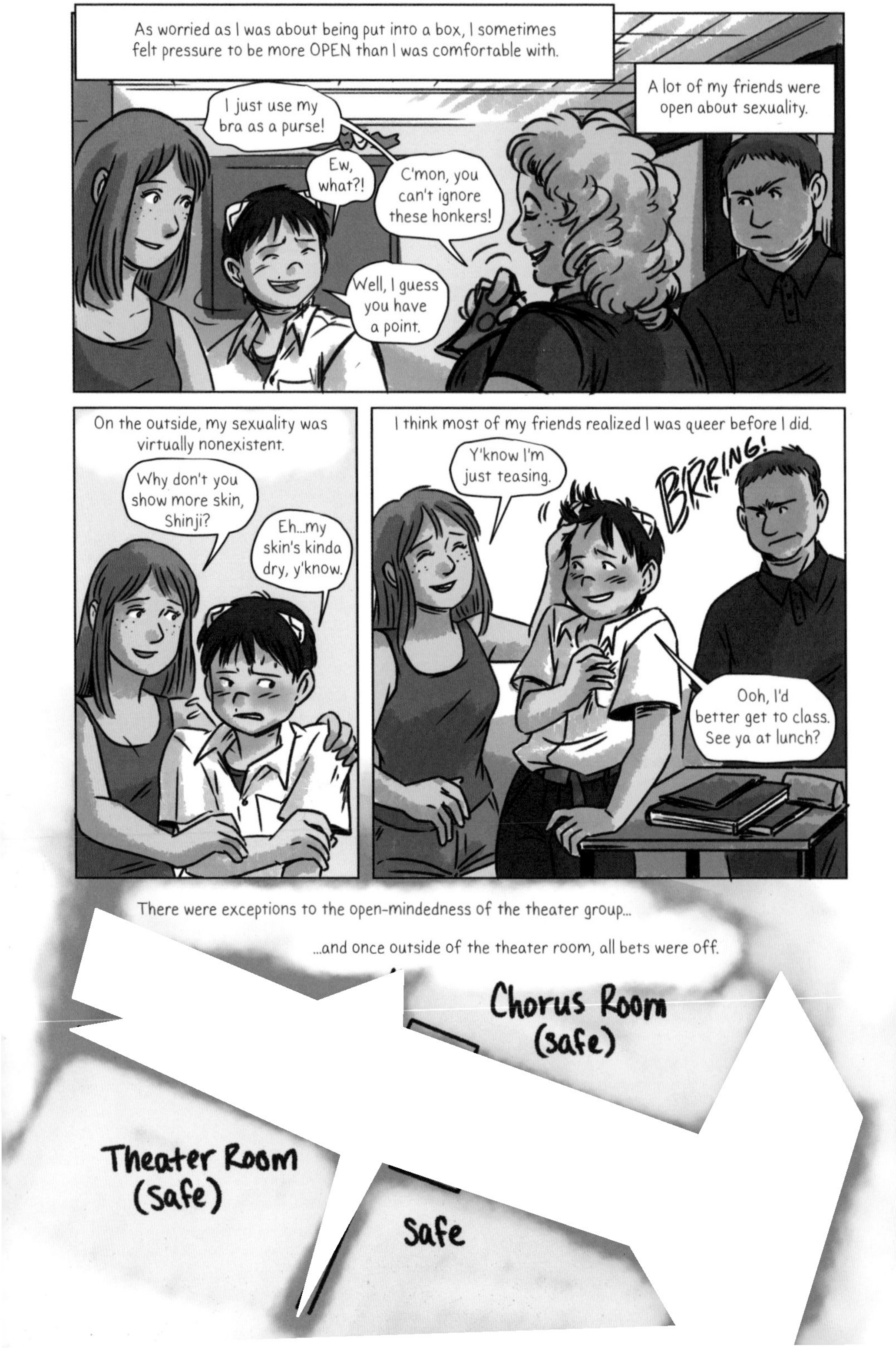
As worried as I was about being put into a box, I sometimes felt pressure to be more OPEN than I was comfortable with.
A lot of my friends were open about sexuality.
I just use my bra as a purse!
Ew, what?!
C'mon, you can't ignore these honkers!
Well, I guess you have a point.
On the outside, my sexuality was virtually nonexistent.
Why don't you show more skin, Shinji?
Eh...my skin's kinda dry, y'know.
I think most of my friends realized I was queer before I did.
Y'know I'm just teasing.
BRRING!
Ooh, I'd better get to class. See ya at lunch?
There were exceptions to the open-mindedness of the theater group...
...and once outside of the theater room, all bets were off.
Chorus Room (safe)
Theater Room (safe)
Safe

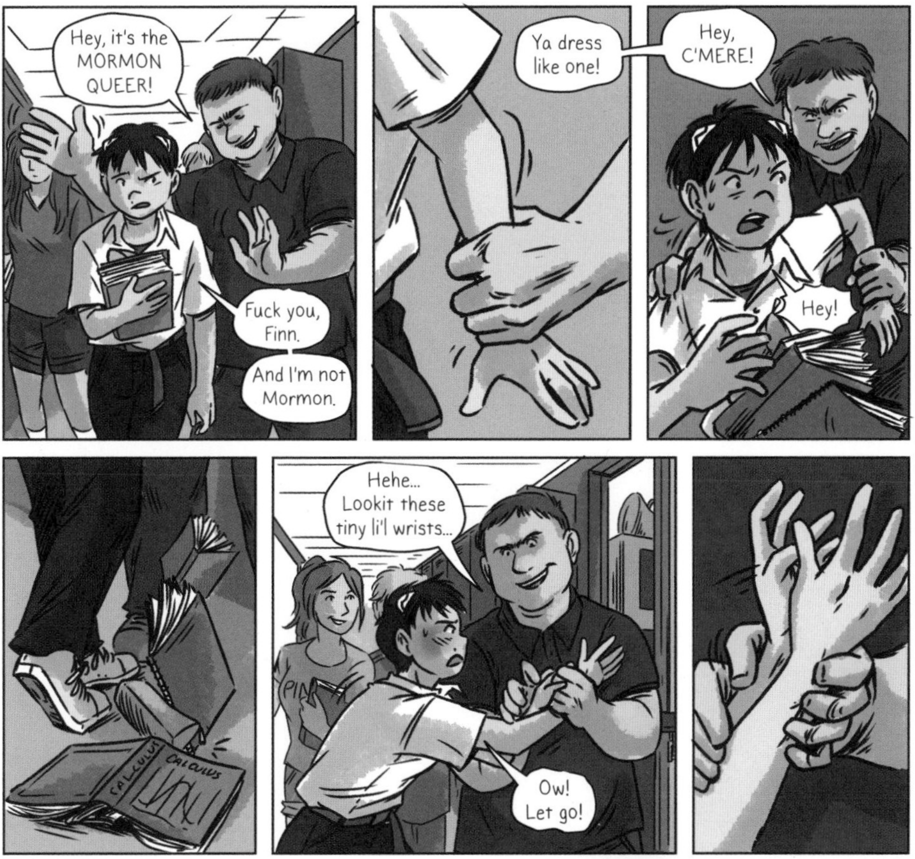
Hey, it's the MORMON QUEER!
Fuck you, Finn.
And I'm not Mormon.
Ya dress like one!
Hey, C'MERE!
Hey!
Hehe... Lookit these tiny li'l wrists...
Ow! Let go!

I didn't know Finn well, but I'd still seen him around in the theater department.

It felt like a betrayal.

Being objectified wasn't a new concept to me.

Only...

Before, it had been mostly verbal, with the perpetrator citing my "weirdness" as their excuse.

But this was PHYSICAL.

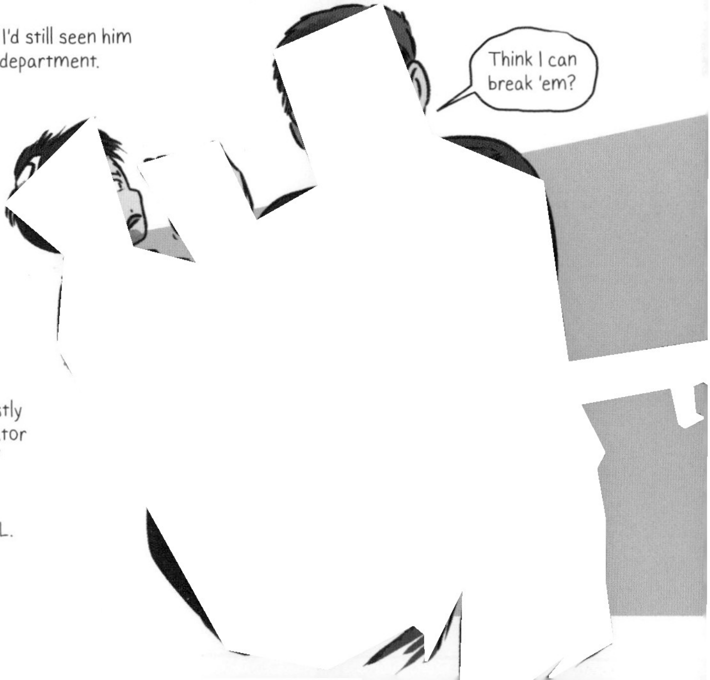
Think I can break 'em?

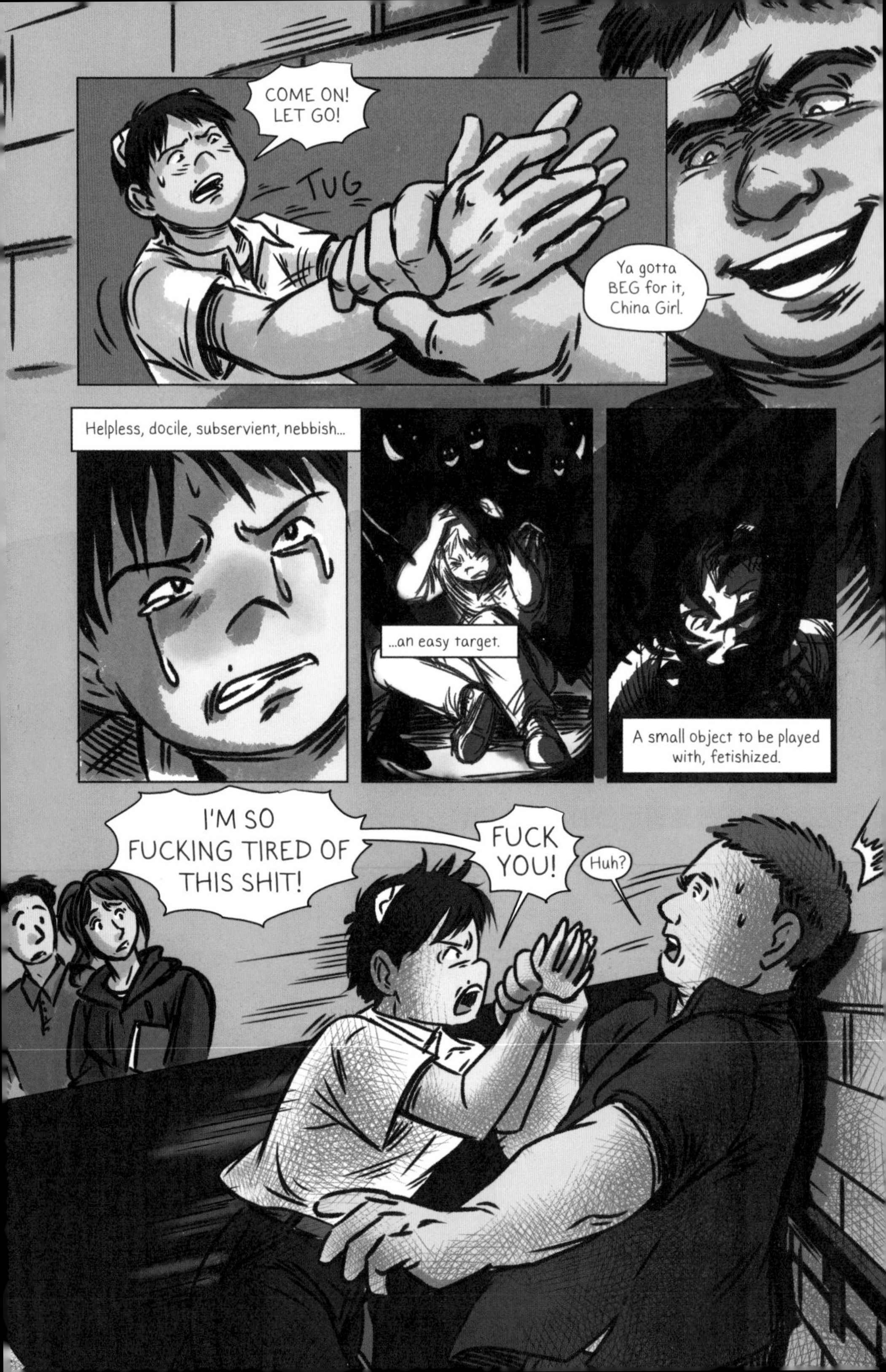
COME ON! LET GO!
TUG
Ya gotta BEG for it, China Girl.
Helpless, docile, subservient, nebbish...
...an easy target.
A small object to be played with, fetishized.
I'M SO FUCKING TIRED OF THIS SHIT!
FUCK YOU!
Huh?

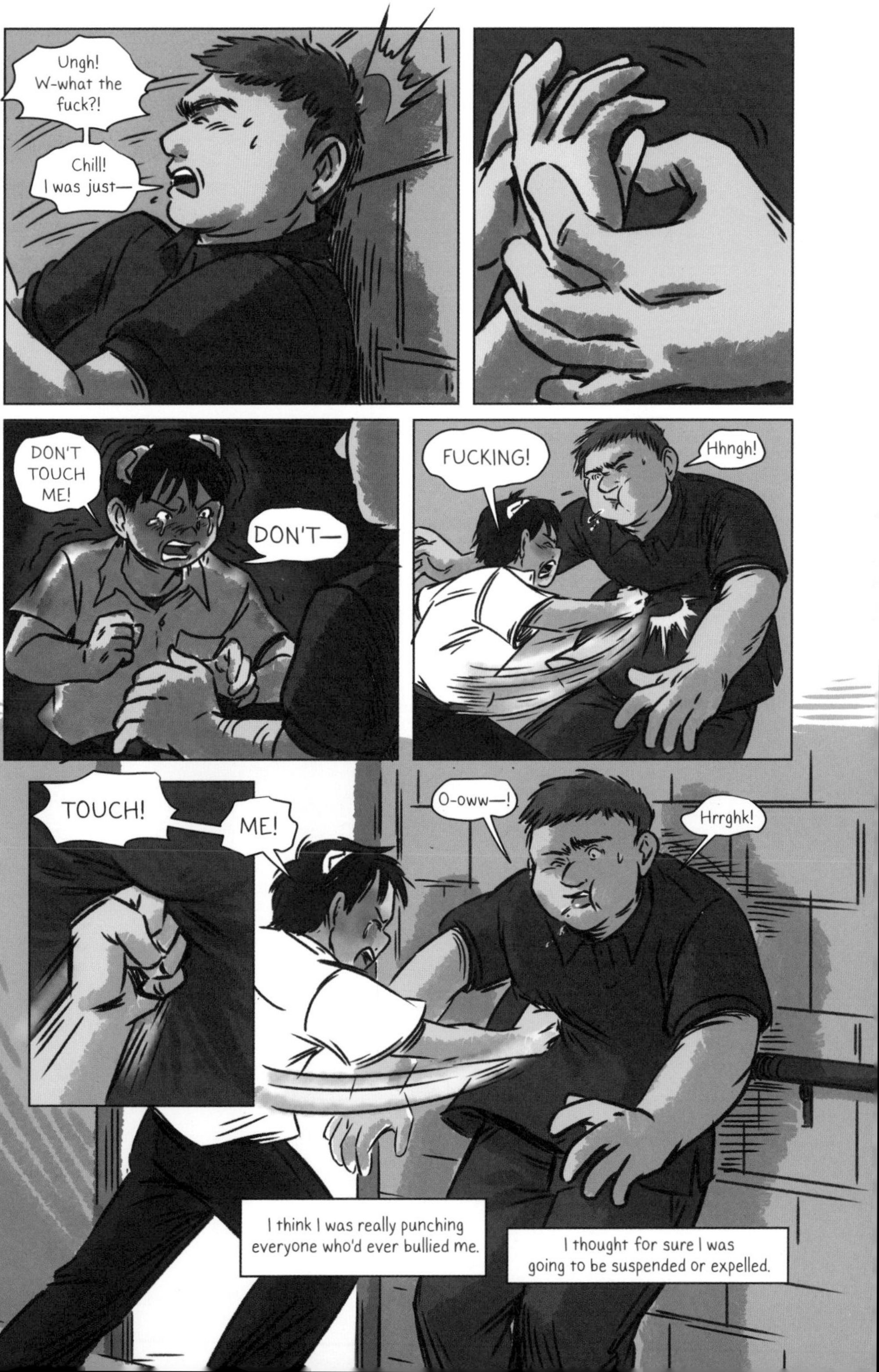
Ungh! W-what the fuck?!
Chill! I was just—
DON'T TOUCH ME!
DON'T—
FUCKING!
Hhngh!
TOUCH!
ME!
O-oww—!
Hrrghk!
I think I was really punching everyone who'd ever bullied me.
I thought for sure I was going to be suspended or expelled.

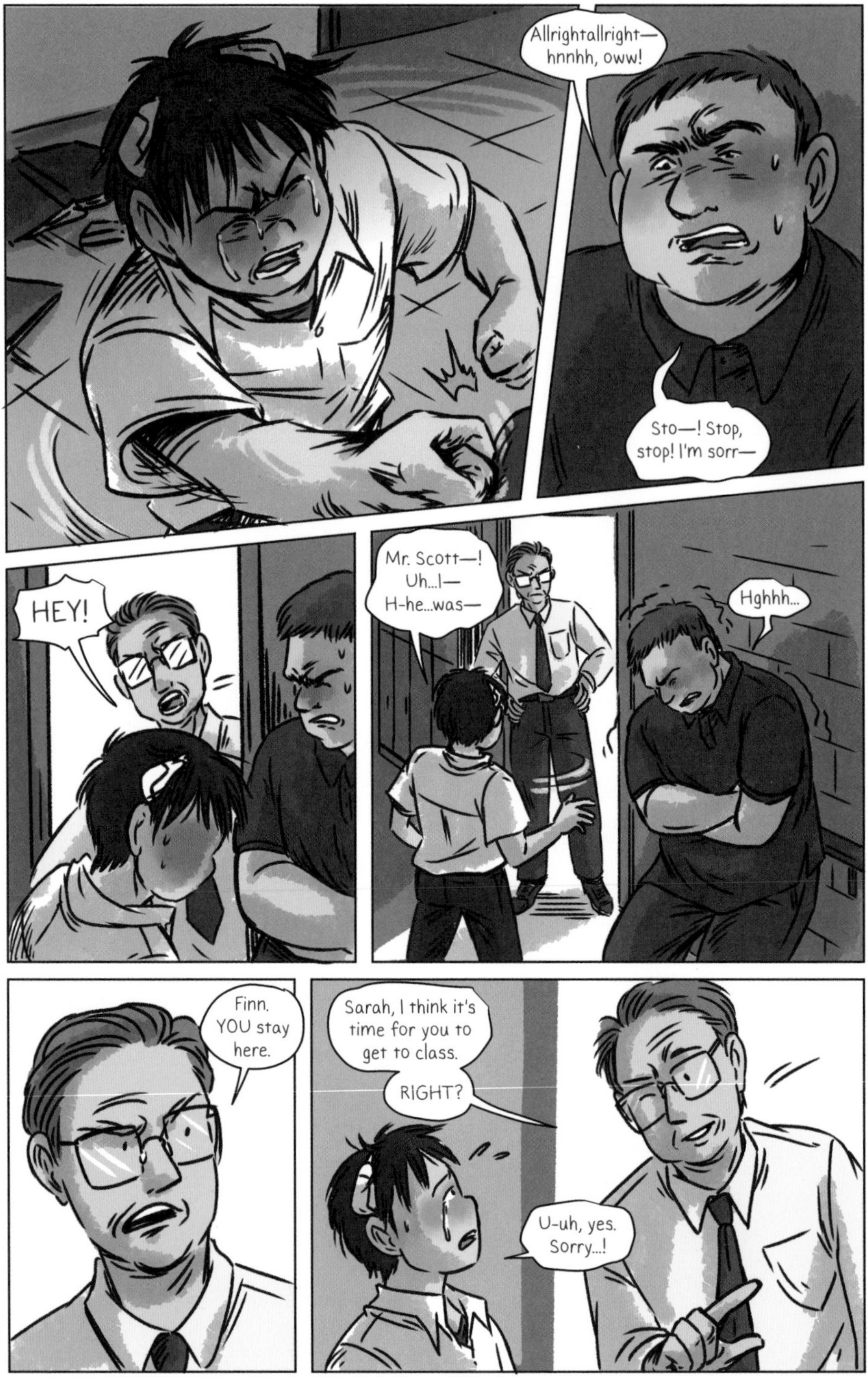
Allrightallright—
hnnhh, oww!
Sto—! Stop,
stop! I'm sorr—
HEY!
Mr. Scott—!
Uh...I—
H-he...was—
Hghhh...
Finn.
YOU stay
here.
Sarah, I think it's
time for you to
get to class.
RIGHT?
U-uh, yes.
Sorry...!

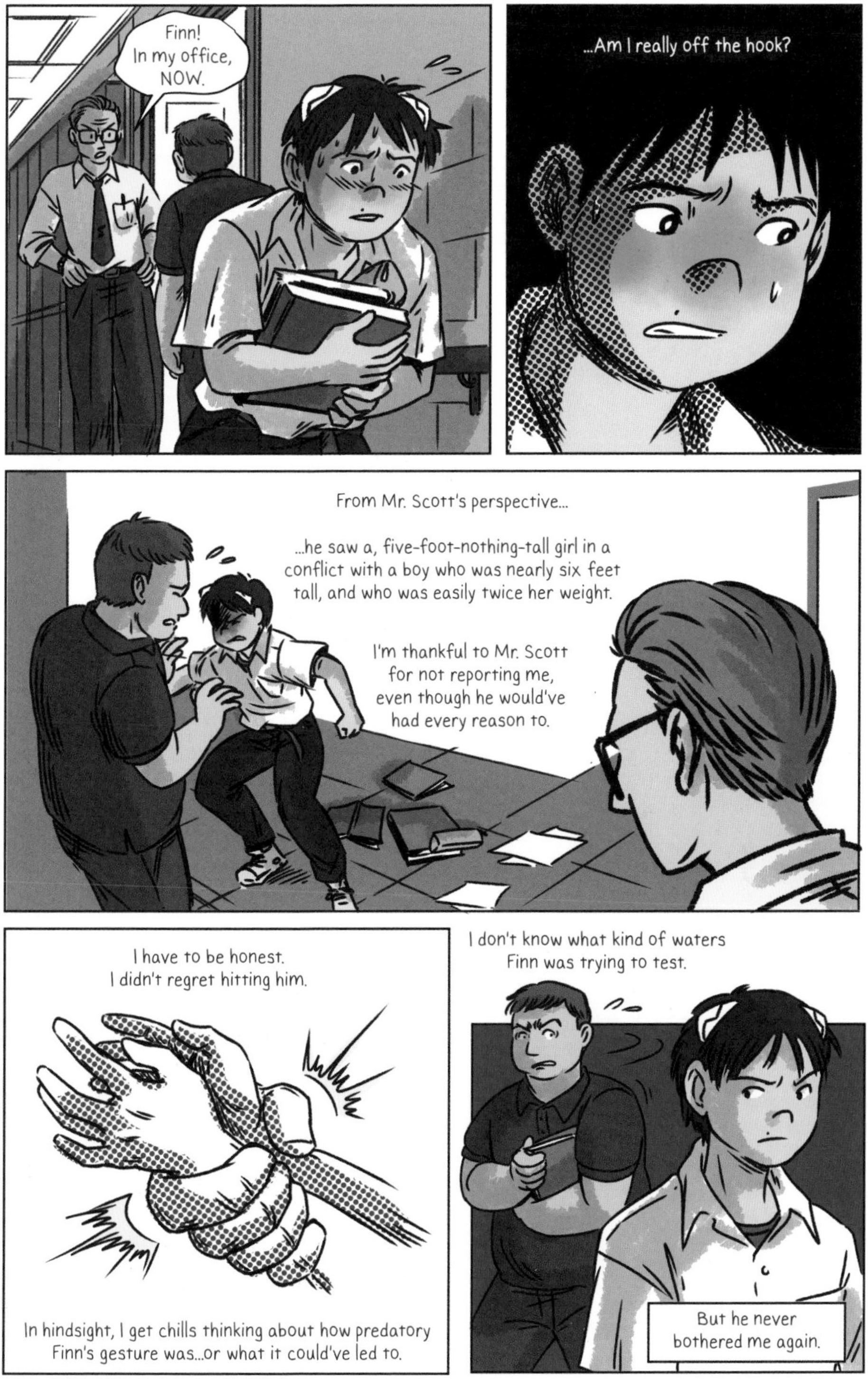
Finn!
In my office,
NOW.
...Am I really off the hook?
From Mr. Scott's perspective...
...he saw a, five-foot-nothing-tall girl in a conflict with a boy who was nearly six feet tall, and who was easily twice her weight.
I'm thankful to Mr. Scott for not reporting me, even though he would've had every reason to.
I have to be honest.
I didn't regret hitting him.
In hindsight, I get chills thinking about how predatory Finn's gesture was...or what it could've led to.
I don't know what kind of waters Finn was trying to test.
But he never bothered me again.

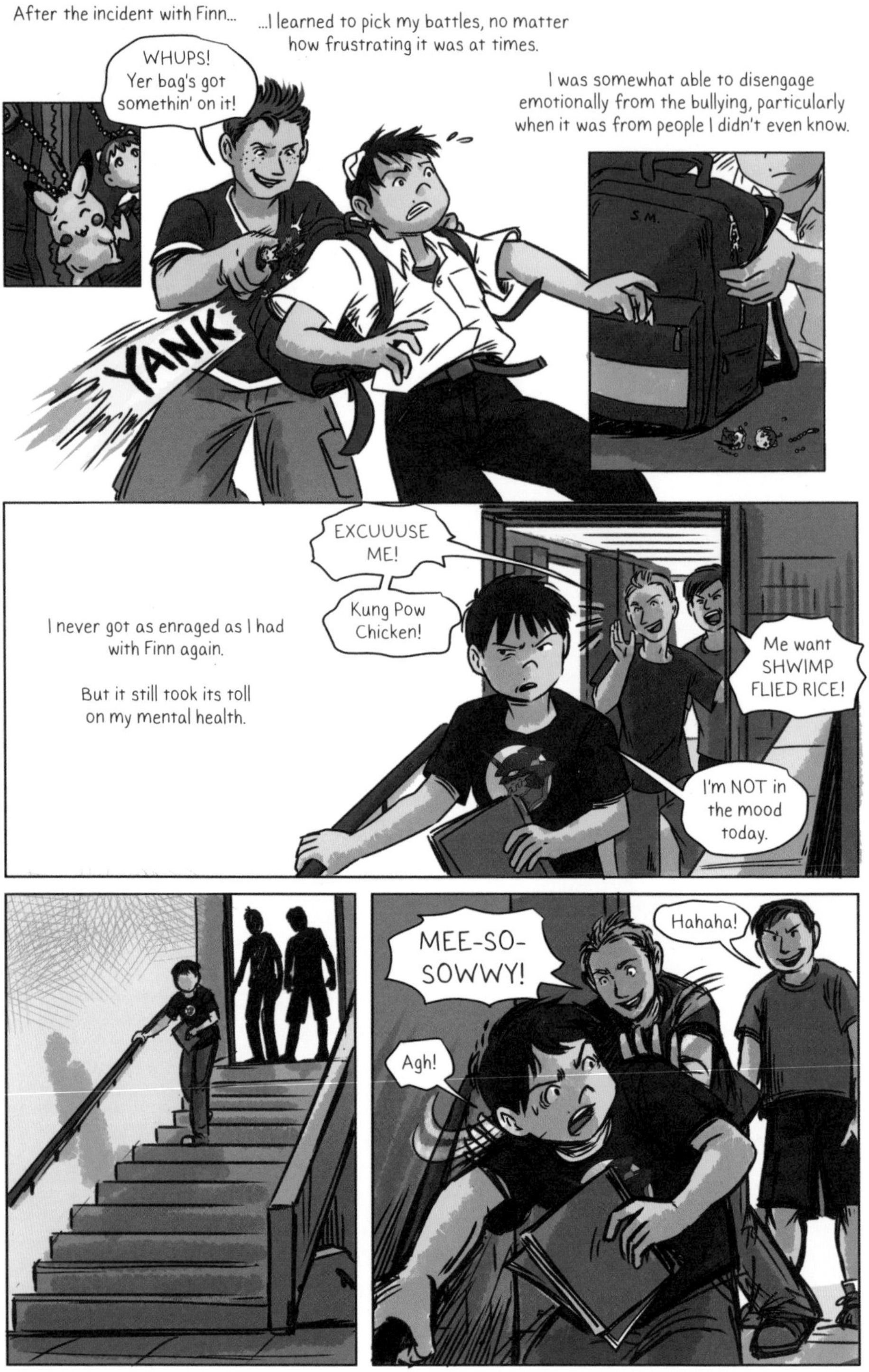
After the incident with Finn...
...I learned to pick my battles, no matter how frustrating it was at times.
WHUPS! Yer bag's got somethin' on it!
YANK
I was somewhat able to disengage emotionally from the bullying, particularly when it was from people I didn't even know.
S.M.
I never got as enraged as I had with Finn again.
But it still took its toll on my mental health.
EXCUUUSE ME!
Kung Pow Chicken!
Me want SHWIMP FLIED RICE!
I'm NOT in the mood today.
MEE-SO-SOWWY!
Hahaha!
Agh!

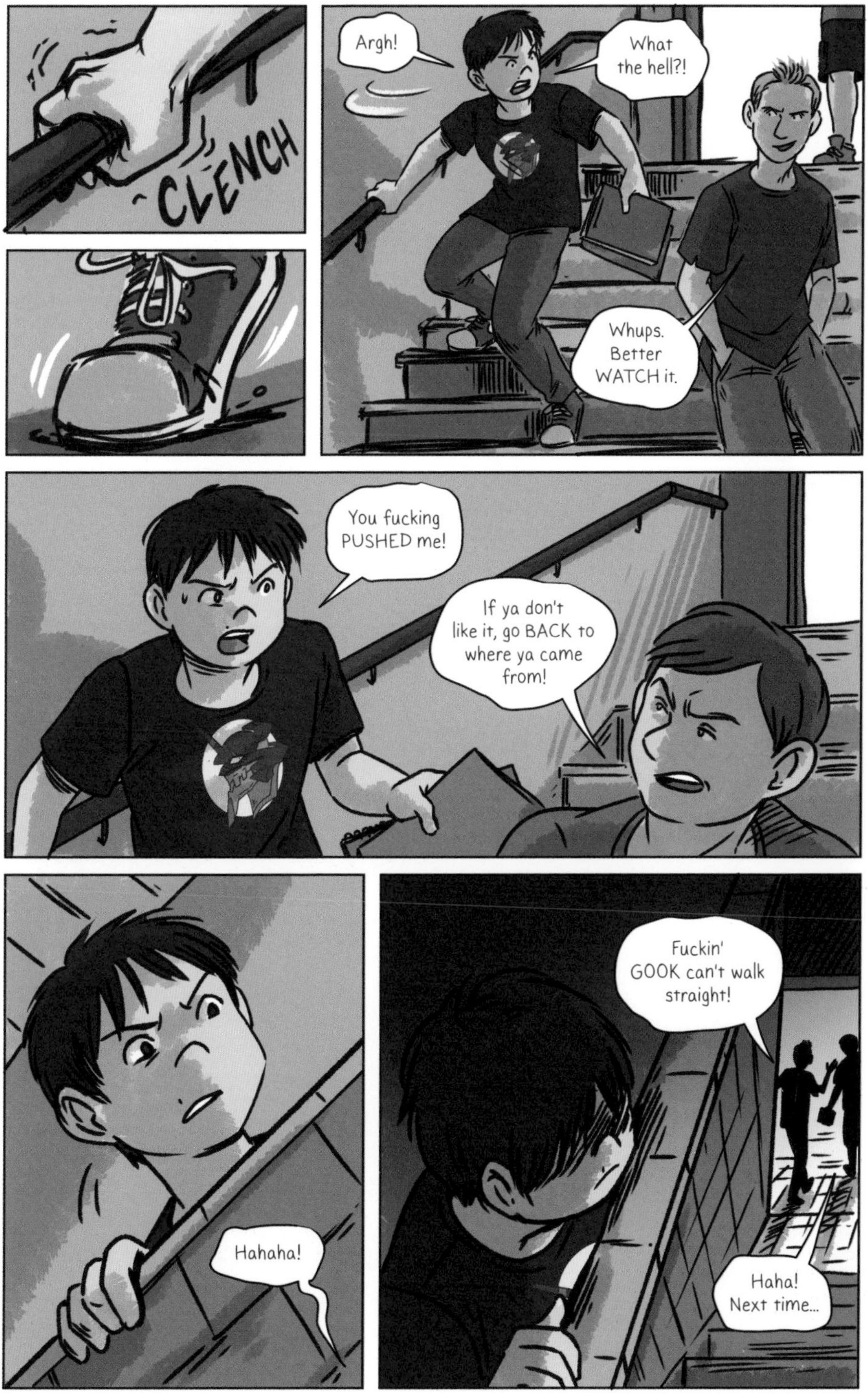
CLENCH
Argh!
What the hell?!
Whups. Better WATCH it.
You fucking PUSHED me!
If ya don't like it, go BACK to where ya came from!
Hahaha!
Fuckin' GOOK can't walk straight!
Haha! Next time...

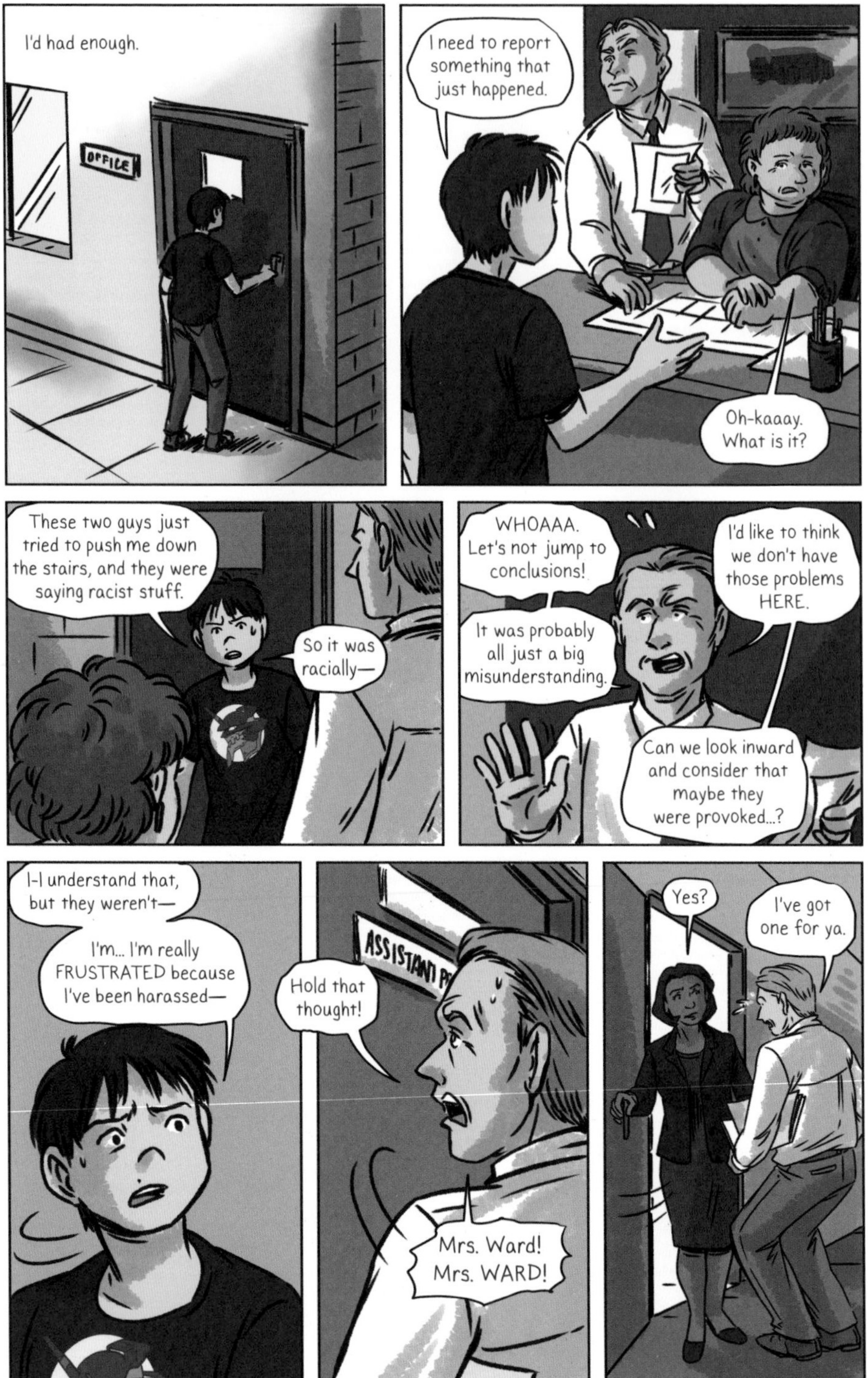
I'd had enough.
OFFICE
I need to report something that just happened.
Oh-kaaay. What is it?
These two guys just tried to push me down the stairs, and they were saying racist stuff.
So it was racially—
WHOAAA. Let's not jump to conclusions!
It was probably all just a big misunderstanding.
I'd like to think we don't have those problems HERE.
Can we look inward and consider that maybe they were provoked...?
I-I understand that, but they weren't—
I'm... I'm really FRUSTRATED because I've been harassed—
Hold that thought!
Mrs. Ward! Mrs. WARD!
Yes?
I've got one for ya.

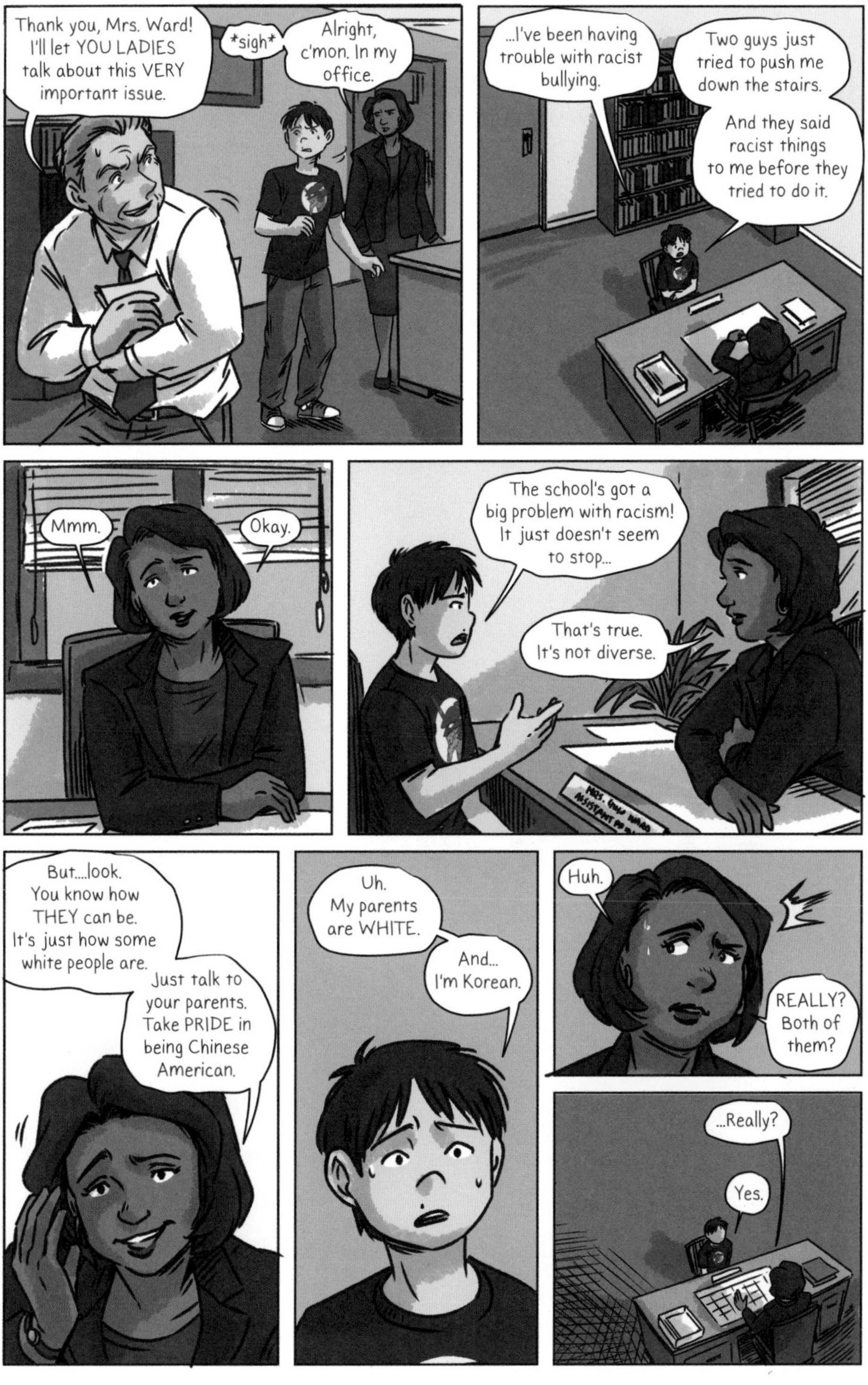
Thank you, Mrs. Ward! I'll let YOU LADIES talk about this VERY important issue.
sigh
Alright, c'mon. In my office.
...I've been having trouble with racist bullying.
Two guys just tried to push me down the stairs.
And they said racist things to me before they tried to do it.
Mmm.
Okay.
The school's got a big problem with racism! It just doesn't seem to stop...
That's true. It's not diverse.
But....look. You know how THEY can be. It's just how some white people are.
Just talk to your parents. Take PRIDE in being Chinese American.
Uh. My parents are WHITE.
And... I'm Korean.
Huh.
REALLY? Both of them?
...Really?
Yes.

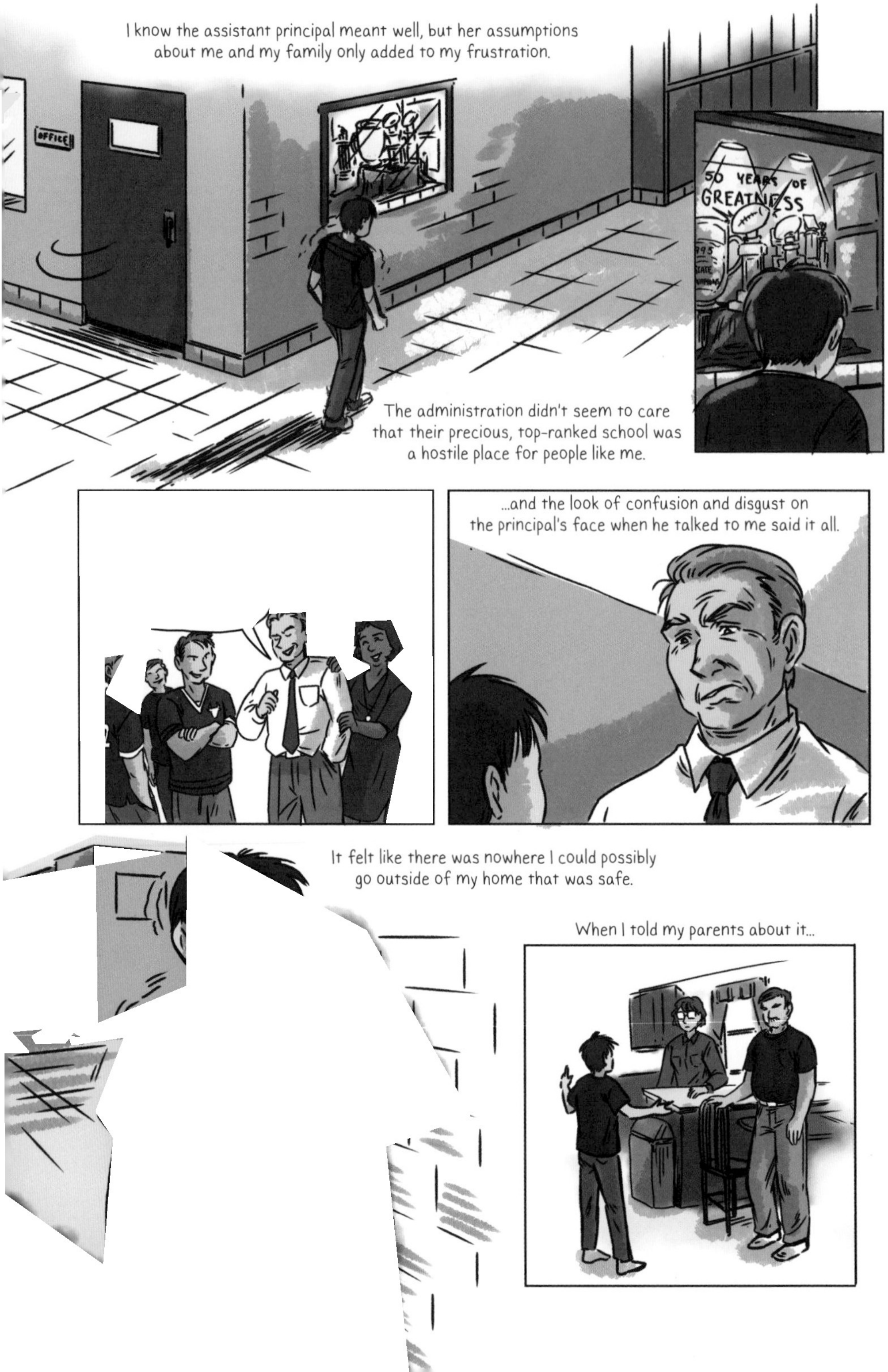
I know the assistant principal meant well, but her assumptions about me and my family only added to my frustration.
OFFICE
50 YEARS OF GREATNESS
The administration didn't seem to care that their precious, top-ranked school was a hostile place for people like me.
...and the look of confusion and disgust on the principal's face when he talked to me said it all.
It felt like there was nowhere I could possibly go outside of my home that was safe.
When I told my parents about it...

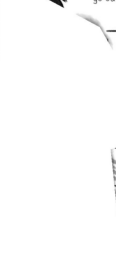

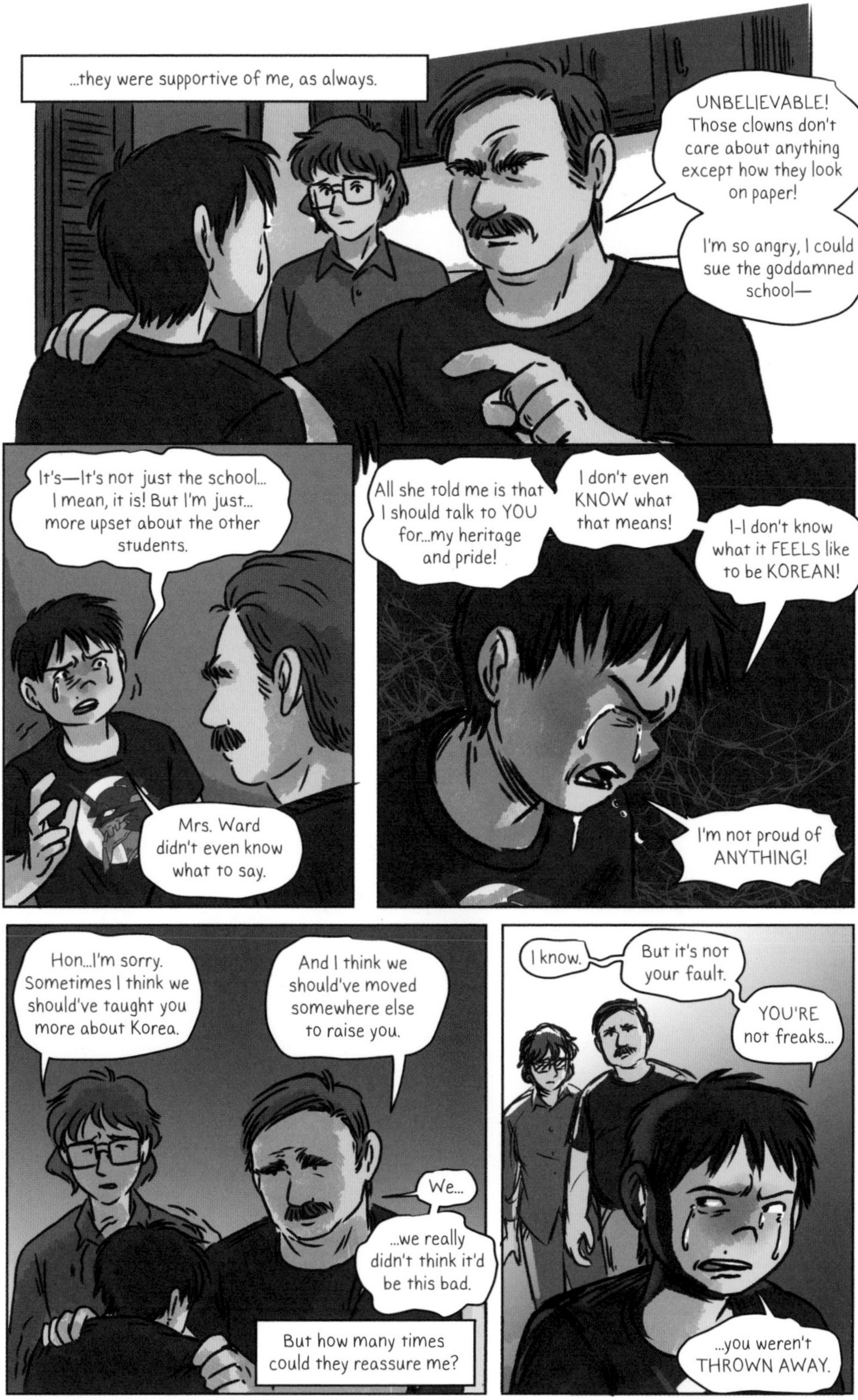
...they were supportive of me, as always.
UNBELIEVABLE! Those clowns don't care about anything except how they look on paper!
I'm so angry, I could sue the goddamned school—
It's—It's not just the school... I mean, it is! But I'm just... more upset about the other students.
Mrs. Ward didn't even know what to say.
All she told me is that I should talk to YOU for...my heritage and pride!
I don't even KNOW what that means!
I-I don't know what it FEELS like to be KOREAN!
I'm not proud of ANYTHING!
Hon...I'm sorry. Sometimes I think we should've taught you more about Korea.
And I think we should've moved somewhere else to raise you.
We...
...we really didn't think it'd be this bad.
But how many times could they reassure me?
I know.
But it's not your fault.
YOU'RE not freaks...
...you weren't THROWN AWAY.

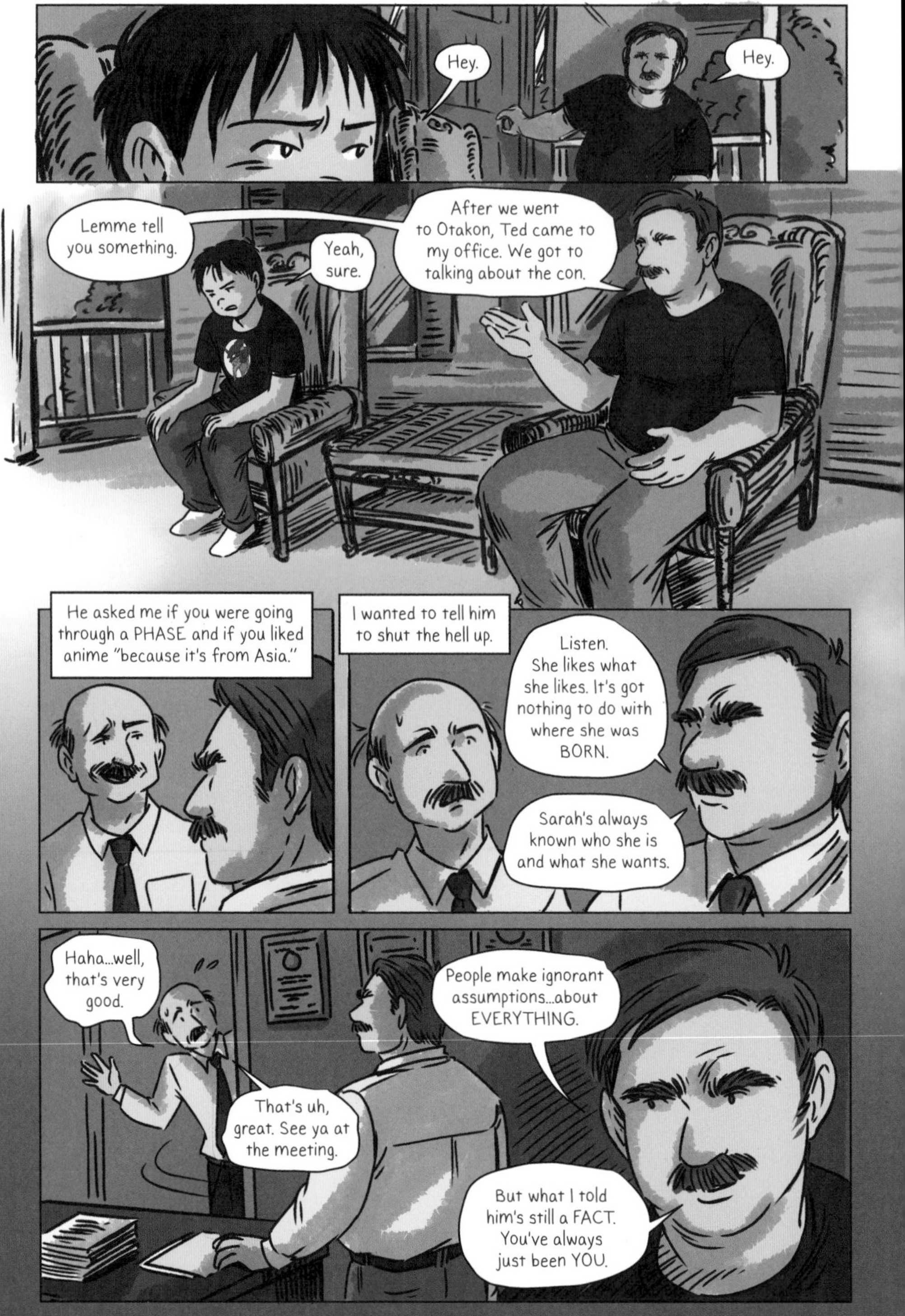
Hey.
Hey.
Lemme tell you something.
Yeah, sure.
After we went to Otakon, Ted came to my office. We got to talking about the con.
He asked me if you were going through a PHASE and if you liked anime "because it's from Asia."
I wanted to tell him to shut the hell up.
Listen. She likes what she likes. It's got nothing to do with where she was BORN.
Sarah's always known who she is and what she wants.
Haha...well, that's very good.
That's uh, great. See ya at the meeting.
People make ignorant assumptions...about EVERYTHING.
But what I told him's still a FACT. You've always just been YOU.

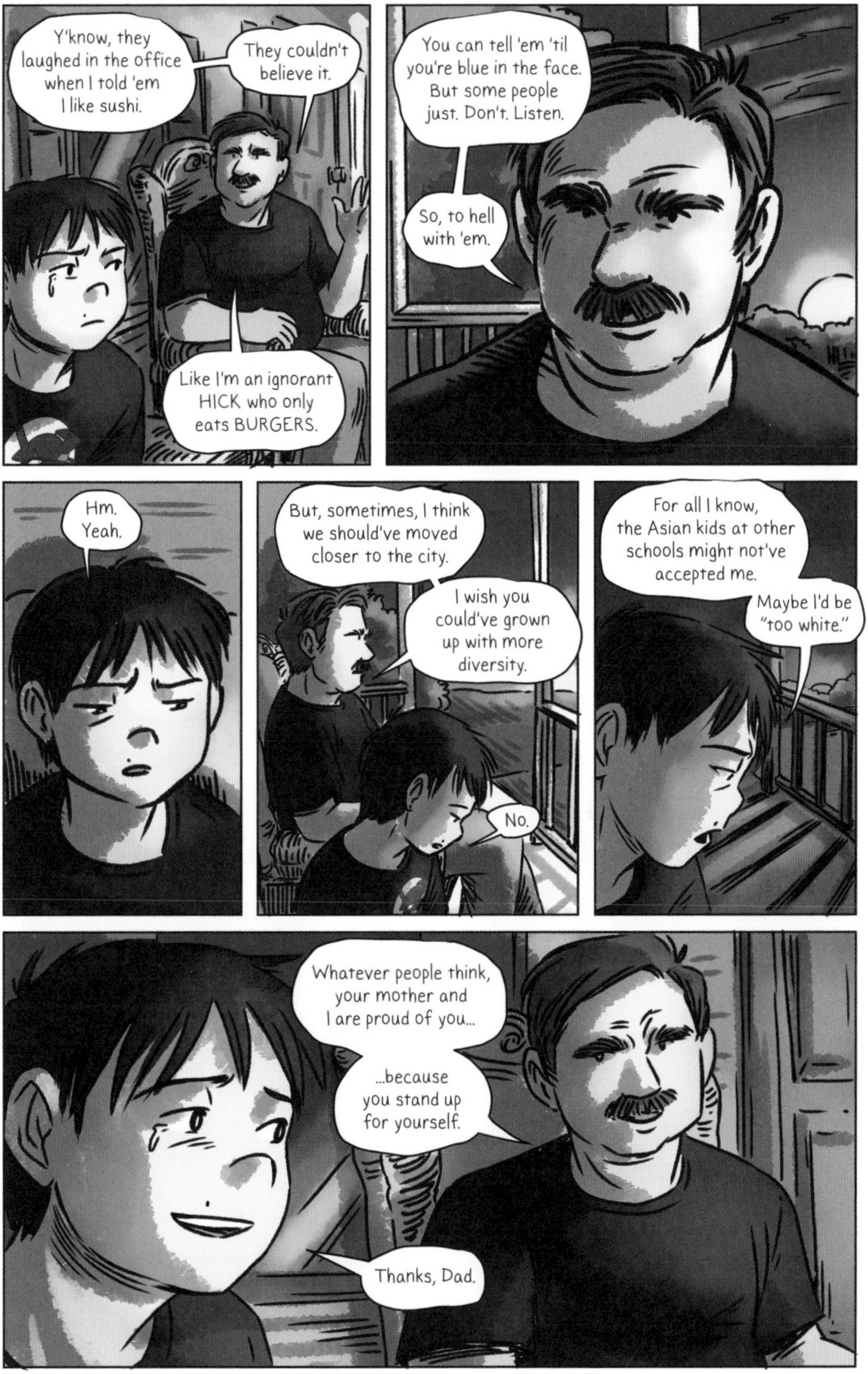
Y'know, they laughed in the office when I told 'em I like sushi.
They couldn't believe it.
Like I'm an ignorant HICK who only eats BURGERS.
You can tell 'em 'til you're blue in the face. But some people just. Don't. Listen.
So, to hell with 'em.
Hm. Yeah.
But, sometimes, I think we should've moved closer to the city.
I wish you could've grown up with more diversity.
No.
For all I know, the Asian kids at other schools might not've accepted me.
Maybe I'd be "too white."
Whatever people think, your mother and I are proud of you...
...because you stand up for yourself.
Thanks, Dad.

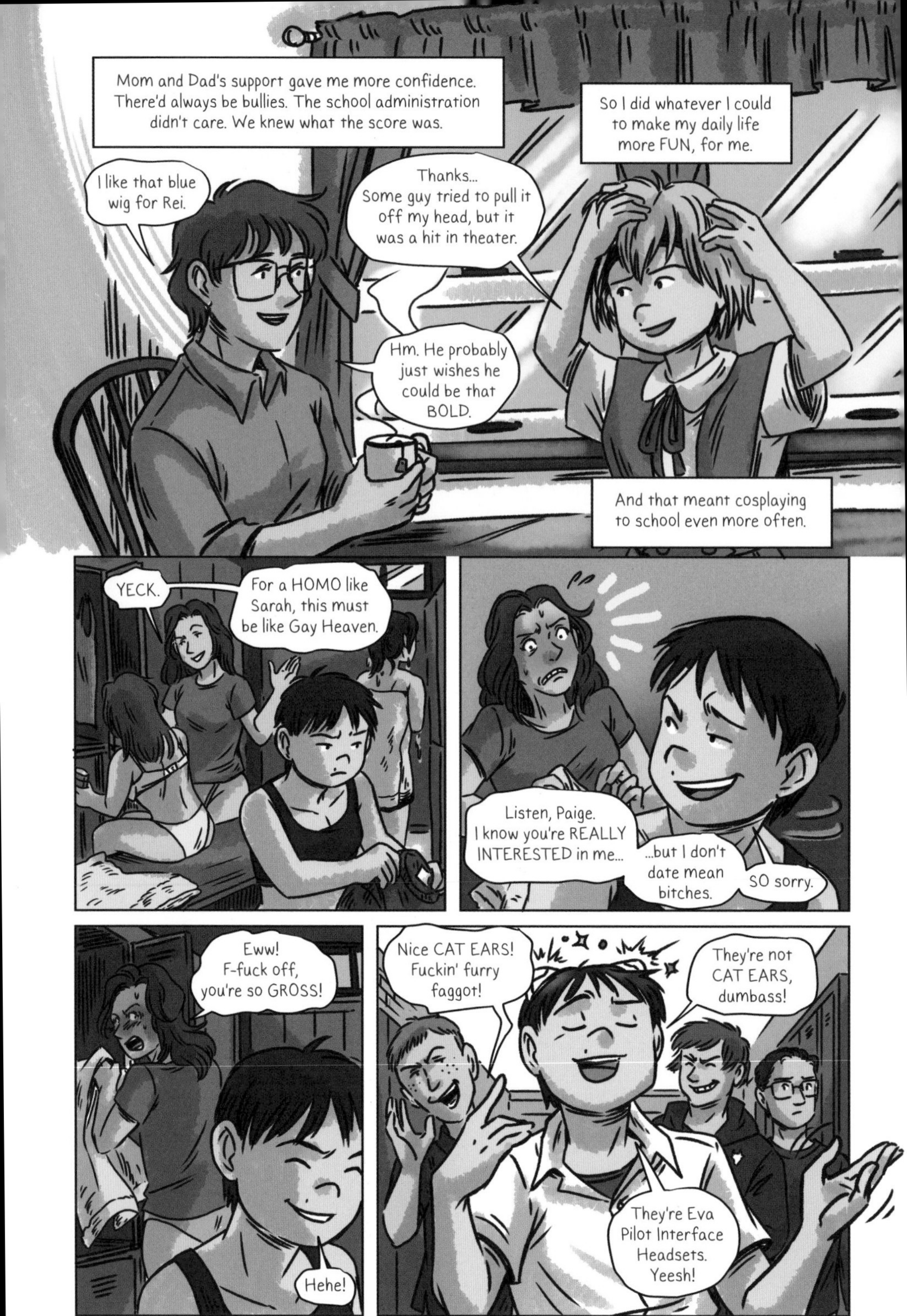

Mom and Dad's support gave me more confidence. There'd always be bullies. The school administration didn't care. We knew what the score was.
So I did whatever I could to make my daily life more FUN, for me.
I like that blue wig for Rei.
Thanks... Some guy tried to pull it off my head, but it was a hit in theater.
Hm. He probably just wishes he could be that BOLD.
And that meant cosplaying to school even more often.
YECK.
For a HOMO like Sarah, this must be like Gay Heaven.
Listen, Paige. I know you're REALLY INTERESTED in me...
...but I don't date mean bitches.
SO sorry.
Eww! F-fuck off, you're so GROSS!
Hehe!
Nice CAT EARS! Fuckin' furry faggot!
They're not CAT EARS, dumbass!
They're Eva Pilot Interface Headsets. Yeesh!

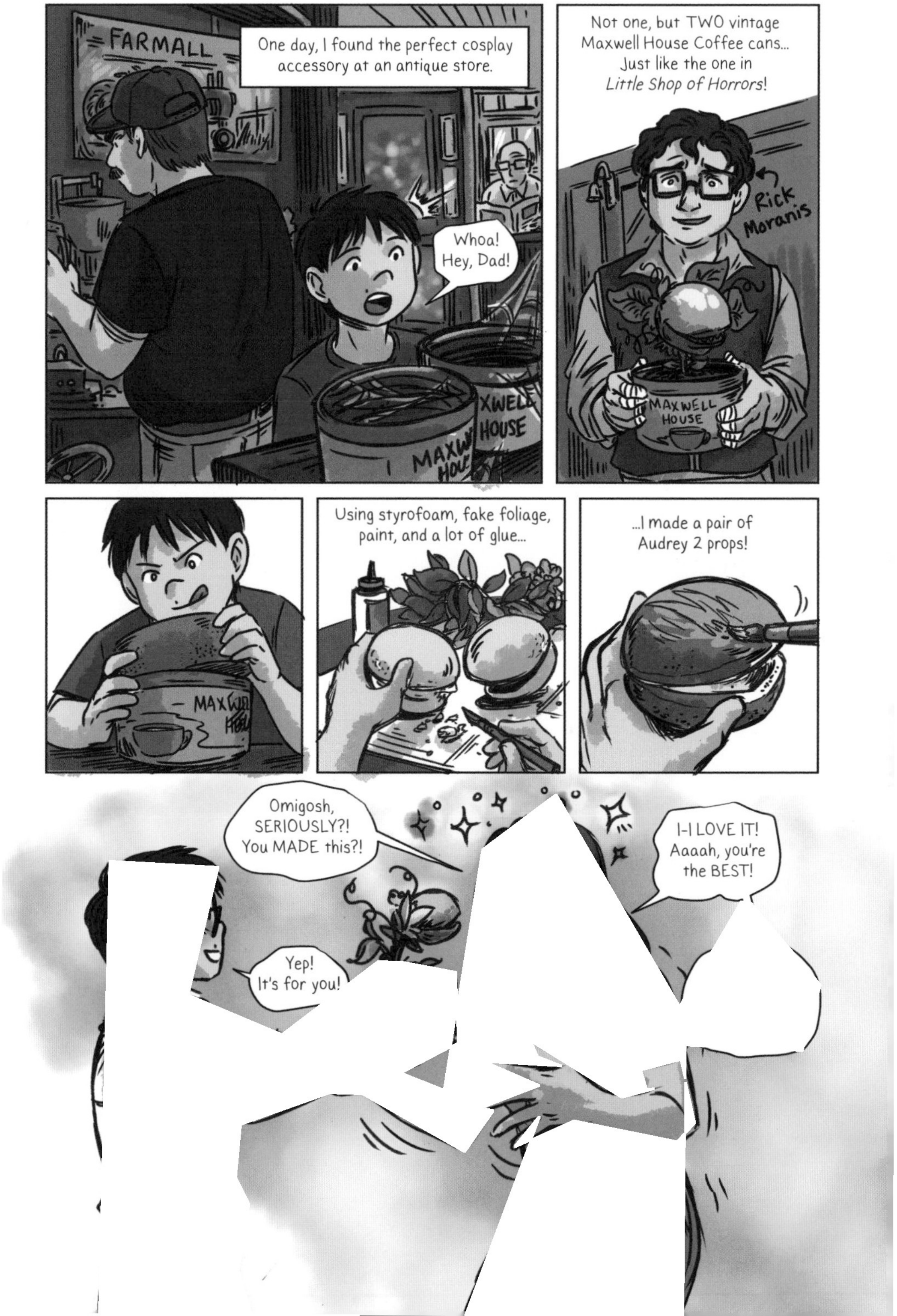
One day, I found the perfect cosplay accessory at an antique store.
FARMALL
Whoa! Hey, Dad!
Not one, but TWO vintage Maxwell House Coffee cans... Just like the one in *Little Shop of Horrors*!
Rick Moranis
MAXWELL HOUSE
Using styrofoam, fake foliage, paint, and a lot of glue...
...I made a pair of Audrey 2 props!
Omigosh, SERIOUSLY?! You MADE this?!
Yep! It's for you!
I-I LOVE IT! Aaaah, you're the BEST!

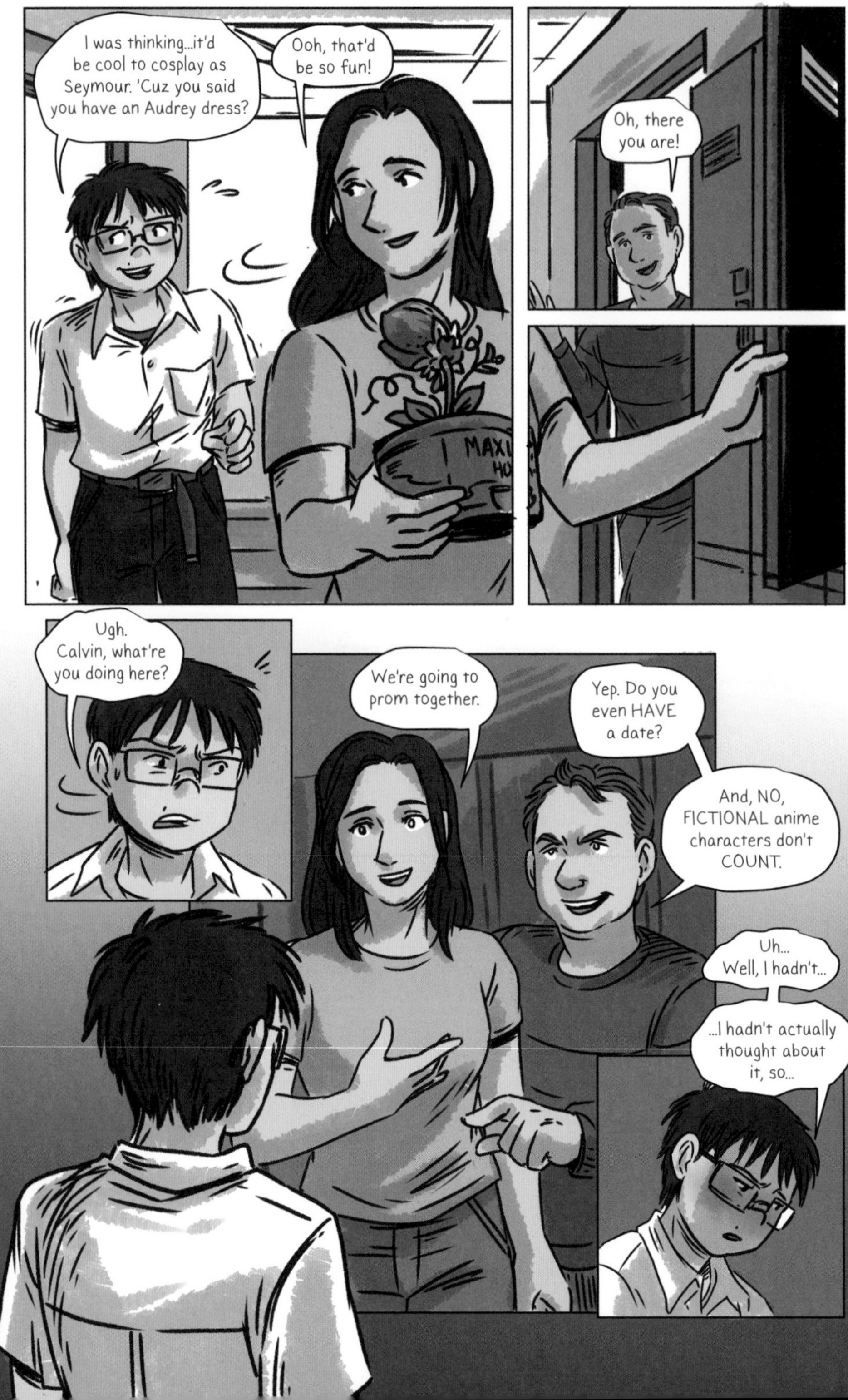
I was thinking...it'd be cool to cosplay as Seymour. 'Cuz you said you have an Audrey dress?
Ooh, that'd be so fun!
MAXI
Oh, there you are!
Ugh. Calvin, what're you doing here?
We're going to prom together.
Yep. Do you even HAVE a date?
And, NO, FICTIONAL anime characters don't COUNT.
Uh... Well, I hadn't...
...I hadn't actually thought about it, so...

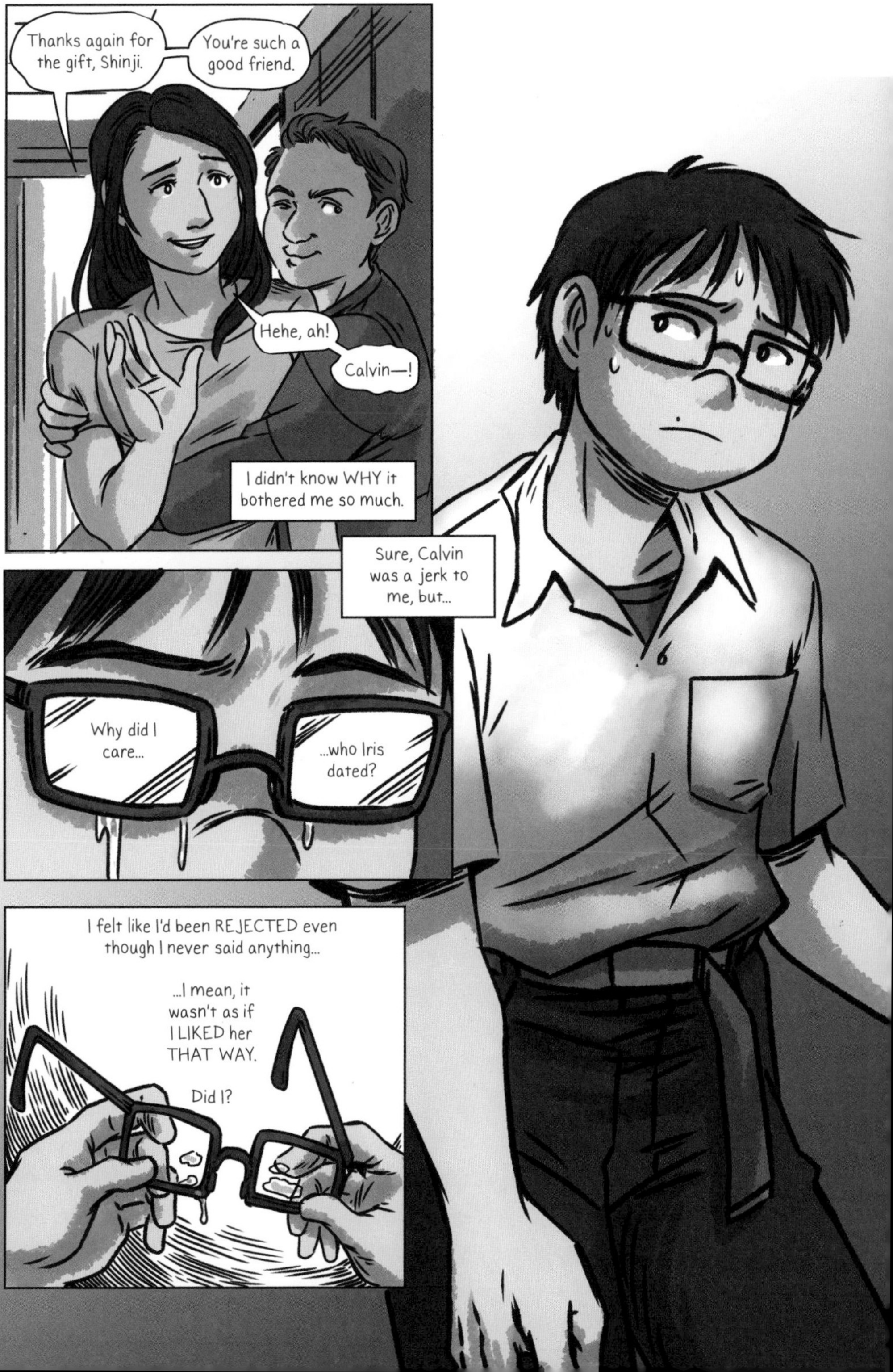
Thanks again for the gift, Shinji.
You're such a good friend.
Hehe, ah!
Calvin—!
I didn't know WHY it bothered me so much.
Sure, Calvin was a jerk to me, but...
Why did I care...
...who Iris dated?
I felt like I'd been REJECTED even though I never said anything...
...I mean, it wasn't as if I LIKED her THAT WAY.
Did I?

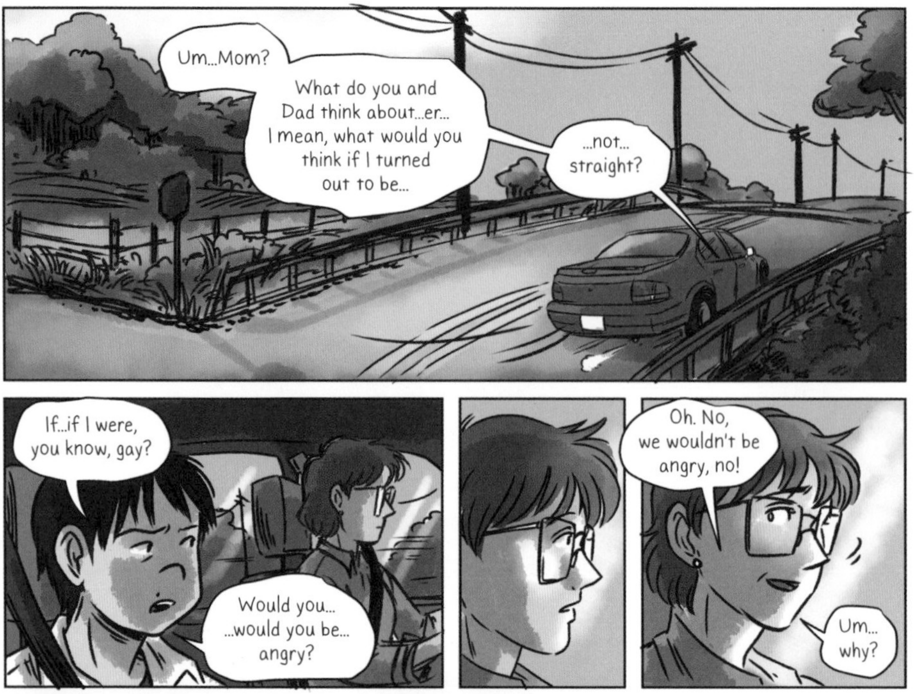
Um...Mom?
What do you and Dad think about...er... I mean, what would you think if I turned out to be...
...not... straight?
If...if I were, you know, gay?
Would you... ...would you be... angry?
Oh. No, we wouldn't be angry, no!
Um... why?

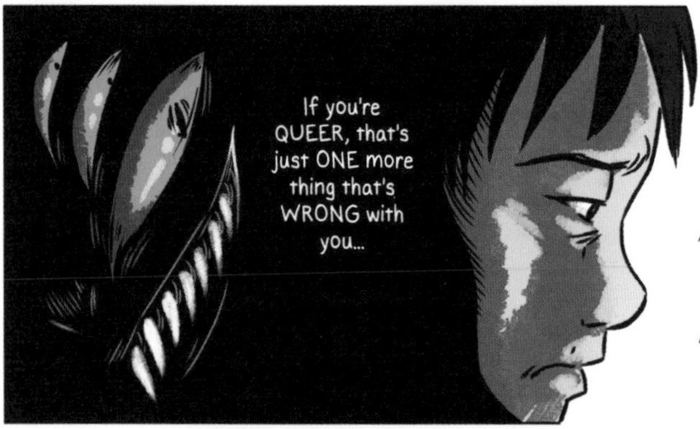
If you're QUEER, that's just ONE more thing that's WRONG with you...

Again, this was the early 2000s.

I hadn't even heard terms like "transgender" or "nonbinary" to describe gender identity yet.

"Bisexual" was a foreign concept to most people in my small town.

"Gay" was an insult at school.

I was AFRAID to be gay.

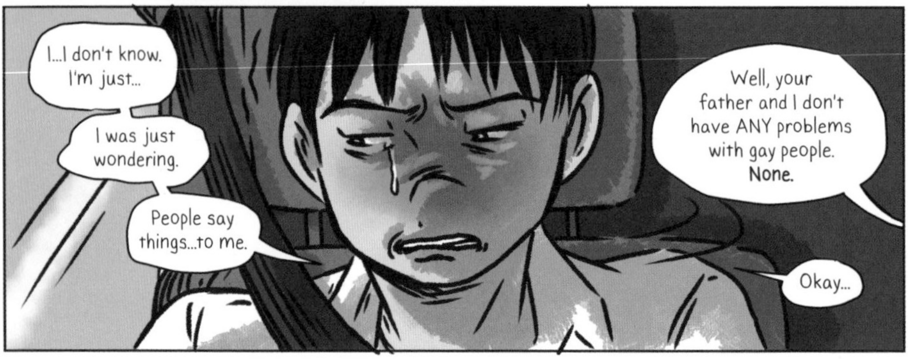
I...I don't know. I'm just...
I was just wondering.
People say things...to me.
Well, your father and I don't have ANY problems with gay people. **None.**
Okay...

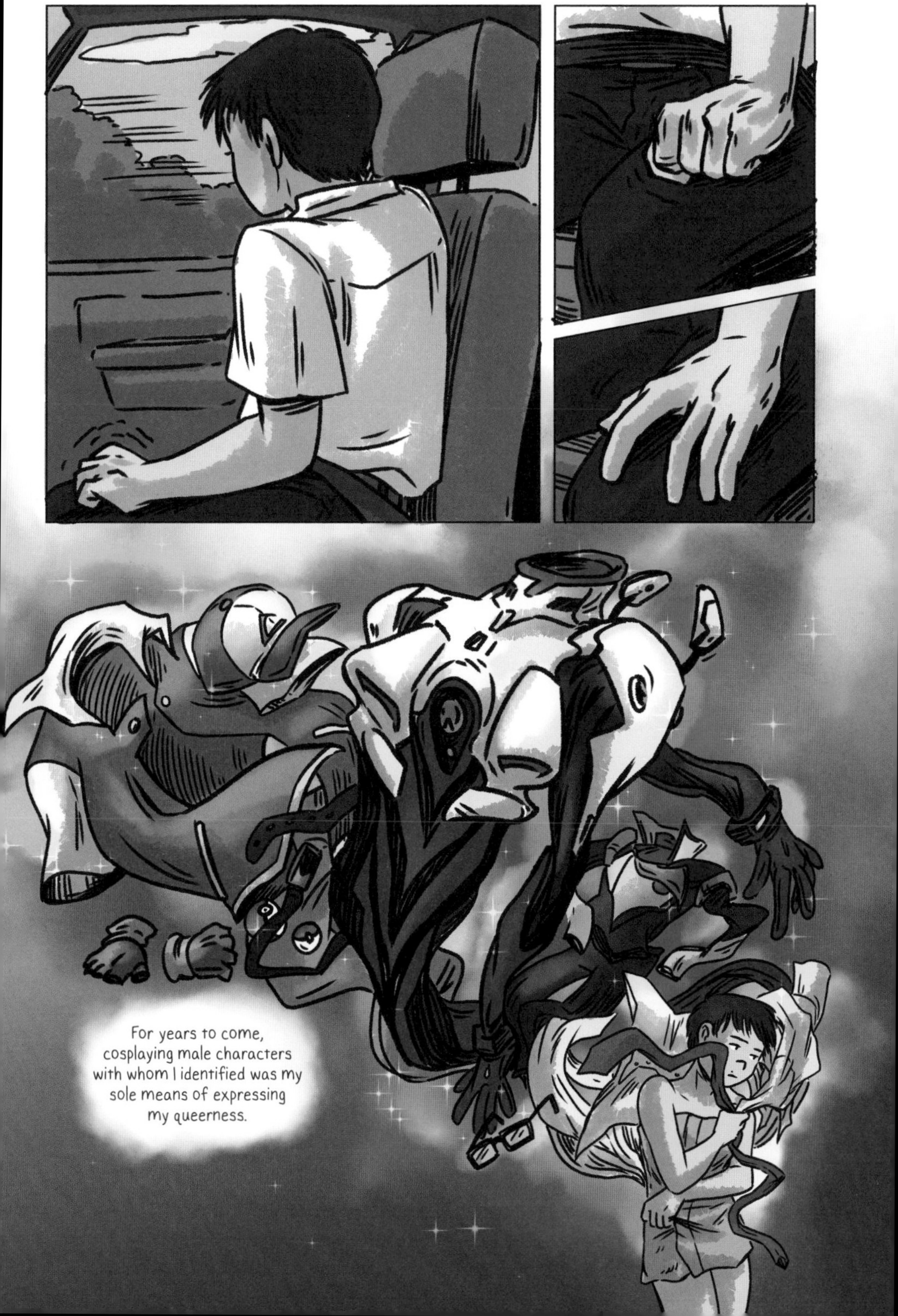
For years to come, cosplaying male characters with whom I identified was my sole means of expressing my queerness.

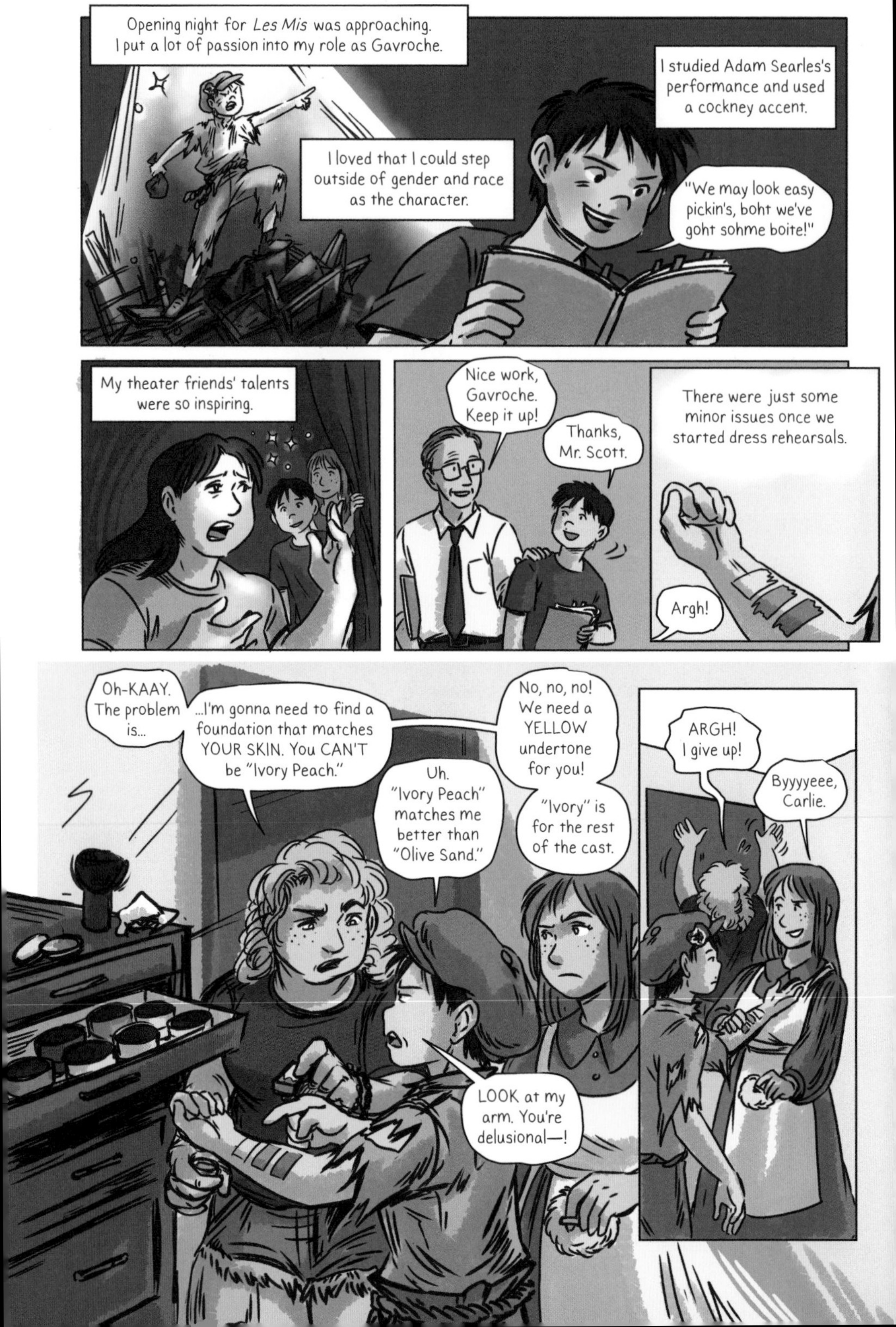

Opening night for *Les Mis* was approaching. I put a lot of passion into my role as Gavroche.
I studied Adam Searles's performance and used a cockney accent.
I loved that I could step outside of gender and race as the character.
"We may look easy pickin's, boht we've goht sohme boite!"
My theater friends' talents were so inspiring.
Nice work, Gavroche. Keep it up!
Thanks, Mr. Scott.
There were just some minor issues once we started dress rehearsals.
Argh!
Oh-KAAY. The problem is...
...I'm gonna need to find a foundation that matches YOUR SKIN. You CAN'T be "Ivory Peach."
Uh. "Ivory Peach" matches me better than "Olive Sand."
No, no, no! We need a YELLOW undertone for you!
"Ivory" is for the rest of the cast.
LOOK at my arm. You're delusional—!
ARGH! I give up!
Byyyyeee, Carlie.

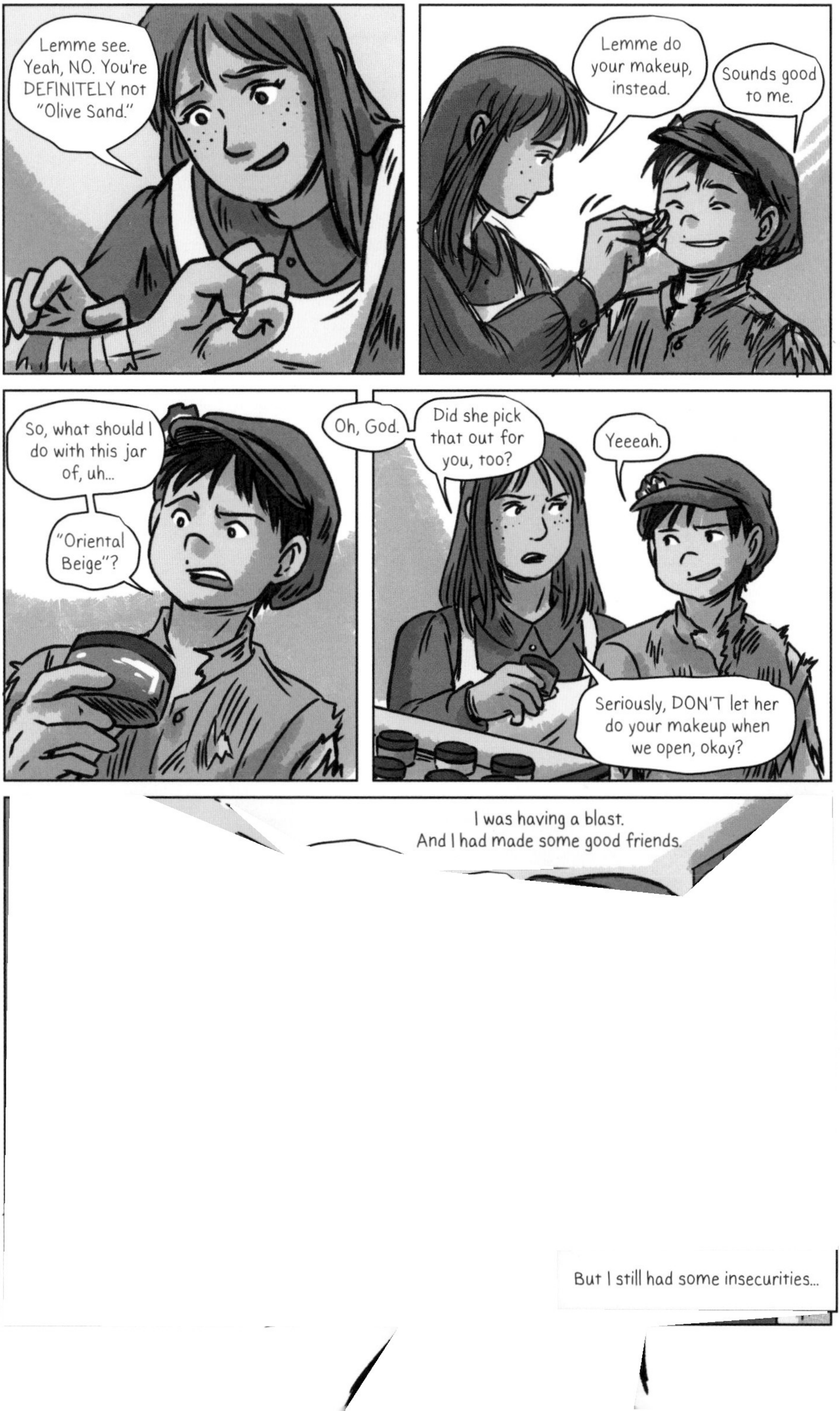
Lemme see. Yeah, NO. You're DEFINITELY not "Olive Sand."
Lemme do your makeup, instead.
Sounds good to me.
So, what should I do with this jar of, uh...
"Oriental Beige"?
Oh, God.
Did she pick that out for you, too?
Yeeeah.
Seriously, DON'T let her do your makeup when we open, okay?
I was having a blast.
And I had made some good friends.
But I still had some insecurities...

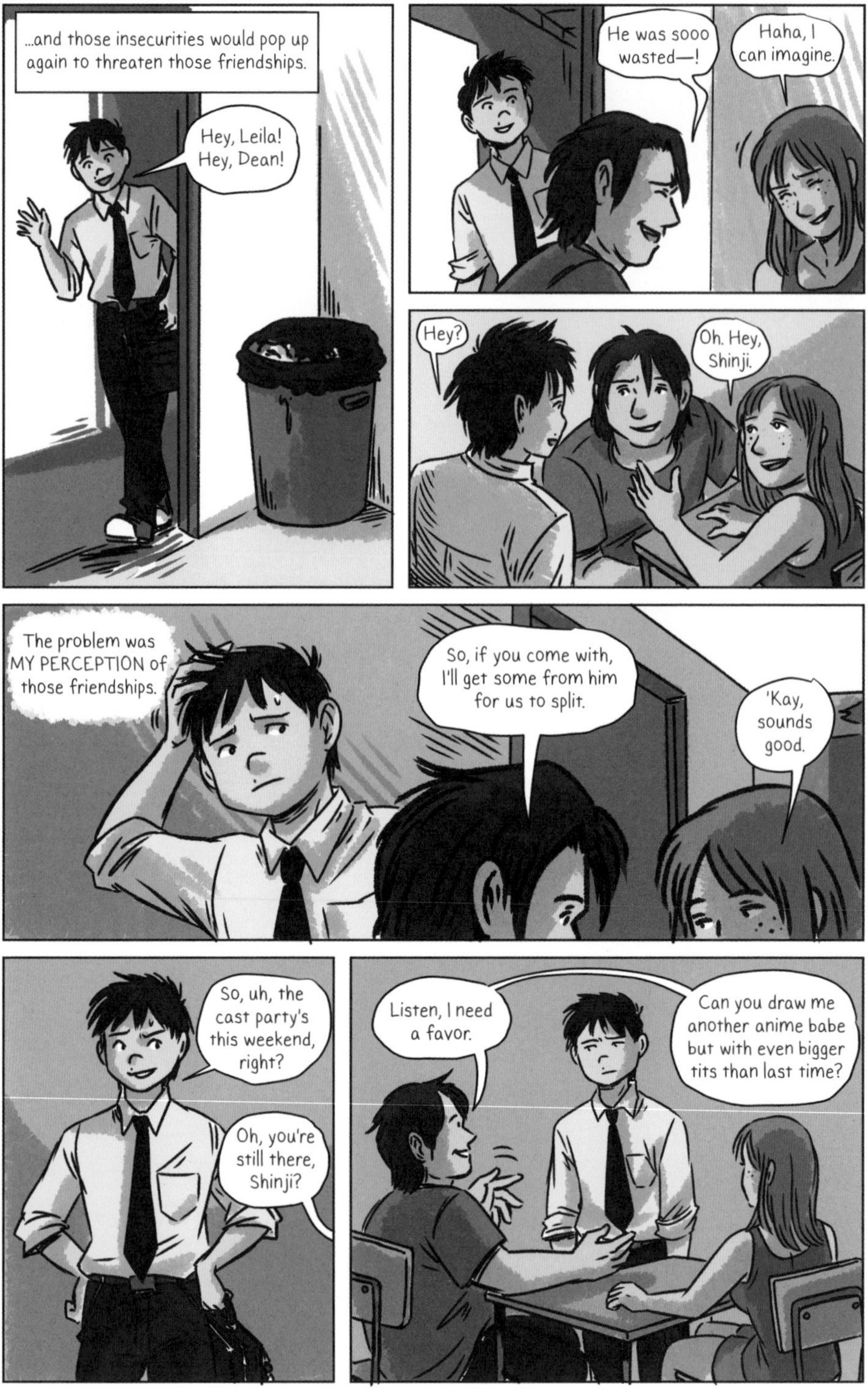
...and those insecurities would pop up again to threaten those friendships.
Hey, Leila! Hey, Dean!
He was sooo wasted—!
Haha, I can imagine.
Hey?
Oh. Hey, Shinji.
The problem was MY PERCEPTION of those friendships.
So, if you come with, I'll get some from him for us to split.
'Kay, sounds good.
So, uh, the cast party's this weekend, right?
Oh, you're still there, Shinji?
Listen, I need a favor.
Can you draw me another anime babe but with even bigger tits than last time?

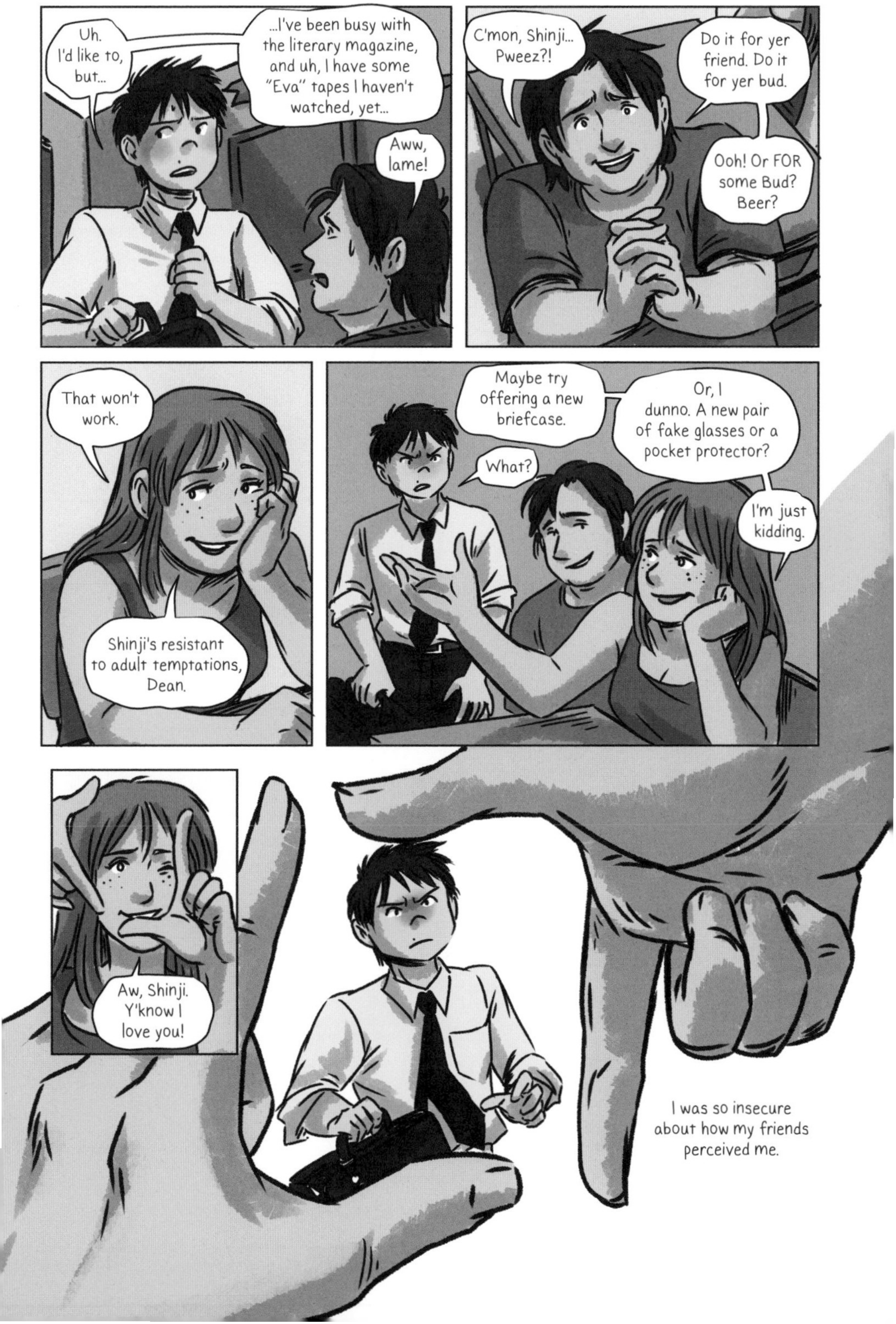
Uh. I'd like to, but...
...I've been busy with the literary magazine, and uh, I have some "Eva" tapes I haven't watched, yet...
Aww, lame!
C'mon, Shinji... Pweez?!
Do it for yer friend. Do it for yer bud.
Ooh! Or FOR some Bud? Beer?
That won't work.
Shinji's resistant to adult temptations, Dean.
Maybe try offering a new briefcase.
Or, I dunno. A new pair of fake glasses or a pocket protector?
What?
I'm just kidding.
Aw, Shinji. Y'know I love you!
I was so insecure about how my friends perceived me.

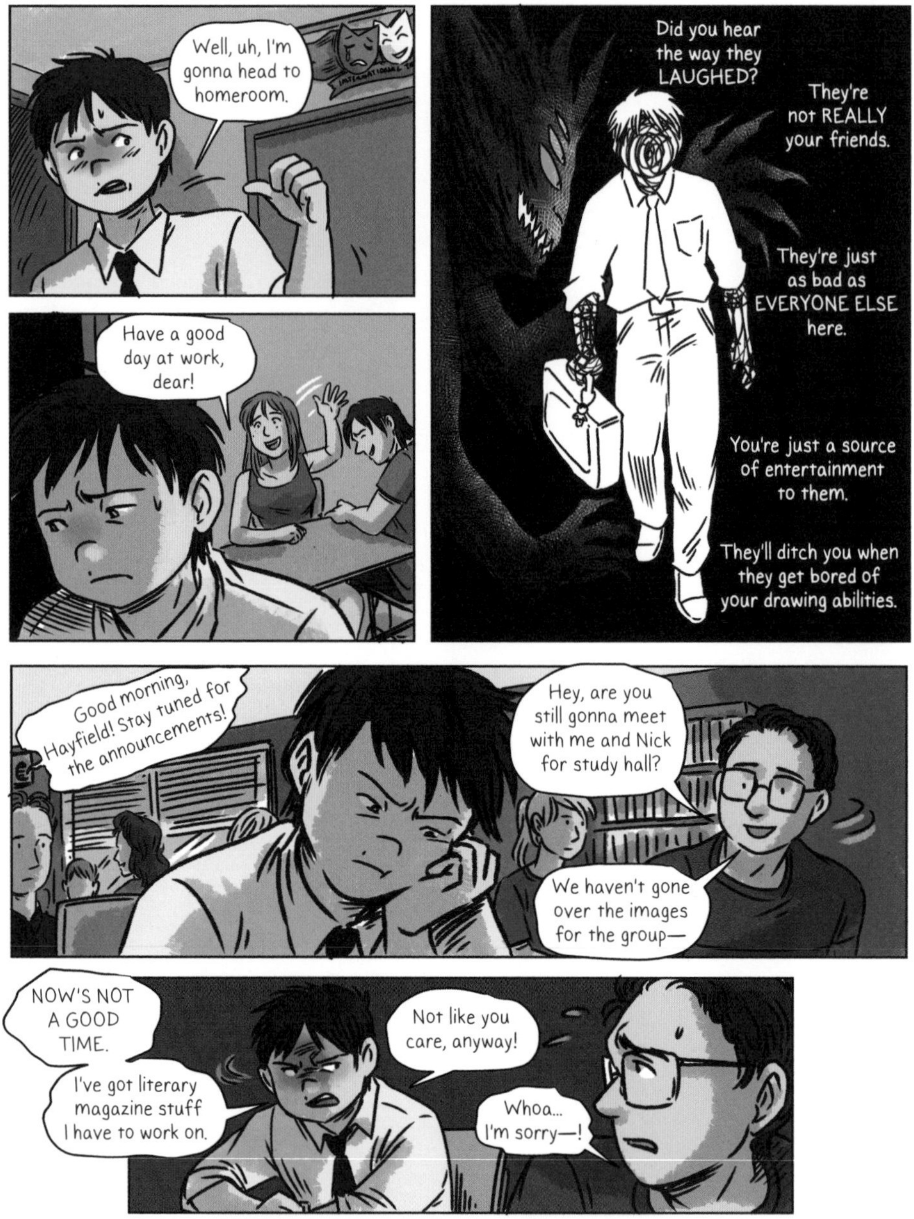
Well, uh, I'm gonna head to homeroom.
Did you hear the way they LAUGHED?
They're not REALLY your friends.
They're just as bad as EVERYONE ELSE here.
You're just a source of entertainment to them.
They'll ditch you when they get bored of your drawing abilities.
Have a good day at work, dear!
Good morning, Hayfield! Stay tuned for the announcements!
Hey, are you still gonna meet with me and Nick for study hall?
We haven't gone over the images for the group—
NOW'S NOT A GOOD TIME.
I've got literary magazine stuff I have to work on.
Not like you care, anyway!
Whoa... I'm sorry—!

When I had something plaguing my mind, I got TUNNEL VISION.

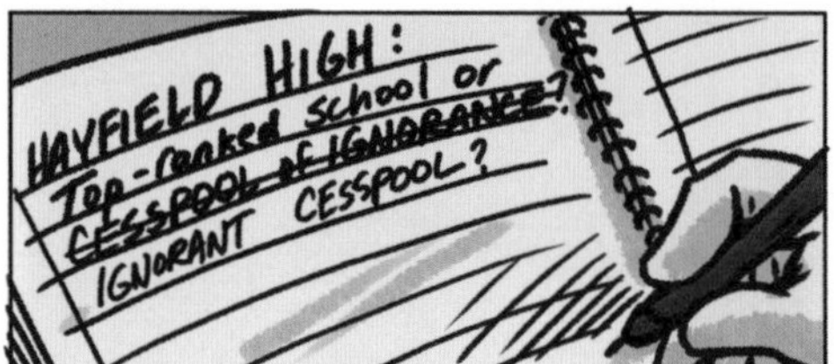
HAYFIELD HIGH:
Top-ranked school or
CESSPOOL of IGNORANCE?
IGNORANT CESSPOOL?

I failed to notice benign aspects of my life, like the kind friends and classmates I DID have.

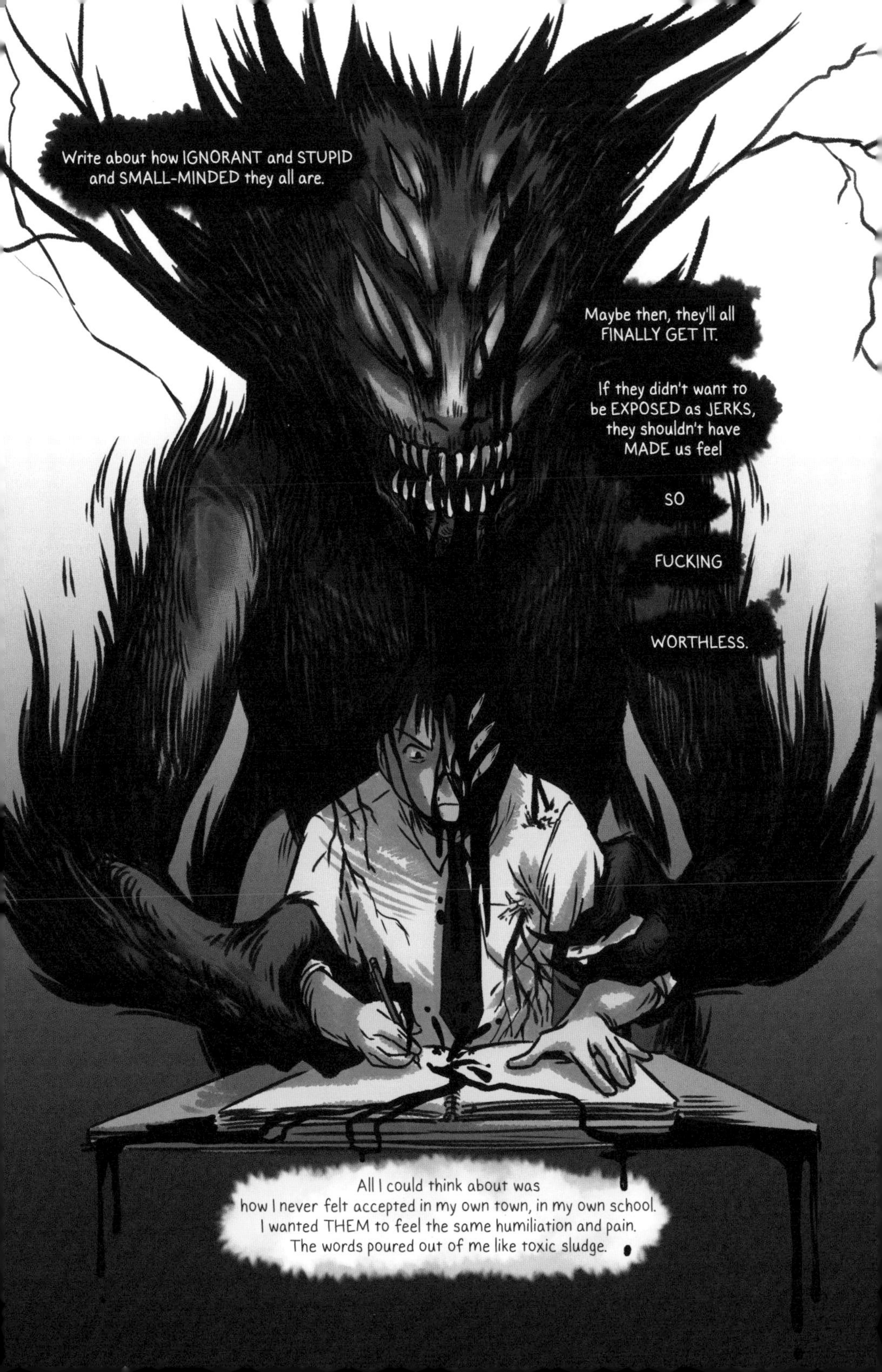
Write about how IGNORANT and STUPID and SMALL-MINDED they all are.
Maybe then, they'll all FINALLY GET IT.
If they didn't want to be EXPOSED as JERKS, they shouldn't have MADE us feel
SO
FUCKING
WORTHLESS.
All I could think about was how I never felt accepted in my own town, in my own school. I wanted THEM to feel the same humiliation and pain. The words poured out of me like toxic sludge.

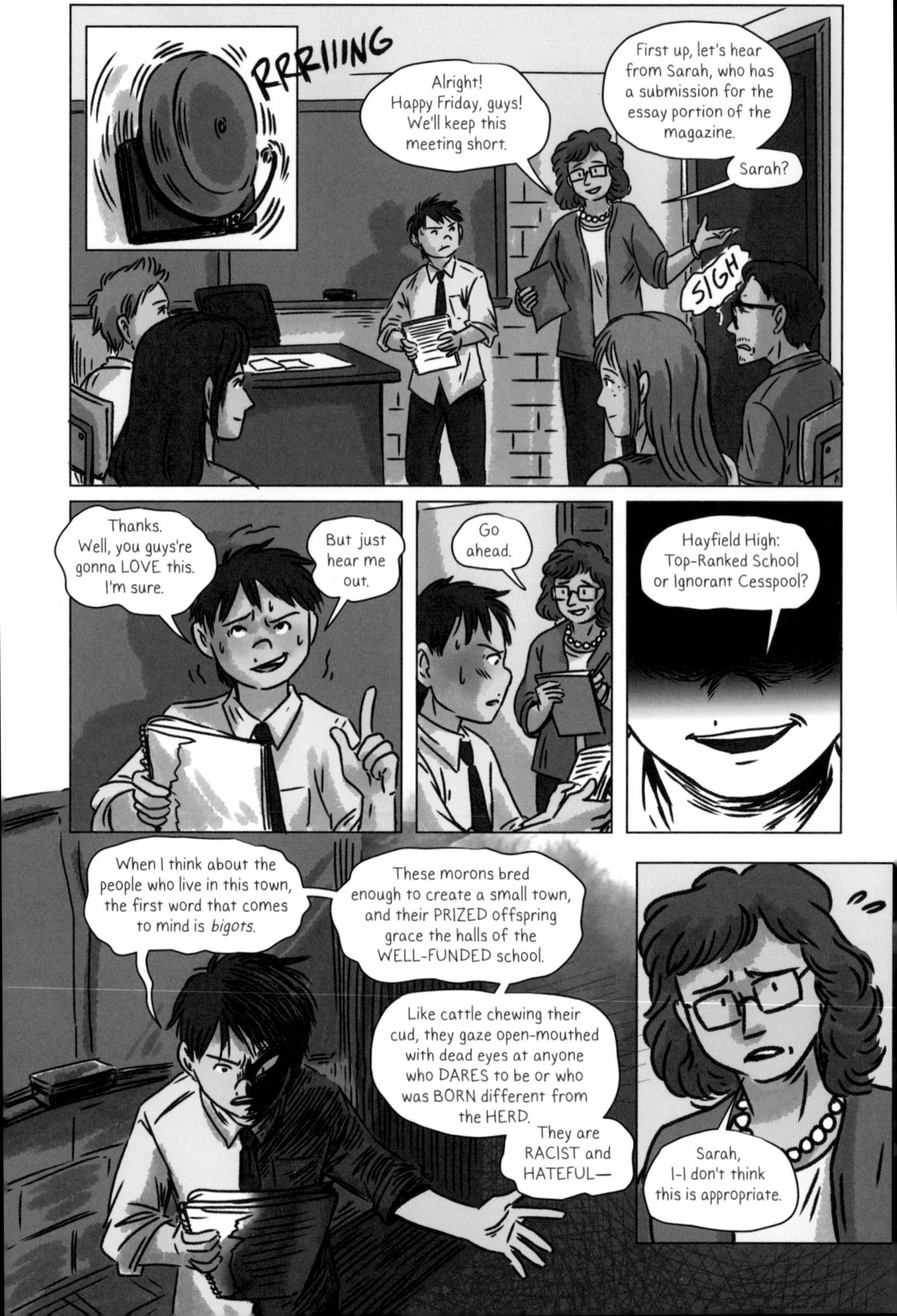
RRRIIING
Alright! Happy Friday, guys! We'll keep this meeting short.
First up, let's hear from Sarah, who has a submission for the essay portion of the magazine.
Sarah?
SIGH
Thanks. Well, you guys're gonna LOVE this. I'm sure.
But just hear me out.
Go ahead.
Hayfield High: Top-Ranked School or Ignorant Cesspool?
When I think about the people who live in this town, the first word that comes to mind is *bigots*.
These morons bred enough to create a small town, and their PRIZED offspring grace the halls of the WELL-FUNDED school.
Like cattle chewing their cud, they gaze open-mouthed with dead eyes at anyone who DARES to be or who was BORN different from the HERD.
They are RACIST and HATEFUL—
Sarah, I-I don't think this is appropriate.

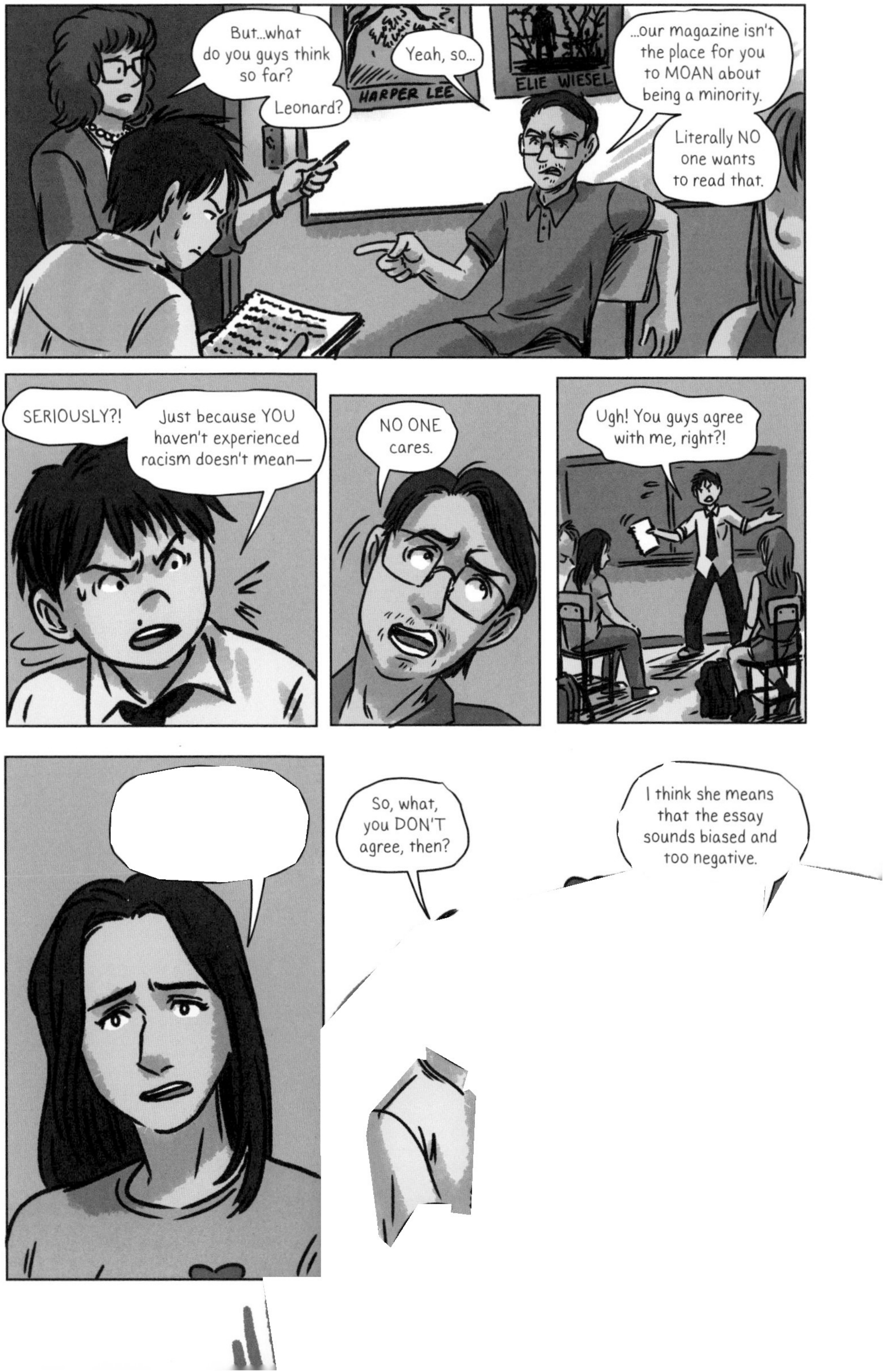
But...what do you guys think so far?
Leonard?
HARPER LEE
Yeah, so...
ELIE WIESEL
...our magazine isn't the place for you to MOAN about being a minority.
Literally NO one wants to read that.
SERIOUSLY?!
Just because YOU haven't experienced racism doesn't mean—
NO ONE cares.
Ugh! You guys agree with me, right?!
So, what, you DON'T agree, then?
I think she means that the essay sounds biased and too negative.

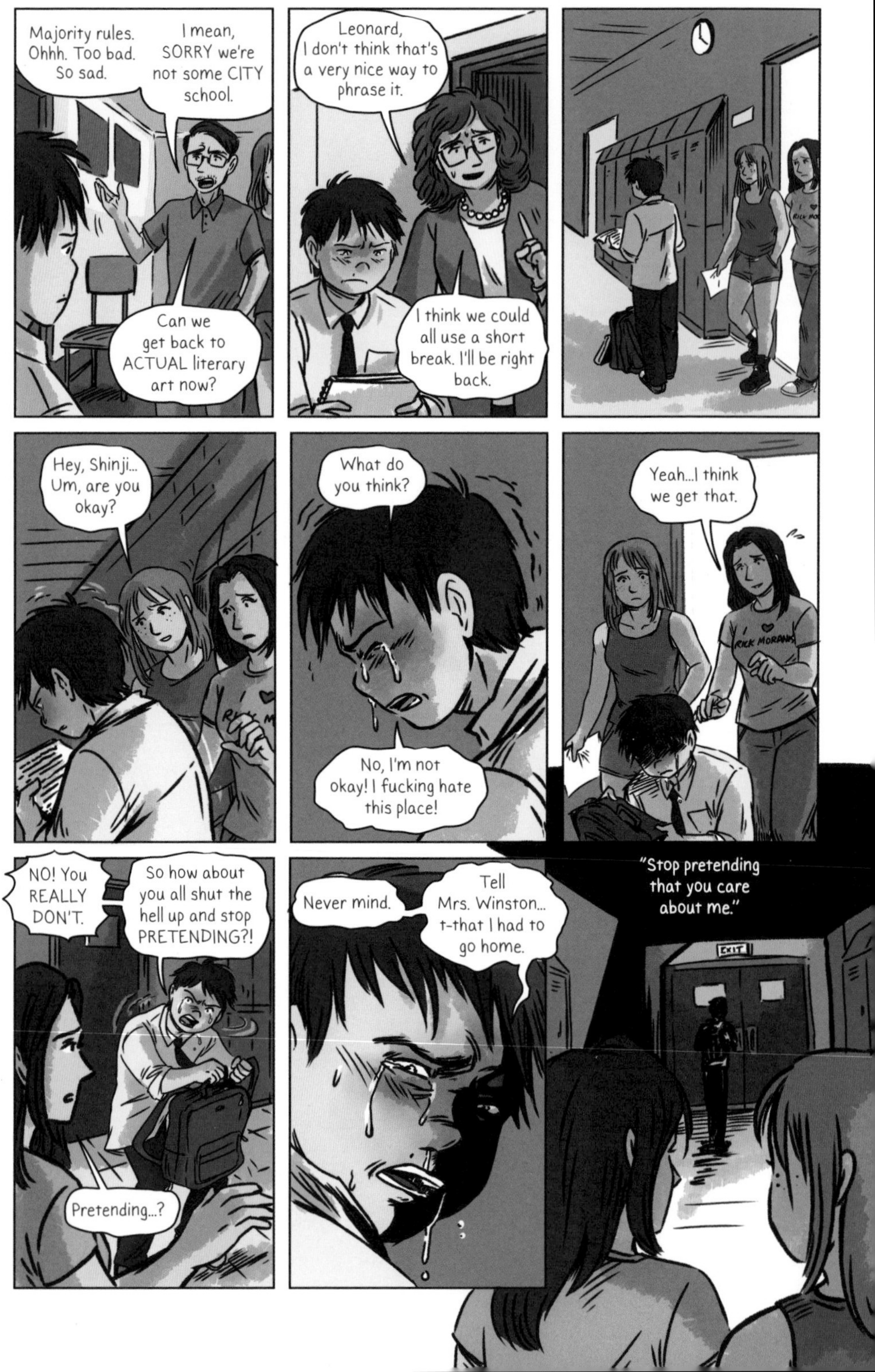
Majority rules. Ohhh. Too bad. So sad.
I mean, SORRY we're not some CITY school.
Can we get back to ACTUAL literary art now?
Leonard, I don't think that's a very nice way to phrase it.
I think we could all use a short break. I'll be right back.
Hey, Shinji... Um, are you okay?
What do you think?
No, I'm not okay! I fucking hate this place!
Yeah...I think we get that.
I ♥ RICK MORANIS
NO! You REALLY DON'T.
So how about you all shut the hell up and stop PRETENDING?!
Pretending...?
Never mind.
Tell Mrs. Winston... t-that I had to go home.
"Stop pretending that you care about me."
EXIT

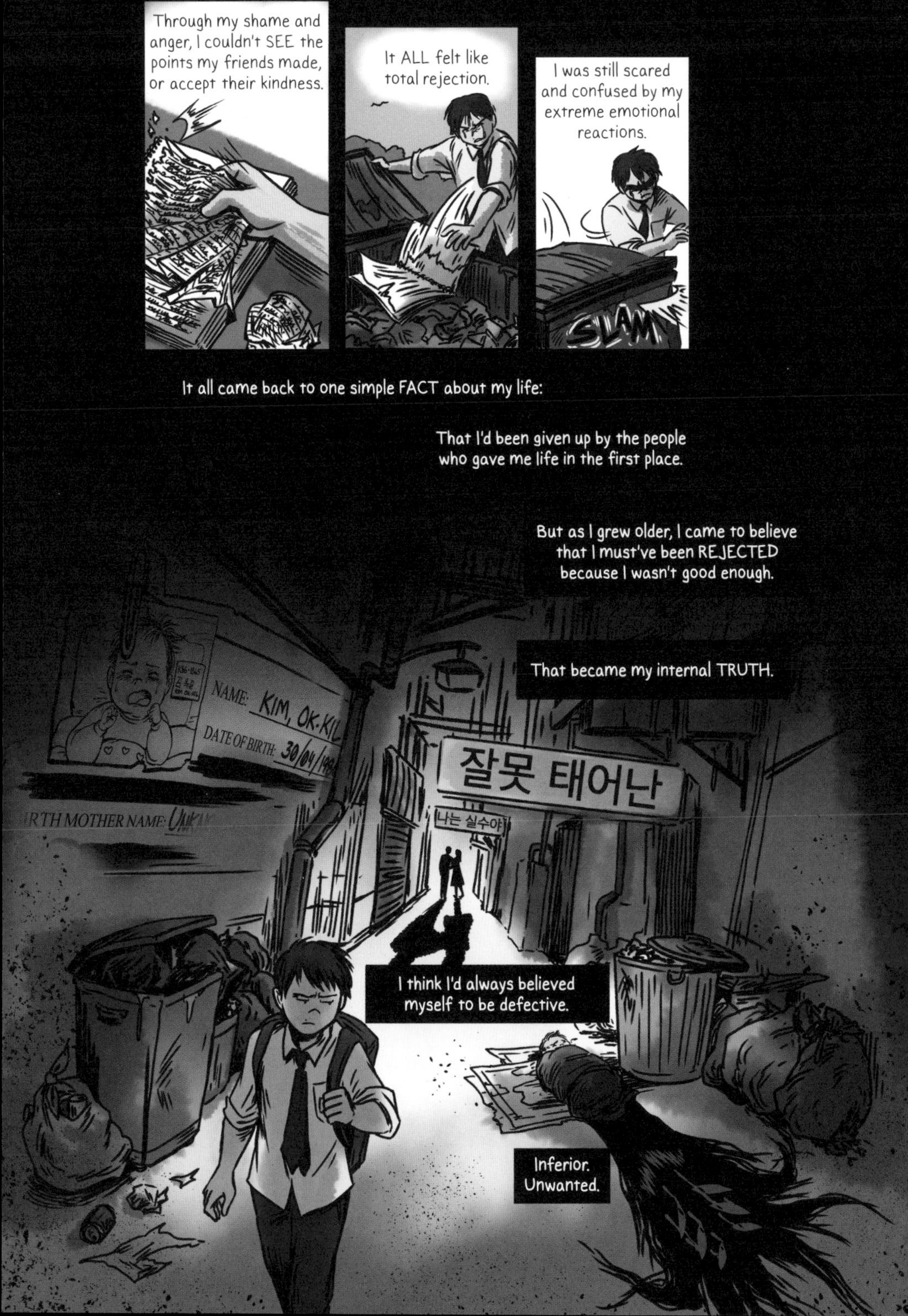
Through my shame and anger, I couldn't SEE the points my friends made, or accept their kindness.
It ALL felt like total rejection.
I was still scared and confused by my extreme emotional reactions.
SLAM
It all came back to one simple FACT about my life:
That I'd been given up by the people who gave me life in the first place.
But as I grew older, I came to believe that I must've been REJECTED because I wasn't good enough.
NAME: KIM, OK-KIL
That became my internal TRUTH.
잘못 태어난
나는 실수야
I think I'd always believed myself to be defective.
Inferior. Unwanted.

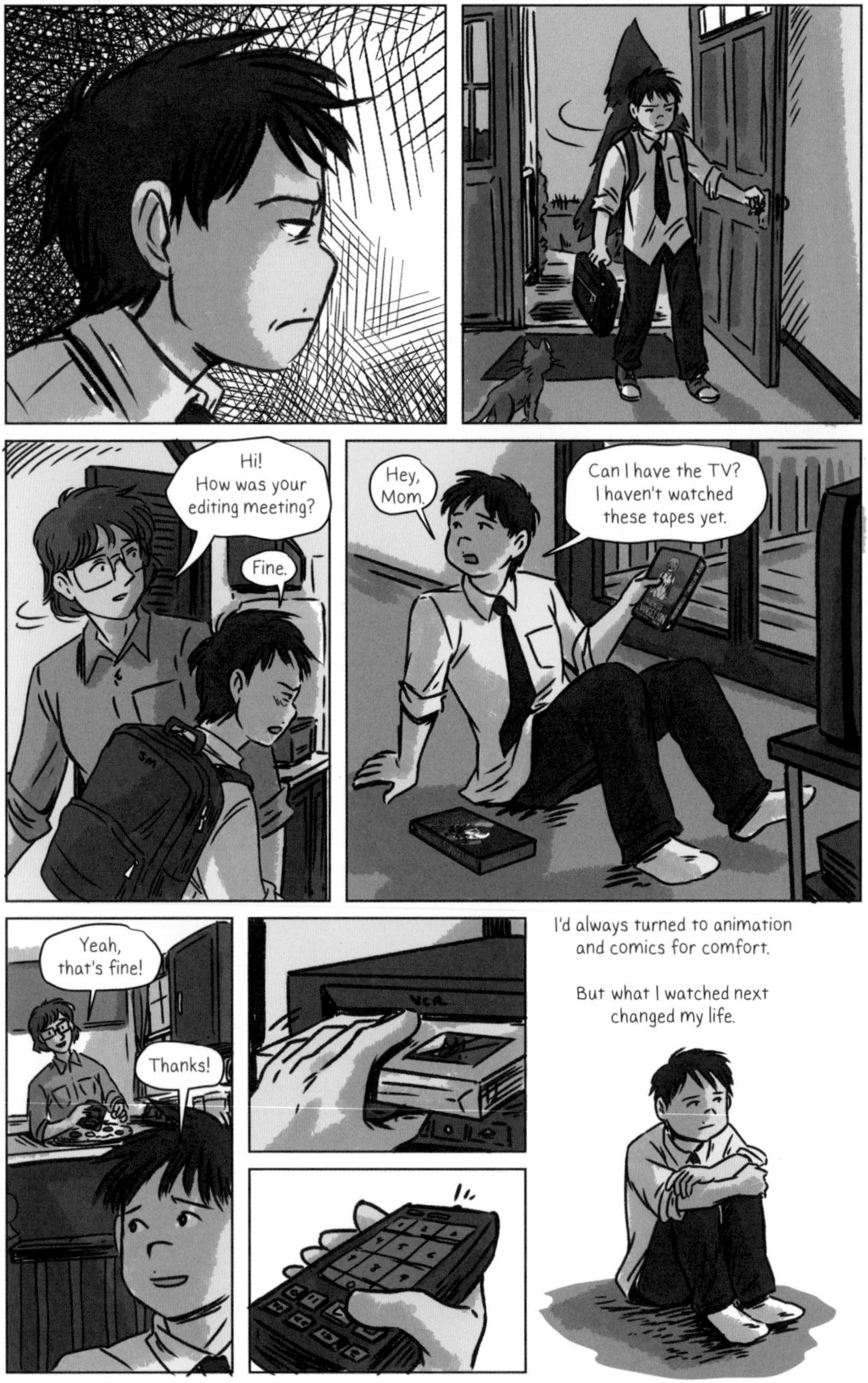
Hi!
How was your editing meeting?
Fine.
Hey, Mom.
Can I have the TV? I haven't watched these tapes yet.
Yeah, that's fine!
Thanks!
VCR
I'd always turned to animation and comics for comfort.
But what I watched next changed my life.

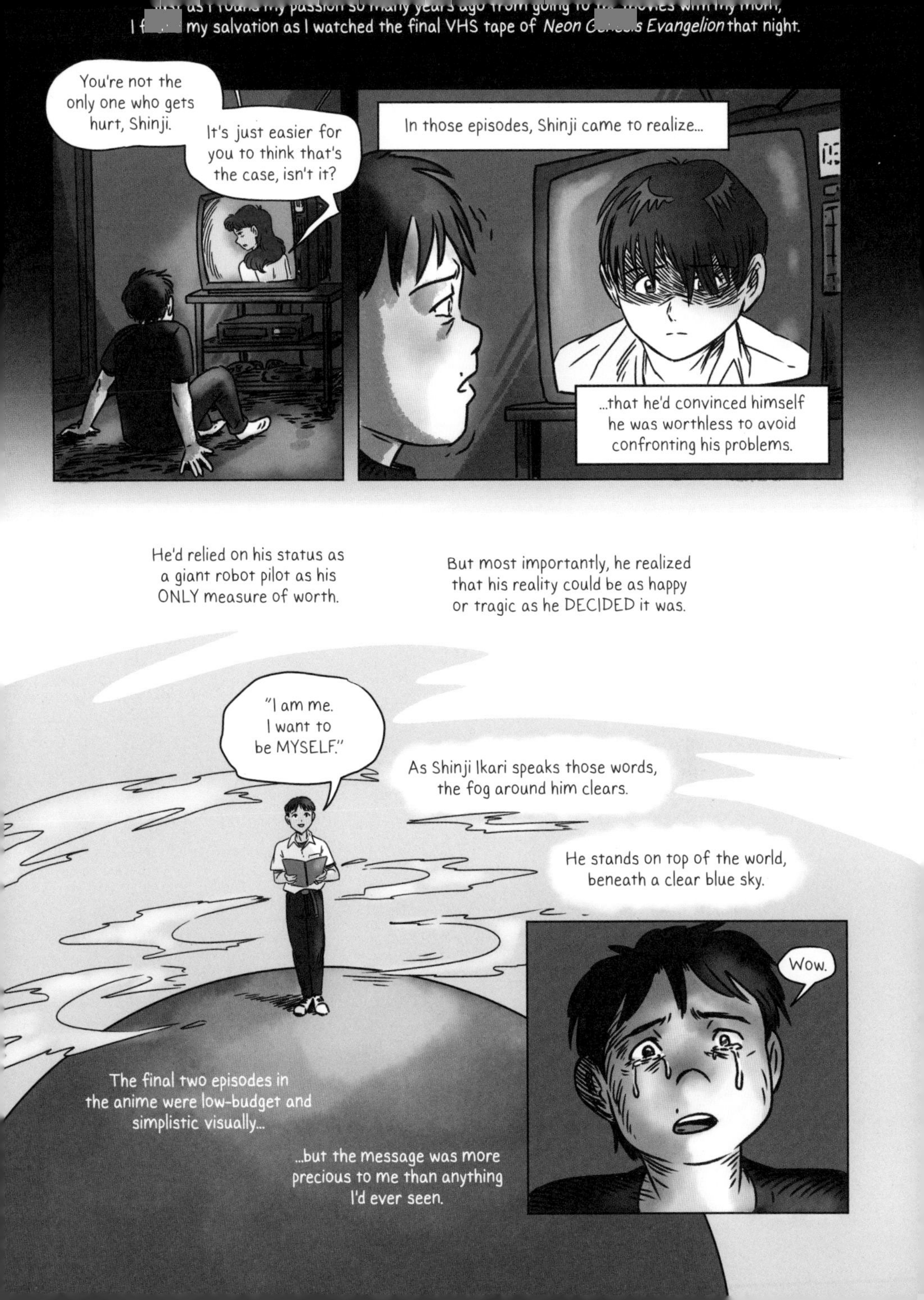

...st as I found my passion so many years ago from going to [redacted] movies with my mom,
I f[redacted] my salvation as I watched the final VHS tape of *Neon G*[redacted]*s Evangelion* that night.
You're not the only one who gets hurt, Shinji.
It's just easier for you to think that's the case, isn't it?
In those episodes, Shinji came to realize...
...that he'd convinced himself he was worthless to avoid confronting his problems.
He'd relied on his status as a giant robot pilot as his ONLY measure of worth.
But most importantly, he realized that his reality could be as happy or tragic as he DECIDED it was.
"I am me. I want to be MYSELF."
As Shinji Ikari speaks those words, the fog around him clears.
He stands on top of the world, beneath a clear blue sky.
Wow.
The final two episodes in the anime were low-budget and simplistic visually...
...but the message was more precious to me than anything I'd ever seen.

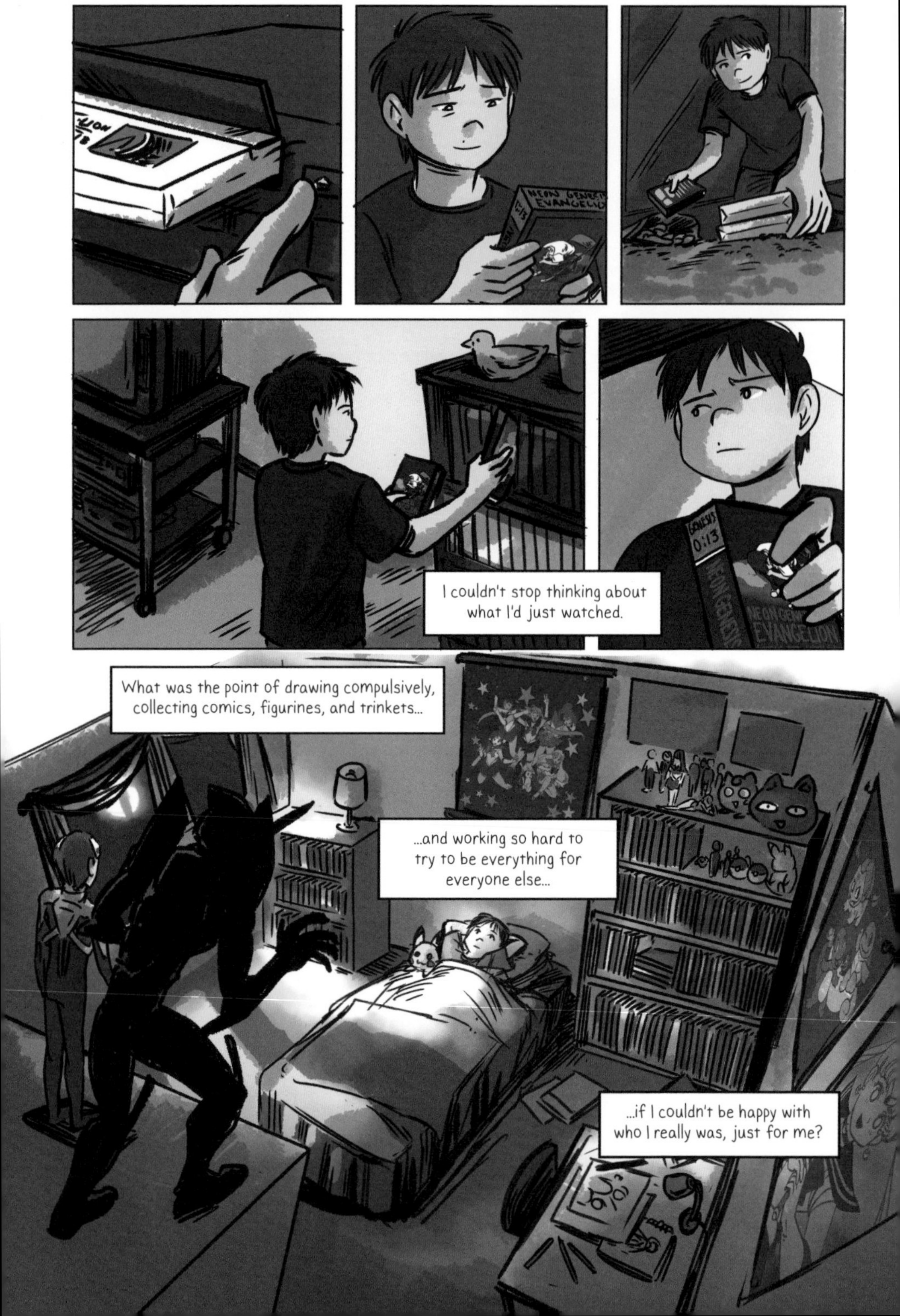
NEON GENESIS EVANGELION
GENESIS 0:13
I couldn't stop thinking about what I'd just watched.
What was the point of drawing compulsively, collecting comics, figurines, and trinkets...
...and working so hard to try to be everything for everyone else...
...if I couldn't be happy with who I really was, just for me?

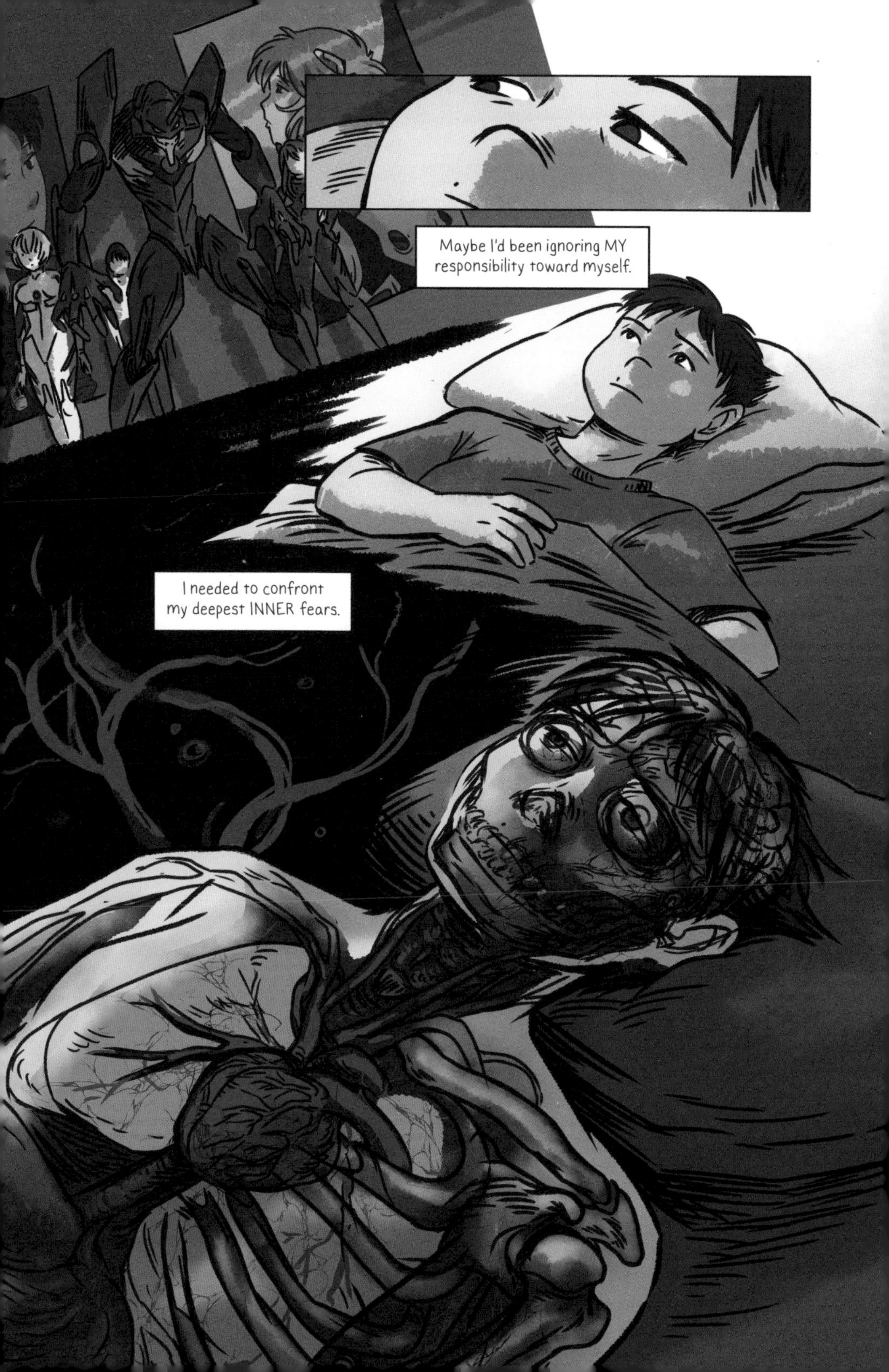
Maybe I'd been ignoring MY responsibility toward myself.
I needed to confront my deepest INNER fears.

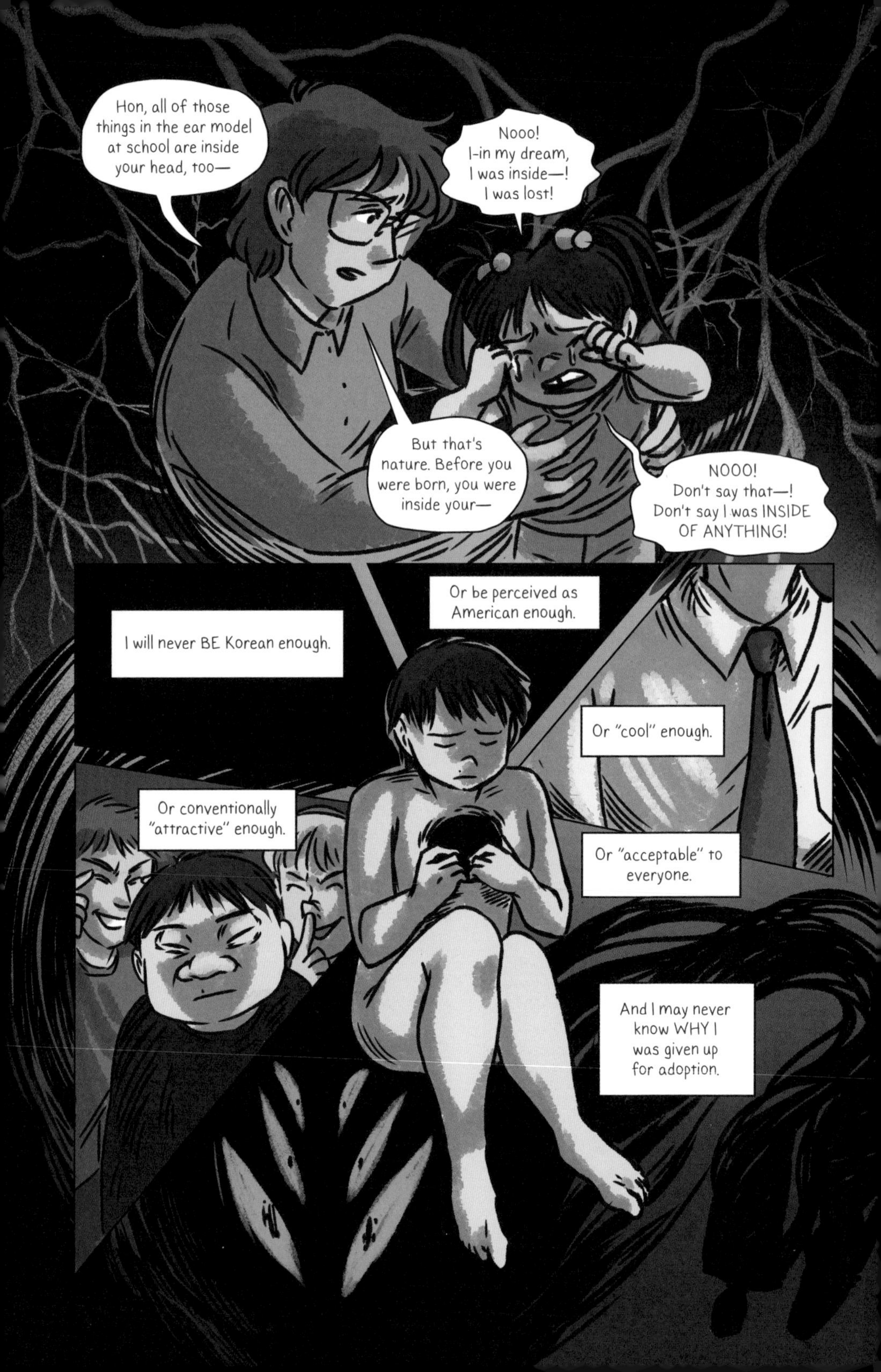
Hon, all of those things in the ear model at school are inside your head, too—
Nooo! I-in my dream, I was inside—! I was lost!
But that's nature. Before you were born, you were inside your—
NOOO! Don't say that—! Don't say I was INSIDE OF ANYTHING!
I will never BE Korean enough.
Or be perceived as American enough.
Or "cool" enough.
Or conventionally "attractive" enough.
Or "acceptable" to everyone.
And I may never know WHY I was given up for adoption.

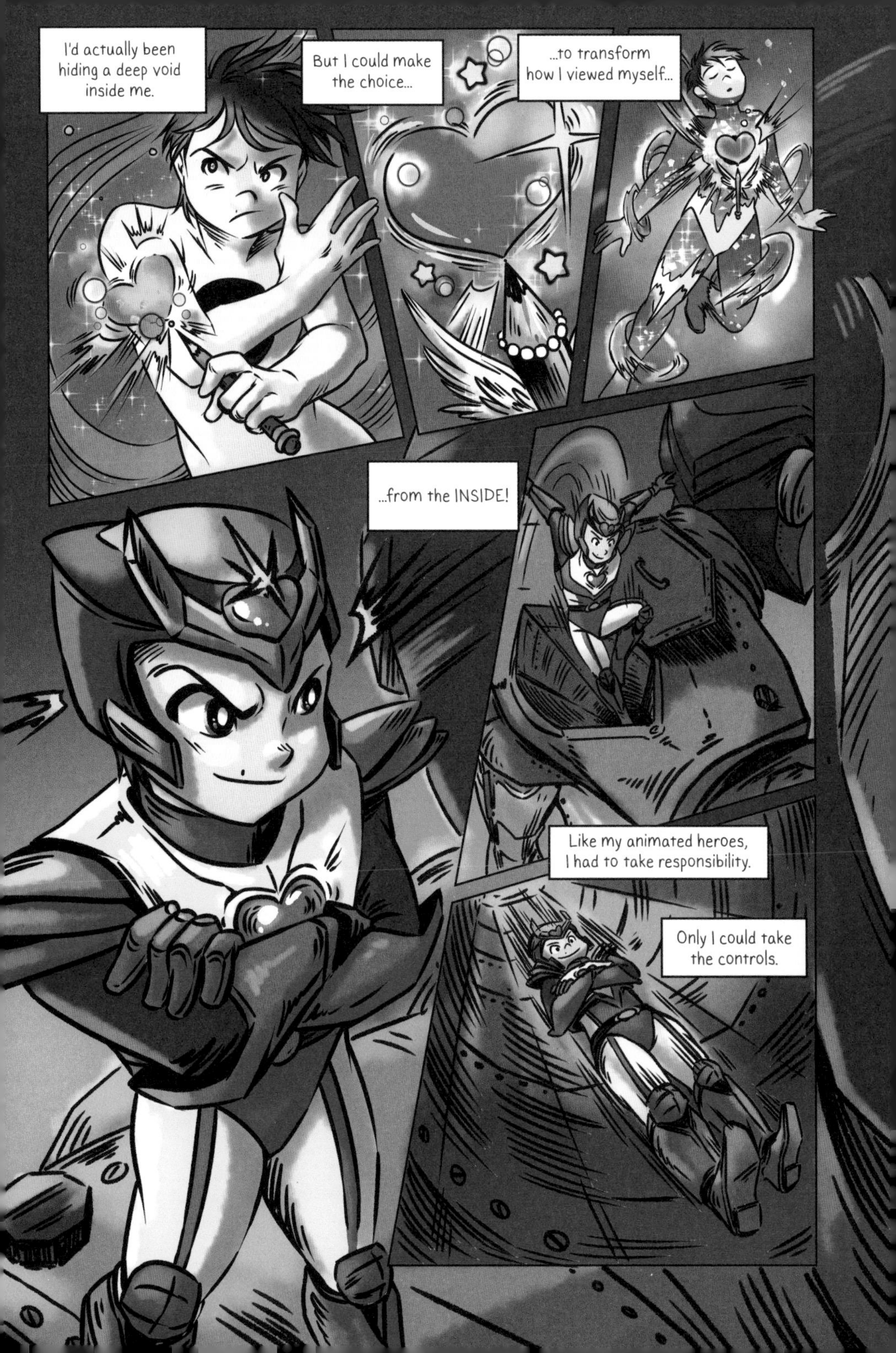
I'd actually been hiding a deep void inside me.
But I could make the choice...
...to transform how I viewed myself...
...from the INSIDE!
Like my animated heroes, I had to take responsibility.
Only I could take the controls.

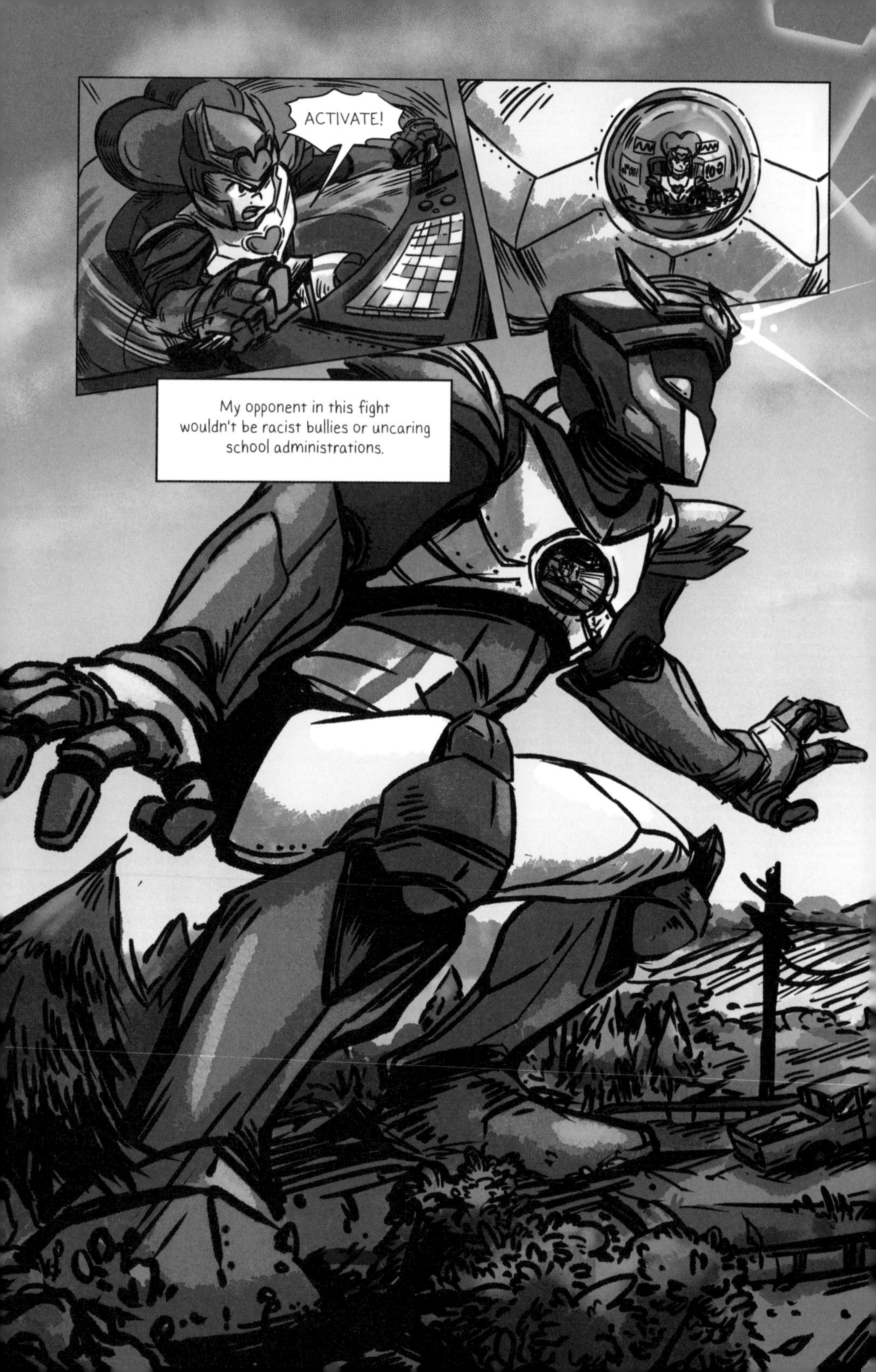
ACTIVATE!
My opponent in this fight wouldn't be racist bullies or uncaring school administrations.

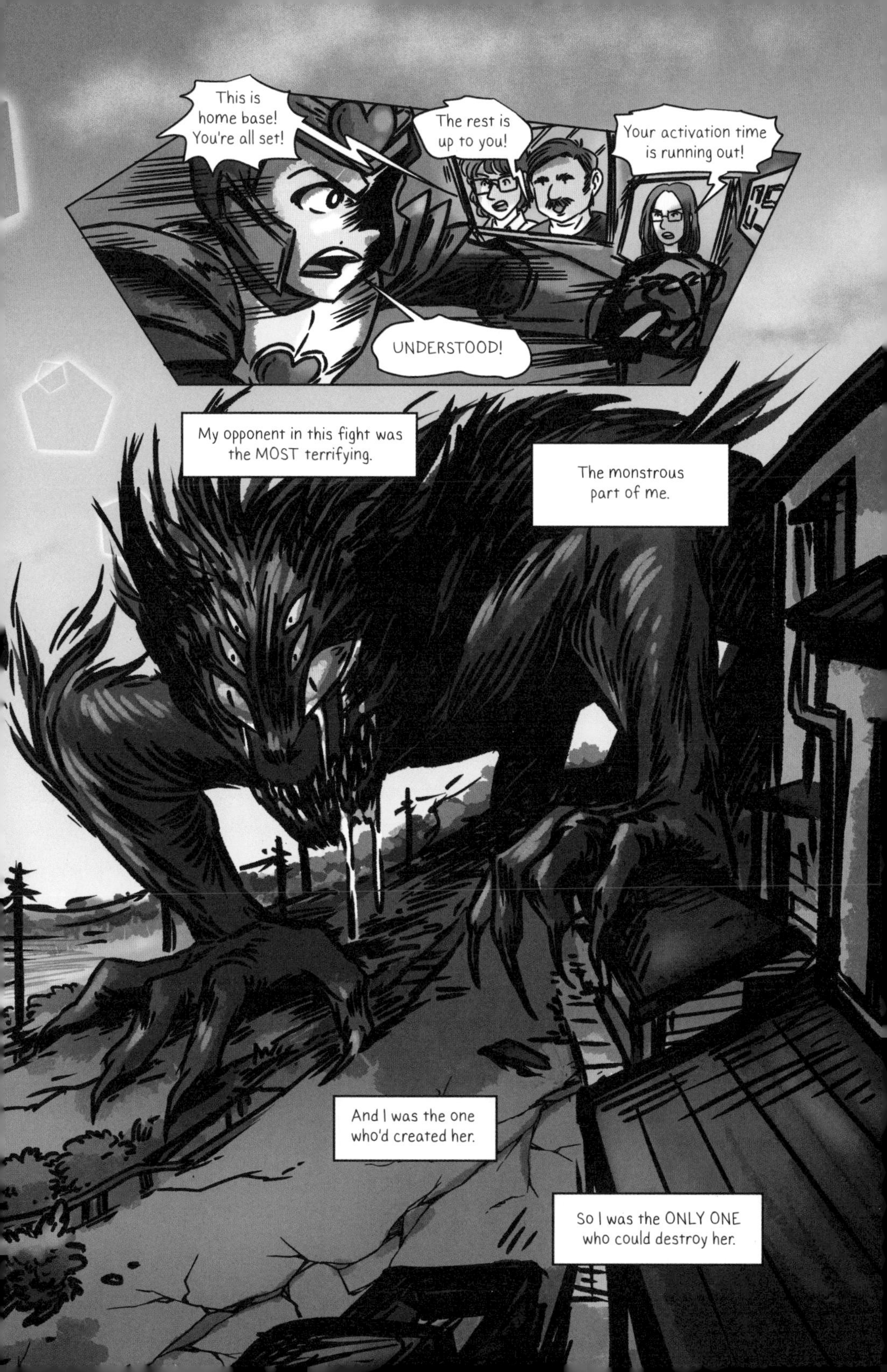
This is home base! You're all set!
The rest is up to you!
Your activation time is running out!
UNDERSTOOD!
My opponent in this fight was the MOST terrifying.
The monstrous part of me.
And I was the one who'd created her.
So I was the ONLY ONE who could destroy her.

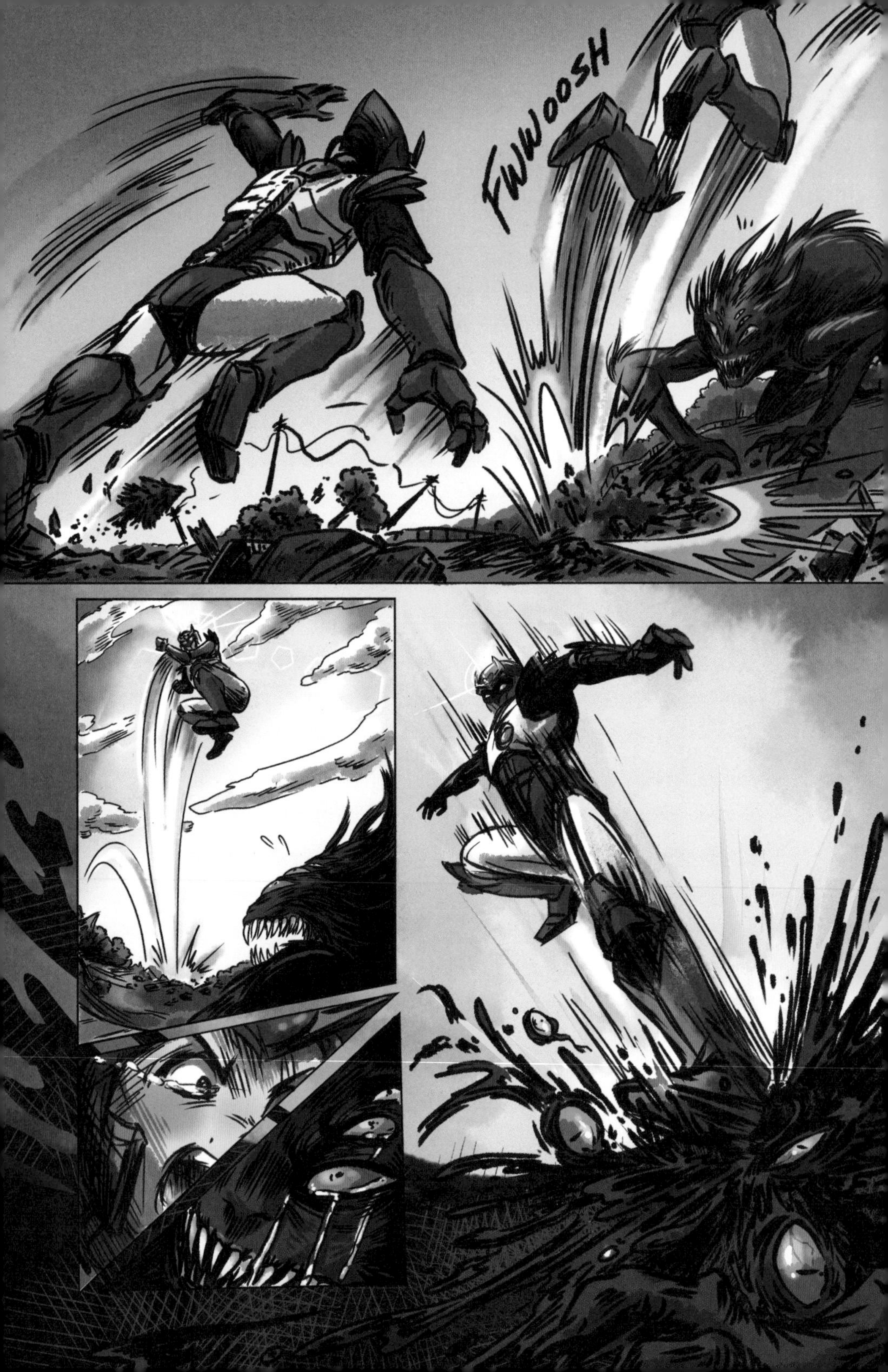
FWWOOSH

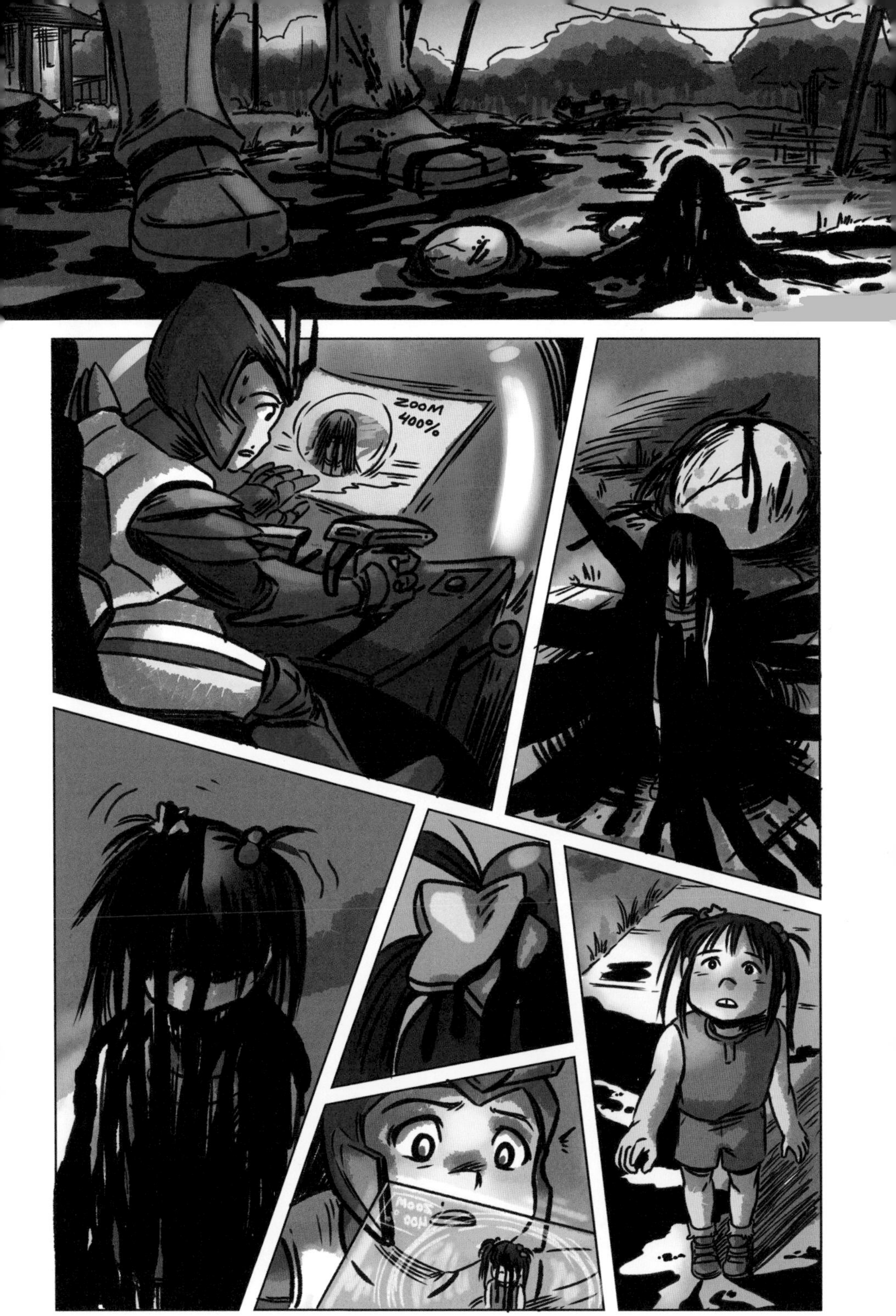
ZOOM
400%

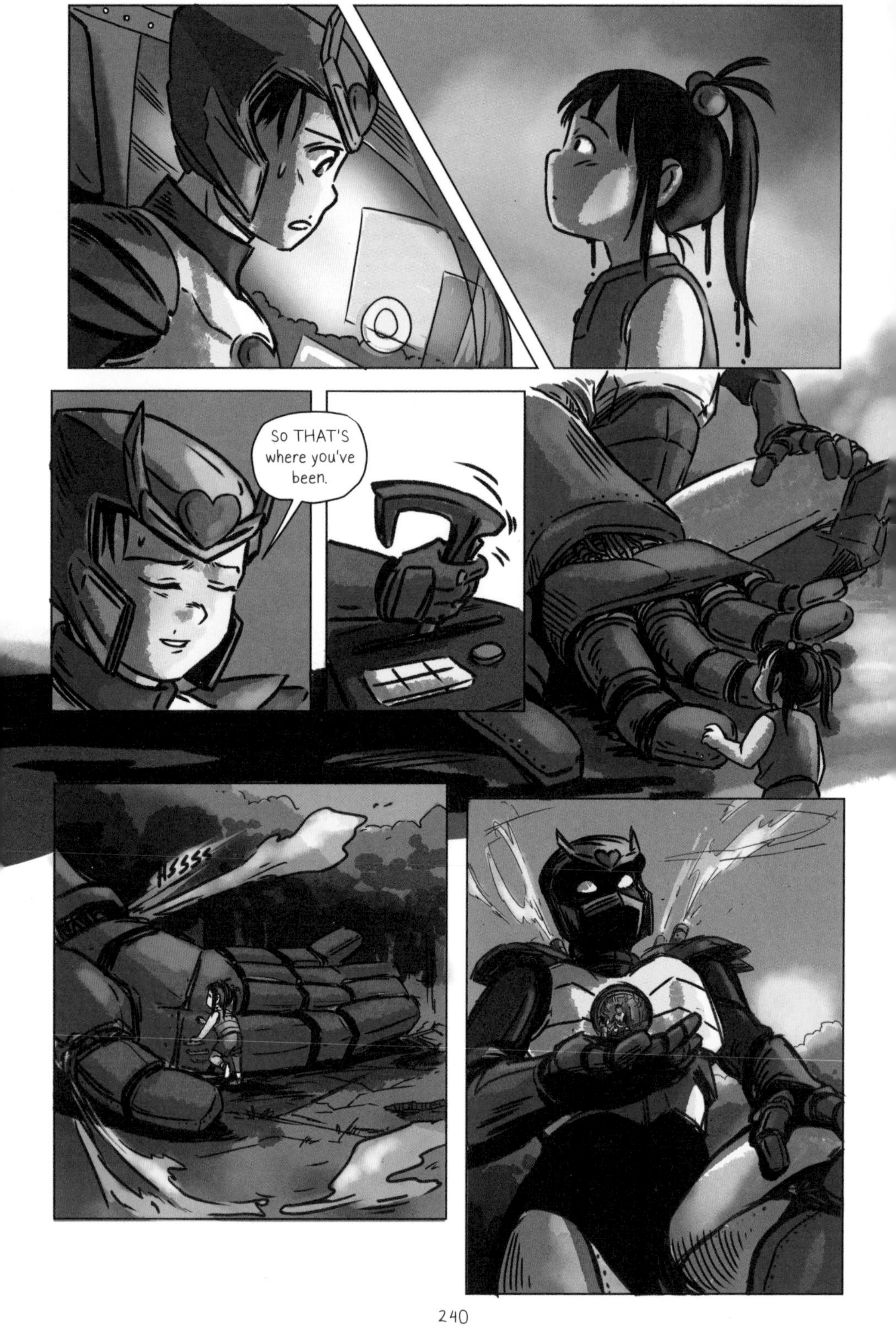
So THAT'S where you've been.
HSSSS

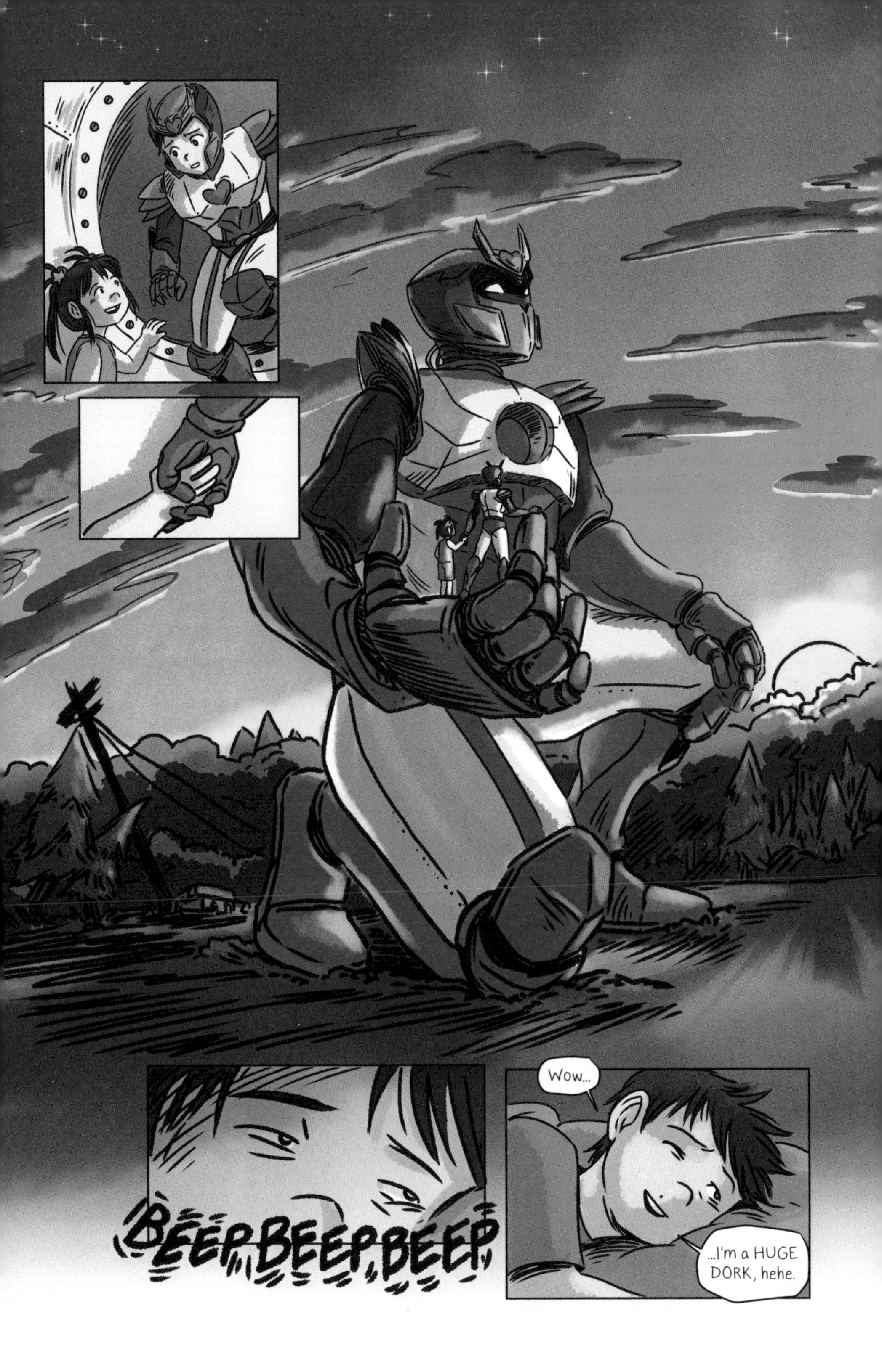
BEEP BEEP BEEP
Wow...
...I'm a HUGE DORK, hehe.

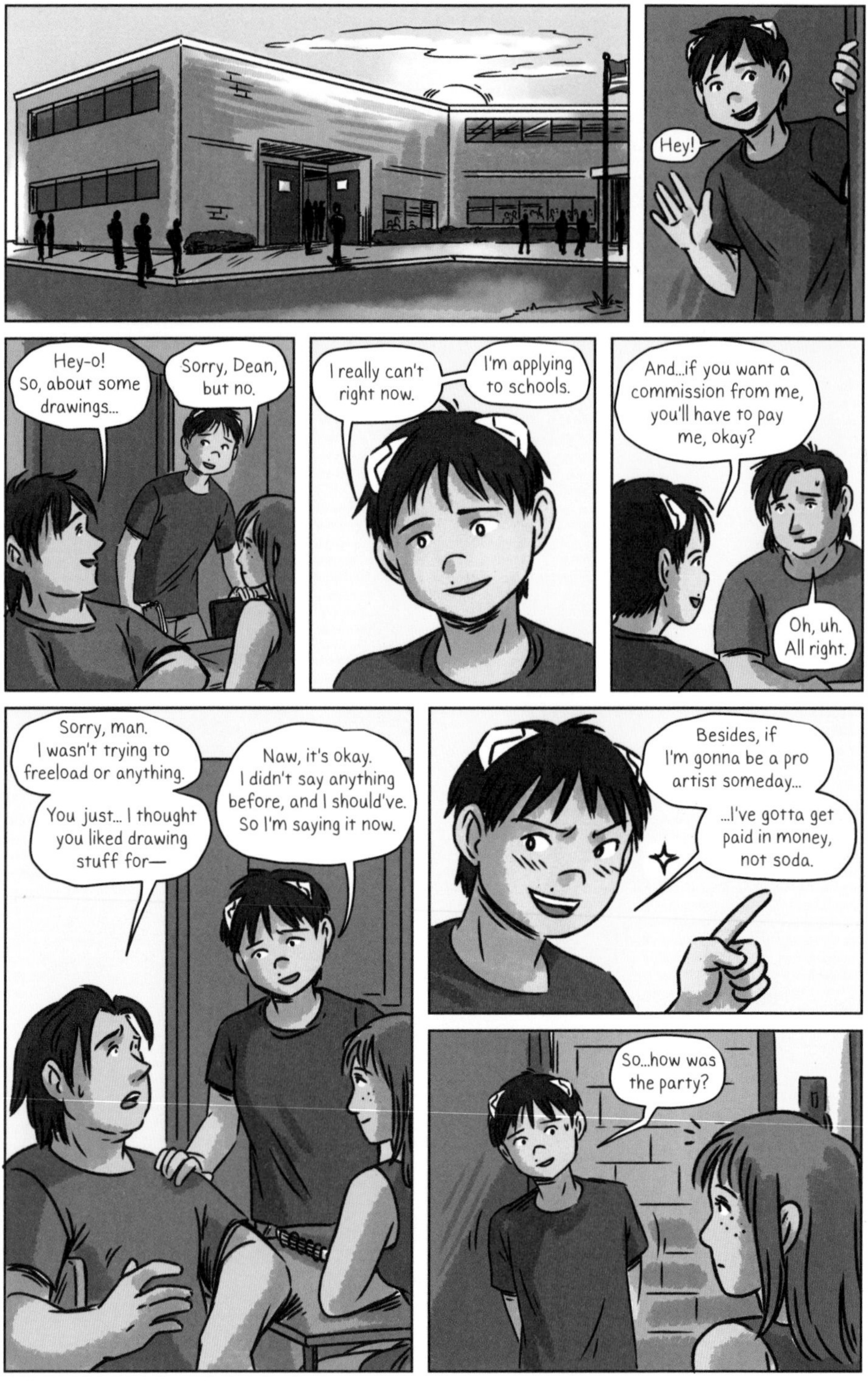
Hey!
Hey-o! So, about some drawings...
Sorry, Dean, but no.
I really can't right now.
I'm applying to schools.
And...if you want a commission from me, you'll have to pay me, okay?
Oh, uh. All right.
Sorry, man. I wasn't trying to freeload or anything.
You just... I thought you liked drawing stuff for—
Naw, it's okay. I didn't say anything before, and I should've. So I'm saying it now.
Besides, if I'm gonna be a pro artist someday...
...I've gotta get paid in money, not soda.
So...how was the party?

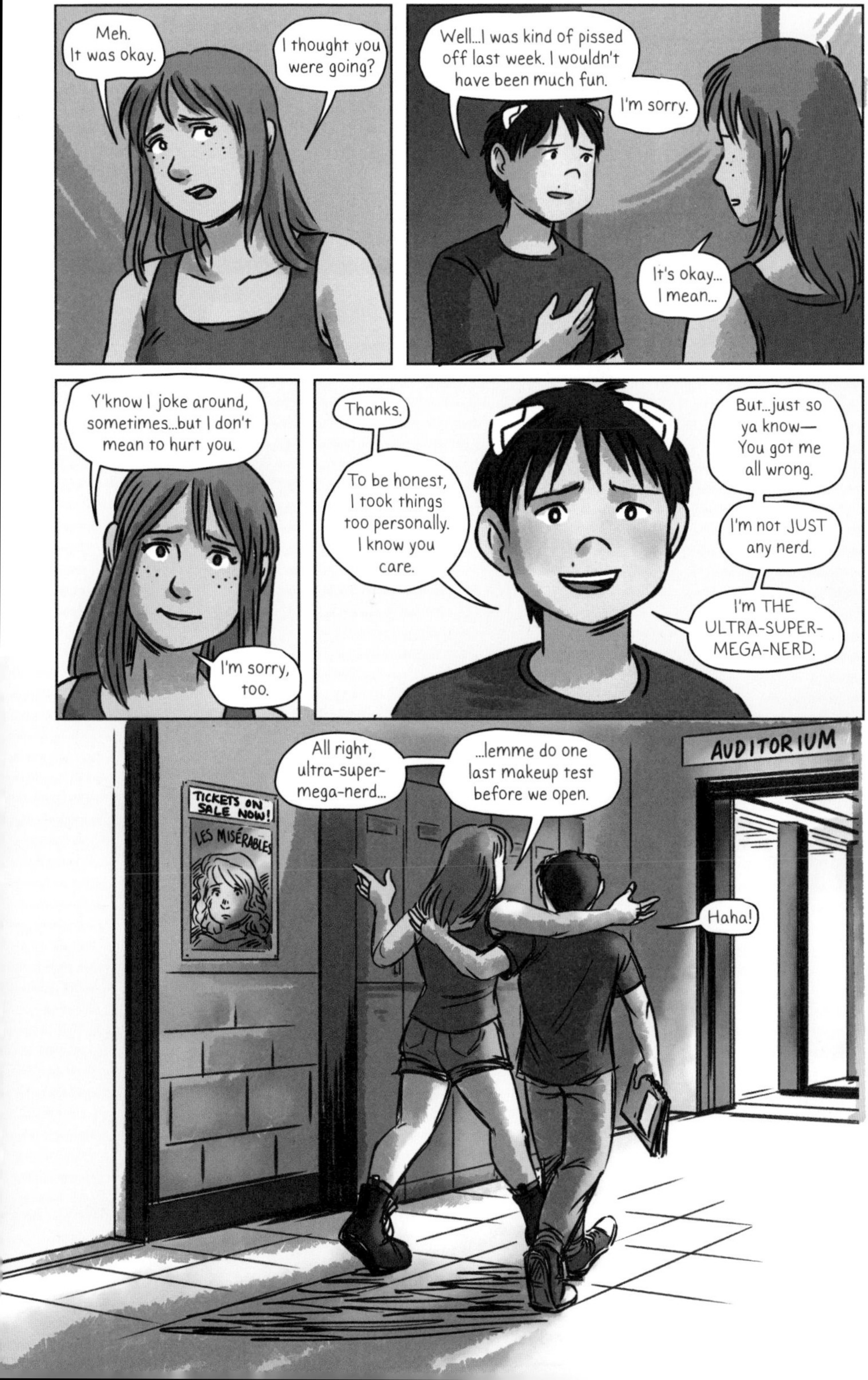
Meh.
It was okay.
I thought you were going?
Well...I was kind of pissed off last week. I wouldn't have been much fun.
I'm sorry.
It's okay... I mean...
Y'know I joke around, sometimes...but I don't mean to hurt you.
I'm sorry, too.
Thanks.
To be honest, I took things too personally. I know you care.
But...just so ya know—You got me all wrong.
I'm not JUST any nerd.
I'm THE ULTRA-SUPER-MEGA-NERD.
TICKETS ON SALE NOW!
LES MISÉRABLES
AUDITORIUM
All right, ultra-super-mega-nerd...
...lemme do one last makeup test before we open.
Haha!

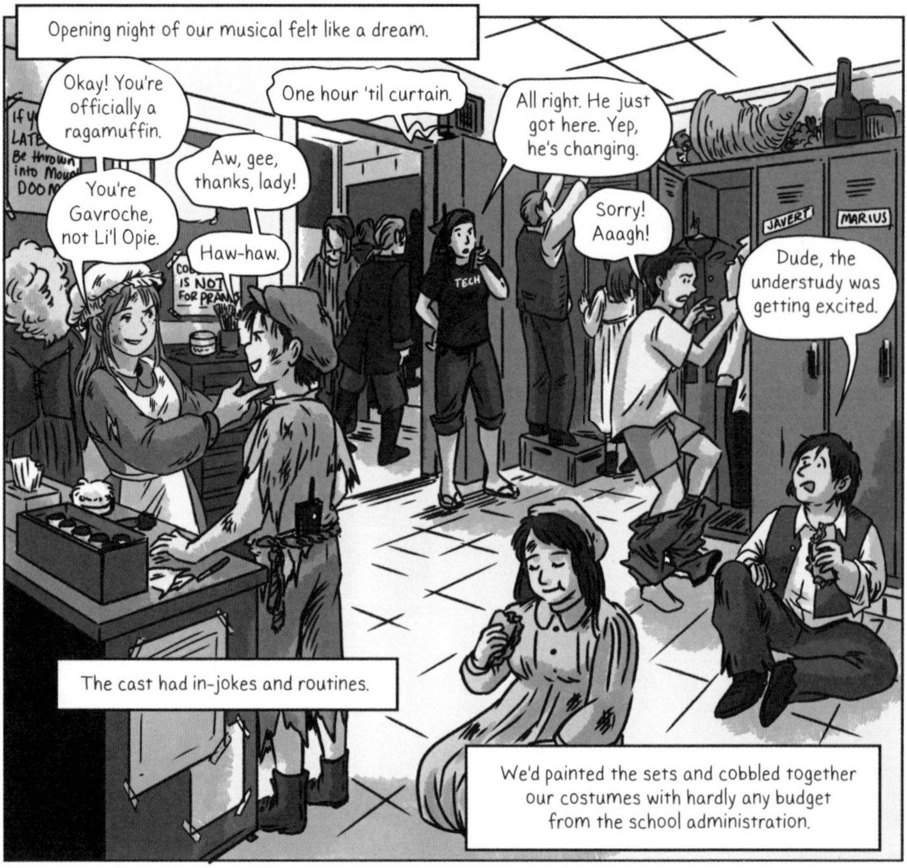

Opening night of our musical felt like a dream.
Okay! You're officially a ragamuffin.
You're Gavroche, not Li'l Opie.
Aw, gee, thanks, lady!
Haw-haw.
One hour 'til curtain.
All right. He just got here. Yep, he's changing.
TECH
Sorry! Aaagh!
JAVERT
MARIUS
Dude, the understudy was getting excited.
The cast had in-jokes and routines.
We'd painted the sets and cobbled together our costumes with hardly any budget from the school administration.

I actually liked who I saw in the mirror on opening night.

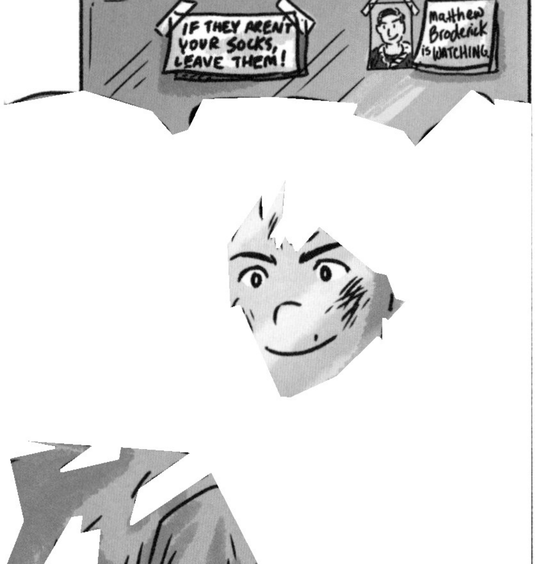

IF THEY AREN'T YOUR SOCKS, LEAVE THEM!
Matthew Broderick is WATCHING

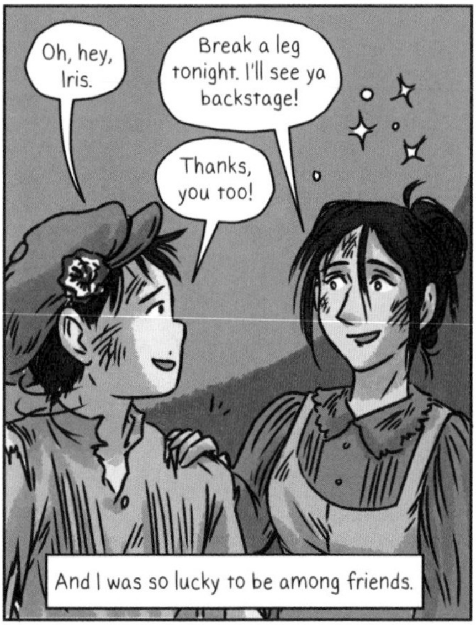

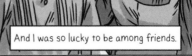

Oh, hey, Iris.
Break a leg tonight. I'll see ya backstage!
Thanks, you too!
And I was so lucky to be among friends.

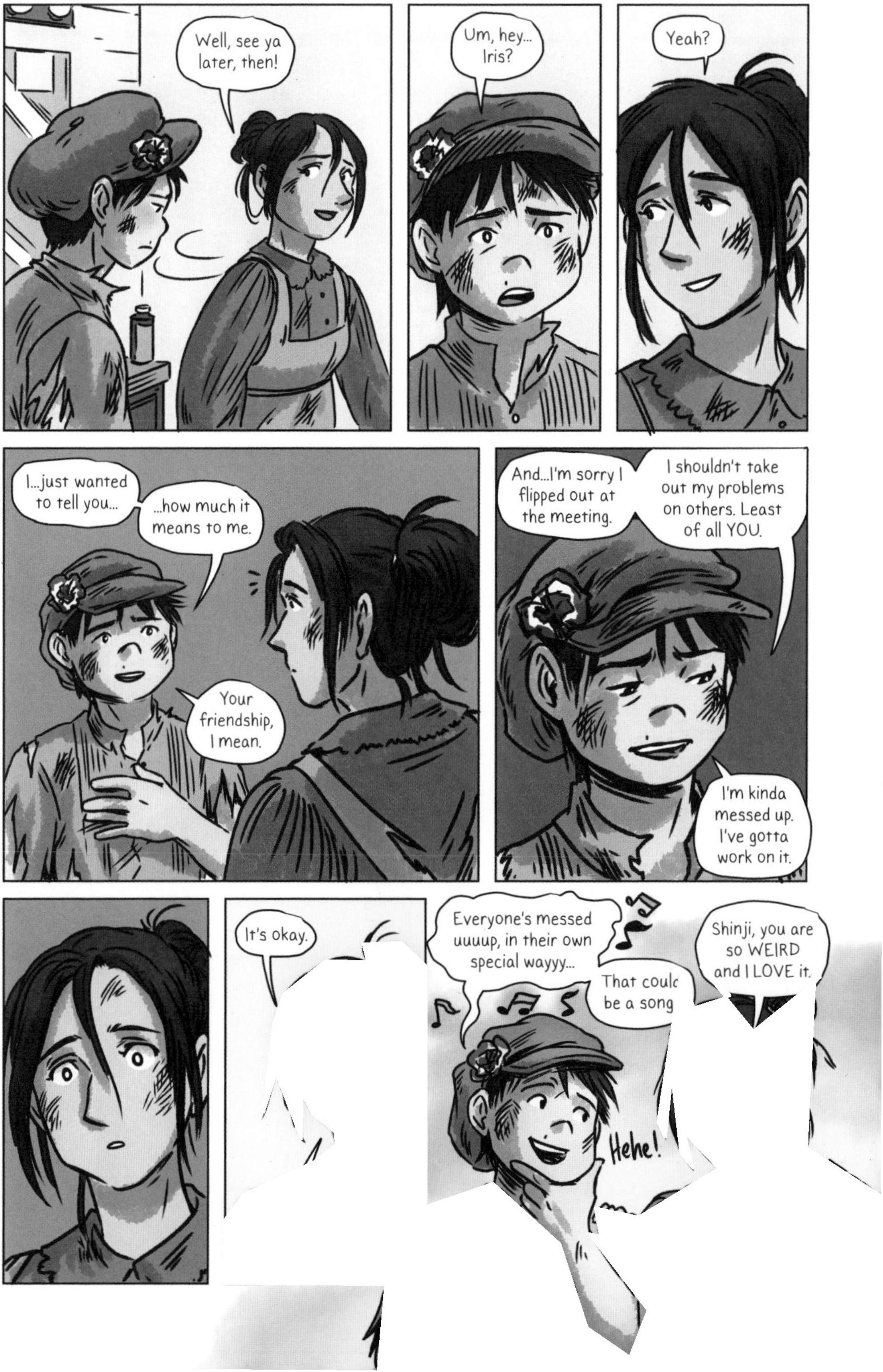
Well, see ya later, then!
Um, hey... Iris?
Yeah?
I...just wanted to tell you...
...how much it means to me.
Your friendship, I mean.
And...I'm sorry I flipped out at the meeting.
I shouldn't take out my problems on others. Least of all YOU.
I'm kinda messed up. I've gotta work on it.
It's okay.
Everyone's messed uuuup, in their own special wayyy...
That coulc be a song
Hehe!
Shinji, you are so WEIRD and I LOVE it.

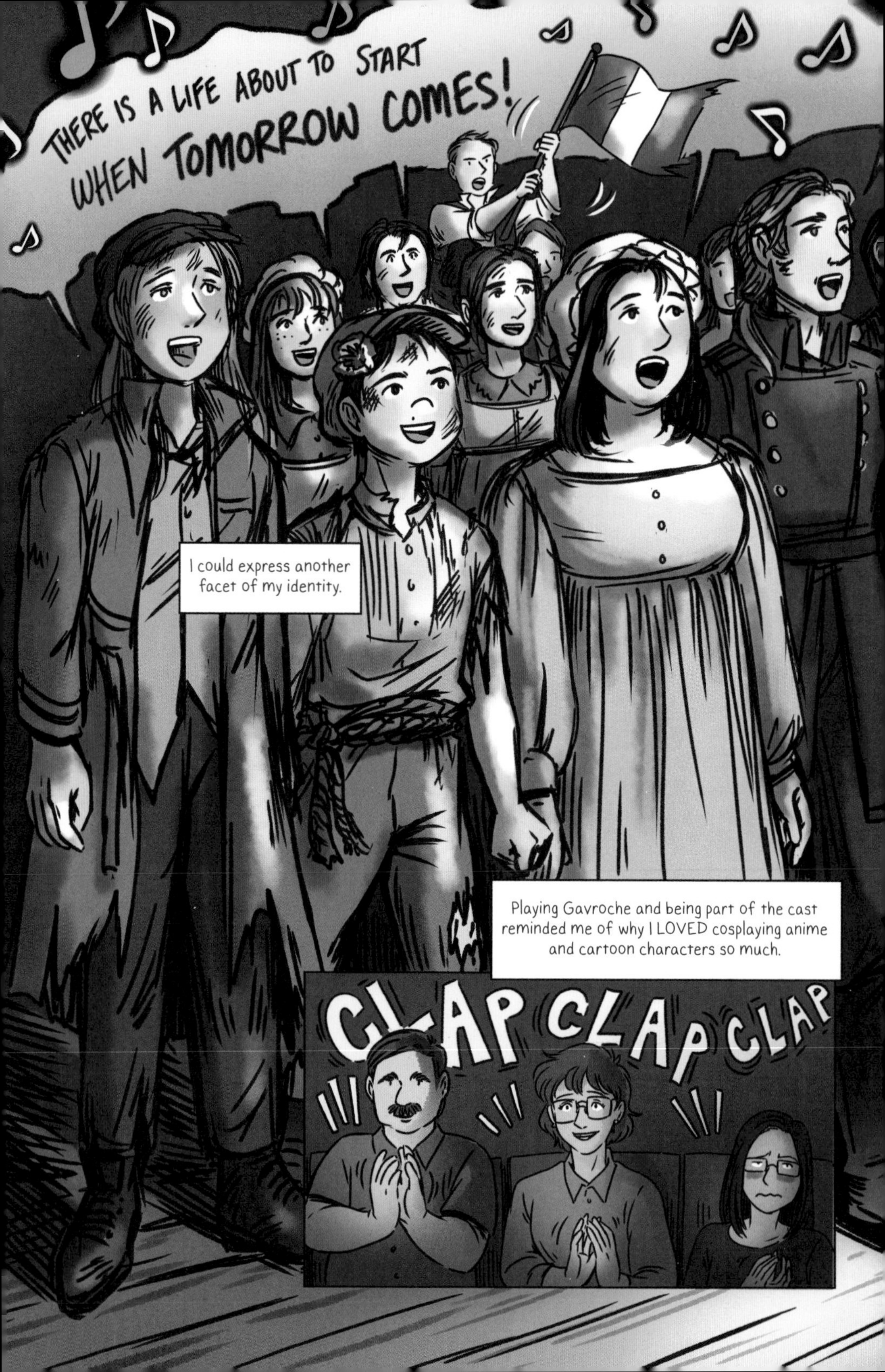
THERE IS A LIFE ABOUT TO START
WHEN TOMORROW COMES!
I could express another facet of my identity.
Playing Gavroche and being part of the cast reminded me of why I LOVED cosplaying anime and cartoon characters so much.
CLAP CLAP CLAP

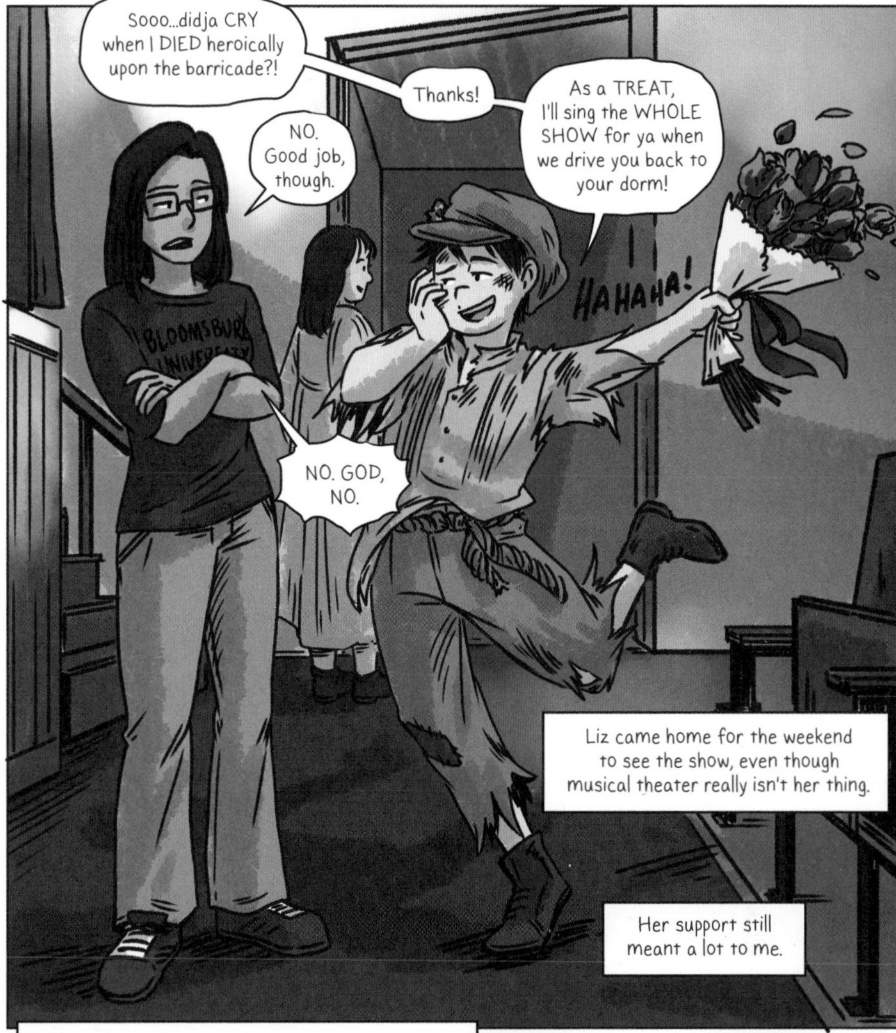
Sooo...didja CRY when I DIED heroically upon the barricade?!
NO. Good job, though.
Thanks!
As a TREAT, I'll sing the WHOLE SHOW for ya when we drive you back to your dorm!
HAHAHA!
BLOOMSBURG UNIVERSITY
NO. GOD, NO.
Liz came home for the weekend to see the show, even though musical theater really isn't her thing.
Her support still meant a lot to me.

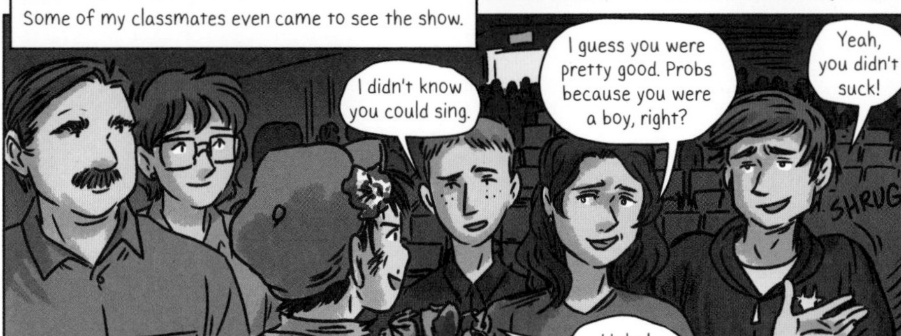
Some of my classmates even came to see the show.
I didn't know you could sing.
I guess you were pretty good. Probs because you were a boy, right?
Yeah, you didn't suck!
SHRUG
Haha! Thanks, guys.

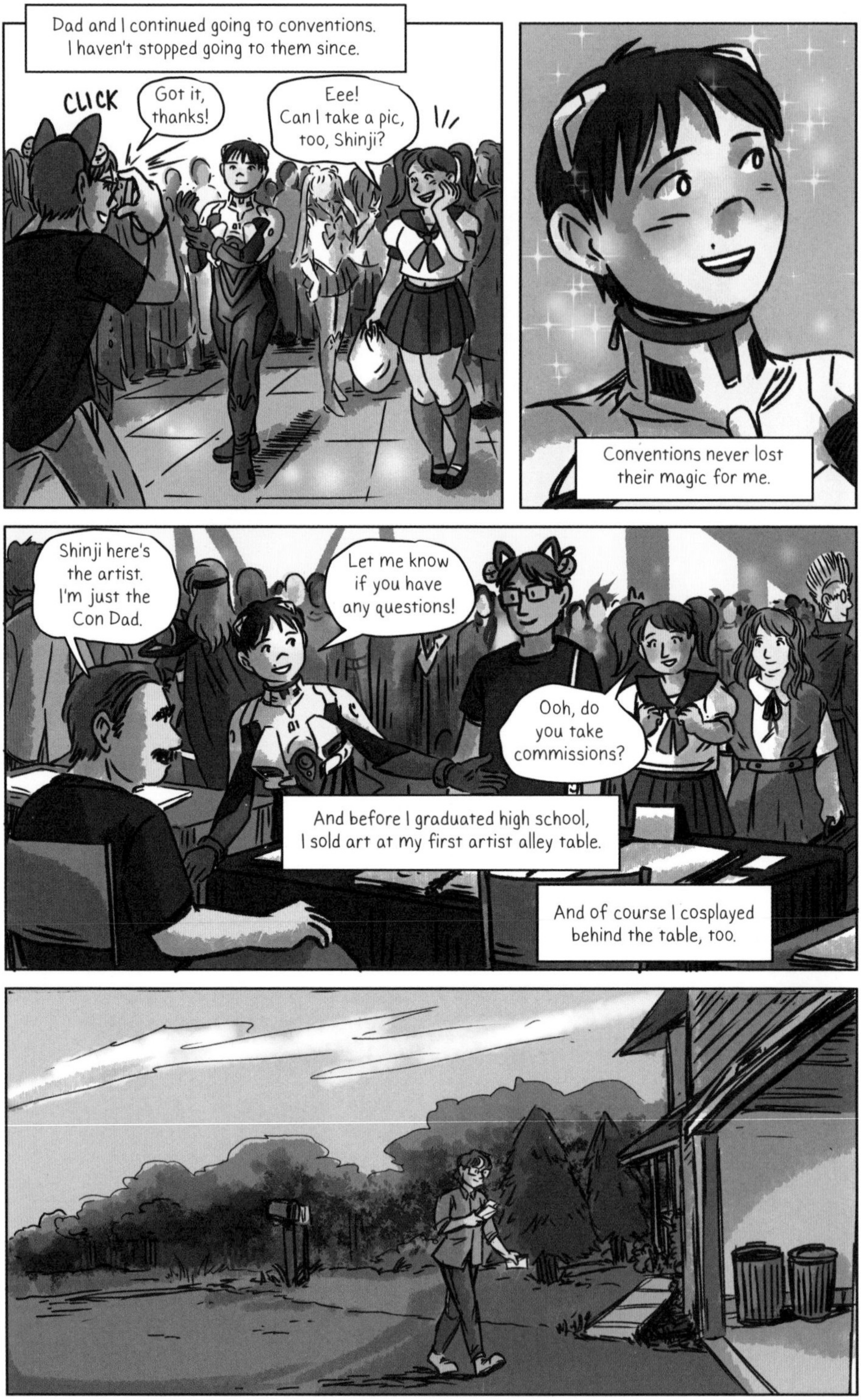
Dad and I continued going to conventions.
I haven't stopped going to them since.
CLICK
Got it, thanks!
Eee! Can I take a pic, too, Shinji?
Conventions never lost their magic for me.
Shinji here's the artist. I'm just the Con Dad.
Let me know if you have any questions!
Ooh, do you take commissions?
And before I graduated high school, I sold art at my first artist alley table.
And of course I cosplayed behind the table, too.

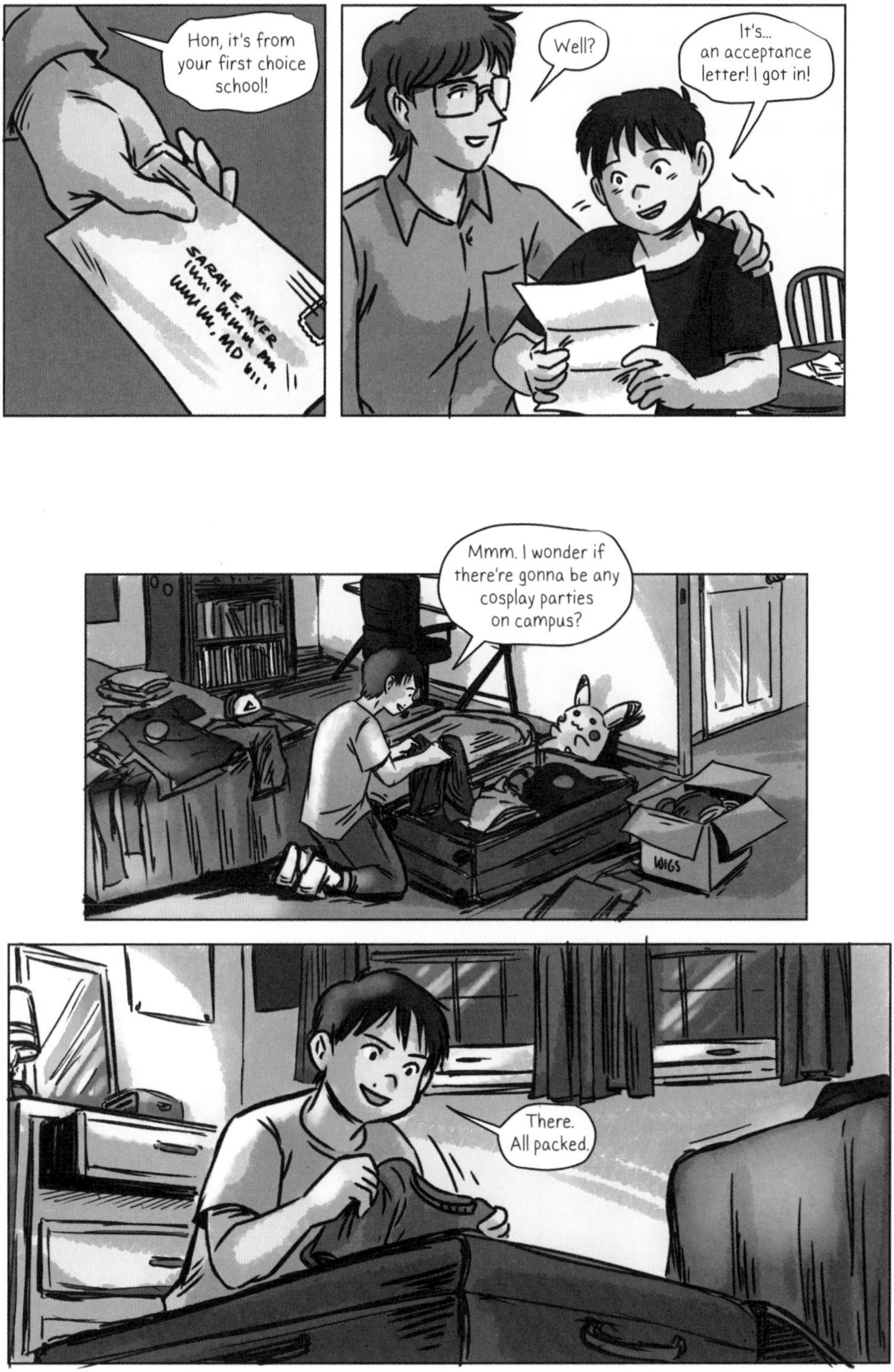
Hon, it's from your first choice school!
SARAH E. MYER
Well?
It's... an acceptance letter! I got in!
Mmm. I wonder if there're gonna be any cosplay parties on campus?
WIGS
There. All packed.

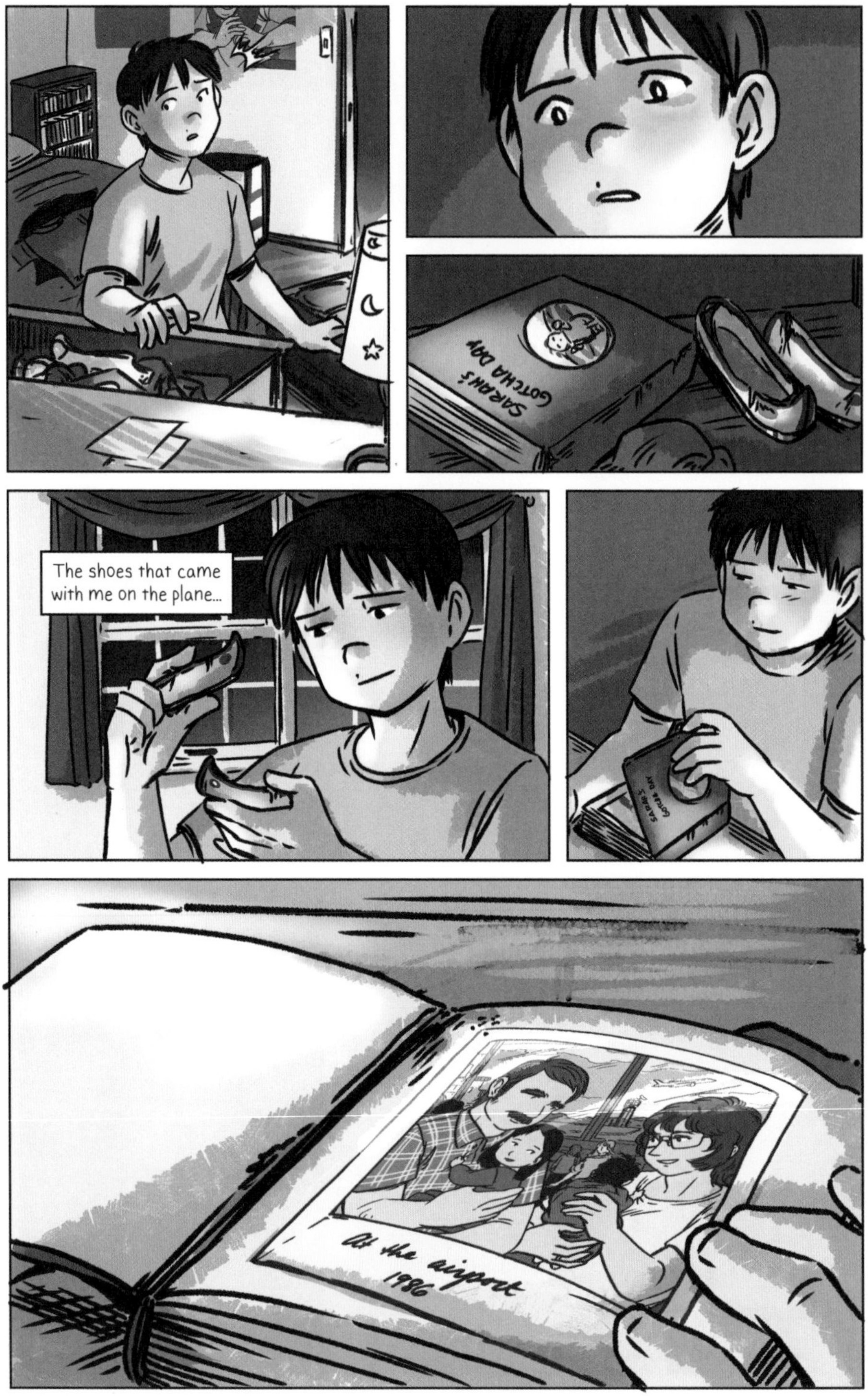
SARAH'S GOTCHA DAY
The shoes that came with me on the plane...
At the airport 1986

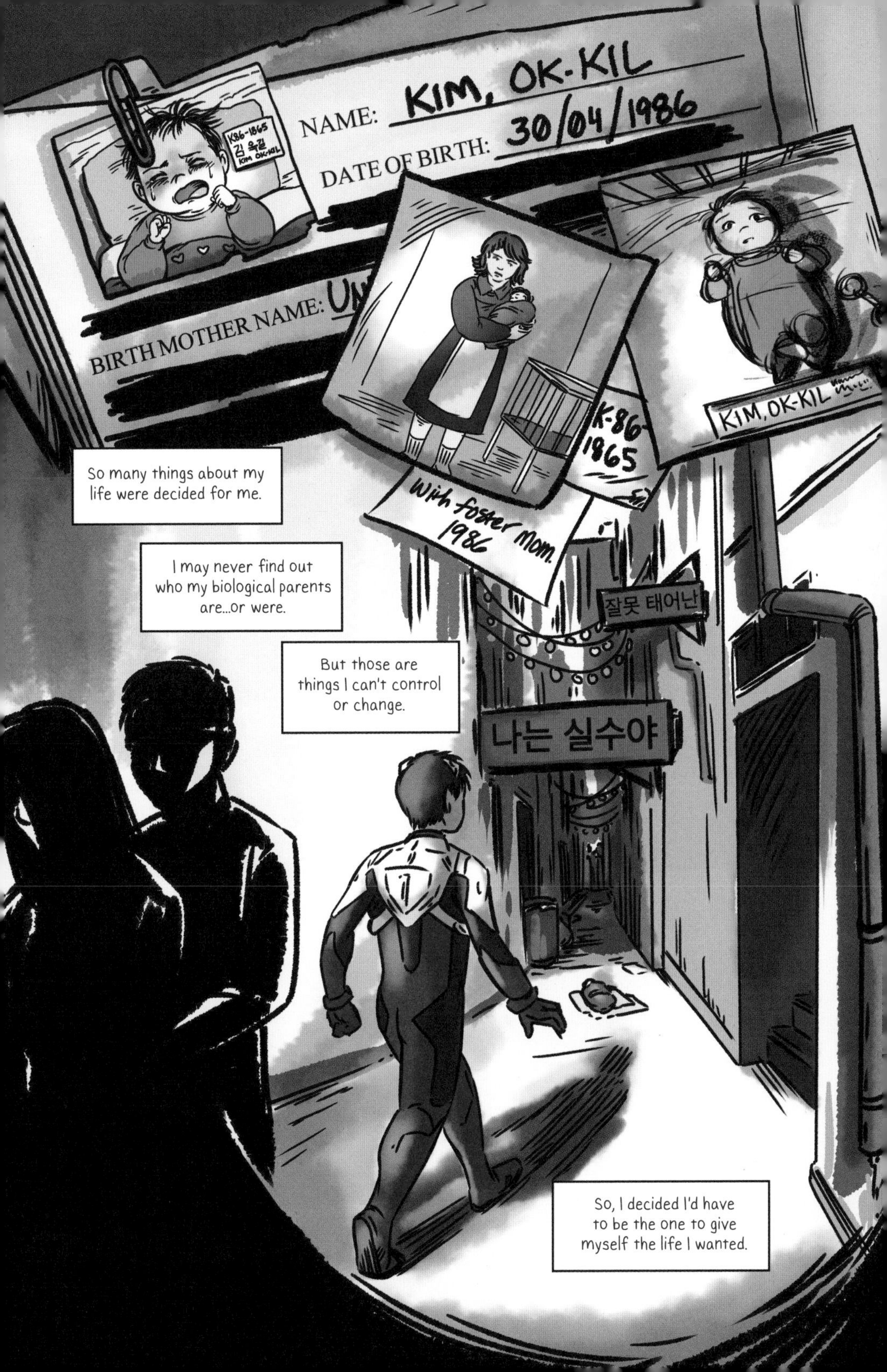

K86-1865
김옥길
KIM OK-KIL
NAME: KIM, OK-KIL
DATE OF BIRTH: 30/04/1986
BIRTH MOTHER NAME:
With foster mom. 1986
K-86-1865
KIM, OK-KIL
So many things about my life were decided for me.
I may never find out who my biological parents are...or were.
But those are things I can't control or change.
잘못 태어난
나는 실수야
So, I decided I'd have to be the one to give myself the life I wanted.

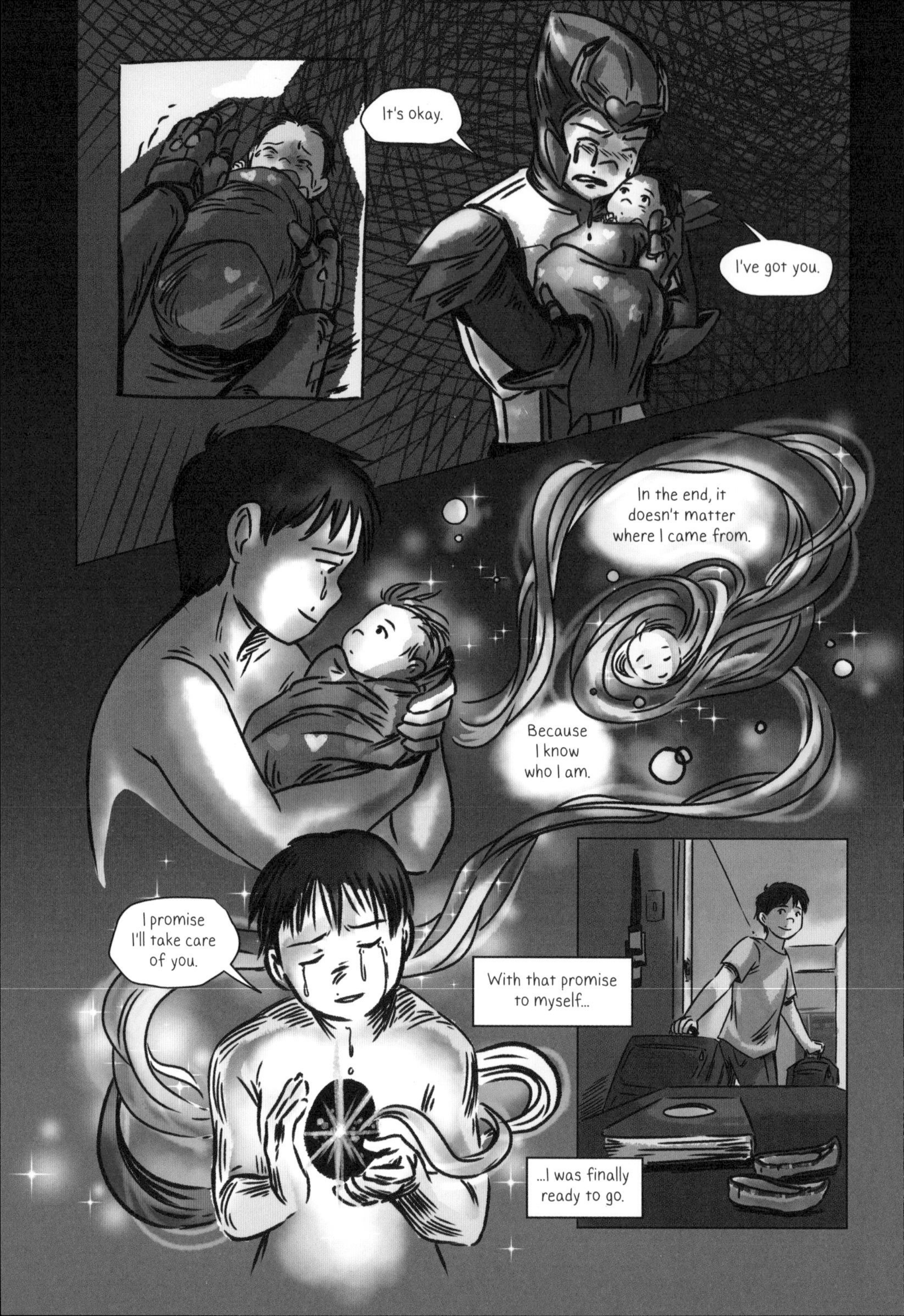
It's okay.
I've got you.
In the end, it doesn't matter where I came from.
Because I know who I am.
I promise I'll take care of you.
With that promise to myself...
...I was finally ready to go.

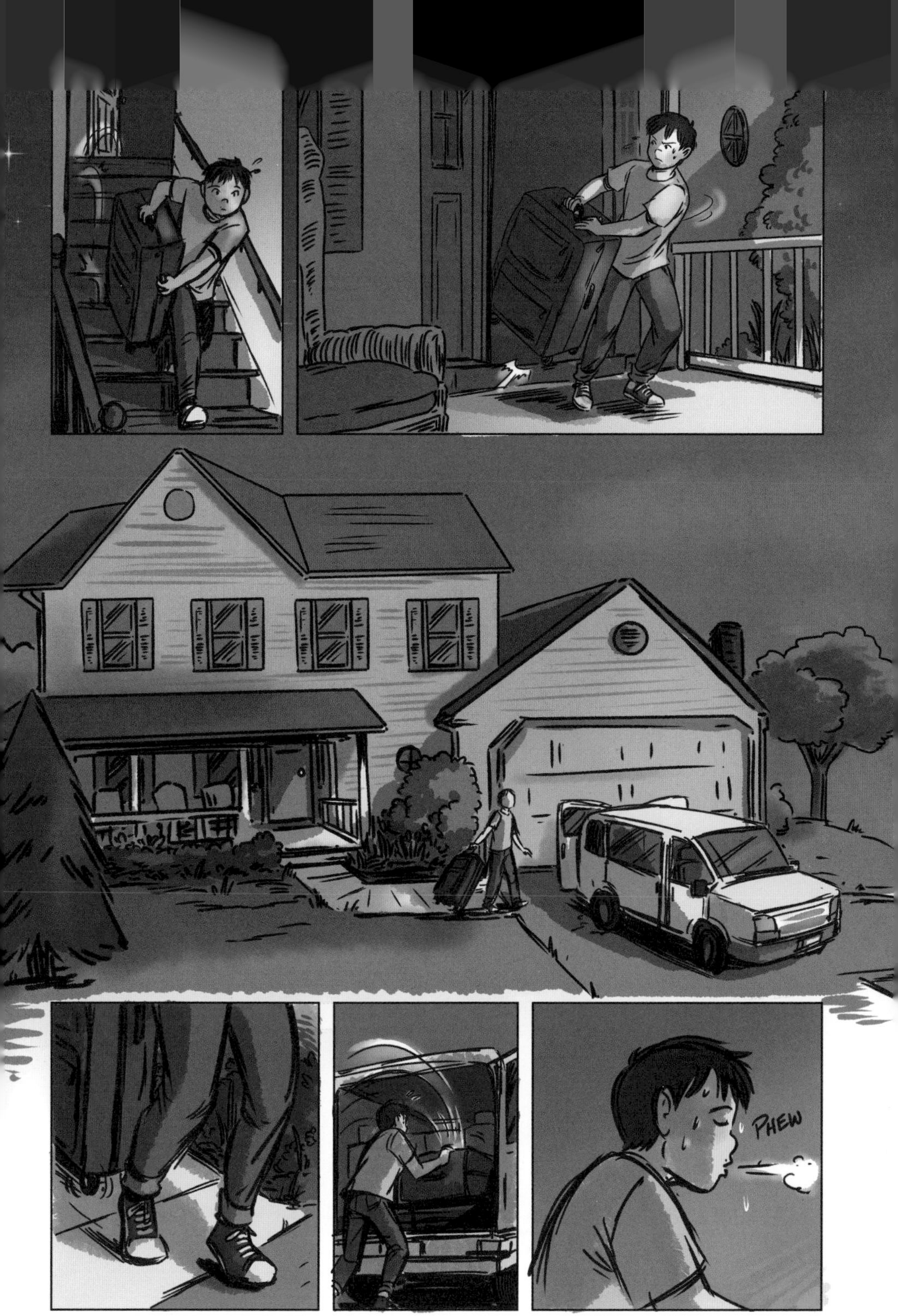
PHEW

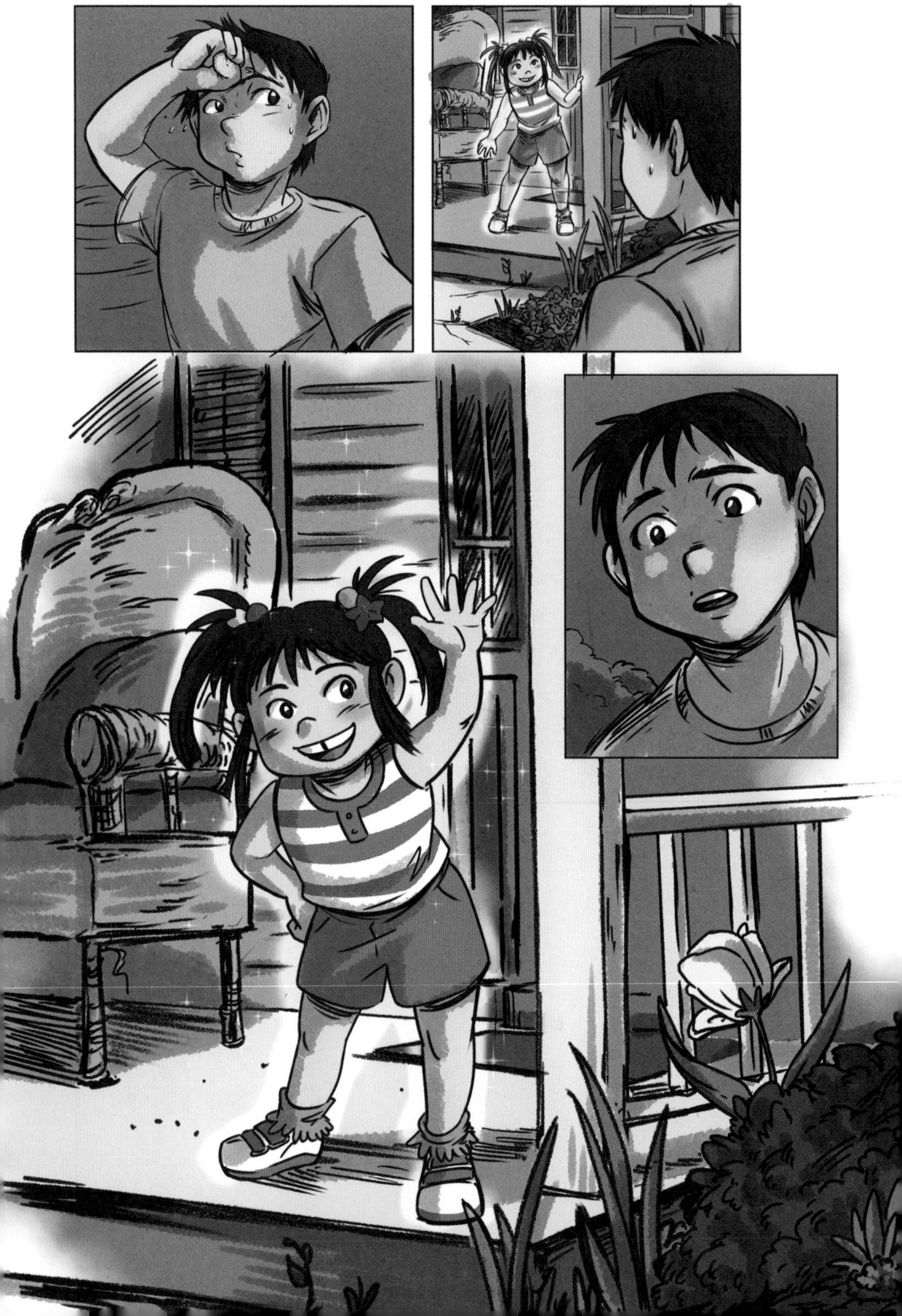

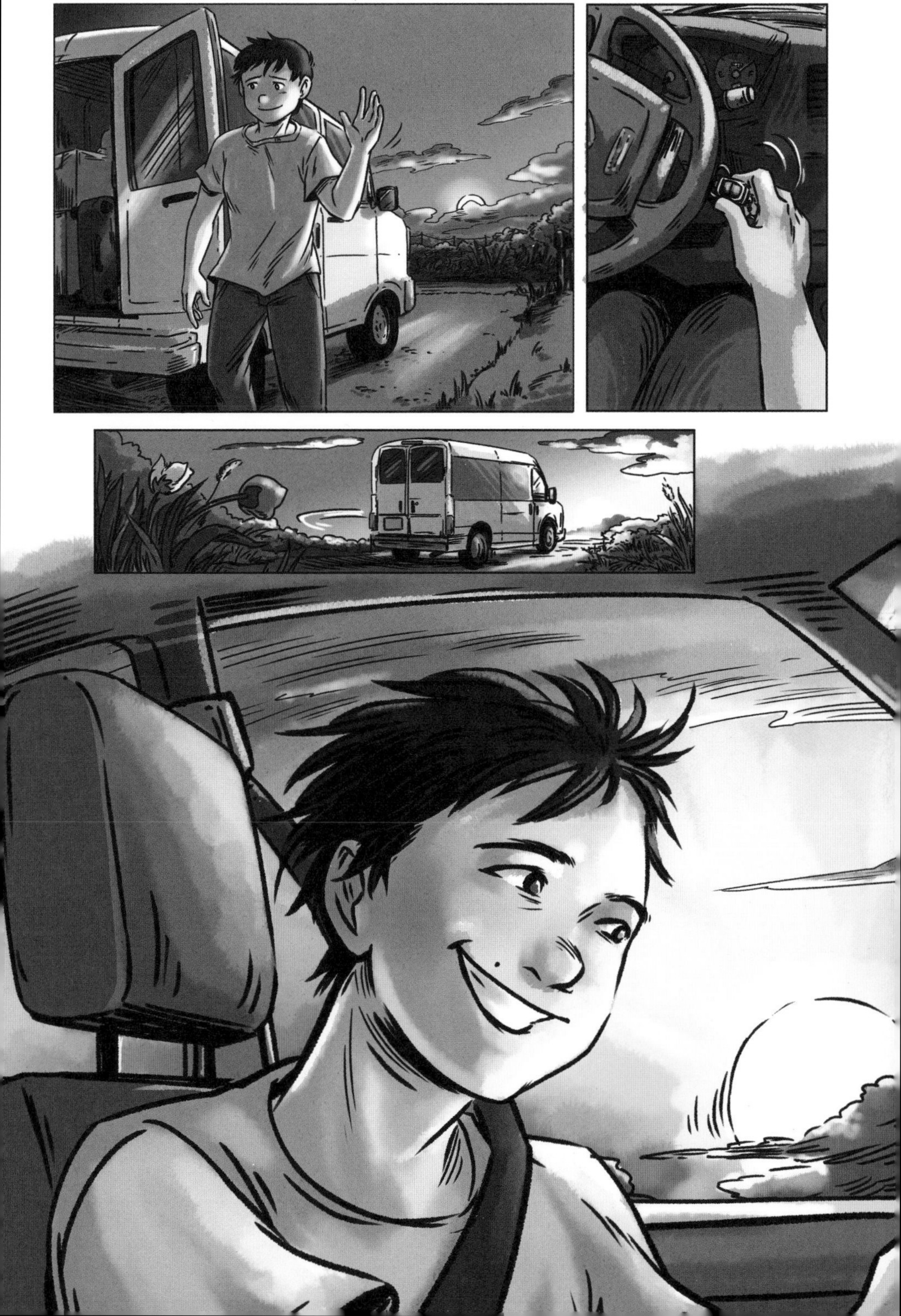

RESOURCES AND SUPPORT

dearadoption.com

Dear Adoption is a platform for adoptees to connect with one another and share their stories. The website collects resources and books for and, most importantly, by adoptees in order to give visibility to their narratives and touchstones for those looking to see themselves represented.

wearekaan.org

The Korean American Adoptee Adoptive Family Network is dedicated to community outreach, advocacy, and post-adoption support for Korean American adoptees. It holds an annual conference with specialized programming for adoptees, their families, and the general audience.

ikaa.org

The International Korean Adoptee Association is a global network of Korean adoptees with organizations in fourteen cities and nine countries. Its goal is to create opportunities for adoptees to connect with one another and share resources on a global scale.

stopbullying.gov

This resource provides educational tools for students, teachers, and parents to help them identify and prevent bullying in its many forms. The organization works with agencies in the US government to coordinate policy, research, and education on bullying topics, with a special focus on cyberbullying.

advancingjustice-aajc.org

Voter hotline: 1-888-API-VOTE

Asian Americans Advancing Justice is a collection of five organizations that advocate for the civil and human rights of Asian Americans and Pacific Islanders in the US. It offers direct legal services and counsel to API community members, and its voter hotline offers support in nine different Asian languages.

centerracialjustice.org

The Center for Racial Justice in Education equips teachers with the tools to address racial justice in educational spaces, giving young people of all backgrounds room to learn and thrive. It offers training seminars and coaching and works one-on-one with schools and other organizations to bring radical equality to classrooms.

asianprideproject.org

Asian Pride Project is a platform for Asian and Pacific Islander LGBTQIA+ individuals and their families to share their experiences though the arts, including film, video, photography, and literature. These narratives are a form of advocacy, calling for greater love and understanding while speaking out against discrimination and hate.

familyequality.org

Family Equality advocates for LGBTQIA+ families and provides resources on a number of topics, including foster care and adoption, antidiscrimination protections, and transgender rights. Its virtual peer-support hub, the Neighborhood, helps families connect with and support one another.

nami.org

NAMI HelpLine: 1-800-950-NAMI
24/7 crisis text line: text NAMI to 741-741
The National Alliance on Mental Illness offers support, advocacy, and educational programming for individuals and families. It offers live help via phone or chat, access to support groups, and advice on how to navigate a mental health crisis or emergency.

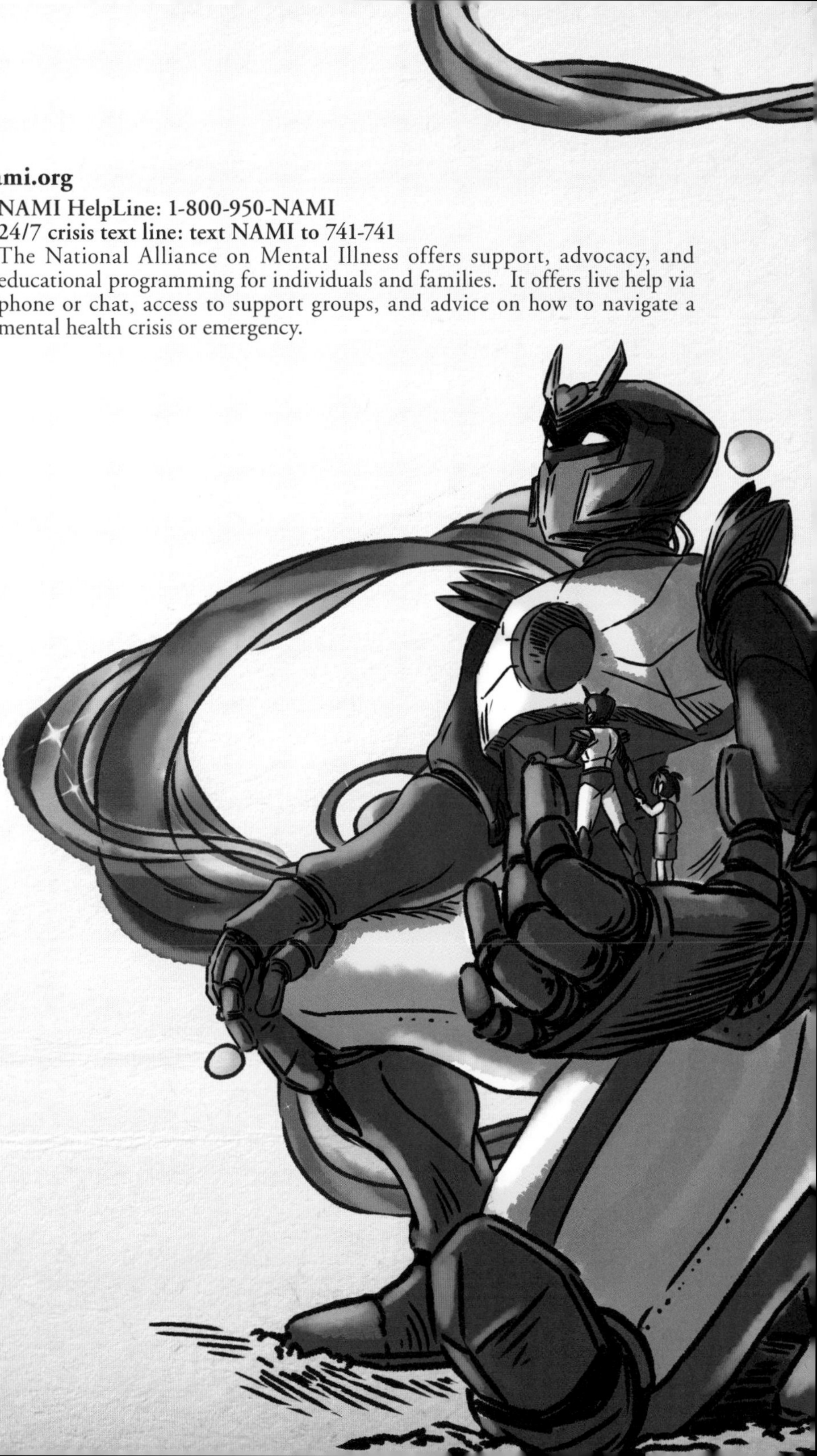

AUTHOR'S NOTE

I was probably seven or eight when I tried to squeeze my feet into the pair of small Korean shoes that had accompanied me on my flight to the US as an infant. Supposedly, my foster mother in Seoul gifted them to me, but who knows what actually happened and why.

I remember being upset that my feet were too big. These tiny shoes didn't fit me like the bright pink, sparkly jellies I wore at the time. Disappointed, I put them back in my dresser drawer.

Now, years later, those shoes are cracked, crumbling, and browned from years of humid Maryland summers with no AC and cold, dry winters. Because I don't know exactly why they were sent with me, nor who sent them, they symbolize the unanswered questions about my origins. Did my birth parents want me to have them so that their child would own a piece of their Korean heritage? Did they dream I'd wear them with a beautiful silk hanbok someday? Did a charity in Korea donate them, with the notion that they were showing an abandoned child an act of kindness?

In the most bitter recesses of my mind, I imagine that the organization that facilitated my adoption had a bin full of cheap plastic shoes and they shipped off a pair with each infant. Almost as if they were completing the item on their checklist: "Gave Child Symbol of Heritage, Not Responsible for What Happens Next. Due Diligence Complete. Hanbok Included? Y/N." Or perhaps they were just thrown in with me because it made the whole adoption feel a little less like a transaction and gave the illusion that I was given gifts and showered with attention before boarding my flight to meet my parents.

Whatever the truth is, because I haven't tossed them out like any other piece of ruined or damaged clothing, they also symbolize my recognition that the unanswered questions still deserve to be revisited from time to time.

When I first began searching for answers, I was absolutely terrified, yet I was so excited that I couldn't look away once I began. I think I was too afraid to hope for a birth parent reunion, but I can't deny the hope was there. It might still be there, but since then I've become less optimistic.

And I don't expect answers anymore, either. Since the events portrayed in this book transpired, I've learned so much about the Korean American adoptee experience from my fellow Americans also adopted from Korea. Don't get me wrong—despite learning a lot about adoption, that doesn't mean I know all the answers.

In fact, what I discovered in the past five or six years raises even more questions: contradictory birth records; adoption agencies approximating or fabricating birth names, dates, and even the birthplace; and, most hauntingly, children being kidnapped from their birth parents and sold into adoption under the lie that they were abandoned or orphaned. Honestly, I don't know how I would feel if I ever found out my adoption circumstances were falsified, but if I had the choice between learning a harsh truth or remaining in the dark about it, I'd pick the former.

Learning about the cultural views toward blood and family lines within Korea has also given me some perspective. There is massive stigma in Korea toward unwed mothers, interracial relationships, and extramarital affairs. As a result, children who are products of those circumstances are still seen by much of Korean society as evidence of something shameful or embarrassing. I'm of two different minds when it comes to these discoveries: understanding that my birth parents had to make these difficult choices in the face of social stigma has soothed some of the anger I've felt toward them. But I don't know if I have any desire to visit Korea, because I fear I would not be welcome in the same way that other Americans might.

Further complicating my feelings about these findings was the rise in popularity of Korean pop music in the US in recent years. It wasn't always easy to hear people excitedly describing Korean stars and culture as beautiful and glamorous and cool while knowing that adoptees like me are seen as a national embarrassment within that same culture. I went through a period, I think, of mourning, too: My younger self might not have felt so alien if K-pop idols were known and loved in the US back then.

The adoption agency told my parents that I was placed for adoption due to monetary reasons, citing my birth parents' inability to afford raising me. I may never find out whether or not this is true. I still feel waves of sadness, anger, and confusion, but every time, it only reminds me to value what I **do** know: I'm here, right now.

The point of this book, however, isn't **just** to talk about these issues as an adoptee. I wanted this book to illustrate the ways in which I was just like any other American kid of my generation: wanting to find my own way, trying to fit in, and struggling with whether or not social status was really worth wearing JNCO jeans or bucket hats as the millennium neared.

Like many human beings, my personal story is about discovering who I am and not giving in to the false and irresponsible belief that I am forever going to be a victim. Being a visible, transracial adoptee only brought these universal issues to the forefront at an earlier age for me . . . and, yes, it gave me more time to figure them out. Every negative thing that I experienced as a result of racism, bullying, or my own mental health and self-esteem issues had the potential to stop me. But, luckily, I eventually saw the real challenge for what it was, is, and always will be: taking responsibility for my own happiness.

I did my best to portray certain events in my life accurately, but I fictionalized some details to protect the identity of those involved. While it is true that there were very few ethnic minorities in my hometown, I chose to avoid including in this narrative those who I knew growing up. I did not feel it was my place to speak for them in this book, and I'm aware that they may have had different experiences or perceptions of the social environment than I did.

I also want to make it clear that some of the people who did and said unkind things when they were younger did so twenty-plus years ago. In many cases, they've changed and grown to be wonderful people who would never dream of doing or saying those things now. I was not always a kind person when I was younger and made my share of mistakes. I still make plenty of them, but I'll always try to do better!

Some people reading this book may be adoptees, Korean American, or ethnic minorities just like me. Some of you may be able to identify with the insecurities I had about my physical appearance, or my troubling experiences with bigotry. Some people reading this book may be trans, and know the pain and confusion that comes when how you look on the outside doesn't match who you are on the inside. Or maybe you are

LGBTQIA+ and can identify with the fear of coming out or with others thinking they can label you and put you in a box. Some of you may not be adopted at all, but belong to a diverse family and can perhaps relate to being on the receiving end of stares, whispers, and judgment. This book may also be picked up by a lonely kid who loves anime or who is picked on at school for whatever reason.

My point is that this story doesn't just belong to me—it is for all who feel or have felt like an outsider.

I hope that it will bring you some comfort and empowerment. The shoes you thought you were supposed to wear might not fit you now. It doesn't matter if they ever did or will, as long as you keep walking toward where you want to be.

Thank you for reading.

-Sarah

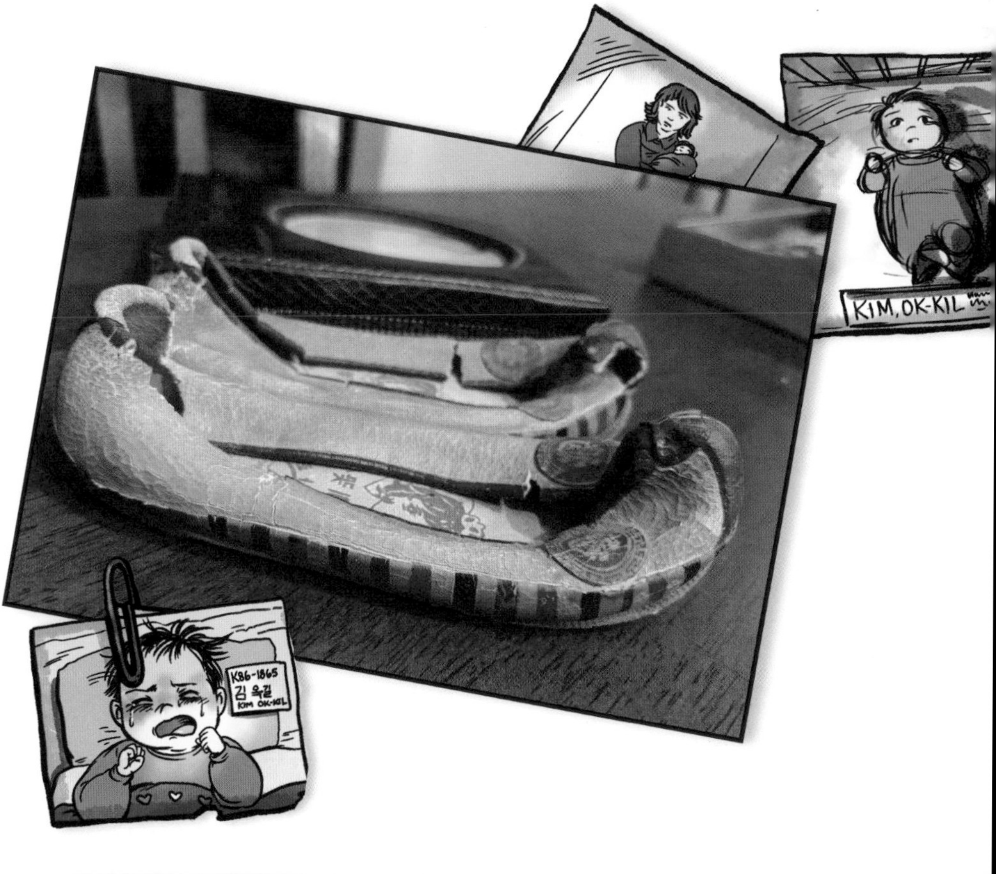
KIM, OK-KIL
K86-1865
김 옥길
KIM OK-KIL

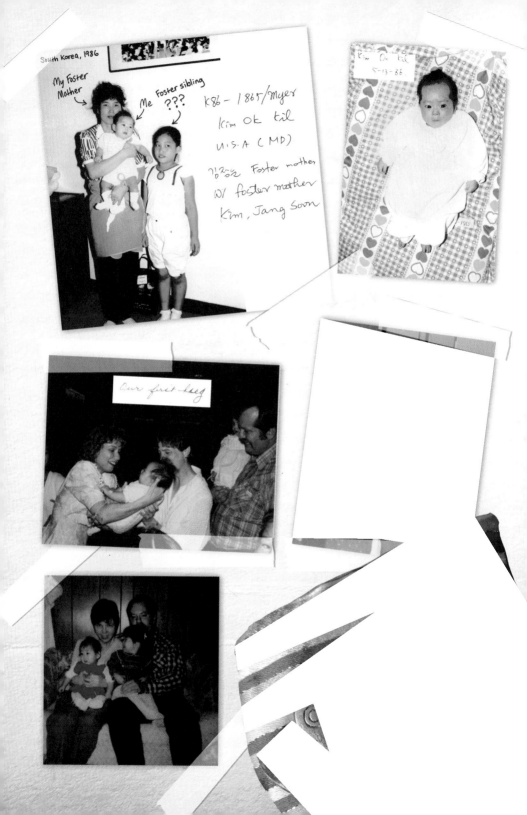

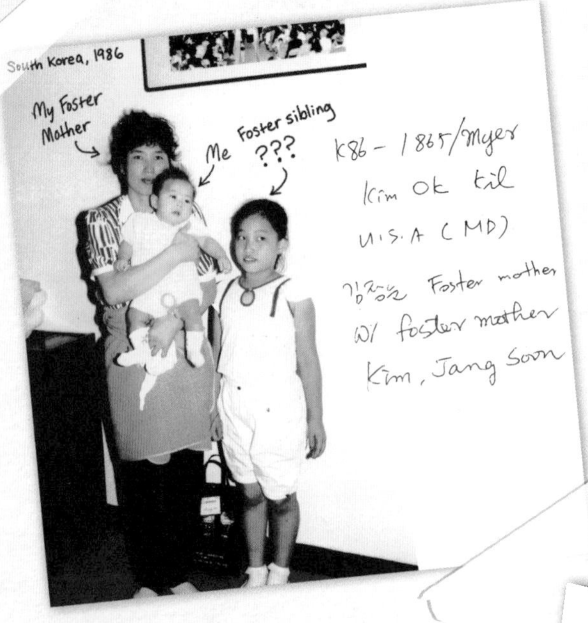
South Korea, 1986
My Foster Mother
Me
Foster sibling
???
K86 - 1865/Myer
Kim Ok til
U.S.A (MD)
Foster mother
W/ foster mother
Kim, Jang Soon

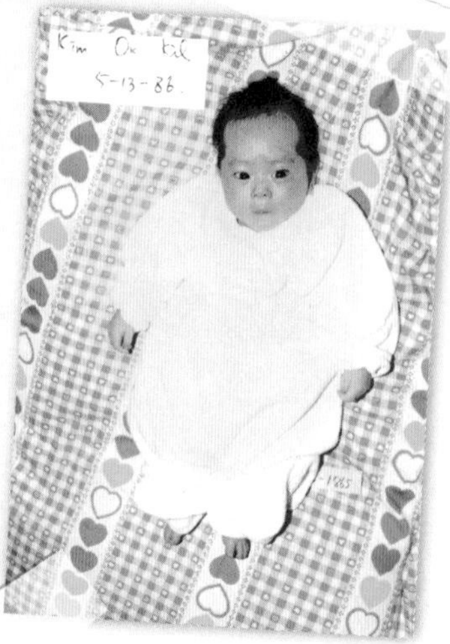
Kim Ok til
5-13-86.

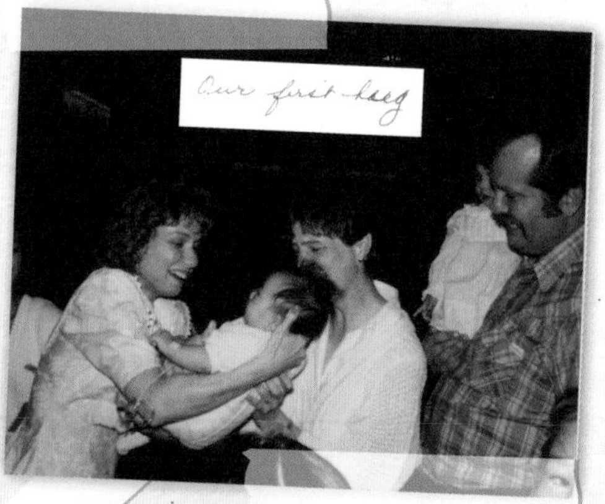
Our first hug

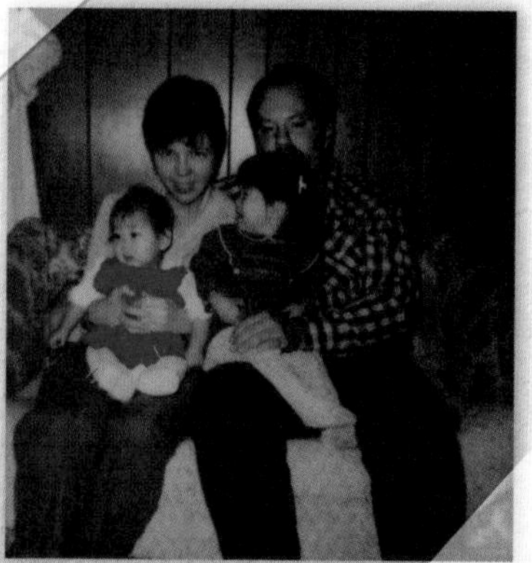

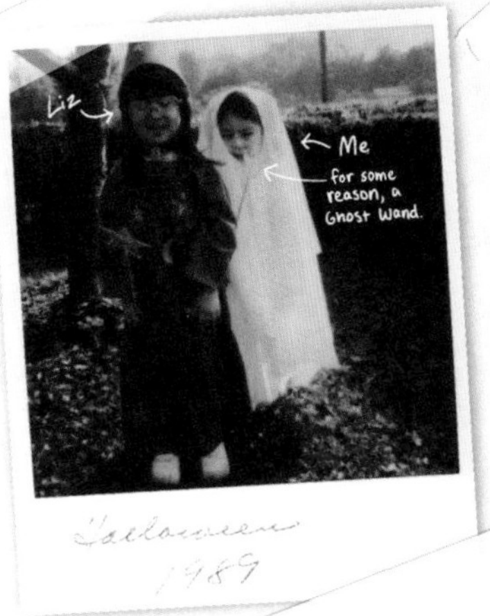
Liz
Me
for some reason, a Ghost Wand.
Halloween 1989

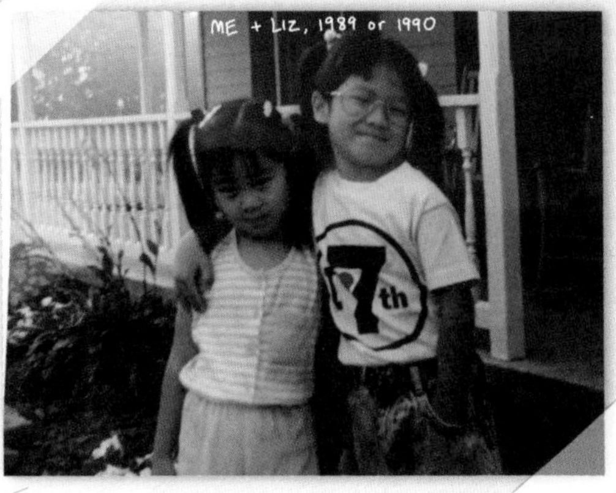
ME + LIZ, 1989 or 1990

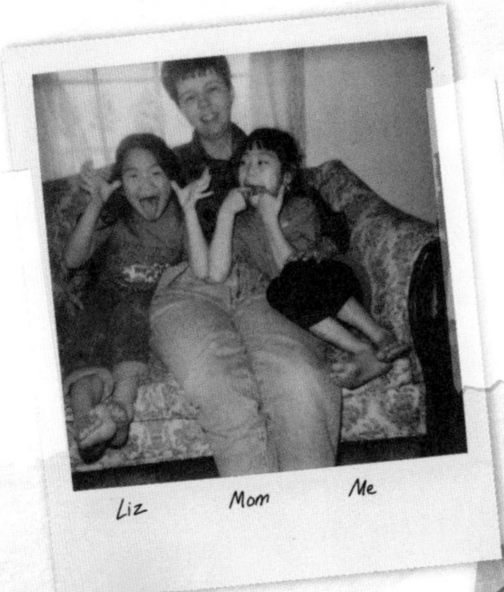
Liz
Mom
Me

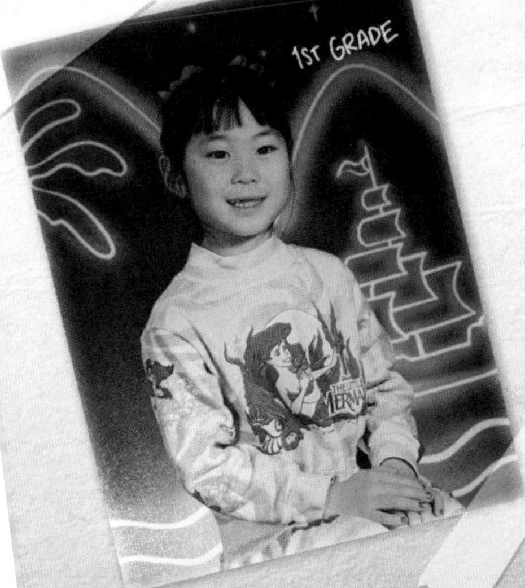
1ST GRADE

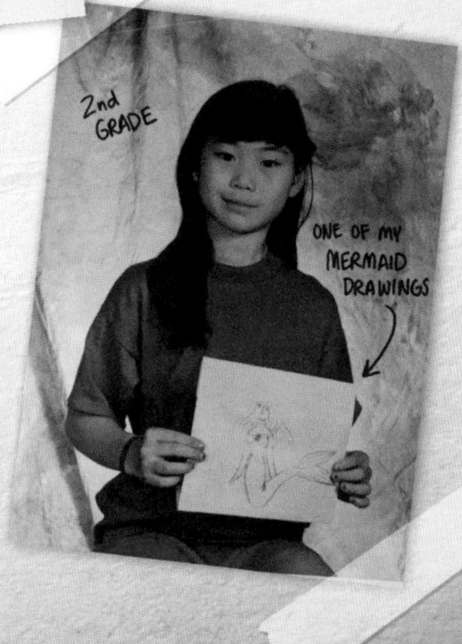
2nd GRADE
ONE OF MY MERMAID DRAWINGS

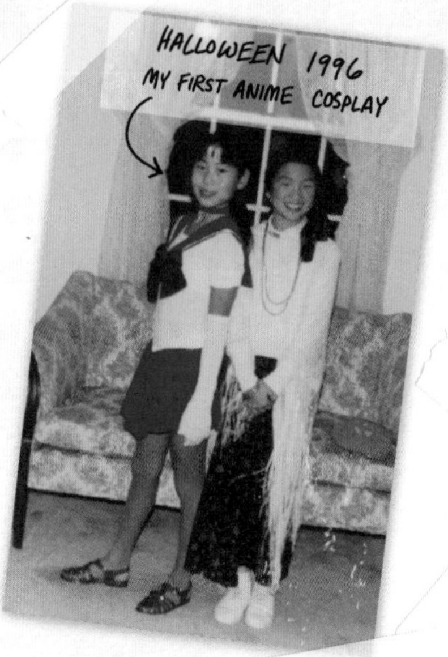
HALLOWEEN 1996
MY FIRST ANIME COSPLAY

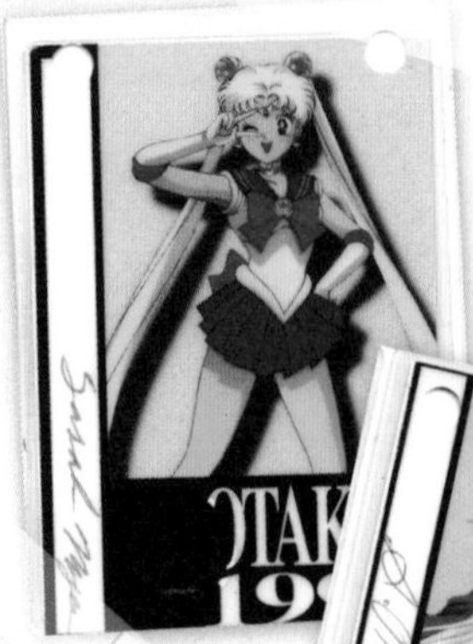
OTAK
199

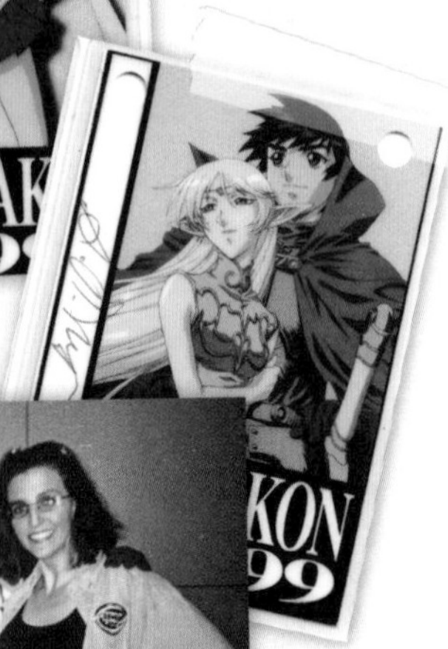
KON
99

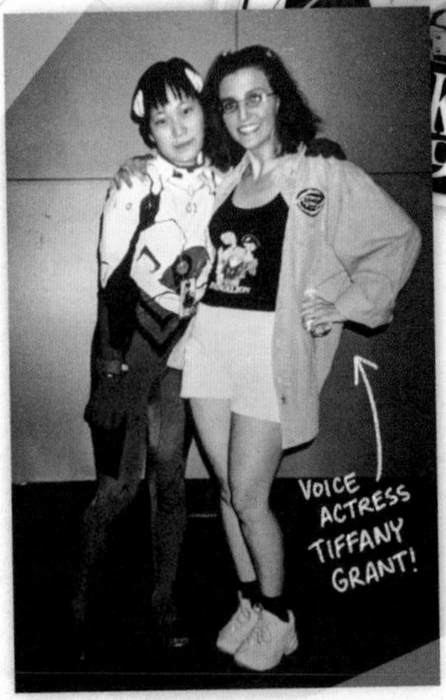
VOICE
ACTRESS
TIFFANY
GRANT!

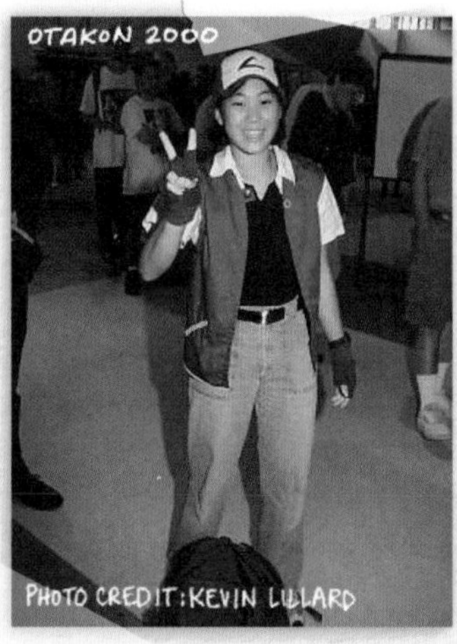
OTAKON 2000
PHOTO CREDIT: KEVIN LILLARD

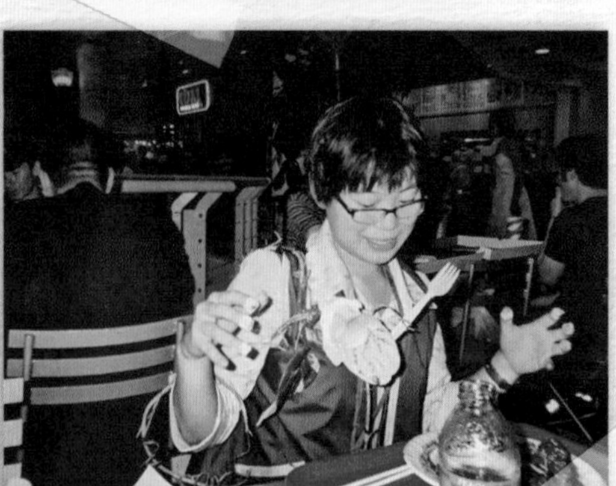

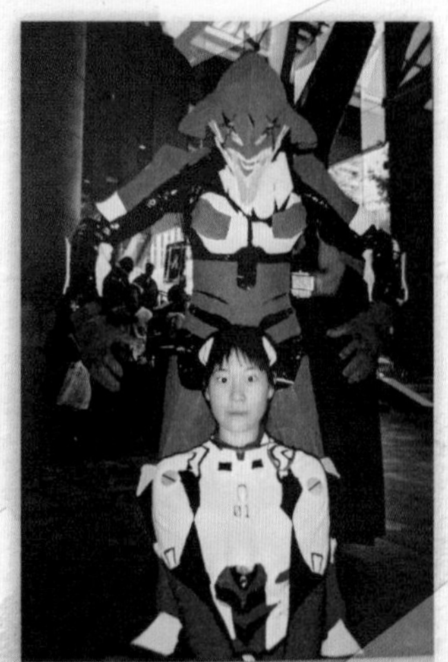

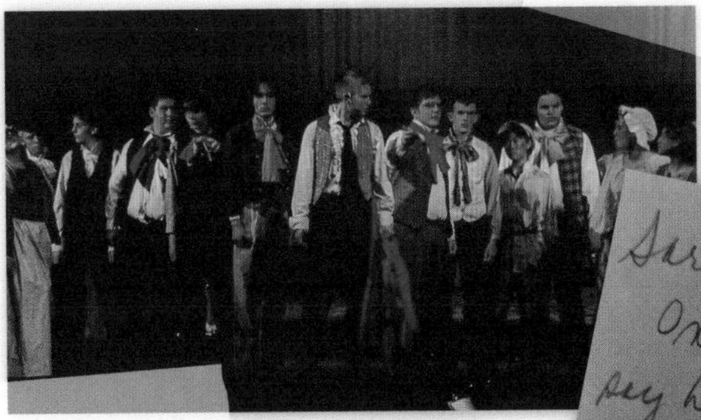

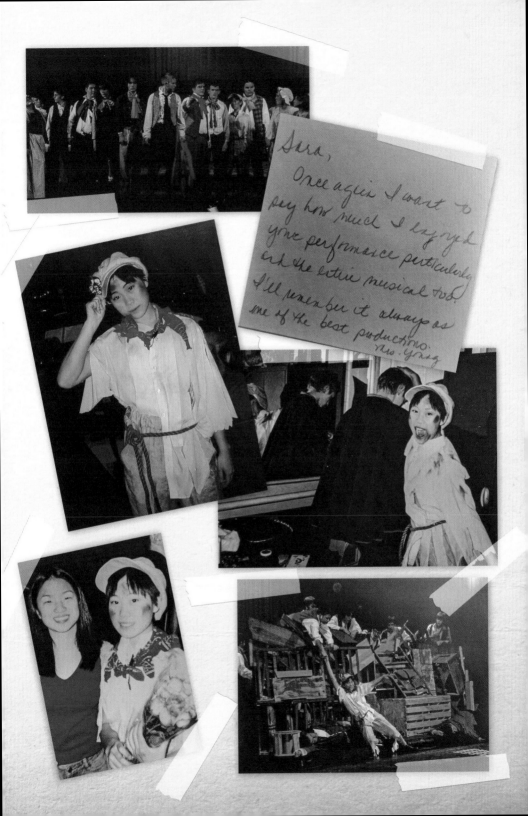

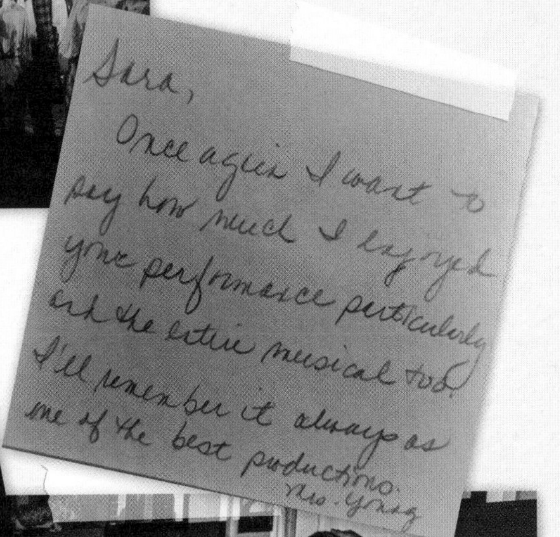
Sara,
Once again I want to
say how much I enjoyed
your performance particularly
and the entire musical too!
I'll remember it always as
one of the best productions.
Mrs. Ying

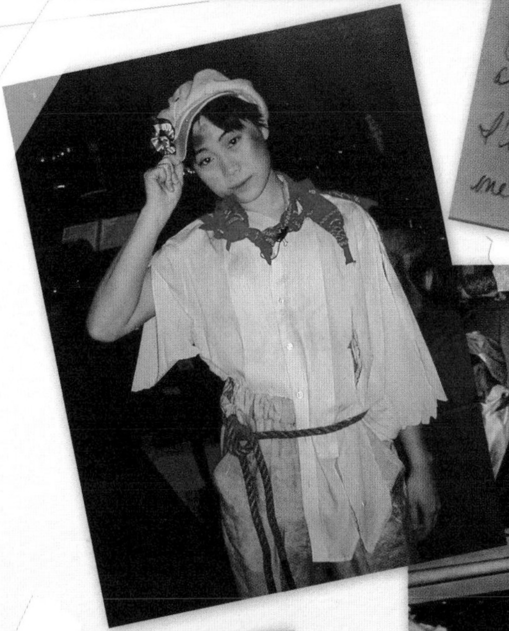

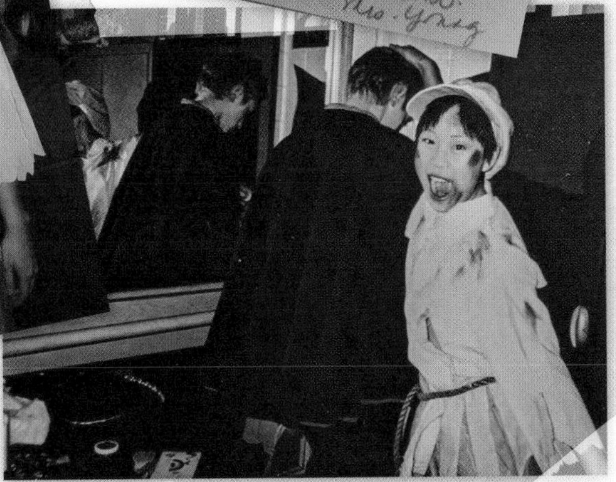

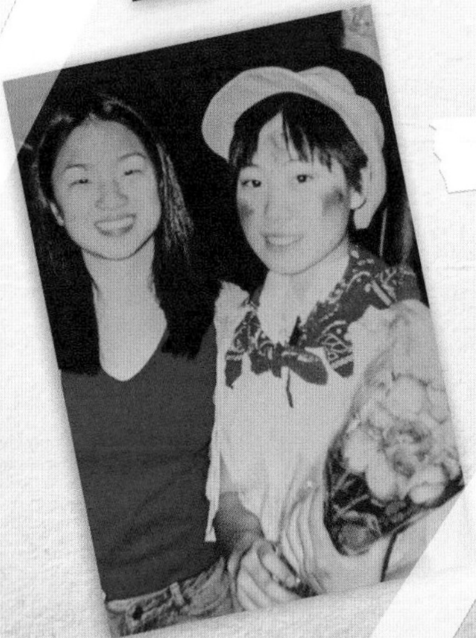

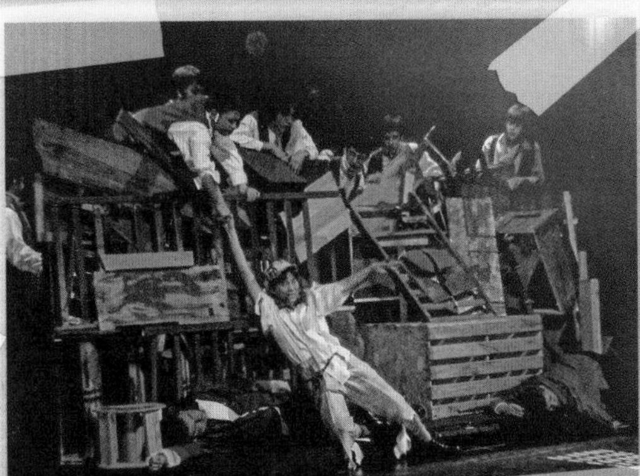

ACKNOWLEDGMENTS

I would like to thank and acknowledge my parents, Mary Ann and Steve Myer, for always championing and supporting my improbable career goal of being someone who draws cartoon characters to tell stories for a living; you never tried to suppress my particular brand of weirdness, even when it was taxing.

I am grateful for the incredible education I received from a variety of wonderful teachers: Mrs. Lemon, Mrs. Cantwell, Mrs. Galinski, Mrs. Lietzel, Mrs. Stickney, Mrs. Benson, Mr. Woodward, Mrs. Emge, Mrs. Diven, Coach Migliarini, Mr. and Mrs. Smith, Mr. Zaldivar, Professor Kneece, Professor Pendarvis, Professor Deems, Professor Yacoub, Professor Inamdar, Professor Phillips, and Professor Silva.

To my fandom and convention friends, thank you for changing my life and for showing me that there are others out there who also love running around dressed as anime and comic book characters.

Thank you to my best friend, Emma Ravenel, for going on so many adventures with me.

And thank you, Robyn Chapman, Michael Moccio, Kirk Benshoff, Molly Johanson, Sarah Gompper, Kelly Markus, Amanda F. Gutierrez, Jennifer Sale, and the entire team at First Second, for your patience, invaluable insight, and support while we worked on this book together. The opportunity you've given me to tell this story is truly once in a lifetime, and one for which I will always be grateful.

If you are struggling with your mental health and anger issues like I did, I urge you not to repeat my mistakes. Lashing out, violently or otherwise, is never the answer. If you are struggling, please do not hesitate to seek professional help.